A Guide to Marxian Political Economy

Teinosuke Otani

A Guide to Marxian Political Economy

What Kind of a Social System Is Capitalism?

Springer

Teinosuke Otani
Tokyo
Japan

The Work was first published in 2001 in Japanese by Sakurai-Shoten Publishers, Tokyo with the following title: Zukai Shakai Keizaigaku: Shihonsyugi towa Donoyouna Shakai System ka?

ISBN 978-3-030-09757-8 ISBN 978-3-319-65954-1 (eBook)
https://doi.org/10.1007/978-3-319-65954-1

Softcover re-print of the Hardcover 1st edition 2018

Printed on acid-free paper

This Springer imprint is published by Springer Nature
The registered company is Springer International Publishing AG
The registered company address is: Gewerbestrasse 11, 6330 Cham, Switzerland

Preface

Everyone knows that the social system known as «capitalism» constitutes the bare bones of modern society. However, if asked to explain what «capitalism» is, it soon becomes clear that the answer is not easy to provide. Political economy—a scientific current that flowed from the *Classical school of political economy* into *Marxian political economy*—has struggled to answer this question since the time that the capitalist social system first emerged. The aim of this book is to convey to readers the answers that Marxian political economy has provided.

The etymology of the term «political economy», incidentally, throws light on its proper meaning. The term «economy» can be traced back to the Greek word οικονομια (oikonomia); it is a combination of the words οικος (oikos), which means «house or place to live in», and νομος (nomos), which means «to manage», so when combined the meaning is roughly «management of a household». The term was later applied to the financial policies of the Greek city-state, πολις (polis), thus creating the term πολιτικη οικονομα (politike oikonomia), which is the direct source of the English term «political economy». It is clear, then, that the word «political» in «political economy» does not refer to politics, but rather a «social» aspect; in other words, political economy should be understood as the science that takes the «economy of society» as its object of investigation.[1]

Given the existence of numerous books dealing with Marxian political economy, I should point out the three aspects of this book that I think set it apart.

First, diagrams are used throughout the book to illustrate concepts. The characteristic point, however, is not so much the large number of diagrams, as the consistent use of shapes, symbols, and terminology in them, which make it possible for the reader to grasp the overall gist of the book through perusing the diagrams. The reader should be aware, of course, that the diagrams only cover a portion of the issues discussed and that the more simplified ones could lead to peculiar conceptions if taken on their own. But as long as these limitations are kept in mind, I trust that the diagrams will contribute to an understanding of Marxian political economy.

1 As I will discuss soon after, «political economy» can be distinguished from «economics», which is a term coined by *Henry Dunning Macleod* (1821–1902), *William Stanley Jevons* (1835–1882), and *Alfred Marshall* (1842–1924) to refer to a field of study that they wanted to set apart from the «political economy» of the Classical era. This gave birth to the odd view that «economics»is a pure science, whereas «political economy» is «politically biased».

The second key characteristic of the book is that it avoids the all-too-typical approach of lining up facts and presenting them as fragmentary, common-sense knowledge in a bid to capture the reader's interest. My aim, instead, is to convey a sense of the appeal and vibrancy of a systematic theoretical development. A person who remains within the realm of conventional thinking is not able to naturally arrive at an awareness of the problems *concerning the totality of society* even if that person is disturbed by the self-interested behaviour encountered everyday in the world. We become able to gain a clear awareness of the problems that require elucidation when we move from the visible surface to uncover the truths concealed underneath and then make use of that understanding to explain the surface phenomena. Solving such problems is the means of advancing our understanding of society, step by step, which makes us aware of the power of political economy as a science. I hope that my book can serve as a map indicating to the reader the route of our ascent and that together we can strive to scale the «*luminous summits*»[2] while experiencing both the hardship and joy of the steep climb.

The third characteristic worth noting is that the book's Part I–III basically correspond to Vol. I–III of *Capital*, so it can also serve as a guide to that great work by Marx. Although *Capital* is far from being light reading, needless to say, it is certainly not the case that every part of it is difficult to understand. Yet there are difficult hurdles for first-time readers, and more than a few have given up as a result. Given this overall difficulty, I have tried to provide an easy-to-understand explanation of the aspects that might hinder the progress of readers so they can make their way through the entirety of *Capital*. Of course, to those whose interest in Marx's work is piqued through reading this book, or who wish to arrive at a deeper understanding of its content, I would heartily recommend going straight to the source and reading *Capital* for themselves.

I will often be quoting from Marx in this book. Passages quoted from the three volumes of *Capital* will be based on the editions published by Penguin Books (Vol. I, 1976; Vol. II, 1978; Vol. III, 1981). Quotations from other works of Marx will refer to the volumes of the *Marx/Engels Collected Works*, Vol. 1–50, issued by Progress Publishers, Lawrence and Wishart, and International Publishers (1975–2005). Translations will on occasion be amended by the author.

---

2 In his preface to the French edition of *Capital* (which was originally a letter to the publisher of that edition, *La Châtre*), Marx wrote: «*The method of analysis which I have employed, and which had not previously been applied to economic subjects*, makes the reading of the first chapters rather arduous, and it is to be feared that the *French public, always impatient to come to a conclusion, eager to know the connection between general principles and the immediate questions that have aroused their passions*, may be disheartened because they will be unable to move on at once. / That is a disadvantage I am powerless to overcome, unless it be by forewarning and forearming those readers who zealously seek the truth. *There is no royal road to science, and only those who do not dread the fatiguing climb of its steep paths have a chance of gaining its luminous summits*» (*Capital*, vol. I, p. 104; my emphasis).

In the case of quotations from Vol. I of *Capital*, I have added italics to *indicate* whatever emphases Marx provided using spaced letters in the first German edition. These emphases were removed from subsequent editions of *Capital*, but they are worth including here to better understand what Marx considered to be particularly important.

Please note that in the text of this book I use **boldface** to indicate terms that need to be assimilated and *italics* to emphasise parts that bear special attention.

The questions my book addresses about the nature of the capitalist social system pertain to the future direction of this society, which has already existed for over three centuries, the manner in which it will change, and how it will give birth to a new society. Today, at the outset of our new millennium, I sincerely hope that the reader will join me in thus giving serious thought to the future of humanity.

Teinosuke Otani
Tokyo, Japan

Acknowledgements

I would like to thank my friends *Michael Schauerte* and *Kohei Saito* for their role in bringing this book to the public. Several years ago, *Michael* took an interest in my book *Zukai Shakai-keizaigaku* (Tokyo, 2001) and expressed his desire to bring it to the attention of readers outside of Japan. Towards that end, he set about translating the book and seeking a publisher. *Kohei* also took an interest in this project and began his own search to find a publisher, which met with success when Springer agreed to issue the book. Following that decision, *Michael* worked to polish his original translation and assist me in the final work needed to edit the main text and diagrams. I am grateful for the efforts of *Michael* and *Kohei*, without which this publication would not have been possible. Let me also take this opportunity to thank *Hideto Akashi, Ryuji Sasaki, and Soichiro Sumida*, who assisted me with *Michael* and *Kohei* in the final proofreading process.

Contents

III Various Forms of the Total Process of Capital

Symbols Used in This Book

a	Material costs of commercial capital
ap	Average profit
ap′	Average rate of profit
ar	Absolute rent
b	Personnel costs of commercial capital
C	Commodity/commodity capital
C′	Augmented commodity capital
c	Constant capital
cf	Fixed capital
CG	Gold as commodity
Cp	Cost price
Ct	Capitalist
cw	Value of wear and tear of fixed capital
cz	Circulating constant capital
ΔC	Added commodity capital
ΔM	Added money capital
δc	Increment in C′
δm	Increment in M′
g	Commercial capital
I	Production Department I
II	Production Department II
K	Total advanced capital
k′	Organic composition of capital (c/v)
κc	Consumption fund in commodity form
κm	Consumption fund in money form
Lp	Labour-power
Lt	Labour-time (amount of abstract labour)
M	Money/money capital
M′	Augmented money capital
Mc	Means of consumption
ML	Means of labour
Mp	Means of production
N	New value
n′	New value rate
OL	Objects of labour
P	Productive capital
P′	Augmented productive capital/rate of annual profit
p	Profit
p′	Rate of profit
Pp	Production price
Pr	Product
Rp	Requisite product
Rt	Requisite labour-time
s	Surplus-value
s′	Rate of surplus-value
sa	Accumulated surplus-value
sc	Added constant capital from surplus-value
sk	Surplus-value consumed by capitalist
Sp	Surplus product
St	Surplus-labour time
sv	Added variable capital from surplus-value
v	Variable capital
W	Wages/total value of total commodities
Wr	Worker
z	Circulating capital

List of Figures

List of Tables

Introduction: The Conception of Society Based upon Labour and the Tasks of Political Economy

T. Otani, *A Guide to Marxian Political Economy*,
https://doi.org/10.1007/978-3-319-65954-1_1

1.1 Theme of This Introduction and Path of Investigation

Preparation for the Main Discussion

Political economy's primary task is to clarify the economic structure of *modern society*, with its object of study thus being the economy of *modern society*. But what time period does the term «modern society» correspond to, and which of the complexly intertwined aspects of society does political economy address?

Everyone is aware that the economic structure is subject to constant change and development, so we need to ponder how political economy endeavours to grasp such a changing and developing object. We also need to consider: What is the position of *modern society* within the overall history of the types of societies humanity has experienced? What procedure should we follow in investigating the modern economy? And what is the distinctive character of political economy as a science?

A preliminary understanding of these problems will prove useful in orienting ourselves once we have entered the main discussion of political economy. Without an overall awareness of where we are situated, the most fundamental parts of the book may strike the reader as a world of theory that bears little relation to reality. The aim of this introduction, therefore, is to provide some preparation for the main body of the book.

Modern Society and Political Economy

The following ► Sect. 1.2 briefly considers the questions: What era corresponds to the modern economy investigated by political economy? What has been the trajectory up to now of political economy? What is demanded of political economy today?

Labour and Production

► Section 1.3 examines fundamental issues regarding *labour*, which has sustained every society and been the formative element of its various aspects, and the production that is carried out through labour.

Modes of Production and Their Replacement

► Sectoin 1.4 begins by looking at labour as a production cost, which is indispensable when considering the productive power necessary to obtain products from nature. The two key concepts here are the *twofold character of labour* and the *distinction between labour and labour-power*. Based upon this, ► Sect. 1.4.2 provides an overview of how social reproduction is carried out for society to continue to exist, and what results from the development of productive power within social reproduction. In ► Sect. 1.4.3, the focus shifts to the relations of production, which are the social relations that people enter into within production. We will look at how the respective laws of social reproduction operate within the different historical relations of production that humanity has experienced up to now or will likely experience in the future. Finally, ► Sect. 1.4.3 touches on how the experience of human history up to now (that developed through the process of a new society replacing the former one) is a law-like process whose starting point is the changes within the economy. Today's capitalist society, which is the object of political economy, cannot escape this general law of social development either.

Fundamental Nature of Political Economy

In ▶ Sect. 1.5.1, the object of political economy is summarised along with its unique characteristics and tasks. This is followed in ▶ Sect. 1.5.2 with a brief explanation of the meaning of political economy as a science and the procedure of its investigation and presentation.

1.2 Modern Society and Political Economy

The Specific Character of Modern Society Consists in Its Social Form «Capitalism»

People expect an economic investigation to suggest solutions to problems related to the *modern era*. But when did the period known as the «modern era» actually begin? We know that imperialism appeared toward the end of the nineteenth century, that World War Two came to an end in 1945, and that the system of so-called «actually-existing socialism» began to collapse in 1989, thereby dissolving the Cold War system. But what about the beginning of the modern era?

In the field of history, the term «modern» refers to what gave birth to the form of society we inhabit today, so there is no need to reset the starting point of modern history from a new point along with the passage of time. Even if new, groundbreaking events occur, as long as they do not alter the fundamental form of society, such events remain within the framework of «modern» society.

In short, the historically specific form of society known as **capitalism** constitutes the forms and characteristics of modern society. Because modern society is a **capitalist society**, the infinite number of new incidents occurring every day are determined by this society's fundamental nature and remain within its framework.

Over time new problems continually appear that require clarification, but the most fundamental problems of the modern era—the question of what capitalism is, what sort of social form it is, and the nature of its movement—have not changed at all. Moreover, far from disappearing with the collapse of «actually existing socialism», these fundamental problems now appear in an even more acute form. Anyone seeking to trace back to its source any one of the infinite number of difficulties facing humanity today will necessarily confront the social system of capitalism, because it is the most developed form of society today and we find ourselves confronting a system of global capitalism.

1

Political Economy Must Clarify the Characteristics of the Capitalist Economy

In order to understand what capitalism is and the nature of its movement, we must grasp various aspects as a totality, including the productive powers of society, industrial structure, industrial location, economic organisation, political structure, legal systems, and social consciousness. In discussing these issues, however, we need to focus above all on the economic mechanism of society. This approach is perfectly natural since what qualitatively determines capitalism is the distinctive nature of its economic structure. So **political economy** must explain what capitalism is and how it moves. Upon this basis, it must then analyse the phenomena and forms in which capitalist society manifests itself today and address the new problems that confront us. In this sense, political economy in the modern era is necessarily the political economy of the distinctive society known as capitalism.

Two Currents in the Study of the Economy: Political Economy and Economics

Two main currents exist within the study of the economy, *Marxian political economy* and *modern economics*, but these two currents are in fact sub-currents of the more comprehensive tendencies of *political economy* and *economics*.

Political economy includes the primary current of *Classical political economy* as well as the subsequent tendencies, most notably *Marxian political economy*. Based on a labour theory of value, political economy grasps modern society as a single, complexly intertwined totality composed of historically formed elements that include the economy, politics, law, morality, and social consciousness. Political economy seeks to elucidate the economic structure that constitutes the base of society in close relation to the other social aspects.

Economics includes the various tendencies of modern economics, beginning around the 1870s with the emergence of the *marginal utility school* that inherited one aspect of Classical political economy. Economics also includes the *neo-classical school*, *Keynesianism*, *neo-classical synthesis*, *neo-conservative (neo-liberal) economics*, and other sub-currents. Economics rejects the labour theory of value and instead «purely» analyses the economic aspects of modern society, setting aside other social aspects and the issue of historical particularity. Economics insists that its own scientific aspect involves grasping, as accurately as possible, quantitative laws and causal relations.

Formation and Demise of Classical Political Economy and the Emergence of Marx's Critique of Political Economy in *Capital*

Initially, political economy was a technique for governments to administer the national economy, which is to say, a field of study to clarify government policy. In the process whereby capitalist society was established, however, a great shift came about in the outlook of political economy. *François Quesnay* (1694–1774) and *Adam Smith* (1723–1790) advocated a laissez-faire approach based on the view that governments should not intervene in the economic process since the capitalist economy is equipped with a mechanism of expansion that naturally develops national wealth. According to this view, the task of political economy was to clarify that natural mechanism, and the outcome of this approach was **Classical political economy**.

The key characteristic of Adam Smith's doctrine is that it was based on a **labour theory of value**. *David Ricardo* (1772–1823), who then brought Classical political economy to its completed form, viewed the opposition of class interests within capitalist society as a natural social phenomenon and emphasised the positive aspects of this society.

In the 1830s, various contradictions of capitalist society came into clear view, as emphasised by *Jean Charles Léonard Simonde de Sismondi* (1773–1842). His work brought to a close the era of Classical political economy, which was characterised by the belief that capitalism is the ultimate, perfect form of social production. The effort of *John Stuart Mill* (1806–1873) to harmoniously balance the theories of the Classical school and the demands of the working class was a declaration of the bankruptcy of political economy based on the standpoint of the capitalist class.

In response, some economists defended capitalism and nakedly represented the interest of the capitalist class by investigating the economy in a way that was nothing more than a plausible systematisation of common-sense thought. Political economy of this sort is derogatorily referred to as **vulgar political economy**.

There were also «socialist» views that emerged, such as the position of *Thomas Hodgskin* (1787–1869), who drew on Ricardo's labour theory of value to defend the interests of workers. But such efforts were inadequate from the perspective of scientific analysis.

The **critique of political economy**[1] of *Karl Marx* (1818–1883) salvaged the scientific achievements of Classical political economy and opened the path to a comprehensive analysis of capitalist society. In *Capital*, his chief work, Marx clarified

---

1 For Marx the ***Critique* of political economy** was not only a critique of the theories of preceding economists but also of the system of capitalist economy itself. In 1858, he wrote: «The work I am presently concerned with is a *Critique of Economic Categories* or, if you like, a *critical exposé of the system of the bourgeois economy*. It is at once an exposé and, by the same token, a *critique of the system*» (Marx 1858: Marx 1983, p. 270; Marx's emphasis).

the particularity of the capitalist form of production on the basis of a thoroughly scientific method. He consistently developed a conception of society based on labour and clarified that the analysis of the economic structure is the basis for grasping society as a whole.

Formation, Development, and Crisis of Modern Economics

In the 1870s, an economic doctrine founded upon the **marginal utility theory of value** of *William Stanley Jevons* (1835–1882), *Carl Menger* (1840–1921), and *Marie Esprit Léon Walras* (1834–1910) was advanced, marking the beginning of what came to be known as **modern economics**. The fundamental characteristic of modern economics is its complete rejection of the labour theory of value. That theory is replaced with the notion that economic phenomena are the combined outcome of subjective choices made by abstract individuals (i.e. individuals without individuality), and that free competition between these individuals brings about equilibrium within the economy as a whole. This current of thought, referred to as the **neo-classical school**, focuses on the analysis of various economic quantities. *Alfred Marshall* (1842–1924), whose ideas are a direct extension of this school, described his own study of the economy as **economics**, in an attempt to distinguish it from **political economy**, and this term gradually gained currency within the field of modern economics.

In the twentieth century, the unrealistic nature of equilibrium theory was exposed by reality itself. At that point, *John Maynard Keynes* (1883–1946) came to the fore. He argued that even in cases where there is underemployment, under conditions of insufficient effective demand (i.e. even in a situation where the unemployed exist), equilibrium can be established, with the state being able to break through a recession and achieve full employment by means of policies to create effective demand. Subsequently, it seemed that the phenomena of crisis had been alleviated through governments implementing Keynes' policies, and that the theories of the **Keynesian school** were now the mainstream of modern economics.

However, the equilibrium theory of the neo-classical school regained popularity once with the recovery of capitalist states after World War Two and the relatively stable growth of the economy. The most popular view was **neo-classical synthesis**, advanced by *Paul Anthony Samuelson* (1915–2009). He argued that as long as a government coordinates the total quantity of effective demand via Keynesian policies, equilibrium can be brought about through a laissez-faire approach.

In the late 1960s, however, fiscal policies proved ineffective in overcoming the severe stagflation that confronted the advanced capitalist countries. This struck a severe blow to both the Keynesian school and the theory of neo-classical synthesis. During this period, a grouping of **radical economists** emerged who criticised capitalism itself and advocated a shift to socialism. But the **neo-conservative (neo-liberal) economists** also appeared, who were critical of both Keynes and neo-classical synthesis, including such tendencies as *monetarism*, *rational expectation hypothesis theory*, *supply-side economics*, and *public choice theory*. These tendencies fiercely criticised the «welfare state» and «big government» that utlised Keynes' policies. Conservative governments in various countries adopted these new theories to implement severe deflationary policies, cut welfare benefits, and sharply reduce taxation. But the neo-conservative policies soon collapsed, signifying a decisive setback for the political influence of this tendency as well. This did not mean, however, that there was the prospect that Keynesian policies could resolve economic difficulties. And within this situation, the bankruptcy of neo-conservative economics also became clear. So, today, economics seems to be once again fervently seeking a new paradigm.

Political Economy Is What Elucidates the Modern Era

There are enormous problems throughout the world (such as the North-South divide, environmental destruction on a global scale, national conflicts, accumulated debt, trade friction, disparities in revenue, and so on), and many capitalist countries are suffering from recession and unemployment as well. In fundamentally investigating such problems, we have no choice but to examine the social system known as *capitalism*. Today, once again, capitalism—i.e. our «modern era»—is being reconsidered. The investigation of the economy that clarifies capitalism is precisely *political economy*. It grasps the historical character of capitalist society on the basis of the labour theory of value and seeks the social framework that determines the actions of the various economic subjects. In other words, political economy is the **modern science of economy** that elucidates the modern era.

Here we will begin our systematic explanation of the structure of capitalism, as clarified by political economy, starting with the most fundamental matters before proceeding to other phenomena visible to the eye.

1.3 Labour and Production

1.3.1 Foundation of Political Economy: Conception of Society Based on Labour

Political Economy Is Founded on the Conception of a Society Based on Labour

Political economy **grasps society with labour as the foundation**. It views human society as a process arising from within the natural history that has existed from time immemorial. According to political economy, the foundation of human society at its deepest level is the uniquely human form of metabolism between human beings and nature, involving the acquisition of products via labour. The gist of what it means to grasp the mechanism of society with labour as the foundation will be explained in ► Sect. 1.4, but first ► Sect. 1.3 will look at the inherent nature of labour and production, while also considering the significance of labour for individuals and for society.

1.3.2 The Production of Products Through Labour

Human Individuals Produce Material Wealth Through Labour

The living human **individuals** who make up society—whatever form it may take—are the starting point of our analysis. These individuals live by **consuming** the **material wealth** that they **produce** through **labour** (*see* ◘ Fig. 1.1).

Consumption of Material Wealth as a Means of Consumption (Original Consumption)

The material wealth individuals consume to sustain themselves is referred to as the **means of consumption** (consumption goods). The consumption of material wealth as a means of consumption includes consumption carried out by various individuals within society, i.e. **individual consumption**, and consumption carried out in some manner or another by a large group of individuals, i.e. **social consumption**.

Consumption of Material Wealth as a Means of Production

In addition to **original consumption**, there is consumption of material wealth *within production*. Here material wealth is consumed for the sake of production (**productive consumption**). The material wealth consumed within this sort of production process is referred to as the **means of production** (production goods) (*see* ◘ Fig. 1.2).

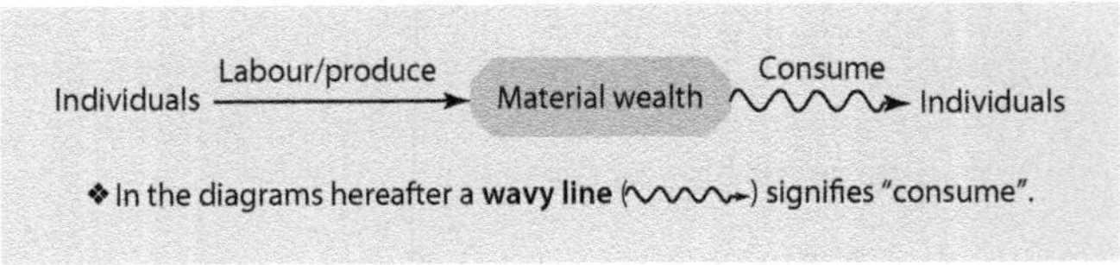

◘ **Fig. 1.1** Labour and production are the fundamental conditions for the existence of individuals and the continuance of society

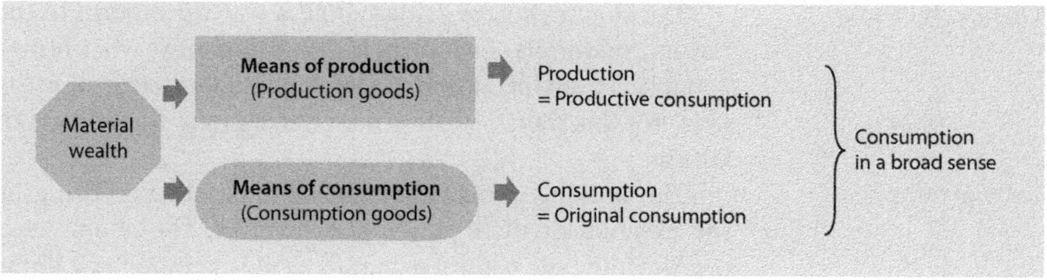

Fig. 1.2 Means of production and means of consumption; original consumption and consumption in a broad sense

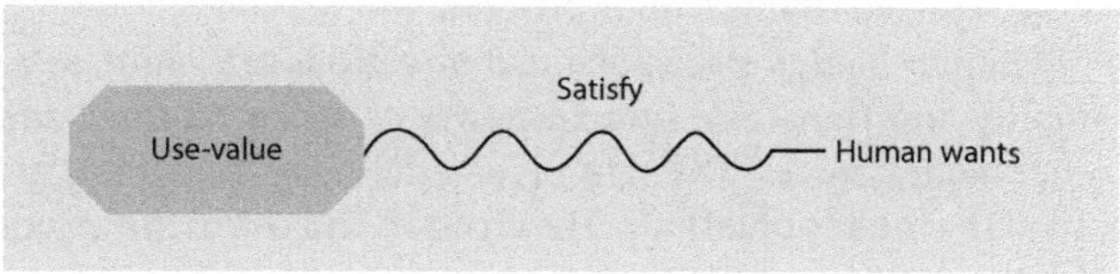

Fig. 1.3 Satisfying wants of individuals through a use-value

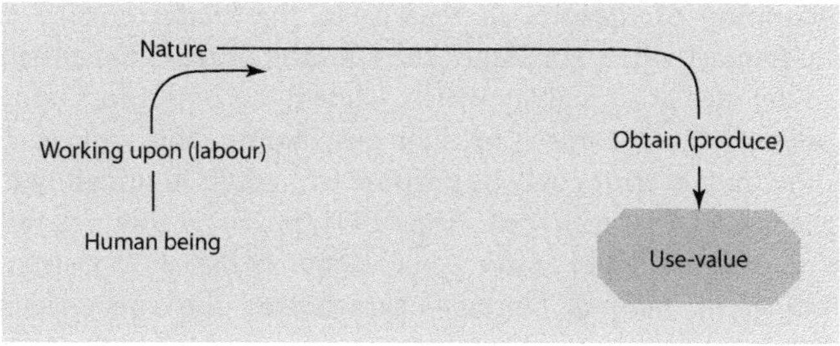

Fig. 1.4 Labour as the working upon nature to obtain a use-value

Use-Value

The quality of material wealth satisfying some human want is called a **use-value**. This is the quality of being able to satisfy a human **want** by means of some natural attribute of material wealth, whether a physical, chemical, physiological, or other attribute. When material wealth has a use-value, the *material wealth itself* is called a use-value (*see* Fig. 1.3).

Labour as the Conscious Control of a Natural Process

Human beings work upon nature and obtain use-values from it that satisfy wants, with the waste product after the consumption of the use-value returning to nature. This is the total process of the **metabolism** unique to human beings. The human activity within this process to **produce** a use-value is **labour** (*see* Fig. 1.4). The unneeded materials, called **waste**, often bring about an unintended transformation of nature (pollution, environmental destruction, etc.), and this human activity that necessarily accompanies productive activity constitutes one important object of political economy.

1

Objects of Labour

The labour process brings about a **transformation** in the **natural materials.** Labour is first and foremost what brings about this **transformation.** Natural materials that become the object of this transformation are referred to as the **objects of labour.**

Labour-power

The working upon nature carried out by human beings is the exertion of their power and involves: (1) labour itself transforming the natural materials as the operation of a physical force, and (2) labour operating a natural force that brings about a transformation of the natural materials. In both cases, the blanket term **labour-power** is used to refer to the human power exerted in this labour process.

Means of Labour

Human beings also make use of various transmitters to amplify and transform human power as a natural force and other natural forces. The natural materials used in this way are called the **means of labour.** The creation and use of the means of labour is something that characterises the labour process particular to human beings.

«The Cunning of Reason»

Georg Wilhelm Friedrich Hegel (1770–1831) spoke of the «**cunning of reason**» in regards to the characteristics of human activities. For Hegel, the cunning of reason «consists in the mediating activity which, while it lets objects act upon one another according to their own nature, and wear each other out, executes only its purpose without itself mingling in the process» (Hegel 1840: Hegel 1991, p. 284). Labour as this sort of «cunning of reason»—i.e. *labour as the conscious control of a natural process*—characterises the metabolism between human beings and nature, and is particular to human beings (*see* ◘ Fig. 1.5).

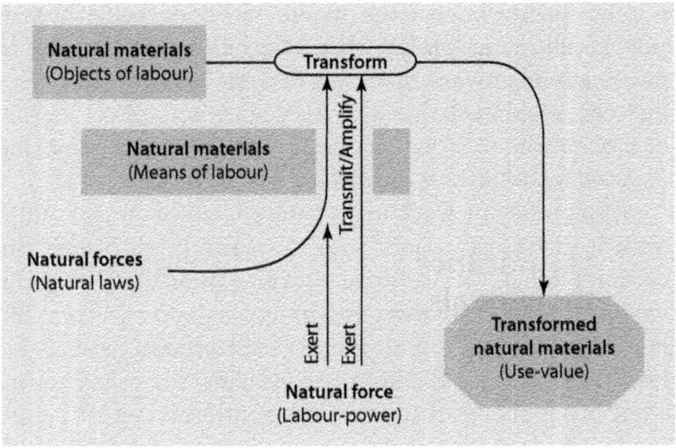

◘ **Fig. 1.5** Labour process as a natural process controlled by human beings

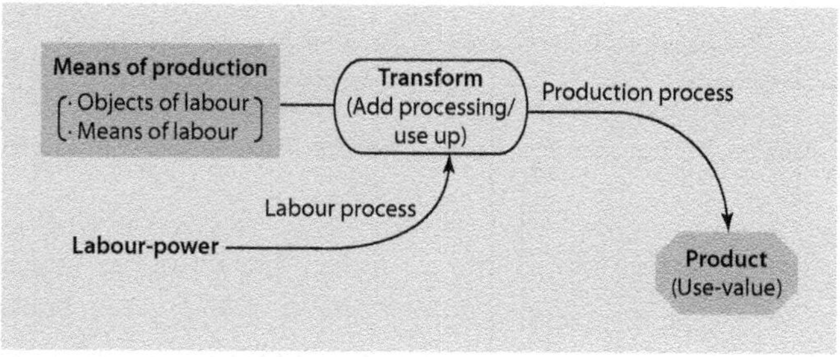

Fig. 1.6 Labour process and production process

Labour Process and Production Process

Labour seen as *a process that proceeds over a certain period of time* is the **labour process.** When the labour process is viewed as *a process that brings about a product* as its outcome it is at the same time the **production process** (*see* Fig. 1.6).

Factors of the Labour Process and Factors of the Production Process

The three *elementary factors of the labour process*, as noted above, are *labour itself*, the *objects of labour*, and the *means of labour*. Within Among the means of production, the objects of labour are processed and the means of labour undergo wear-and-tear, which are both transformations for the sake of producing a product. The objects of labour are divided into materials of nature that exist naturally and have not been processed by human beings (i.e. *natural resources*) and natural materials that have undergone previous processing (i.e. *raw materials*). The means of labour include—in addition to *labour instruments* such as machinery and tools—such things as *containers* and *transport pipelines*, as well as *land, roads, canals*, and *buildings*. If the factors of the labour process are viewed as the *elementary factors of the production process*, labour is the *productive labour* that brings a product into existence, while the objects of labour and the means of labour are the means for the production of products, i.e. *the means of production* (*see* Fig. 1.7).

Simplified Diagram

The production process and its various factors will be consistently depicted throughout the book using the following sort of diagram, so please note its shape and the abbreviations used (*see* Fig. 1.8).

1.3.3 Significance of Labour for Both Individuals and Society

Labour Is the Source of Wealth and the Fundamental Condition for Human Life

Labour, along with *nature*, is the *source of material wealth*, and therefore the *fundamental condition for human life*. In every form of society, labour has been the primary requisite for the survival of human beings and the continued existence of society. And this will necessarily remain the case in the future as well.

Factors of labour process	Factors of production process
(Labour-power ⟹) Labour itself	**Productive labour**
Conditions of labour **· Objects of labour** Raw materials Natural resources **· Means of labour** Skeletal and muscular system of production (tools and machines) Vascular system of production (pipes, tubes, baskets, jars, etc.) Spatial conditions of labour (the earth, workshops, canals, roads, etc.)	**Means of production**

Fig. 1.7 Factors of the labour process and of the production process

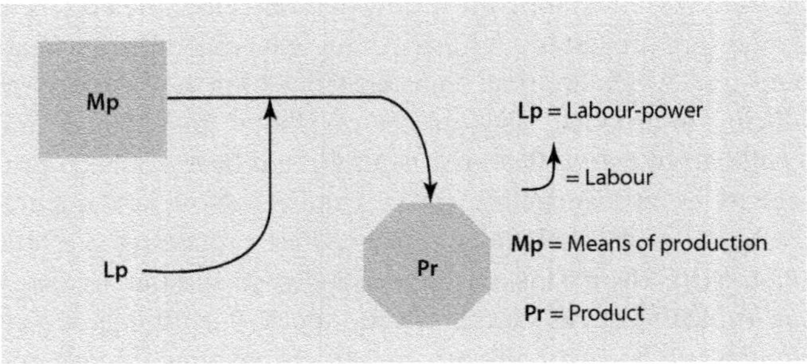

Fig. 1.8 Production process (simplified diagram)

Labour Is the Indispensable Condition for the Development of Individuals as Human Beings

Through their labour people alter the nature that lies outside of themselves, while at the same time *altering their own human nature* through the natural force of their own physical constitution, putting into motion their arms and legs, brainpower, and hands. In other words, they manifest a force latent within themselves, thereby developing themselves as human beings. Without labour, the individual's human development is not possible.

Labour Creates Human Beings Themselves

Labour played a pivotal role within the process that transformed a particular species of primates into *homo sapiens*. The emergence of mankind within natural history would not have been possible without labour. Indeed, it is *labour that created human beings themselves*.

Labour Is the Fundamental Form of Human Praxis and the Primary Existence-form of Human Beings

The essence of human activity is the activity of individuals as subjects who *consciously and intentionally* alter reality as their object, i.e. it consists of **praxis**. Human beings *satisfy their* wants, achieving their aims through praxis. Of all our practical activities, labour is the *most fundamental praxis*, and it even constitutes the *primary existence-form of human beings*. This means that human individuals—both fundamentally and essentially—are **labouring individuals**.[2]

Labour Seems Unattractive in Modern Society

Labour that satisfies wants through the accomplishment of an objective must have originally been *joyful* and *attractive*, so *labour itself* would have been the *object of human desire*. But in modern society labour does not generally appear as such. Far from being a joy, labour is often the source of pain and anguish. A great number of labouring individuals *would like to get along without labour*, if possible. Why is this now the case? Here we have a question that political economy needs to answer.

1.4 Mode of Production and the Change from One Mode to Another

1.4.1 Productive Powers of Society

Productive Powers and Relations of Production; Mode of Production

Productive Powers of Society and the Relations of Production

The capacity of human beings to control nature within production is referred to as **productive powers**. At the bedrock of each historical era has always been the productive powers, at a particular level of development. In contrast, the **relations of production** refer to the social relations of human beings within production. The differences between forms of society are determined by the differences in the relations of production (*see* ◘ Fig. 1.9).

Mode of Production

Actual production is always production carried out with productive powers at a historically specific developmental stage, under relations of production of a historically specific form. The term **mode of production** refers to the particular method of production carried out under productive powers of a historically specific developmental stage and the historically specific relations of production corresponding to these powers. As we shall see in ► Sect. 1.4.3, there is a close relation between the developmental stage of productive powers and the relations of production (*see* ◘ Fig. 1.10).

2 I frequently use the expression «**labouring individual**» in this book to stress the importance of grasping the acting subjects of every society as *individuals*. The term «labourer» literally means a *labouring person in general*, but is now commonly used in to mean «*a person doing unskilled manual work for wages*». So I will use the term «**worker**» when dealing with a *person working for wages*, instead of «labourer».

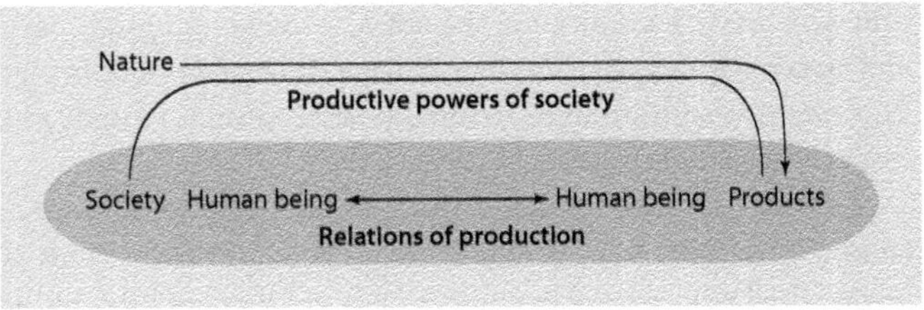

Fig. 1.9 Productive powers of society and relations of production

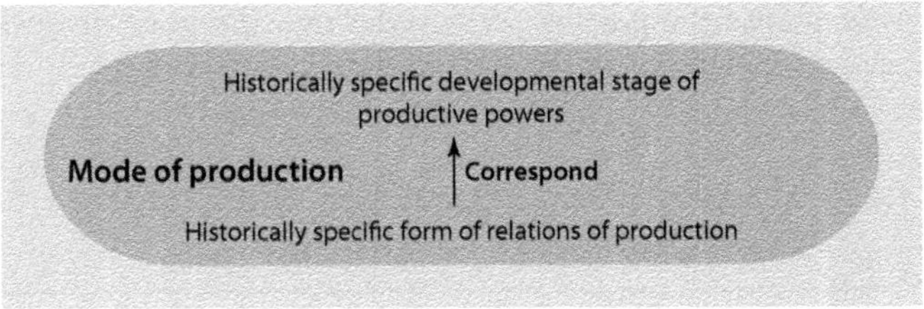

Fig. 1.10 Mode of production as a historically specific social form of production

Let's begin by considering the *productive powers of society and the development of these powers.*

Productive Powers of Society and Labour as Its Motive Force

Productive Power of Labour and the Productive Powers of Society

The productive powers of society are determined by the **productive power of labour**, which is the capacity of labour to produce products. Meanwhile, the capacity of society as a whole to control nature within production is referred to as the **productive powers of society**. The productive powers of society are fundamentally determined by the general level of the productive power of labour within society.

Labour Is the Motive Force of Productive Power

The two factors that actually constitute the productive powers of society are the means of production and productive labour, and they determine the developmental level of productive powers. However, without the operation of labour, the means of production could not carry out any functions and would lose their use-value in the meantime. In contrast, labour not only maintains the productive powers, but develops them. Labour is thus *the* motive force of productive powers, and its level of development determines the level of the productive powers.

Labour as a Production Cost

The Concept of Production Cost Is Indispensable for Grasping the Developmental Level of Productive Power

In considering the developmental level of productive power, one indispensable concept is the cost necessary to produce a product, referred to as **production cost.**

Fundamental Cost of Production Is Labour

Individuals cannot produce products without labour. Thus labour is the *fundamental cost of production* for human beings. Production cost, which is the cost needed for human beings to produce a product, comes down to the quantity of *labour expended in the production of the product.*

Means of Production Constitute a Cost, Provided Their Production Has Required Labour

The means of production are necessary to produce a product, but the means of production only become a cost for human beings to the extent that they themselves require labour. Things to which no labour has been added, such as the natural materials available in nature and the natural environment, do not entail any cost for human beings. The degree to which the means of production represent a cost corresponds to the amount of labour needed for their production. Thus, the cost of a given product is the quantity of labour necessary for its production, which is the sum of the *labour for the current production of the product* and the *past labour necessary for the production of the means of production* employed in the production of the product.

Labour Takes on a New Meaning When Viewed as the Cost of Production

In addition to the meaning of labour in terms of transforming or processing natural materials to obtain a product, mentioned earlier, it comes to have *another meaning* when viewed *from the perspective of being the cost of producing a product.* This is the significance of labour as the cost necessary to produce each product. Regardless of the form of society, when labour is considered as the cost of the product it always involves the *transforming and processing of natural materials* and at the same time *the cost of production for human beings.* Therefore, we must now consider labour from these *two aspects.*

Labour Must Be Treated as Having Two Aspects

Generally, it is not possible to consider production in society without taking into account labour as the production cost of a product. Thus, when *political economy* raises the question of labour—*regardless of the form of historical society in question*—it must always be dealt with as *something with those two aspects.*

Transforming Action and Expenditure of Labour-power

Now let's take a look at the two aspects of labour. Expressed in simple terms for now, the two aspects are the *qualitatively different aspect of the transforming action* and

1

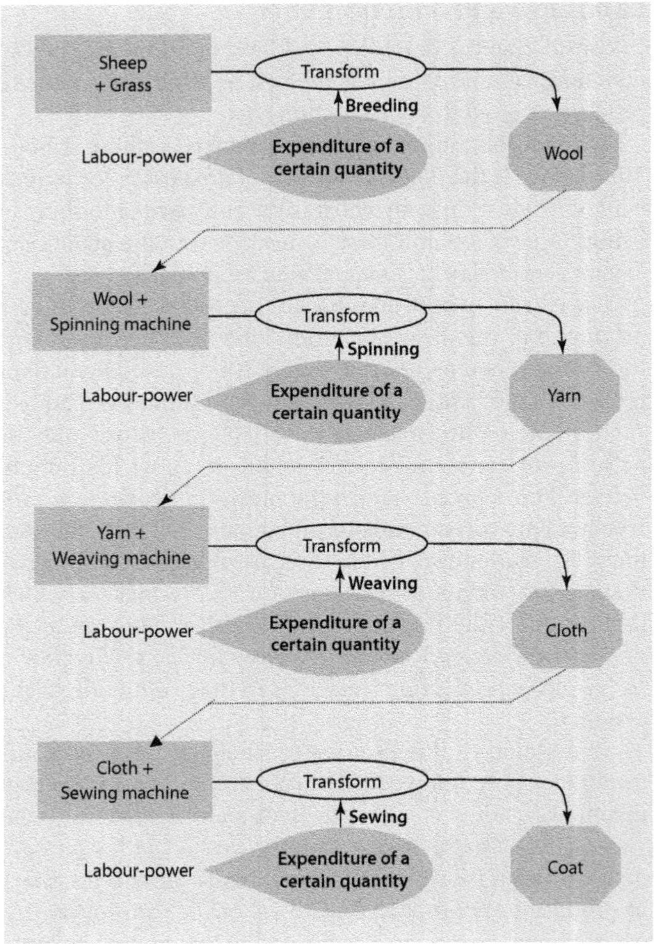

Fig. 1.11 Two aspects of labour: transforming action and expenditure of labour-power

the *quantitatively different aspect of the expenditure of labour-power* (*see* Fig. 1.11).

Concrete
Labour = Useful Labour

Labour as a transforming action is an *activity exercised with a definite purpose, to produce a specific use-value by employing the specific means of production in a specific manner*. People use the word «labour» in that sense when they say, for instance, «That person's labour is different than my labour»; «My labour yesterday is different than my labour today»; or «The labour to produce this thing is different from the labour to produce that thing». Labour in this sense refers to labour in a specific concrete form, and is thus called **concrete labour**. And since this is labour that produces some

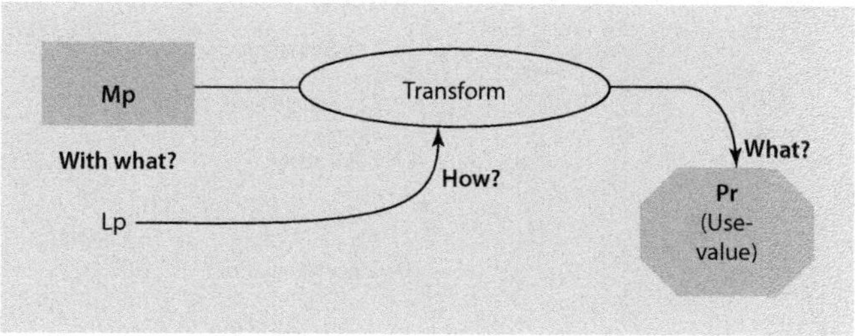

Fig. 1.12 Concrete labour = useful labour

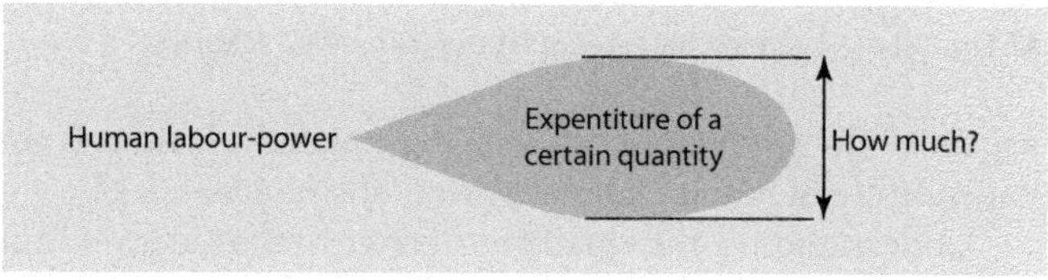

Fig. 1.13 Abstract labour = human-labour

sort of useful thing, it is also referred to as **useful labour** (*see* Fig. 1.12).

Abstract Labour = Human-labour

Labour as the expenditure of labour-power is an *activity viewed as the expenditure or exertion of the power of human beings*. People use the word «labour» in this sense when they say: «He laboured a lot but I did not labour that much» or «It requires a lot of labour to produce this thing but only a little is necessary to produce that thing». Labour in this sense is labour abstracted from the various concrete forms that actual labour takes, as the common quality of being an expenditure of labour-power. It is thus called **abstract labour**.[3] And since this common quality is the expenditure of human labour-power, it is also referred to as **human-labour**. Abstract labour can be measured in a quantity of continuous time. In this case, units of time (e.g., hour, minute, etc.) are the measurement unit (*see* Fig. 1.13). When we speak of the «labour of human beings» or «human labour», this generally indicates the labour carried out by human beings that has the dual aspect of being concrete labour and abstract labour, whereas *adding the hyphen*, to speak of «human-labour», indicates only a single

3 **Abstraction** *here* refers to *extracting* a specific aspect or aspects *within one's thought*, from the many aspects of a *real thing*, while setting aside other aspects. Abstraction is a decisively important means of thought within human cognition, particularly scientific cognition.

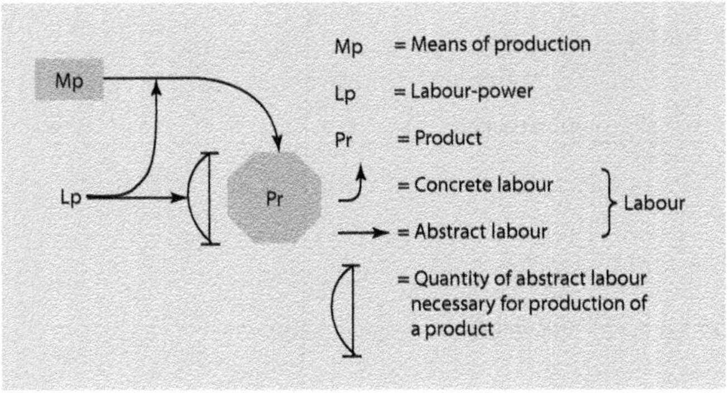

Fig. 1.14 Twofold character of labour (simplified diagram)

aspect of the labour of human beings; namely, labour as the expenditure of human labour-power (abstract labour).[4]

Twofold Character of Labour as the Pivot of Political Economy

Understanding the duality of labour, referred to as the **twofold character of labour**,[5] is the *pivot of political economy*. Throughout this book, the twofold character of labour will be indicated using the diagram above (*see* Fig. 1.14). As it will appear very frequently, it is useful to memorise its meaning and the symbols used.

Labour and Labour-power

In the diagram above, a distinction is made between labour and labour-power. We need to consider how the two differ as well as the relation between them.

The information in Table 1.1 is taken from the *Survey on Labour-power* published annually by the Statistics Bureau of the Japanese Government. Here the labour-power population is divided into the population that is labouring (the employed) and the population that is not labouring (the unemployed).

4 «**Human labour**» in the sense of the «labour of human beings» is a translation of Marx's German term *die menschliche Arbeit* (definite article «die» attached), whereas «**human-labour**» is a translation of his term *menschliche Arbeit* (no article attached), and the distinction between the two is clear.

5 There is a persistent and widespread misconception that the «**twofold character of labour**» is a concept peculiar to commodity production, even though in every society, where wealth must be produced through labour, that labour needs to be considered from the two aspects of being a transforming action and an expenditure of human labour. Those who hold this misconception—when dealing with the decrease in the quantity of labour necessary to produce a product that accompanies the development of productive power of labour and the distinction between requisite labour and surplus labour discussed in ▶ Sect. 1.4.2—do not perceive that this is the expenditure of human labour regardless of differences in the concrete transforming act of labour. What could this be called if not «abstract labour»?

Table 1.1 Labour-power population and non-labour-power population

Overall population of Japan	110.78 million	
Non-Labour-Power Population	44.23 million	Not in possession of labour-power
Labour-Power Population	66.48 million	In possession of labour-power
Employed	64.40 million	Labouring
Fully Unemployed	2.08 million	Not labouring

Statistics for the population 15 years of age or older in 2016 (Statistics Bureau Japan 2017)

From the statistics in the table, we can see that the population that possesses labour-power, or *labour-power population*, includes those who are not labouring (the unemployed). In other words, a distinction is made between *possessing labour-power* and actually *labouring*. **Labour-power** refers to the entirety of those physical and mental capabilities existing in a living human body (consisting of sensory, cerebral, locomotive, and other organs), which are put into operation to produce a use-value. *In terms of its relation to labour-power*, **labour** is the human activity of exerting, fluidising, and expending labour-power. The difference between labour-power and labour is the same as any difference between a force and its actual exertion, such as the difference between an engine's horsepower and its actual operation, the explosive power of a nuclear bomb (expressed in megatons) and its actual explosion, or linguistic ability and the use of a language (*see* ◘ Fig. 1.15).

Abstract Labour as the Production Cost of a Product

Labour as a production cost is the abstract labour needed to produce a product. Labour as the production cost of any product is the labour of the same quality that is quantitatively comparable and can also be calculated. Such labour is precisely abstract labour (*see* ◘ Fig. 1.16).

Past Labour and New Labour as the Production Cost

The means of production consumed in the production of a product only signify the product's production cost when they are the product of a production process carried out prior to the current production, and when a certain quantity of labour was necessary to produce them.

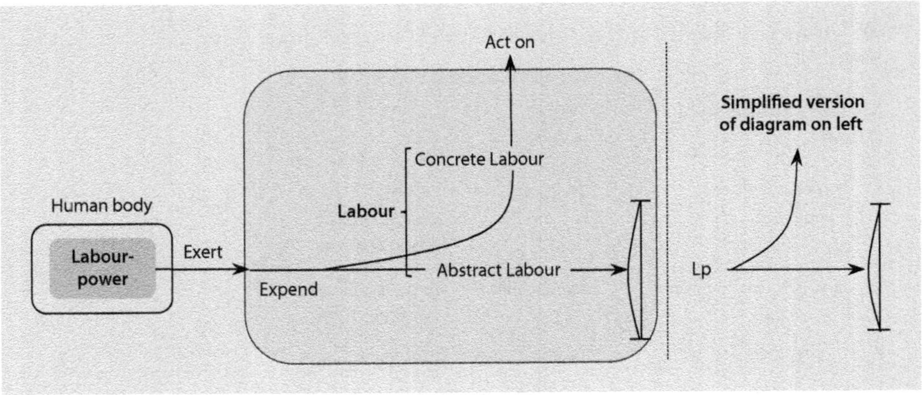

Fig. 1.15 Labour-power and labour as its exertion and expenditure

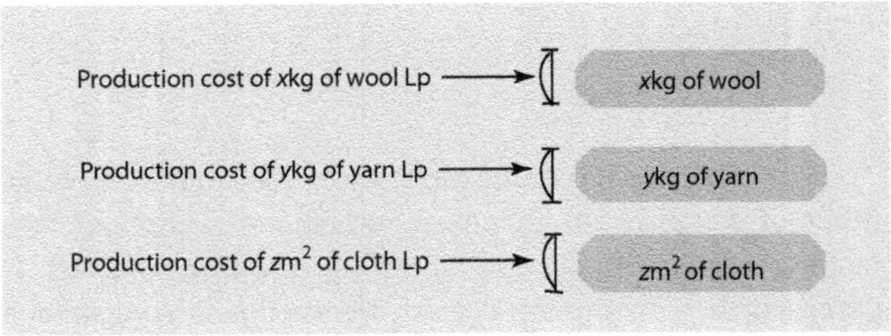

Fig. 1.16 Labour as the production cost = quantity of abstract labour

Labour as the production cost of a product is therefore the amount of **new labour** needed for the production of the product, plus the **old labour** needed for the production of the means of production consumed in its production. New labour is also called **current labour** or **living labour**, while past labour can also be referred to as **past labour** or **dead labour** (*see* Fig. 1.17).

If we add new labour and past labour to the simplified figure of labour as the production cost already presented, we arrive at the following simplified diagram (*see* Fig. 1.18).

Productive Power of Labour

The Productive Power of Labour Is the Productive Power of Concrete Labour

The quantity of products can be different even if the quantity of labour (abstract labour) that is necessary to produce them is the same. Differences in the quantity of products arise from differences in the degree of effectiveness of labour. These are differences in the concrete forms when labour is expended, the differences in the rates at which useful things are generated: in other words, differences in concrete labour. The capacity of labour to produce products, known as the **productive power of labour**, is in fact the productive power of *concrete labour* (*see* Fig. 1.19).

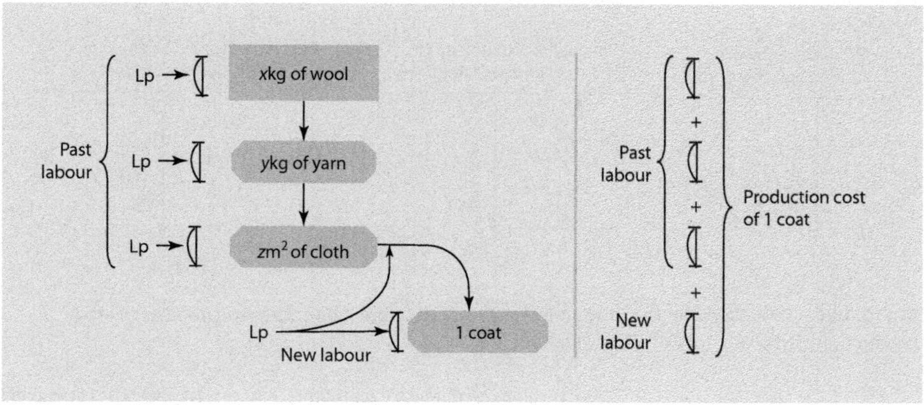

Fig. 1.17 Production cost of a product = new labour + past labour

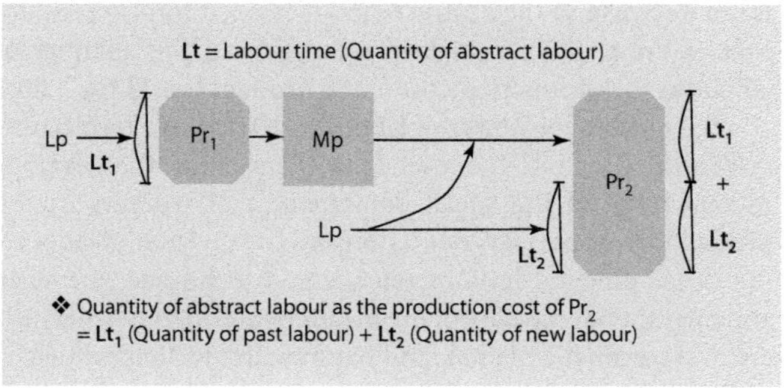

Fig. 1.18 Quantity of abstract labour as the production cost (simplified diagram)

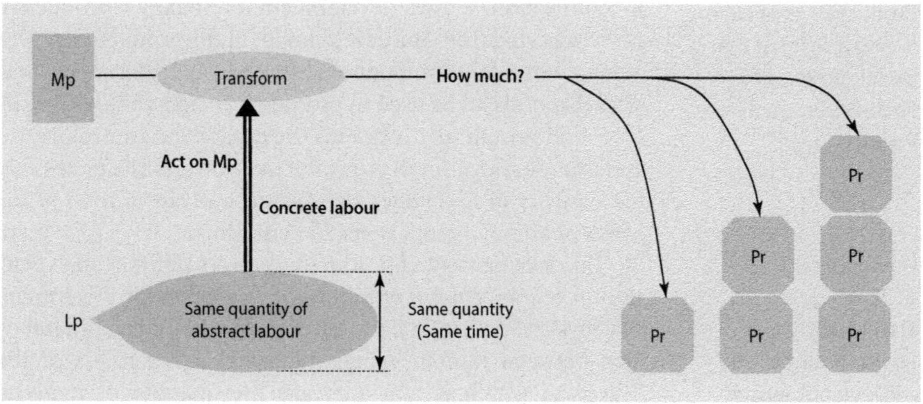

Fig. 1.19 Quantity of products can differ despite the same quantity of abstract labour

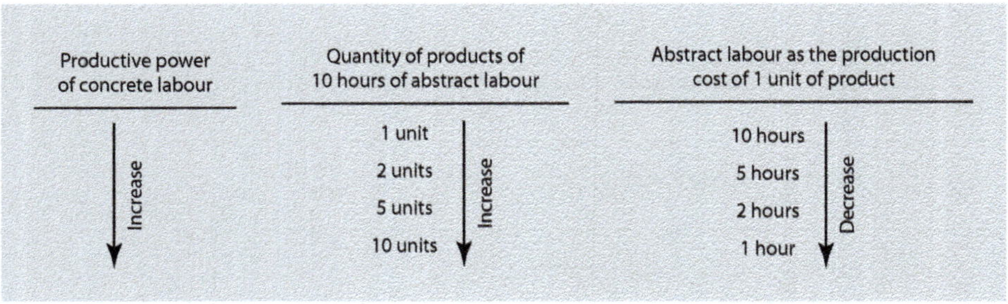

Fig. 1.20 An increase in the productive power of concrete labour causes a decrease in the production cost = quantity of abstract labour

An increase in the productive power of labour (concrete labour), brings about an increase in the quantity of products that can be produced with the same quantity of labour (abstract labour); but if viewed in terms of each product unit, it is a decrease in the abstract labour needed for the production of the product, which is a decrease in the quantity of labour as the production cost of the product (*see* Fig. 1.20).

Circumstances That Determine the Productive Power of Labour

The productive power of labour is determined by circumstances that include the level of workers' skills, the developmental stage of the social combination of workers in the production process (co-operation and the division of labour), the developmental level of science and technique, the scale and operational capacity of the means of production (machinery and automatic plants), and natural circumstances such as soil fertility and climate.

What Can and Cannot be Called a «Development of Productive Power»

Product Diversification Is Also a Form of the Development of Society's Productive Powers

In connection to the development of society's productive powers arising from the development of the productive power of labour, the same amount of abstract labour that society has at its disposal can be used to produce a *greater variety of products*. And this, in turn, expands the capacity to control nature and thus develops society's productive powers. The *increase in the varieties of use-values* also means a *diversification of the wants* of human beings that can be satisfied.

Development of Techniques That Destroy the Environment Is Not a «Development of Productive Powers»

The development of productive powers signifies an expansion in *human control of nature*, so if a developed technique destroys the environment and impedes the normal metabolism between human beings and nature (regardless of the degree to which it may increase the quantity of material wealth), it cannot be considered a «development of productive powers». In this sense, it is conceptually mistaken to say that, «productive power has been developed too far, to the point of destroying the environment». A society that is *unable*

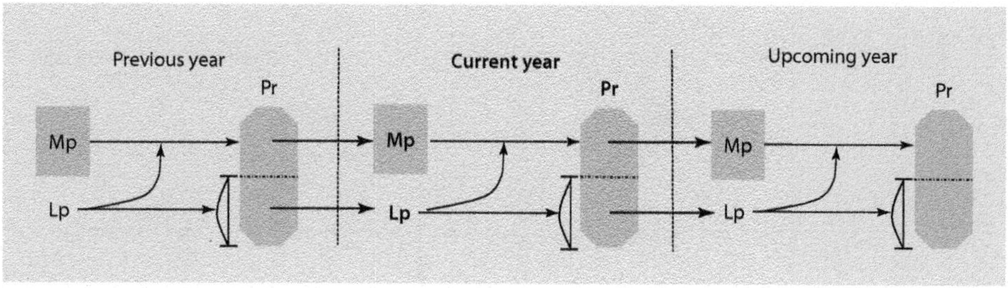

■ **Fig. 1.21** Reproduction of means of production and labour-power through the yearly products

to achieve an ecological harmony with nature is one that has *not yet developed its productive powers* to the point where it has sufficient powers at its disposal to control nature.

1.4.2 General Laws of Social Reproduction and Development of Productive Powers

The Existence of a Society Is Made Possible Through Its Reproduction

Production, regardless of the social form it takes, must always be carried out repeatedly. Just as society cannot cease consumption, it cannot cease production either. Production carried out repeatedly, or **reproduction**, is the means through which society can continue to exist.

Here we will look at the **general laws of social reproduction** that operate in every society, based on the premise of **simple reproduction**—i.e. reproduction at an unchanged scale of production. For the time being we will assume that a single production process encompasses society's production over the course of a year, and that the productive powers of labour do not undergo any change.

Means of Production and Labour-powers Must Be Reproduced

First of all, the yearly products must include the means of production and labour-powers needed for the following year's production (*see* ■ Fig. 1.21).[6]

Products Must Include the Means of Production and Means of Consumption

In addition to the means of production, the annual product must include the means of consumption for the reproduction of labour-powers so that the labour-powers can be readied for the following year's production (*see* ■ Fig. 1.22).

Total Product = Reappearing Means of Production + New Product

The total product of society is made up of various products (use-values), but in order for the same production to be repeated on the same scale, the **total product** of the current year must include the means of production consumed during the course of the year, which is to say, those means of production must reappear in the yearly products. These **reappearing**

6 Here we assume that the yearly products, not only the means of consumption but also the means of production, are used up in the following year.

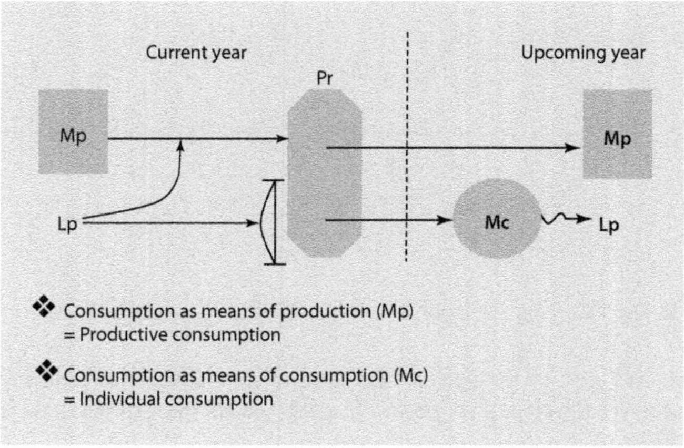

Fig. 1.22 Reproduction of means of production and means of consumption for the reproduction of labour-power

means of production are the things produced with past labour that reappear within the products of the current year.

The production cost of the total product, as we have seen, is the sum of the new labour of the current year and the past labour that was necessary for the means of production consumed. Within the total product of the current year, the quantity of labour necessary to reproduce the reappearing means of production is the amount of past labour necessary for the production of the consumed means of production, so if we deduct the reappearing means of production from the total product, the production cost of the remaining products is the new labour for the current year. In other words, the current year's new labour produces these products, which can be called the **new products** of the current year. The total product minus the reappearing means of production thus equals the new product (*see* Fig. 1.23).[7]

7 Here, for the sake of simplification, we assume the *productive power of labour does not change*. But what would be the case if the productive power of the current year rose compared to the previous year? If the quantity of total labour for the current year (lt_2) is the same as that of the previous year, there would naturally be an increase in the quantity of the new product produced through the same quantity of labour. However, the new labour (lt_2) that is a production cost within the total product of the current year, which has become materially greater than the previous year, is the same as the previous year (i.e. the quantity of total annual labour is the same as the previous year). If the entirety of the new product of the current year is consumed during the current year, the quantity of products consumed will be greater than in the previous year, so that a surplus product that

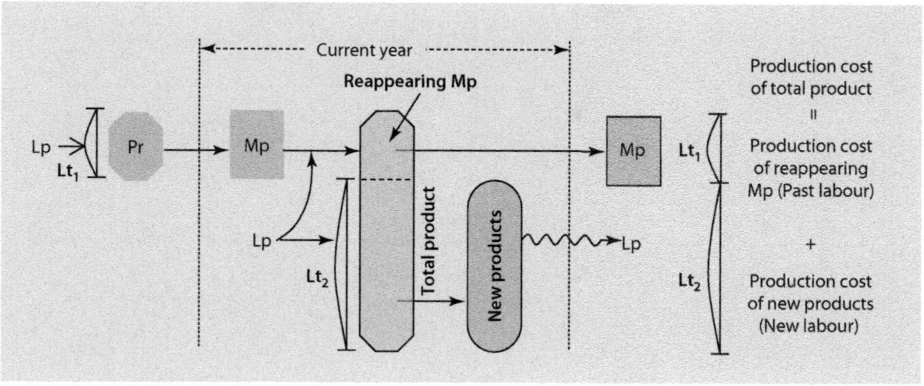

Fig. 1.23 Total product consists of the reappearing means of production and the new products

Requisite Means of Livelihood and Requisite Labour

The new products must include the products for the reproduction of labour-powers. The term **requisite means of livelihood**[8] refers to products that are indispensable to the reproduction of labour-powers (including the raising of a family by the possessor of labour-power), and is also called the **requisite product** or **labour fund**[9]; while the abstract labour necessary to produce the requisite means of livelihood is called

---

is not consumed will arise if the quantity of products consumed are the same as in the previous year. This means that there is an emergence or increase of surplus labour, as we will soon discuss. Also, with the development of productive power, there was a decrease compared to the previous year in the quantity of labour necessary for the production of the various means of production that reappear in the same material form, but *since the means of production consumed in the current year are produced with the labour-power of the previous year, the production cost of the reappearing means of production is the quantity of labour necessary to produce them in the previous year.* When the reappearing means of production enter into the production for the following year, however, their production cost is the quantity of labour necessary to produce them under the productive power of the current year, so it will decrease compared to the production cost for them calculated for the current year.

8 Usually the terms «*necessary* means of livelihood» (*necessary* product) or «*necessary* labour» (*necessary* labour-time) are used instead of «*requisite* means of livelihood» (requisite product) and «*requisite* labour» (*requisite* labour-time), but in the body of this book the term «*necessary* labour-time» is used in the sense of the «labour-time necessary to produce *a commodity*», so to avoid confusion I have adopted this new terminology.

9 The term «**fund**» that will appear repeatedly refers to goods or money of a certain magnitude that must carry out a certain use or be prepared. Also, goods or money secured for some aim are called a «fund».

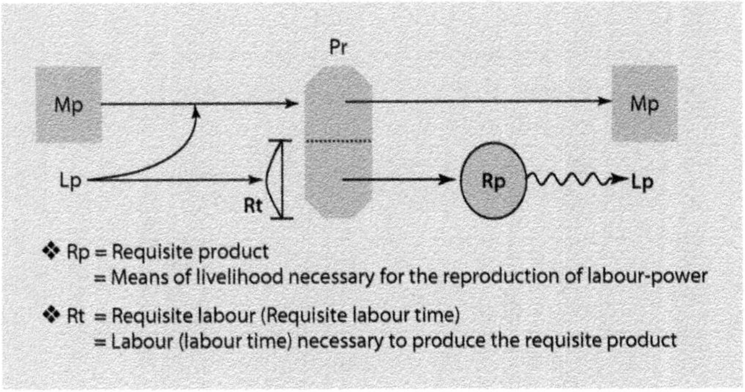

Fig. 1.24 Requisite means of livelihood and requisite labour

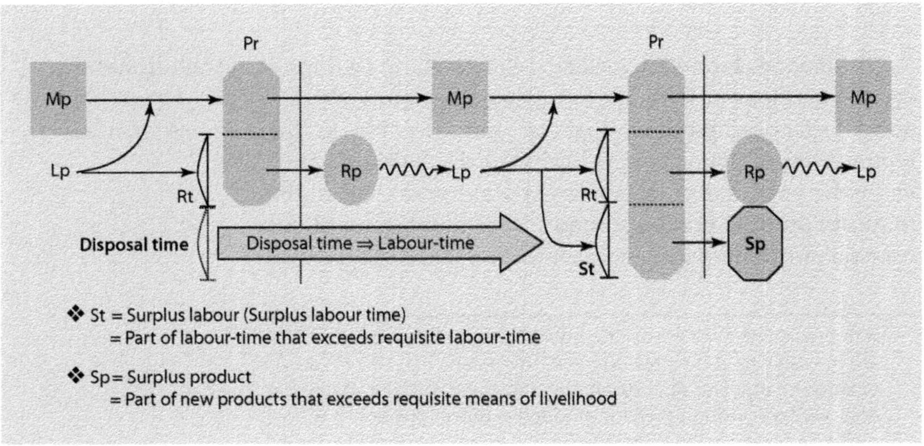

Fig. 1.25 Surplus labour and surplus product

requisite labour (**requisite labour-time**) (*see* Fig. 1.24). (For the moment, past labour as the production cost of the reappearing means of production will be omitted from the diagrams that follow.)

Surplus Labour and Surplus Product

If the labouring individuals, in addition to requisite labour-time, also have time they can freely dispose of (**disposal time**), and carry out labour during this time as well, products are produced that exceeds the requisite means of livelihood. The part of labour-time that exceeds requisite labour-time is called **surplus labour** (or **surplus labour-time**). The products produced during this surplus labour-time—i.e. the excess part of the new products that exceeds the requisite means of livelihood—are called the **surplus product** (*see* Fig. 1.25).[10]

10 In order for the individuals convert their freely disposal time to labouring time some «historical circumstances» were necessary. Marx

Surplus Products Must Be Produced in Any Society

The word «surplus» in the term «surplus product» signifies a surplus that exceeds the means of livelihood, not something superfluous that one can do without. Leaving the primitive age aside, surplus products must be produced to some extent in order for society to continue to exist.

1. First of all, regardless of the form of society, surplus products in excess of the requisite means of livelihood must exist to fulfill the following uses:
    1. Expansion of production (accumulation fund)
    2. Saving for emergencies (reserve fund)
    3. Consumption fund for population other than direct producers
        1. Consumption fund for population involved in unproductive labour
        2. Consumption fund for non–labour-power population not supported by the direct producers
    4. Fund for non–productive consumption carried out socially (fund for construction of public buildings, etc.)
2. Furthermore, in societies where a *non-labouring class* exists, surplus product is exploited from the *labouring class* and consumed by this non-labouring class. Without surplus product, class society is not possible.[11]

writes: «Favourable natural conditions can provide in themselves only the possibility, never the reality of surplus labour, nor, accordingly, the reality of ... a surplus product ... Suppose now that an East Indian bread-cutter ... requires 12 working hours a week for the satisfaction of all his needs. Nature's direct gift to him is plenty of leisure time. Before he can apply this leisure time productively for himself, a *whole series of historical circumstances* is required; before he spends it in surplus labour *for others, compulsion* is necessary» (Marx 1872: Marx 1976, pp. 650–651; my emphasis).

11 Needless to say, different social forms will have markedly different ways—both quantitatively and qualitatively—of distributing products to the requisite means of livelihood and to the surplus product. Particularly in the case of class-divided societies, the requisite means of livelihood are inevitably meager in both quantity and quality compared to the surplus product. However, the content of the requisite means of livelihood is certainly not something fixed, but rather subject to change depending on changes in the power relation between classes. The crux of the matter is that, *in any form of society*, the total product of society is divided into one part that enters into the reproduction of the labouring individuals, and another part that exceeds it. The significance of this point is overlooked by those who think that the distinction between requisite labour and surplus labour only pertains to class-divided society.

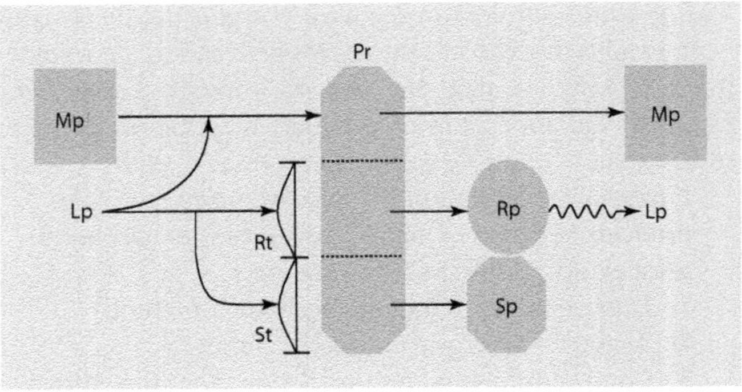

■ **Fig. 1.26** General law of reproduction (simplified diagram)

The above concerns the **general laws of social reproduction** that operate in any society, regardless of its form, as can be diagrammed in simplified form as above (*see* ■ Fig. 1.26).

Increase of Surplus Labour Through Development of Productive Power

Without surplus products, neither an expansion of production nor an increase in population is possible. An increase in surplus products is thus essential to the development of society. The quantitative expansion of the surplus products can be carried out by either an expansion in production or an increase in the labour-power population, but the most decisive factor is an *augmentation of surplus products through the development of the productive power of labour*. Unless there is a change in the quantity and extent of the requisite means of livelihood, a development of the productive power of labour will decrease the labour-time needed to produce the requisite means of livelihood (requisite labour-time). If the total labour-time is unchanged, a decrease in the requisite labour will increase surplus products (*see* ■ Fig. 1.27).

A Decisive Condition for Expansion of Freedom for Individuals Is Shortening of the Working Day Through the Development of Productive Power

An increase in the **disposal time** (time that can be freely disposed of) is crucial to satisfying expanding and diversifying wants. For the *overall development and blossoming of the individuality and abilities of individuals*, therefore, it is indispensable that there be a *high development of productive powers* and a *broad shortening of the working day* (daily labour-time).

Need for the Social Division of Labour and the Distribution of the Total Social Product

Regardless of the form of society, labouring individuals live by obtaining products to satisfy their wants from among the total social product produced through their overall labour. For this to happen, the total labour of society must take the form of various kinds of *concrete labour* to produce various products required by society. So the total social labour, *as abstract labour*, must be **distributed** in different quantities to the various departments of *concrete labour* that produce different use-values. This constitutes the **division of labour**. Since the division of labour is

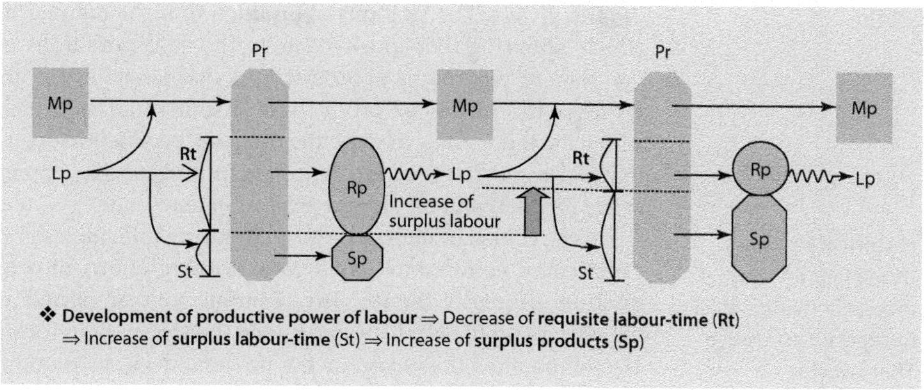

Fig. 1.27 Increase of surplus labour through development of the productive power of labour

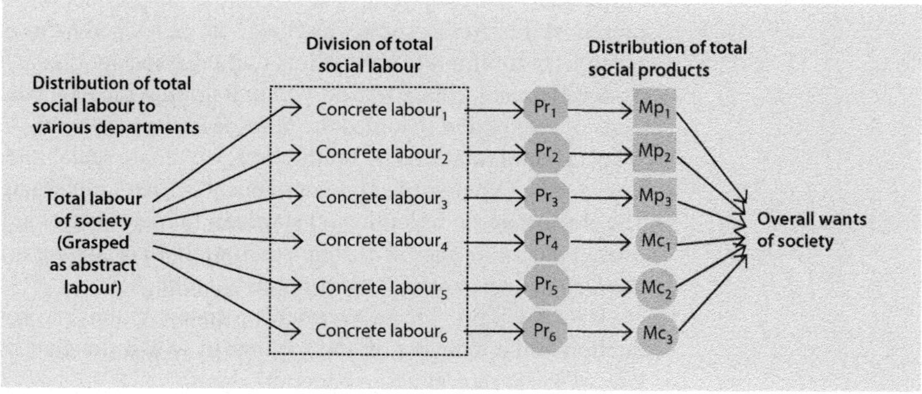

Fig. 1.28 Division of total social labour and distribution of total social products

a dividing up of labour within society as a whole—as opposed to a division or dividing up of labour within a given workshop or factory—it is referred to as the **social division of labour.**

Furthermore, the various kinds of products produced must, in some way or another, be **distributed** to the labouring individuals and other members of the society (*see* Fig. 1.28).

1.4.3 Relations of Production

Relations of Production Determine the Social Form of Human Life

In the social production of life, human beings enter definite relations that correspond to a given stage in the development of productive powers of society. These are the **relations of production**, which form the basis of all social relations between human individuals.

Relations of Production: Relations Between Human Beings Within the Social Production of Life

1

The pivot of the relations of production is the manner in which labouring individuals relate to the vital conditions of their labour (i.e. means of production), and how they labour vis-à-vis the means of production. The manner in which labouring individuals relate to the means of production determines the way that the individuals constituting society *appropriate products and the surplus product in particular*.

Historical Forms of the Relations of Production and Social Reproduction Under These Forms

In the course of human history, labouring individuals first experienced community-based **communal relations of production**: primarily the primitive community that existed as the starting point of human society and then the various forms of communities that arose in the process of its dissolution. This was followed by the appearance of **relations of commodity production,** wherein people are connected through money rather than the community. The relations of production in present-day capitalist society are the most developed form of relations of commodity production. Capitalist society, through its development, comes to bear within its womb the new relations of production that must be born. Here I am referring to **associational relations of production**, which are social relations formed voluntarily and consciously by free individuals. The three major developmental stages in human history are, thus, *communal relations of production*, *relations of commodity production*, and *associational relations of production*.

Here I will provide an overview of these relations of production while focusing on the manner in which the general laws of social reproduction penetrate them.

Main Relations of Production Within History and Social Reproduction Therein

(A) Community-based Relations of Personal Dependence

The first relations of production experienced by humanity were the *relations of production based upon the primitive community and the various community forms that arose from the process of its dissolution*. Here labouring individuals belong to some sort of community and are connected as community members through **relations of personal dependence**, with the conditions of labour (i.e. the means of production) belonging in common to the community. What characterises the relations of community members within social production is that they are either relations of mutual personal dependence or relations of domination and servitude whereby non-labouring individuals personally dominate the labouring individuals.

(A)-(1) Communal Relations of Production

The fundamental relations of production here involve a spontaneously formed primitive community composed of labouring individuals and the community's ownership of the means of production. These individuals relate to each other as

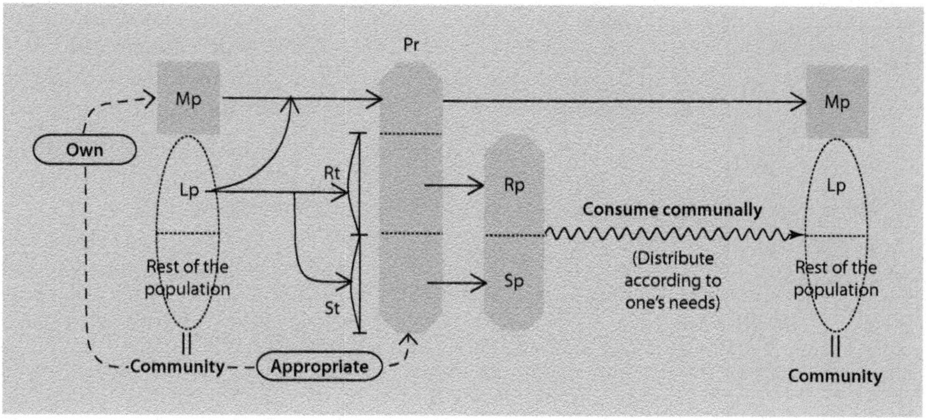

Fig. 1.29 Social reproduction under the primitive community

members of a community that owns the means of production. What connects the labouring individuals is the community, based upon primitive relations of personal interdependence, and the community members are governed by spontaneously generated relations of personal dependence. Submerged within the community, the members do not stand out as individuals. The common labour they carry out is performed directly to satisfy the community's needs, i.e. directly social labour. Therefore, all of the products of labour are distributed among the community members according to their needs (*see* Fig. 1.29).

With the development of productive powers, private ownership emerges among the individuals of the community and develops, and along with this the community is gradually dissolved. *The community forms seen within this dissolution process* (depending on the development level of private ownership) are the **Asiatic form** where private property barely develops at all, the **Greek-Roman Form** where communal and private property exist alongside each other, and the **Germanic form** where communal ownership is only a supplement to private ownership.[12]

(A)-(2) Relations of Personal Domination and Servitude

With the process of the community's dissolution, antagonistic relations between individuals emerge, and **relations of direct domination and servitude** within a hierarchical order

12 The adjectives, «Asiatic», «Greek-Roman», and «German» are used to distinguish these forms from each other according to the region where each form was observed *in its typical shape* within history. But all of the forms existed, to a greater or lesser extent, in regions throughout the world.

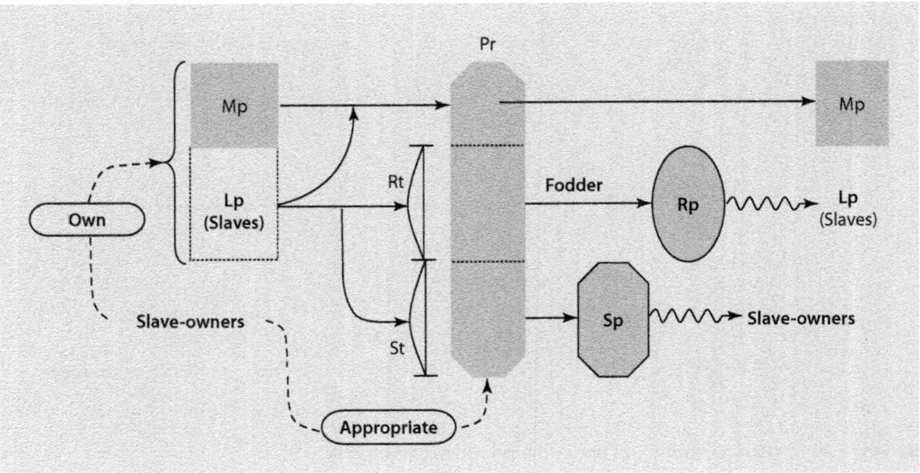

Fig. 1.30 Social reproduction under the ancient slavery system

are established. However, the labouring individuals, even though they are labouring for others, do not yet engage in private labour but rather directly social labour as before.

The main relations of domination and servitude that humanity has experienced up to now are: (a) the Asiatic slavery system established upon the foundation of the Asiatic community, (b) the ancient slavery system based upon the foundation of the Greek-Roman community, and (c) the feudal system established upon the foundation of the Germanic community.

(A)-(2)-(a) Asiatic Slavery System

The Asiatic Slavery System arose upon the foundation of the Asiatic community. The **despot**, who personally represents the community, comprehensively dominates the community and all its members. Individuals relate to the means of production as members of the community, but they are *slaves* personally subordinated to the despot, who dominates the community as a whole and exploits via the community the surplus product from the products of the members' directly social labour.

(A)-(2)-(b) Ancient Slavery System

The Ancient Slavery System arose within the process of the dissolution of the Greek-Roman community. **Slaves**, who labour under the direction and superintendence of the **slave owners'** *villicus*, relate to the means of production as the property of others (slave owners), and are treated as non-human entities no different than livestock. The slave owners appropriate the entire product, foddering the slaves with the part that constitutes the requisite means of livelihood, much like «animal feed» (*see* Fig. 1.30).

(A)-(2)-(c) Feudal System

The feudal system consists of the relations of personal domination and servitude constructed on the foundation of the Germanic community built upon the ruins of the Greek-Roman community. This system can be divided into the two stages: (i) the serfdom system and (ii) the *villein* system.

(A)-(2)-(c)-(i) Serfdom System

In the system of serfdom, the **serfs** (labouring individuals) are personally subordinated to the **lords**, who are the **feudal landowners**. There are two ways in which serfs relate to the land that constitutes the main means of production. On the **peasant holdings**, serfs relate to the land as basically means of production belonging to themselves and appropriate products from this land. On the **seigniorial domain**, meanwhile, serfs relate to the land as something belonging to another person, and the entire product of that land is appropriated by the lord. In the former case, labour is a subjective activity carried out by the serfs themselves to acquire their requisite means of livelihood, whereas in the latter case it is forced labour by means of **extra-economic compulsion** under the direction of supervisors who embody the will of the lord. Surplus labour is exploited in the latter case in the form of **labour rent** (*corvée*) (*see* ◘ Fig. 1.31).

(A)-(2)-(c)-(ii) *Villein* System

With the development of productive power, the serfdom system comes to be reorganised into the *villein* system. In this system, **peasants** (*villein*) relate to the land as basically autonomous owners and appropriate all of the products of the land, with labour being their own subjective activity. However, the lords who personally dominate them use *extra-economic compulsion* to obtain **rent in kind** (product rent), and later **money rent** (*see* ◘ Fig. 1.32).

(B) Reified Relations of Interdependence Among Individuals Mediated by Money

The *capitalist mode of production* fundamentally overturns both the naturally generated communal relations of production and the relations of personal domination and servitude, replacing them with *reified relations* (i.e. relations via *res* or «thing») of interdependence between individuals. At the core of capitalist relations of production is the unique production relation known as the capital/wage-labour relation. This production relation is established on the foundation of **relations of commodity production**, which are **relations of reified interdependence between individuals**, and it is completely concealed by the relations of commodity production.

(B)-(1) Relations of Commodity Production

In the relations of commodity production, labouring individuals relate to the means of production as **mutually autonomous private individuals**, and labour is directly private labour. However, private labour in society forms the total labour of society, and is mutually dependent as spontaneously generated branches of the social division of labour. For directly private labour to become social labour, the products

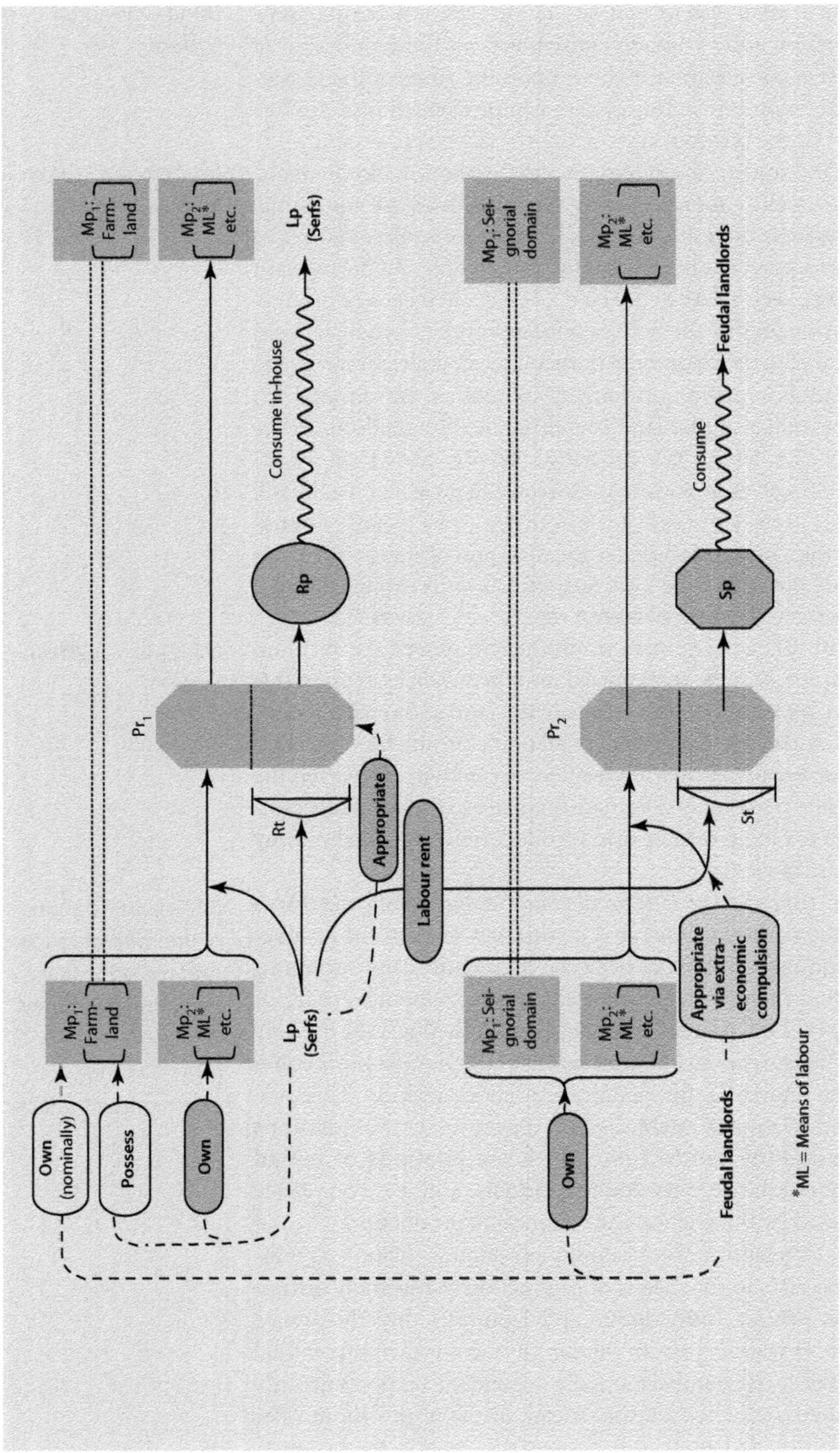

Fig. 1.31 Social reproduction under the serfdom system

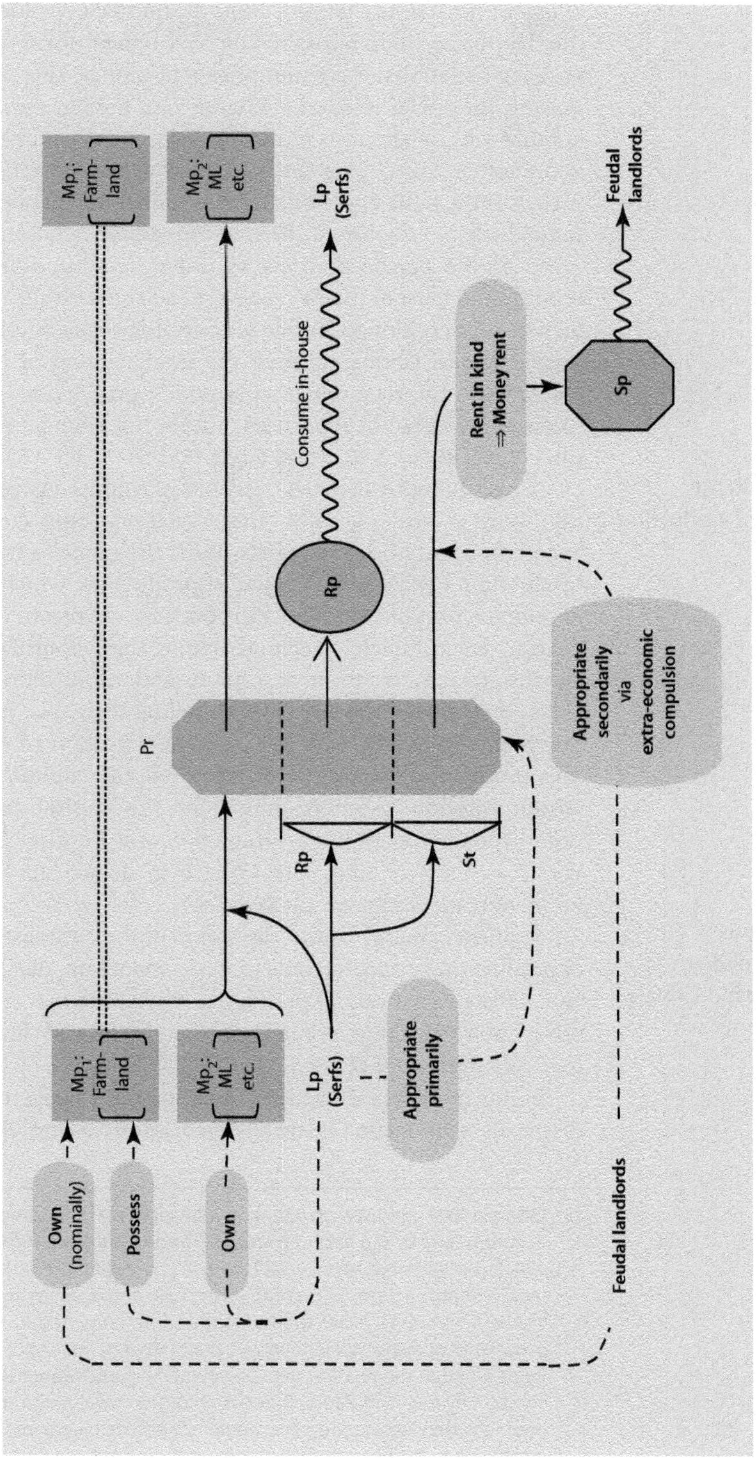

Fig. 1.32 Social reproduction under the *villein* system

of labour must be exchanged. Thus, the mutual dependence of the labouring individuals takes the reified form of the exchange relations of commodities and money, thereby disguising the social relations between one human being and another within labour as a social relation between one thing and another thing. This sort of reified dependence of individuals is the basis upon which the personal independence of individuals is established. Private individuals relate to each other as the personifications of things (commodities and money) and must mutually recognise each other as the private owners of these things. In this manner, the social relations of people within labour generate the legal relation of private ownership (The relations of commodity production will be discussed in detail in ► Sect. 2.4, but for the moment readers can consult ◘ Fig. 2.32 and ◘ Fig. 2.33).[13]

(B)-(2) Capitalist Relations of Production

In pre-capitalist societies, relations of commodity production only existed partially. These relations only come to encompass the entirety of society under the capitalist mode of production. In the case of capitalist production, which is the developed form of commodity production, the means of production are completely separated from the labouring individuals, taking the form of capital, and these individuals become **wageworkers** who live by selling their own labour-power to **capitalists**, who are the personification of capital. This production relation is referred to as the **capital/wage-labour relation** or more simply as the **capital relation** (The capitalist relations of production will be discussed in Part I as a whole, and in ► Chap. 6 in detail, but for the moment readers can consult ◘ Fig. 8.1).

(C) Conscious Personal Relations of Associated Individuals (Association)

Moments emerge within the womb of the capitalist mode of production, as the outcome of its development, that negate and sublate this mode of production itself. The new form of production that these moments indicate is an **association** of free individuals (*see* ◘ Fig. 1.33).

In this mode of production, labouring individuals relate to the means of production as **socially associated free individuals**.

13 Ownership is premised on labour in a society based on some form of community or the **petty producer's mode of production** in which production is carried out by those possessing their own means of production, so that the owners are at the same time workers, whether it is ownership via the community or the ownership of dispersed individuals. But in the relations of commodity production the relation between ownership and labour is completely reversed. At the foundation of the social-relation of people within labour, the legal relation of private ownership is established. This point will be discussed in ► Sect. 2.4.3.

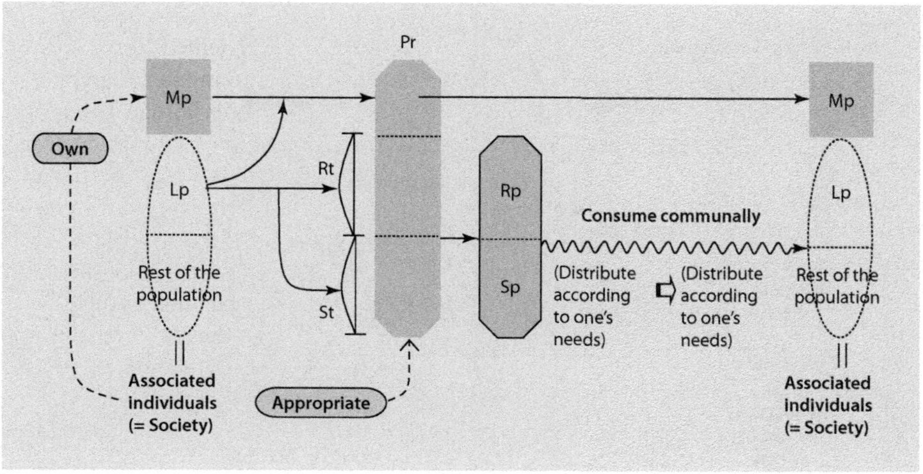

Fig. 1.33 Social reproduction under association

Labour is a process whereby these individuals, holding the means of production in common, consciously expend their own labour-power as social labour-power, so that it is directly social labour. The production process comes under the *conscious and planned control of individuals* as the outcome of freely socialised individuals, achieving a high development of productive powers. At the same time, the reduction in the requisite labour-time brought about by the high development of productive powers leads to a reduced working day, thus expanding the free time for individuals to fully develop their individuality and abilities. (Association will be discussed in ► Sect. 11.2.2).

Formation of Society and Social System

Society Consists of a Foundation (Economic Structure) and a Legal-Political Superstructure

Whatever the form of actual historical society, various relations of production exist that are complexly intertwined, combining the old and the new, the undeveloped and the developed. This totality forms the **economic structure of society** (i.e. the «**economy**»). Upon this economic structure, there arises a **legal and political structure**. In other words, the economic structure is the **foundation** and the legal-political structure is the **superstructure** that is restricted by this foundation. The foundation and the superstructure form a single organic whole called the **formation of society**.

The totality of a certain level of productive powers and a specific social structure based on relations of production corresponding to these powers constitutes a **social system** (or a **social production organism**). This is a certain historical, organic system that is formed and continually reproduced by

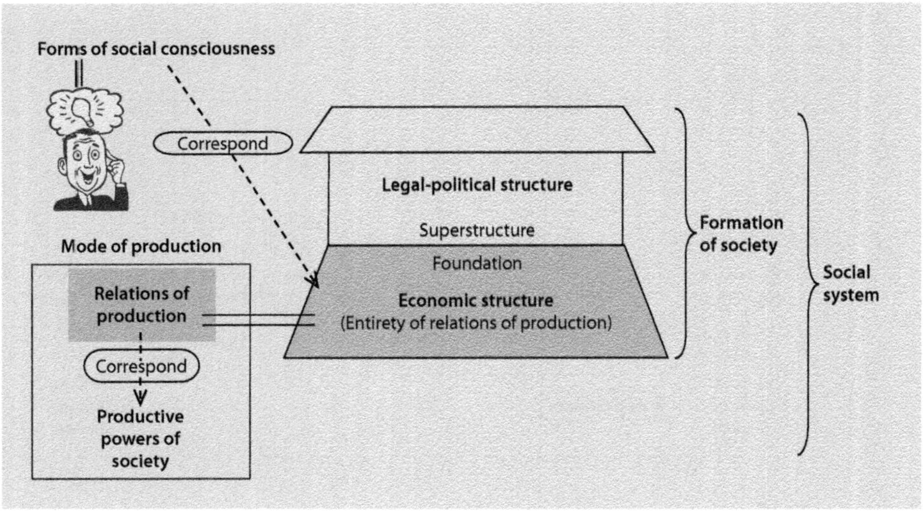

Fig. 1.34 Mode of production, formation of society, and social system

labouring individuals within their reciprocal relations via a metabolism with nature.

Forms of Social Consciousness Also Correspond to the Economic Structure

Various forms of human consciousness regarding society exist within it, including social psychology; philosophy, science, art, ethics, legal ideas, political doctrines, religions, and other ideologies. These **forms of social consciousness** necessarily correspond to the economic structure that is the foundation of society (*see* Fig. 1.34).

General Law of Development of the Society

Human History Is a Synthetic Result of the Actions of Human Beings Equipped with Consciousness and Will

History is created by the actions of human individuals equipped with consciousness, interests, and will. However, if human consciousness and will were not subject to any limitations, history would be a mere composite outcome of various actions of individuals, arbitrarily veering in every sort of direction, and thus amounting to nothing but a random collection of accidents. Is this indeed the case?

Productive Powers of Society and Relations of Production That Limit Human Actions Have a Material Character

As we have already seen, at the core of human life is praxis in pursuit of definite aims. In order to achieve an aim, human beings must follow objective laws. In the case of society as well, as we have seen, various laws are in operation. Thus, when individuals act within society, their consciousness and will is necessarily limited by social laws, just as in the case where they work upon nature.

Society's production (mode of production) is the unity of productive powers and the relations of production, but with the development of productive powers, it becomes unavoidable that the relations of production are replaced. The economic structure of society is thus an objective entity—independent of subjective moments such as human consciousness and will—that corresponds to the developmental stage of material productive powers. Individuals are unable to intentionally choose which form of society they will be born into. And there is a correspondence between the legal-political superstructure *created through the given social consciousness* and the objectively existing relations of production. This means that the state of the material life of human beings, which is to say the mode of production at a given time, limits the social, political, and mental life of people in a given era. *Rather than the consciousness of people determining their existence, it is the social existence of people that determines their consciousness.*

However, the fact that society is composed in this manner, with an economic structure (i.e. the foundation) and the legal-political superstructure that stands upon it, as well as the fact that people's social existence determines their consciousness, only comes to be fully understood for the first time *once we are familiar with the process whereby a form of society is replaced,* with a new social structure taking its place. So here I would like to outline this process.

Replacement of a Formation of Society Takes Place Through a Social Revolution

The process of replacing a formation of society is a **social revolution**. The economic structure of an actual historical society is a composite of numerous relations of production. Apart from a period of social revolution, this economic structure is made up of the **dominant relations of production** and other **subordinate relations of production**, with the dominant relations determining the character of the superstructure, and therefore determining the character of the society (*see* ◘ Fig. 1.35).[14]

---

14 ◘ Figure 1.35 depicts the «**petty proprietor's mode of production**», which refers to the production of individual producers who own and administer their own land and other means of production. This mode of production, as depicted in the diagram, exists more or less within any society before Association, and was particularly widespread during the transitional period from feudal society to capitalist society, but *it never formed dominant relations of production within history*. Capitalism is established by separating individuals who carry out labour *qua* owners from their means of production, thereby steadily wiping out the petty proprietor's mode of production.

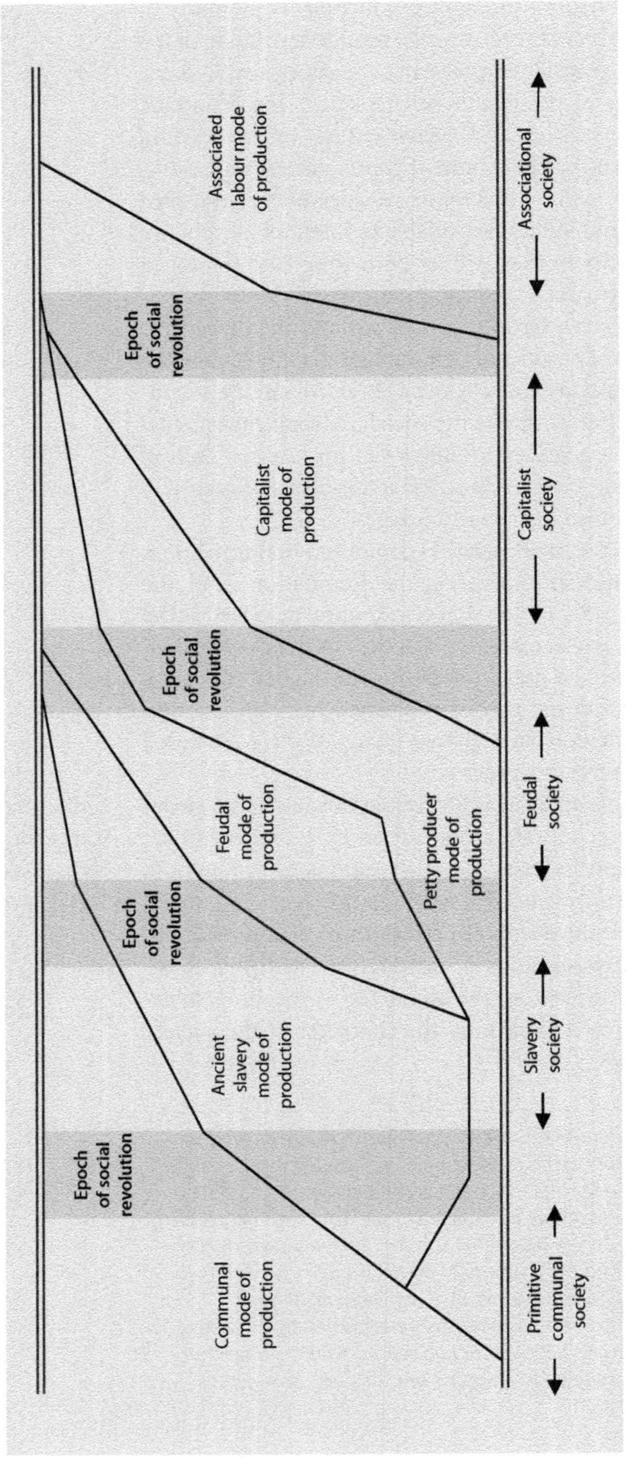

Fig. 1.35 Development of social form = replacement of a mode of production (excluding the asiatic slavery system)

A social revolution progresses as a continuous process whereby new relations of production begin to be generated within the old society, followed by the establishment of a new legal-political superstructure that corresponds to these new relations (i.e. a *political revolution*), and then, finally, the new relations of production expand rapidly under the new superstructure to become the dominant relations of production (i.e. an *economic revolution*). Here I would like to sketch this process a bit further (*see* ◘ Fig. 1.36).

Productive powers in any given society gradually expand and develop (*see 1* in ◘ Fig. 1.36). As this development progresses, the productive power comes into contradiction and collision with the dominant relations of production (*see 2*). As a result, the dominant relations of production become a fetter to the productive powers, generating every sort of friction (*see 3*). Meanwhile, new relations of production suitable to the development of the productive powers emerge and begin to develop. The bearers of the new relations of production perceive the old superstructure as a barrier to their economic activities, and set out to overthrow the political power (*see 4*). The ruling strata seek to maintain the existing system but are unable to stop the changes in the foundation, resulting in an increasingly conservative and fragile superstructure (*see 5*).

The frictions and changes in the economic structure are reflected in people's social consciousness. A desire for revolutionary change emerges among them, and **revolutionary thought** is born, in the form of the ideas of progressive individuals and groups (*see 6*). Ideas that suit the demands of the age and anticipate the direction of change win people's hearts, and the current of a revolutionary movement comes into existence. Those who were ruled in the former society wage a struggle against their rulers, and the class representing the new relations of production struggles against the old ruling class, reaching the extreme point of a **class struggle** against the old ruling class. This culminates in a **political revolution** to replace political power, followed by a change in the legal-political superstructure (*see 7*).

A class comes to power that represents the interests of the development of new relations of production, and it removes the legal and political limitations that impede the development of the new relations of production and rapidly expands these relations. This is an **economic revolution** (*see 8*). The new economic structure is the form for developing productive powers (*see 9*). Under this structure, the productive powers can develop in an unrestrained manner (*see 10*).

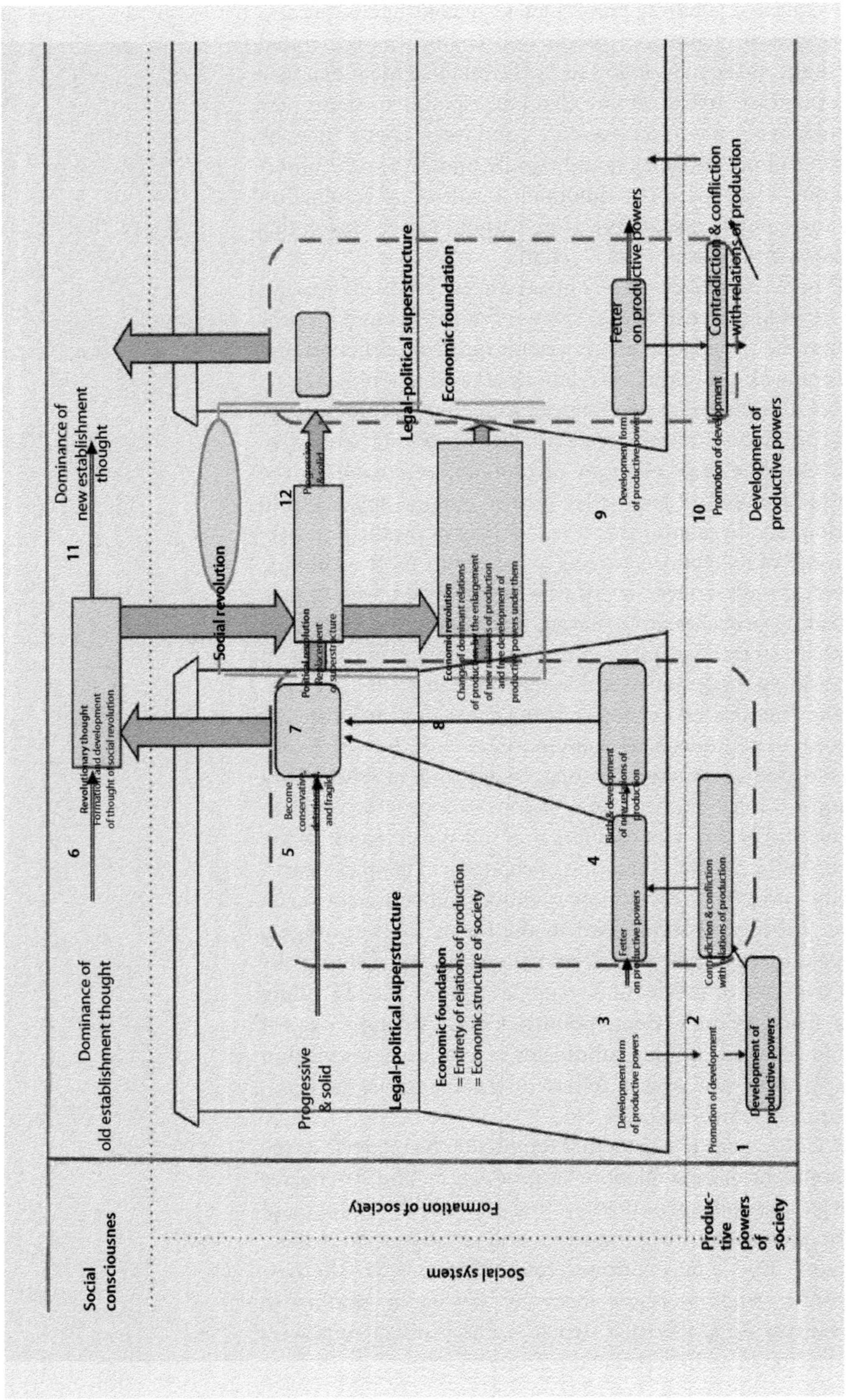

Fig. 1.36 Social revolution = replacement of a formation of society brought about by development of productive powers of society as motive power

The revolutionary thought that gave birth to the new society, gradually becomes the dominant, establishment thought that supports the new society (*see 11*). This new establishment thought, as well as the superstructure it supports, corresponds to the development of the productive powers and to the changes in the relations of production, and is therefore progressive and able to solidify its dominance (*see 12*).

In this way, history is created precisely through the actions of individuals equipped with consciousness, interests, and will, but the basis for such an historical process, which is the totality of the intentional actions of individuals, is the development of the material productive powers and changes in the economic foundation, which precede and determine the individuals' consciousness, interests, and will.

General Law of Social Development

This movement of society progresses as follows: development of productive powers → contradiction and collision with the relations of production → genesis and development of new relations of production → formation and development of revolutionary thought → political revolution → economic revolution → development of productive powers. This is the **general law of social development** that operates throughout every society before Association. However, in each particular historical society, this law operates in a different form, and each society has its own *particular laws of genesis, development, and extinction*. Elucidating the *law of the genesis, development, and extinction of capitalist society* is a matter that concerns the *fundamental theory of* political economy, which clarifies the economic structure of this form of society.

1.5 Fundamental Character of Political Economy

1.5.1 The Object and Tasks of Political Economy

The Object of Political Economy

Political economy's **object of study** is the **capitalist mode of production**.

Political economy was established as an independent science by *William Petty* (1623–1687) and then developed by *Adam Smith* and *David Ricardo*. These Classical political economists studied the economic structure of the capitalist society that lay before their eyes and established political economy as a science that took as its object the economic structure of capitalist society.

Karl Marx inherited the scientific aspects of classical political economy and developed them further. He clarified that capitalist society is one form of society within history that must be distinguished from other societies, and he clarified its laws of motion, which is to say the laws concerning its genesis, development, and extinction.

Political Economy in a Broad Sense and in a Narrow Sense

Political economy as the investigation of the capitalist mode of production is **political economy in the narrow sense**, whereas political economy as a whole, including the investigation of modes of production other than the capitalist mode of production, is referred to as **political economy in the broad sense**. However, the object necessary for a systematic theoretical development is only the capitalist mode of production, which is concealed by reified relations; whereas the elucidation of the economic structure of prior societies is substantially encompassed within the study of economic history.

Uniqueness of Political Economy

The object of study for social sciences other than political economy, fundamentally speaking, concerns the forms of social consciousness, or the intentionally formed legal and political superstructure, and the social actions of human beings or groups of human beings equipped with social consciousness. A scientific cognition of these objects requires an understanding of the economic foundation of society, and so these other social sciences must be premised on the theory of the economic structure of capitalist society, i.e. a theory of political economy.

Political economy deals directly with the economic interests of individuals and classes within society. Thus, political economy requires a cool-headed analysis characterised by a thoroughly critical spirit that does not fear attack from private interests.

Tasks of Political Economy

Political economy clarifies the nature of the capitalist mode of production, its mechanism, and manner of reproduction. However, political economy also elucidates how this mode of production came into being, changes with the development of productive powers, becomes a fetter upon productive powers, and prepares the way for new relations of production. In short, political economy clarifies the **laws of motion of capitalist society**, i.e. the **laws** of its **genesis, development, and extinction**.

1.5.2 Method of Political Economy

Method of Political Economy

The **method of political economy** is an issue that pertains to the **investigative method** of the object of political economy and the **presentation method** of that investigation's results. However, since it is unlikely that a person could understand an abstract explanation of this method without some image of the overall content of political economy, here I would like to touch on the issue of method in relation to the question of *why everyday economic phenomena do not appear all at once as the starting point of the theory of political economy.*[15]

Political economy is a science. First and foremost, **science** is *human beings' systematic cognition of objective laws*, and scientific **theory** is the *system of these cognised laws.*

The reason human beings can consciously transform nature and society through their activities is that the world is governed by laws that are independent of human consciousness and will. A **law** is a *general, internal, and essential relation between things or matters.* What is given to our senses is the appearance of law, i.e. **phenomena**. This means that science, above all, must grasp the **essence** or law that is concealed behind phenomena.

The essence or law underlying phenomena, however, is often manifested in a completely opposite form. A cognised law often takes a form that is completely different from the phenomena that are at the starting point. *Science* thus *systematically grasps the law from phenomena, and upon this basis develops (explains) phenomena from the law.* Without this development (explanation), the law (essence) that has been grasped, and the thing or matter that is still a given thing or matter as phenomenon, would remain separate from each other, so that the phenomena would not yet be understood. In order for science to grasp objective reality, it is necessary to follow two courses: the path «**from phenomena to essence**» *and then* the path «**from essence to phenomena**» (*see* ◘ Fig. 1.37).

Method of Investigation

In the case of political economy, the posited thing or matter to be analysed is *intertwined within the complexity of the economic structure of society, assuming a confused appearance.* The investigation begins from the given phenomena and grasps the various essential relations and laws that underlie it. Then, upon this basis, the relations and laws are used to develop and explain the various phenomena that are given to our ordinary senses.

Relations Between Phenomena and Essence Multiply Overlap

The actual economy is a totality consisting of multitiered relations of «essence → phenomena» (*see* ◘ Fig. 1.38).

---

15 Although decisively important for the method of political economy, I will not touch on the **dialectical method** here. An object must be grasped within its **dialectical movement** for the theoretical development of political economy, but an abstract explanation of this, before the reader has come into contact with the concrete setting in which dialectics appears, would invite misunderstanding. Although I have set aside discussion of the dialectical method, readers with an interest in the issue can consult footnote 14 of ► Chap. 2.

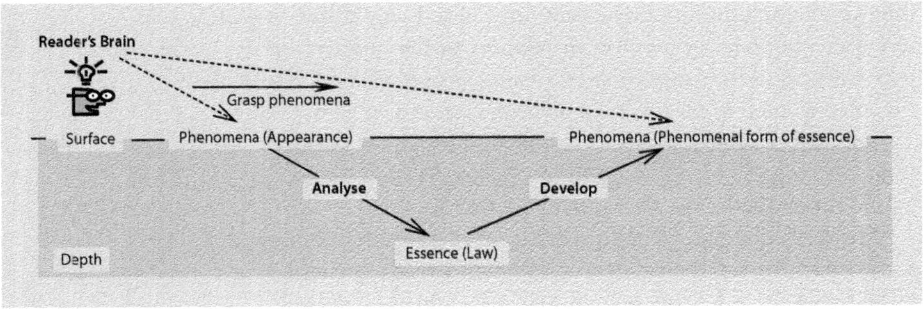

■ **Fig. 1.37** Analysis (phenomena → essence) and development (essence → phenomena)

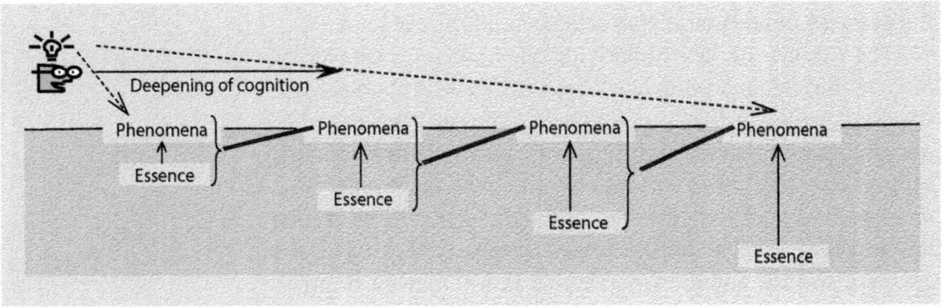

■ **Fig. 1.38** Multitiered structure of phenomena and essence

The investigation in political economy involves correctly grasping each of the relations and clarifying the connections between them. If this is accomplished, the confused appearance of the object at the starting point is transformed into a coherent totality consisting of numerous laws and relations.

Descending Path and Ascending Path

The investigation and the presentation of its results must fundamentally follow two paths: the descending and the ascending path. The first involves starting out from the confused appearance on the most superficial layer to pursue the essence until one arrives at the essence at the deepest layer (**descending path**). This fundamentally corresponds to the first half of the operation of «phenomena → essence → phenomena». For the second path, which starts from the *essence grasped at the deepest layer*, one must progressively clarify the phenomenal forms, until arriving again at the totality of the most superficial layer (**ascending path**). This is fundamentally the latter half of «phenomena → essence → phenomena» (*see* ■ Fig. 1.39).

What is decisively important *for the investigation* is the descending path, which determines success or failure, and the process of research is, overall, the descending path. However, this path is not a one-directional, straight descent, but rather an

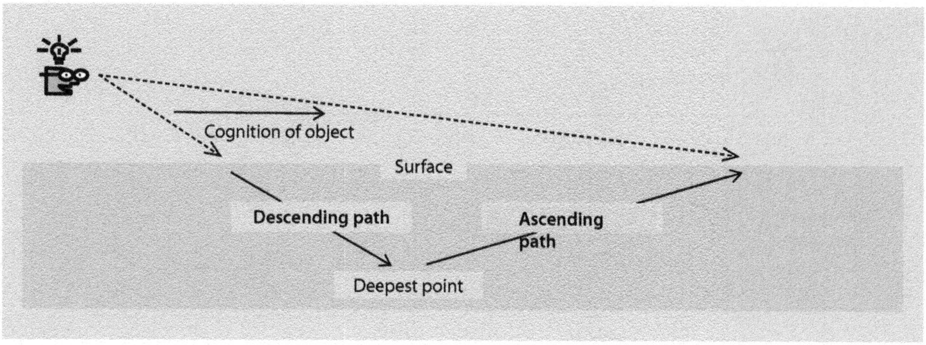

Fig. 1.39 Descending path and ascending path

overall downward process that encompasses back-and-forth processes. In the case of a child who takes apart a clock but is unable to put it back together again, the disassembly is merely a one-directional downward path that involves removing one part after another. But the adult who takes apart a clock to learn how to reassemble it must be careful to consider how each part relates to the other parts. In this case, the adult takes apart the clock while repeatedly seeing how the detached parts fit back together. It is by means of this downward path that includes a partial recomposition, and thus partial movements upwards, that a person is able for the first time to mentally reproduce the structure of the entire clock properly, and to thus be able for the first time to reassemble the watch starting from the separated parts.

Method of Presentation

The **presentation** (description) of the results of the investigation *demonstrates the correctness of cognition*. This demonstration is completed when one successfully *reproduces the totality of the object within the mind of the reader* by means of passing through the process of developing the concrete phenomenal forms, one after another, starting from the most abstract essence at the deepest layer, until ultimately arriving at the most superficial layer. This means that the *presentation (demonstration)* is fundamentally the ascending path.

Yet in order to show that the *subject matter newly dealt with* at each stage of moving upwards *actually exists within the economic structure*, within the presentation itself this object must *be grasped from the economic structure*. In other words, the presentation must include the analysis from phenomena to essence, meaning that there is always a *partial downward movement included within its progression* (*see* ◘ Fig. 1.40).

At the starting point of the presentation of political economy (the ascending path), the most simple and general objects are dealt with and analysed; therefore, at the outset of the pre-

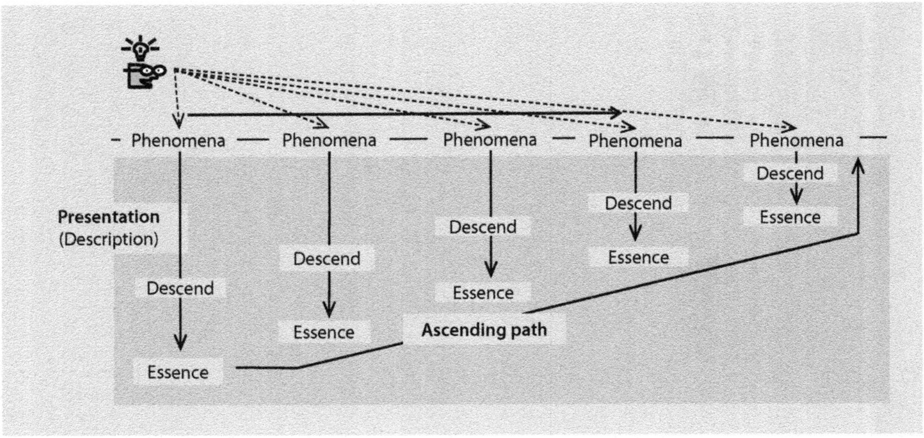

■ **Fig. 1.40** Method of presentation

sentation, the entirety of the everyday economic phenomena do not appear together all at once. However, in the course of the unfolding upward trajectory, concrete phenomena progressively appear, and the relations and connections between phenomena are explained in turn, until one draws closer to the everyday phenomenal world as it appears on the surface.

References

Hegel GF (1840) Encyclopädie der philosophischen Wissenschaften im Grundrisse. Erster Theil. Die Logik. In: Werke. Vol. 6. Berlin. English edition: Hegel GF (1991) The encyclopaedia logic (trans: Geraets TF et al.). Hackett Publishing Company, Indianapolis/Cambridge

Marx K (1872) Das Kapital. Kritik der politischen Oekonomie. Bd. 1. Buch 1: Der Produktionsprocess des Kapitals. 2. verb. Aufl. Hamburg. English edition: Marx K (1976) Capital. A critique of political economy. Vol. 1 (trans: Howkes B). Penguin Books

Marx K (1858) Letter to Ferdinand Lassalle, 22 February 1858. English edition: Marx K (1983) Marx-Engels Collected Works. Vol. 40. Progress Publishers et al. New York

Statistics Bureau Japan (2017) Survey on labour-power in 2017. Tokyo

The Process of Production of Capital

Contents

2

Commodity and Money

T. Otani, *A Guide to Marxian Political Economy*,
https://doi.org/10.1007/978-3-319-65954-1_2

2.1 The Theme of Part I and the Path of Investigation

Examining Commodity and Money Prior to Capital

Here we will begin looking at the theory of political economy that deals with the capitalist mode of production. The keyword pertaining to the capitalist economy is certainly «capital», but the analysis of capital is premised on a correct understanding of the commodity and money.

Commodity and Money as Well as the Relations of Commodity Production That Generate Them

In ► Chap. 2, where we examine the commodity as it actually appears on the market, the commodity's two constituent elements (use-value and value) will be extracted and investigated in detail. This will be followed by an analysis of the independent form assumed by value, where the completely social element of value is expressed in a quantity of a natural thing: the use-value of another commodity. This analysis teaches us that the emergence of money is the ultimate outcome of the development of this form taken by value, while at the same time it clarifies the nature of money. This understanding in turn forms the basis for the subsequent investigation of why labour products assume the commodity form and why money emerges out of commodities. The reason is that human beings enter historically peculiar relations of production: the relations of commodity production. We will see that these relations of production are necessarily manifested as relations between things, and that these relations between things are represented by human beings who come into relations with each other as persons. Finally, this chapter will clarify the functions money performs under relations of commodity production.

Secret of the Valorisation of Capital

Once we have equipped ourselves with the necessary knowledge regarding the commodity and money, we will go on to analyse capital in ► Chap. 3, which begins by confirming that capital is self-valorising value and then pursues the question of how capital is augmented. We will see that this augmentation is possible because the holder of money can purchase a human capacity known as labour-power and then utilise that capacity. This is followed by a look at how value can be augmented through the utilisation of labour-power. ► Chapter 3 thus unravels the riddle of the valorisation of capital, uncovering the essence of the augmented value known as «surplus-value». This chapter is a central pillar of the book because our subsequent investigation unfolds on the basis of that understanding.

Two Ways To Increase Surplus-value

► Chapters 4 and 5 examine the two ways that capital increases surplus-value; with the former analysing the method of increasing surplus-value by extending the workers' daily labour-time and the latter focusing on how surplus-value is augmented by cheapening the commodities that determine workers' wages on the basis of an increase in labour's productive power. The latter investigation involves, at the same time, an examination of the development of production methods under capitalism; or, more concretely, the development under manufacture from simple co-operation to co-operation based on a division of labour, and then the establishment of large-scale industry through the generalisation of the use of machinery. It will become clear that this development involved the subordination of wageworkers to capital under capitalist production (and the various suffering resulting from this), while at the same time we will see the positive roles played by capital within human history.

Capitalist Relations of Production as the Root of the Valorisation Movement of Capital

► Chapter 6 provides an outline of the capitalist relations of production that are the root of the valorisation process of capital seen up to that point, clarifying that workers under these relations of production are completely integrated within capital and subjected to it, which brings about circumstances for the labouring individuals that correspond to the term «alienation of labour».

Distorted Form of Wages as Remuneration for Labour

The analysis of the valorisation process of capital already makes clear that the essence of the wage a worker receives in return for his commodity is the value of his labour-power. But this necessarily takes the completely distorted form of remuneration for labour, or more accurately, the «value or price of labour», as ► Chap. 7 will discuss.

Reproduction of Capital and Capital Accumulation

In our investigation up to ► Chap. 7, the existence of capital and labour-power is premised, and upon this basis we look at the mechanism of valorisation. But capitalist production itself is always generating new capital, with labour-power never ceasing to enter the labour market. This point can be well understood by examining the reproduction process whereby capital is repeatedly produced. ► Chap. 8 analyses the reproduction of capital, clarifying that, within the progression of reproduction, capital changes to be a congelation of surplus-value. This is followed, in ► Chap. 9, with an examination of the accumulation of capital, which is a process whereby the obtained surplus-value is converted into capital so as to augment capital itself. This shows us that the appropriation of surplus-value by capital is nothing but the appropriation by congealed surplus-value.

Influence of Capital Accumulation on the Working Class

► Chapter 10 addresses the influence exerted by capital accumulation on the working class; namely, its influence on wages and the employment situation. The chapter clarifies that capitalist production, in order to exist, must constantly produce a surplus population (i.e. unemployed population).

Historical Formation Process That Is the Starting Point of Capital

The investigation up to this point has raised awareness of the fundamental aspects of the mechanism of capitalist production, but the premise has been a *situation where there is a separation of the labouring individuals from the material conditions of labour, and that these labour conditions take the form of capital*. However, considering that labouring individuals in pre-capitalist societies had been united with the conditions of labour, there must have been some *process* whereby a separation occurred. This historical process is referred to as «primitive accumulation». ▶ Chapter 11 looks back on this historical process, clarifying the original genesis of capitalist production. This makes it possible for us to now grasp the historical tendency underlying the genesis, development, and extinction of capitalist production.

Toward the Study of the Circulation Process of Capital

The most essential content of capitalist *production* concerns the examination of the *production* process of capital, which is completed in Part I. The knowledge thus obtained is then applied to the study of the circulation process of capital in Part II. Once we are familiar with both the production and circulation of processes of capital, we can turn in Part III to the concrete shapes of capital and surplus-value that confront us in reality.

2.2 The Commodity

2.2.1 Capitalist Production as Commodity Production

Common Image of the «Cyclical Flow» of the Economy

What would be the bird's-eye view of capitalism for someone with no knowledge of political economy? The following diagram is an attempt to depict the common image that people have of the capitalist economy (*see* ◘ Fig. 2.1).

The grasp of capitalism depicted in ◘ Fig. 2.1 corresponds perfectly to the ultimate conclusions reached through the investigation carried out by modern economics. In contrast, for political economy, this sort of view of the capitalist economy is only the investigation's starting point. That is, we are dealing with nothing more than the common or superficial viewpoint easily arrived at by those who gaze at the surface of the capitalist economy without engaging in any special economic analysis. The precise task for political economy as a science is to seek out the deeper layer beneath that surface.

Political economy clarifies the essential relations that underlie the phenomena that posit the common image of the economy. But this work cannot be carried out all at once. Rather, it involves

2

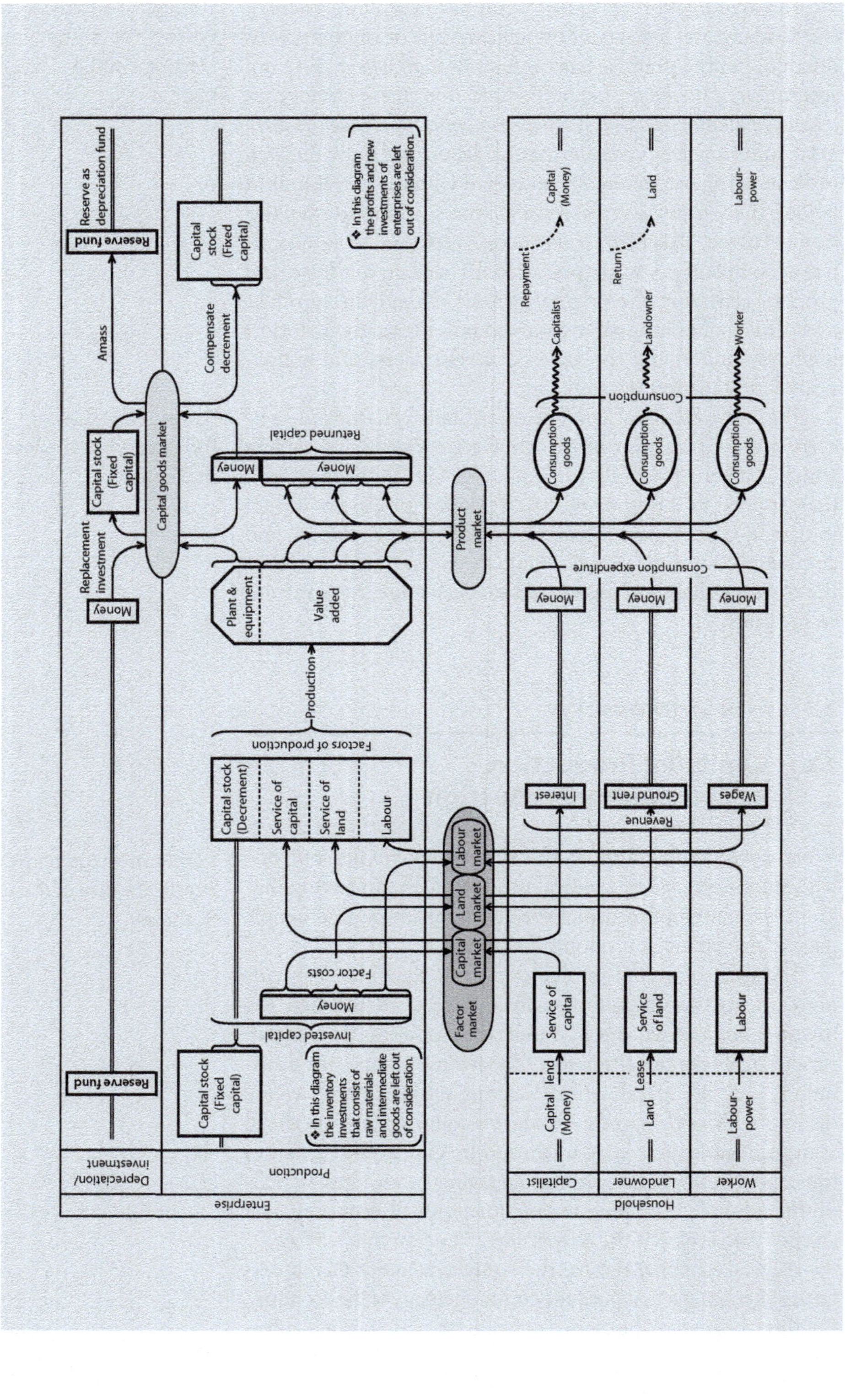

Fig. 2.1 Common image of the «circular flow» of the economy

the method of beginning from the simplest and most abstract, and working gradually upwards toward the more complex and concrete, until ultimately arriving at a transformed image of the whole that is fully explained in accordance with the structure and laws at its deepest layer. Later we will have the opportunity to carefully compare the view that we finally arrived at with the common image that was the starting point (*see* ◘ Fig. 2.2).

Market Economy and Commodity Production

The most general matter regarding the capitalist economy is the relations involving the sale and purchase of commodities, and further (if we set aside how this relation is mediated by money) the exchange-relations between commodities. The capitalist economy is therefore generally grasped to begin with as a «**market economy**».

In a capitalist economy, the labour-produced **wealth**[1] *of society that supports the survival of human beings and the*

---

1 The term «**wealth**» here clearly refers to the products produced by labour that support the continued existence of human beings and society. Even a junior-high student would know that human beings and society cannot continue to exist without labour, and that it is only through labour that we can obtain physical wealth from nature. In any society, therefore, human beings must, in one way or another, think about the labour needed to attain that wealth. This is not a «hidden truth» that has to be clarified ultimately by political economy. Political economy thus takes these facts as self-evident premises, rather than starting without any premises at all.

The following quote from Marx (1868) offers us invaluable suggestions as to «exchange-value» as well as «value» discussed hereafter: «The unfortunate fellow does not see that, even if there were no chapter on «value» at all in my book [i.e. *Capital*], the analysis I give of the real relations would contain the proof and demonstration of the real value relation. The chatter about the need to prove the concept of value arises only from complete ignorance both of the subject under discussion and of the method of science. Every child knows that any nation that stopped working, not for a year, but let us say, just for a few weeks, would perish. And every child knows, too, that the amounts of products corresponding to the differing amounts of needs demand differing and quantitatively determined amounts of society's aggregate labour. It is *self-evident* that this *necessity* of the *distribution* of social labour in specific proportion is certainly not abolished by the *specific form* of social production; it can only change *its form of manifestation*. Natural laws cannot be abolished at all. The only thing that can change, under historically differing conditions, is the *form* in which those laws assert themselves. And the form in which this proportional distribution of labour asserts itself in a state of society in which the interconnection of social labour expresses itself as the *private exchange* of the individual products of labour, is precisely the *exchange-value* of these products» (Marx 1868. Marx 1988, p. 68; Marx's emphasis and brackets).

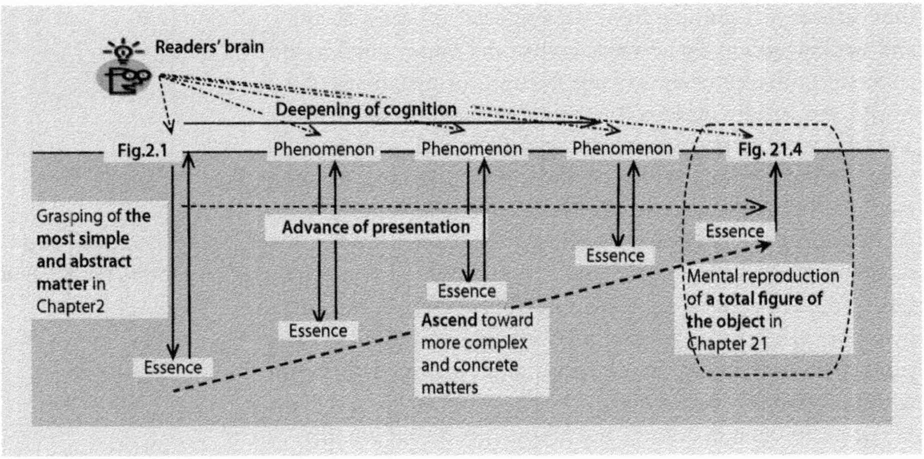

Fig. 2.2 Starting point and arrival point of the presentation

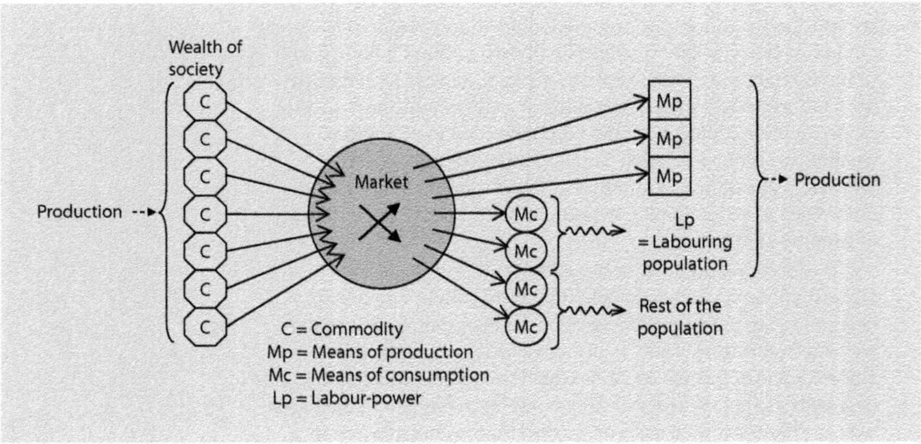

Fig. 2.3 Wealth in capitalist society takes the commodity form

continued existence of the society presents itself as an immense collection of commodities. In other words, wealth takes the form of the commodity. The fact that products of labour take the form of the **commodity** is the *most general, simple, and abstract matter concerning the capitalist economy* (*see* Fig. 2.3).

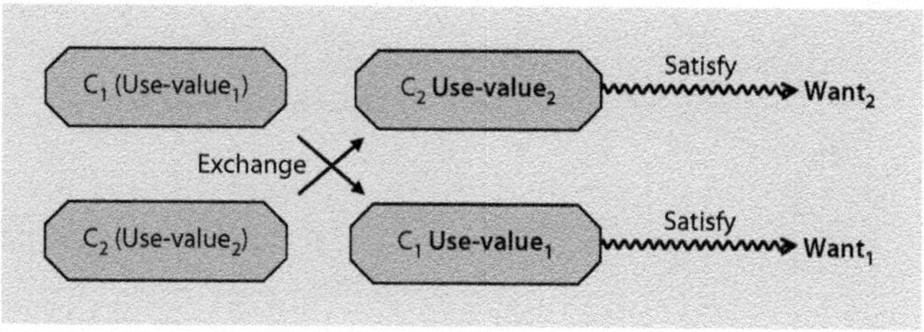

Fig. 2.4 Commodity must have a use-value

We must begin, therefore, by analysing the commodity[2] to grasp its nature and particular social character. Consequently, our main discussion of political economy must begin with an examination of the commodity as the particular form that products of labour take in a capitalist society.

Commodity's Use-value and Exchange-value

A commodity must first of all possess some sort of **use-value** that satisfies a particular human want (*see* Fig. 2.4).

The most essential aspect of a commodity, however, is its **exchange-value**. This concerns the quantity of other com-

---

2 When money is used, anything can be exchanged with money and *thus* become a «**commodity**». *All sorts of things* are sold, whether it be a vote in an election, a bid for a public works project, a membership list, a tip for a horse race, etc. One book on economics, for example, lists up all sorts of «economic goods», such as, space exploration, education, national defense, recreation, time, entertainment, clean air, a pleasant environment, pleasant working conditions, more productive resources, or leisure (Gwartney et al. 1982, p. 5). This, in other words, is a random list of anything that can be currently sold. If one were to seek what these things have in common, the answer would be the completely shallow observation that «they are things that are sold because people want them». This is a mere tautology because the things listed that are currently sold would of course not be sold if no one wanted them.

The commodities that we are dealing with here are the commodities within the market economy that people have to bring to the market to sell every day in order to continue living and commodities as the particular form taken by the wealth that supports the continued existence of human beings and society. In other words, the commodities that are produced every day with one portion of the total labour of society and are then exchanged on the market to satisfy a portion of the aggregate needs of society for productive and individual consumption. These are commodities whose prices fluctuate depending on the relation of supply and demand, and the producers increase or decrease the quantity of production using these price fluctuations as their barometer. Thus there are things that are sold at stores, such as used books or other used items, that are placed outside of consideration here. The price and value of those «commodities» not produced by labour, or «commodities» that are absolutely unique or whose prices are determined solely by the buyer's capacity to pay, can only be understood once we have first clarified the commodity and money in the original sense.

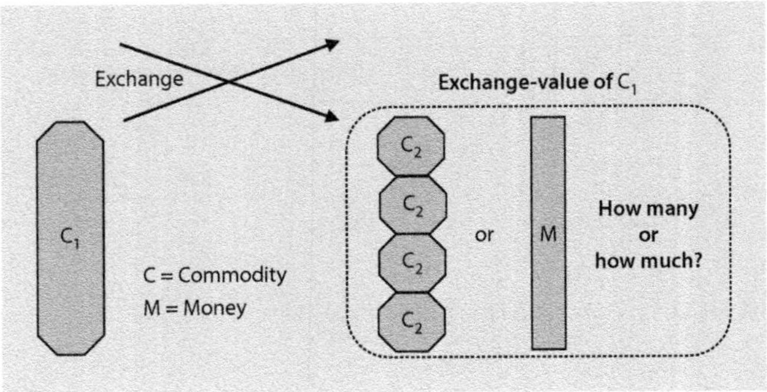

Fig. 2.5 What is crucial to commodity is exchange-value

modities—or the quantity of money, once it has emerged—for which the commodity can be replaced (*see* Fig. 2.5).

A given commodity—say five meters of cotton cloth—can have different expressions depending on the various kinds of commodities for which it is exchanged. But the exchange-value of the five meters of cotton cloth is determined by the relation between a certain quantity of something intrinsic to a single unit of cotton cloth and a certain quantity of something intrinsic to a single unit of that other commodity, whether it is a coat, tea, rice, gold, iron, etc. This «something» is precisely what determines exchange-value, which is the most essential aspect of the commodity. This is referred to as the «worth» of a commodity or its **value**[3] (*see* Fig. 2.6).

---

3 **Value** is not something that was first discovered by political economy after a difficult struggle. Long ago it was perceived in the marketplace by the buyers and sellers of commodities that one's own commodity or that of another person had a certain magnitude of «worth» that should be socially recognised, and that if the price of the commodity were higher than its «worth» it would be to the advantage of that commodity, just as if the price were lower it would be to its disadvantage. And based on decisions with regard to such factors, one would decide what to produce and bring to market, and in what quantity. This «worth» was called «*value*» by both the buyers and the sellers as well as the Classical economists. What political economy had to uncover is what exactly determines this «value». *Adam Smith* and the Classical economists proposed the «**labour theory of value**», according to which, the quantity of labour constitutes the value of commodities. *Marx* developed this labour theory of value to make it more precise. Against that theory is the view of the «**utility theory of value**», which says that value is determined by utility, and this view spread through the efforts of vulgar economists. But because it was difficulty to respond to doubts about the subjective and arbitrary nature of utility in the original form of that theory, *William Jevons, Léon Walrus, Carl Menger* in 1871 each developed theories of «marginal utility» based on the marginal

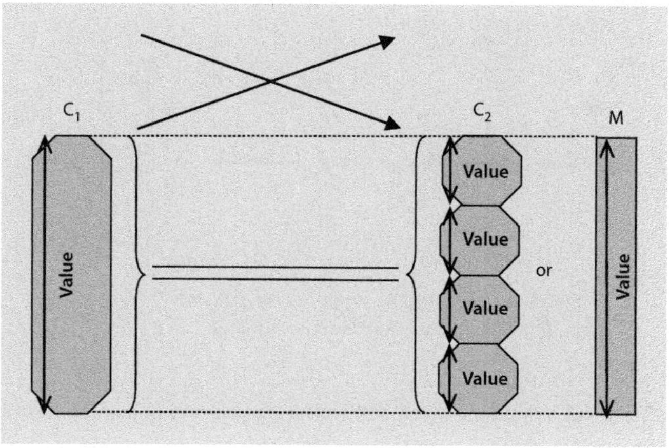

Fig. 2.6 The value of a commodity determines the magnitude of its exchange-value

2.2.2 Value of a Commodity[4]

The Value of a Commodity Is the Abstract Labour Objectified in It

What is this value commodities have in common that determines their ratio of exchange? It cannot be use-value, as commodities are exchanged precisely because their use-values differ. This means that we must place use-value out of consideration. If we do so, the only common attribute that remains is that commodities are all the product of labour. Moreover, «labour» in this case cannot be anything other than abstract labour. In other words, *abstract labour* is the **substance of value**.

Abstract labour, however, is a characteristic that actual labour in every sort of society possesses in common—and abstract labour as such is an active state of human beings. But here, abstract labour becomes an attribute of the things that are commodities, a social attribute. That is to say, abstract

principle. However, the dominant «theory» for contemporary economics is that concepts such as «value», even in the case of the theory of utility, are not necessary because it is a «metaphysical argument».

4 Readers who are already familiar with the Marx's extraction and analysis of value in the chapter on the commodity in *Capital* may feel that the elucidation here is too brief and rough to convey his brilliant reasoning there. However, since we already touched on what Marx grasped there (above all the *twofold character of labour: concrete labour* and *abstract labour*) in the Introduction (1.4.1.3), it is possible here to simplify the discussion of the content the second time around.

2

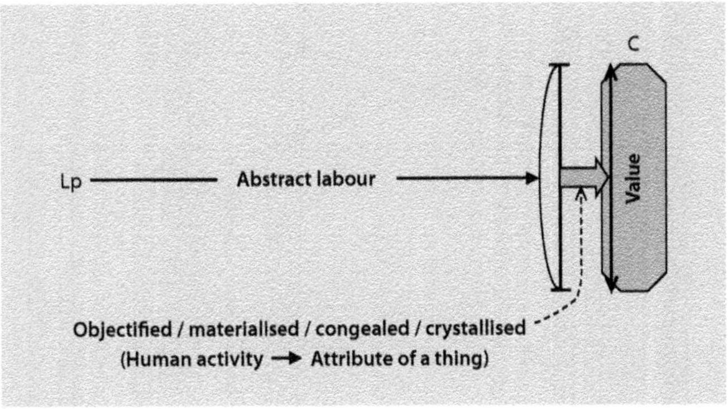

Fig. 2.7 Value of a commodity is the abstract labour objectified in it

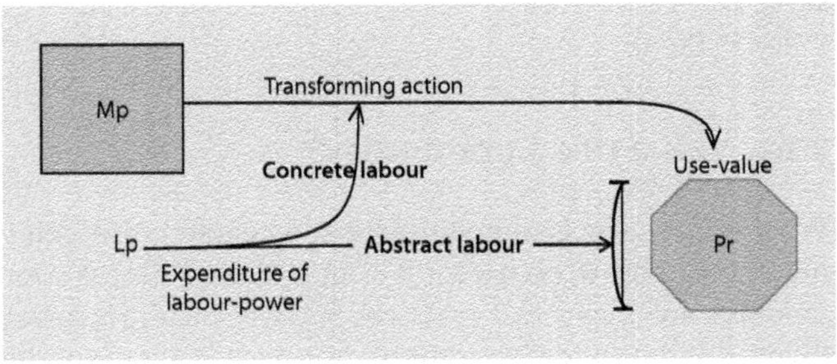

Fig. 2.8 Twofold character of labour

labour as *human activity* is **objectified**, **materialised**, **congealed**, and **crystallised** within *things*, becoming an *attribute of things*. Value is thus precisely *abstract labour objectified in a commodity* (*see* Fig. 2.7).

Twofold Character of Labour Is Manifested in the Form of the Two Factors of the Commodity

The **twofold character of labour** (*see* Figs. 1.11, 1.12, 1.13, and 1.14) is something common to the labour of every form of society (*see* Fig. 2.8).

Under commodity production, the twofold character of labour assumes the particular form of the **commodity's two elements**. That is to say, concrete labour takes the form of use-value for other people, while abstract labour takes the form of value. Here the twofold character of labour presents itself as the *dual aspects of the outcome of labour* (*see* Fig. 2.9).

As we have seen, regardless of the form of society, the production cost of a product comes down to the quantity of abstract labour necessary for its production (*see* Figs. 2.16, 2.17, and 2.18). Setting aside for a moment the production cost of the means of production, which is explained at the end of this section, the following figure depicts abstract labour as the production cost of a product (*see* Fig. 2.10).

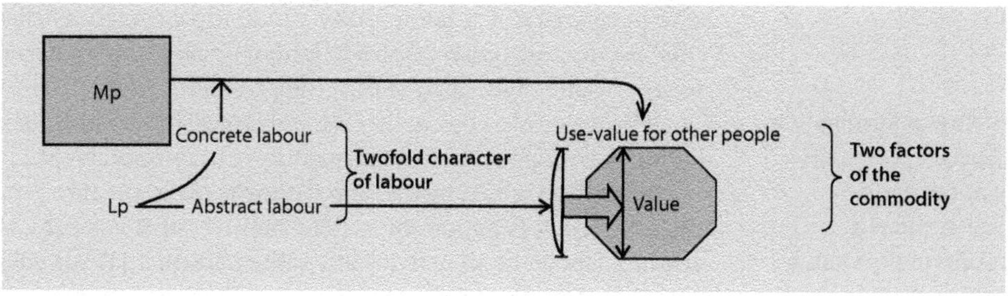

Fig. 2.9 Twofold character of labour is manifested in the particular form of the two factors of the commodity

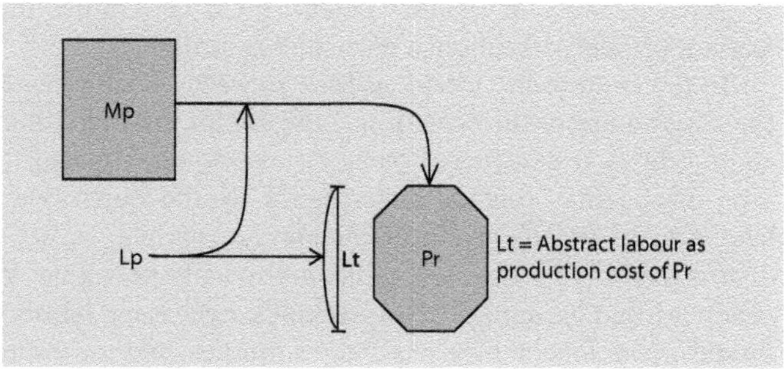

Fig. 2.10 Abstract labour as production cost

When we say that the value of a commodity is the abstract labour objectified within it, this at the same time means that the value of a commodity is nothing but the *production cost of the product common to every sort of society but manifesting itself in the peculiar form of being a product's attribute*[5].

---

5 The doctrine according to which the value of a commodity is determined by its «utility», which is to say, determined by the degree to which it satisfies a human need, is called the «**utility theory of value**». Because this doctrine states that the value of a commodity is decided by the degree of its utility in satisfying a human need, it implies that the amount of labour necessary for the commodity's production has no relation to its value. Thus, the world in which commodity owners exchange commodities that only have «value» in this sense is thought to be composed of sellers who are concerned solely with the degree to which the commodities of others might satisfy their own needs and completely indifferent to the cost required for their own commodities that they bring to market. In other words, it is a world of spoiled brats who bring the toys they no longer want to exchange them for ones they do. This is completely different from the world of real commodity producers who make decisions every day regarding what and how much to produce, while keeping a constant eye on the production cost of their own commodity and the market price.

The peculiarity of a commodity production society is that this production cost (abstract labour) takes the material form of value objectified within the product.

Value-determination: Socially Necessary Labour-time Determines a Commodity's Value

If the value of a commodity is the abstract labour objectified within it, it might seem that the quantity of a commodity's value would be determined by the labour-time actually spent to produce it. Here it is important to note, however, that value is not abstract labour in an active state; rather, abstract labour *congealed in the material form* of a commodity becomes its attribute. Value is an attribute of a «thing» so that the commodity of the same kind has the same quantity of value. What has value is the *commodity*—not labour or the labouring human being.

What quantity of abstract labour, then, determines the amount of value per unit of a particular commodity?

In the commodity world, as long as we are dealing with the commodity of the same kind, any one of the individual commodities is considered to be an **average sample** of it. This means that value is determined by the quantity of labour necessary to produce this average sample; i.e. it is determined by the quantity of labour socially necessary to produce the commodity. This «**socially necessary labour-time**»[6] is the *labour-time required to produce any use-value under the conditions of production normal for a given society and with the average degree of labour skill and intensity prevalent in that society*. The abbreviated term **value-determination** is used to describe the determination of the quantity of a commodity's value by socially necessary labour-time (*see* ◘ Fig. 2.11).

The necessary labour-time for the production of a use-value is always fluctuating with changes in the productive power of labour. As a result, the socially necessary labour-time for a given commodity—under socially normal conditions of production—will increase or decrease along with changes in the productive power of the labour that produces it.

The socially normal conditions for the production of a commodity are constantly fluctuating due to improvements in the production conditions of the producers who produce that commodity and due to alterations in the quantitative

6 «**Necessary labour-time**» is different from the *requisite labour-time* mentioned in 1.4.2 (though the latter is usually also called «necessary labour-time»). The term «necessary labour-time» here refers to the labour-time needed to produce a commodity, whereas requisite labour-time refers to labour-time needed to produce the *requisite means of livelihood*. The reader should be careful to not confuse the two!

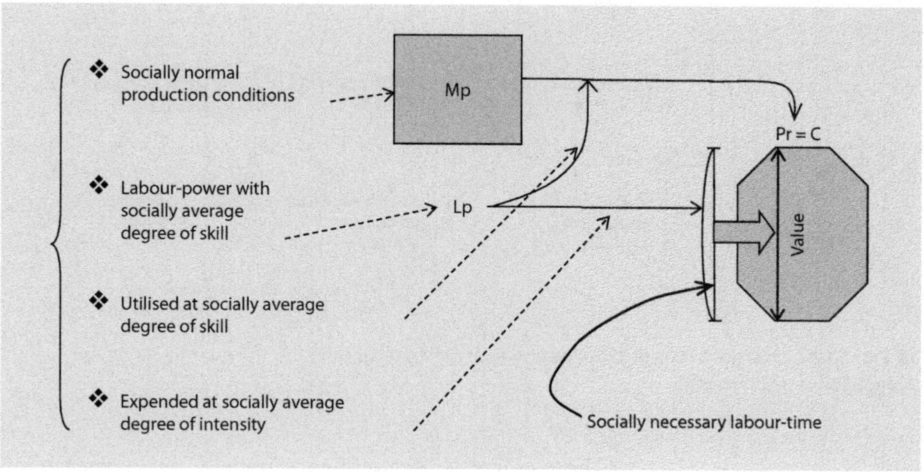

Fig. 2.11 The value of a commodity is determined by socially necessary labour-time (value-determination)

combination of varied production conditions under a large number of producers, so socially necessary labour-time is far from being fixed or technically determined. The value of a commodity differs completely from the natural-scientific attributes the commodity has as a natural material. It is rather a purely *social* quantity that—despite being an attribute of the commodity—is not a natural attribute but a completely *social* attribute.

Among the conditions that influence socially necessary labour-time, a clear distinction must be made between the intensity of labour and the other conditions.

Difference in the Intensity of Labour Is a Difference in the Quantity of Abstract Labour

A difference in the **intensity of labour** concerns a difference in the density of the expenditure of abstract labour within the same duration of physical time. Generally speaking, the degree of the difference in the intensity of labour can be grasped by comparing the quantity of the products of the particular labour to the quantity of products produced under a normal intensity of labour. Therefore, other conditions being the same, labour of a higher intensity can be easily converted into the labour of normal intensity (as the expenditure of labour-power of a density so many times greater than the normal intensity of labour) by looking at the greater or lesser degree of labour-time needed to produce a use-value compared to the socially necessary labour-time, although there are various types of concrete labour that do not produce quantitatively measurable material products.

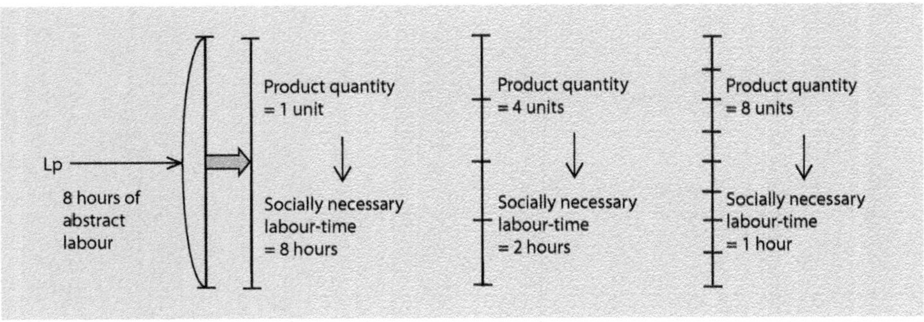

Fig. 2.12 Changes in the productive power of concrete labour after the quantity of labour objectified in a commodity

The conditions that influence socially necessary labour-time—apart from the intensity of labour—all concern the **productive power of labour** (so-called labour productivity).

Difference in the Productive Power of Labour Is a Difference in the Degree of Effectiveness of Concrete Labour

We already saw in 1.4.1 (*see* Fig. 1.19) that the productive power of labour is the productive power of concrete labour, which is determined by factors that include the degree of labour skill, the developmental level of science and its technical applications (science and technology), the social combination of the production process (co-operation and division of labour), the extent and effectiveness of means of production (machinery and automated factories, etc.), and physical conditions (climate, soil fertility, etc.). With the exception of the degree of workers' skill, which is a subjective condition pertaining to the labouring individuals themselves, all of these are objective conditions of production. And all of these conditions, taken together, increase or decrease the necessary labour-time for the production of use-values by influencing the degree of effectiveness of concrete labour (*see* Fig. 2.12).

We have already in 1.4.1 seen that in any form of society an increase in the productive power of concrete labour leads to a decrease in the abstract labour that is the product's production cost (*see* Fig. 1.20). In a commodity production society, a change in productive power manifests itself in the form of a decrease or increase in the value of commodities.

If the productive power of a particular labour is higher or lower than the productive power of the concrete labour needed to produce a given commodity according to the socially necessary labour-time, how would this be evaluated in commodity production?

Labour of Different Degrees of Skill Is Reduced to Labour of the Average Degree According to the Quantity of Products

Here, out of the various factors that determine the productive power of concrete labour, let's consider a difference in the **degree of skill** of labour that *produces the same kind of*

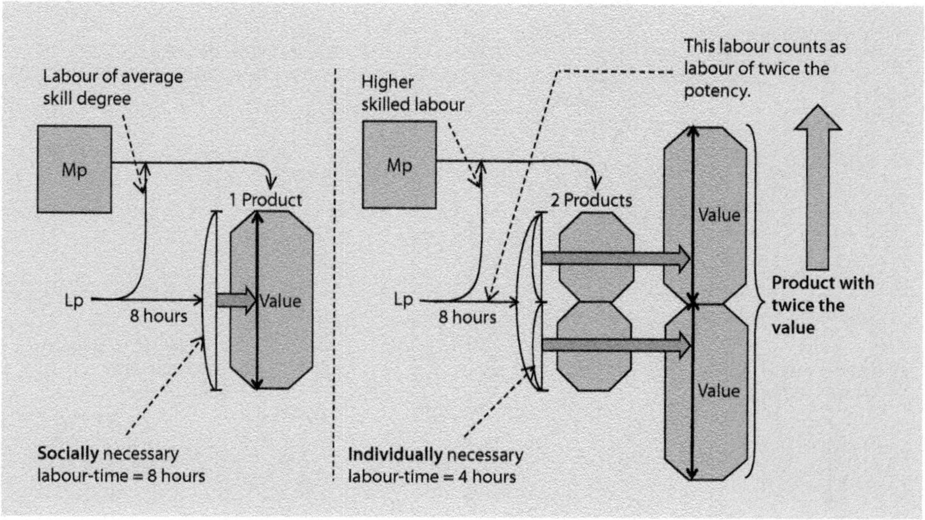

Fig. 2.13 Individual labour of a higher skill degree counts as labour of higher potency

commodity. The value of the commodity is determined by the labour-time necessary to produce it with a socially average degree of skill. Given this, how would a labour of a higher or lower skill degree that produces this commodity be evaluated? This is actually quite simple. Whether labour of a higher, lower, or average degree of skill, all of the labours produce the same kind of commodity, so by measuring the difference in the quantity of commodities produced in the same time span, we can see how labour of a higher or lower skill degree is abstract labour of so many times greater or lesser capacity than the case of labour of normal productive power. That is, we can definitely measure the degree to which the skill level of labour exceeds the average skill level of labour according to the degree to which use-values are produced in the same time span (*see* Fig. 2.13), although again we should bear in mind that there are concrete labours that produce no quantitatively measurable material product.

Complex Labour Reduced to Simple Labour

In terms of concrete labour, there is not only **simple labour**, which is the concrete labour performed using the labour-power an *ordinary individual physically possesses without any special development*, i.e. **simple labour-power**; but also **complex labour**, which is concrete labour performed using **complex labour-power** that requires special education or training and therefore *a special* **training cost**.

Differences in the skill degree of labour are differences in the degree of effectiveness of concrete labour, which can be uni-

2

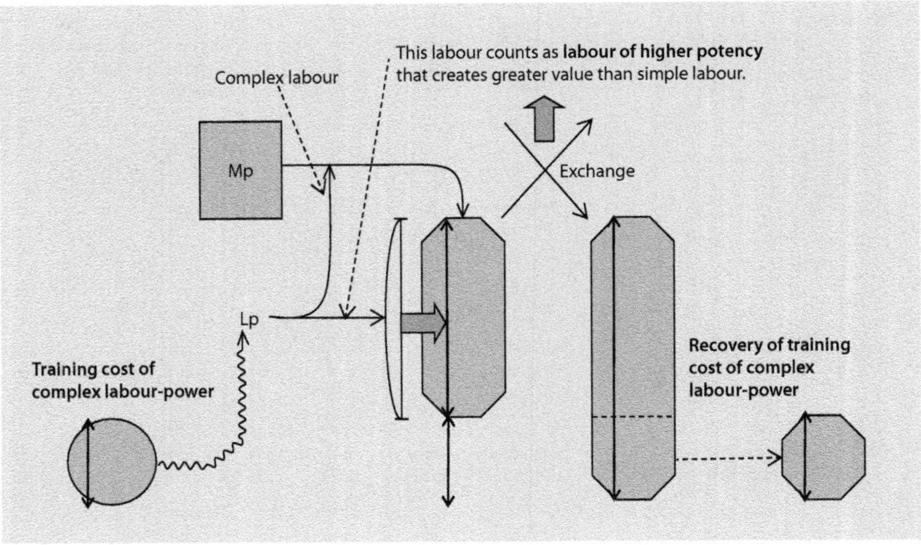

Fig. 2.14 Training cost of complex labour-power can only be recovered through the value of the commodity

formly evaluated by the greater or lesser quantity of products; whereas the distinction between simple labour and complex labour is a matter that concerns whether or not the labour-power exerted requires special training cost—bearing *no relation to the degree of effectiveness of the labour* performed using the labour-power. Moreover, complex labour is concrete labour that cannot be attained by simply piling up simple labour, so the products of complex labour are of a different kind than products of simple labour; this means that one cannot measure the degree of complexity through the quantity of products.

How is this distinction considered *in a society of commodity production*?

In a commodity production society, when the owner of a commodity has labour-power that necessitates a special expenditure for training, the cost is expended *privately* by that person. Moreover, *the person cannot recoup the training cost without exchanging the commodity he provides*. Thus, as long as complex labour is required in this society, the possessors of complex labour-power must recover the cost of training via the exchange of commodities (*see* Fig. 2.14).

The product of one hour of complex labour thus counts as something with more value than the product of one-hour of simple labour. If one hour of complex labour is reduced to simple labour, it would be equivalent to a period of time greater than that of simple labour. In other words, *complex*

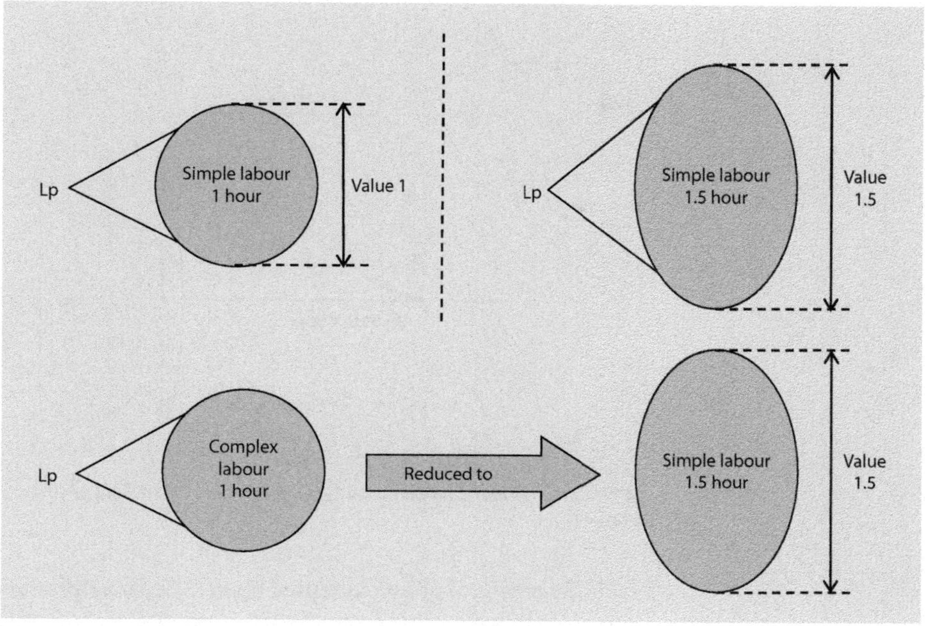

Fig. 2.15 Any kind of complex labour is reduced to simple labour

labour counts as labour of higher potency than simple labour, and can therefore *be reduced to so many times the amount of simple labour* (*see* Fig. 2.15).

In this way, the degree of the potency of complex labour is ultimately determined by the amount of training costs for the labour-power necessary to perform the labour.

From our everyday experience, we can see immediately that this conversion of complex labour to simple labour is always carried out. However, in capitalist society, the conversion is not only realised as the outcome of a long-term process accompanied by continual trial and error, but is also carried out via a complicated process through buying and selling of labour-power (which we will examine in the next chapter); therefore, the rate of conversion of various sorts of complex labour to simple labour is determined behind the backs of the producers or is posited by custom.

Hereinafter, complex labour will be reduced to simple labour and all labour-power will be seen as simple labour-power.

Transfer of the Value of the Means of Production; New Value and Old Value

The value of a commodity is determined by the labour-time socially necessary to produce it. This is, first and foremost, the new abstract labour added to the means of production (means of labour and objects of labour) transformed into products or consumed in this process. (*see* Fig. 2.16).

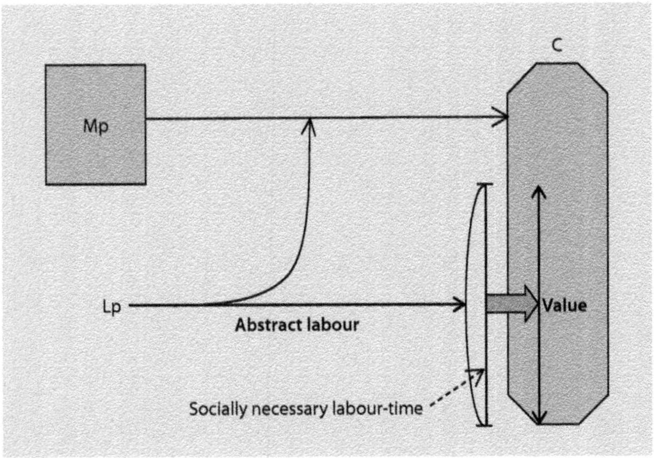

Fig. 2.16 Value of a commodity is determined by socially necessary labour-time

If the means of production used up in the current production already have value from the prior production—so that they contain abstract labour objectified from the preceding production—this value will enter into the commodity produced in the current production, forming one part of its value. The value of the commodity is thus the sum of the **old labour** contained in the means of production and the **new labour** created and added through the current production. In this way, the **transfer** and **maintaining** of the value of the means of production within the product occurs through the purposeful consumption of the means of the production within the process of production, but such purposeful consumption is performed by the aspect of concrete labour within the twofold character of labour. In other words, *concrete labour transfers the value of the means of production to the product and thereby maintains that value within the product* (*see* Fig. 2.17).

Just as the value formed in production is determined by socially necessary labour-time, the quantity of the transferred value is also only that which is of a social average[7]. The labour

7 Strictly speaking, the value of the means of production transferred during production is the value at the time that production starts, which is to say the magnitude of value determined by the labour-time socially necessary for production at that point in time. For this reason, labour-time is neither the individual labour-time that is actually expended to produce the means of production that are consumed in this production, nor is it the labour-time necessary under the socially average production conditions at the time of the production to be carried out. *The magnitude of the value of the means of production consumed is already determined prior to that*

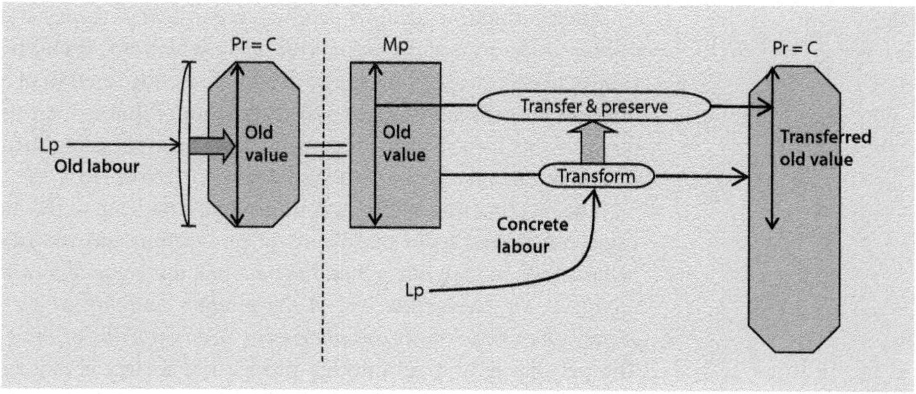

Fig. 2.17 Transfer of the value of the means of production via concrete labour

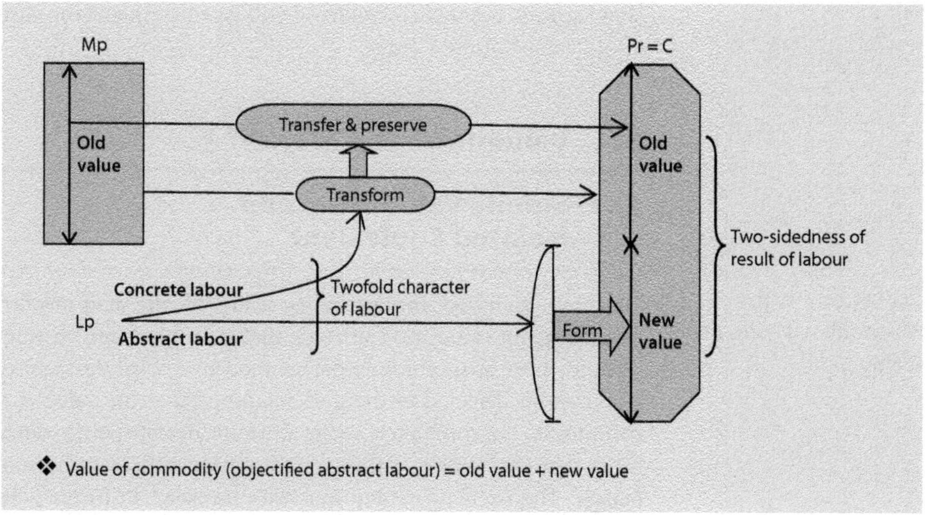

Fig. 2.18 Twofold character of labour and new and old value of the commodity

that produces a commodity has simultaneously the aspect of *concrete labour*, on the one hand, which involves the transfer and maintaining of the value of the means of production, and the aspect of *abstract labour*, on the other hand, which involves the formation of the value within the product. Thus, the *twofold character of labour* is further manifested here as the *twofold character of the outcome of labour*—as old value on the one hand and new value on the other (*see* Fig. 2.18).

production, so that it is not affected at all by the productive power pertaining to that production. This theoretically vital premise is dismissed by more than a few mathematical economists in their discussions of Marx's theory of value.

The production cost of a product, regardless of the form of society, is the sum of the old labour (abstract labour) that is the production cost of the means of production consumed in production plus the new labour (abstract labour) that is the production cost for the transformation of the product using these means of production—as explained in 1.4.1 (*see* ◘ Fig. 1.18).

The fact that the value of a commodity is made up of the old value transferred from the means of production and the new value added to it signifies that, here as well, the *value of a commodity is the production cost of the product common to every society, manifested in the peculiar form of an attribute of things.* The peculiarity of a commodity production society is that the new and old labour (both abstract labour) that is the production cost takes the form of the value objectified in the product.

When speaking of the «value» of a commodity—unless some special mention is made—I will be referring to the sum of old value and new value.

2.3 Value-form and Money[8]

2.3.1 Simple Value-form and Isolated Equivalent

Value-form as the Phenomenal Form of Value

We have analysed the exchange-value of the commodity, extracting out value and clarifying that it is objectified abstract labour whose magnitude is determined by socially necessary labour-time. This led to the understanding that the value of a commodity is a completely social attribute, despite being something that «pertains to a thing» existing separate from human beings. The exchange-value that we examined to begin with (*see* ◘ Fig. 2.5) is in fact nothing but value's phenomenal form. The **value-form of the commodity** is the *form in which the value of a commodity is manifested* or the *form in which the commodity manifests its own value*. Thus, the first thing we grasped as exchange-value was the value-form of the commodity. By means of analysis, we proceeded from the phenomenon of exchange-value to grasp value as its essence. So we now need to once again return to exchange-value (but based on the knowl-

8 ► Sections 2.3 to 2.5 deal with problems concerning the genesis of money, which Marx discusses in *Capital* in rather difficult but extremely brilliant and interesting passages. *See* Kuruma 1979 (Kuruma 2017) and Kuruma 1979–1985.

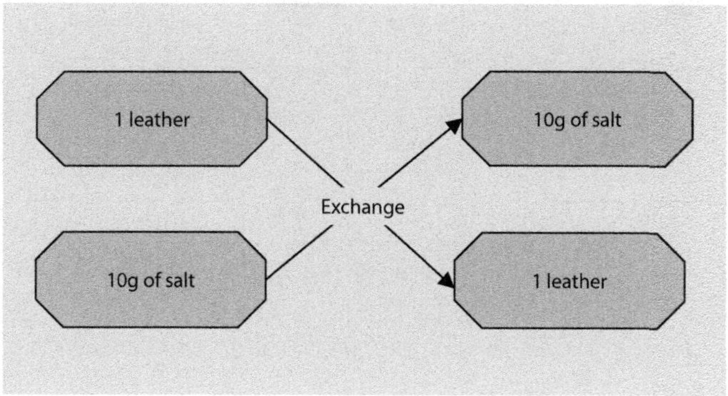

■ **Fig. 2.19** Simplest exchange-relation

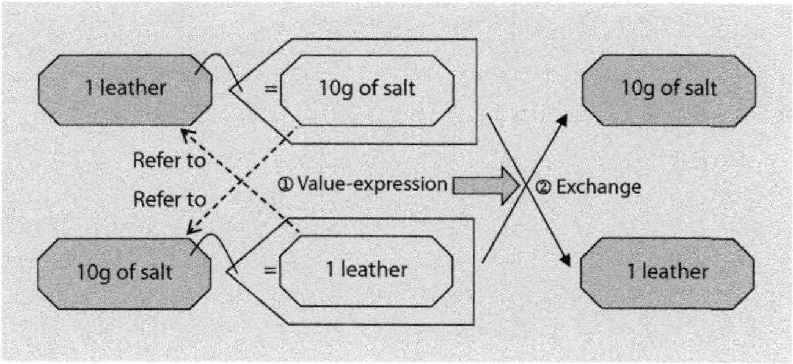

■ **Fig. 2.20** Value-expression precedes exchange of commodities

edge of value already obtained) in order to investigate the form that this essence takes, which is the phenomenal form of value.

The Simple Value-form of One Commodity and the Isolated Equivalent

As long as production is geared toward one's own demand, exchange is rare, only occurring for this or that object that those involved in exchange happen to have left over. Exchange between leather and salt, for instance, is at first is carried out at a random ratio of magnitude. But with the repetition of this exchange, the exchange ratio comes to be gradually settled, so that one piece of leather is exchanged for a given quantity of salt (*see* ■ Fig. 2.19).

However, in order for this exchange to actually be carried out, the leather, using the voice of its holder, must say, to begin with: «My value is the same as 10 g of salt, so if 10 g of salt are offered, I recognise the exchange immediately». Meanwhile, the 10 g of salt, using the voice of its holder, would say: «My value is the same as one piece of leather, so if it is offered, I recognise the exchange with it immediately» (*see* ■ Fig. 2.20).

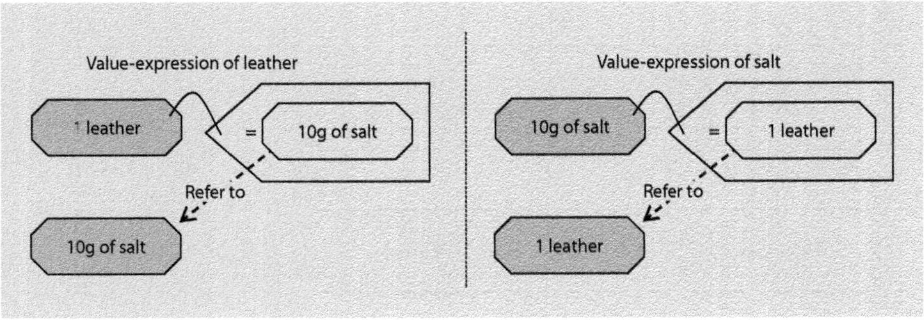

Fig. 2.21 Value-expression or value-form within the simple exchange relation

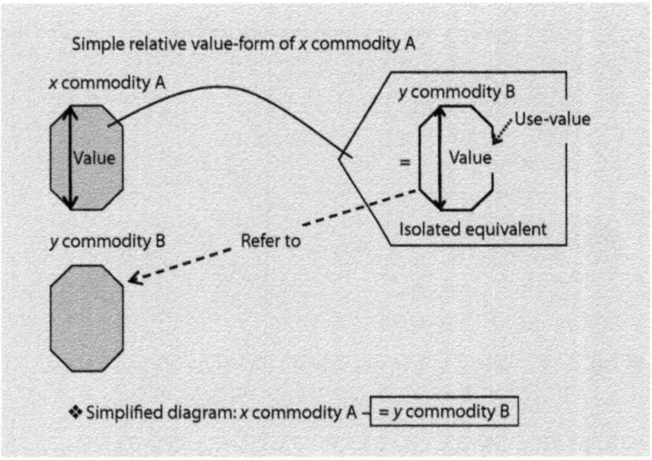

Fig. 2.22 Simple value-form and isolated equivalent

In short, both the leather and the salt are expressing their own value through another commodity. A *commodity expressing its own value in another commodity in this manner* is called **value-expression**. The value-expression of the leather and of the salt both have exactly the same form as a single commodity expressing its value in a single other commodity. This is the simplest form of value-expression (*see* Fig. 2.21).

Here an identical expression of value can be extracted from the case of either the leather or the salt by observing the commodity on the left as A and the commodity on the right as B (*see* Fig. 2.22).

We need, first of all, to keep in mind that this value-expression is the *value-expression of Commodity A* on the left (*x* quantity of Commodity A), and is an expression carried out by that commodity to express its own value; whereas

Commodity B on the right (*y* quantity of Commodity B) becomes the *material for that value-expression* of Commodity A. The diagram makes clear that Commodity A is an actual tangible commodity that is expressing its value. In contrast, Commodity B in the diagram could be written down as a «tag» (the embryonic form of a «price tag» indicating money) or conveyed through spoken language. Indeed, «*y* quantity Commodity B», whether written or spoken, is not the tangible Commodity B, but an ideal (or imagined) commodity depicted in a person's mind. Since a commodity cannot directly express its own value as «such-and-such labour-time», Commodity A expresses its own value in terms of «being equal to *y* quantity of Commodity B». As you can see, the commodity cannot express its own value by itself, but rather has to take another commodity as its equivalent. This peculiar manner to express the value of commodity is called the **roundabout way of value expression.**

Meanwhile, by Commodity A having had this value-expression, Commodity B assumes a special form that it otherwise could not take on. As long as Commodity A says that, «*y* quantity of Commodity B can immediately exchange with me because it is of equal value to myself», Commodity B will count as «something of equal value» (**equivalent**) with regard to Commodity A in particular. So Commodity B will have the power of unmediated, direct exchangeability with Commodity A. Thus, Commodity B is posited by Commodity A in the *form of being the equivalent of Commodity A* (**equivalent form**), and if Commodity B (through its holder as its personification) wishes to enter into exchange with Commodity A, the exchange could be carried out immediately. However, this is value-expression that Commodity A carries out on its own at its own discretion, regardless of Commodity B; so even if Commodity B has the special form as the equivalent, it is up to Commodity B whether the special power of this form vis-à-vis exchange with Commodity A will be exercised or not. It is akin Person A saying to Person B, «You are an appropriate spouse for me», so that B is capable of playing the role of spouse for A; but it is actually up to B whether or not this role will be performed.

It is thus by means of the value-expression of Commodity A that Commodity B becomes its equivalent. Commodity B, first of all, plays the role of making the value of Commodity A visible, becoming a sort of *mirror that reflects value* (**value-mirror**). Second, Commodity B *counts as immediate value* vis-à-vis Commodity A, so that *its corporal self is the direct incarnation of value* (**value-body**). In short, Commodity B, as the equivalent for Commodity A, is both its value-mirror and its value-body.

The form whereby *one* commodity expresses its own value in *one* other commodity is called the **simple value-form** of the commodity, and the commodity that serves as the equivalent is called the **isolated equivalent** because *only a single commodity* is the equivalent in this case.

2.3.2 Total Value-form and Particular Equivalent

Total Value-form of a Commodity and Innumerable Particular Equivalents

With the development of the exchange-relation, a higher stage is reached. Consider the historical example of a Siberian hunting tribe. Nearly the only item such a group had for exchange was leather. They had to travel to various places to exchange leather for other items (such as knives, bows, vodka, salt, etc.).

The point to note here is that, while the hunting tribe exchanged leather for many other sorts of products, the other tribes it encountered only exchanged their commodities for the tribe's leather; i.e. this exchange-relation, from the perspective of the other tribes, was the simple exchange-relation just elucidated.

◘ Figure 2.23 deals with these exchange-relations and the value-expressions that they are premised upon.

Each of the value-forms for other tribes' commodities depicted in the diagram is nothing more than the simple value-form, while the leather that is the equivalent of those commodities is still the isolated equivalent of each. From the perspective of the *hunting tribe's leather*, however, *all of the commodities of the various other tribes serve as its equivalent.* That is to say, *from leather's perspective*, we are dealing with a *new value-form*, called the **total value-form**. In this case, each of the commodities that are useful as the equivalent is *a single commodity among many equivalents*, and each equivalent is referred to as the **particular equivalent** (*see* ◘ Fig. 2.24).

The value of the leather is now expressed in innumerable particular equivalents, so that it comes to have manifold expressions. When value is thus expressed in so many other commodities, it becomes customary for the hunting tribe to view the value of leather separately from its use-value. At the same time, because it becomes necessary to gauge the same value in a continually increasing number of different equivalents, the determination of the magnitude of the value of leather gradually becomes fixed. That is to say, compared

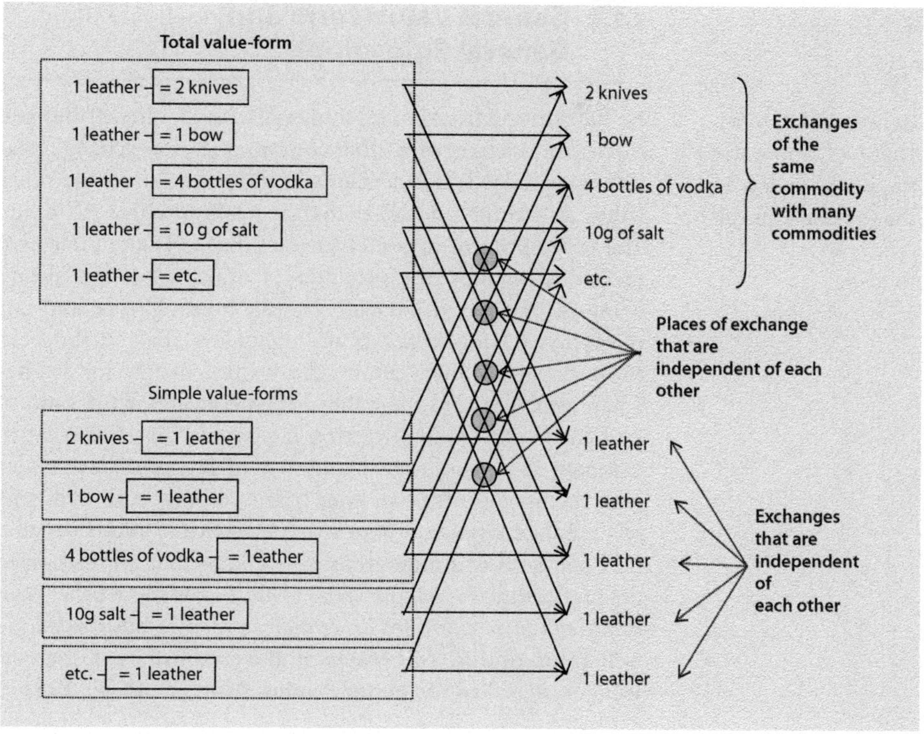

Fig. 2.23 Exchange-relations including the total value-form

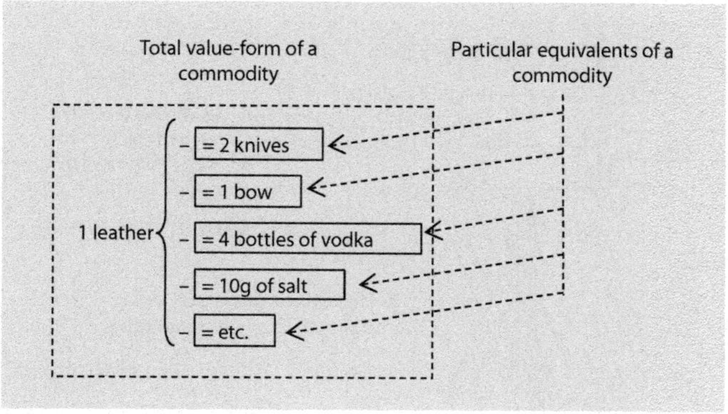

Fig. 2.24 Total value-form and innumerable particular equivalents

to the previous case of product exchange carried out separately, the value of leather has a much clearer shape, and therefore the leather itself takes on more of a character as a commodity.

2.3.3 General Value-form and General Equivalent

General Value-form That All Commodities Have in Common and the General Equivalent

As the hunting tribe comes into contact with other tribes and carries out exchange for other commodities, its exchange relation with those tribes develops to the point where the other tribes also come into an exchange relation with each other. The tribes become aware of the fact that not only their own products, but also the products of other tribes are always being exchanged for the leather of the hunting tribe, and this raises the *exchange relations* to a higher level. Every tribe seeks to exchange its own commodities immediately for leather when available, and the tribes become aware of the ratio of exchange with leather, making it possible for each tribe to compare the magnitude of their own commodities' values with the magnitude of another tribe's commodities. This sort of exchange relation—*from the perspective of the tribes* that now stand on common ground—signifies that, in relation to the hunters in Siberia, the *value of any one of those tribes' own commodities is expressed in leather*, and that both sides are well aware of this. This results in the establishment of a *new value-form*, called the **general value-form** (*see* ◘ Fig. 2.25).

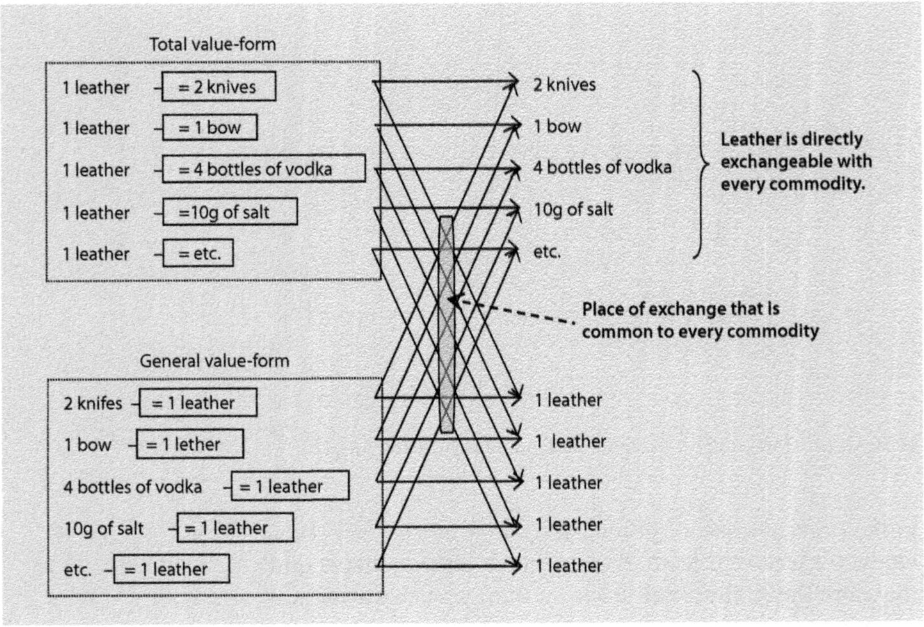

◘ **Fig. 2.25** Exchange-relations including the general value-form

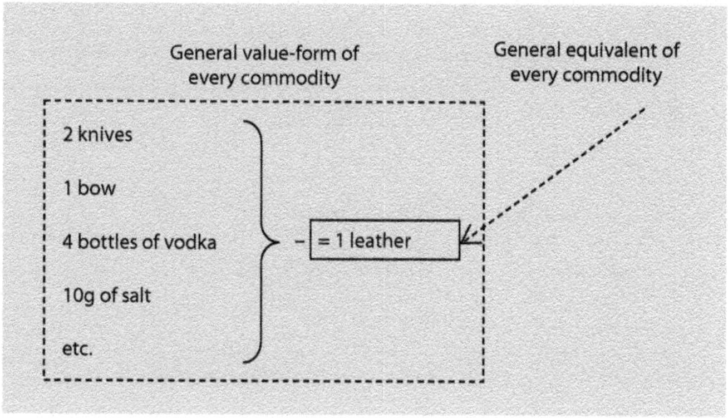

Fig. 2.26 General value-form and general equivalent

The general value-form is the *form* in which *all of the commodities* within the same «**commodity world**» *express their respective values* in *a single commodity* that is excluded from that world. The commodity positioned as the equivalent in the general value-form not only has *direct exchangeability with all of the commodities* of other people, but also *is useful for the common value-expression* of *all of the commodities* of these other people; therefore, it *serves as a means to measure and compare value*. For this reason, it is called the **general equivalent** (*see* Fig. 2.26).

In the figure above, all of the commodities within the commodity world express their own values generally, so that these commodities now can be mutually compared; i.e. the products have fully entered into a reciprocal relationship as commodities. *All of the commodities within the commodity world* have made a single commodity the general equivalent by means of their *joint action* (rather than as the result of the power of individual commodities); and in ► Sect. 2.5.1 we will see what it is that must carry out that joint action.

2.3.4 Money-form and Money

Money-form of Commodities and Money

With the development of the exchange-relations and the expansion of the commodity world, one commodity at any given time might play the role of general equivalent (within whatever the world's narrow or broad boundary might be), while a different commodity might play that same role at a different time. But once commodity exchange had become generalised, the role shifted everywhere to gold and silver, which are *the commodity type best suited to the role*. Gold and silver, and ultimately gold, thus became *money*, with direct

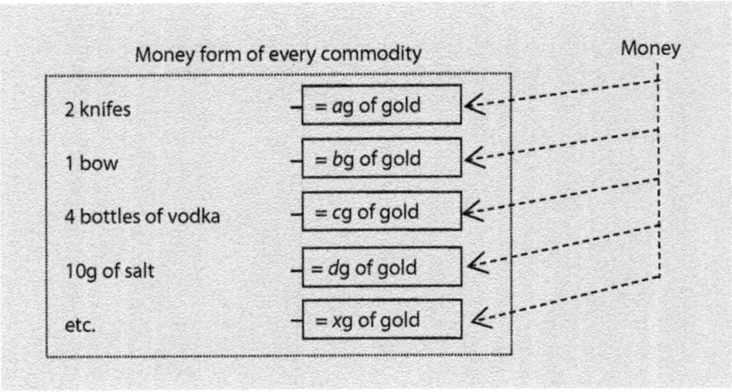

Fig. 2.27 Money-form and money

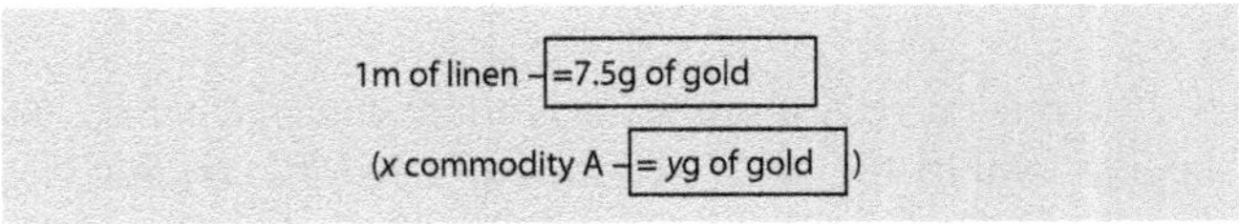

Fig. 2.28 Price-form of a commodity

exchangeability vis-à-vis every other commodity. This meant that all the other commodities became able to express, gauge, and compare their own values together.

Money is the *commodity to whose tangible form the function of general equivalent adheres and is conjoined*, thus becoming a *commodity that socially monopolises the function of general equivalent*. The *value-form whereby commodities express their own value in money* is called the **money-form**.

With the emergence of money, all the commodities within the commodity world express their own values in money, and if money is offered they are prepared to immediately be exchanged for it. Money, meanwhile, always has the power to be immediately exchanged for all the other commodities, supplying the material for their value-expression (*see* Fig. 2.27)

Price-form of Commodities

The value of a commodity expressed in money is called its **price**. Here a commodity takes price-form. For instance, the value of five meters of cotton thread is expressed in price terms as ⊣ =7.5g of gold (this frame symbolises a price tag). Here, the five meters of cotton thread *has the price*: 7.5 g of gold (*see* Fig. 2.28).

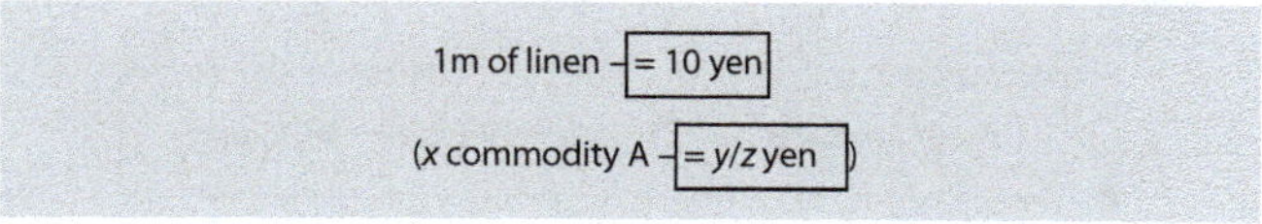

Fig. 2.29 Indication of price in a money name

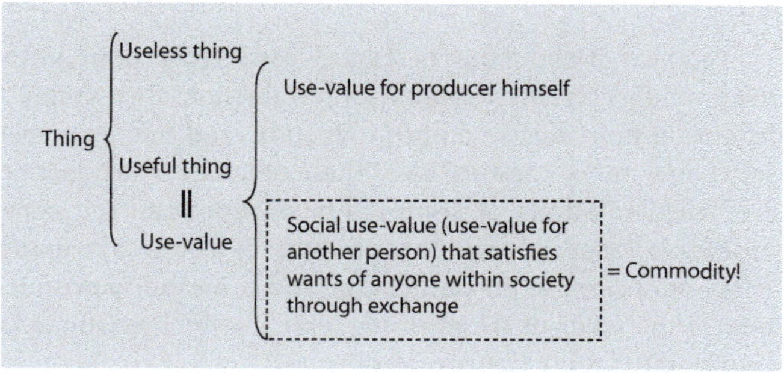

Fig. 2.30 Commodity is a particular social form of labour products

If 750 mg (or *z* mg) is set as the unit to measure the monetary quantity, and the **money-name** «yen»[9] is attached to this quantity, the price of the commodity would be expressed as above (*see* Fig. 2.29).

The expression of the value of a commodity in gold is its money-form or price. A *single equation now suffices to express the value of the commodity in a socially valid manner* because the equivalent commodity, gold, already possesses the character of money.

2.4 Relations of Commodity Production and their Peculiar Character

2.4.1 Relations of Commodity Production

The Commodity Is the Particular Social Form of Labour Products

The commodity is the particular social form taken by products of labour. A commodity's use-value must be a use-value for other people (a **social use-value**) and its value is a completely social attribute that is determined socially. The commodity is therefore a thoroughly social entity (*see* Fig. 2.30).

9 I will refer to money units in Japanese «*yen*» because Japan uses the easy-to-understand *decimal system* for its monetary system and its measuring system in general.

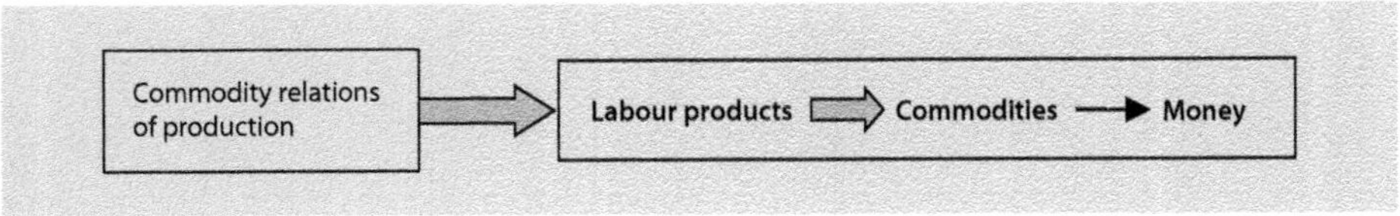

Fig. 2.31 Under relations of commodity production labour-products become commodities and money emerges out of commodities

Products of labour only necessarily assume the commodity-form under certain relations of production that connect labouring individuals within production; and money comes into being out of commodities. These relations of production are called **relations of commodity production**. The **commodity** is the social form that products of labour take under relations of commodity production, and **commodity production** is the form of social production in which relations of commodity production are dominant.

Products of labour assuming the commodity-form under relations of commodity production, and money emerging from out of this, concerns an objective law that asserts itself independently of people's will and desire, with this law instead determining that will and desire (*see* Fig. 2.31).

Relation of Private Labours to Social Labour Takes a Peculiar Form

We saw in 1.4.2 that any form of society requires a *social distribution of the total labour* (**social division of labour**) and a *distribution of the aggregate product* (*see* Fig. 1.28). For relations of production other than commodity production, the social division of labour and social distribution of products are consciously decided on in advance based on the intentions of human beings, and the manner in which this is done is immediately clear. In the case of Association in particular, this is plainly carried out as diagrammed on the following page (*see* Fig. 2.32).

In the case of commodity production as well, a system must be formed to carry out a social division of labour corresponding to the total needs of society, and the aggregate product must be distributed in line with these needs. Under commodity production, however, labouring individuals carry out production in complete accordance to their own free will, judgment, responsibility, and calculations. The labour that is the expenditure of their labour-power is **private labour** exerted privately by each producer. Therefore, directly speaking, labour itself has absolutely no social character. Likewise, the products produced are **privately appropriated** by each producer, with the producers legally recognising each other as the private owners of products belonging to them personally (*see* Fig. 2.33).

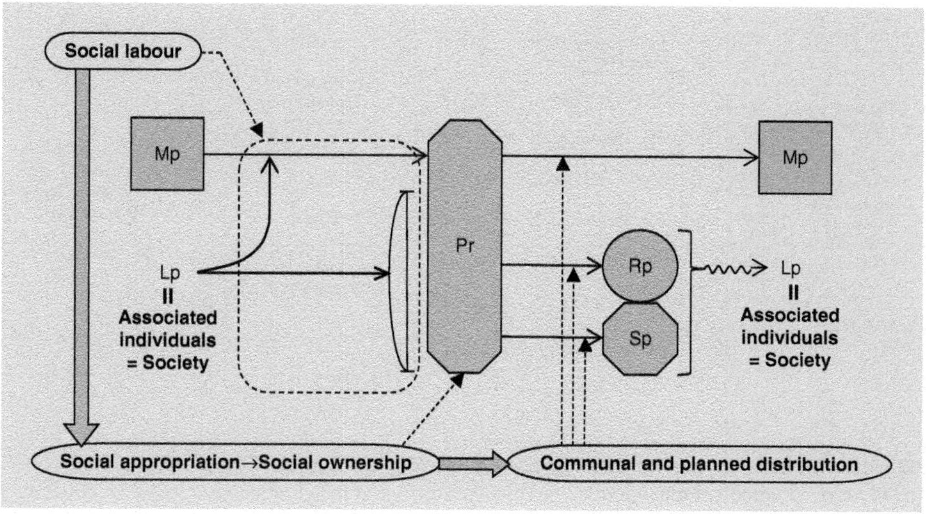

Fig. 2.32 Social labour, social appropriation, and social ownership under Association

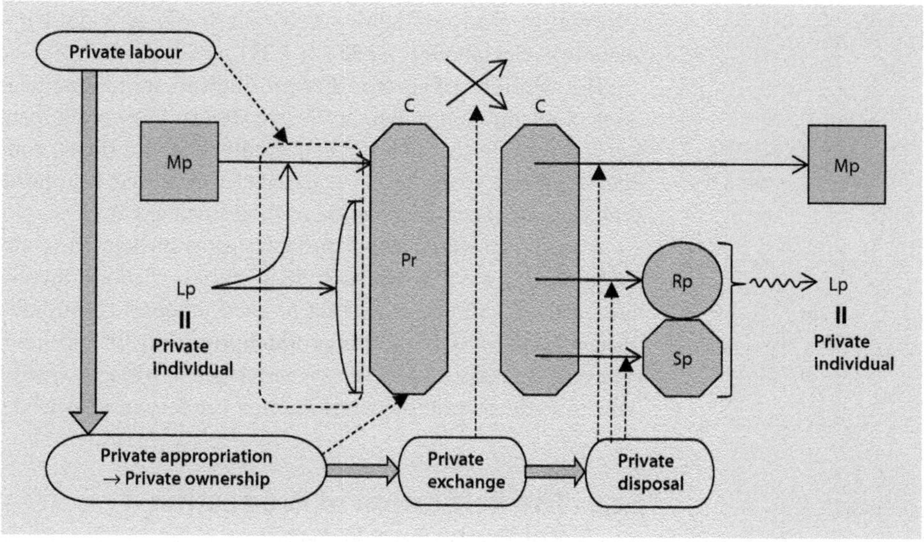

Fig. 2.33 Private labour, private appropriation, and private ownership under commodity production

How is it possible, then, for commodity production to exist as a system of social production? The fact is that, even though the commodity producers do not directly form relations of production between each other (as human beings), they are connected via the detour of exchanging their own products as commodities. The characteristic point here is that even if products that are produced by private labour appear

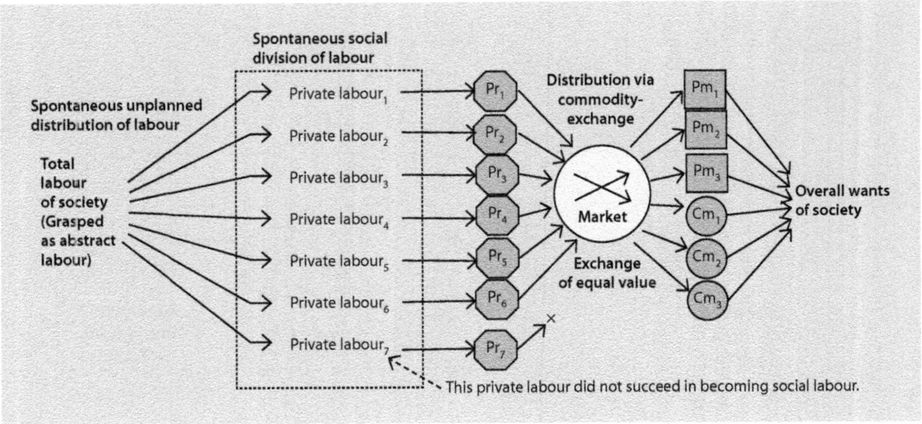

Fig. 2.34 Relations of production between commodity producers are established through relations of commodity exchange

on the market as commodities, the private labour only satisfies a social need if a product can be exchanged for another commodity (and any labour that fails to do so would not become social labour) (*see* Fig. 2.34).

The **relations of commodity production** are unique relations of production in which the private producers first form a social relation through the commodity-form of their products of labour, with their private labour only first becoming social labour through the value of their products[10].

A society in which labour products generally take the commodity-form, so that the dominant social relations involve human beings mutually relating to each other as commodity owners, is called a **commodity production society**. In fact, however, only capitalist society is such a society. We will see why this is the case when we subsequently examine capital (*see* ▶ Sect. 6.1).

2.4.2 The Reification of Production Relations and Fetishism

The Peculiar Social Character of Private Labour Is Reflected in the Minds of Commodity Producers

The peculiar social character of private labour, just discussed, becomes visible to people at the place of exchange. The social connection between the private labours of the producers manifests itself, as far as they are concerned, not as a direct

10 The passage from Marx quoted in Footnote 1 of this chapter addresses this issue of how the relations of commodity production are the specific form in which the division of social labour and the distribution of total social products assert themselves.

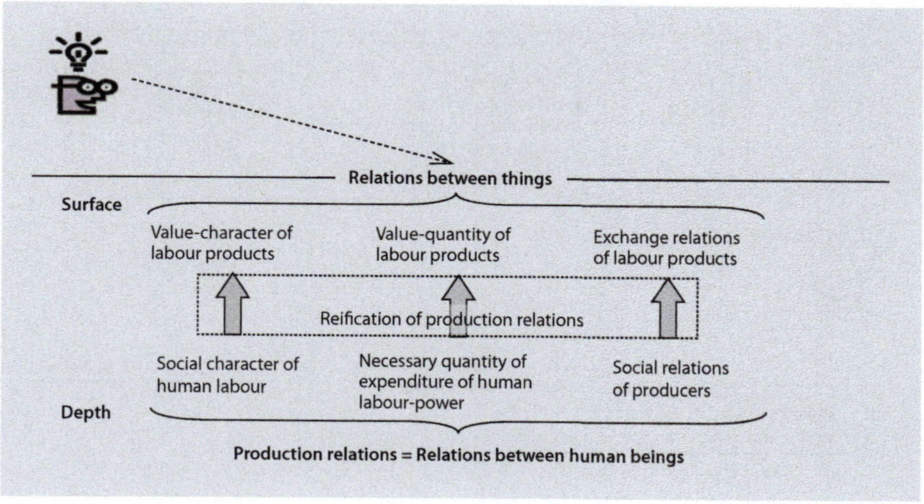

Fig. 2.35 Reification of relations of production: relations between human individuals appear as relations between things

social relation that connects the labours, but as *material relations between people* or *social relations between things*.

Under commodity production, where labour products assume the commodity-form, the social character of people's own labour is reflected within their minds as the material character of the labour products themselves, i.e. as a socio-natural property of a thing. In this way, their own social relation to the total labour is mentally reflected as a social relation between things that lie outside of them. This is the **reification of relations of production**, where a relation between human beings appears to be a relation between things (*see* Fig. 2.35).

Fetishism

People completely lose sight of the relations between human beings because those relations (production relations) present themselves as relations between things (material relations). It appears as if the products in the hands of human beings are in a relationship with each other and also in a relationship with human beings. This manner in which people are deceived by the objective, material appearance of the social character of labour, is exactly like worshiping and being under the sway of a **fetish** (such as a *totem pole*), which is thought to have mystical powers despite actually being something created by human beings. This *distorted consciousness* and the *actions based upon it* are referred to by the term **fetishism** (*see* Fig. 2.36).

Fetishism arises as soon as products of labour assume the commodity form. An outward appearance arises where

2

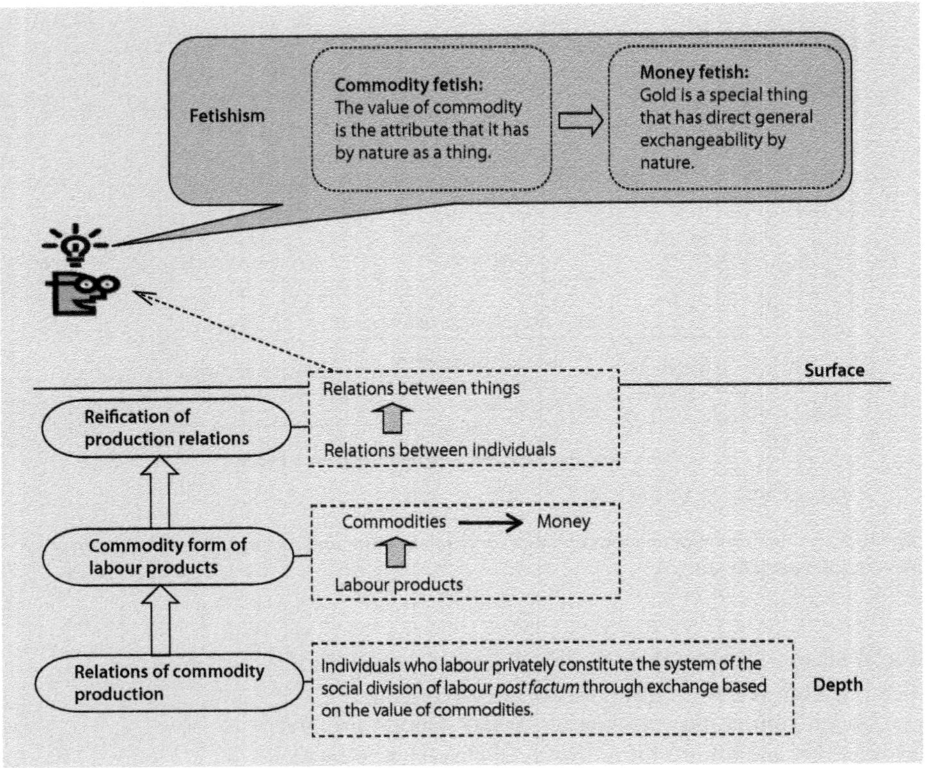

Fig. 2.36 Reification of relations of production and fetishism are inevitable under commodity production

the commodity seems to inherently have a value that gives it the power of exchangeability with another commodity, thereby generating the illusion that the commodity is a sort of enigmatic thing with special powers. The commodity thus comes to **dominate human beings** as a **commodity fetish**.

Within the commodity world, the specific commodity gold becomes money, making it possible for every commodity to express its value in money. This means that gold's particular natural body, in its given state, counts as a mass of value, thereby completing the shape of fetishism. Gold has direct exchangeability with every commodity because all the other commodities excluded gold from the commodity world, making it the general equivalent. But people imagine that gold's property of direct exchangeability is an inherent attribute of gold, like its weight or luster, and that other commodities generally express their value in gold because it is inherently money. Thus, as soon as it is extracted from the bowels of the earth, gold is already the *direct embodiment of human labour*.

Here we have the source of the worship of gold or **mammonism**. Money acquires the overwhelming power to **dominate human beings**, known as the **money fetish**. This is how people become absorbed in a thing—money. In short, money comes to dominate human individuals.

2.4.3 The Personification of Things and Property Laws of Commodity Production

Exchangers Must Recognise Each Other as Commodity Owners

Under relations of commodity production, the relations of production are penetrated by reification, so that people are dragged around by things—commodities and money. But commodities are unable to bring themselves to market, nor can they enter exchange with each other on their own. And the desires the commodities are meant to satisfy pertain to human attributes, not to the commodities themselves.

For products of labour to enter a mutual relation as commodities, they thus need living human beings to play a role as their representatives. Until now, the **persons**[11] who carry out this role refers concretely to the commodity holder and the money holder, i.e. the seller and the buyer. These persons come into a mutual relationship as representatives of commodity and money. The commodity holder, on the one side, is only able to hand over his own commodity and come into possession of the other person's commodity on the basis of the consent of the commodity holder on the other side, which is to say through an **intentional act** of both parties; so they must recognise each other as **private owners** of commodities. **Private ownership** must be *socially recognised*, in other words.

11 The word «**person**» is of course used to indicate an individual human being, an individual personality, or an individual as distinguished from a thing or animal. But in political economy it means, in particular, *a social character or role that is socially recognised or has social validity*. The English word «person» stems from Latin *persōna*, which refers to the masks worn by stage actors (*dramatis persona*). In our case, the person «seller» and «buyer» refers to the role played part in the market to represent a commodity and money, respectively, regardless of which individuals happen to be playing each role. *The very same individuals* who come into contact with each other as labouring individuals at the more profound level of society are concerned with each other as a «person» representing the thing commodity or money when they interact at the surface level in the marketplace. Persons within commodity production also appear legally as a person (natural person and legal person) who is the subject of rights and duties.

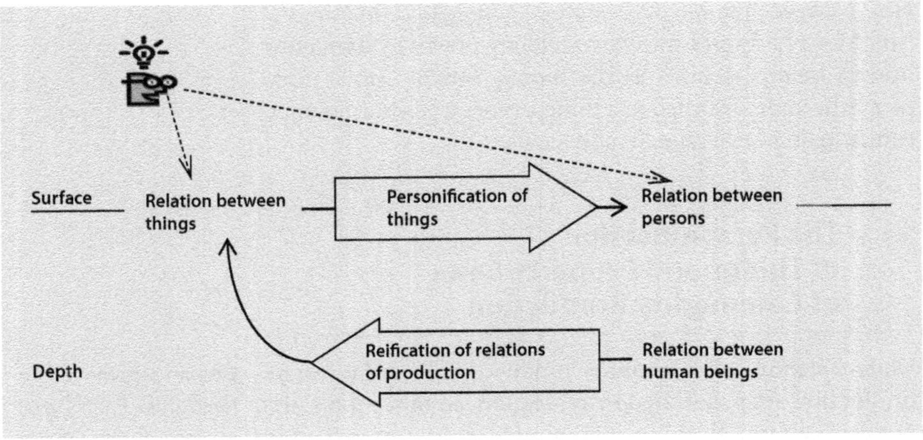

Fig. 2.37 Personification of things: Things are represented by persons

This **legal relation** which takes the form of a *contract* between the persons concerned, is a **relation of will** between them, and its content is posited by their economic relation. In commodity exchange, various kinds of human beings exist only as persons representing commodities or money, i.e. as commodity owners or money owners. Thus, *the things that bear economic relations are necessarily represented by various persons*, and we can refer to this as the **personification of things**.

Commodity production, through the reification of relations of production, signifies not only that social relations between human individuals are manifested as relations between things, but also that these things come to be represented by persons (*see* Fig. 2.37).

Property Law of Commodity Production

In the sphere of commodity exchange, commodity holders recognise each other as private owners. But in so doing, the person on one side cannot see the economic relations under which the other person became a commodity holder. One can only assume that this other person *legally* came into possession of the commodity through his own labour—rather than obtaining it in some illegal manner. In this world, *it is assumed that the* **ownership title** *of private owners stems from their,* **own labour** *and this assumption gains social currency socially as a law*, referred to as the **property law of commodity production**[12].

12 Private labour and the social division of labour are what turn products of labour into commodities, and money emerges from out of this. But in the market, where commodities and money are exchanged, one has no idea how the holders of commodities and

2.4.4 *Homo Oeconomicus* Illusion

Commodity World: A World of Liberty, Equality, Private Property, and Self-Interest

Under commodity production, what is visible to people are only the relations between economic things and the relations between the persons who represent these things. If one focuses on the former relations alone, the commodity world will appear as a *world of fetishism*; whereas if the latter relations are the focus, it will seem that *it is a world in which mutually equal private owners*, as ***homo oeconomicus***[13], *behave themselves like moving molecules, taking their own self-interest as the sole principle*. In viewing the commodity world with a fetishistic eye, people admire the astounding power of things, and they are satisfied with their freedom from their perspective as *homo oeconomicus*.

In this world, everyone is self-concerned, and the power that posits them in relations with each other is simply the power of their own self-interest, personal gain, and private interests. Here the idea is established that precisely because each person, as *homo oeconomicus*, is only concerned with himself and gives no thought to others, their mutual profit or

---

of money came into their possession; nor does one inquire into each particular case. One can only say, simply, that in all cases the commodities and money were produced by the private labour of each holder. That is, one can only assume that everyone is the owner of the commodity based on his own private labour. However, as we shall see later, *under capitalist production* the labouring individuals are separated from the means of production and do not possess them at all, so that ownership and labour are completely separated. Despite this, the sales and purchases on the market are carried out based on contracts between private owners, and therefore, on that surface level of the exchange of commodities, the property laws of commodity production still hold sway. In fact, however, people have come into possession of commodities and money, not through their own labour, but as the crystallisation of the labour of others that is rendered independent of the labouring individuals. This means that the property laws of commodity production are a mere external appearance, concealing the capitalist appropriation underneath. However, when capitalist production is viewed from the angle of reproduction, this hidden fact is revealed. This point will be looked at in ► Chapts. 8 and 9, but here it is at least worth noting the occurrence of this inversion.

13 According to economics (or the neo-classical school), human beings are often said to ultimately act in accordance with their own economic interests, essentially speaking, in pursuit of maximum economic benefits at the minimum cost. This premise of this view is a society consisting solely of such individuals, so that their arguments unfold quite separate from reality. The Latin term «***homo oeconomicus***» refers to a human being conceived of in this manner.

the overall profit—the «commonweal»—can be achieved as the outcome of a pre-established harmony between their actions or thanks to the perfect providence of a divine «invisible hand» (Smith 1776: Smith 1937, p. 423).

Homo Oeconomicus Illusion

I use the term ***homo oeconomicus* illusion** to refer to the illusion that the *behaviour of human beings as the personification of things arises from an inherent human nature*. This illusion, like fetishism, is the inevitable product of relations of commodity production.

Human Beings Become Visible by Stripping Away Fetishism and the *Homo Oeconomicus* Illusion

Not only are social relations between labouring individuals (relations of production) reflected in people's minds as relations between things, but the relations of production between labouring individuals are concealed further by the fact that relations between things are manifested as relations between the persons representing those things (*see* ◘ Fig. 2.37). The only relations between human beings that enter people's minds are the relations between *persons* on the **surface layer**, and in their everyday life they cannot perceive the social relations between producers at the **deeper layer**. The «common sense» regarding the economic phenomena of capitalist society is an awareness of the visible outward appearance of relations between things as well as relations between persons. For political economy as a science, it is vital to explain this outward appearance on the basis of a familiarity with and knowledge of the deeper layer.

Once we are aware of the *reification of production relations* peculiar to commodity production and of the *fetishism* that arises from it, as well as the *personification of things* and the *homo oeconomicus illusion* that emerges from this situation, we can perceive the relations between human beings (production relations) that underlie the relations between things that are visible on the surface of commodity production. Furthermore, we can become familiar with the social situation particular to commodity production, where the production process controls human beings, rather than human beings controlling the production process.

At the same time, through this understanding, *it becomes possible to understand which sorts of human consciousness and actions* within capitalist society—out of the variety of human consciousness and innumerable actions based upon it—*are determined and limited by commodity production, making it possible to separate such determined consciousness and actions from those that are not determined by commodity production.*

For example, the mode of behaviour of people who will do anything for money can be said to be completely determined by relations of commodity production. But, at the same time, we can see various modes of behaviour, even in capitalist society, where a person ignores personal benefit to work for the sake of others. Relations of commodity production do not essentially determine such behaviour. In most cases it would be a manifestation of a **species essence** that *individuals possess as human beings*. The awareness that human beings under commodity production are generally dominated by money, provides us with the ability to perceive such modes of behaviour as a **universal human nature** that exists within the *actions of such individuals*, rather than simply dismissing such actions as exceptional or saintly.

Conscious Actions of Those Involved in Production and Economic Laws

Relations between people are manifested as relations between things under commodity production relations, but since economic things are represented by legal persons, every economic phenomenon is mediated by the intentional acts of those involved in production. Both the changes in the supply and demand of commodities, and the resulting price fluctuations, arise through the intentional actions of those actors. However, when political economy deals with economic phenomena (as is the case in economics), it does not deal with such intentional actions because they are determined by the underlying economic relations. For instance, if price rises, it can be simply said that «supply will increase and demand decrease» because one knows that the price rise will cause those involved in production to increase supply, thereby reducing demand.

The reason political economy does not deal with the particular behaviour of individual human beings is not because it ignores human beings, but rather because it deals with the behaviour of human beings within social production, where the production process governs them. One should not mistake the fact that human beings do not directly appear as meaning that political economy is a field of study in which human beings do not exist. Indeed, it is only when one supposes a completely abstract image of human beings along the lines of *homo oeconomicus*—so as to think that the purest economic process results from the unrestricted behaviour of this *homo oeconomicus*—that one ends up ignoring the undeniable social framework that restricts actual human beings, thus shutting out the real human beings.

2.5 Necessity of the Genesis of Money

Section Structure

As seen in ▶ Sect. 2.3, the value-form develops along with the development of exchange-relations. The development from the simple value-form to the total value-form corresponds to an expansion of exchange-relations, where a single commodity actively involves itself with other commodities, and this development can occur without a reliance on the power of other commodities. This development corresponds to the development from the isolated equivalent to the particular equivalent. Next, the total value-form develops into the general value-form, in which every commodity equates a single other commodity to itself, so that the particular equivalent develops into the general equivalent. This development is already something that cannot be brought about by the power of individual commodities on their own; rather, it is achieved for the first time through the *joint action of all of the commodities in the commodity world*. When the general equivalent adheres to the tangible form of a specific commodity, this commodity comes to be a special commodity that monopolises the function of general equivalent, i.e. it becomes money. Historically speaking, the commodities that become money are gold and silver, and ultimately gold alone.

With the genesis of money, the following three questions arise: (1) Why must all the commodities in the commodity world carry out a joint action to exclude one commodity, thereby turning it into the general equivalent? (2) Why is it that a specific commodity monopolises the function of general equivalent, so that its tangible form and this function adhere to each other? (3) Why is the specific commodity gold and silver, and ultimately gold alone?

2.5.1 What Brings About the Joint Action that Gives Birth to the General Equivalent

First Question

The decisive breakthrough in the formative process of money is the formation of a general equivalent, but the general equivalent—and therefore the general value-form as well—is first formed by all the commodities in the commodity world jointly excluding a single commodity from this world, forcing upon it the role of general equivalent. What exactly, then, causes this *joint action of the commodity world* to inevitably arise?

Internal Contradiction of Commodity-producing Labour

As we have seen, the labour of commodity producers is carried out directly as private labour, with the labour in itself having absolutely no social unity. However, in order for social production to be feasible, the producers' labour must, in some way or another, demonstrate that it is a constituent part of the total labour of society, as something that forms the system of the social division of labour (*see* ◘ Fig. 2.34).

It is clearly a **contradiction** for exclusively private labour to also have actuality as social labour, but such a contradiction is inherent to the labour carried out under relations of commodity production[14].

Contradiction of Labour Takes the Material Form of the Commodity's Contradiction

The **mediation**[15] **of this contradiction** cannot possibly be carried out by labour itself. It is carried out, rather, through the exchange of products that the labour creates. Thus, under relations of commodity production, just as social relations between human beings within labour take the material form of relations between labour products, the **contradiction inherent to labour**, takes the form of a **contradiction of the commodity** as a unity of use-value and value—not the direct form of a contradiction of labour itself. In other words, it appears in the material form of the commodity's contradiction.

Contradiction of the Commodity: Contradiction Between Use-value and Value

What does it mean to say that the unity of use-value and value constitutes a «contradiction»? This is referring to the fact that a given commodity as *use-value* is the *product of useful private labour that occupies only one of the branches of the social division of labour* that is spontaneously generated; whereas as *value* it seeks to be *recognised as a value-body and*

14 In the objective world of reality, not only does every thing contain aspects that are in mutual opposition, but it is precisely through such internal opposition that the thing itself can exist. The opposition constitutes the thing's motive force, generating its various forms. The term «**dialectic**» refers to this state of things in the objective world. A *dialectical view of the world* had already emerged in Ancient Greece, and *Hegel* later deepened and systematised this view. *Hegel* used the term «**contradiction**» to indicate the internal opposition that brings about the movement and development of things and concepts. *Marx* inherited the correct content of Hegel's dialectic and made it his own. The *core of the dialectic* is that the motive force of the movement and development of a thing, and what gives birth to the its various forms, is its own *internal opposition*. In this sense, the term dialectic must be clearly distinguished from a logical contradiction in terms.

If a thing is a perfectly harmonious existence, containing no opposition within itself, then its movement can only be brought about by some outside force. If everything were that sort of harmonious existence, the world would be in a completely stagnant situation. In fact, however, every thing in the world is in a state of constant change and development, and within each thing is its motive force for movement. And that force consists of the *contradictions that actually exist*.

Within the labour that exists under relations of commodity production there is the contradiction where private labour must become social labour. This is the objective contradiction that exists within this real world.

The term «contradiction» that will occasionally appear in this book always signifies an objective contradiction.

15 The «**mediation**» **of a contradiction** means to act as the intermediary between the two oppositional elements, but this intercession does not integrate the two elements. Rather, it *creates a new form* so that the two elements can coexist.

2

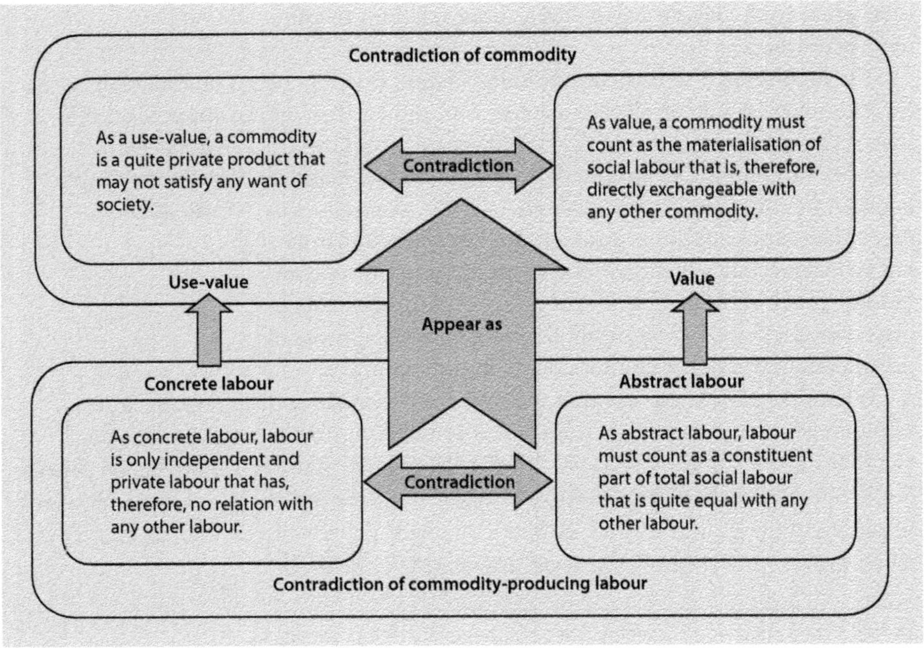

■ **Fig. 2.38** Contradiction of commodity-producing labour appears as the contradiction of the commodity

to be exchanged with any other commodity as the objectification of abstract human-labour (*see* ■ Fig. 2.38).

Contradiction of the Exchange Process

The contradiction of the commodity, as we grasp through our analysis, is not manifested in a form that is visible to everyone. However, when commodities seek to be mutually exchanged, this contradiction becomes visible as the **contradiction of the exchange process**.

A Commodity Must Demonstrate That It Is a Use-value

The exchange process is a process in which commodities are actually in motion and come into the hands of different commodity holders. First and foremost, it is a process through which commodities pass from the hands of those for whom they are not use-values to the hands of those for whom they are. Thus, the commodity must first of all encounter another commodity holder who desires its use-value and then pass into the hands of this other person. When the commodity thus finds another commodity holder who desires it, and passes into this person's hands, we refer to this as the «**realisation of the commodity as use-value**». This is how the commodity *demonstrates that it is a use-value for another person*.

A Commodity Must Demonstrate That It Is a Value

Even if a given commodity comes across a commodity possessor who desires it, this commodity holder will not immediately just hand over the commodity. This is because the person is offering a commodity for exchange to obtain in

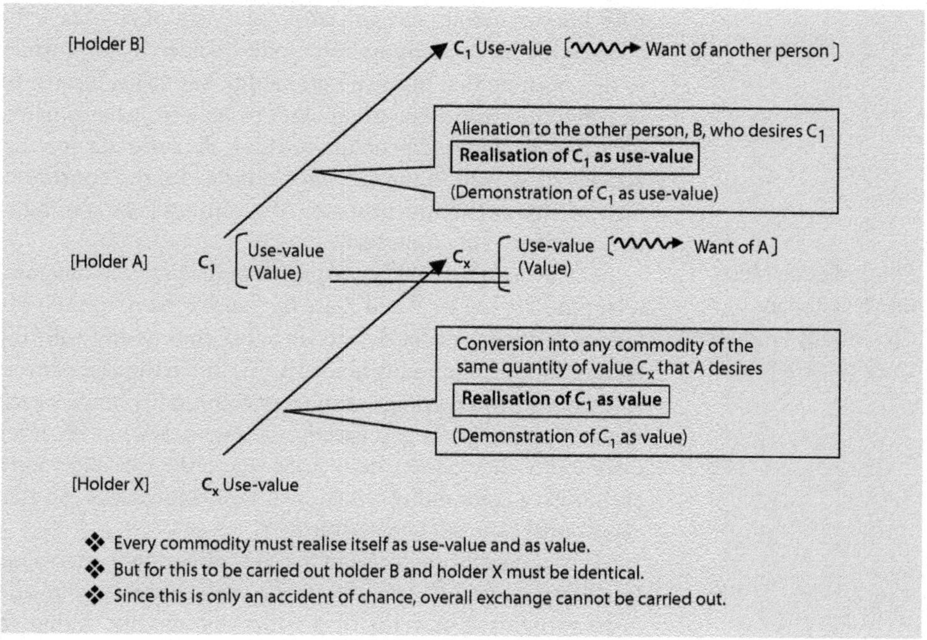

Fig. 2.39 Contradiction of the exchange process: Contradiction between the two realisations of the commodity

return the commodity he desires. He is only able to obtain another commodity in exchange for his own when his commodity counts vis-à-vis this other commodity as the value-body, and when any other commodity recognises his commodity as value. If this is expressed from the commodity's perspective, it can be said that the commodity must *demonstrate that it is value*. We refer to this as the «**realisation of the commodity as value**».

In order for a commodity to pass into the hands of the other commodity holder who desires it, so that the commodity is realised as use-value, the holder of this commodity must, prior to this, obtain the particular commodity he desires in exchange for this. However, in order for this commodity holder to be able to obtain a given commodity in exchange for his own commodity (and for the commodity to thus be realised as value) it must be demonstrated, prior to this, that his own commodity is a thing that satisfies some need (so that it is realised as use-value).

The exchange process is thus, simultaneously, a process of the realisation of the commodity as use-value and as value. However, *both of the realisations mutually presuppose and exclude each other* (*see* Fig. 2.39). On one hand, for commodity holder A to hand over his commodity to commodity holder B, he must

Contradictory Relation of the Realisation of a Commodity as Use-value and Realisation as Value have his commodity recognised as value, and then obtain the commodity he wants from commodity holder X. Meanwhile, to demonstrate that his own commodity has value, it must be shown to be a use-value for another person, by actually handing it over to commodity holder B. This is the contradiction that actually exists within the exchange process, i.e. the **contradiction of the exchange process**—the commodity's contradiction manifested in visible form.

Contradiction Must Be Mediated for Commodity Production To Be Generalised

As can be immediately grasped from the previous diagram, if commodity holder B and X are the same person, commodity holder A can immediately exchange his commodity with the commodity of commodity holder B = X. But in the case of overall exchange, where a large number of commodity holders each want to exchange their respective commodities for whatever commodity they desire, such cases where the two sides want each other's commodity would be a rare coincidence. So that exceptional case will be set aside here.

The commodity as a real material form is only a use-value. But every commodity seeks to make itself count as value and to be recognised as value by another commodity. Although every commodity wants to be recognised as value, these commodities will not necessarily recognise that another commodity counts as value. This means that commodities are not able to come into a mutual relation as value, and therefore cannot enter a mutual relation as commodities. Somehow *this contradiction must be mediated* so that overall commodity exchange can be carried out, thus allowing *for general commodity production*. How can a way out of this blind alley be found?

Contradiction Is Mediated Through the Formation of a General Equivalent

The mediation or breakthrough is in fact contained within the development of the value-form that we examined in ► Sect. 2.2. That is, if *all of the commodity holders come into a relation with a single other commodity that is in the position of* **general equivalent** *vis-à-vis their own commodities*, their own commodities can relate to each other as value, and therefore as commodities.

Concretely speaking, the following occurs. A given commodity holder, rather than immediately seeking to exchange his own commodity for a commodity with the specific use-value he desires, first seeks to exchange it for the general equivalent. In this process, all that is necessary for the commodity holder is to be able to find a person holding the general equivalent who desires his commodity. If he can demonstrate that his own commodity has a use-value for another person, by handing over his commodity to the holder of the general equivalent, which is received in return, he can come into possession of the commodity he wants by exchang-

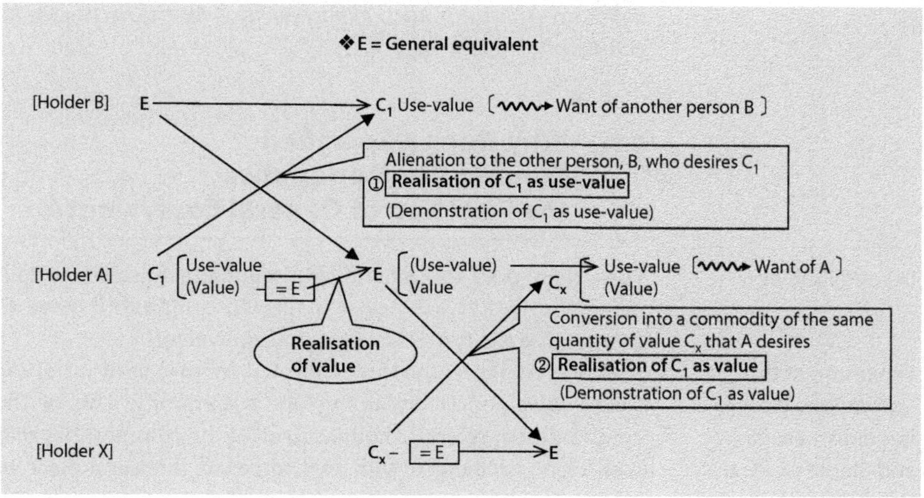

Fig. 2.40 Mediation of the contradiction of the exchange process through the general equivalent

ing for it the general equivalent, which has direct general exchangeability. Thus, once the general equivalent has been formed within the commodity world, every commodity can shed its material form (as use-value) by realising itself as use-value by becoming the general equivalent that is the incarnation of value vis-à-vis every other commodity, and then realise its own value by being transformed into the particular commodity that the commodity holder wants. This is how the contradiction of the exchange process is mediated, making possible the overall exchange of commodities. Fig. 2.40 depicts how the general equivalent (E) mediates the exchange process.

Contradiction of the Exchange Process Generates the Joint Action of the Commodity World

For overall commodity exchange to be carried out, commodities must jointly make one commodity the general equivalent. This is something that the commodity holders, who are the personification of commodities, have to do for their commodities. They act together in excluding a specific commodity from the commodity world, making this commodity bear the role of general equivalent. This mediates the contradiction of the exchange process so that overall commodity exchange can be carried out.

Thus, if one poses the question of why all of the commodities in the commodity world jointly exclude one commodity that becomes the general equivalent, the answer would be that it occurs «through the contradiction of the exchange process». The *contradiction inherent to the commodity is manifested within the exchange process as a contradiction between the realisation of the commodity as use-value and its realisation as value*, and *this contradiction necessarily gives rise to the general equivalent.*

2.5.2 Why Does a Specified Commodity Monopolise the Function of General Equivalent?

Second Problem

How, then, does the general equivalent attach itself to a specific commodity? Why does a specific commodity come to monopolise the function of general equivalent?

Expansion of the Commodity World Requires a Fixed and Stable General Equivalent

The general equivalent is formed by means of *all of the commodities* jointly excluding one commodity. «All of the commodities» refers, of course, to all of the commodities that seek to be exchanged with each other at the same place of exchange. These commodities form the same «**commodity world**». This means that the various commodity worlds, of different sizes, in accordance with their own particularities, give birth to general equivalents that count as such to a certain extent. Any commodity world that is temporarily formed generates its own general equivalent. Historically speaking, these commodity worlds of various sizes—in various locations, through various ways, and across various time periods—necessarily pass through a process of generation, transformation, and extinction. Along with this, general equivalents are formed by attachment to this or that commodity, are then subsequently perish. However, with the development of commodity exchange, the general equivalent comes to adhere to a specified commodity. This is the crystallisation of the money-form.

In short, the *expansion and deepening of the commodity world through the development of commodity exchange demands a general equivalent that is fixed and socially stable.* The general equivalent ultimately comes to be limited to a single, special kind of commodity that is excluded from the commodity world. This commodity monopolises the function of general equivalent, resulting in the formation of money.

2.5.3 Why Is Gold the Commodity that Monopolises the Function of General Equivalent?

Third Problem

Historically, gold and silver, and ultimately gold alone, became money, monopolising the position of general equivalent. Why was this the case?

Marx's Explanation

Marx (1872) offers a clear explanation of this point:

«With the development of exchange the general equivalent fixes itself firmly and exclusively onto *particular* kinds of commodity, i.e. it crystallises out into the *money form*. The particular kind of commodity to which it sticks is at first a matter of accident. Nevertheless there are two circumstances which are by and large decisive. The *money-form* comes to be attached either to the most important *articles of exchange from outside*, which are in fact the primitive and spontaneous forms of manifestation of the exchange-value of local products, *or* to the object of utility which forms the chief element of indigenous *alienable wealth*, for example cattle. Nomadic peoples are the first to develop the money-form, because all their worldly possessions are in a *movable* and therefore directly alienable form, and because their mode of life, by continually bringing them into contact with foreign commodities, encourages the exchange of products…. In the same proportion as exchange bursts its local bonds, and the *value* of commodities accordingly expands more and more into the material embodiment of *human labour as such*, in that proportion does the money-form become transferred to commodities which are by nature fitted to perform the social function of a general equivalent. Those commodities are *precious metals*. / The truth of the statement that «although gold and silver are not by nature money, money is by nature gold and silver», is shown by the appropriateness of their natural properties for the functions of money…. Only a material whose every sample possesses the same *uniform* quality can be an adequate form of appearance of value, that is a material embodiment of abstract and therefore equal human labour. On the other hand, since the difference between the magnitudes of value is purely *quantitative*, the money commodity must be capable of purely quantitative differentiation, it must therefore be divisible at will, and it must also be possible to assemble it again from its component parts. Gold and silver possess these properties by nature» (Marx 1976, pp. 183–184: Marx's emphasis as in the first German edition).

General Equivalent Settles upon a Commodity with the Attributes Suited to Its Function

It is gold and silver therefore—particularly gold—that have the *natural attributes best suited to perform the function of general equivalent* and the *functions of money*, since money, as we shall see in the next section, is not simply the function of general equivalent but also includes other functions. Gold, then, comes to monopolise the function of general equivalent because it *has natural attributes well suited to money*.

Completion of the Money Fetish To View Gold as Money by Nature

As seen in the previous section, however, once gold has monopolised the position of general equivalent so as to have direct exchangeability in general, the social character of the general equivalent, which counts as value for every other commodity, adheres to the glittering natural form of gold. The

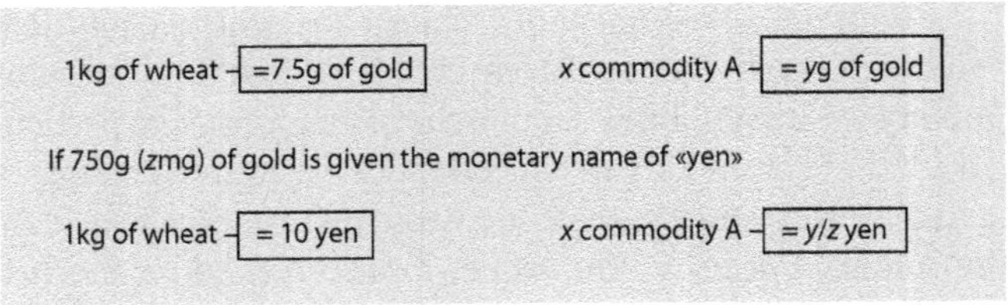

Fig. 2.41 The commodity's value-expression and its price

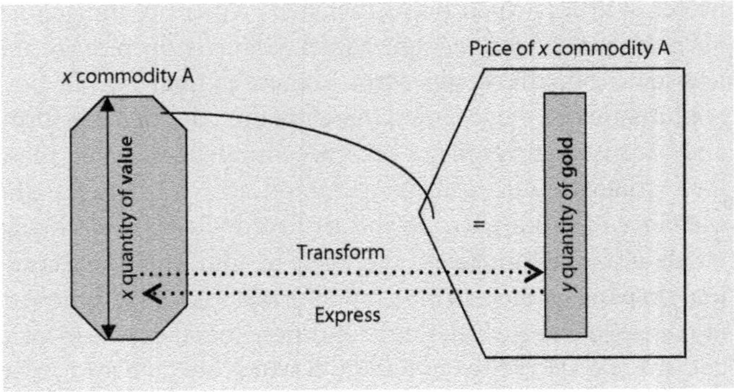

Fig. 2.42 Function of money as measure of value

result is that people view gold as having a mysterious inherent force that other commodities lack, making it irresistible. The «magical character of gold» is generated, where gold everywhere is seen as money in people's eyes.

2.6 Functions of Money

2.6.1 Functions of Money

Function of Money as Measure of Value and as Standard of Price

Value-expression of Commodities and Function of Money as Measure of Value

Commodities that appear on the market must first of all express their value in money. The *value of a commodity expressed in money* is a commodity's **price**. For example, the value of 1 kg of wheat is expressed in the price: 1 kg of wheat – = 7.5 g of gold , or in the price: 1 kg of wheat – = 10 yen in the case where 750 mg of gold is given the **money-name** of «yen» (*see* Fig. 2.41).

Here gold, which is money, functions as **measure of value**. The function of money as measure of value is the first function of money (*see* Fig. 2.42).

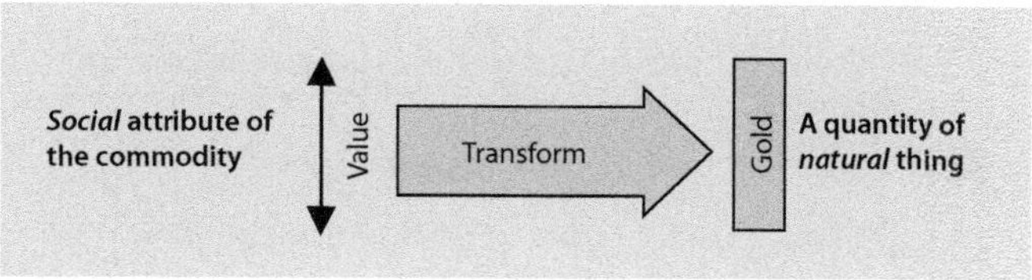

Fig. 2.43 Quality of the measure of value

Quality of the Measure of Value

Value is a completely social attribute of the commodity that cannot be grasped sensually, and therefore cannot be visualised. But in the case of price, this value takes the form of gold, which is sensual and visualisable. Value thus takes the form of a quantity of a natural thing that can be represented. *This transformation of the commodity's completely social attribute of value into a quantity of a natural thing* is the most essential qualitative content of the *measurement of a commodity's value* by money; in other words, this is the **quality of the measure of value** (*see* Fig. 2.43).

Price Indicates Actual Gold

Price is a quantity of gold, which is a natural thing, but in price this natural thing is merely represented, so that the actual thing is not present. What we have is merely the gold indicated by the price tag of a commodity, not actual gold. Yet actual gold is in fact indicated. It is precisely because gold, which is excluded from the commodity world to become money, actually exists and confronts commodities that it can be indicated in price. Thus, money as the measure of value is *ideal money that is represented*, but what is represented and indicated is *actual gold* (*see* Fig. 2.44).

Value of the Money-commodity Is Grasped Only by Reading the Price List Backwards

How, then, can the value of gold itself, which is money, be expressed? The value of gold, which is determined (as in the case of other commodities) by the labour-time socially necessary for its production, is quite unable to be expressed by gold itself. Its value can only be expressed in the quantity of another commodity that is equated to gold. Ordinary commodities express their own value in price, which is represented in a quantity of gold, but it is not possible for gold to equate gold to itself. Since the prices of ordinary commodities are all an equation to a quantity of gold of the same value, the magnitude of gold's value must be also reflected in the equation. Indeed, if the list of commodity prices (*price list*) is read from the side of gold, rather than the commodity side, the magnitude of the value of money is expressed in every sort of commodity (*see* Fig. 2.45).

Standard of Price

Commodities express their own value in a quantity of gold that is represented in price, which means that they can be compared with each other. In order for these various quantities of

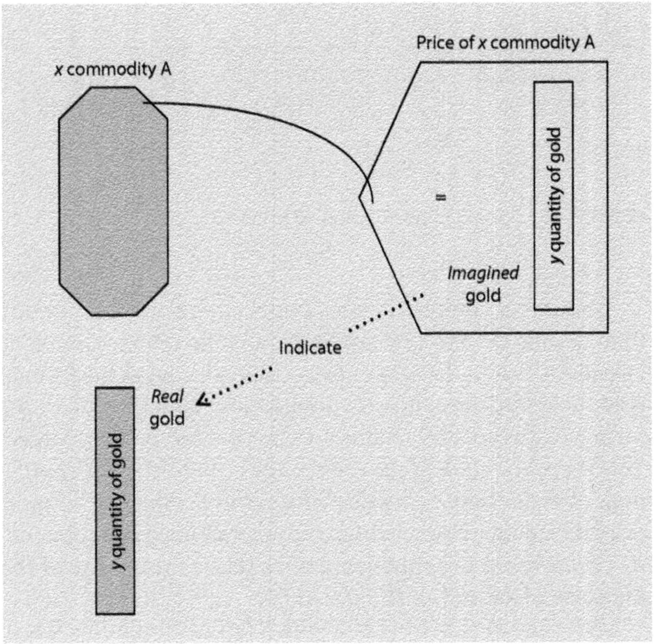

Fig. 2.44 The price of a commodity and the real money it indicates

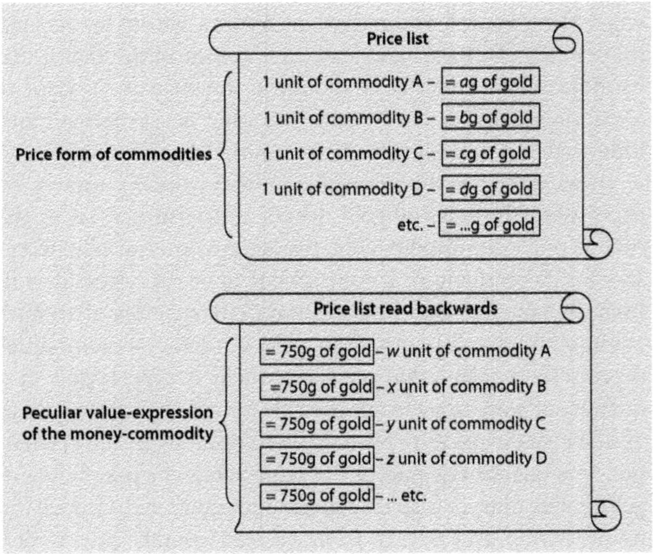

Fig. 2.45 Peculiar value-expression of the money-commodity

gold to be measured and expressed using identical nomenclature, a technical need arises for a given quantity of gold to be fixed as the **measure unit of price**.

There were weight-based units to measure gold prior to it becoming money, such as *pounds* or *grams*, and these units are in turn divided into sub-units such as *ounces* or *milligrams*. Together, these units and sub-units form a single measurement standard or system of measurement.

Initially this weight-based measurement system was used as the standard to measure the quantity of metal (gold or silver) that represented price, thus serving as the **measure standard of price**—or the **standard of price**, for short. Due to various factors, however, the money-names expressing the weight of the money-commodity began to diverge from the weight-based measurement system, so that it became customary to use something other than the weight names. Even in cases where the weight-names evolved into the money-names, the gold weight expressed by the money-name differed from the weight expressed by the weight-name.

The standard of price measures not only the ideal quantity of gold that is price, but also the *actual gold that is money*, so it is the **standard of money** as well. This serves as a sort of ruler to gauge the quantity of gold. Whether we are dealing with gold represented in the price of a commodity or actual gold as money, the gold can be said to function as **money of account** when certain quantities of it are turned into a measurement system in order to express amounts of gold.

At first, various monetary names were customarily used, but the need for a widely recognised money-name within a given commodity world led countries to legally establish a standard of price or standard of money. In Japan, for instance, Article 2 of the Coinage Law (established in 1897 and abolished in 1990) made 750 mg of pure gold in weight the unit of price, labeling this «**yen**», and under Article 4 of the law the calculation of money was based on the decimal system, so that for quantities under 1 yen, 1/100 was designated as «*sen*» and 1/10 of sen as «*rin*». This meant that the price of 1 kg of wheat -[= 7.5 g of gold], when expressed by the money-name «yen», became 1 kg of wheat -[10 yen] (*see* ◘ Fig. 2.46).

Quality and Quantity of Price

The price of a commodity is thus, *qualitatively* speaking, a matter of expressing the objectified abstract human labour that constitutes commodity-value in a quantity of gold that is money *qua* measure of value. *Quantitatively* speaking, this

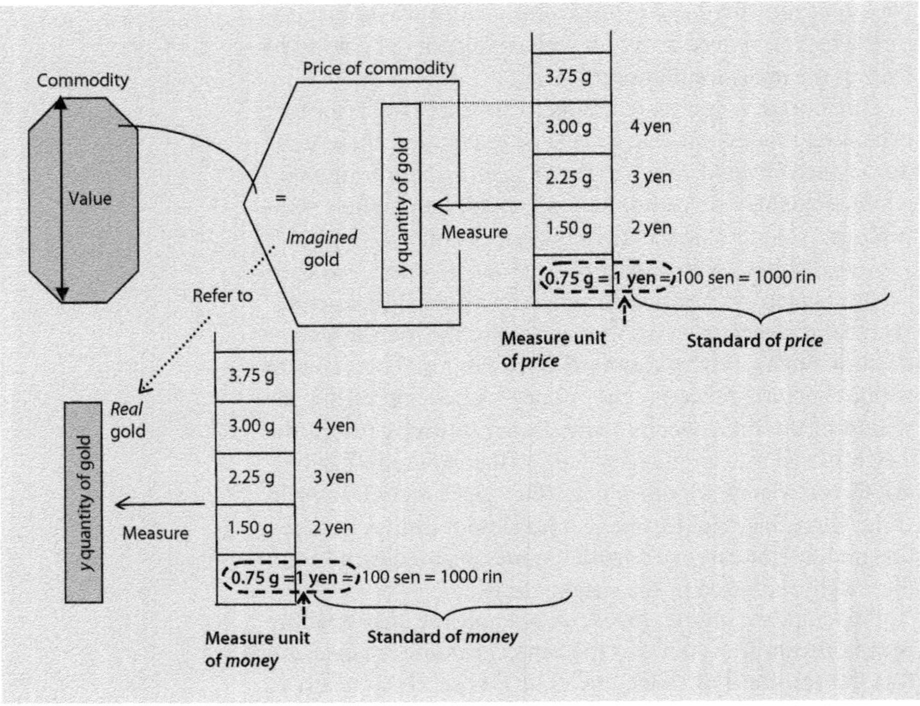

Fig. 2.46 «Yen» as the measure-unit of price (and of money)

involves the quantity of gold being measured in an amount of gold that serves as the standard of price.

Price Does Not Necessarily Accurately Express Value

Price is something that expresses value, so there would of course be cases where price squarely equates with value, so that the commodity's price is represented by a quantity of gold of equal value. However, no one is able to grasp the absolute magnitude of either the value of a commodity or the value of gold. This is precisely why the same commodity can have numerous prices. Even if there is a quantitative difference between the «**asking price**» that the seller of the commodity wants, the «**bid price**» of the purchaser, and the «**agreed price**» or «**selling price**» that seller and buyer ultimately agree upon, qualitatively speaking they are all prices that express the value of a commodity in a quantity of gold. Moreover, the price that constantly fluctuates even when the value of a commodity is unchanged, qualitatively remains the price of a commodity no matter how much it may change quantitatively. The price of a commodity, therefore, *by its very nature*, does not necessarily accurately express the value of a commodity (*see* Fig. 2.47).

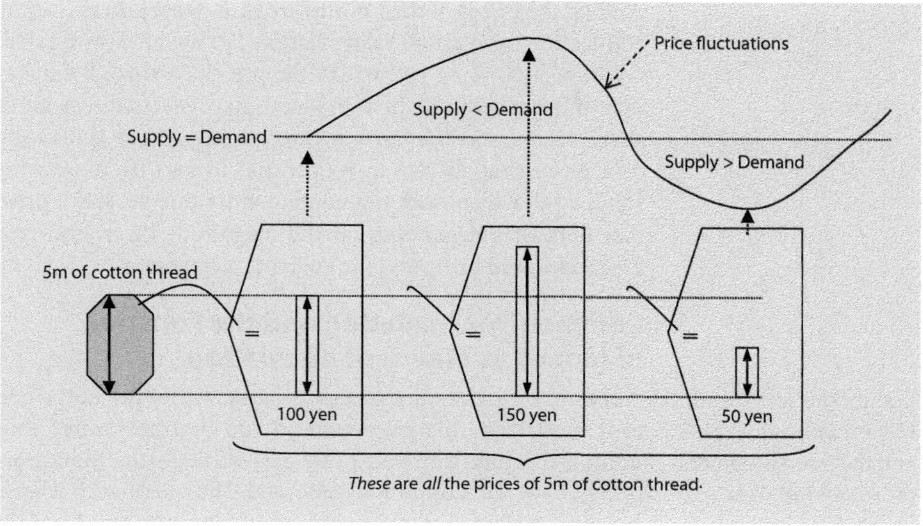

Fig. 2.47 Price does not necessarily accurately express value

Divergence of Price from Value Is an Inescapable Moment of Commodity Production

The possibility that value will not be in agreement with price—i.e. the possibility of a divergence of price from value—is inherent to the form itself. The possibility of this divergence, however, is not a defect in the price-form, but rather *an important moment that makes commodity production, which can only exist as anarchical production, feasible as social production.*

If value diverges above or below value, sooner or later this will trigger a fluctuation in the supply of a commodity and in demand for it, so that the price then changes in the opposite direction. Price, which is always fluctuating through changes in supply and demand, is in fact able to conversely regulate the supply and demand of a commodity *through its divergence from value*, and this sort of fluctuation in price is necessarily a *fluctuation that is restricted by value.* Fluctuations involving price bring about a supply of the commodity that coincides with social demand. By means of this, for the first time, it becomes possible for the production scale for commodities, which are all produced anarchically by private labour, to accommodate the everchanging demands of society.

Things Without Value Can Also Have Price

Given the character of price, which is able to diverge from value, not only can something with just a small amount of value be sold for an extremely high price, but even *something with no value at all*—i.e. *something that is not a product of labour—can have price and be sold as a commodity.* Some examples include conscience, honor, a job position, virtue, and the chance to attain wealth (such as «financial commodities»).

Among the prices of such things are cases where there is some connection to an actual value relation. For instance, as we shall see in ► Sect. 19.2.7 in Part III, the price of a stock fluctuates due to the magnitude of a dividend that reflects the profit of share capital and the current interest rate. There is also the case, as we shall discuss in ► Sect. 20.5 in Part III, of uncultivated land, which does not contain any value yet has a price that fluctuates depending on the magnitude of ground-rent the land would bring and the current interest rate.

Commodity Circulation and the Function of Money as Means of Circulation

Commodity Metamorphosis C–M–C and the Intertwinement of Metamorphoses

A commodity that appears on the market with a price attached to it must have this price realised and be transformed into money. In other words, it must pass through the **metamorphosis C–M** (i.e. **C**ommodity–**M**oney). The *commodity-holder*, as seller, must sell his own commodity. However, this C–M, or the **sale** for the seller, is the first half of the commodity metamorphosis, which must be complemented by **M–C** (i.e. **M**oney–**C**ommodity), a **purchase** for the buyer. Since the *metamorphosis of the commodity* is **C–M–C**, the *action of the commodity-holder* is the process of a sale for the sake of a purchase, or selling and then buying.

The sale of the commodity involves handing it over to the money-holder who desires it, in exchange for the amount of money indicated in its price. This is the ***salto mortale*** «fatal jump» for the commodity. This feat must be achieved—since the commodity may cease to exist as such if it fails. But success or failure depends on the situation of the social division of labour, wherein the production of each individual commodity is carried out independently in a spontaneous and anarchical manner. If C–M, or the sale, is carried out successfully, the commodity is stripped of its commodity form, to be transformed into the money-form that is the figure of its value. Since money is the general equivalent, it possesses direct exchangeability with every commodity, and the process whereby it displays this capability, so as to transform itself into a given commodity, is M–C, which is a purchase for the commodity-holder. This means that the second transformation, the purchase (M–C), is not a process that entails the difficulty seen in the sale (C–M); rather, it is easily done as long as the desired commodity is on the market.

The sale of a commodity (C–M) always corresponds to a purchase of another commodity (M–C). The M in M–C is always the figure of the value of the commodity that **shed its skin** in C–M (casting off the slough of use-value), and therefore M–C is the *second* metamorphosis for this commodity.

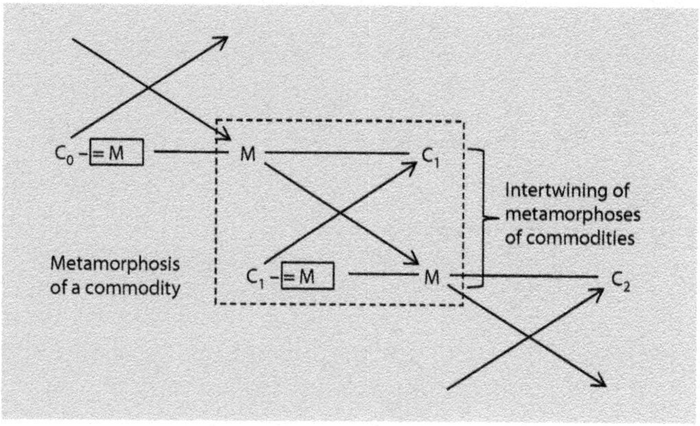

■ **Fig. 2.48** Metamorphosis of a commodity and intertwining of metamorphoses of commodities

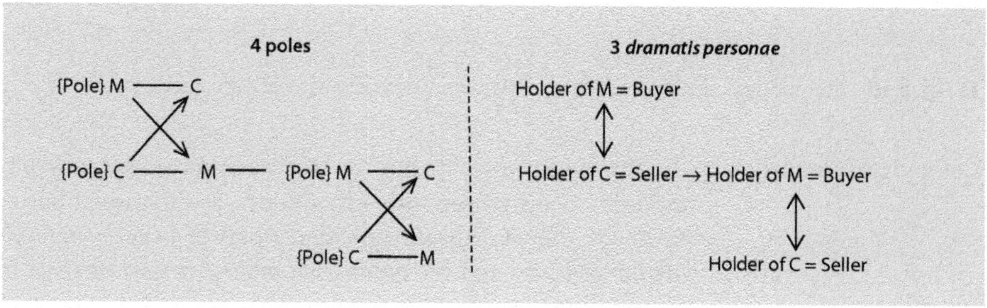

■ **Fig. 2.49** Four poles and three *dramatis personae* in the metamorphosis of a commodity

One commodity's metamorphosis is therefore necessarily intertwined with the metamorphoses of another commodities. A single process has two aspects: a sale from the side of the commodity-holder and a purchase from the side of the money-holder (*see* ■ Fig. 2.48).

Four Poles and Three *Dramatis Personae*

In the metamorphosis of one commodity, C–M–C, there are four poles and three *dramatis personae*. First, there are the two opposing poles, with the commodity on one side and the money that is the figure of the commodity's value on the other side (in a person's pocket); here a commodity-holder confronts a money-holder. Next, if the commodity is transformed into money, we have the two opposing poles of this money and the commodity of another person that is the figure for use; here a money-holder confronts a commodity-holder. The seller (persnonification of commodity) in the first act becomes the buyer (personification of money) in the second, where he confronts a third commodity-holder who is the seller (*see* ■ Fig. 2.49).

2

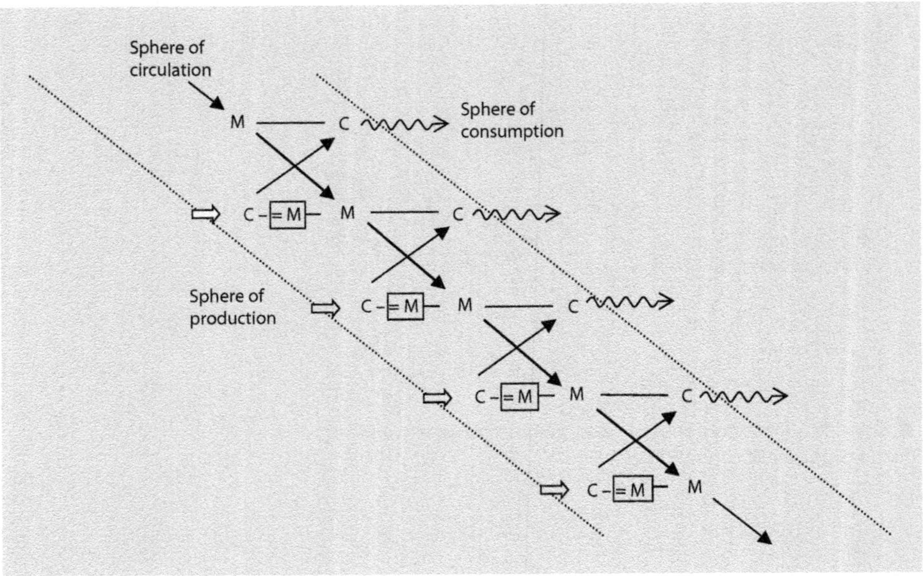

Fig. 2.50 Commodity circulation and circulation of money as means of circulation

Commodity Circulation

The intertwined totality of the metamorphoses of commodities forms **commodity circulation**. In the case of barter exchange, there is a direct coincidence between *one's own product handed over* and *the product of another person received* in return. But in commodity circulation the two moments within barter exchange are *split into the two acts of sale and purchase*, so that they are separated from each other, temporally and spatially. The two acts can be carried out at different locations and can also be separated temporally. *Commodity circulation thus breaks through the temporal and spatial limitations of barter exchange, thereby developing the metabolism of human labour.*

Function of Money as Means of Circulation

Money, as the medium of commodity circulation, acquires the function of **means of circulation**. Within commodity circulation, money as means of circulation fills in for the commodities that are constantly falling out of circulation, passing from the hands of one commodity-holder to another, thus mediating the **social metabolism** within commodity-production society (*see* Fig. 2.50).

Money Circulation

The intertwined metamorphoses of the commodity, C–M–C, make money flow from the hands of the buyer to the seller. This movement of money visible to everyone is **money circulation**, which is distinguished from commodity circulation.

Function of Money as Means of Purchase

The circulation of money presents itself as the ceaseless repetition of the same process. The money in the hands of the buyer always appears as the means of purchasing the com-

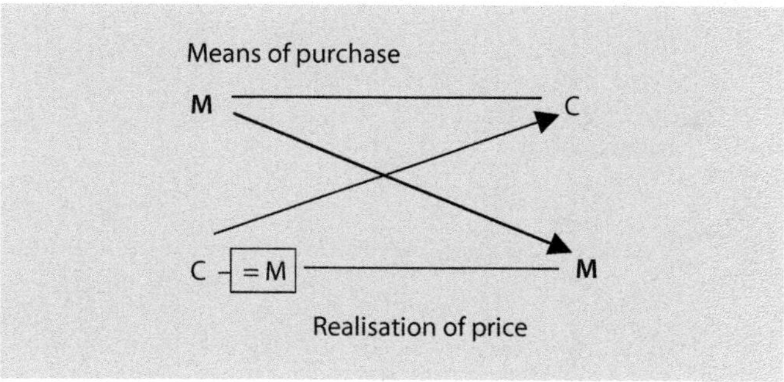

■ **Fig. 2.51** Function of money as means of purchase

modity in the hands of the seller, thereby realising the commodity's price. Here money functions as means of purchasing the commodity by realising the commodity's price; which is to say, it functions as **means of purchase** (*see* ■ Fig. 2.51).

Money, when functioning as means of purchase, passes into the hands of one commodity holder after another, in endless repetition. Even though the circulation of money is a manifestation of the intertwined metamorphoses of commodities and the result of the movement of commodities, *if we focus on the movement form of money as a means of circulation, it appears conversely as if money as a means of purchase is what causes commodities to move.*

Coin and Its Circulation

Gold as means of circulation initially was **money by weight**, where its weight was measured with the purity ascertained at the time a sale was made. However, since it was troublesome to test and measure gold at every transaction, the development of commodity circulation led to the gradual emergence of coins with a certain stamp and shape. **Coin** is a piece of gold that, by means of its stamp and shape, expresses that it contain a certain quantity of gold, which bears a monetary name such as *yen, pound, dollar,* etc. The technical operation of turning **gold bullion** into coins, i.e. **coinage**, just like the establishment of a standard of price, is carried out by the state, which guarantees the **purity** and **weight** of the gold included in its coins (*see* ■ Fig. 2.52).

Reduction in a Coin's Actual Gold Quantity Through Abrasion

As gold coins circulate, however, they gradually *wear away* through abrasion, so that the **real gold weight** of a coin comes to be less than the **nominal gold weight** indicated on the coin's face (*see* ■ Fig. 2.53).

Worn-down Coins Can Still Function as Means of Circulation

Worn-down coins can still function as means of circulation, provided the degree of abrasion is not too great. This is possible—even though the coin that comes into the hand of the seller is the figure of his commodity's value and the independent indication of value—because this is a temporary state

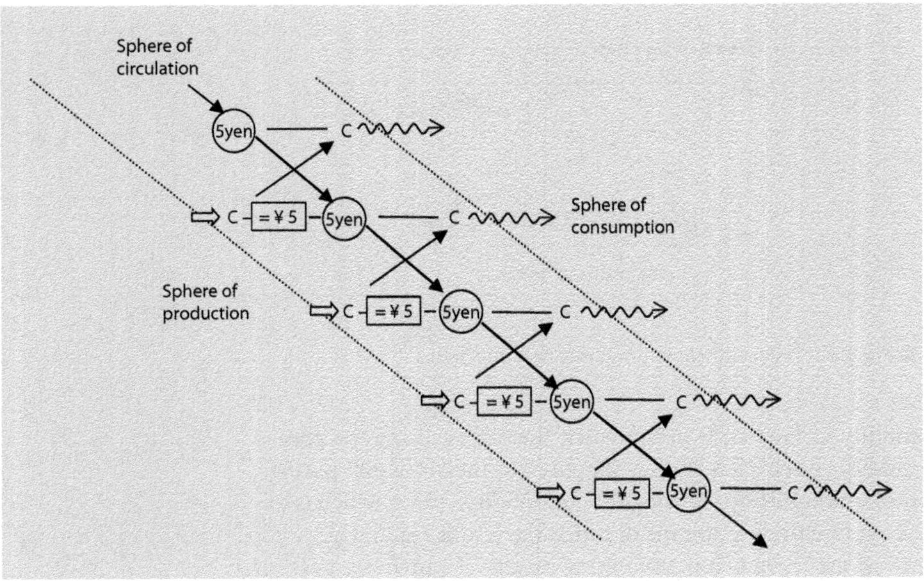

Fig. 2.52 Coin circulation

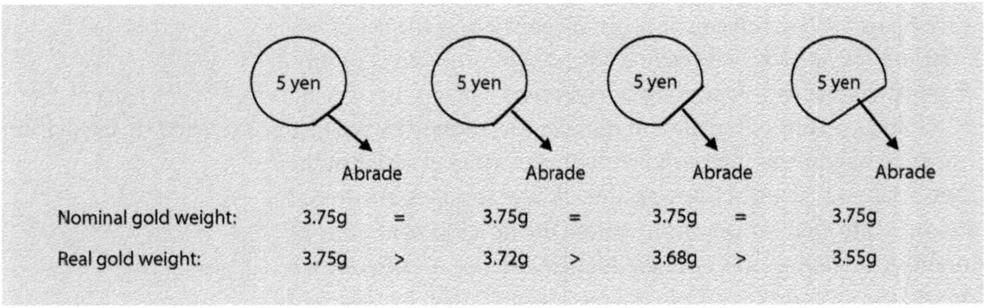

Fig. 2.53 Deviation of coin's real gold weight from its nominal weight through abrasion

that dissolves when the subsequent purchase is made. Thus, as long as a worn-down coin is able to circulate as its nominal value, the coin's abrasion will have no significance whatsoever for the person involved. Since we are solely dealing with the function as means of circulation, therefore, it can fully be performed even *by something that is a mere symbol of money.*

Subsidiary Coin

Because a symbol can perform the function as means of circulation, gold coins are replaced by coins containing metal of lesser value in the sphere of circulation, where gold coins are rapidly worn out by the constant repetition of small-scale purchases and sales. For example, the smallest gold coins of insignificant denominations are replaced by *tokens* made of

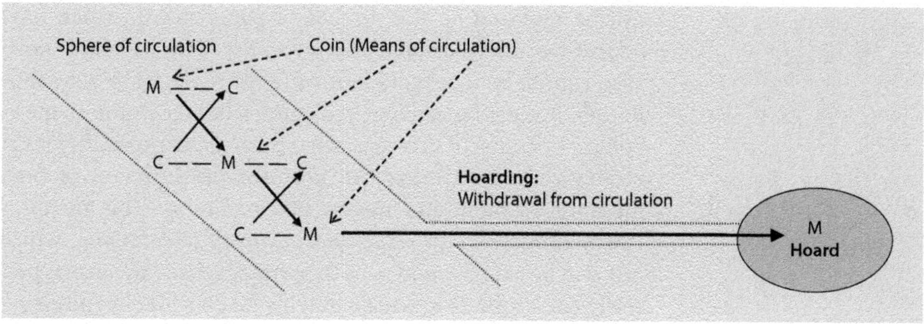

Fig. 2.54 Hoarding and hoard

copper or some other metal. These are **subsidiary coins**, distinguished from the **legal tender** that consists of gold as measure of value.

State Paper Money

There are also things with almost no intrinsic value that are stamped as money and symbolically express a certain quantity of gold, such as **paper notes**. The classic example is the paper notes issued by the state, or **state paper money**, which is given **forced currency** through the legal compulsion of requiring them to be accepted as payment.

Hoarding and Money in Its Proper Sense

Hoarding and Hoard

When a sale (C–M) is carried out, the commodity is temporally dormant in the money-form for a greater or lesser period of time, before then re-entering circulation to transform itself into another commodity; but after a sale (C–M), if the realised price, or M, is withdrawn from circulation and locked up, it becomes a **hoard**, and this act is known as **hoarding** (*see* Fig. 2.54).

Money in the Proper Sense

A hoard is value that becomes independent by being set free from commodities and takes the form of a thing—gold. This is *«money» in the strict sense of the term* or **money in the proper sense.**

Thus far we have separately observed the roles money plays when commodities appear within circulation: first the function as measure of value and then the function as means of circulation. However, the same commodity, gold, which was chosen by the commodity world to become money, performs both functions. We divided and analysed those two functions performed by gold as money in accordance with the movement of commodities. Both functions, observed separately, could be performed even if gold *qua* money does not actually appear. Money, as measure of value, is always ideal gold that is merely imagined, while as means of circulation, it can be replaced by the symbol of paper notes, which have almost no intrinsic value. Money in the form of hoard, however, cannot be ideal gold, nor can it be replaced by a symbol. Rather, it must be *genuine, real gold*, whether in the shape of bullion or coins. In this case, what must appear in reality is the money-commodity that can perform the function of both measure of value and means of circulation. This means a «*unity of measure of value and means of circulation*», which can also be called «money in the proper sense» because it precisely corresponds to what can truly be considered «money».

Money as Wealth in Its General Form

All sorts of common commodities, precisely because they possess only a specific sort of use-value, must be transformed into money, which is the shape of their value. In absolute contrast to this, the real, genuine money-commodity can not only be transformed into some other commodity in the commodity world, to whatever extent its quantity allows, and it can under certain circumstances even make things that are not originally commodities assume the commodity-form in order to transform itself into those things. Its unique use-value is its capacity to be transformable into any sort of use-value in its existence as congealed value, which is to say, as value in the form of a thing and the materialisation of abstract labour. This means that the real money-commodity can represent the use-value of every conceivable commodity and encompass all of the concrete labour that gives birth to those commodities, as the «**embodiment of abstract labour**», the «**material representative of the wealth of society**», and «**wealth in its general form**». This is money in the proper sense.

Original Hoarding

Thus, if the metamorphosis of the commodity stops after C–M, so that money is withdrawn from circulation to form a hoard as money in the proper sense, this is the formation of wealth in its general form. As long as one is unaware of how capital is augmented by putting money into movement, the only way to augment one's wealth is to amass a hoard by repeating the process of hoarding. Indeed, prior to the generalisation of capitalist production, wherever there were commodities and money, hoarding was always carried out. Hoarders sought to sell as much as possible without buying, and their motto was diligence, frugality, and stinginess. This was the **original hoarding**.

Money Hoard Under Capitalist Production

Under capitalist production, as we shall discuss later, money holders put that money into motion as capital rather than amassing it as a hoard. They let go of money in order to augment it. In this sense, original hoarding becomes an exception. However, the valorisation movement of capital itself requires that hoarding be carried out in a new form. The typical case is the amassment of amortisation funds and of accumulation funds, which will be discussed in more detail when we look at capital (► Sects. 14.3.4 and 14.4.3).

Function of a Hoard as Reservoir of Circulating Money

From a social perspective, the hoard formed in the hands of individual commodity holders plays an very important role for commodity circulation as a whole as a reservoir of circulating money, which makes it possible to increase or decrease the quantity of circulating money. We will soon touch on this role in ► Sect. 2.6.2, when we examine the quantity of circulating money.

Sale on Credit and Function of Money as Means of Payment

Sales and Purchases on Credit

As we have seen, the sale and purchase intertwined in the metamorphoses of two commodities involves a cash transaction in which a commodity is handed over and money is paid in return. With the development of commodity circulation, however, various situations unfold where there is a temporal gap between the handing over of the commodity and the realisation of a commodity's price (payment of money). For instance, there may be a case where the purchaser seeking a commodity cannot yet secure the needed money due to the situation regarding the production or sale of his own commodity, but if it can be confirmed that he will obtain the money after a certain period of time, the seller of the commodity can allow the payment of money to be temporarily delayed. There thus arises a new transaction form in which a commodity is handed over and the money payment is made later—referred to as **sales and purchases on credit**. The sale becomes a sale on credit, and the purchase is likewise a purchase on credit (*see* ◘ Fig. 2.55).

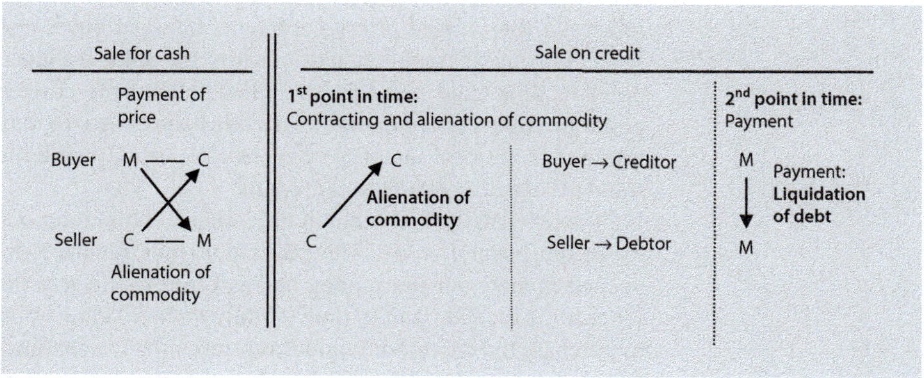

◘ **Fig. 2.55** Sale for cash and sale on credit

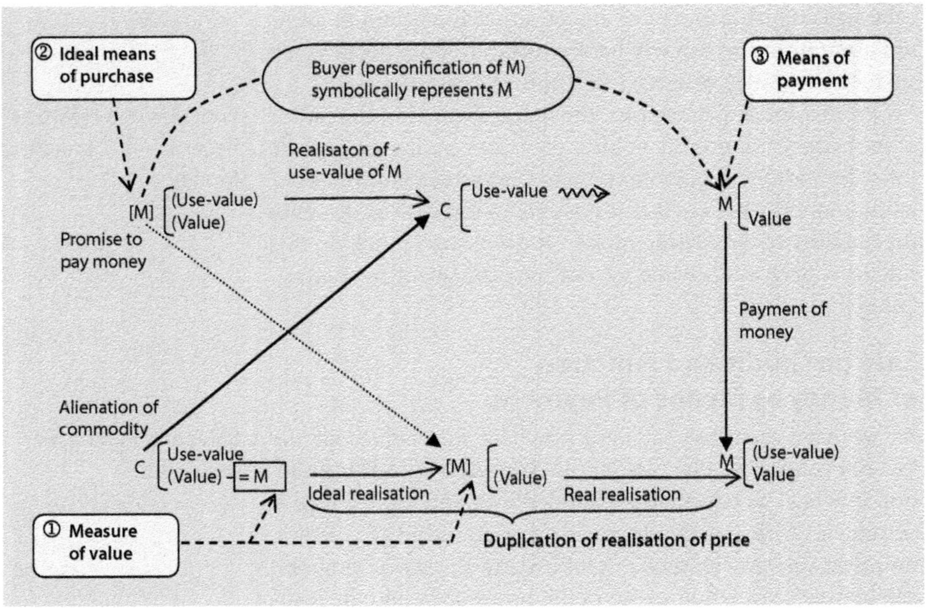

Fig. 2.56 Intertwining of the metamorphoses of commodities and the functions of money in a sale on credit

At the first point of this transaction, when the commodity is handed over, the seller becomes a creditor and the buyer a debtor. But when money is paid at the second point in time, the relation of claim and debt is dissolved.

Functions of Money Within Sale/Purchase on Credit

In the case of purchases and sales on credit, the function of money is somewhat complex (*see* Fig. 2.56).

As in the case of a cash transaction, money functions in sales and purchases on credit as a **measure of value** expressing the value of a commodity as **price** (*see* ① in Fig. 2.56). Let's assume that this price is not the «asking price» of the seller, but the «agreed price» contracted between buyer and seller. The buyer *promises to pay money* to the seller at a given point in time (2nd point in time) that follows the current point in time (1st point in time). This «**promise to pay money**» is an ideal quantity of money measured using the standard of price or money of account.

The seller, at the first point in time, alienates his commodity to the buyer (*see* ②). The buyer does not yet have the needed money, but the money he has promised to pay the seller at the second point in time («*future money*») allows him to purchase the commodity, and this future money now functions as **means of purchase**, which is to say, it only functions ideally. By means of this, the *formal use-value that the future* *money should have as money* is now realised, and the buyer is able to obtain the use-value that satisfies his want. The seller has alienated the commodity, but not yet received real money. He does, however, have the buyer's «*promise to pay money*». This is not the case of a mere price of his commodity, that may or may not be realised, but something that represents the money that *will* be paid at the second point in time (as long as the contract is respected). Thus, the price of his commodity has already been realised, albeit ideally, becoming a *promise to pay money*. This promise to pay money for the seller is a *claim*, while for the buyer it is a *debt*. From this point in time, the seller is a *creditor* and the buyer a *debtor*.

The only thing that remains is for the debtor (buyer) to pay money to the creditor (seller) at the second point in time, thereby settling the debt (*see* ③). At that second point in time, money enters circulation as **means of payment**. From the perspective of the seller (creditor), the price of his commodity is ultimately transformed into real money through this payment; which is to say, the price of the commodity is actually realised. For the buyer (debtor), the *money* that *had its use-value realised* by functioning as means of purchase at the first point in time, is now handed over to the creditor, and thus his debt is settled.

Circulation of Money as Means of Payment

Within the functions of money for sale on credit, there appears for the first time the function played by money when the debtor pays the creditor at the second point in time. This money paid on the basis of a promise-to-pay, *which settles the debt, thus bringing to an end the creditor-debtor relation*, is **money as means of payment**. At the second point in time, money *enters circulation* as means of payment.

Here it is clear that money circulates from the debtor to the creditor but this is not as means of circulation, i.e. not as currency. Here money is different from the medium of circulation that is the temporary shape of a commodity's value. And since this is a form in which the debtor hands over *value itself* to the creditor, it is originally a function that only money in the proper sense can perform. However, with the development of money-forms (such as banknotes) that can take the place of gold *qua* money in the proper sense, these representatives are able to circulate as means of payment.

Genesis of Credit

In ◘ Fig. 2.56, [M] represents a *promise to pay money*, which is a *claim* for the seller and a *debt* for the buyer. This is an indication that the seller trusts the buyer's promise-to-pay. In this transaction, the seller gives **credit** to the buyer, with [M] expressing the magnitude of the credit. Thus, in **sale and purchase on credit**, the seller and buyer give and receive

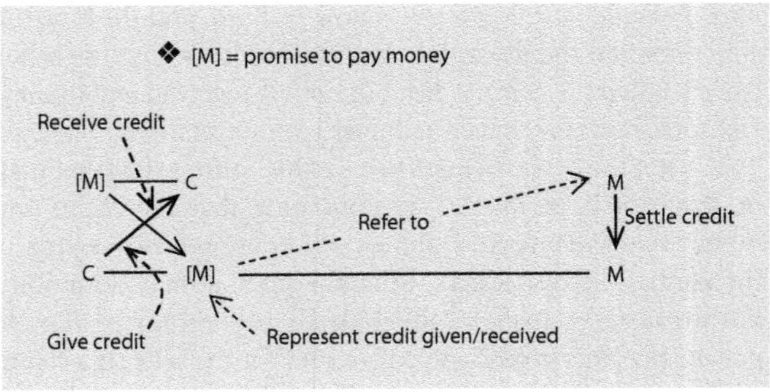

Fig. 2.57 Credit is given/received in sale/purchase on credit

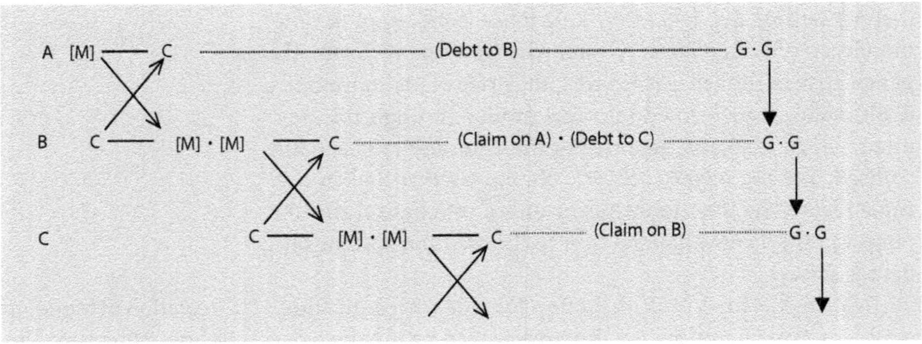

Fig. 2.58 Chain of credit and the chain of the flows of the means of payment

credit. Later, in ► Sect. 19.2 in Part III, we will see that within developed capitalist production an elaborate credit system develops, so that various credit transactions are carried out. Credit establishes such transactions, as well as the system of credit itself, and it is one of the most fundamental social relations within the relations of commodity production. But credit is precisely spontaneously generated out of credit-based sales and purchases (*see* Fig. 2.57).

Chain of Credit and Chain of Payment

With the development of sales on credit, commodity holders who have given credit, make their own purchases of commodities on credit, based on the money to be received on the payment date. A *chain of transactions* is thus formed among commodity holders. The diagram above (*see* Fig. 2.58) shows how B sells his commodity to A on credit, and then buys a commodity from C on credit, relying upon the payment to be received from A on the settlement date, while C does the same thing in turn, etc. We can see that the intertwined commodity metamorphoses and *chain of credit* are

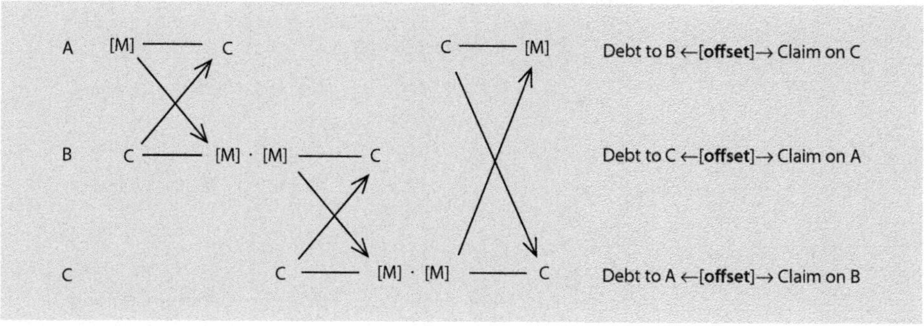

Fig. 2.59 Offsetting of claims and debts

spontaneously formed. When the promised date of payment arrives, money goes into circulation as means of payment, from A to B, then B to C, and from C to the next commodity owner, and so on. This chain of a *flow of means of payment* is thus a manifestation of the previously formed *chain of sales/purchases*, and therefore of the *chain of credit* as well.

Offsetting Claims and Debts

Let's suppose that in the intertwined commodity metamorphoses and the chain of credit, depicted in the diagram above, C buys a commodity from A, and that the three concerned parties (A, B, and C) are aware of all transactions (purchase of A from B, purchase of B from C, and purchase of C from A). Then, at the point where C buys a commodity from A, the three debts (of A to B; of B to C; of C to A) are **offset** by the three claims (of A on C; of B on A; of C on B), so that they are all eliminated (*see* Fig. 2.59).

In this case, the payments that were supposed to be made on the settlement date for the first two transactions, come to an end without the means of payment entering circulation at this point in time. A sale/purchase on credit is a transaction formed on the basis of credit used for the payment of money on the date of payment; therefore, it is a transaction premised on the function of money as means of payment. Despite this, on the settlement date, the payment of money—and therefore money as means of payment—does not enter circulation, and the sale/purchase is carried out without this payment, with the claims and debts being settled.

Circulation of Bills

Credit in its most elementary form can be a verbal promise, but in commercial transactions there is at the very least some written proof, expressed in a «bond». Furthermore, by indicating a proof of an obligation received from a third party, a person demonstrates that he is holding a claim, and this proof of the promise of money to settle the claim can at the same time be used to purchase a commodity on credit.

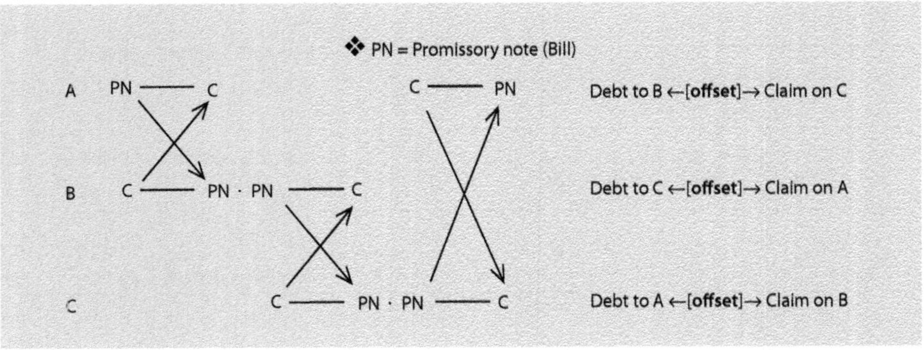

Fig. 2.60 Offsetting of claims and debts via the circulation of bills

Taken still further, credit is widely expressed using the proof of a *promise-to-pay* that can be handed over in a certain form during a certain period of time. *Negotiable (transferable) bonds or promissory notes with a fixed payment-due date* are called **bills**.

Now let's consider a case where A purchases a commodity from B using a bill, while B uses this bill to buy a commodity from C, and then C, in turn, uses the bill to buy a commodity from A (*see* Fig. 2.60).

Even if A is unaware that B and C have carried out a transaction, all claims and debts will still be cancelled out with the final transaction. In this case, money does not enter circulation as means of payment, and all transactions are completed solely with the «circulation» of bills. Thus, the bill itself functions as means of purchasing a commodity, and therefore as means of circulation. *Bills that perform the function of money in this manner* are called **commercial money**. Bills come in two forms: **promissory notes** that are *drawn (issued) by debtors* and **bills of exchange** *drawn (issued) by creditors* and accepted by debtors, but they are not fundamentally different in nature as *written promises-to-pay*.

Development of Institutions for Offsetting of Payments

With the development of sales on credit, the circulation of bills spreads widely, resulting in the development of artificial methods and corresponding institutions for gathering the securities that express various claims and debts to one place where they can be compared and offset to the greatest extent possible. Such institutions already existed in Ancient Rome. With the further development of these institutions, the sum of money actually used to settle accounts, i.e. the quantity of money circulating as means of payment, decreases compared to the total sum of claims and debts. In the modern age, such facilities are known as a **clearing house**.

Banknotes and Cheques

At the heart of the credit system formed under capitalist production is the banking system, and upon the basis of the circulation of commercial bills as commercial money, banks give birth to the special bills that represent the bank's promise-to-pay, which come to circulate widely as money. In other words, these are the **banknotes** (originally convertible into gold as money in the proper sense) that are *promises-to-pay issued by the bank as debtor*, and **cheques**, which are the *promises-to-pay of banks issued by depositors as creditors*. These are *bank bills*, but of these, banknotes in particular are called **credit money** in the strict sense. Credit money in the broad sense includes the totality of commercial securities and bank securities as well, which will be discussed in the section on the banking system (► Sect. 19.2 in Part III).

World Market and World Money

World Market

The commodity circulation we have examined up to now has been within a given country, demarcated by certain boundaries and governed by a single state, and the functions of money have also been within this framework. In reality, however, not only does commodity circulation extend beyond a nation's boundaries, but commodity exchange actually first took place between different communities and thus transcends national boundaries by its very essence. Value becomes the objectification of human labour in the true sense, without any distinctions, when the social metabolism that commodity circulation mediates spreads throughout the world. And capitalist production, as we shall see, necessarily develops a **world market**, that forces itself upon those countries and regions with pre-capitalist production forms.

World Money

In the world market, money is stripped of all the different national uniforms that states can dress it up in, and must assume the shape of having currency for people throughout the world. In other words, the standard of price that the money names of various countries have, and the various types of coins particular to a given country that bear these money names, do not count as such in the world market. In the world market, the weight-based measurement system is used, as is, as the standard of price, with the money-commodity, gold, appearing in the shape of *bullion*. In the world market, money must take a shape that is appropriate to this realm, and money functioning as such on the world market is **world money**.

Two Flows of Gold

There are two flows of gold in the world market. The first starts from those countries that have domestic sources of gold production, i.e. *the steady movement from the gold-producing countries to the world market*, where gold becomes money that circulates within each country or is congealed as a hoard. This movement, seen from the perspective of the gold-producing countries, is the direct barter exchange between the gold as commodity that these countries produced, and the commodities of the non-gold-producing countries; while from the perspective of the non-gold-producing countries, this is a process where the price of their own commodities is realised in the gold of the gold-producing countries, i.e. a sale. In the world market, the second flow of gold is the *constant back-and-forth* movement *between the circulation realms of each country.* It is through this second flow that even non-gold-producing countries that do not sell commodities to gold-producing countries are able to get hold of gold in exchange for their own commodities.

Functions of Money as World Money

The function that money plays between non-gold-producing countries is, first of all, for the purchase and sale of commodities carried out between them; which is to say, money as means of payment to settle the claims and debts that arise through imports and exports. This is the function of money as **means of international payment**, which is the most fundamental—and common—function played by world money. Second, in those cases where the import and export of commodities between countries is immediately settled using cash, money is paid as means of purchase in exchange for the commodity. This is the function, in other words, as **means of international purchase**, and this sort of transaction arises when commodities are bought and sold between countries in a hostile relation toward each other, for example. Third, there is the case where wealth must be transferred from one country to another, taking the original form of money as the representative of social wealth, i.e. the form of raw gold. In this case, the gold transfer is the **absolute form of wealth**. One such example would be a case where a country defeated in a war pays reparations to the victor. The movement of gold in the world market and the functions of world money can be diagramed as follows (*see* ◘ Fig. 2.61).

Contemporary «International Currency»

In the contemporary world market, what circulates is not gold, but rather money wearing the national uniform of a specific country, i.e. the dollar. This is the «**international currency**». This sort of situation is premised on the development of a global credit system, but an understanding of this requires knowledge of not only the credit system but also the concrete historical development of international trade, which goes beyond the scope of this book.

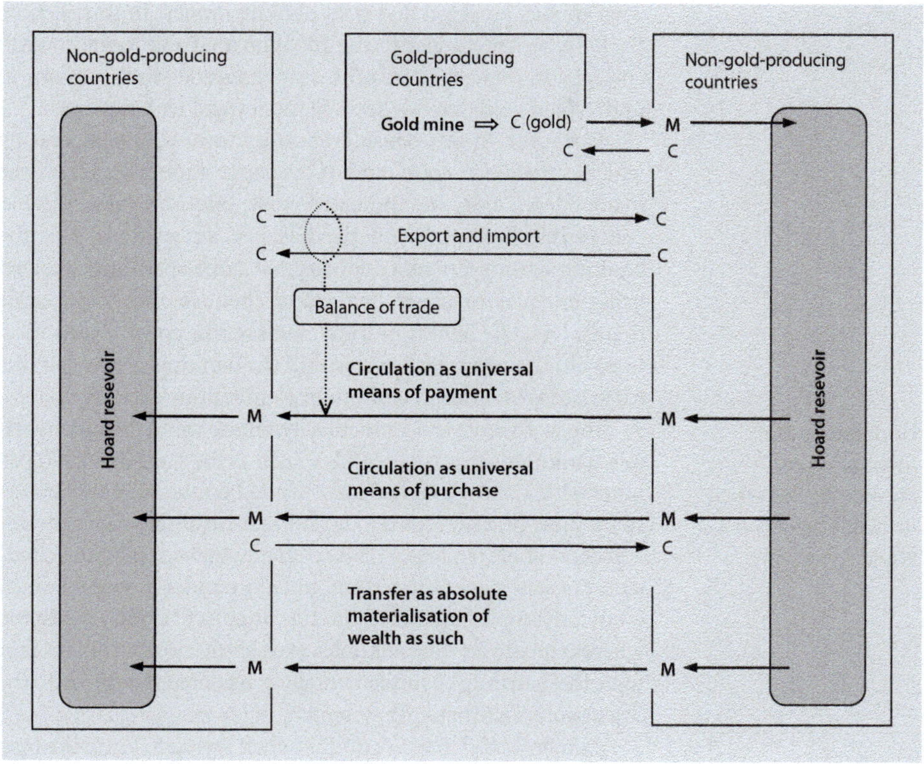

Fig. 2.61 Movements of gold in the world market and the functions of world money

Forms of Money Under the Inconvertibility System

Knowledge of the Functions of Money Under Metal Money Circulation Is Indispensable to Understanding Contemporary Forms of Money

Up to now, we have looked at the functions of money for gold as money. In the past, it was well known that gold circulated as bullion or coins, but the various types of money that we are conscious of in our own everyday lives do not include gold coins (not to mention gold bullion). Why then, instead of the sort of money that we see in daily reality, did we examine the functions of money in the case of gold money, which seems to have ceased to exist some time ago?

This is because the various kinds of money today emerged from out of the functions of money under the «**metal circulation**» in which gold also circulated as coins. In order to clarify the basis for what continues to exist today, it is essential to first correctly understand the functions of gold under metal circulation. Already in ► Sects. 2.2, 2.3 and 2.4, we saw how, why, and through what money emerged and gold became money. In this section, we have sought to clarify the function that the money which emerged in that way performs, so naturally it was necessary to understand gold that has become money and its functions.

Moreover, in our consideration up to now, the process by which subsidiary coins and state paper money emerge was made clear, and we indicated that one can first discuss convertible banknotes on the basis of an awareness of the banking system. Current deposits that can be paid and received using cheques or credit cards, and cheques and credit cards themselves, like banknotes, are credit money, or the indication to pay it, that emerges from within the banking system, so this topic cannot be raised without explaining the banking system.

Understanding Inconvertible Banknotes Requires Knowledge of the Banking System

The word «money» immediately calls to mind the **inconvertible banknotes** that we use today, such as the 1000 or 10,000 yen notes with «Bank of Japan Note» printed on them. But to understand these notes we need to be familiar with state paper money and convertible banknotes. Subsequently, in discussing the circulation of state paper money and inflation under it, we will touch on inconvertible banknotes, but the «**inconvertibility system**», wherein inconvertible banknotes exclusively circulate, is another topic that can only be fundamentally considered in relation to the discussion of the banking system.

As mentioned in ▶ Sect. 1.5.2, when trying to grasp the economic structure of society from its foundation, one cannot raise all at once all of the concrete phenomena that are visible to the eye. Rather, one must start with the analysis of the most essential and simple phenomena, and then move upwards, step by step (*see* ◘ Fig. 1.40). The same is true when dealing with money. Our study of money up to now has already provided us with the most fundamental knowledge regarding money. Using this as our basis, we can gradually gain a more concrete understanding of money, while advancing our study of the fundamental system of capitalist production and the banking system.

2.6.2 Quantity of Circulating Money and Money Reservoir

Quantity of Circulating Money

Our examination thus far has revealed that gold is excluded from the commodity world to become money, so that all commodities express their own value in this money. All commodities, through the mediation of money, are generally handed over, forming the circulation of commodities. Sales on credit also come to be carried out, so that gold enters circulation as means of payment. Within a given country, therefore, the means of circulation that mediate cash transactions and the means of payment to settle the balances of credit transactions are always circulating, and money necessary for this circulation also exists. But we still need to touch on the *quantity of money circulating within a country in the sphere of circulation.*

In the domestic circulation of a given country, there are individual commodities C_1 to C_n, each having quantities q_1 to q_n, and these are sold at various prices of $-\boxed{=M_1}$ to $-\boxed{=M_n}$. Here «price» refers to the price at the actual time of sale, which is to say the realised price—not the «asking price». Let's assume that these sales and purchases are all completed at the same time parallel to each other, with each requiring payment using separate money (coins). Each sale/purchase requires money for the prices that are indicated from $-\boxed{=M_1}$ to $-\boxed{=M_n}$. Here the **quantity of money necessary for circulation** is equal to the total sum of the commodity prices that are to be realised—i.e. Σ ($-\boxed{=M}\times q$). What this simple example directly indicates is that the most fundamental determinate of the quantity of circulating money is the *total sum of the prices of commodities* (the sum of the prices of individual commodities and the quantity of each sale/purchase). Rather than an increase or decrease in the quantity of money determining a rise or fall in the commodity prices, *it is the prices and quantity of the circulating commodities that determine the quantity of the money necessary to realise their prices.* This is the *most fundamental law* regarding the *quantity of circulating money*[16] (*see* ◘ Fig. 2.62).

Sales/purchases carried out at the same time, side by side, require separate money for each transaction, but in the case of sales that are carried out sequentially, the same piece of money can mediate different sales/purchases, passing from the hand of one person to the next. The following diagram depicts a single 10-yen coin mediating three transactions in a single day (*see* ◘ Fig. 2.63).

In the course of 1 day, a single 10-yen coin mediates 3 sales/purchases of 10-yen commodities. So 30 yen in total

---

16 Economics, particularly of the neo-classical school, is overwhelmingly dominated by the opposite view that the quantity of circulating money decides the prices of commodities. On the basis of this view, contemporary capitalist states often carry out the futile policy of aiming to overcome «deflation» by increasing the amount of currency supplied by the central bank. This upside-down view, referred to as the «**quantity theory of money**», was first advocated by *David Hume* (1711–1776) and was later refined by *Ricardo*. The theory's decisive fault is that it overlooks the role played by widely scattered hoards as a reservoir of money, thereby ignoring the increase and decrease in the quantity of currency that accompanies its flow out of and into this reservoir—as we will examine soon hereafter.

2

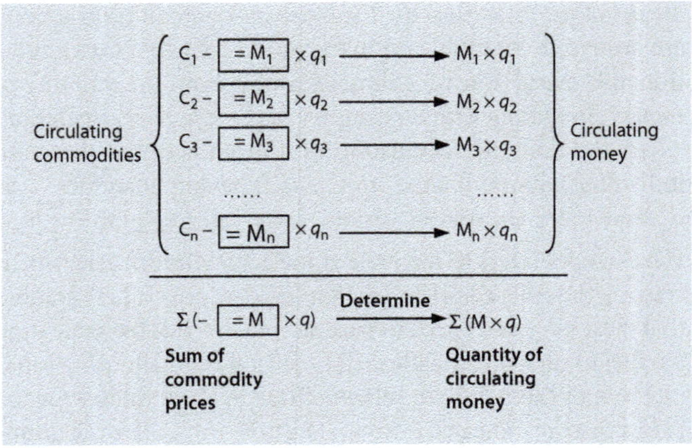

Fig. 2.62 Quantity of means of circulation mediating side-by-side commodity metamorphoses

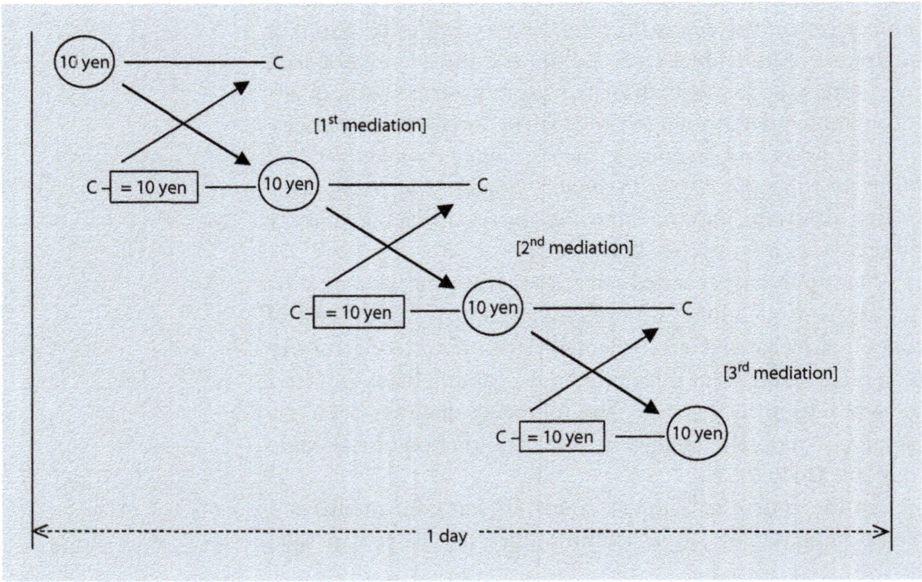

Fig. 2.63 Quantity of means of circulation mediating sequential commodity metamorphoses

prices has been realised with one 10-yen coin. We can see, then, that within a given period the sum of prices realised by a single piece of money is proportional to the times the piece of money realises a price within that period, i.e. it is proportional to the **circulation times of a piece of money**. Thus, the quantity of pieces of money necessary to realise the same sum of prices in a given period is inversely proportional to the times a piece of money circulates. An increase in the circulation times of a piece of money within a fixed period of time, is an increase in the velocity of that money's circulation or the **circulation velocity of a piece of money**. Therefore, if the circulation velocity of a piece of money increases, the money needed to realise the same sum of prices will decrease. The *quantity of circulating money* here is proportional to the sum of commodity prices, and *inversely proportional to the circulating velocity or circulating times of the same piece of money*. If we express the average circulating turnover of the same denomination of money during a fixed period of time as n, the following relation of determinacy becomes clear.

$$\frac{\text{sum of prices of circulating commodities}}{\text{average circulation times of pieces of money}} = \frac{\Sigma(-\boxed{\equiv M} \times q)}{n}$$

$$\xrightarrow{\text{determines}} \textit{quantity of circulating money } (M)$$

In this equation, the crux of the matter is that the sum of the commodities prices is the factor that determines the quantity of circulating money, rather than the quantity of circulating money determining the price of commodities, and this relation of determinacy is indicated by the arrow.

In thinking about the quantity of circulating money, we have assumed that all of the sales/purchases are cash transactions, with money circulating solely as means of circulation. However, as we have already seen, when sales and purchases on credit come to be carried out, money circulates as means of payment that settles balances between claims and debts, and this *money circulating as means of payment* also forms a part of the circulating money. Included in the sum of sales and purchases on credit (i.e. the sum of the products of the prices of the individual commodities bought and sold on credit and the total quantity of each transaction) are the total obligations that must be settled, and among them the offset obligations do not require any payment in reality. Also, as means of payment, it is possible for the same piece of money to repeatedly pass from the hands of one person to another within a certain period of time. So *the quantity of money as means of payment circulating to settle sales and purchases on credit* is decided as follows.

$$\frac{\text{sum of obligations to be paid} - \text{sum of offset payments}}{\text{circulating velocity of means of payment}}$$

$$\xrightarrow{\text{determines}} \textit{quantity of circulating means of payment}$$

2

The quantity of money circulating during a certain period of time in the circulation of a country is the sum of the money circulating as means of circulation and as means of payment. This is carried out, for example, by a given amount of money realising the price of a commodity as means of circulation, and then circulating as means of payment to settle an obligation, so that the *circulating money fulfills both functions* and does not have to be calculated twice but rather is subtracted from the total of the two above-mentioned functions. This means that, ultimately, the **total quantity of money circulating as means of circulation and means of payment** is determined by the following formula.

$$\frac{\text{sum of commodity prices to be realised}}{\text{circulating velocity of means of circulation}}$$

$$+\frac{\text{sum of obligations to be paid} - \text{sum of offset payments}}{\text{circulating velocity of means of payment}}$$

– *sum of pieces of money functioning as both means of circulation and means of payment*

$\xrightarrow{\text{determines}}$ *quantity of circulating money (total quantity of money circulating as means of circulation and means of payment)*

This *relation of determinacy* is called the **law of the quantity of circulating money**. Incidentally, *all of the circulating money*—money as means of circulation and money as means of payment—are called the «means of circulation». In this case, the term has a broad meaning, so that «*means of circulation in the broad sense = means of circulation in the original sense + circulating means of payment*».

Original Formation of Circulating Money

When money of a quantity necessary for commodity circulation is circulating in a given country, how is it that this precise quantity of money comes to exist? The money-commodity gold, to begin with, is something produced as a product of labour at the production source of gold, and then enters the sphere of circulation. As noted in our discussion of world money, if we are dealing with a non-gold-producing country without any gold mines, the gold circulating in the country is all produced by in countries that mine gold, obtained directly through trade with those gold-producing countries or indirectly through trade with non-gold-producing countries. This gold thus enters after crossing national borders. If a country has gold mines, the gold that is mined by its gold producers enters circulation. How does this occur? As indicated simply in the discussion of world money, gold producers exchange their own product of labour for other commodities. This exchange, *from their perspective*, is the *direct*

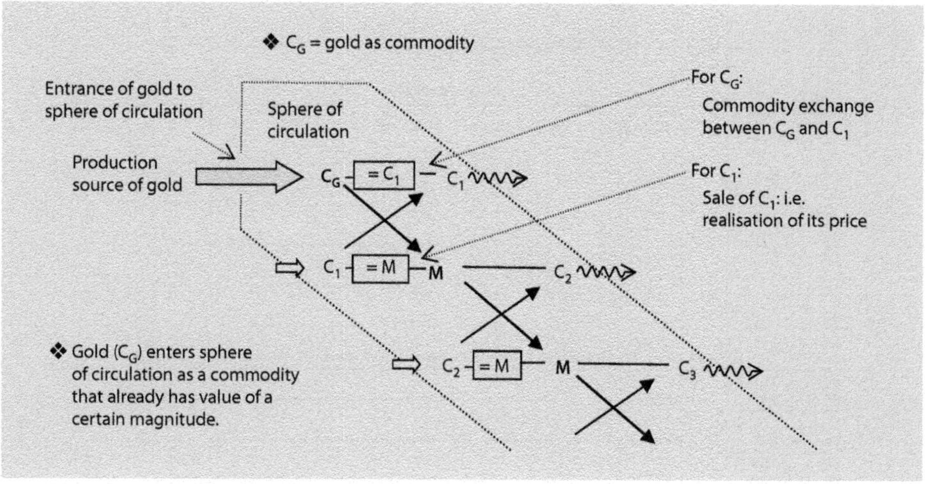

Fig. 2.64 Influx of gold into the sphere of circulation from its production sources

barter exchange of their own product gold for other commodities, but *from the perspective of the owners* of the other commodities for which the gold is exchanged, this is a *sale of commodities.* Here we have a unique transaction of **sale without purchase**, which results in the gold that has appeared as a commodity becoming a realised price, and then subsequently circulating as money. In this way, there is a hole or entrance in the circulation realm *through which gold qua money enters,* and *once it has entered it becomes money* (*see* Fig. 2.64).

Circulating Money and Coin Reserve

The commodity metamorphosis is C–M–C, but between the first metamorphosis of the commodity through which it turns into money (C–M, or the sale), and the second metamorphosis in the money-form (M–C, or the purchase), a stationary period of long or short duration is possible. During this stationary period preparations are made for subsequent purchases, since the seller who has turned his commodities into money may not immediately purchase the commodities desired to satisfy his own needs. Money in this static state is called a **coin reserve**. Money in the form of this coin reserve is the *provisional money-form* taken by a commodity *in a temporary resting state that will subsequently seek to transform itself into another commodity.* A clear distinction must be made between this coin reserve and the hoard (money in the proper sense) that is taken out of circulation and enters an immobile state (*see* Fig. 2.65).

So where, exactly, is the money that circulates? The period of time in which M as the means of purchase passes from the hands of the buyer to the seller is so short that it can basically

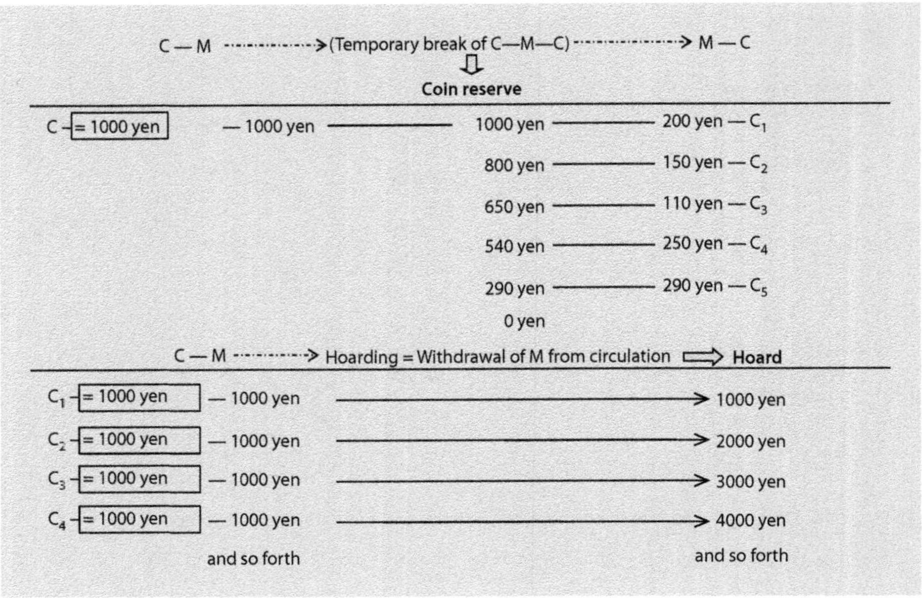

Fig. 2.65 Coin reserve and hoard

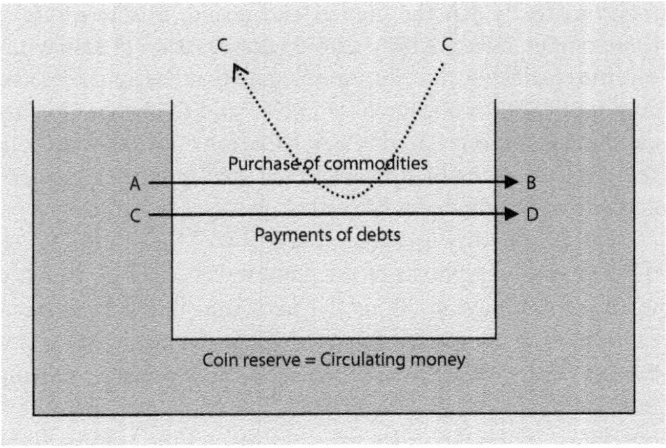

Fig. 2.66 Circulating money and coin reserve are the same thing seen from a different perspective

be ignored. Even if this transfer does take a moment to be carried out, it can be thought of temporally as a zero quantity. Thus, the circulating money is ultimately always in the hands of someone in the form of a coin reserve, passing from the hands of the seller to the buyer at some point in time. In other words, the coin reserve is **circulating money** *seen from the perspective of remaining in someone's hands*, and its substance is the same as that of circulating money (*see* Fig. 2.66).

Circulating money is thus the totality of the money for purchasing that is temporarily in wallets, cash registers, vaults, and the like. And the coin reserve similarly includes the money the debtor has temporarily shelved in expectation of payment as a means of payment.

Increase or Decrease in Quantity of Circulating Money and Hoard Reservoir

The quantity of circulating money changes constantly through changes in the price level of commodities, changes in the quantity of commodities bought and sold with cash or on credit, changes in the circulating velocity of money, etc. In what manner, then, is the quantity of circulating money, which must constantly fluctuate, able to increase or decrease?

First and foremost, this occurs through a reservoir formed from a hoard. The transfer of circulating money to a hoard decreases the quantity of circulating money, while increasing the level of the **hoard reservoir**. Conversely, when the hoard is again transformed into circulating money, the quantity of circulating money increases, while the level of the hoard reservoir is lowered. This sort of flow in and out of the reservoir is how the quantity of circulating money can always increase or decrease (*see* ◘ Fig. 2.67).

The quantity of the circulating money or hoard can also increase by gold entering circulation—from the domestic and foreign sources of gold production (or generally from *foreign countries*). Meanwhile, the gold flowing out to a *foreign country* can lead to a decrease in the quantity of the circulating money or hoard.

In this way, the quantity of circulating money is always able to be appropriate to the needs of circulation (*see* ◘ Fig. 2.68).

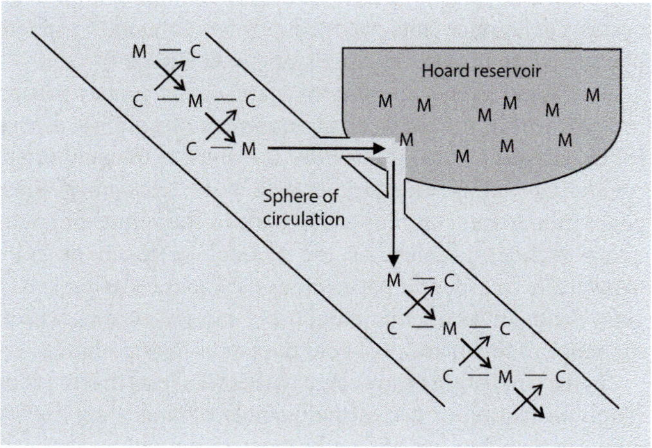

◘ **Fig. 2.67** Efflux from the sphere of circulation to the hoard reservoir and influx from the latter to the former

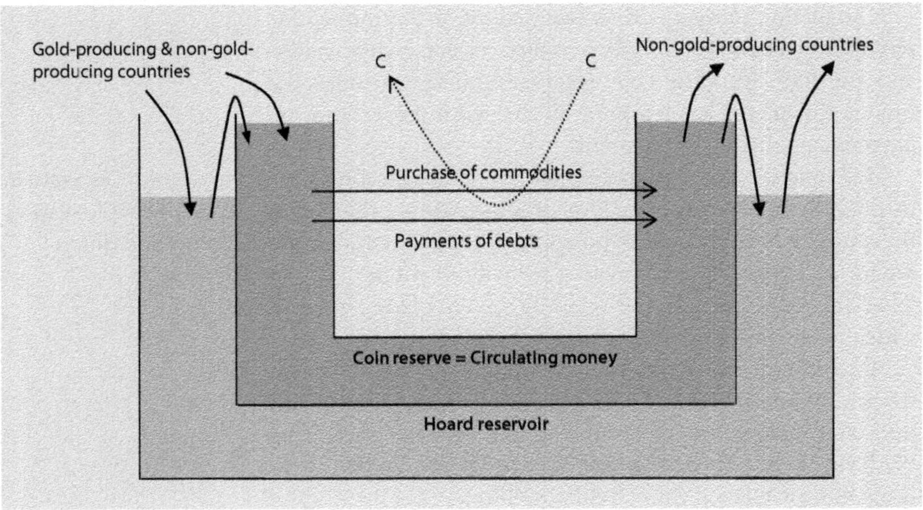

Fig. 2.68 Control of quantity of circulating money through hoard reservoir and influx from and efflux to abroad

Circulation of State Paper Money

As we have seen, in the process of circulation nearly valueless piece of paper can circulate as symbols expressing a certain quantity of gold. Thus, the state issues **state paper money** that is given a forced power of currency.

State paper money can only circulate to the extent that it represents the M between C–M and M–C, which is the momentary independent form of value. But this certainly cannot become a hoard. Moreover, there is no exit from the sphere of circulation for this paper money, apart the very exceptional method of a state forcefully siphoning it off to be destroyed. So once state paper money has entered the sphere of circulation, it must remain there (*see* Fig. 2.69).

However, if the amount of state paper money issued remains within the range of the **quantity of gold necessary for circulation**—i.e. *if it is within the range of the quantity of circulating money necessary if gold were circulating*—state paper money can continue to circulate in the sphere of circulation without problem as the symbol or token of gold. Conversely, in order for paper money to function as a token of gold, the quantity of circulating paper money must be within the range of the quantity of gold necessary for circulation.

In the circulation of any country, there is a level that the constantly increasing or decreasing quantity of circulating money does not go below, which can be grasped through experience. This is the **minimum quantity of money necessary for circulation**. As long as the amount of paper money issued by the state

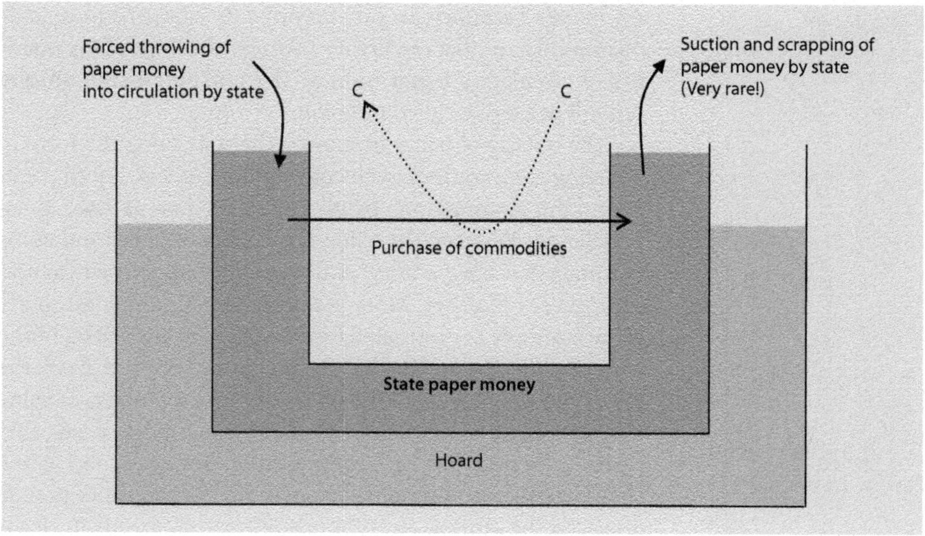

Fig. 2.69 No exit from the sphere of circulation for state paper money

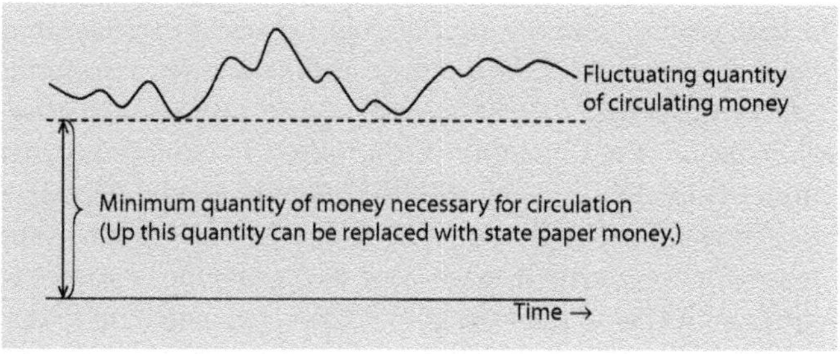

Fig. 2.70 Fluctuations in the quantity of circulating money and the minimum quantity of money necessary for circulation

remains at or above this minimum, the quantity of circulating money will not exceed the quantity of gold necessary for circulation, provided it is always circulating to function as **token of gold**. The increase or decrease in the quantity of circulating money is carried out through the influx and efflux of gold coins that circulate along with state paper money (*see* Fig. 2.70).

Inflation

The state, however, can throw value-less paper money, easily printed on a rotary press, into the sphere of circulation, to withdraw from the sphere of circulation commodities with value *qua* objectified abstract human labour. That is, it is possible to continue issuing paper money while ignoring the limit of the circulation of paper money. As a result, a situation arises in which the total sum of money expressed by the *state paper money issued exceeds the minimum quantity of circulat-*

ing money necessary. In other words, the state, from outside commodity circulation, breaks through the limit of the quantity of circulating paper money. The outcome is the **unique type of price rise** called *inflation*.

The issuing of paper money by the state takes the form of it buying commodities from commodity holders, but the reality of this transaction, from the state's perspective, is an «exchange» between the value-less scraps of paper and commodities that have a price of the quantity of gold written on these pieces of paper. More precisely, the sum of commodity value is simply expropriated by the state. For the sellers of the commodities, however, the paper money received from the state is no different than the paper money *qua* tokens of value that are already circulating, so the transaction is a sale that realises the price of their commodities. Thus, as soon as the state is handed commodities from the seller, the paper money is exactly the same as any other paper money already in circulation up to this point, and as such becomes one part of the quantity of circulating paper money. When the increasing quantity of circulating paper money breaks through its limits in that way, so that *the sum of gold expressed by circulating paper money exceeds the quantity of the necessary circulating gold*, it must trigger a counter-reaction. A process thus arises whereby the total quantity of the *inflated* circulating paper money is forcibly equated with the quantity of gold necessary for circulation. Simply put, this is the process whereby the denomination borne by each note of paper money comes to represent less gold than the gold it had represented up to that point, so that the *quantity of gold represented by the total amount of circulating paper money is compressed to be the same as the quantity of gold necessary for circulation*. Since the quantity of gold represented by each note of paper money is *commonly* called the «value of paper money», the decrease in the represented quantity of gold is called the **depreciation of paper money**. Once this depreciation of paper money occurs, the prices of commodities generally rise in reaction.

Let's suppose that *yen* is the monetary name of 750 mg of gold, and that 75 t of gold are necessary for circulation. The monetary name of this quantity of gold would be 100 million yen. And up to now, the maximum of the 1-yen paper money has been 100 million circulating notes. Let's also assume that there is no gold money circulating. Despite this, the quantity of circulating paper money just manages to stay within the limit, with each 1-yen note able to circulate as the proxy for 750 mg of gold.

Now, suppose that the state throws into circulation 100 million value-less notes with 1-yen printed on them, which are used to withdraw commodities from the sphere of circulation with a combined price of 100 million yen. The circulating money has been increased to 200 million notes, with the money-name they bear being 200 million yen. There is now 100 million yen in excess in terms of the money-name up to now of a quantity of gold necessary for circulation of 100 million yen, and this excess expresses the unilateral appropriation of value by the state. However, there is no difference at all between each of the 200 million yen circulating notes. Here a process arises whereby the totality of this 200 million of circulating paper money is equated with the 75 t of gold necessary for circulation. So the quantity of gold represented by 1 yen, which had been 750 mg, decreases to 375 mg. *If this process is completed*, the quantity of gold represented by the total sum of 200 million yen, borne by the 200 million 1-yen notes, is compressed to 75 t. By means of this the quantity of gold expressed by *yen* is reduced from 750 mg to 375 mg. As a result, a commodity that previously represented 750 mg of gold in the price of – = 1 yen would need to have a price of – = 2 yen to express the same quantity of gold. Since all commodities are in the same situation, sooner or later prices would have to rise two-fold. This is the same effect as if the *legal determination* of the standard of «yen» had been reduced from «750 mg of gold» to «375 mg of gold». So a manner of understanding arises where «a de facto devaluation in the standard of price» is thought to cause a price rise.

We must first bear in mind, however, that in this sort of price rise there is an extremely complex *spreading process* that unfolds, from the moment when the throwing of 100 million yen by the state has been perceived up to the point where prices ultimately double; this process is accompanied by an increased demand for commodities, so that the prices of all commodities do not rise in unison. Secondly, the rate of the price rise varies greatly among commodities, so it cannot be seen as identical to a legal change in the standard of price.

This sort of price rise, which simply put is *a price rise* via *the depreciation of paper money*, is called **inflation**.

The typical price rise we see today is also inflation. Moreover, the essence of today's inflation, as a «price rise via the depreciation of paper money», is the same as above. However, present-day paper money is not simply state paper money, but rather *inconvertible banknotes issued by central banks* that have more or less of a national character. Even though the characteristic as a price rise via the depreciation of paper money is the same, inconvertible banknotes—although they cannot be converted into gold—are banknotes nonetheless, and as such *their issuance involves a manner of lending* that must be reimbursed in the end. So, there are many points where the characteristics of inflation differ between inconvertible banknotes and pure state paper money. However, this cannot be understood without knowledge of the structure of capitalist production and an overview of the banking system.

References

Gwartney JD et al (1982) Essentials of economics. Academic Press, New York

Kuruma S (1979–1985) Lexikon der Politischen Ökonomie, vol 10–15. Tokyo, Otsuki-Shoten Publishers

Kuruma S (1979) Kahei-ron. Otsuki-Shoten Publishers. Tokyo. English edition: Kuruma S (2017) Marx's theory of the genesis of money (trans. Schauerte M). Brill Publishers, Leiden et al.

Marx K (1872) Das Kapital. Kritik der politischen Oekonomie. Bd. 1. Buch 1: Der Produktionsprocess des Kapitals. 2. verb. Aufl. Hamburg. English edition: Marx K (1976) Capital. A critique of political economy. Vol. 1 (trans: Howkes B). Penguin Books

Marx K (1868) Brief an Ludwig Kugelmann, 11. Juli 1868. English edition: Marx K (1988) Letter to Ludwig Kugelmann, 11 July 1868. Marx-Engels Collected Works. Vol. 43. Progress Publishers et al. New York

Smith A (1776) An inquiry into the nature and causes of the wealth of nations. In 2 vols. London. New edition: Smith A (1937) An inquiry into the nature and causes of the wealth of nations. Modern Library edition. New York

Capital and Surplus-value

T. Otani, *A Guide to Marxian Political Economy*,
https://doi.org/10.1007/978-3-319-65954-1_3

3.1 Process of Valorisation

3.1.1 Riddle of Capital

Examining the Common Image of Capital Based on the Knowledge Obtained Thus Far

Now that we have familiarised ourselves with the commodity and money, we are in a position to begin analysing capital. We need to first examine the common image of capital based on our understanding of the commodity and money in order to grasp its core concept. Then we will need to be aware of—and solve—a riddle within this concept that cannot be understood on the sole basis of the knowledge gained up to now.

The Form of Circulation of Money *qua* Capital: Augmentation of Value

First of all, capital appears as money, but this is money that moves in a form that contrasts absolutely with that of commodity circulation.

Simple commodity circulation, as we saw, is C–M–C, where the aim of the process is to obtain a specific use value (*see* ◘ Fig. 3.1).

By contrast, capital is money that moves according to the following form (*see* ◘ Fig. 3.2).

Money is both the starting point and the arrival point. Therefore, the money at the starting point is not finally expended in exchange for a commodity, but only advanced[1] with the expectation of a reflux to the point of departure. In addition, this process can only have meaning if M at the arrival point is of greater magnitude than the initial M. The term «capital» is used, in everyday life, to refer to the movement of money that results in a greater quantity at the end

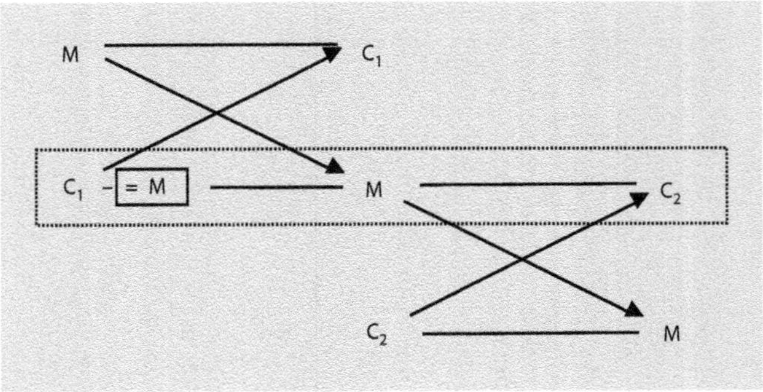

◘ **Fig. 3.1** Simple commodity circulation: C–M–C

1 When a money holder *pays out* his money, *expecting a reflux of the money after a time*, it is said that he *advances* the money. The term **advance** relates overwhelmingly to paying out *money as capital*, but there is also a peculiar case relating to *money as means of circulation*, as we shall see in ► Sect. 14.3.2 in Part II.

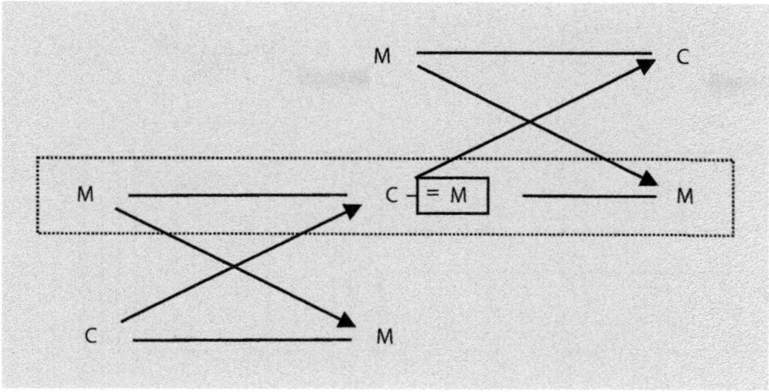

■ **Fig. 3.2** Circulation form of money as capital: M–C–M

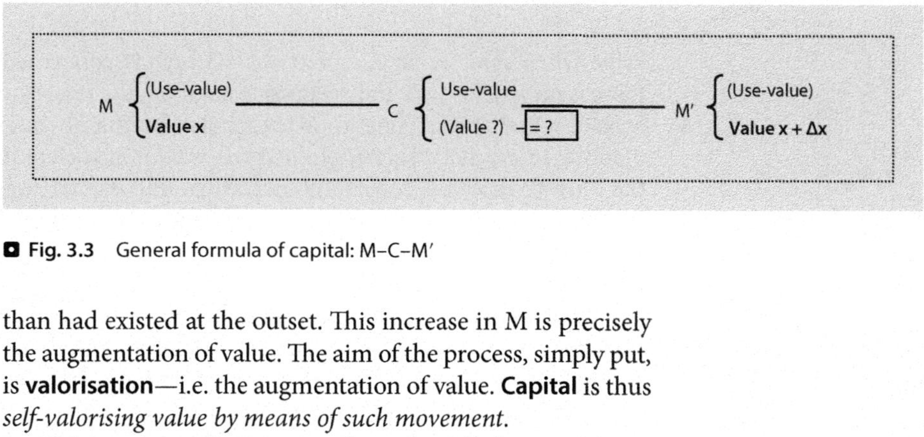

■ **Fig. 3.3** General formula of capital: M–C–M′

than had existed at the outset. This increase in M is precisely the augmentation of value. The aim of the process, simply put, is **valorisation**—i.e. the augmentation of value. **Capital** is thus *self-valorising value by means of such movement.*

If the augmented money is indicated as M′, the circulation-form of capital is M–C–M′. This is the general movement-form of capital and can thus be called the **general formula of capital** (*see* ■ Fig. 3.3).

Riddle of Capital: From Where Does Augmented Value Arise?

If we assume that commodities are bought and sold at their value, it is not possible for value to be augmented in either the purchase (M–C) or the sale (C–M). How, then, does the augmented part or increment of M (ΔM) arise? (*see* ■ Fig. 3.4) This is the riddle that we must solve: the **riddle of capital**.

In actual transactions, price and value are usually not in agreement. But when a transaction is carried out at a price that diverges from value, there is merely a transfer of the difference in value from one side to another side between the seller and purchaser (either in the commodity form or money form); whereas the total amount of value of the sold commodity and the money paid remains completely unchanged after the sale is completed. A gain on one side would be a loss on the other. So no matter how much commodities may diverge from their

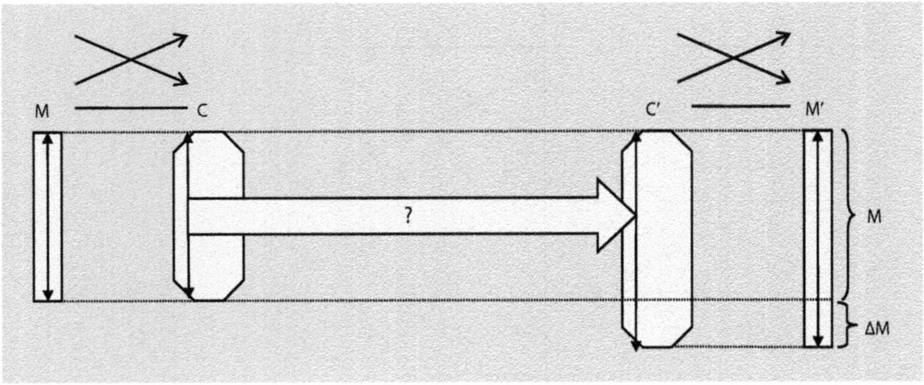

Fig. 3.4 Riddle of capital: From where does augmented value arise?

value when sold, as far as society as a whole is concerned, there is no way for such transactions to augment the total sum of value. Yet, as everyone knows, capital is constantly augmenting in capitalist society, so that the wealth of society in the form of capital is constantly increasing. This capital augmentation must occur, therefore, regardless of whether the prices of commodities diverge from their values. Even if every transaction were carried out in line with value, the augmentation of value would have to take place somewhere, through some process or another. It is sufficient, then, and indeed necessary, *to assume that all commodities are sold at their value* when trying to unravel this riddle of how capital is augmented.

3.1.2 Key to Solving the Riddle: The Use-value and Value of Labour-power as a Commodity

A Commodity Must Exist Whose Use-value Creates Value

It is only possible for a change in the quantity of value to occur in the process of M–C–M if the consumption of C (which is the outcome of M–C) generates value, and if, moreover, the quantity of newly generated value is greater than the value of the commodity consumed. This can only occur, in other words, if a special sort of commodity exists (*see* Fig. 3.5).

For this to be possible, something must exist with a *unique use-value whose consumption generates value*, and it must *be sold as a commodity on the market.*

Under Commodity Production, the Consumption of Labour-power Generates Value

We know that such a thing does indeed exist: **labour-power**.

The consumption of labour-power is its exertion, which is to say, labour itself. And that labour has two aspects: concrete labour and abstract labour (*see* Fig. 2.8).

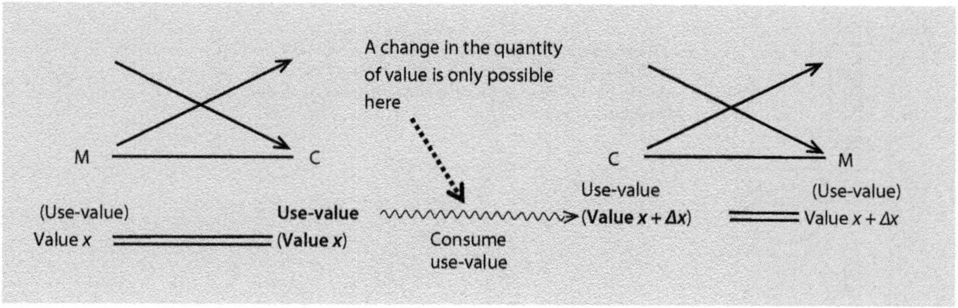

Fig. 3.5 Exclusive possibility for a change to arise in the quantity of value

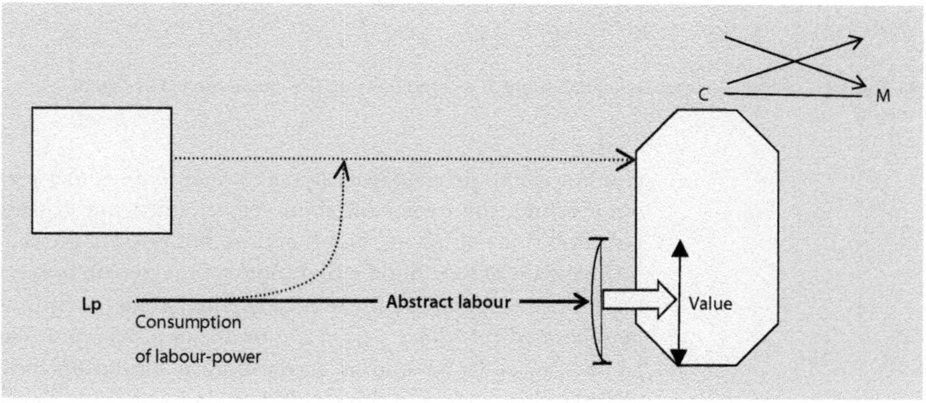

Fig. 3.6 Labour-power creates value through its consumption

Concrete labour transfers the value of the means of production to a product, so there is no change in value at all (*see* Fig. 2.17). Abstract labour, in contrast, forms the new value that is objectified within a product. So when a product becomes a commodity, abstract labour creates the new value (*see* Fig. 2.18).

Under commodity production, therefore, labour-power has the *quality of generating new value through the aspect that labour (consumption of labour-power) has as abstract labour.* Labour-power thus has the unique use-value of creating value when consumed (*see* Fig. 3.6).

Labour-power Is Bought and Sold as a Commodity in Capitalist Society

Labour-power is in fact bought and sold as a commodity in the «**labour market**» (*see* Fig. 3.7).

Unlike the case of slaves, labour-power is not sold in a bodily form, in its entirety, to *another person.* Rather, it is a transaction in which a wageworker (seller) sells *his own* labour-power *for a definite period of time* to a capitalist (purchaser).

Two Conditions for Labour-power To Be Sold

Two conditions must be met for labour-power to be sold. First, the owners of labour-power must be *personally free*

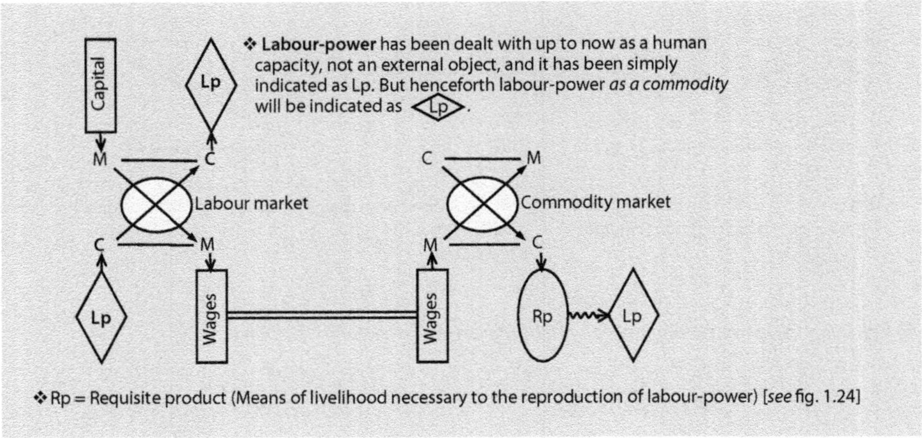

Fig. 3.7 Labour-power is sold and bought as a commodity on the labour market in capitalist society

and not bound personally as slaves or serfs to any other person. Second, the owner of labour-power must not possess the conditions of labour, and therefore not possess the requisite means of livelihood either; nor can the person possess the money to purchase those means. The person must thus be *separated* (or «*free*»[2]) *from the means of production.* For labour-power to be sold as a commodity, **labouring individuals who are free in this double sense** must exist.

3.1.3 Sale and Purchase of Labour-power

Labour-power Is Sold Temporarily

The relation between the buyer and seller of labour-power is a relation between two persons on an equal legal footing, namely: the possessor (holder) of labour-power and the holder of money. For the possessor of labour-power[3] to be able to sell labour-power as his own possession, his labour-power must be sold only *temporarily for a definite period of time,* rather than in its entirety.[4]

---

2 The word «**free**» in this case signifies «removed or forced out from a position».

3 At the starting point of the analysis of capital the adult male workers must be posited as the possessors of labour-power. This is certainly not meant to suggest gender discrimination, but rather is historically as well as theoretically necessarily. Later (in ► Sect. 5.4.3), we shall see how capitalist production massively incorporates women and children into the labour market.

4 Marx (1865) first clearly stated the crux of this issue in his report in English at the meetings of the Working Men's International

Temporary Sales and Purchases Are Common

In fact, **sales and purchases according to time (hour, day, month etc.)** are common.[5] The typical form of this sort of transaction is a «**lease**».[6] The characteristic of such transactions is that they are a special form of *sale and purchase. The seller hands over his commodity to the purchaser and allows the latter to freely dispose of it for a certain period of time; but the seller does not hand over the right of ownership of the commodity itself, and therefore after the time has elapsed, it is returned from the purchaser to seller.* This transaction form is also common to «rent» and «charter».

For sales on a temporary basis,[7] the purchase price is for the time during which a person is entrusted with the commodity. But how is this price, known as **rent**, determined?

Association held on 20 and 27 June, 1865: «What the working man sells is not directly his *labour*, but his *Labouring Power*, the temporary disposal of which he makes over to the capitalist» (Marx 1985, p. 128; Marx's emphasis). He writes in *Capital* (Marx 1872): «He [proprietor of labour-power] must constantly treat his labour-power as his own property, his own commodity, and he can do this only by placing it at the disposal of the buyer, i.e. handing it over to the buyer for him to consume, *at all times only temporarily, for a definite period of time*» (Marx 1976, p. 271; my emphasis and brackets).

5 Marx (1872) writes: «Suppose that a *capitalist pays for a day's worth of labour-power;* then the *right to use that power for a day* belongs to him, *just as much as the right to use any other commodity, such as a horse he had hired for the day*» (Marx 1976, p. 292; my emphasis).

6 The transaction-form of «**lease**» is commonly considered as a sort of lending and borrowing of money. In terms of industry classification, leasing enterprises also often belong to financial institutions. Lending and borrowing of money are almost the same insofar as their *legal forms* are concerned, but, as we shall see later (► Sect. 19.1.1 in Part III), they have thoroughly different characteristics from leasing. Lending and borrowing takes the *form of selling and buying a commodity* (the peculiar commodity of money as capital). *In capitalist society, every possible transaction between economic partners necessarily takes the form of commodity sale and purchase.* Thus, we should clearly distinguish between the *rent* paid for leasing and the *interest* paid for lending (*see* the following footnote 7).

7 In capitalist society, the practical transaction of leasing is related to the lending of money. This is because what is paid as rent involves the interest for the time period involved, in addition to the price of temporarily using the commodity. (It should go without saying that such an addition would never arise in the case of the sale of labour-power.) But to grasp the lease transaction in a pure form we must abstract from this side of lending—and therefore from interest. Once we have severed the link to lending, we can clearly see what kind of transaction leasing is. For example, however low the interest rate may fall, the leasing industry still must recover the value of leased commodities via rent, and as far as being able to do so this industry can continue to exist regardless of interest.

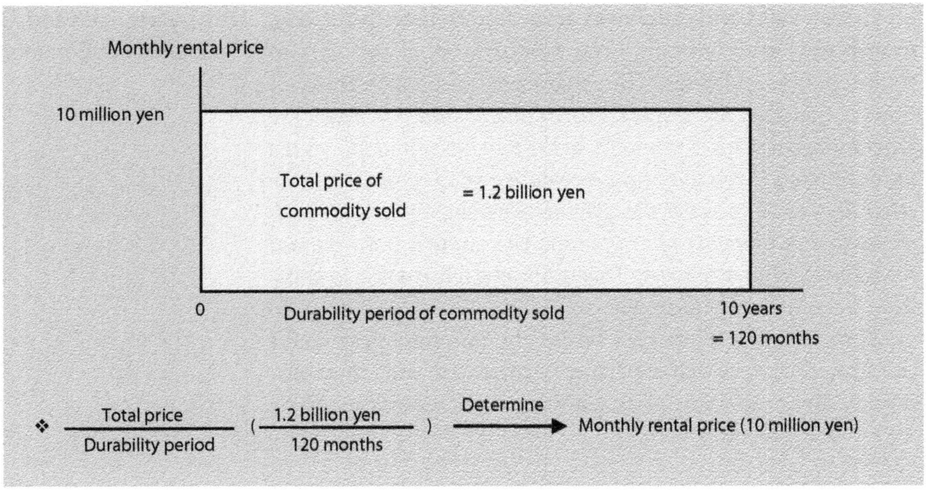

Fig. 3.8 How is the price per time-unit determined for a commodity sold on a temporary basis?

Let's consider the case of a machine leased by the month. A one-month rental of the machine would be based on the following calculation.

Assume that the total price of the machine is 1.2 billion yen and the machine lasts for 10 years (120 months), which is also the period during which it can be leased. The one-month rental fee for the machine in this case would have to be such that 120 months would equal to 1.2 billion yen (*see* Fig. 3.8). Here the «price» of the rented commodity is an expression of its value.

Crucially important to this calculation is the total price of the machine that expresses its *total value* and its *period of durability* (sales period), which are both givens to begin with. This is the basis upon which the rent for a time-unit (rental price) can be calculated. The rent is certainly not determined by the degree to which the machine is useful to the leaser (buyer) during a one-month period or the manner in which the leaser uses the machine; which is to say, rent is absolutely not determined by the machine's «utility» or its use-value.[8]

Also in the case of the labour-power commodity, we first must grasp the *total value* of this commodity and its *period of durability* (sales period), and then determine the rent for a unit-period on that basis. What corresponds here to rent is the daily, monthly, or weekly wages, or annual salary and the like.

---

8 The simple example of house rent highlights this point. Whether a tenant actually uses the rented house or not, he must unconditionally pay the rent. The monthly rent is paid for the right to use it for a month, not for the «utility» that it brings to the tenant.

The Primary Time Unit for the Sale of Labour-power Is a Single Day

Labouring individuals, as living creatures, require rest and sleep *every day*. Thus, the sale of labour-power for a definite time period, in normal cases, takes the form in which the purchaser (capitalist) uses labour-power for a limited period of time *every day*. One might think, therefore, that the hour would be adoptable as the unit of time for the sale of labour-power, but that unit is above all the *single day*.

The day as such a unit for the sale and purchase of labour-power for a definite period of time came to be known in England as the «**working day**». Although hereafter this word is also used to express the labour-time of 1 day performed by wageworkers, i.e. the working hours in a day, it still remains crucially important to grasp that the *fundamental unit of sale and purchase of labour-power is, above all, the working day.* Even when the unit of a contract is the week or month, it is still the day that is the basis for calculation.[9]

Value of Labour-power Is Determined by the Social Reproduction Cost of Labour-power

What determines the **value of labour-power** as a commodity? Like other commodities, its value is determined by the socially necessary labour-time to produce it. However, since labour-power is produced and reproduced within the process of an individual's consumption of the requisite means of livelihood, the *socially necessary labour-time for the production of labour-power* resolves itself into the *socially labour-time for the production of the requisite means of livelihood,* which are *the means of livelihood indispensable to the reproduction of labour-power.*

Included in the requisite means of livelihood are (1) «**living costs**» – which are the means of livelihood indispensable to the maintaining of the labouring individual in a normal state of existence, and (2) «**familial costs**» – which are the means of livelihood needed to replenish the labour-power that disappears from the market by being worn out or due to deaths (i.e. the cost of raising the children of workers). In addition to those two expenses, the production of labour-power requires, to a greater or lesser extent, (3) «**education or training costs**»—which are the costs and items needed to foster the particular developed labour-power in a specific department of labour through the acquisition of skills and expertise. The value of labour-power is thus determined by the socially necessary labour to produce those three factors. This is the reproduction cost of labour-power.

---

9 In practice, wages are paid by the hour. We shall elucidate the reason and the manner of this form of payment in ► Chap. 7. Here it is only necessary to understand that, whatever their hourly wages may be, wageworkers must be able to live a day on their daily wages.

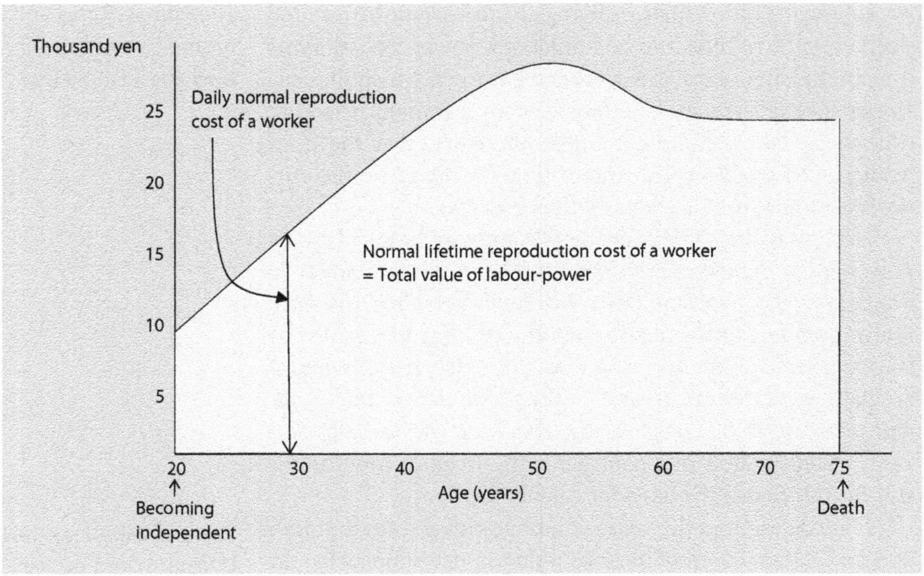

Fig. 3.9 Total value of labour-power

Total Value of Labour-power is the Reproduction Cost for the Entire Life of the Worker

What would be the total value of labour-power? This is akin to a machine's total value, which was the basis for calculating rent in our earlier example. In short, the value of labour-power is the *cost from the time the worker begins independently selling his own labour-power until the time of his death.* In other words, *the total sum of the reproduction cost necessary to keep the worker in a normal condition as a working individual throughout his life—from the time he leaves his parent's household until his death.* Here we have the **total value of labour-power** (*see* Fig. 3.9).

The total value of labour-power is the *total value of the means of livelihood that are socially indispensable to a life that can be considered to have a socially normal life cycle.* The term «normal» here means that a person in a given society is able to live as a physically and mentally healthy and stable labouring individual. This would be reflected, for example, in the calculation of «lifetime expenditures» that is often seen in advertising pamphlets for life insurance companies.

Daily Value of Labour-power Is Determined by Its Total Value and the Number of Days It Is Sold

The sales price of labour-power, with a working day as its value-unit, is decided by the *value of a day's labour-power*—or the **daily value of labour-power**, for short.

Labour-power's daily value is the sum of its total value divided by the number of days it is sold. The number of days that labour-power is sold is the socially average number of days that a worker sells his labour-power throughout his life.

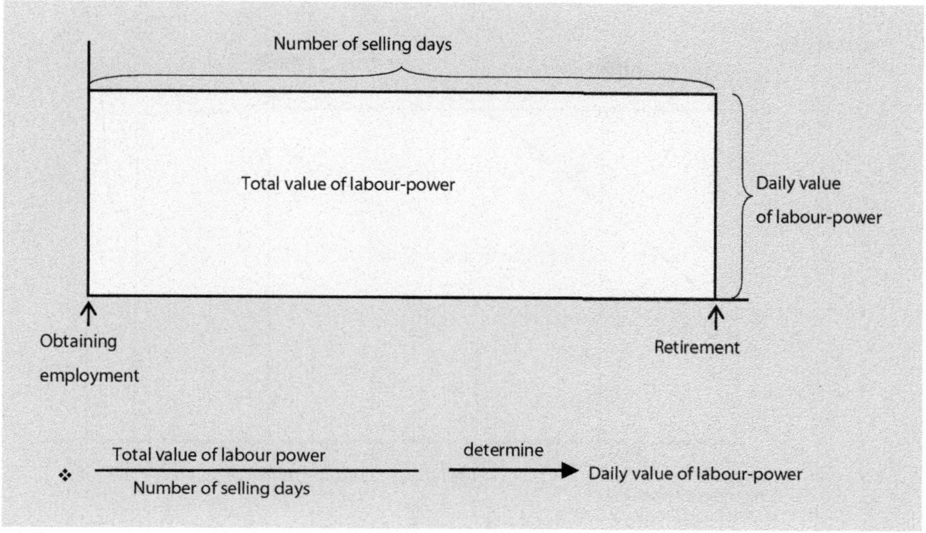

Fig. 3.10 Daily value of labour-power is determined by its total value and the number of selling days

The contract between capitalist and worker involves a worker providing one working day and the capitalist paying the value (in the form of money) for labour power's daily value (*see* Fig. 3.10).

The sum of money that a worker actually obtains throughout his lifetime through the sale of labour-power is called «*lifetime wages*», which forms his «*lifetime revenue*». Naturally, the worker's *lifetime expenditures* are covered by the *lifetime revenue* obtained through *lifetime wages,* as also seen in life-insurance pamphlets. This common calculation vividly expresses the essential fact that the reproduction cost of labour-power is the total value of labour-power, which in turn determines the wages (price of labour-power) sold on a temporary basis. The relation between the total value of labour-power and the daily value of labour-power can be illustrated as follows (*see* Fig. 3.11).

Let us assume, simply, that workers on average begin to sell their labour-power at age 20 and retire at age 60. The costs necessary for a worker increase from the time he is single and begins working to when he gets married and has children who are then educated. These costs peak out at around the time a worker is in his early 50s, and then begin to decrease as his children become independent. Then, after a period of retirement in which he ceases to sell his labour-power, the worker and spouse die. So they would have required living costs until the age of around 75. If we depict this 55-year, *socially standard «life cycle»*, and calculate the *total socially average costs it*

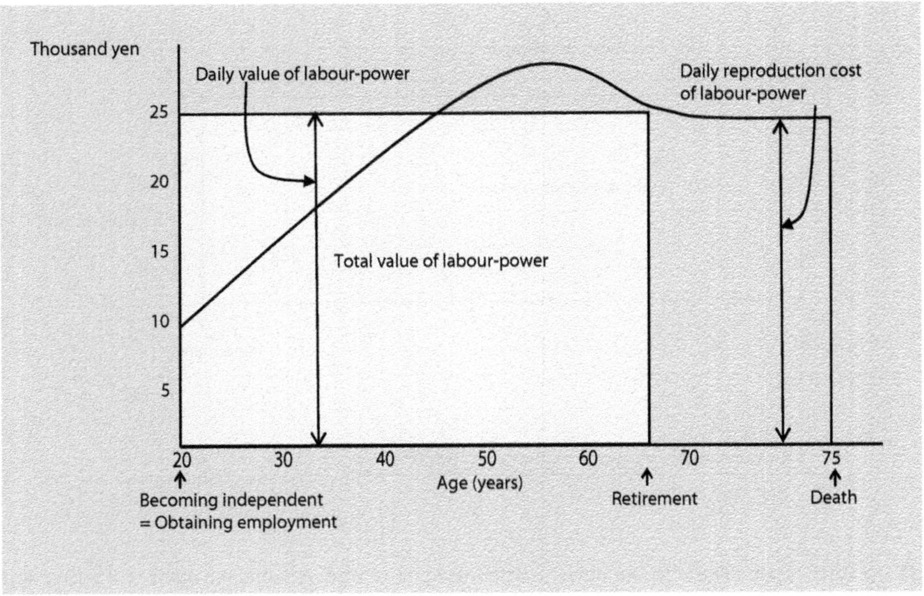

Fig. 3.11 Total value of labour-power and daily value of labour-power

requires (referred to more popularly as «*lifetime expenditures*»), it can serve as an estimate of the total value of labour-power (whereas the costs up to age 20 are included within the familial costs of the worker's parents). The worker must cover this total value through the sum of the value of the labour-power sold every day over a period that (in our example) spans the 40 years from age 20 to 60. This is the worker's «*lifetime wages*» or «*lifetime revenue*». We thus arrive at the daily value of labour-power by dividing the total value by the number of days in which labour-power can be sold during a 40-year span.

Reproduction Cost of Labour-power Is Nothing More than the Requisite Labour-time

As we saw in the Introduction (► Sect. 1.3.2), a certain quantity and range of the means of livelihood are indispensable for the reproduction of labour-power, regardless of the form of society. And the (abstract) labour for the production of these requisite means of livelihood (labour fund) is the requisite labour (labour-time) (*see* Fig. 1.24). Thus, the *reproduction cost of labour-power that determines the value of labour-power is the requisite labour (labour-time) for the reproduction of labour-power, which is common to every society.* The value of labour-power is the requisite labour (labour-time) that indispensable in any society to the reproduction of labour-power. But this only takes on a completely unique material form when the human capacity of labour-power is sold as a commodity (*see* Fig. 3.12).

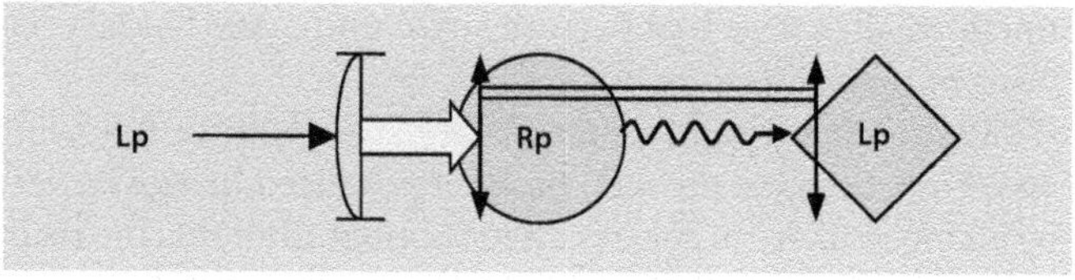

Fig. 3.12 Reproduction cost of labour-power determines the value of labour-power

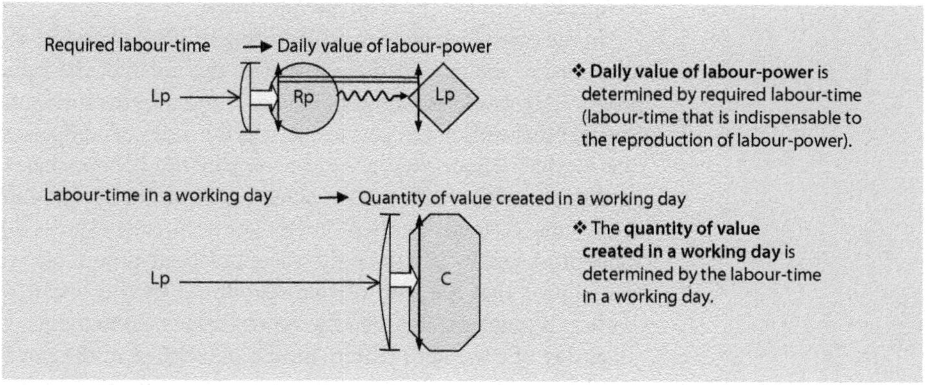

Fig. 3.13 Daily value of labour-power and value created in a working day

3.1.4 Secret of the Valorisation Process

The daily value of labour-power is determined by the requisite labour-time, but the value that labour-power creates in 1 day is determined by the daily labour-time of the worker; there is *absolutely no necessary relation* between the two. The daily cost of maintaining labour-power and the daily expenditure of labour-power are *two completely different quantities* (*see* Fig. 3.13).

Daily Value of Labour-power and the Quantity of Value Created by Labour-power in a Working Day Are Two Different Things

Surplus-Value: Difference Between the Value Created in a Working Day and the Daily Value of Labour-power

As noted in ► Sect. 1.4.2, **surplus labour** (labour-time) is the part of labour (labour-time) carried out beyond the requisite labour (labour-time). And the product produced by this surplus-labour is the **surplus product**. In any society, surplus products must be produced, to a greater or lesser extent (*see* Figs. 1.25, 1.29, 1.30, 1.31, 1.32, and 1.33).

Capitalist production not only started off, originally, with productive power clearly exceeding the productive power under the feudal relations of production, but then also developed productive power at a faster tempo than in any other previous epoch. Under capitalist production, given this productive power, the proportion of requisite labour within the daily labour-time of a worker is clearly

3

much smaller than had been the case under the feudal relations of production.

We could envisage contemporary society in the following way. First, imagine the total product produced in a given year by all the workers in society; then subtract from this the reappearing means of production that compensate for those used up in productive consumption. What remains is the new product of the given year. Out of this new product, the products that are bought back and consumed by the workers who produced them are the requisite products.

In the case of Japanese manufacturing in 2014, if we take the total sum of «value added» in a year as the index of the value produced by workers' labour in that year, and take the total sum of wages that workers receive in a year as the index of compensation for their labour-power, we can compare the «labour share», i.e. the ratio of the former to the latter (*see* ◘ Table 3.1). The data in the table certainly neither directly nor accurately express the value produced by labour or the value of labour-power, but we can still see that the sum of value produced by the labour of workers is much greater than the sum of value paid to them.

A **day** of a worker's labour-time is objectified in the product to become its value, while the requisite labour-time within

◘ **Table 3.1** Value added, wages, labour share (Japan 2014)

Number of personnel (scale of enterprise)	Value added (1 million yen)	Wages (1 million yen)	Labour share (%)
4–9	3,080,909	1,465,055	47.6
10–19	5,005,471	2,264,004	45.2
20–29	4,996,279	2,116,396	42.4
30–49	5,355,902	2,254,124	42.1
50–99	10,097,322	3,898,069	38.6
100–199	12,417,669	4,439,147	35.7
200–299	8,587,525	2,630,952	30.6
300–499	9,916,084	3,232,304	32.6
500–999	11,451,906	3,841,891	33.5
Over 1000	21,379,804	6,544,257	30.6

Ministry of International Trade and Industry, Japan (2016)

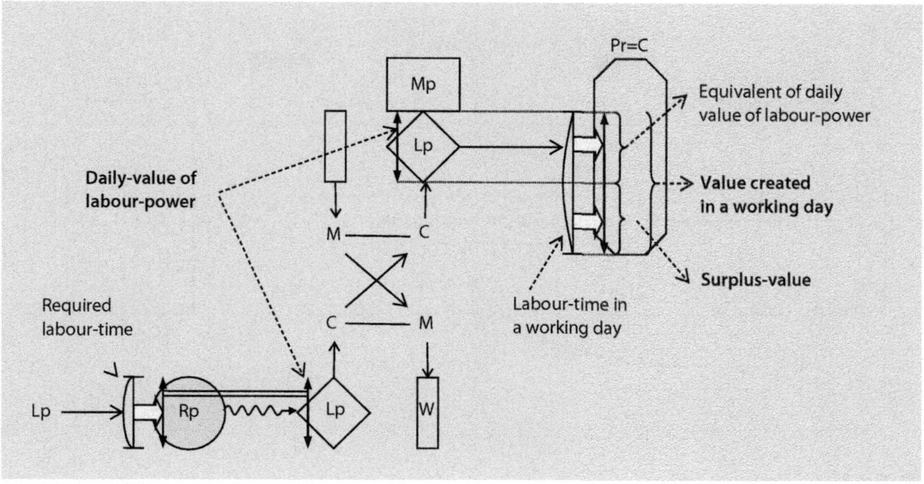

■ **Fig. 3.14** Surplus-value is the difference between the value created in a working day and the daily value of labour-power

that produces an equivalent for the labour-power. **Surplus-value** (*s*) is produced by the surplus labour-time that exceeds this requisite labour-time (*see* ■ Fig. 3.14).

Value of Labour-power Is the Objectified Requisite Labour and Surplus-value Is the Objectified Surplus Labour

Of the labour a worker performs in a day, the part of the labour (labour-time) that reproduces the daily value of labour-power is the requisite labour (labour-time), and the labour that exceeds this is the surplus labour (labour-time). This requisite labour and surplus labour—as mentioned in ► Sect. 1.4.2—*are merely the particular capitalist forms of the requisite labour and surplus-labour that can be seen in any form of society* (*see* ■ Fig. 1.26).

3.1.5 Constant Capital and Variable Capital

Constant Capital

As explained near the end of ► Sect. 2.2.2, in the case where the means of production already include value, the value of those means of production are transferred and thus maintained within the product through concrete labour that transforms and processes them (*see* ■ Figs. 1.57 and 1.58). In the course of the production process, the value included within the means of production is not altered at all quantitatively. Therefore, the part of capital advanced in the means of production remains completely unchanged quantitatively from its initial money-form to its final money-form, and is thus called **constant capital (c)** (*see* ■ Fig. 3.15).

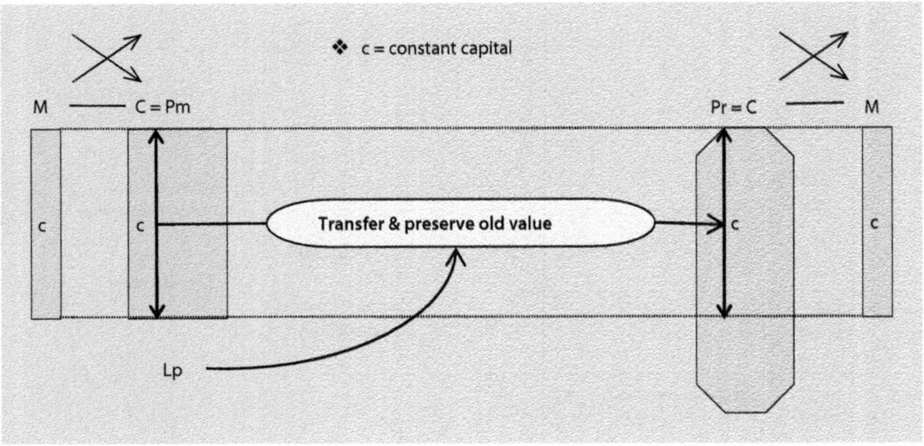

Fig. 3.15 Constant capital

Partial Transfer of the Value of Machinery

In the case of those durable means of production that can be used to produce a large quantity of products until they wear out (e.g., machinery or factory buildings), their total value is transferred through that production to the total products produced. In line with how the means of production wear away little by little, their value is also transferred bit by bit to the product. For example, the following quantity of value would be transferred to, and maintained within, the product of 1 day:

$$\begin{aligned}&\text{Daily transferred value}\\&=\text{Total value of the means of production}\\&\times\frac{\text{Daily quantity of products}}{\text{Total quantity of products produced until means of production wear out}}\end{aligned}$$

In this case as well, needless to say, the transfer in value from the means of production to the products does not involve any change in the quantity of value. Since the capital advanced for such means of production is fixed in the production process until they wear out, it is called *fixed capital*. In Part II (▶ Sect. 13.2), we will look at the distinction between **fixed capital** and the other part of capital (**circulating capital**).

Variable Capital

Capital is able to appropriate surplus-value because labour-power can create a greater magnitude of value in a day than its own daily value. Thus, the part of capital advanced in labour-power increases in magnitude by the sum of the surplus-value. Since this part of capital that brings about valorisation is able to change in the production process, it is

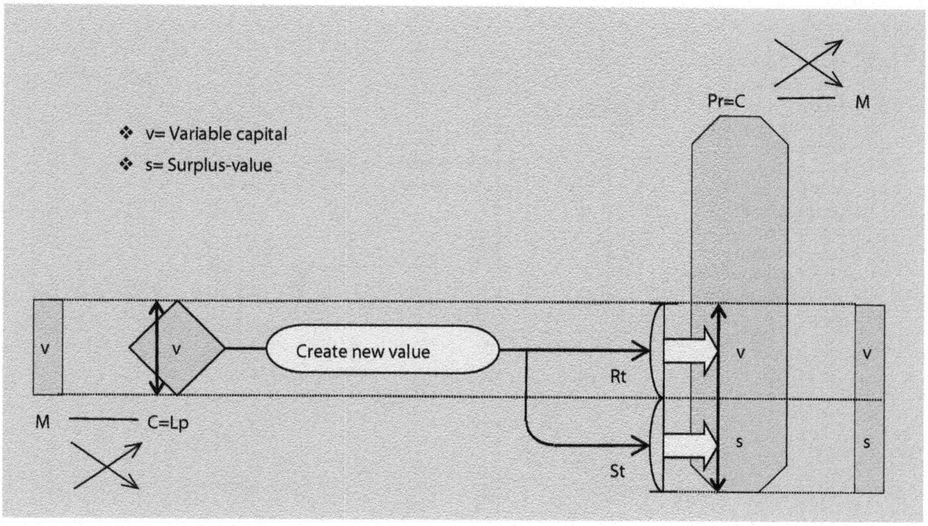

■ **Fig. 3.16** Variable capital

called *variable capital* (*v*). In the production process, *variable capital (v)* augments to the magnitude of **variable capital (v)** *plus surplus-value* (*s*) (*see* ■ Fig. 3.16).

Valorisation Process: Production of Surplus-value Based on Sale and Purchase of Labour-power

As noted already, under capitalist production, capital purchases the labour-power commodity on a temporary basis, and by consuming it obtains more value than that contained in the labour-power itself. This value exceeding the variable capital advanced is **surplus-value.** *The secret of valorisation is capital's appropriation of surplus-value based on the commodification of labour-power* (*see* ■ Fig. 3.17).

■ Figure 3.17 is worth consulting later any number of times because it deals with the *essential core of capitalist production.* So, here let's examine each part of I-VI of the diagram in detail.

(I) Determination of the Value of Labour-power

I. The value of labour-power is determined by the value of the requisite means of livelihood (means of livelihood necessary for the reproduction of labour-power), and therefore by the labour-time necessary to their production.

(II) Purchase of Labour-power (Capital Is Advanced in Labour-power)

II. Capitalists purchase labour-power on the labour-market from workers on a temporary basis and pay wages in return (but only after the labour has been completed).

(III) Purchase of the Means of Production (Capital Is Advanced in the Means of Production)

III. Capitalists purchase the means of production on the commodity-market from other capitalists.

(IV) Consumption of Labour-power

IV. Capitalists consume the labour-power within the contracted period of time, making the workers labour under their direction and superintendence. This consumption process of labour-power is the labour process, on the one hand, and the valorisation process, on the other.

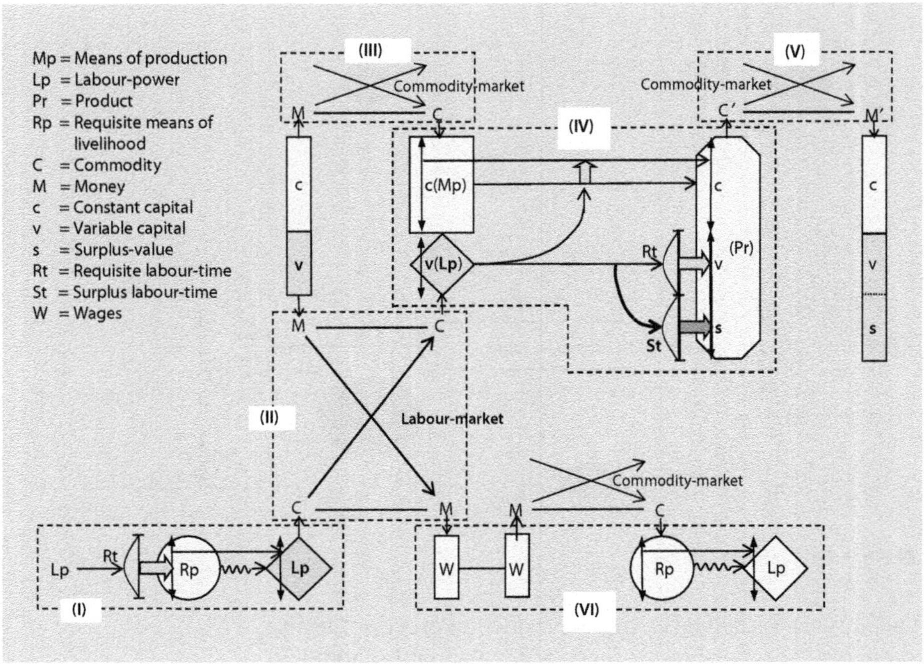

Fig. 3.17 Valorisation process (production of surplus-value)

(IV–1) Labour Process

Concrete labour, which is one aspect of workers' labour, produces the product by transforming (processing or using up) the means of production.

(IV–2) Valorisation Process

(IV–2–a) Transfer of the Value of the Means of Production

Concrete labour transfers the value of the means of production (old value) to the product. Therefore, the value-amount of the capital component advanced in the means of production (constant capital) is solely preserved through this process, with its magnitude remaining unchanged.

(IV–2–b) Reproduction of the Equivalent of the Value of Labour-power and the New Production of Surplus-value

Abstract labour, which is the other aspect of workers' labour, becomes the new value that is objectified within commodities. That is, *first* the value of the labour-power is reproduced (requisite labour-time), and *then* the surplus-value exceeding that value is newly produced (surplus labour-time). Therefore, the value-amount of the capital component advanced in labour-power (variable capital) is not only changed but also augments in this process.

(V) Realisation of Surplus-value Through the Realisation of the Value of Commodities

V. Capitalists sell their commodities on the commodity-market, thereby realising the value of those commodities (conversion into money). By means of this, they realise the surplus-value that is contained within that value (conversion into money) at the same time.

VI. Workers obtain wages in payment for their labour-power, which are used to purchase the requisite means of livelihood

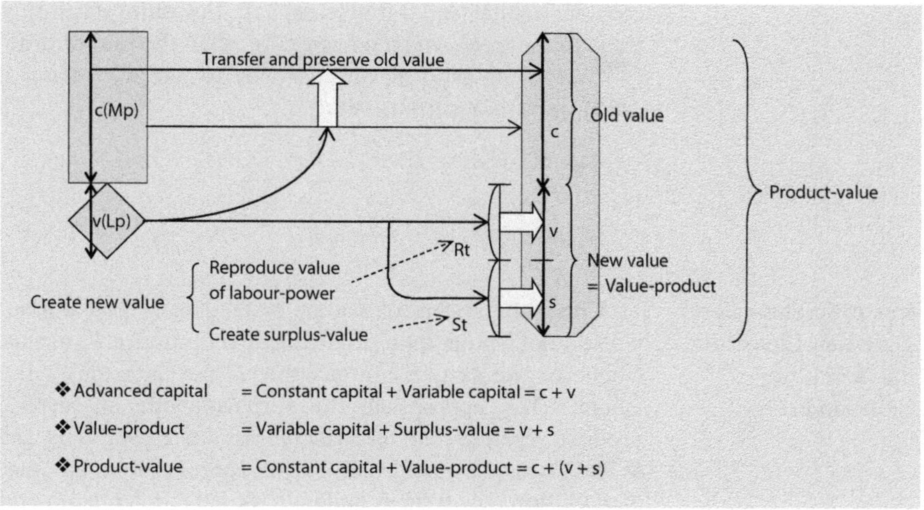

Fig. 3.18 Product-value and value-product

from capitalists on the commodity-market. And through the consumption of those means the workers reproduce their labour-power.

(VI) Reproduction of Labour-power

Product-value and Value-product

The value of the product of labour of a day is the sum of the **old value** (constant capital) transferred that day from the means of production to the product, and the **new value** (variable capital + surplus-value) created that day. This is the **product-value**, of which the new value produced in the process (variable capital + surplus-value) is called the **value-product**. *Product-value* and *value-product* are *two different concepts* that need to be clearly distinguished (*see* Fig. 3.18).

In the production process of capital, there is the value of the means of production that forms the old value transferred to and maintained within the product via concrete labour, and at the same time the abstract labour that is objectified to become new value, including both the **equivalent of the value of labour-power** and the **surplus-value** that exceeds it.

3.2 Rate of Surplus-value

3.2.1 Rate of Surplus-value = Rate of Exploitation of Labour-power

Two Rates That Express Degree of Valorisation: Rate of Profit and Rate of Surplus-value

The degree to which advanced capital is augmented is expressed by the ratio between advanced capital and its increment, i.e. surplus-value. The advanced capital is composed of constant capital and variable capital. The ratio of surplus-value to the *total capital advanced* is called the **rate of profit** (p'), while the ratio of surplus-value to *variable capital* is called the **rate of surplus-value** (s').

- Rate of surplus-value: $s' = \dfrac{s}{v}$
- Rate of profit: $p' = \dfrac{s}{c+v}$

Rate of Surplus-value Accurately Expresses the Degree of Exploitation

Under the system of slavery or feudalism, non-workers who do not labour appropriate the direct producers' surplus-labour or the surplus-product that is the outcome of this labour. They appropriate the surplus-labour or surplus-product *regardless of the will of the direct producers* (see ◘ Figs. 1.30, 1.31, and 1.32). This appropriation is called **exploitation**. The term *exploitation* is used to refer to *any case where a non-labouring individual makes the direct producers labour in excess of the requisite labour-time, through some type of personal or material (economic) compulsion, in order to appropriate this surplus-labour.*

Capitalist relations of production are covered by the relations of commodity production, wherein material relations between people are manifested as spontaneous, free and equal mutual relations between *homo oeconomicus* pursuing their respective self-interest. Yet the capitalist appropriates surplus-value, and therefore surplus-labour, from the wageworkers *regardless of their will*. Capital seeks to appropriate as much surplus-labour from labour-power as possible. Moreover, there is no way for the labouring individuals to live unless they perform surplus-labour of this nature for another person. Objectively speaking, this surplus-labour is coerced from the labouring individuals, so that exploitation is clearly being carried out.

The degree of exploitation can best be expressed by the ratio between the magnitude of requisite labour and the magnitude of surplus-labour that must be carried out in excess of the requisite labour; i.e. surplus-labour divided by requisite labour.

Under capitalist production, «surplus-labour divided by requisite labour» takes the form of «surplus-value divided by the value of labour-power»—i.e. «surplus-value divided by variable capital». The ratio of the absolute quantity of surplus-value (s) to the value of labour-power or variable capital (v) is called the **rate of surplus-value** (s'). The rate of surplus-value most precisely expresses the degree of the exploitation of workers by capital, i.e. the **rate of exploitation**.

Workers receive as an equivalent for their labour-power the value that is equal to the value that their requisite labour creates. But all the surplus-value created by their surplus-labour comes into the capitalist's possession. So *nothing at all is paid to the workers from surplus-labour. From this perspective,* requisite labour can be called «**paid labour**», while surplus-labour can be referred to as «**unpaid labour**». This means that the rate of surplus-value also expresses the ratio of *unpaid labour* to *paid labour.*

$$\text{Rate of surplus-value}(s') = \frac{\text{surplus-value}(s)}{\text{variable capital}(v)} = \frac{\text{surplus-value}}{\text{value of labor-power}}$$
$$= \frac{\text{surplus-labor}}{\text{requisite labor}} = \frac{\text{unpaid labor}}{\text{paid labor}}$$

In contrast, the rate of profit ($p' = \frac{s}{c+v}$) indicates how much was augmented vis-à-vis the total capital advanced by the capitalist. This is an important ratio that has direct interest for capitalists. Yet this ratio does not accurately express the degree of exploitation. In fact, the ratio conceals the true degree of exploitation or makes it appear smaller than it actually is. We will investigate in detail the rate of profit (p') in ► Chap. 15 in Part III.

3.2.2 Various Ways to Represent Product-value

Value-constituents of the Total Product Can Be Represented in Various Ways

The value-constituents of the total product of 1 day—which are constant capital (c), variable capital (v), and surplus-value (s)—can be represented in various ways.

Let's take a given capital for the production of bread (*see* ◘ Fig. 3.19).

How Is the Value of the Total Product of a Day Formed?

To begin, let's assume that 1 hour of abstract labour (1 hour of labour-time) forms 10 yen of value. We will also assume that the daily value of labour-power is 30 yen, and the working day is 6 hours. Given this, the worker reproduces the 30-yen daily value of labour-power in 3 hours, so the 30 yen of surplus-value is produced in the remaining 3 hours.

We assume that the machinery utilised transfers 5 yen of its value to each loaf of bread through its wear and tear, whereas we can here take no account of the magnitude of its total value. Let us say that the capital produces 6 loaves of

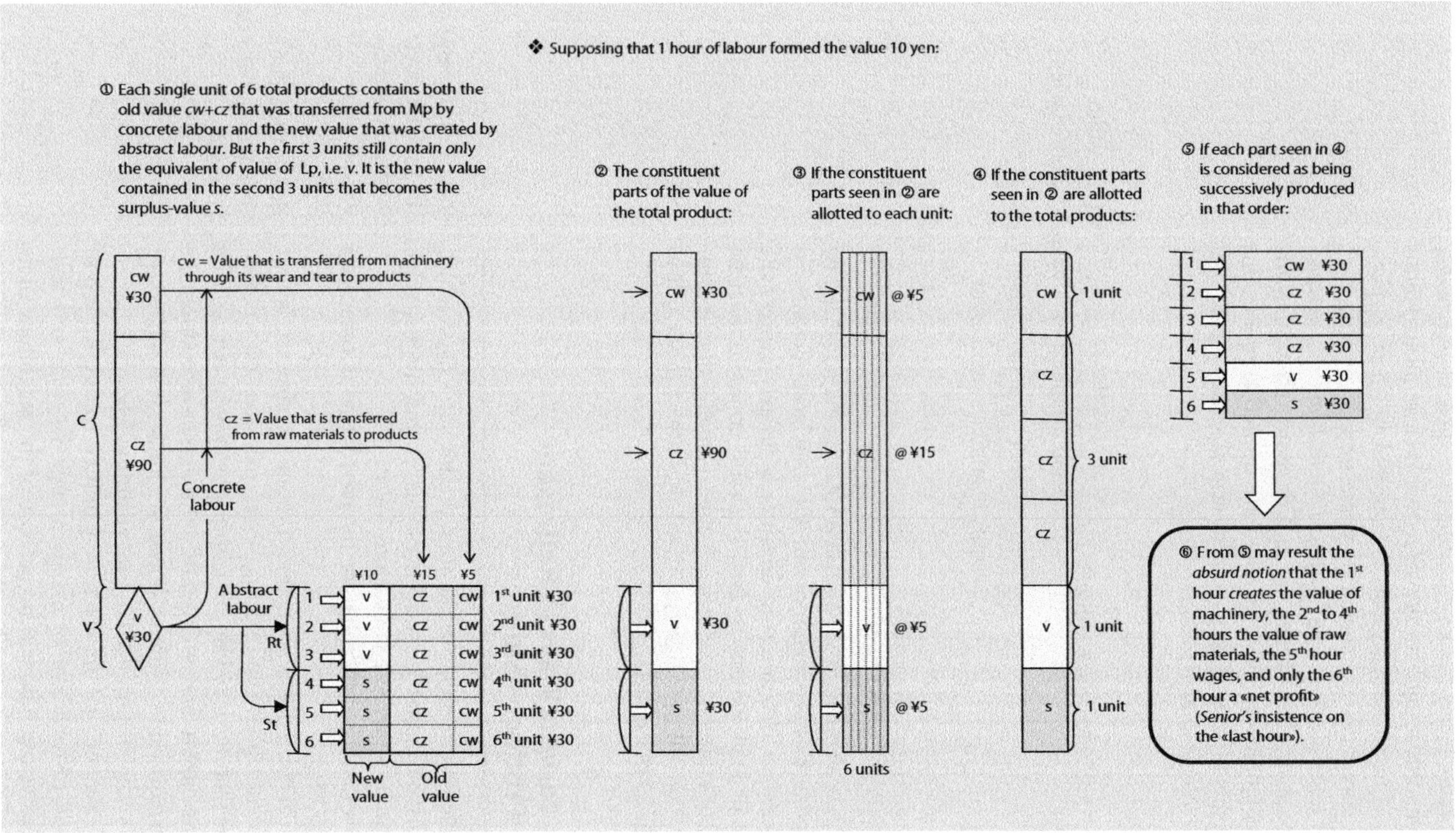

Fig. 3.19 Various ways of representing the value-constituents of the total product of a working day

bread in a day, using 90 yen of flour and other ingredients (raw materials), along with labour-power that has a daily value of 30 yen. This means that 1 hour of labour-time is used to produce 1 loaf of bread.

When capital produces 1 loaf of bread, 1 hour of labour-time is objectified in that loaf, with 10 yen of new value created. Each loaf contains 10 yen of this new value, 5 yen of transferred value from the machinery (*cw*), and 15 yen of transferred value from the ingredients (*cz*), for a total of 20 yen in old value and 30 yen in overall value.

Of the 6 hours in the working day, the worker makes 3 loaves of bread in the first 3 hours. But the 30 yen of new value included in these 3 loaves merely equates to the daily value of labour-power, so through this the capital only collects the variable capital advanced. If the production process were to be halted at this point, the capital would only get back the variable capital advanced and would thus be unable to obtain surplus-value. Conversely, any labour performed after this point is surplus-labour, and the 10 yen of new value produced every hour is all surplus-value. This means that the 10 yen of new value contained in each of the 3 loaves produced in the final 3 hours is surplus-value for the capital. The capital thus comes to obtain a total of 30 yen in surplus-value.

The discussion above, which is the process of valorisation examined up to now, is represented in the diagram as ①.

Examining the Value-constituents of the Overall Product

The total value of the 6 loaves of bread, which are the overall product of 1 working day, is made up of the following four parts: (i) 30 yen of value transferred from the machinery (*cw*); (ii) 90 yen of value transferred from the raw materials (*cz*); (iii) 30 yen of new value equivalent to the daily value of labour-power (*v*); and (iv) 30 yen of surplus-value (*s*) (indicated as ② in the diagram).

Value-constituents Can Be Proportionally Allotted to Each Product

The overall product produced in 1 working day is made up of 6 loaves of bread, with each loaf being exactly the same product. *Each loaf can be seen as one equal part of the totality of 6 loaves.* And if we *equally allot* (proportionally distribute) *the 4 value-constituents included in the 6 loaves*, each loaf would include 5 yen of *cw*, 15 yen of *cz*, 5 yen of *v*, and 5 yen of *s* (indicated as ③ in the diagram).

Value-constituents Can Be Proportionally Allotted to the Total Quantity of Products

Furthermore, if we *proportionally allot the 4 value-constituents included in the 6 loaves of bread, so as to express this in a number of loaves, it would be 1 loaf as* value transferred from the machinery (*cw*), *3 loaves as* value transferred from the raw materials (*cz*), *1 loaf as* daily value of labour-power (*v*), *and 1 loaf as* surplus-value (*s*) (indicated as ④ in the diagram).

The two ways above of representing the value-constituents—insofar as each product unit is dealt with as an aliquot part of the overall product of 1 working day—are both *theoretically correct and practically carried out every day.*

A False Notion Arises of Viewing Proportionally Allotted Parts as Sequentially Produced

In the final method, which is ④ in the diagram, the bread that represents the four value-constituents is premised on the overall product of a 6-hour working day, and a *completely mistaken notion* will be generated if we overlook that this is proportionally allotted to the total quantity of products—imagining instead that the first loaf only including the value of *cw*, the next three loaves produced (loaves 2–4) only contain the value of *cz*, the fifth loaf only includes *v*, and the sixth and final loaf only includes *s*.

From that perspective, for the totality of value included in each loaf (30 yen), it appears that the 1 hour of labour that creates the first loaf would generate the value of *cw*, the 3 hours of labour that produce loaves 2–4 generate the value of *cz*, the 1 hour of labour that produces the fifth loaf generates the value of *v*, and the 1 hour of labour that produces the final loaf generates the value of *s* (indicated as ⑤ in the diagram).

«The Final One Hour Produces Surplus-value»?!

According to this line of thought, only the last hour produces surplus-value. Therefore, if the working day, i.e. the daily labour-time of workers, were reduced by 1 hour (from 6 to 5 hours, in our example), a capitalist would not acquire any surplus-value. The vulgar economist *Nassau William Senior* (1790–1864) utilised this argument in 1836 to oppose the movement seeking a reduction in labour-time (indicated as ⑥ in the diagram).

The *error* in this way of thinking is that it overlooks—or pretends to be unaware of—the fact that *cw* and *cz* are value originally included within the machinery and raw materials, which is then *transferred* to the product. This means that the value of the first four loaves can only be seen as the value of *cw* and *cz* insofar as the old value of *cw* and *cz*, included within each of the 6 loaves forming the overall product, is made to mentally represent loaves 1 through 4, so that the entirety of *cw* and *cz* could be seen as being transferred to these 4 loaves alone. This would mean that one is obliged to consider the 4 hours of labour (abstract labour) as being included, not in these 4 loaves, but only in the remaining 2 loaves.

The portions of product-value can be expressed as proportional parts of the product, and it is necessary to be accustomed to this manner of calculation. But we should not forget that each of the parts can only play this sort of role insofar as they are divided parts of *a given overall quantity of products.*

References

Marx K (1865) Lohn, Preis und Profit. English edition: Marx K (1985) Value, price and profit. Marx-Engels Collected Works. Vol. 20. Progress Publishers et al. New York

Marx K (1872) Das Kapital. Kritik der politischen Oekonomie. Bd. 1. Buch 1: Der Produktionsprocess des Kapitals. 2. verb. Aufl. Hamburg. English edition: Marx K (1976) Capital. A critique of political economy. Vol. 1 (trans: Howkes B). Penguin Books

Ministry of International Trade and Industry, Japan (2016) Census 2014. Census of manufacture. Tokyo

Extension and Shortening of Working Day

T. Otani, *A Guide to Marxian Political Economy*,
https://doi.org/10.1007/978-3-319-65954-1_4

4.1 Working Day and Its Limits

Working Day

As mentioned earlier (in ► Sect. 3.1.3), the daily labour-time of a worker is referred to as the «**working day**»—this means, for instance, an 8-hour working day, 1 day in which 8 hours of labour are carried out, or 8 hours of labour carried out in a single day.

4

Minimum and Maximum Limits of a Working Day

The length of the working day can change, but there is a **minimum limit** beyond which it cannot be shortened, as well as a **maximum limit** beyond which it cannot be extended. Under capitalist production, the minimum limit is not zero, but rather the requisite labour-time, while the maximum limit is set by the physical limitations of the worker and social limitations. Both limitations are *quite elastic*, allowing for great fluctuation. The working day is of varying lengths, at any point between those minimum and maximum limits (*see* ◘ Fig. 4.1).

Capitalist Insists on Rights *qua* Purchaser

A capitalist, by purchasing labour-power for the period of 1 day, is able to use that labour-power during that day. The capitalist, i.e. capital personified, buys the labour-power in order to obtain living labour through it, and thus seeks to extend the working day to its maximum limit. Moreover, making use of the fact that the physical and mental limitations that mark this maximum limit are *elastic*, he will also estimate the worker's requirements as being as little as possible. As the purchaser of labour-power, the capitalist must try to extend the working day to its maximum limit. Here we have *the capitalist's insistence on his rights as purchaser.*

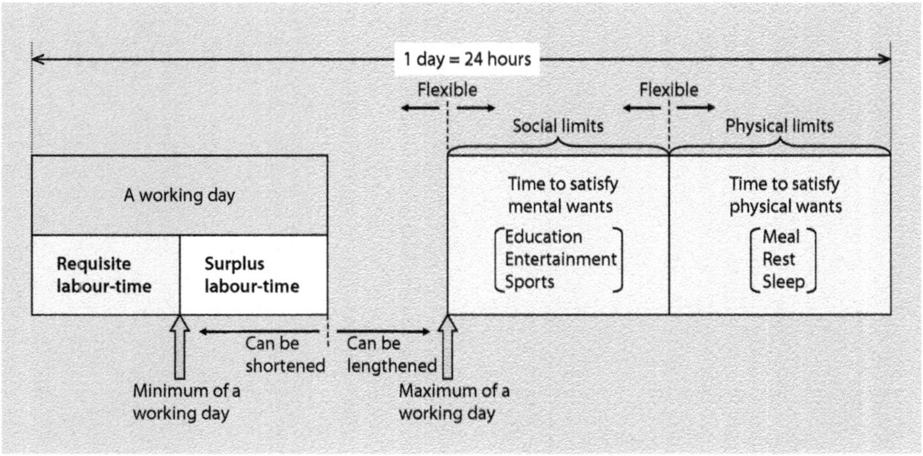

◘ **Fig. 4.1** Limits of the working day

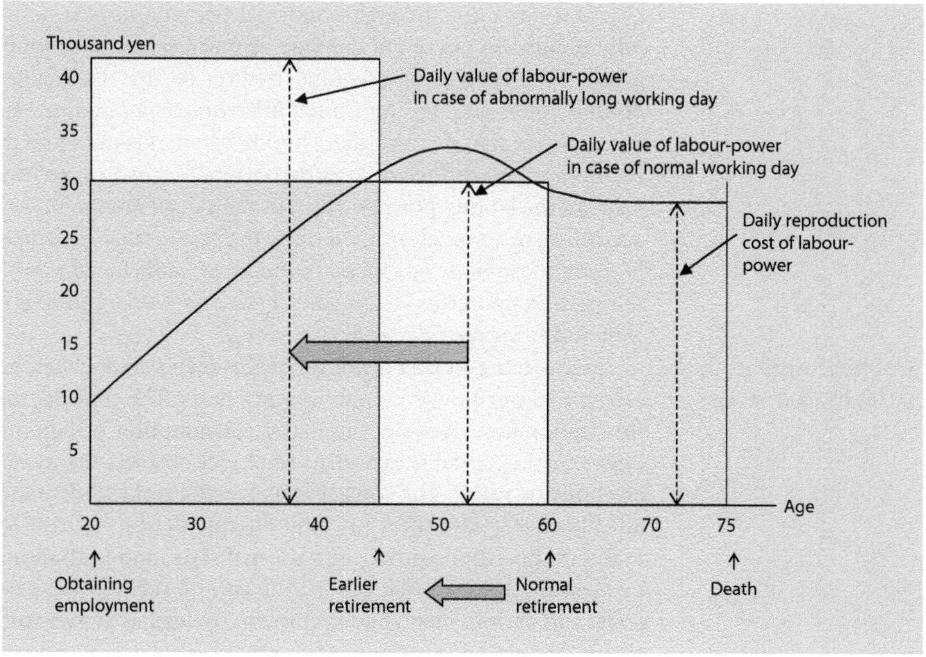

■ **Fig. 4.2** Abnormally long working day leads to sharp rise in the daily value of labour-power

Extravagant Working Day Leads to a Rapid Increase in the Daily Value of Labour-power

What would occur, then, if the working day in a society were generally extended to an extravagant point? In such a case, labour-power is abnormally worn out, resulting in the early deaths or the premature obsolescence of workers. Meanwhile, additional reproduction costs would be needed for labour-power that is considerably worn out to recover, resulting in a sharp rise in the costs needed to reproduce labour-power, and shortening the period during which labour-power could be sold to recover the reproduction costs indispensable to a worker leading a normal life, i.e. reducing the period of recovering the total value of labour-power. Due to these two factors, there will inevitably be a sharp rise in the daily value of labour-power (*see* ■ Fig. 4.2).

If the capitalist does not pay for this additional value, the worker would not be able to recover the value of his own commodity, resulting in an unequal exchange between capitalist and worker. Does that mean that no problem would arise as long as the capitalist pays for that increased value?

Normal Use Is Presupposed for Sales on a Temporary Basis

What is decisively important here is that the sale of labour-power is a sale on a temporary basis. Temporary sales, such as leasing, generally presuppose that the purchaser will use the object in a normal manner, and if the object is damaged through abnormal use, the user is naturally obliged to cover the damage or pay a penalty. Labour-power is an object of a special nature, in that the *owner himself suffers damage if it is used in an abnormal manner*. In a case where that owner suffers bodily harm, it is not enough to merely pay sufficient compensation (according to the value of the labour-power). Thus, in the sale of labour-power according to a predetermined time, the *contractual condition of normal use must be strictly maintained*, and the worker—in insisting upon this—*is making a fair and proper claim as a commodity owner.*

Worker's Insistence on Rights *qua* Seller

In short, the worker is not selling his own person when he sells his labour-power on a temporary basis. The contract for this transaction does not allow the consumption of labour-power by the capitalist to destroy or render obsolete the worker's body or mind. The worker thus has the right to demand adequate sleep to renew his vital energy, periods of rest to maintain his labour-power in a normal state, and limitations on working time so that other time can be secured for personal cultivation, mental development, societal activities, and social interaction (i.e. the opportunity to display his physical and mental capabilities).[1] The worker, as the seller of labour-power, demands a working day that will secure such time, i.e. a «**normal working day**». Here we have the worker's *insistence on his right as a seller.*

The Working Day Is Determined by Struggle Between Workers and Capitalists Over Its Limits

Therefore, *based on the laws of commodity exchange, a conflict between two equal rights arises, with the buyer and seller each insisting on their respective rights.* This is a struggle between two equal rights that can only be decided by force. During the history of capitalist production, it has been this **struggle over the working day** between collective capital (capitalist class) and collective labour (working class) that has set the limits on the working day, established a normal working day, and led to the subsequent shortening the normal working day.

---

1 In Marx's English report to the Working Men's International Association (Marx 1865), quoted from earlier, he also states: «*Time is the room of human development*. A man who has no free time to dispose of, whose whole lifetime, apart from the mere physical interruptions by sleep, meals, and so forth, is absorbed by his labour for the capitalist, is less than a beast of burden. *He is a mere machine for producing Foreign Wealth, broken in body and brutalised in mind*» (Marx 1985, p. 142: my emphasis).

4.2 Production of Absolute Surplus-value

Absolute Surplus-value

If the magnitude of the value of labour-power (and therefore of variable capital) does not change, surplus-value can be increased by extending the working day. If the requisite labour-time, which is bound by the magnitude of the value of labour-power, is deducted from the working day, what remains is surplus labour-time. Since the objectification of this time is surplus-value, if the working day is extended without any change in the value of labour-power, surplus-value will expand in proportion to the extension. *Surplus-value produced through extending the working day* is called **absolute surplus-value** (*see* ■ Fig. 4.3).

Production of Surplus-value Is Above All the Production of Absolute Surplus-value

In the case where absolute surplus-value is produced through the extension of a working day that *already* contains surplus-labour, we will see an *increase* of surplus-value. But since surplus-value is, to begin with, produced by *extending the working day* beyond the requisite labour-time, the *production of surplus-value itself* is originally the production of absolute surplus-value.

The other method of increasing surplus-value, which occurs without extending the working day, shall be discussed in the next chapter.

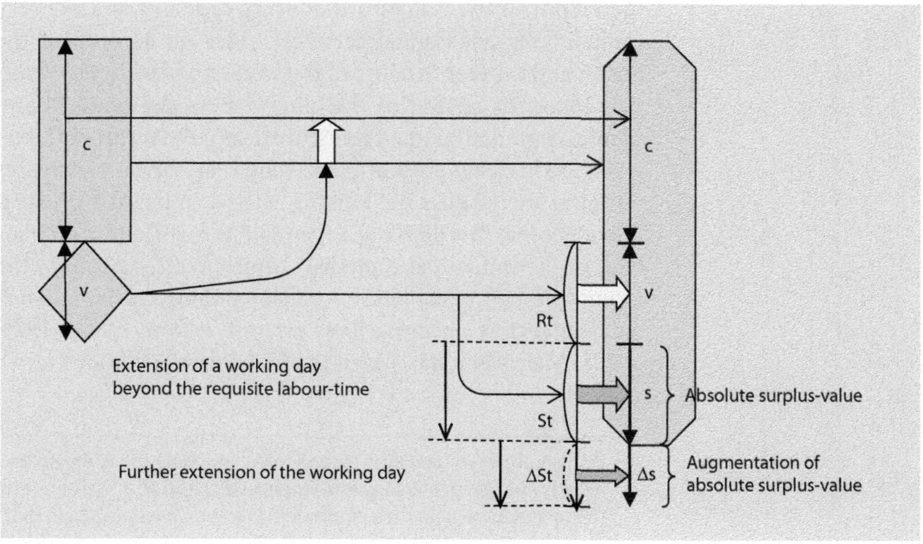

■ **Fig. 4.3** Production of absolute surplus-value (increase of surplus-value through extension of working day)

4.3 Struggle Between Capital and Labour over the Working Day

Driving Force for Capital Is the Augmentation of Surplus-Value

The driving motive and determining purpose of capitalist production is the greatest possible self-valorisation of capital, i.e. the greatest possible production of surplus-value. This means the greatest possible exploitation of labour-power by the capitalist. So the *augmentation of surplus-value* is the **nature of capital** and the **essential driving force for capital**.

Limitless Extension of Working Day by Individual Capitals

As long as there are no social restraints in place, *individual capitals* will try to extend the labour-time of the workers employed to the greatest extent possible. This coercive extension of labour-time by *individual capitals* undermines the health of workers, curtailing their lives. However, as long as new material for exploitation can be found on the labour market, this is a matter of indifference as far as those individual capitals are concerned. Thus, a point will soon be reached where the source of a nation's vitality is threatened. From the perspective of the *total capital of society* this signifies a depletion of the normal quality of labour-power, which is the material for exploitation.

«After Me the Flood!»

However, as Marx (1872) writes: «In every stock-jobbing swindle everyone knows that some time or other the crash must come, but everyone hopes that it may fall on the head of his neighbour, after he himself has caught the shower of gold and placed it in secure hands. *Après moi le déluge!* [After me the Flood!] *is* the watchword of every capitalist and of every capitalist nation. Capital therefore takes no account of the health and the length of life of the worker, *unless society forces it to do so.* Its answer to the outcry about the physical and mental degradation, the premature death, the torture of over-work, is this: Should that pain trouble us, since it increases our pleasure (profit)? But looking at these things as a whole, it is evident that this does not depend on the will, either good or bad, of the individual capitalist. Under *free competition,* the *immanent laws of capitalist production* confront the individual capitalist as a *coercive force external to him*» (Marx 1976, p. 381; Marx's emphasis as in the first German edition).[2]

2 If any number of capitalists extend the working day, they are able to increase not only their absolute surplus-value but also their share of the market by selling their commodities somewhat cheaper. In that case, the rest of capitalists cannot sit idly by and must also make an effort to extend the working day, because *otherwise they would be defeated in the competition between capitalists*. Here we can see the *law* of capital striving inevitably to maximise the working day to increase absolute surplus-value, which holds whether a capitalist

Establishment of the Normal Working Day Through Pressure of the Labour Movement

For capital as a whole, it becomes necessary to end the atrophy of labour-power caused by the limitless exploitation of labour-power. However, the establishment of the **normal working day** by the capitalist state, as the representative of capital as a whole, is not a voluntary endeavour. Rather, it comes about through the struggles of the working class, which is to say the social compulsion of pressure from the labour movement.

Let's consider the case of England, to begin with. The working day there was extended by law during the period from the fourteenth century to the end of the seventeenth century. As capitalist production was emerging it had to be drilled into the workers' heads, through the power of the state, that an entire day had to be worked in return for the sale of labour-power on a daily basis. With the development of capitalism, particularly the establishment of large-scale industry through the Industrial Revolution, extremely long labour-time was widespread.

The struggle of workers for a normal working day was tenaciously carried out, starting from around 1802. For roughly 30 years, the concessions wrung by the working class remained purely nominal. They managed to get five factory laws passed by Parliament, but there were no clauses to ensure enforcement. Finally, starting in 1833, the normal working day began to steadily spread to various branches of industry. In 1838, the demand for a 10-hour working day was widely raised, and by 1844, working time for all women over 18 years of age was restricted to 12 hours. The Factory Law of 1847 initially limited the working day to 11 hours for women and youth aged 13–18, and the following year restricted it further to 10 hours.

The capitalists «rebelled» against this law, openly flaunting it. This, in turn, exhausted the patience of workers, who forced the capitalists to compromise, in the form of the Factory Law of 1850. A considerable number of workers remained outside of the law, but from that time legislation gradually restricted the length of the working day.

In the case of France, the February Revolution of 1848 created, in a single blow, a 12-hour working day.

---

likes it or not as the driving motive of his operations and is exercised through the *pressure of competition* among capitalists. In ▶ Sect. 5.1 and then in ▶ Sect. 16.1 of Part III we shall again see how *competition* is the *force that realises the imminent laws of capitalist production*.

Meanwhile, in 1866, the International Working Men's Association raised the demand of an 8-hour working day.

Just prior to that call, the General Congress of Labour, in the United States, also called for an 8-hour working day. A general strike was called in the United States on 1 May 1866 to demand the 8-hour working day (and starting in 1890, «May Day» demonstrations have been held around the world on the first of May).

Ever since that time, at least in what are known as the «advanced capitalist countries», the trend has been toward a gradual reduction in the working day, through pressure exerted by the labour movement.

In Japan as well, after the end of the Second World War, the working day was gradually reduced, but its length remains quite long compared to other advanced capitalist countries, as symbolised by the notorious word «*karōshi*» (death from overwork).

Labour-time Under Association

In a society wherein the law of production of surplus-value does not operate, labour-time is decided in a manner completely different from the case of capitalist society.

Consider, for example, the case of the society called Association, which we shall examine in ▶ Sect. 11.2.2. Since the labouring individuals in this society have a high level of needs with regard to their lives, it is obvious that the working day cannot be limited to the labour-time requisite for the reproduction of labour-power. However, labouring individuals are working for their own sake, not for that of non-labouring individuals who are distinguished from them. Moreover, because of the highly developed productive powers that can only be realised by fully developed workers, and also because everyone capable of working is engaged in productive labour, the working day itself would be drastically reduced compared to present-day society. This would mean an expansion of individuals' free time, which could be used as they like for the sake of their own human development.

References

Marx K (1865) Lohn, Preis und Profit. English edition: Marx K (1985) Value, price and profit. Marx-Engels Collected Works. Vol. 20. Progress Publishers et al. New York

Marx K (1872) Das Kapital. Kritik der politischen Oekonomie. Bd. 1. Buch 1: Der Produktionsprocess des Kapitals. 2. verb. Aufl. Hamburg. English edition: Marx K (1976) Capital. A critique of political economy. Vol. 1 (trans: Howkes B). Penguin Books

Methods for the Development of Productive Power

T. Otani, *A Guide to Marxian Political Economy*,
https://doi.org/10.1007/978-3-319-65954-1_5

5.1 Production of Relative Surplus-value

Relative Surplus-value

When the length of the working day is fixed—or when it cannot be extended any further—the only way to expand surplus-labour (and therefore to increase surplus-value) is to reduce the labour-time needed for the reproduction of the value of labour-power, which is the requisite labour-time. If the intensity of labour remains the same, the reduction in requisite labour-time can only be achieved by reducing the value of labour-power. Surplus-value can be expanded through a reduction in the value of labour-power because it results in a *relative* decrease in the portion of variable capital (equivalent to the value of labour-power) within the new value produced in a working day. Surplus-value produced in this way is called **relative surplus-value.**

Decrease in the Value of Labour-power by Increasing Productive Power of Labour

The value of labour-power can only be reduced through a reduction in the reproduction costs of labour-power, which is a reduction in the value of the requisite means of livelihood that labour-power must consume. This reduction in the value of the requisite means of livelihood is a reduction in the socially necessary labour-time for the requisite means of livelihood.

The socially necessary labour-time of the requisite means of livelihood is reduced, first of all, by increasing the productive power of labour engaged in the production of the requisite means of livelihood themselves.

The second way for reducing the value of the requisite means of livelihood is decreasing the value of the means of production that transfer their own value to the requisite means of livelihood. This decrease is possible when the productive power increases for the production of such means of production.

Thus, an increase in the productive power of labour—either in the production of the requisite means of livelihood or the means of production used for their production—leads to a decrease in the value of labour-power, thereby decreasing the labour for the reproduction of that value, i.e. the requisite labour. This, in turn, increases, by the same amount, the surplus-labour and the surplus-value that is its objectification (*see* ◘ Fig. 1.27).

Relative surplus-value is thus the surplus-value produced through the transformation of requisite labour-time into surplus labour-time (*see* ◘ Fig. 5.1).

Increase in the Productive Power of Labour Makes Innovation in the Method of Production Necessary

As we have seen, an increase in the productive power of labour is a rise in the degree of effectiveness of concrete labour (*see* ◘ Figs. 1.20 and 2.12). This is a change in the technical and social conditions of the labour process, which reduces the socially necessary labour-time of commodities by increasing the quantity of use-values that can be produced

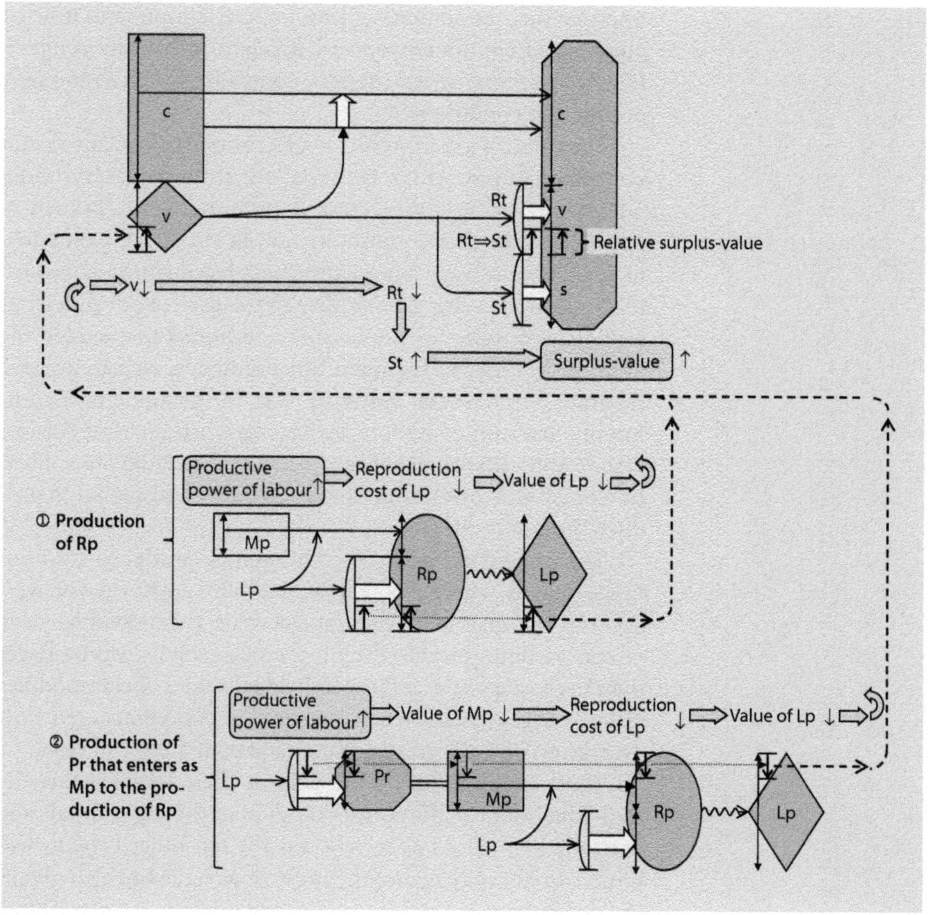

Fig. 5.1 Production of relative surplus-value (increase of surplus-value by shortening requisite labour-time)

using the same amount of abstract labour. When a change of this sort generally occurs within society's production, a change in the manner of production in the technical and social sense must also occur, which is a **revolution in the method of production.**

Competition Among Individual Capitals for Extra Surplus-value

An increase in the productive power of labour for the production of the requisite means of livelihood or the production of the means of production used for that production generates relative surplus-value for all capitals by lowering the value of labour-power. So this is in the overall interest of capital. Yet the reason for this increase in the productive power of labour is an improvement in the production conditions of *each individual capital* that has advanced capital for production. What sort of motive, then, drives these individual capitals to improve their conditions of production? Simply put, it is the outcome of continued pressure brought to bear by *competition between individual capitals*, compelling each to improve production conditions.

The value of a commodity is determined by socially necessary labour-time, which is the labour-time necessary under normal or average production conditions in the branch of production for that commodity (*see* ◘ Fig. 2.11). Compared to socially necessary labour-time, less labour-time is needed to produce the same commodity in the case of advantageous capitals with superior production conditions that exceed the average. In order to highlight this difference, we can use two separate terms: **social value** to refer to the value of a commodity determined by socially necessary labour-time (or real value), and **individual value** to refer to the actual objectification of labour-time required of each individual capital to produce the commodity.

The individual value of commodities produced by mid-range capitals, where production conditions are normal or average, will be nearly identical to social value; the individual value of commodities produced by top-range capitals will be lower than the social value; and the individual values of commodities of low-range capitals, where production conditions are below average, will be of a greater magnitude than the social value.

Thus, if commodities are sold at their social value, the individual value of the commodities of mid-range capitals will basically be realised as is, whereas the *top-range capitals* will be able to not only realise the individual value but also obtain the *difference between social value and individual value*. This is because the individual value of their commodities is lower than the social value. That additional sum of value can be called **extra surplus-value**. Conversely, the low-range capitals—even if able to sell their commodities at their social value—do not realise all of their commodities' individual value. The value that is lost or unrealised can be referred to as **loss in value**.

As a result of the operation of the value-determination of a commodity (an operation expressed commonly as the «law of one price»), where value is determined by the socially necessary labour-time, the high-range capitals obtain extra surplus-value and the low-range ones suffer a loss in value (*see* ◘ Fig. 5.2).

The advantageous capitals that put in place new, superior conditions of production, produce a greater amount of commodities using the same quantity of capital as before. And this increased number of commodities must somehow be sold on

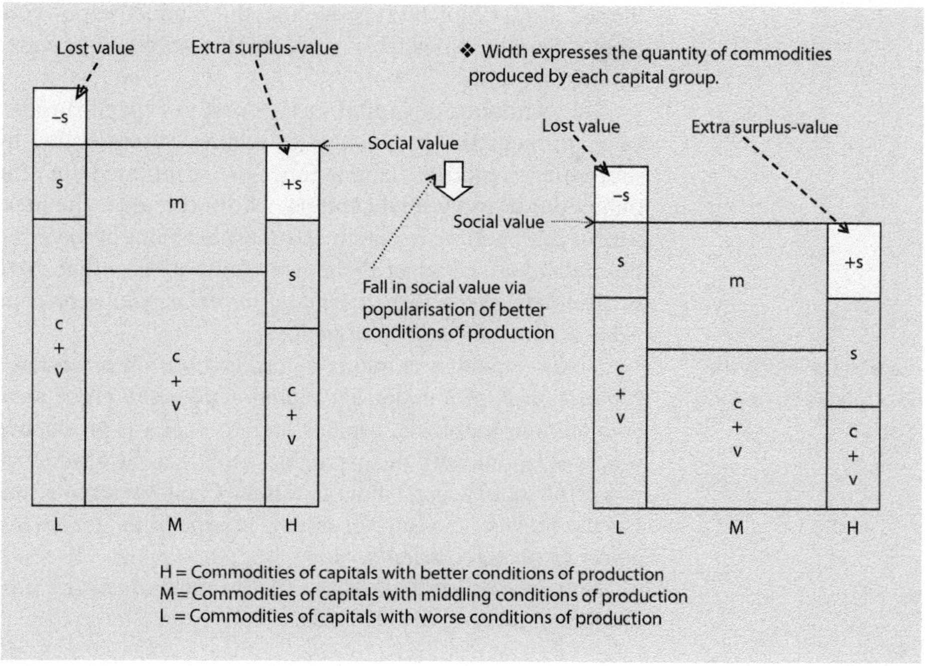

Fig. 5.2 Acquisition of extra surplus-value by capitals with better conditions of production

the market. Given this situation, the capitals seek to expand their market share by selling commodities at a price below social value but higher than individual value. They are still able to realise some of the extra surplus-value—although not all of it. In other words, the lowering of the individual value, made possible by an increase in the productive power of labour, is a weapon for expanding the market share of a commodity. From the perspective of individual capitals, therefore, there is great significance in *raising the productive power of labour so as to lower individual value* (which capitalists are aware of as «reducing costs»).

There is thus a mutual exertion of force among capitals in the same sphere of production to lower the necessary labour-time for one's own commodity by introducing superior production conditions. This *mutual pressure between capitals* is **competition**. That is not to say, however, that in the minds of individual capitalists (who represent individual capitals) the conscious aim is to reduce the value of labour-power by lowering the value of the workers' requisite means of livelihood, as a means of lowering the requisite labour-time and thereby expanding surplus labour-time. Yet this is the way they must act, since those who fall behind risk slipping hopelessly into the red. Under capitalist production, the productive power of labour develops inevitably through this sort of behaviour among capitalists.

This **tendency of capital**—of seeking to expand surplus-value through the production of relative surplus-value by shortening requisite labour-time—is manifested in the **behaviour of individual capitals**, who seek, under the pressure of competition, to obtain extra surplus-value by lowering the individual values of their own commodities. That extra surplus-value is therefore the *unique form that relative surplus-value assumes for individual capitals.*

Capital Develops the Productive Powers of Society

Under capitalist relations of production, all of society's production is production by capital. Under the pressure of competition, individual capitals seek to raise the productive power of labour, with the inevitable result that the productive power of society as a whole is raised. Capitalist production has the *intrinsic tendency of seeking to expand the productive power of society ceaselessly.*

Now we need to look at the special methods of the production of relative surplus-value.

5.2 Co-operation

Co-operation

The first method to produce relative surplus-value—which is to say the primary production method that capital adopts to raise productive power—is co-operation. The term **co-operation** refers to the form of labour in which many people collaborate to carry out labour in a planned manner, either in the same production process or in related production processes.

Benefits of Co-operation

Co-operation raises the productive power of labour by offering the following benefits: (1) Lends to individual labour the character of average social labour (e.g., the outcome of the labour of any five people out of a great number of people will be more or less equal); (2) Economises the means of production by use in common (e.g., production can be accomplished with fewer buildings, containers, tools, equipment, etc.); (3) Creates new productive power, which is intrinsically collective (e.g., moving heavy objects that cannot be moved by individuals); (4) Excites rivalry between individuals and raises their animal spirits; (5) Impresses the stamp of continuity and many-sidedness on similar operations carried out by a number of people (e.g., use of bucket relays can raise the efficiency of movement in many directions during construction work); (6) Performs different operations simultaneously (e.g., the need on a fishing boat to perform many types of different jobs at the same time);

(7) Sets large masses of labour to work at the critical moment (e.g., co-operation is indispensable to work with seasonal limitations); (8) Extends the sphere of action of labour over a greater space (e.g., co-operation is indispensable for reclamation of land or construction of river banks, irrigation, canals, roads, and railways); (9) Contracts the field of production relatively to the scale of production (e.g., a great deal of capital and labour can be concentrated in a relatively narrow plot of land).

Social Productive Power of Labour

The *unique productive power that arises from co-operation* is the **social productive power of labour**—or the **productive power of social labour**. In *planned co-operation* with others, the labouring individuals go beyond their own physical limitations to *display their species capacity as human beings.* However, the manner and scale of co-operation will differ greatly depending on whether it is a conscious and voluntary act of labouring individuals or a combination brought about by external coercion unrelated to their own will.

Social Productive Power of Labour Appears as the Productive Power of Capital

Co-operation is the method first employed by capital to produce relative surplus-value, by raising the productive power of labour. In this case, the *co-operation of labouring individuals is realised by capital that purchases their labour-powers and combines them within the same workplace*—not by the workers themselves. For this reason, the *social productive power of labour* appears as a power that capital possesses by nature, i.e. a **productive power of capital**, and co-operation seems to be a form unique to the capitalist production process.

Functions of Direction and Superintendence Belong to Capital

Social labour carried out by numerous workers requires **direction** and **directors** to carry it out. In the case of co-operation realised by capital, the function of direction belongs to capital. The personal bearer of this function is, above all, the capitalist.

Because labour under capital, as far as workers are concerned, is labour for another person to realise the objectives of capital (rather than labour to realise their own objectives), there is a need for the labour of workers to be **superintended by capital**. This is of course the function of capital, and the superintendent of the workers is first of all the *capitalist as the personification of capital.*

Regardless of the form of society, *direction* is necessary when social labour is performed by a large number of people; whereas *superintendence* is something required in the case of the social form of wage-labour. So we must distinguish the two. In reality, though, *in terms of being functions of capital,* both are completely integrated and are executed by the **capitalist**. As a result, the two functions present themselves as the *single function of* «**direction and superintendence**».

The direction and superintendence function originally performed by the capitalist himself is eventually handed over to *special types of wageworkers*: **managers** (officers) and various **middle-managers** (industrial sergeants).

Meanwhile, because the direction and superintendence necessary for co-operation under capital is carried out through the capitalist, *the distorted view emerges that co-operation in general requires capital and the capitalist;* and that, because these functions are performed by specific sorts of workers, *not only direction but superintendence as well is necessary for social labour in general regardless of the form of society.*

Simple Co-operation

Developed forms of co-operation include not only manufacture, as co-operation based on a division of labour (examined in the next ▶ Sect. 5.3), but also large-scale industry (examined in ▶ Sect. 5.4). The term **simple co-operation** is used to refer to co-operation that involves neither a division of labour nor the use of machinery. It is this simple co-operation that capitalist production first employs to produce relative surplus-value.

5.3 Division of Labour and Manufacture

Division of Labour

The second method for producing relative surplus-value is the **division of labour within a workshop**. Arising out of simple co-operation is the division of labour at a workshop, which characterises the *manufacturing period.*

Manufacturing Period in the Proper Sense of the Term

The period during which *manufacture was the dominant form of the capitalist mode of production* in England was from the middle of the sixteenth to the last third of the eighteenth century. This is the «**manufacturing period in the proper sense of the term**», when political economy debuted as a specific science. *Adam Smith*, who could be called the comprehensive economist of the manufacturing period, examined the capitalist mode of production, with an emphasis on the division of labour.

Social Division of Labour and Division of Labour Within a Workshop

In relation to the division of labour, there is both a *social division of labour* and a *division of labour within a workshop*. The two have many points in common and connections, insofar as both involve the dividing of labour, but they must also be clearly distinguished. The **social division of labour** refers to the total labour of all workers in society being divided into the various sorts of concrete labour (*see* ◘ Figs. 1.28 and 2.34). In contrast, the **division of labour within a workshop** involves dividing the labour of workers within a single production process for a product or group of products. Under capitalist production, the former division of labour is fundamentally characterised by being *spontaneous and anarchic*, whereas the latter is *thoroughly conscious and planned*. In this sense, there is an essential difference between them. The division of labour that is here at issue, in terms of what increases the productive power of labour, is the division of labour within a workshop. That division of labour is first manifested as the **division of labour in manufacture**, and subsequently (once the use of machinery is generalised) as the **division of labour in a factory**.

Division of Labour in Manufacture and Its Benefits

Manufacture is a total productive mechanism whose organs are human beings, with the foundation of production being handicraft skills. The labouring individuals only perform a specialised, partial function, and for their entire lives are merely one organ of this total structure. The division of labour increases the productive power of labour through the following benefits: (1) It saves time needed to alter the place of production or tools; (2) raises significantly the level of skills and expertise; (3) simplifies, improves, and diversifies tools.

Two Origins of Manufacture

Manufacture emerges from two origins: the combination of separate handicrafts or the specialisation of the same handicraft. (*see* ◘ Fig. 5.3).

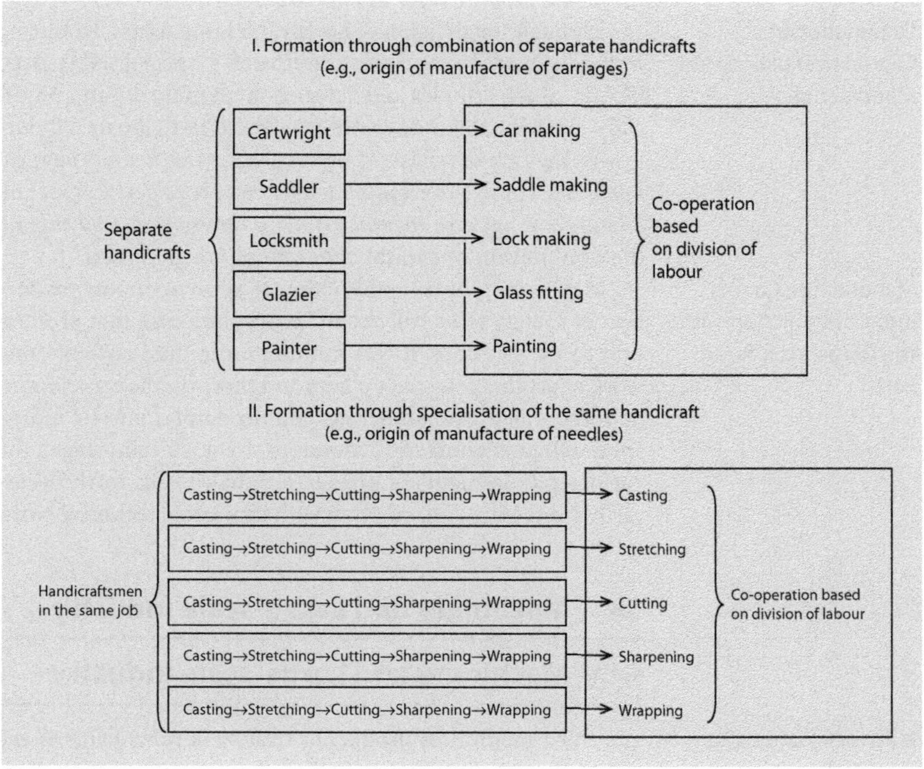

◘ **Fig. 5.3** Two origins of manufacture

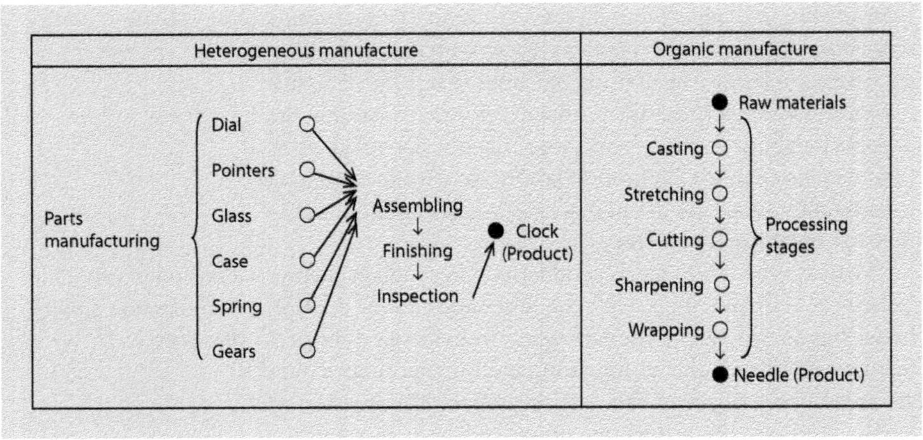

Fig. 5.4 Heterogeneous manufacture and organic manufacture

Two Fundamental Forms of Manufacture

Manufacture has two fundamental forms that are essentially different in kind: *heterogeneous manufacture* and *organic manufacture*. This double character arises from the *nature of the article produced* (*see* Fig. 5.4).

Domination of Capital over Labour in Manufacture

Through the division of labour in manufacture, labouring individuals are compelled to perform a specialised, partial labour, which cripples and deforms them mentally and physically. And if capital does not buy these individuals' labour-power, they are of no use. Many workers, as *exclusively physical labourers*, come to be *dominated by those who perform mental labour*; and because *mental labour is appropriated by capital*, the **domination of capital over labour** is established.

Manufacture Comes into Contradiction with the Demands It Brings Forth

Manufacture was unable either to seize upon the production of society to its full extent, or revolutionise that production to its very core. It was nothing more than an economic work of art that towered up here and there on the broad foundation of the town handicrafts and the rural domestic industries. Once manufacture develops to a certain stage, the various requirements of production that it calls forth necessarily come into contradiction with its narrow technical basis.

5.4 Machinery and Large-scale Industry

5.4.1 Machinery and Large-scale Industry

Machinery and Large-scale Industry

The third method of producing relative surplus-value is the **use of machinery**. The capitalist mode of production developed from manufacture based on the division of labour into

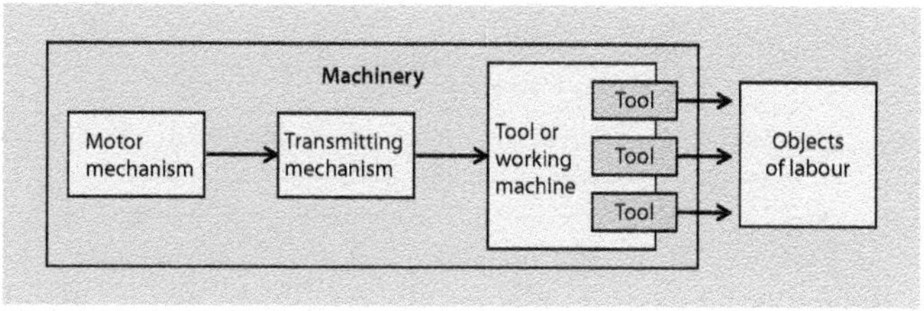

Fig. 5.5 Developed machinery

large-scale industry, obtaining the technical foundation of machinery through revolutions in the means of labour.

Three Constituent Parts of Machinery

Fully developed machinery consists of three essentially different parts:

- **Motor mechanism:** Acts as the driving force of the mechanism as a whole.
- **Transmitting Mechanism:** Regulates the motion, changes its form, and distributes it among the working machines.
- **Tool Machine or Working Machine:** Seizes on the object of labour and transforms it in the *way* fitted to the given purposes.

Whereas a *tool* is a means of labour that is directly used by human beings, **machinery** is a means of labour that processes the object by putting in motion the tool machines that are equipped with tools (*see* Fig. 5.5).

Appearance of Tool Machine → Revolution in Motor Mechanism → Improvement in Transmitting Mechanism

The starting point of the **Industrial Revolution**, which began in late eighteenth century England, was the appearance of the tool machine or working machine that simultaneously operated either a large number of the same type of tool or different types of similar tools. The expansion of the use of tool machines called forth inventions of motor mechanism—from human-, horse-, wind-, and water-power to the steam engine of *James Watt* (1736–1819)—and the revolution in motor mechanism in turn led to *improvements in and the invention of transmitting mechanisms*, as well as the development of the means of transport.

Simple Co-operation of Machines → Machinery System → Automatic System of Machinery

The initial form of a machinery-based factory is **simple co-operation of tool machines**, which involves combining various tools to create an entire product.

Next, there is the appearance of a **machinery system** composed of a *combination of separate tool machines that handle different operation stages*. This is what could be called the co-operation by division of labour *among machines*.

When a tool machine or working machine becomes able to perform all of the movement necessary to process the raw

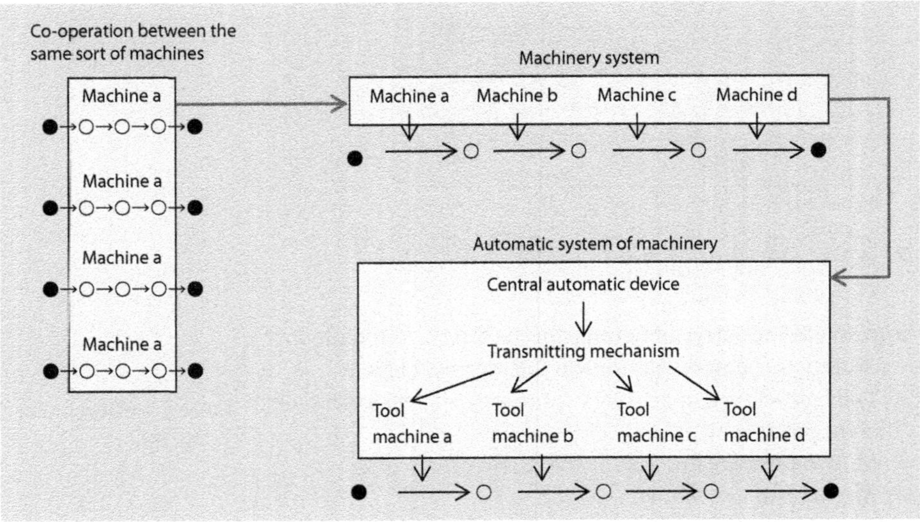

Fig. 5.6 Co-operation of the same sort of machines → machinery system → automatic system of machinery

material, with the aid of human beings who only attend to the machine, we have an automatic system of machinery. The **automatic system of machinery** is an *organised system of machines to which motion is communicated through a transmitting mechanism from a central automaton* (*see* Fig. 5.6).[1]

Transfer of Value from Machinery to the Product and the Capitalist Limits of the Adoption of Machinery

Individual capitals adopt machinery because its use raises the productive power of labour, making the individual value of the commodity produced lower than its social value, so that extra surplus-value can be obtained and market share expanded on the basis of lowering prices. However, if the adopting of machinery becomes generalised, the social value of the products produced with it will itself be lowered. Therefore, *the adoption of machinery lowers the value of products.*

How, then, does the adoption of machinery lower a product's price?

---

1 Marx (1872) vividly depicts this system as follows: «An organised system of machines to which motion is communicated by the transmitting mechanism from an *automatic centre* is the developed form of production by machinery. Here we have, in place of the isolated machine, a mechanical monster whose body fills whole factories, and whose demonic power, at first hidden by the slow and measured motions of its gigantic members, finally bursts forth in the fast and feverish wheel of its countless working organs» (Marx 1976, p. 503: Marx's emphasis as in the first German edition).

What is clear, first of all, is that if the part of value transferred to the product is excluded, machinery is something utilised free of charge—such as natural powers or sciences.

The quantity of products produced using machinery is far greater than that produced using tools; and because the period of durability for machinery is longer, the total quantity of products to which the total value of one machine is distributed is enormous. So even though the value of machinery is much greater than tools, relatively little value is transferred to each individual product. However, because the value of the machinery is high, the quantity of this value transferred from the means of labour can be greater than the case when tools are employed.

Through the use of machinery a far greater quantity of products can be produced than using the same amount of live labour (abstract labour) employing tools. Thus, there is a definite decrease in the amount of new labour objectified in each individual product.

On the other hand, whether tools or machinery, as long as there is no change in the raw materials that are turned into an individual product through transformation, there will be no change in the absolute quantity of value of raw materials transferred to the individual product. Thus, with the arrival of machinery-based production, there is not much change in the value of transferred raw materials within the value of an individual product.

However, since the living labour objectified in the product decreases sharply, the value of an individual product will decrease through the use of machinery even if *there is an increase in the value of machinery transferred to the product compared to the previous value transferred from tools—as long as this increase is smaller than the amount of objectified living labour*, so it will be advantageous for capital to adopt machinery in that case (*see* ◘ Fig. 5.7).

As long as the labour necessary for the production of the machinery itself is less than the labour replaced through its use, the use of machinery will bring the benefit of cheapening a product by decreasing the quantity of abstract labour it contains.

For the capitalist, however, this use is still more limited. This is because capital does not pay *for the labour* used, but rather *for the value of the labour-power* used. The limit for the utilisation of machinery, as far as capital is concerned, is posited by *the difference between the value of a machine and the value of the labour-power that it replaces.*

In a society of associated individuals, where the capitalist limits on the use of machinery no longer exist, the scope of

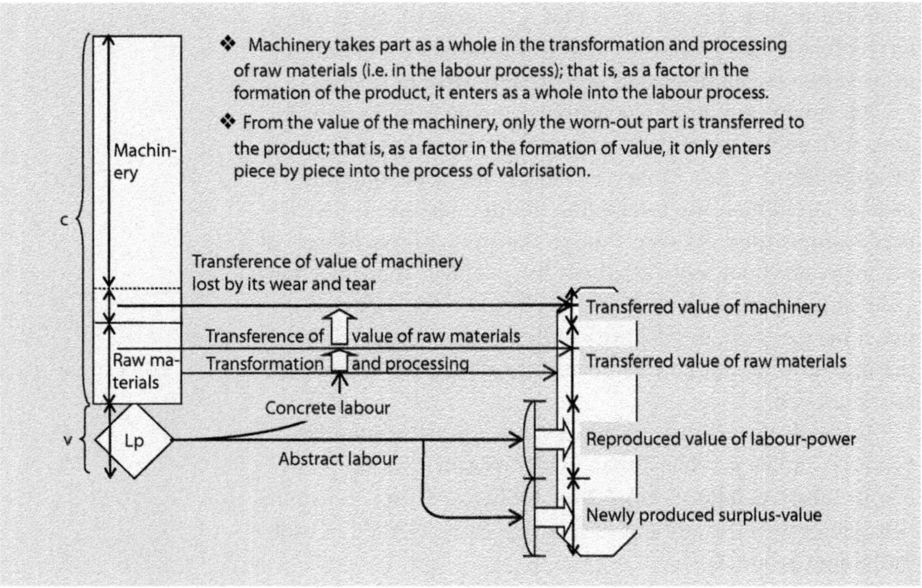

Fig. 5.7 Machinery as a factor in product formation and in value formation

the activity of machinery is completely different from that of capitalist society.

Significance of Machinery Use from the Human-historical Perspective

There is *enormous human-historical significance* in the fact that machinery comes into general use in production carried out under conditions of large-scale industry.

First of all, one indispensable moment for large-scale industry is the *conscious technical application of natural science to the production process*. Regardless of how the concrete form of industry may change in the future, it is only able to develop through natural science and its technical application in the production process. The production process begins to be transformed, through large-scale industry, into a process whereby nature is scientifically controlled.[2]

2 Marx (1872) writes: «Large-scale industry tore aside the veil that concealed from men their own social process of production and turned the various spontaneously divided branches of production into riddles, not only to outsiders but even to the initiated. Its principle, which is to view each process of production in and for itself, and to resolve it into its constituent elements without looking first at the ability of the human hand to perform the new processes, brought into existence the whole of the modern science of technology. The varied, apparently unconnected and petrified forms of the social production process were now dissolved into conscious and planned applications of natural science, divided up systematically in accordance with the particular useful effect aimed

Secondly, the labour process under large-scale industry that employs vast means of production is a *profoundly social process that can only be formed through co-operation involving a large number of workers*, i.e. *social labour*. Thus, the labour process is transformed from a dispersed and isolated process into a social process.[3]

Under capitalist production, however, because the means of production take the form of capital, and machinery is only employed to the extent that it is useful for the production of surplus-value, the human-historical significance of the use of machinery presents itself in the **distorted form** of *machinery dominating the labouring individuals.*

5.4.2 Effects of the Capitalist Application of Machinery on the Worker

Means of Labour Dominate Workers

The large-scale industry that characterises capitalist production developed in the nineteenth century with the expansion in the use of machinery and the production of machines by machinery, thus overwhelming handicraft and manufacture to achieve rapid growth. Workers had previously controlled their means of labour (tools), but that development meant that *the*

at in each case. Similarly, technology discovered the *few grand fundamental forms of motion* which, despite all the diversity of the instruments used, apply necessarily to every productive action of the human body, just as the science of mechanics is not misled by the immense complication of modern machinery into viewing this as anything other than the constant re-appearance of the same simple mechanical processes. / Modern industry never views or treats the existing form of a production process as the definitive one. Its technical basis is therefore revolutionary, whereas all earlier modes of production were essentially conservative» (Marx 1976, pp. 616–617; Marx's emphasis as in the first German edition).

3 Marx (1872) writes: «As machinery, the instrument of labour assumes a material mode of existence which necessitates the replacement of human force by natural forces, and the replacement of the rule of thumb by the conscious application of natural science. In manufacture the organisation of the social labour process is *purely subjective*; it is a *combination* of specialised workers. Large-scale industry, on the other hand, possesses in the machine system an entirely *objective* organisation of production, which *confronts* the worker as a pre-existing material condition of production … Machinery … operates only by means of associated labour, or labour in common. Hence the *co-operative character* of the labour process is in this case a *technical necessity dictated by the very nature of the instrument of labour*» (Marx 1976, p. 508; Marx's emphasis as in the first German edition).

means of labour (machinery) came to dominate human beings, with the worker turning into a mere appendage of the machine.

Under capitalist production, because both the means of labour and the object of labour are forms that capital assumes, factories with automatic system of machinery represent the completion of the *rule of labour by capital within the labour process itself.*

Moreover, the emergence of machinery also swept aside the broad sector of skilled workers, who had limited the rule of labour by capital. This is another sense in which the rule of labour by means of labour was completed.

Male Labour Replaced by Female and Child Labour

The appearance of machinery makes it possible to utilise workers without great muscular strength or those whose bodies are not fully developed but who are physically pliable; i.e. *the broad utilisation of female and child labour.* The worker's entire family thus came under the rule of capital, *increasing the number of wageworkers. Distributing the familial costs once included solely within the labour-power of the adult male worker to all family members lowered the value of the worker's labour-power.* Machinery, by adding an overwhelming number of women and children to the working population, finally broke the resistance that male workers had put up against the despotism of capital during the era of manufacture. Workers thus became increasingly subordinate to capital.

Lengthening the Working Day Through the Capitalistic Application of Machinery

Machinery, whether used or not, materially deteriorates and suffers a loss in value through the «moral depreciation»[4] resulting from decline in the price of machinery. The capitalist thus seeks to use up a machine in the shortest period of time possible. For this reason, a capitalist seeks to expand the working day to the greatest extent possible. Indeed, it was during the period in which large-scale industry was being established in England that labour-time was extended to an extreme point. Machinery, *which makes it possible for workers to produce more in less time, creates—in the hands of capital—new incentives to limitlessly extend the working day.*

Intensifying Labour Through the Capitalist Use of Machinery

When a society in which the very foundation of workers' lives has been threatened by the limitless extension of the working day decides to establish a normal working day, capital strives to exploit labour-power in the most intensive manner possible. With the shortened working day, *the velocity of machines is accelerated, and the superintendence of workers*

---

4 Marx uses the term «*moral depreciation*» to refer to the depreciation of fixed capital due to the obsolescence of means of labour caused by social conditions, particularly as a result of a rise in the productive power of labour lowering the value of the means of labour.

heightened, thus raising the intensity of labour. In England, just a few years after the working day was shortened, the number of workers employed in industry decreased remarkably. This was because the labour squeezed out of the individual worker had increased. This intensification of labour in turn led to a stronger demand on the part of workers for a further shortening of the working day.

Factory as Purgatory

In factories where machinery had been introduced, the rank-based system of manufacture, which was composed of workers with various skill levels, was dissolved. The fate of workers was to be used by machinery their whole lives. The means of labour that have become an automatic system of machinery already confront the workers as capital—i.e. as dead labour that dominates and soaks up living labour-power. In factories, where the *despotic control of workers* predominates, capital makes use of labour superintendents and *barrack-like regulations*. Inside the hot and dusty factories, workers are exposed to dangers to life and limb, among machines crowded together and deafening noise. Here we have the scene of the factory as Purgatory!

Workers Rebel Against Machinery

Given this situation, it was natural that for a long period of time workers fought ferociously against machines, often focusing their energy on the physical destruction of machines (e.g., the «Luddite movement» in the 1810s in Nottingham). Their error was the inability to perceive that the hardships brought to them by the use of machinery were not inherent to the machinery itself, but rather resulted from their capitalistic use.

Repulsion and Attraction of Workers Through the Development of Machinery-based Production

The capacity for sudden and enormous expansion of the factory system, and the system's dependence on the world market, brings about a period of feverish production, but the outcome of this is overproduction and crisis, and the resultant stagnation. *The repulsion and attraction of workers, in and out of different industrial sectors, results from this industrial cycle*, creating in extremely unstable life and employment conditions for workers.

5.4.3 Large-scale Industry Develops the Moments for Social Upheaval of Society and the Elements for Forming a New Society

Unfolding of Contradictions Ferment the Transformation of Capitalist Production

Large-scale industry is constantly transforming the technical foundation of production, while at the same time transforming the functions of workers and social combinations in the labour process. This is also a constant transformation of the social division of labour, continuously throwing huge amounts of capital and large numbers of workers from one production sphere to another. In this way, large-scale industry necessitates the *conversion of labour*, fluidisation of functions, and overall mobility of workers. At the same time, however, large-scale industry under capitalism is always reproducing the age-old division of labour by specialising and fixing many workers into a specific kind of labour, so that individual workers are not able to easily transfer to a different production sphere. This is *a serious contradiction of capitalist large-scale industry*, and because of it, an unneeded population is generated made up of those who are separated from the means of production through unemployment and stripped of their means of livelihood. This, in turn, strips workers' living conditions of stability and security, subjecting the working class to constant sacrifice and limitless wasting of labour-power. These are the *negative aspects* of capitalist large-scale industry.

However, there is a recognition—through a period of crisis or stagnation—of the need to change over the labour of workers; and therefore a recognition of the need for workers to have *versatile labour capacities*. That is, large-scale industry calls for *workers who are able to perform any sort of labour necessary*, and thus demands the sort of *fully-developed individuals* who are able to take on various social functions, one after another, as their various modes of activity. The capitalist form of production, on the one hand, seeks to discard the old division of labour and to do so must generate *such an enzyme that revolutionises the form of production itself*, but, on the other hand, the *economic relations of workers* that correspond to this production form are *in direct contradiction with this tendency*.

The *development of these contradictions* inherent to the capitalist form of production prepares the way for the dissolution of that form of production and the emergence of a new form to take its place. Large-scale industry *ferments the revolutionary upheaval* of capitalist production.

Combined Labour of Men and Women Within Large-scale Industry Alters Completely To Become a Source of Human Development

Capitalist production makes use of the manifold discrimination that exists between labouring individuals for the sake of augmenting capital, including the gender discrimination inherited from previous social forms. Capitalist production seeks to preserve and make use of gender discrimination, but at the same time the development of capitalist large-scale industry necessarily brings forth *a new economic foundation for a higher form of the family and gender relations by allotting a decisive role to women and children in the production process* socially organised beyond the realm of housekeeping.

The fact that the working population integrated into co-operation by capital is composed of male and female workers of an extreme variety of ages often becomes the source of decay or slave-like conditions precisely because it takes place under the capitalist form of production. But under relations where the production process is for the sake of workers themselves, this conversely turns into a source of human development. In this sense, capitalist large-scale industry *cultivates the enzymes that ultimately will dissolve gender discrimination.*

The Education of the Future Sprouts Within the Factory System

The development of large-scale industry, by leading to the destruction and exhaustion of labour-power within the production process, inevitably calls forth the **factory legislation** that included clauses to protect workers. The factory laws represent the first consciously planned action by society to counter the spontaneously generated shape of the production process. The English factory laws included clauses that merit attention. One example was the *educational clauses*, which was the first concession wrenched from capital. The factory law made it compulsory for the children of factory workers to receive an elementary education *as a necessary precondition to work.* This demonstrated for the first time that it was possible to link mental and physical education to physical labour. Here we can see *the education of the future sprouting from the factory system.* This is education that seeks to connect instruction and gymnastics to productive labour for *all children* above a certain age. Marx (1872) viewed this sort of education as «the only method of producing fully developed human beings» (Marx 1976, p. 614). Today, however, despite elementary education being compulsory in developed capitalist countries, there is not yet education that is combined with productive labour.

Generalisation of Factory Legislation Matures the Moments for Social Upheaval and the Elements for Forming of a New Society

The extensive development of large-scale industry and the factory system necessitates that the factory laws be generalised into laws governing all social production. This *generalisation of the factory legislation* provided a great stimulus for the development of the production process of capital, while *developing the contradictions* contained therein. Within individual factories, this reinforced uniformity, order, and savings, and socially transformed the small-scale dispersed production process into a large-scale, integrated one—thus generalising the rule of the factory system, which in turn promoted the concentration of capital. The restriction and regulation of the working day greatly stimulated the introduction of new techniques and the intensification of labour, thus enhancing the anarchy of capitalist production as a whole and thereby increasing the factors underlying overproduction.

The factory laws crushed small-scale production and domestic labour by forcing strict compliance with clauses protecting workers, while also destroying antiquated and transitional forms, replacing them with the *direct, naked rule of capital.*

However, eliminating the old spheres and forms that had absorbed excess workers, also destroyed the safety-valve for the entire social mechanism, which enhanced the hostility between worker and capital and *generalised the workers' struggle against the rule of capital.*

Thus, the *generalisation of the factory laws*, which were inevitably generated by capitalist large-scale industry, *developed contradictions and antagonistic relations intrinsic to the capitalist form of the production process, while putting in place the material conditions of the production process necessary for forming a new society and maturing the association of labouring individuals within the production process.* In other words, the development of large-scale industry under capitalist production has generated the various elements needed for forming a new society, while also *maturing various moments that are indispensable to the upheaval of society.*

Environmental Destruction Indicates the Necessity of a Socially Controllable Production Process

Large-scale industry began to turn the production process into a process that scientifically controls nature, but this did not mean that the production process had been transformed into a process of ecologically controlling the *metabolism between human beings and nature* in a way that simultaneously protects the environment. As long as each production process is carried out by individual capitals, with the aim of appropriating surplus-value, it is only possible through overall social compulsion (i.e. legal regulations and the like) to control social production process so as to also preserve the environment. But capitalist large-scale industry, through the paradoxical outcome of a *process controlled by science destroying the environment*, demonstrates to the labouring individuals *the need for the production process to be converted from its capitalist form to a form in which it can be socially controlled*, and *for society in the meantime to exercise coercion vis-à-vis individual capitals.*

Marx noted that the development of productive powers under capitalist production inevitably destroys the natural environment, and necessarily damages the *metabolism between human beings and nature and their ecological relationship*, thereby compelling human beings «to restore it systematically as a regulating law of social production, and in a form adequate to the full development of the human race».[5] He was prescient in foreseeing the gravity of the pollution and environmental destruction of the modern era, and the need for people to engage in an international social effort to address the problem.

References

Marx K (1872) Das Kapital. Kritik der politischen Oekonomie. Bd. 1. Buch 1: Der Produktionsprocess des Kapitals. 2. verb. Aufl. Hamburg. English edition: Marx K (1976) Capital. A critique of political economy. Vol. 1 (trans: Howkes B). Penguin Books

Saito K (2017) Karl Marx's Ecosocialism: Capital, Nature, and the Unfinished Critique of Political Economy. New York

5 The following is a compendium of what Marx (1872) wrote on this point: «Through the development of the large-scale capitalist production that employs machinery in the sphere of agriculture the *conscious, technological application of science* replaces also here the previous highly irrational and slothfully traditional way of working. The capitalist mode of production thus *creates the material conditions for the union of agriculture and industry putting an end to the period of their antagonistic isolation.* / On the other hand, however, *the capitalist production disturbs inevitably the metabolism between man and the earth*, i.e. it prevents the return to the soil of its constituent elements consumed by *man* in the form of food and clothing; hence it hinders the operation of the eternal natural condition for the lasting fertility of the soil. All progress in capitalist agriculture is a progress in the art, not only of robbing the worker, but of robbing the soil. All progress in increasing the fertility of the soil for a given time by the capitalist farmer is a progress towards ruining the more long-lasting sources of that fertility. / In modern agriculture, as in urban industry, the increase in the productive power of the mobility of labour is purchased at the cost of laying waste and debilitating labour-power itself. At the same time it destroys the physical health of the urban worker, and the intellectual life of the rural worker. / *Capitalist production,* therefore, *only develops the techniques and the degree of combination of social process of production by simultaneously undermining the original sources of all wealth—the soil and the worker.* / But at the same time *by destroying the circumstances surrounding that metabolism, which originated in a merely natural and spontaneous fashion, it compels its systematic restoration as a regulating law of social production, and in a form adequate to the full development of the human race*» (Marx 1976, pp. 637–638; my emphasis).

With regard to how Marx's views on ecology deepened along with the development of his critique of political economy, the detailed and lucid study of Saito (2017) is very thought-provoking.

Capitalist Relations of Production and the Alienation of Labour

T. Otani, *A Guide to Marxian Political Economy*,
https://doi.org/10.1007/978-3-319-65954-1_6

6.1 Capitalist Relations of Production

The Capital Relation is the Fundamental Relation of Production That Determines Capitalist Production

Capitalist production is a particular form of production in which, as we have seen, capital is able to obtain new value of greater magnitude than the value of the labour-power purchased—by means of consuming labour-power purchased on the labour market and means of production purchased on the commodity market—and augment itself through the appropriation of that surplus-value, which is the difference between those two magnitudes. The overall character and movement of this form of production are determined by the relation of production called the capital/wage-labour relation.

6

Primary Moments Within the Capital Relation

In this relation, labouring individuals are completely separated from the means of production, becoming wageworkers unable to survive without selling their labour-power as a commodity. Meanwhile, the means of production produced and all the labour-products in general become autonomous as capital, personified by the capitalist who does not labour. The production process in which the capitalist consumes the labour-power purchased is carried out under the command of capitalists. Among the products of this process, the workers are only able to buy back and make their own the requisite means of livelihood, whereas the surplus products in their entirety belong to the capitalists, to say nothing of the products that compensate the means of production. Labour takes the form of wage-labour, while the means of production take the form of capital. This relation of production is the **capital/wage-labour relation** (abbreviated as the **capital relation**). The *primary moments included within the capital relation* are as follows.

- The means of production (or conditions of labour) are separated from the labouring individuals to become independent.
- The means of production (or conditions of labour) become capital, and labour-power is commodified.
- The capitalist personally represents capital and the wageworker labour-power.
- The capitalist advances capital to purchase labour-power from the wageworkers.
- Production is carried out by the wageworkers under the direction and superintendence of the capitalist.
- The capitalist appropriates the surplus products, while the wageworkers buy back the requisite means of livelihood.
- The capitalists who possess the means of production (or conditions of labour) and the wageworkers who only possess labour-power are reproduced.

Capital Relation: Estranged Relationship of Labouring Individuals Toward the Conditions of Labour

As we saw in ► Sect. 1.4.3.1, the pivot of the relations of production concerns the manner in which labouring individuals relate to the means of production, and how they carry out labour in connection to those means of production. In the capital relation, *the labouring individuals*, who are completely separated from the conditions of labour, enter a relation *in the production process* with the *means of production*, which are the conditions of labour, *as something belonging to another person*, the outcome of which is that the products come to be appropriated by this other person—i.e. they are appropriated by the capitalist who personally represents the means of production. The *capitalist* who appropriates the products is thus able *to act as the owner of the means of production*, while the labouring individuals must again appear on the market as the sellers of labour-power.

In short, whereas the relations of commodity production examined in ► Sect. 2.4.1 involved a social relation between human beings in which society's total labour is spontaneously divided and the labour or production of the labouring individuals becomes private labour, the **capitalist relations of production** examined here involve *a social relation between human beings in which the labouring individuals are separated from the means of production, becoming property-less, with the means of production taking the form of capital and dominating the labouring individuals*. The capital relation represents the *fundamental relations of production* that determine the totality of relations of production under capitalist production, which is to say the totality of capitalist relations of production.

Reification of Relations of Production: Reified Relation Between Capital and Labour-power

In this way, *the social relation between human beings within labour*—i.e. the capital relation—presents itself as a *relation between things* (*capital and the labour-power as commodity*). This is nothing more than the development of the *reification of production relations* within the relations of commodity production, where the social relations between the private labour of labouring individuals take the reified form of the commodity/money relations, as examined in ► Sect. 2.4.2 (*see* ◘ Fig. 2.35).

Personification of Things: Capitalist and Wageworker

Furthermore, since capital and the labour-power commodity, which are the reification of the capital relation, come into a mutual relationship on the market and then in the production process, they need to be represented by *persons equipped with will*. The **capitalist** is the *personification of capital* and the **wageworker** is the *personification of labour-power*. The two enter a relationship on the market as the contracted parties who buy and sell labour-power, while in the production process they enter a relationship as persons in the different position of being either the director and superintendent or the workers combined to work under the capitalist. The things capital and labour-power are represented in the person of the capitalist and the wageworker. This is a development of the *personification of things*, wherein commodity as well as money are represented in the person of the commodity-holder (seller) and the money-holder (buyer), as discussed in ► Sect. 2.4.3 (*see* ◘ Fig. 2.37).

Capitalist Relations of Production Are the Relations of Commodity Production Determined by the Capital Relation

Where the capital relation prevails, products of labour generally take the commodity form, which means that commodity production is generally carried out.

In capitalist society, since the labouring individuals do not own the conditions of labour, they cannot carry out private labour as their own labour. Instead, the capitalists who purchase those individuals' labour-power and consume it are private producers, and the totality of the labour of individuals working under one capitalist confronts the totality of the labour of individuals working under other capitalists, as mutually private labour. Consequently, the products of the labour under each capitalist confront each other as commodities. Under capitalist relations of production, labour is also private labour that in its totality forms the social division of labour, and thus must become social labour through the exchange of commodities according to their value.

Furthermore, the labouring individuals are wageworkers who possess neither the requisite means of livelihood nor the necessary means of production to produce them. They can only rely on their wages, which is the equivalent value of their labour-power, so as to purchase the requisite means of livelihood from the market. *Thus, every possible means of livelihood that the worker requires for his life has to take the commodity form.* Not only do the means of production become capital, so that they are sold as commodities, but also every sort of means of livelihood is commodified. This means that *commodity production must be generalised under the capitalist production.*

Capitalist relations of production, therefore are *relations of commodity production determined by the capital relation.* Meanwhile, since the capital relation is premised on the circulation of commodities as well as money, and is only able to exist and develop upon this basis, commodity production forms the *foundation of capitalist relations of production.* It can thus be said that *capitalist relations of production are made up of relations of commodity production as the foundational relations and the capital relation as the determining relation.*

Commodity Circulation Is the Surface Layer That Covers the Deeper Layer of the Capital Relation

At the beginning of our analysis of capitalist society, we looked at commodity exchange, which is the most general phenomenon of this society, and first examined the commodity before arriving at the capital relation. Now we are aware that it is precisely this capital relation that determines the relations of commodity production. The *circulation of commodities and money*, which we first see, *is the* **surface layer** *of capitalist production*, whereas *the capital relation lies at the* **deeper layer**.

Because of the reification of the relations of production and the personification of things under relations of commodity production, one can only see in the realm of commodity circulation the free, equal relations of self-interest between private owners as *homo oeconomicus*. Underlying that surface layer, however, is a relation between the labouring individuals who do not possess the conditions of labour and the capitalists who possess these conditions but do not labour. Thus, also encompassed in the production process is the relationship between the capitalist who directs and superintends workers to appropriate unpaid labour, on the one hand, and the labouring individuals who work under the direction and superintendence of someone else and must hand over to that person their surplus-labour in the form of surplus-value, on the other hand.

The capital relation at the deeper layer is covered by the commodity circulation at the surface layer. Thus, the true figure of the former is hidden by the latter.

6.2 Subsumption of Labour Under Capital

Subsumption of Labour Under Capital

For the existence of human beings and the society they form, labour and the labour process must be carried out by labouring individuals. This is the process wherein the labour-power of the labouring individuals is consumed, as well as the metabolism between human beings and nature. This process takes various historical forms, depending on the manner in which the labouring individuals relate to the conditions of labour (means of production).

As we have seen, the labour process under the capitalist mode of production is a process whereby capital consumes labour-power to produce surplus-value. The subject of this process is capital, not the labouring individuals. The labour process becomes the process of capital, with labour carried out under the direction and superintendence of capital, and hence becomes the labour of capital. Here *labour and the metabolism between human individuals and nature* via *that labour, which are necessary to the individuals and to human society, are completely taken over by and subordinated to capital.*

Capitalist production is a historical form that emerges after various pre-capitalist forms. The emergence of capitalist production is precisely the transformation of the labour process that had been carried out under the preceding forms into a process of capital. Capital as self-valorising value (i.e. the reification of the capital relation) *incorporates and envelops labour and the labour process within itself, making it its own.* Marx calls this process the «**subsumption of labour under capital**» or the «**subordination of labour to capital**». The production of surplus-value by capital is production carried out through labour subsumed within capital.

The subsumption of labour under capital takes two forms: a formal subsumption and a real subsumption.

Formal Subsumption of Labour Under Capital

In ► Chap. 3 we examined how capital produces surplus-value in the process of valorisation, which is the *form of the production of surplus-value itself.* There we merely looked formally at the valorisation process in which the production process is subsumed within capital, without considering at all the issue of the real mode of labour or the method of production carried out under that form. Thus, regardless of the labour mode under which the labour process is carried out or the degree of its productive powers, when this has become a process for the production of surplus-value by capital (i.e. a process of valorisation), so that it has become a process of the exploitation of workers' labour by the capitalist *qua* director and superintendent, it is referred to as the **formal subsumption of labour under capital**.

Capital can be said to subsume labour when the *capitalist as the personification of capital* directs and superintends workers in the labour process and exploits their surplus-value. For the subsumption of labour under capital to be established, therefore, all of the time during which the capitalist functions as personified capital must be used for appropriating the labour of other people and selling the products of this labour, etc.; therefore, the *capitalist must appropriate a level of surplus-value that allows a livelihood equal to or surpassing that of the worker.* In the case of medieval guilds, the maximum number of workers that a master handicraftsman could utilise was extremely limited, which forcefully prevented the master from becoming a capitalist. Only after the minimum advanced for production far exceeds this medieval maximum, does the money-owner becomes a capitalist. «Here, as in natural science, is shown the correctness of the law discovered by *Hegel*, in his *Logic*, that at a certain point merely *quantitative* differences pass over by a dialectical inversion into *qualitative* distinctions» (Marx 1872: Marx 1976, p. 423; Marx's emphasis as in the first German edition). This is the only thing necessary for labour to be formally subsumed under capital.

Real Subsumption of Labour Under Capital

In ► Chap. 5 we saw that in order for capital to produce relative surplus-value, the productive power of labour must be developed; and that for this to occur there must be a revolution in the mode of labour or production method within the labour process via co-operation, the division of labour, and the utilisation of machinery, resulting in the capitalist mode of production passing through the developmental stages of simple co-operation, manufacture, and large-scale industry. That chapter, in other words, considers the real change and development in the mode of labour and method of production inevitably accompanying the formal subsumption of labour under capital. Thus, the **real subsumption of labour under capital** refers to the case where *capital, which formally subsumes labour and the labour process, innovates the real character and conditions of the labour process for the sake of producing relative surplus-value, and establishes its own mode of production in terms of technique and other points.*

With the real subsumption of labour under capital, **a specifically capitalist mode of production**, which had not existed in any prior labour process, develops by means of a thoroughgoing change in the technical process of labour and the social formations. This is characterised by *large-scale labour within co-operation, a systematic organisation of labour with a division of labour within the factory, and the application of science and machinery to the process of production.*

Relations of production, with a basis in this specifically capitalist mode of production, thus develop between those involved in the capitalist production process, particularly between capitalists and wageworkers. Along with the real subsumption of labour under capital, *the mode of production itself—and therefore the productive power of labour and the relations between capitalist and workers as well—undergoes a complete revolution.*

The mode of production itself, i.e. *productive-power as well as the relations between capitalist and workers, is entirely revolutionised* through the real subsumption of labour under capital.

From Formal Subsumption to Formal as Well as Real Subsumption

Historically speaking, first there was the mere formal subsumption of labour under capital, and then, on that basis the specifically capitalist mode of production was spontaneously generated and developed, so that the real subsumption of labour under capital emerged. Therefore, the formal subsumption of labour under capital is the *general form of the capitalist process of production,* but in the developmental process of capitalist production this takes *the special form* particular to the capitalist mode of production that exists alongside the real subsumption of labour under capital that emerged as a form of the capitalist process of production prior to the generation of the specific capitalist mode of production.

The subsumption of labour under capital clearly shows that under capitalist production *the human necessity of labour and the labour process are subordinated to the subject capital.*

6.3 Transformation of the Social Productive Power of Labour into the Productive Power of Capital

Social Productive Power of Labour in the Specifically Capitalist Mode of Production

Capitalist production highly develops the productive powers in general through co-operation, the division of labour in factories, and the utilisation of machinery, and also through the overall transformation of the production process into a conscious technical application of the natural sciences. This is the *social productive power of labour, the productive power of directly social labour, and the productive power of communal labour and socialised labour*—in contrast to the productive power of labour carried out by more or less isolated labouring individuals. Only such socialised labour can apply science—as *the general product of human social development*—to the direct production process. In turn, the development of science is premised on a certain level of the material production process.

Social Productive Power of Labour Appears as the Productive Power of Capital

This *social* productive power of *labour* (or productive power of *social labour*), however, does not manifest itself as the productive power of individual workers or as the productive power of co-operating workers. It does not, in other words, present itself as the productive power *belonging to labour*. Rather, it is manifested solely as the *productive power of capital*—or, at best, as the productive power of labour as a form assumed by capital.

Because the social productive power of labour manifests itself as the productive power of capital, the social quality of this productive power also presents itself as something obtained by capital, rather than pertaining to the workers. The social quality of collective workers' labour thus comes to confront the workers themselves in the guise of the capitalist, who personifies capital.

This is *a further and more conspicuous development of the mystification inherent to the capitalist relations in general*, which we examined in the case of the formal subsumption of labour under capital.

Historical Significance of Capitalist Production Clearly Manifests Itself

In the case of the real subsumption of labour under capital, *the historical significance of capitalist production* is also first clearly manifested in a specific form by means of the changes in the direct production process itself and the development of the social productive power of labour.

Capitalist production, by developing the specifically capitalist mode of production, *transforms* the control of nature via labour into a *social process* via *the co-operation of a large number of labouring individuals*, while also *transforming this into a process whereby science is technically applied in a conscious manner*. Capital must constantly push this process forward and seek to raise the productive power of society. This is how capitalist production brings humanity a *higher* level of productive power. By so doing, it *prepares the way materially for a new social production organism, the society known as Association, wherein the labouring individuals control the production process rather than being controlled by it* (*see* ► Sect. 11.2.2).

6.4 Alienation of Labour Under Capitalist Production

Alienated Labour

Marx (1844) in *Economic and Philosophic Manuscripts of 1844*, which he wrote soon after beginning his study of political economy, looks to the manner in which individuals labour within this society as the most profound basis of economic reality within capitalist society, and he grasps this using the concept of «**alienated labour**». And we can outline his view as follows[1]:

In this society, the products of workers confront them as an independent, outside power because their labour itself has becomes forced labour for others that is a source of pain for themselves. This manner of labour estranges human beings from their own life activity and species being, so that they are also estranged from each other. The private property that results from this *alienated labour* necessarily brings about the subordination of workers to the proprietors. Therefore, the emancipation of society from private property and subordination can only be achieved through the emancipation of workers, which means at the same time universal emancipation of human beings. Marx's manner of grasping the issue, as just sketched, incorporates ideas of *Ludwig Feuerbach* (1804–1872) in terms of criticising the idealist character of *Hegel's concept of «alienation»*, but at the same time he inherits *Hegel's*

1 *See* Marx 1975, pp. 270–282.

way of grasping labour as a subjective and essential activity of human beings and as a process of the **alienation** *and* **sublation of alienation**,[2] Marx sought to reinvestigate *the results of the analysis of Classical political economy* on the basis of a more fundamental concept of labour.

Deepening the Grasp of the Alienation of Labour

Marx continued this investigation in the form of the «*materialist conception of history*»[3] he developed as a scientific conception of history and society. This bore fruit as his *theory of the revolutionising of society*, wherein the overall liberation of human beings is sought through the realisation of the new Association society. Marx further deepened his ideas through the scientific analysis of capitalist society, which was his *critique of political economy*.

Systematic Development of Alienation of Labour in *Capital*

In his main work *Capital*, above all, Marx (1867) explores in systematic detail the roots and phenomena of the alienation of labour through his analysis of capitalist production. The following is a summary of his theoretical development there: (1) On the ground of a clear grasp of the relations of commodity production and the capitalist relations of production based upon them, (2) and by pursuing the reification of production relations and the personification of things that inevitably arises under relations of commodity production and which develop and reach completion under capitalist relations of production, Marx elucidates that the alienation of labour arises when (3) the means of production under capitalist relations of production become independent of the workers as capital so that the labour process at the same time becomes a process of valorisation, with the subsumption of labour under capital being systematically developed; (4) this fully illustrates that the condition of the labouring individuals merits the term «alienation» and that (5) the development of capitalist production, which is a process of alienation, is also a process that prepares the way for this alienation to be overcome and that enormously develops productive powers and fosters a trained and organised working class.

---

2 Marx (1844) writes: «The outstanding achievement of *Hegel's Phenomenology* and of *its final outcome, the dialectic of negativity as the moving and generating principle*, is thus first that Hegel conceives the self-creation of man as a process, conceives objectification as loss of the object, *as alienation and as sublation of this alienation*; that he thus *grasps the essence of labour* and *comprehends objective man—true, because real man—as the outcome of man's own labour*» (Marx 1975. pp. 332–333; my emphasis).

3 Engels (1859). *See* Engels 1980, p. 469.

Marx thus unfolds, in a concrete and systematic manner, the distorted figure of labour in the specific social form of wage labour («alienated labour»), based upon his theoretical analysis of capitalist production. And this elaborates the content of alienation and its sublation.

Alienation of Labour Fundamentally Explains Why Labour Becomes a Source of Suffering

In the Introduction (► Sect. 1.3.3), we questioned why, in modern society, labour manifests itself as the source of human suffering, even though labour is the fundamental form of human praxis and should be a source of joy for those who satisfy their wants by accomplishing some aim thereby. Now we are able to answer that question: Labour subsumed under capital, i.e. *alienated labour*, is not an activity to realise aims set by the labouring individuals themselves, but rather an activity to realise the aims of capital. Rather than being the activity of labouring individuals as subject, who bring nature under their own conscious control, it is an activity carried out under the command of an other (capital). This *alienation of labour* is the precise source of the *suffering related to labour in modern society*, manifested as activities we must perform against our will.

Domination of Individuals by Commodities and Money Develops into Domination of Individuals by Capital

In this chapter we have seen that the subsumption of labour under capital develops under the capitalist relations of production, thereby completing the alienation of labour. Within this process, the means of production that are the product of the labouring individuals become independent of them by assuming the form of capital, and come to dominate the labouring individuals. In other words, the domination of human individuals by commodity and money—touched on in ► Sect. 2.4.2—has now developed into the **domination of human individuals by capital**.

References

Engels F (1859) [Rezension:] Karl Marx, "Zur Kritik der Politischen Oekonomie". Erstes Heft, Berlin, Franz Duncker, 1859. English edition: Engels F (1980) Marx-Engels Collected Works. Vol. 16. Progress Publishers et al. New York

Marx K (1844) Ökonomisch-philosophische Manuskripte aus dem Jahre 1844. English edition: Marx K (1975) Economic and philosophic manuscripts of 1844, Collected Works. Vol. 3. Progress Publishers et al. New York

Marx K (1872) Das Kapital. Kritik der politischen Oekonomie. Bd. 1. Buch 1: Der Produktionsprocess des Kapitals. 2. verb. Aufl. Hamburg. English edition: Marx K (1976) Capital. A critique of political economy. Vol. 1 (trans: Howkes B). Penguin Books

Wages

T. Otani, *A Guide to Marxian Political Economy*,
https://doi.org/10.1007/978-3-319-65954-1_7

7.1 Essence and Phenomenal Form of Wages

Essence of Wages

The wage a capitalist pays a wageworker is the price of the commodity labour-power that the wageworker sells. This price is the monetary expression of the value of this labour-power commodity. In short, the **essence of the wage** is the **value of labour-power**, the money-expression of which is the **price of labour-power** (*see* ◘ Fig. 7.1).

Phenomenal Form of Wages

However, at the surface level of circulation, which directly enters the field of vision of the capitalist and wageworker actually involved in a transaction, it does not appear at all that labour-power is the commodity being sold. They fall under the sway of the illusion that what is bought and sold is labour, rather. This illusion arises because labour is what the wageworker must actually perform under the capitalist, in line with the sales contract; and what the capitalist actually intends to obtain through the purchase is one day of labour of the wageworker, including surplus labour. The essence of the wage, which is the value or price of labour-power, takes the **phenomenal form** of the **value or price of labour**. Therefore, the market where labour-power is bought and sold is called the «**labour market**» rather than the labour-power market (*see* ◘ Fig. 7.2).

In the case of the wage, which is the phenomenal form of the essence that is the value or price of labour-power, the *daily value of labour-power presents itself as the* **daily value of labour**. The wage is the transformed form of the value of labour-power.

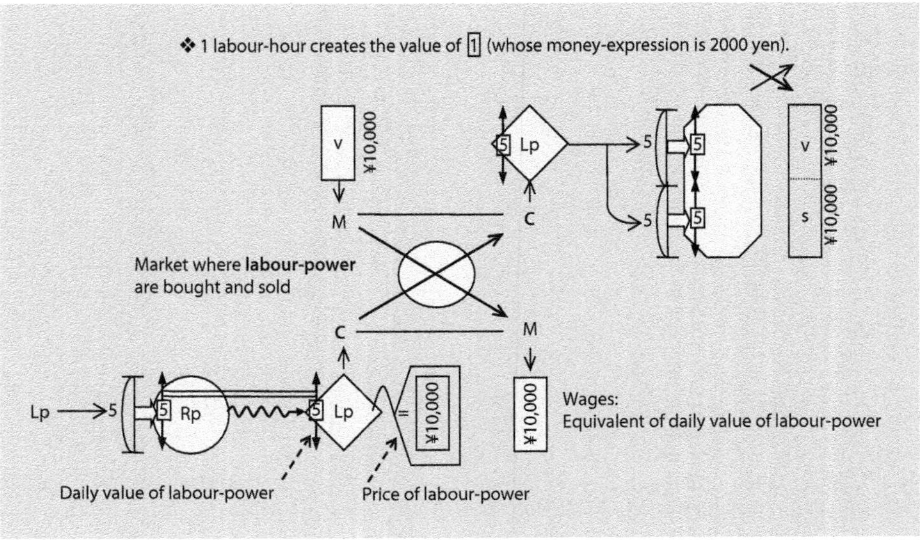

◘ **Fig. 7.1** Essence of wages: Value and price of labour-power

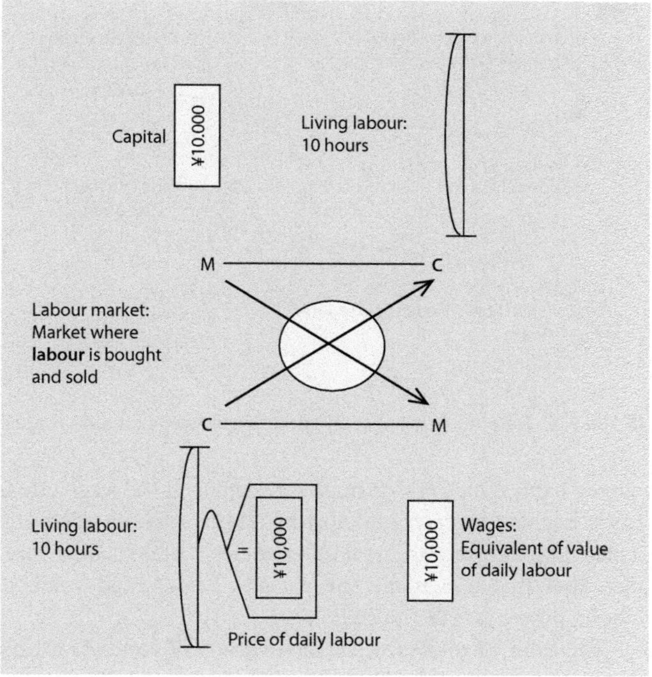

Fig. 7.2 Phenomenal form of the wage = value and price of labour

7.2 Two Fundamental Wage Forms: Time-wage and Piece-wage

Time-wage and Time-wage Rate

The first fundamental wage form is the **time-wage**, which is a wage form in which the quantity of labour is measured by labour-time, so that the wages are paid in the form of «so many yen per hour». The level of the wage per hour of labour is referred to as the **time-wage rate** or **wage rate** for short. For the time-wage, the daily wage of each worker is calculated by multiplying the given time-wage rate by the labour-time the worker expended for that day.

Objective Basis of the Wage Rate

The wage rate fluctuates depending on the power relation between capitalists and wageworkers, but *its objective basis is that the wages determined by means of the wage rate allow the wageworker to recover the daily value of his labour-power through a day of labour*. This is necessary because if it could not be achieved for the social average of wageworkers, regardless of what the wage rate of individual capital might be, they would be unable to normally reproduce their own labour-power.

External Appearance of How the Wage Rate Is Decided

The basis of the daily value of labour-power cannot be directly seen, however. So *it is thought that «one hour of labour itself has a certain quantity of value and that the wage rate is its*

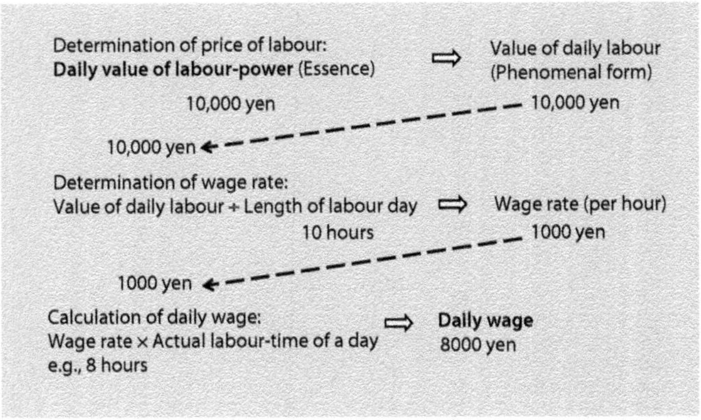

Fig. 7.3 Determination of each worker's daily wage for time-wages

money-expression», which makes it seem as if the wage rate is freely decided by each capitalist by taking into consideration its level up to now and the level in society. There is no awareness that this is actually the socially determined value of labour-power (*see* Fig. 7.3).

Concrete Forms of the Time-wage

The time-wage assumes a wide variety of concrete forms: not only hourly wages but also daily wages, weekly wages, monthly wages, yearly salaries, as well as the base wage, job wages, seniority-based wages, etc.

Piece-wage and the Piece-wage Rate

The second fundamental wage form is the **piece-wage**. In the case of the piece-wage, the quantity of labour a worker carries out is measured by the quantity of products that the labour produces, with the wages paid in line with this quantity. This means that the wages are paid in the form: «1 unit of product is worth so many yen». This is nothing more than the *transformed form of the time-wage*. The level of the wages paid per single unit of product is called the **piece-wage rate** or **wage rate** for short. In the case of piece-wages, the piece-wage rate is decided beforehand, so that the daily wage is calculated by multiplying this rate by the daily quantity of products for each worker in 1 day.

Objective Basis of the Wage Rate

For this piece-wage rate, as well, *its objective basis is that the wages determined by means of the wages rate allow the wageworker to recover the value of his labour-power through a day of labour*. In other words, here as well the basis is the transformation of the daily value of labour-power into the value of daily labour.

External Appearance of the Wage Rate Determination

Even though the rate of piece-wages is essentially determined by the daily value of the labour-power and the daily quantity of products, which is in proportion to the length (in hours) of a working day, the piece-wages-rate is *understood in terms of «the quantity of labour that produces one unit of prod-*

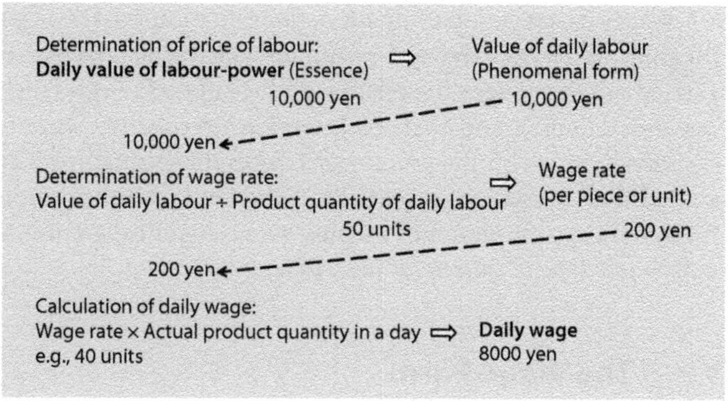

Fig. 7.4 Determination of each worker's daily wage for piece-wages

uct itself having value, so that the wage rate is a monetary expression of this value». There is no awareness of the connection to the determining essence (*see* Fig. 7.4).

Reduction in Wage Rate Through Increase in the Intensity and Skill of Labour

Because the daily quantity of labour products increases along with an increase in the intensity or skill of labour, the piece-wage rate is in inverse proportion to the length of the working day and to the intensity and skill of labour. That is, the piece-wage rate, unlike the time-wage rate, reflects not only the length of the working day, but also the intensity and level of skill of labour. Thus, *if the daily quantity of products increases through an increase in the intensity or skill of labour, the wage rate will fall.*

Piece-wages Lead to a Lowering of the General Level of Wages

Piece-wages allow a great deal of leeway for the individual activity of a worker, since a worker can raise the skill and intensity of his own labour on his own. This means that some workers' wages are higher than the general level, but there are other workers whose wages fall below that level. This *stimulates competition among workers, and by straining labour to an extreme point it has a tendency to lower the general wage level.*

Concrete Forms of Piece-wages

Piece-wages appear in an extremely diverse array of concrete forms, including simple piecework wages, premium pay, experience-based bonuses, efficiency wages, etc.

Wage-Decision-System

The complex combination of the diverse forms of time-wages and piece-wages to determine the sum of wages of an individual worker is called the **wage-decision-system**. In Japan, each individual capital—or more concretely, each private enterprise—has its proper system for determining wages. In fact, such systems *are a means of beating down the price of labour-power, using as its pretext the various differences among workers' concrete labour, the education levels, and various other individual circumstances of workers*. By means of the system for determining wages, the two parties concerned, capitalists and workers, further lose sight of the fact that the value of labour-power is the essence of wages.

Evaluation-based Wages

Wages based on job evaluation, or evaluation-based wages for short, is a wage-payment-system in which «job analysis» is carried out to «gauge» the relative «value» of each «job» (each concrete labour), and then each worker's respective wage is decided in line with the points received in the evaluation. The standard of evaluation, essentially, is the level of contribution to capital's appropriation of surplus-value, so *for capital this is a desirable type of system for determining wages.*

7.3 The Wage Form

Circumstances That Inevitably Generate the Notion of Wages for Labour

Under capitalist production, *the distorted notion inevitably emerges that* «wages are the price of labour». The circumstances that generate this notion are the following:

1. Despite the fact that rent from a temporary sale can only be objectively determined by the aggregate value of the commodity thus sold and the period of durability during which it can be sold in that form—and that there is no way for this to be determined by the quality and quantity of its use—what the buyer actually wants to obtain is not its value but its use. This is why there is the notion in general that «rent is the price (or equivalent) for using an object during its leasing term». Likewise, in the temporary sale of labour-power, what the buyer (capitalist) wants is not the value of labour-power but its use-value, which is labour, as well as the surplus-labour within it. The inevitable result is that the capitalist, who is the buyer, thinks that he has purchased labour.
2. Since the labour-power commodity sold is not a material object, but rather the power within the seller's body, its consumption requires the seller to expend his own power. This is a difference between the temporary sale of labour-power and the general temporary sale of material objects. For the sale of labour-power, the seller (worker) must expend his own power under the direction and superintendence of the buyer (capitalist). It is this expenditure of power (i.e. labour) that the worker does in fact hand over to the capitalist in exchange for wages. Moreover, unlike the case of the temporary sale of a house, for example, where rent is paid prior to use, in the case of the sale of labour-power, the wages that are the equivalent are paid after the labour is completed, as a rule. This means that, in the sale of labour-power, the worker (seller) is obliged to be conscious of selling his own labour.

3. Since wages take the form of either time-wages or piece-wages paid on the basis of a wage rate corresponding to the quantity of labour units, wages increase or decrease in proportion to the actual quantity of labour a worker performs, and differences in wages are also established on the basis on the «level» of «quality» of labour (regardless of the quality of labour-power) in any system for determining wages that is based on the idea of an «equivalent for labour». Thus, the magnitude of the wage each worker receives differs depending on the «quantity and quality of labour», so that both capitalist and worker are obliged to see wages as an equivalent for labour.

The Irrationality of the Wage Form as the Value or Price of Labour

However, the form whereby wages are considered as the value or price of labour is, *from the perspective of political economy*, founded on *an extremely irrational and distorted concept*, as is clear from the following:

1. Since the magnitude of a commodity's value is determined by the quantity of labour, it is a nonsensical tautology to say that «the value of labour itself is determined by labour». This is like saying, for example, that the value of 10 hours of labour is determined by 10 hours of labour; it explains nothing at all.
2. Even if one seeks some meaning in there being an exchange between the same 10 hours of labour—with 10 hours of *living labour* on one side and 10 hours of *dead labour* (objectified labour) on the other—the capitalist in this case would not be a penny richer as the result of this «exchange». Since no profit could be obtained, capitalist production would face extinction «.... a direct exchange of money, i.e. of objectified labour, with living labour, would either supersede the *law of value*, which only begins to develop freely on the basis of capitalist production, or supersede *capitalist production itself*, which rests directly on *wage-labour*» (Marx 1872: Marx 1976, p. 676; Marx's emphasis as in the first German edition).
3. Since labour from the outset is performed under the capitalist who has already purchased labour-power, this labour-power is consumed under his direction and superintendence. So it is quite impossible for the worker to sell to the capitalist each act of concrete labour performed under him.

The Form of Wages as a Pillar of the Trinity Formula

The concept of «wage = value of labour» is thus nonsense from the perspective of political economy, and cannot be made compatible with the labour theory of value. Moreover, it is an undeniable fact that «value added» is of greater value than wages, which is to say, greater than the imagined «value of labour» (*see* ◘ Table 3.1). But a notion emerges *to account for this irrationality and negate the labour theory of value*. This is the idea that, of the added value, only one part is value generated through labour, thus corresponding to the value of labour, while the other parts are not labour but rather value generated by capital (means of production or money) and land.

This is the *distorted concept* of «capital → interest (profit); land → ground-rent; labour → wages», referred to as the **trinity formula**. According to this *three-in-one economic* formula, all of the worker's labour is paid labour, so that no surplus-labour is carried out in capitalist society. In fact, the «common image» presented in ◘ Fig. 2.1 is precisely based on this concept. An overall discussion of the trinity formula is provided in the final chapter of this book (► Sect. 21.3 in Part III).

Everyone involved in the sale and purchase of labour-power in capitalist society (both capitalists and workers) share the same distorted notion of wages for labour, which is phenomenally manifested in a form that is the complete opposite of its essence. This forms the basis of *legal concepts* and becomes *the main pillar of apologetic theories of capitalism*.[1]

References

Marx K (1872) Das Kapital. Kritik der politischen Oekonomie. Bd. 1. Buch 1: Der Produktionsprocess des Kapitals. 2. verb. Aufl. Hamburg. English edition: Marx K (1976) Capital. A critique of political economy. Vol. 1 (trans: Howkes B). Penguin Books

1 Marx (1872) writes: «We may therefore understand the decisive importance of the *transformation* of the value and price of labour-power into the form of *wages*, or into the value and price of labour itself. All the notions of justice held by both the worker and the capitalist, all the mystifications of the capitalist mode of production, all the illusions of this mode of produciton about freedom, all the apologetic tricks of vulgar economics, have as their basis the *form of appearance* discussed above, which makes the actual relation invisible, and indeed presents to the eye the precise opposite of that relation» (Marx 1976, p. 680; Marx's emphasis as in the first German edition).

Reproduction of Capital

T. Otani, *A Guide to Marxian Political Economy*,
https://doi.org/10.1007/978-3-319-65954-1_8

8.1 Chapter Structure

In ► Chaps. 3, 4, 5, and 6, we studied the valorisation process of capital, which is the process whereby surplus-value is produced. In so doing, we assumed that conditions were in place for this process to proceed normally. That is, we assumed the existence beforehand of both the capital that was to be augmented and the labour-power necessary for this augmentation.

However, the existence of capital and the availability of labour-power as a commodity on the market are the results of a previous process. But now, instead of *assuming (as we have up to now) the existence of capital and the labour-power commodity*, we will examine *the process that brings them about.*

Instead of grasping the production process as we have up to now, as a single process that starts off on the basis of the premises just mentioned and then passes through the given process to arrive at a certain result, here we will be looking at a repeating process, where *the result of each process becomes the premise and preparation for the next process.* So what we will be dealing with is the **reproduction process**.

In order to begin the production process, capital must be able to buy means of production and labour-power on the market and then be able, after the end of the production process, to sell its products on the market. Because the reproduction process of capital is a process in which capital value passes through the market, i.e. through the sphere of circulation, and thus encompasses the circulation process, one must enter into an analysis of the *circulation process of capital* to be able to elucidate the concrete conditions of the reproduction process. At this stage, however, where the production process of capital is our object of examination, we will first observe the reproduction process of capital, which centres on the *repetitive process of the production of capital*, before then, in Part II, studying the circulation process of capital and the reproduction process of capital that it encompasses. Therefore, our assumption here will be the *normal (unobstructed) progression of all the movement of circulation* that mediates the reproduction process, so that the capital is always able to purchase means of production and labour-power on the market and also able to sell its products.

8.2 Reproduction of Capital and Capital Relation

8.2.1 Reproduction of Capital

Reproduction Under Capitalist Production Is the Reproduction of Capital

As we saw in the Introduction (▶ Sect. 1.4.2), production must always at the same time be reproduction, regardless of the particular form of society.

If production takes a capitalist form, so too must reproduction. Under the capitalist mode of production, the labour process only appears as a means of the valorisation process. Likewise, reproduction only appears as a means for the capital advanced to be reproduced as capital (i.e. as self-augmenting value). In short, under capitalist production, reproduction also takes the form of the **reproduction of capital**.

8.2.2 Simple Reproduction

Surplus-Value Takes the Form of the Capitalist's Revenue

The existence of capital requires the existence of a person representing capital. The **personification of capital** is the **capitalist**. A given individual is able to continue being a capitalist because his money is functioning as capital. In this sense, he is nothing but the personal representative of the money functioning as capital. For example, if 1000 yen in money is transformed into capital in a given year, generating 200 yen in surplus-value, this same operation would have to be repeated the following year and in the subsequent years. Further, since it is a living individual who performs the role of capitalist, in order for that individual to *continue existing as a capitalist, he must consume the means of consumption*. Thus, surplus-value as the periodic increment to capital value, and as the periodic fruit capital brings about, takes the *form of* **revenue** *for the capitalist*.

Simple Reproduction Is Carried Out if All Surplus-Value Is Consumed as Revenue by the Capitalist

If the capitalist consumes all of the surplus-value he appropriates as revenue, **simple reproduction** is carried out, which means that a production process is repeated on the same scale. Yet even though the process is merely repeated or continued, the process is provided with a *new character*; and this *dissolves* the *apparent character* that the process had up to that point of seeming to be just a single process, *revealing the essential content that had been hidden within the process*.

8.2.3 Reproduction of Capital Is at the Same Time the Reproduction of the Capital Relation

Reproduction of Capital

Social reproduction under capitalist production takes the form of the reproduction of capital. Let us begin by looking at the reproduction of capital as simple reproduction (*see* ◘ Fig. 8.1).

Through this reproduction, not only are the means of production and the requisite products reproduced, first of all, but new surplus products are also repeatedly produced. At the same time, it is a process through which capital—i.e. constant and variable capital—is reproduced along with surplus-value.

Working Class Only Receives the Requisite Products Out of Their Products

The production process is prepared through the temporary purchase of labour-power. This preparation is always renewed when the period of the contract for the sale of labour-power comes to an end. The worker, however, first receives payment after his labour-power has been put into operation and the value of his labour-power and surplus-value has been realised in the commodity. In other words, production is carried out before the variable capital that is the fund for the worker's payment flows into his hands in the form of a wage. And the worker can only utilise this fund insofar as he is always reproducing it. The use of the worker's labour-power today or this month is paid for from his labour the previous day or month.

If, then, we consider the capitalist class and the working class, rather than the single capitalist and the workers that he hires, the illusion generated by the money form immediately disappears. The capitalist class is constantly giving to the working class bills, in the form of money, that represent a portion of the product produced by the latter and appropriated by the former. The workers give these bills back just as constantly to the capitalists and thereby withdraw from the latter their allotted share of their own product.

In this manner, through the simple reproduction of capital, there is a reproduction of *the capitalist class that possesses means of production and a sum of money that can be advanced as capital, and of the working class, which only has labour-power to sell on the labour-market*. Thus, there is a reproduction of *the relation between the two classes, which is the capital relation*.

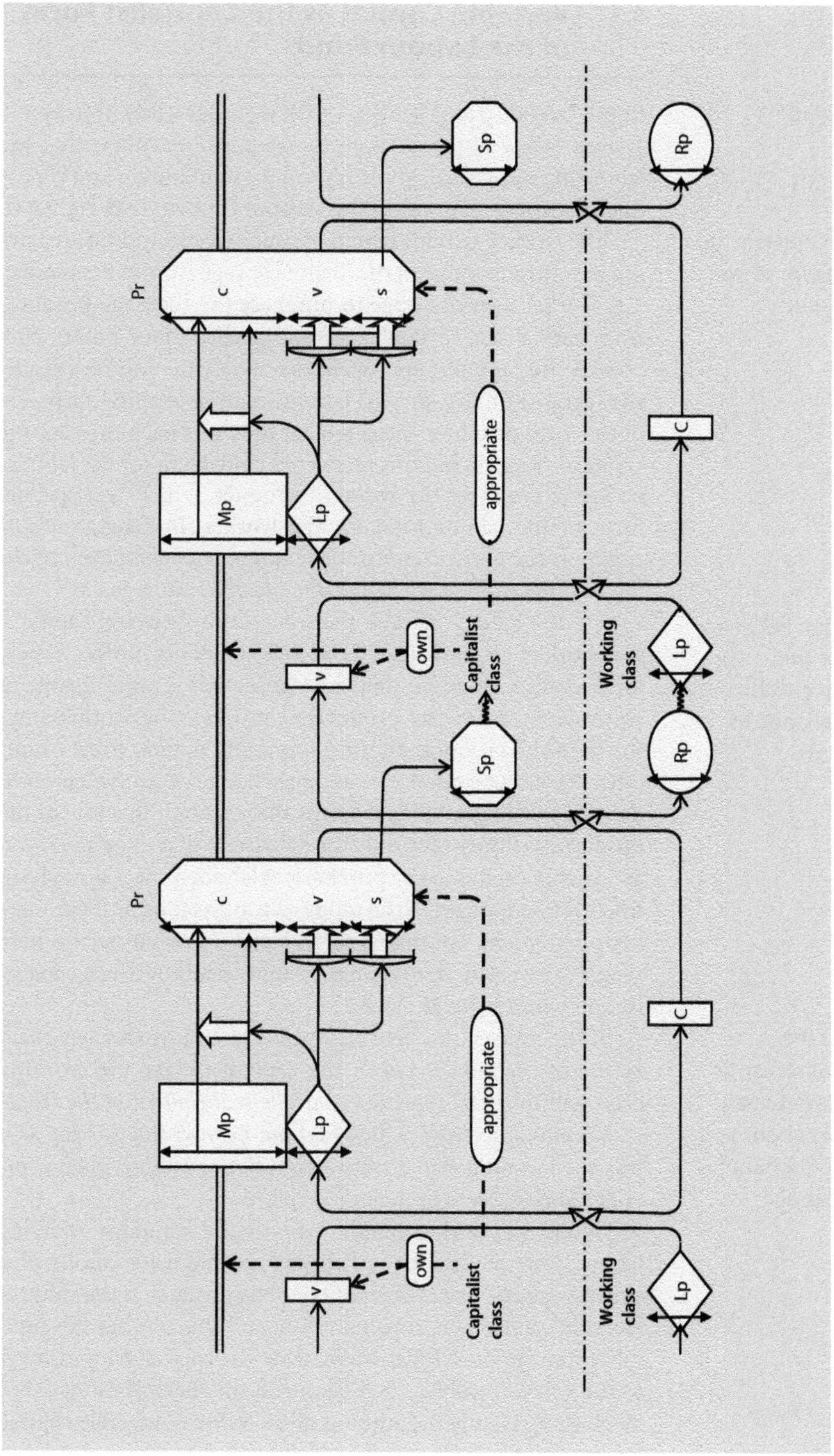

Fig. 8.1 Social reproduction under capitalist relations of production

8.3 Variable Capital as the Capitalist Form of the Labour Fund

Labour Fund

In the Introduction (▶ Sect. 1.4.2), we touched on how, in any system of social production, the requisite products that the labouring individuals must reproduce to maintain and reproduce themselves are called the «**labour fund**» (*see* ◘ Fig. 1.24).

Variable Capital Is the Specific Form of the Labour Fund

The worker sells his labour-power as a commodity, receiving in return its value in the form of a wage from the capitalist. The worker uses the wage to purchase the requisite products from capitalists. Through consuming the labour-power purchased, the capitalist appropriates not only the worker's requisite labour but also surplus labour in an objectified form, i.e. in the form of value. The capitalist thus gets back the variable capital advanced, but this recovered equivalent for the labour-power is precisely the worker's product, which is a specific form of the labour fund for the worker. In short, *variable capital is the particular historical and phenomenal form of the labour fund under the capitalist mode of production.*

Transaction Between Capitalist and Worker Seems to Be an Exchange of Equivalents

On the labour market, the transaction between capitalist and worker, i.e. the sale and purchase of labour-power, is performed at its value, so that the transaction is an exchange of equivalents. After the production process, the worker buys the requisite products on the commodity market from a capitalist. This transaction, too, is an exchange of equivalents. On the side of the capitalist, it seems that through this sale of the products to the worker, only the equal sum of money advanced as variable capital in the purchase of labour-power flows back into his hands again in the money form. As long as these market phenomena are observed in isolation, what occurs here seems to be solely an exchange of equivalents between capitalist and worker (*see* ◘ Fig. 8.2).

Reality of the Transaction Is an Exchange Between Requisite Labour and Requisite Labour Plus Surplus-labour

If the transaction between capitalist and worker is viewed as the transaction between the capitalist class and working class within social reproduction, *the real content of the transaction manifests itself*, which had not been visible as long as it was seen as an isolated transaction between individual capitalists and workers in the marketplace.

What the worker hands over to the capitalist is living labour, but the quantity of this is the requisite labour plus surplus-labour that is objectified to the product as the value of variable capital plus surplus-value, and this is what the capitalist appropriates. Meanwhile, what the capitalist hands over to the worker is objectified labour in the form of money; but its quantity is only the amount of the value of variable capital, i.e. the amount of the requisite labour.

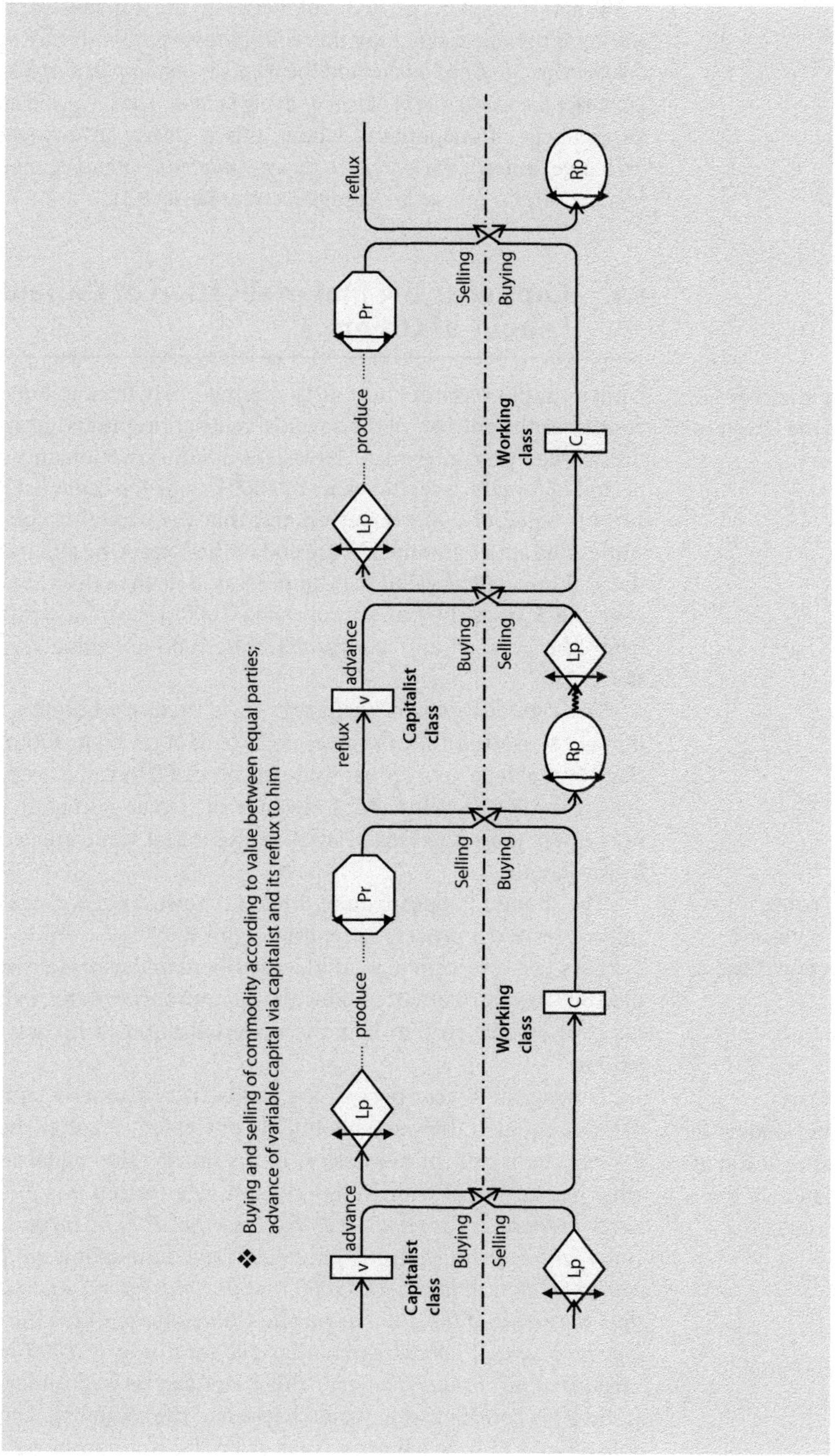

■ **Fig. 8.2** External form of the market transaction between capitalist and worker

What is actually carried out between the capitalist and worker is thus an exchange of the *requisite labour of the worker in the form of objectified labour* and the *requisite labour plus surplus-labour of the worker in the form of living labour*. Thus, viewed as an exchange of quantities of labour, this is clearly an unequal exchange. Indeed, *the worker is always unilaterally handing over his own surplus-labour to the capitalist* (*see* ◘ Fig. 8.3).

8.4 Capital as the Materialisation of Unpaid Labour of Others

Capitalist Insists: «My Capital Is the Result of My Labour»

Under simple reproduction, it is assumed that the capitalist consumes the entirety of the surplus-value appropriated from the worker year after year. Now let's assume that during a period of 5 years, a capital value of 1000 brings the capitalist a surplus-value of 200 every year and that the capitalist consumes this entire amount. At the end of the 5 years, he still has the 1000 in capital value that he possessed at the outset, but over the 5 years, he has appropriated 1000 in surplus-value from the worker and consumed this 1000 in value (*see* ◘ Fig. 8.4).

The capitalist would likely say: «It is precisely because I initially possessed 1000 in value, as the fruit of my own labour, that I was able to appropriate and consume 200 in value every year. The 1000 in value that I advance each year—no matter how many years this is repeated—is the initial value created by my labour».

Situation Looks Different if Viewed as Reproduction Process

The situation appears quite different, however, if we carefully observe the process as repeated reproduction.

Let's take our capitalist at his word here and assume that the 1000 in value he started off with was appropriated through his own labour, so that it is the materialisation of his own labour.

Capital in the Capitalist's Hands After 5 Years Is the Result of Appropriation of the Surplus-value for 5 Years

During the 5-year period, the capitalist consumes a sum of value equal to the value he initially possessed. Yet after the 5 years, he is still in possession of a sum of value equal to what he started off with. Why? What is clear is that *it is precisely because the capitalist has received the 1000 in surplus-value for free that he can still have 1000 in value despite having consumed that amount. The 1000 that he holds after 5 years is thus the result of the 1000 in surplus-value appropriated during the 5 years, merely representing the total sum of 1000 in surplus-value obtained for free*. This point can be well understood if we consider what would happen to the capitalist, who consumes 200 in value every year, if he did not appropriate

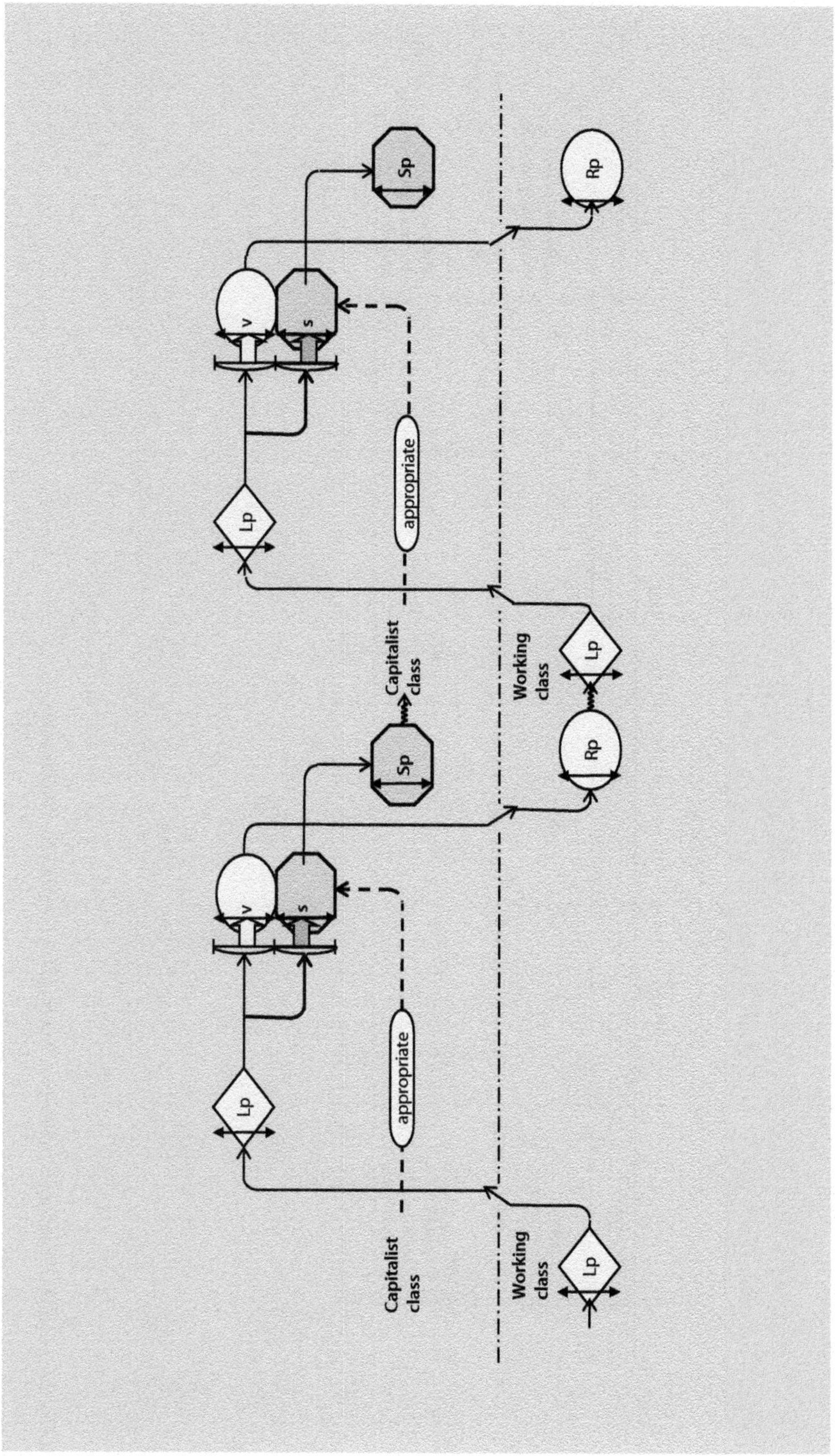

Fig. 8.3 Actual content of the transaction between capitalist class and working class

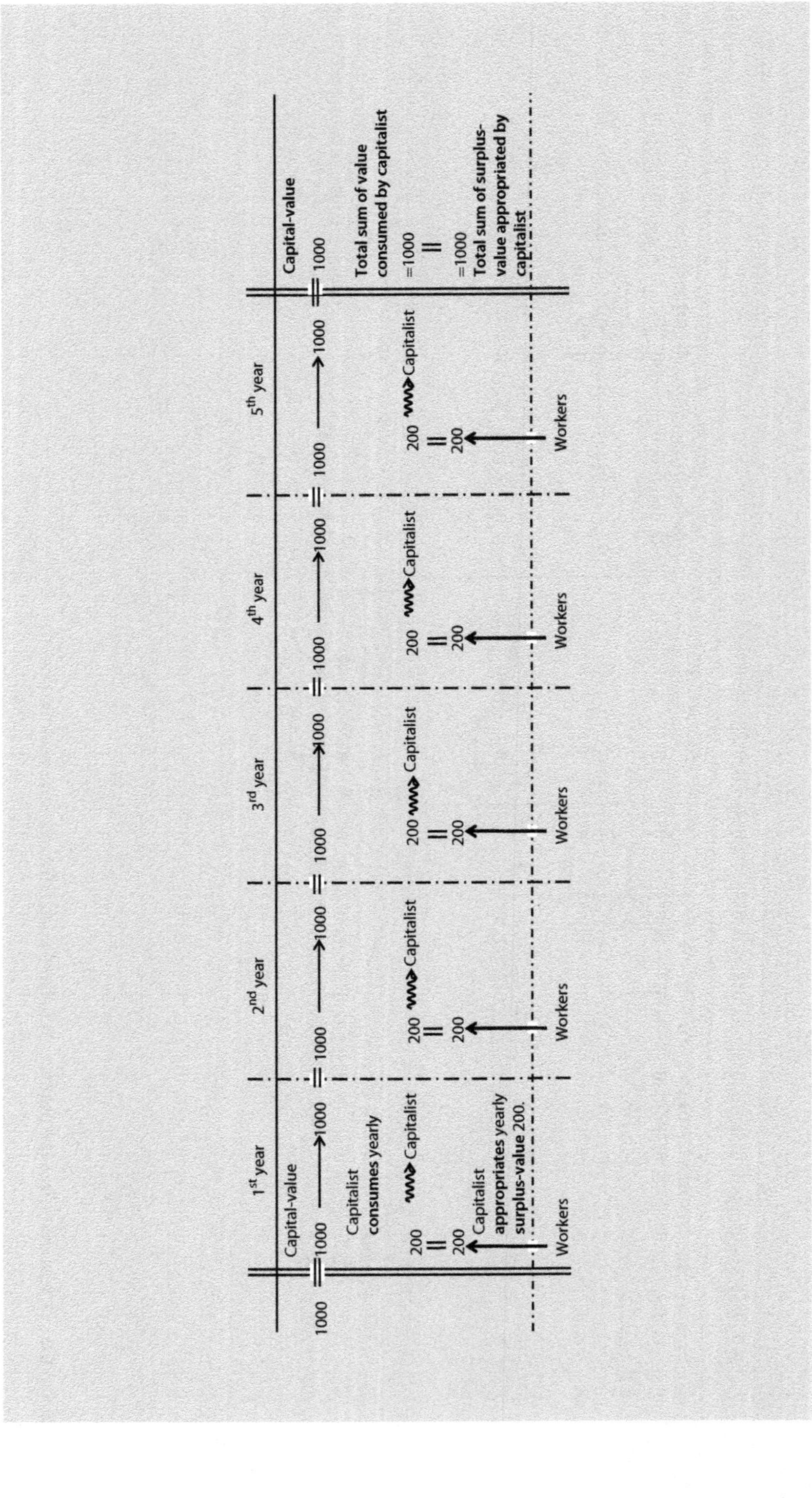

■ **Fig. 8.4** Capitalist consumes the surplus-value appropriated by his capital-value

any surplus-value during those years. In such a case, even if he had 1000 the first year, he would have no alternative but to consume 200 every year, reducing by that amount the sum of money that could be advanced as capital. After 5 years, the sum would reach zero and he would cease to be a capitalist. The fact that he is able to still exist as a capitalist at the end of 5 years, with 1000 in capital, is clearly the outcome of appropriating 200 surplus-value every year over the course of that period.

Capital Value Is Transformed into the Materialisation of the Labour of Others

The capitalist in our example has appropriated the materialisation of 1000 in value from another person's labour during a 5-year period. Since the capitalist is still in possession of 1000 in value after 5 years, having lived by consuming 200 per year, his 1000 is nothing but the materialisation of the labour of others. Even if the capital value the capitalist initially possessed was the materialisation of his own labour, the capital value he is now in possession of after 5 years is the **materialisation of the worker's surplus-value**, which is to say, the **materialisation of the labour of others**. Starting from the sixth year, the capitalist appropriates further surplus-value that is the materialisation of others' labour by means of capital value that is also purely the materialisation of the labour of others (*see* ◘ Fig. 8.5).

8.5 Reproduction of Capital-ownership Through Appropriating the Labour of Others

Surplus-value Must Be Appropriated for the Capitalist to Continue Existing as Such

Capital must be personally represented by a living individual, who possesses consciousness and will. Insofar as the capitalist, who is the personification of capital, is a living human being, he needs a consumption fund to continue to exist as a capitalist as well as a luxury fund to satisfy his desire for pleasure. The fund for his individual consumption and luxury is the surplus-value that he appropriates from the production process. He continues to be *the personification of 1000 of capital* over 5 years only *insofar as this 1000 functions as capital every year.* But *the continued existence of a living individual as a capitalist is the outcome of his continual appropriation of 200 in value from the labour of others in the production process every year.* Indeed, as Marx (1872) wrote: «The economic character mask of capitalist becomes firmly fixed to a man only if his money constantly functions *as capital.*» (Marx 1976, p. 711; Marx's emphasis as in the first German edition).

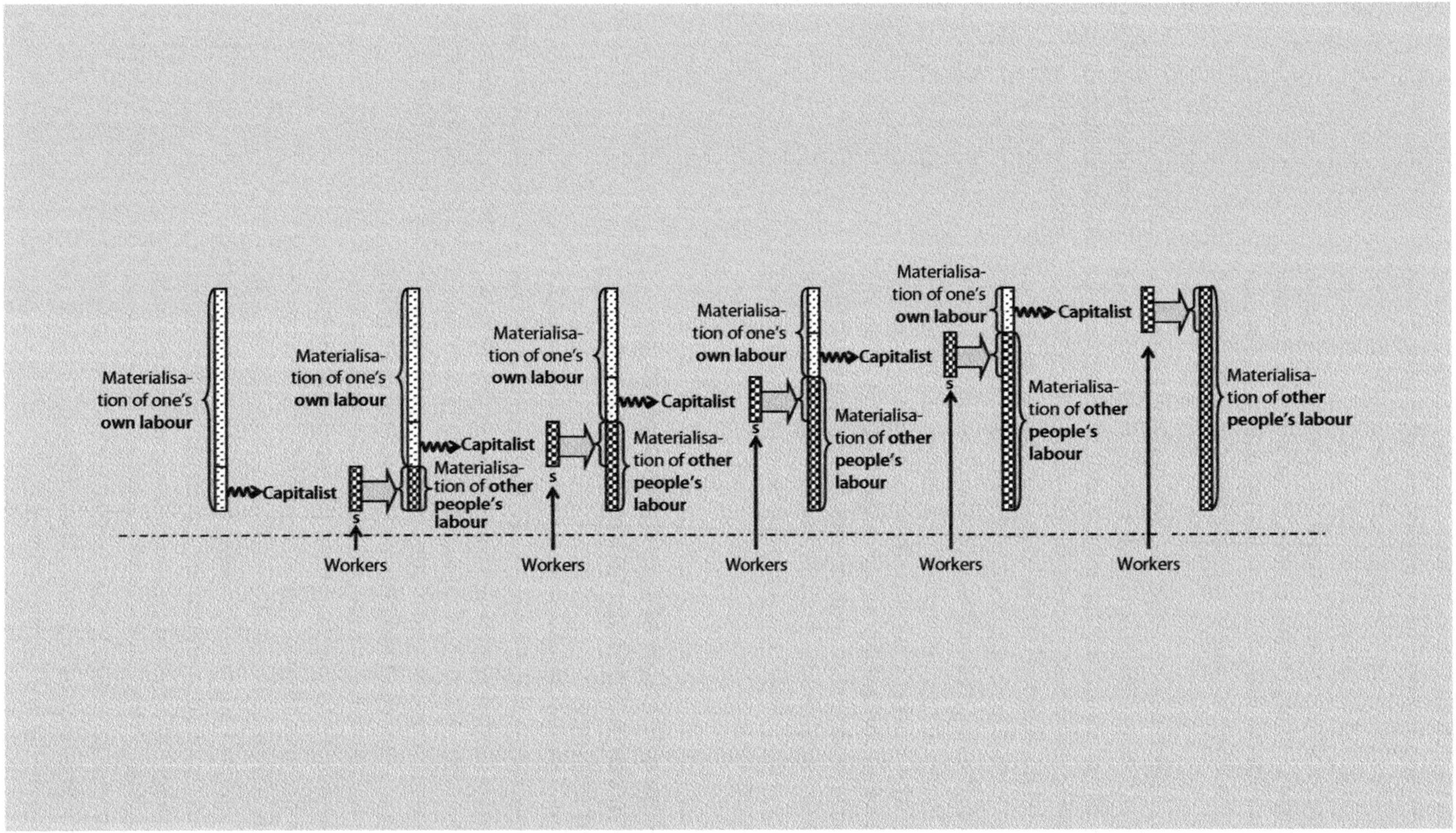

Fig. 8.5 Through the repetition of simple reproduction capital converts itself into capitalised surplus-value

The Capital Relation Itself Continues to Exist by Being Reproduced

At first glance, the capital relation, which is the relation of production between capitalists and workers, seems to continue to exist, as is, year after year. In particular, it seems that the pivot of this continuity is the capitalist's continued possession of capital, which he owned from the outset. In fact, however, as noted in the previous section, the capital relation is not an inorganic entity like a cornerstone, which cannot collapse once put in place unless some outside force is applied, but rather is *maintained by being constantly reproduced and formed through the labour of labouring individuals within the production process*. This is similar to how the human body is maintained by the infinite number of cells that compose it being replaced every day by newly created ones.

Ownership of Capital Is the Outcome of the Capitalist Appropriating Surplus-value

Moreover, the capitalist's *ownership of capital* is a *socially recognised relation between the thing capital, which is the reification of the capital relation, and the capitalist, who is the personification of this thing*. Capital-ownership, therefore, is not merely capital being reproduced as such: it also continues to exist as long as the capitalist, who is its personification, exists. And because this capitalist is a human being, his continued existence is dependent on the continual appropriation of the labour of others. It is through this appropriation that the ownership of capital can be maintained. In other words, *the ownership of capital by the capitalist* is always *being generated anew* by being continually *reproduced* from the *outcome of appropriating surplus-value* in the production process.

The Situation Is Clearer if Borrowed Capital Functions

Now let's imagine that a person with no money borrows 1000 in value from someone (assuming that the loan is free of interest) and makes it function as capital for a 5-year period, during which he appropriates 200 in surplus-value every year and that after 5 years he repays the 1000. Once the loan had been repaid, he would return to his penniless state and cease to be a capitalist. In this case, the fact that he was able to exist as a capitalist for 5 years was not because *he held on to* 1000 in value during the 5 years. Indeed, if the 1000 *had not functioned as capital*, he would have consumed the 1000 during the 5 years, leaving him with nothing but the debt for that amount. The reason the capitalist is instead able to still have 1000, and was able to consume 200 in value every year, is that during those 5 years, he made the 1000 in value *function as capital* and was thus able to appropriate 200 in surplus-value from workers each year. It is precisely because of *appropriating this unpaid labour* that the capitalist is able to exist as a capitalist for a period of 5 years.

Even if, during the 5-year period, he had been able to live without consuming the 200 of surplus-value or had somehow been able to procure a separate consumption fund to last the 5 years, so that even after repaying the 1000 by the end of that period he would have a total of 1000 in value appropriated from workers, it would still be clear that this value is the mass of surplus-value appropriated from the workers.

As Reproduction Progresses Capital-ownership Is Transformed into the Outcome of Appropriating the Labour of Others

In short, the capital value owned by the capitalist must sooner or later, through the progression of reproduction, be transformed into the *materialisation of the appropriated labour of others*, so that the *ownership of capital value by the capitalist* (even if initially the result of his own labour) is transformed *into the outcome of the appropriation of others' labour*, i.e. *transformed into the outcome of exploitation carried out in the production process.*

Reference

Marx K (1872) Das Kapital. Kritik der politischen Oekonomie. Bd. 1. Buch 1: Der Produktionsprocess des Kapitals. 2. verb. Aufl. Hamburg. English edition: Marx K (1976) Capital. A critique of political economy. Vol. 1 (trans: Howkes B). Penguin Books, Harmondsworth

Accumulation of Capital

T. Otani, *A Guide to Marxian Political Economy*,
https://doi.org/10.1007/978-3-319-65954-1_9

9.1 Chapter Structure

In ▸ Chap. 8, we considered the reproduction of capital on the premise of simple reproduction. And now we will consider reproduction on an expanded scale or **expanded reproduction**. Expanded reproduction under capitalist production is carried out by using surplus-value as capital, which is to say, the transformation of surplus-value into capital. The transformation of the surplus-value generated by capital back into capital is the **accumulation of capital**. The study of the accumulation of capital ultimately clarifies how capital is generated from surplus-value. Moreover, since the actual development of capitalist production is carried out as constantly expanding reproduction via capital accumulation, the content of this chapter is an important premise for the topics we will examine subsequently.

9.2 Accumulation of Capital and Expanded Reproduction of the Capital Relation

Surplus-Value → Additional Constant Capital + Additional Variable Capital + Revenue of Capitalist

The accumulation of capital is the transformation of the surplus-value generated by capital back into capital. In other words, the capital advanced is augmented by surplus-value being transformed into the **additional capital** added to the **original capital**.

Capital is composed of the constant capital advanced in the means of production and the variable capital advanced in labour-power, so under normal conditions, the additional capital must be composed of additional constant capital transformed into additional means of production and additional variable capital transformed into additional labour-power.

Let us assume that one part of the surplus-value is accumulated and another part is consumed by the capitalist. In this case, surplus-value must be divided into two parts: the **accumulation fund** and the **capitalist's consumption fund**. When the accumulation fund is advanced as capital, it becomes additional capital.[1]

Additional capital is further divided into **additional constant capital** and **additional variable capital**. If we express

1 The assumption in this chapter is that the accumulation funds are immediately advanced as additional capital. But in ordinary practice, accumulation funds are only advanced as additional capital in the production process once they have been amassed to a certain amount (*see* ▸ Sect. 14.4.3 in Part II).

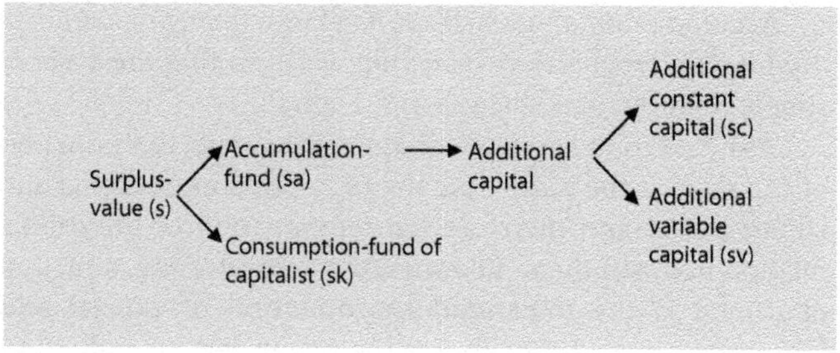

Fig. 9.1 Divided parts of surplus-value

the capitalist's consumption fund as *sk*, the additional capital as *sa*, the additional constant capital as *sc*, and the additional variable capital as *sv*, then the surplus-value (*s*) can be broken down as above (*see* Fig. 9.1).

Assumption that Additional Means of Production Are Available on the Market

It must be possible to transform the additional constant capital—on the market—into the necessary means of production (additional means of production). From the standpoint of individual capital, it is sufficient as long as some other individual capital produces these means of production and offers them on the market as a commodity. Meanwhile, from the perspective of the total social capital, these means of production must exist within the aggregate annual product. And our assumption here is that the means of production are available on the market.

Additional Assumption that Labour-power Is Available on the Labour Market

The additional variable capital must be able to find additional new labour-power on the labour market. From the standpoint of individual capital, it is sufficient as long as labour-power can be purchased on the labour market. Meanwhile, from the perspective of total social capital, there must appear on the market additional workers beyond those workers utilised by the original capital. However, the mechanism of capitalist production provides for this by reproducing the working class as a class dependent on wages, a class whose ordinary wages suffice to not only maintain itself but also increase its numbers. The reproduction costs that determine the value of labour-power (as we saw in ► Sect. 3.1.3) include the socially average familial costs for raising a family, so as to augment the labouring population. Thus, additional variable capital has only to purchase labour-power that additionally appears on the market in this manner. Of course, these additional workers require means of livelihood, which must be found within the aggregate annual product. But since there are surplus products within that aggregate, no problem arises as long as a portion of the surplus products takes the form of the means of livelihood for additional workers.

Accumulation Transforms Capital Reproduction into a Spiral

Accumulation, thus, resolves itself into the *reproduction of capital on a progressively increasing scale*, so that the cycle of simple reproduction changes into a spiral.

Expanded Reproduction of Capital Is the Expanded Reproduction of the Capital Relation

As noted in the previous chapter, the simple reproduction of capital is at the same time the reproduction of capital and labour-power and therefore the reproduction of the capital relation between them. Likewise, the expanded reproduction of capital is the **expanded reproduction of capital and labour-power** and therefore is the **expanded reproduction of the capital/wage-labour relation** (*see* ◘ Fig. 9.2).

9.3 Inversion of the Property Laws of Commodity Production into the Laws of Capitalist Appropriation

The Capitalist Insists: «Capital Was the Result of My Own Labour!»

Our assumption here again will be that a capitalist has advanced 1000 in value and then appropriates 200 in surplus-value, all of which is subsequently advanced as additional capital.

Where does the capitalist get this 1000 in capital? The capitalists and the economists who defend their interests respond in unison that this capital was the fruit of the capitalists' own labour or that of their forbearers. But we have already seen that, even seen from the perspective of simple reproduction, all capital is transformed into a mass of unpaid labour of others through the recurrence of reproduction and that capital-ownership is also reproduced through the appropriation of unpaid labour. But, for now, let us accept the capitalist's view of the situation.

Property Laws of Commodity Production

As we saw in ► Sect. 2.4.3, commodity holders in the sphere of commodity exchange recognise each other as private owners, but in so doing, they do not concern themselves with how the other person came to possess his commodity. Instead, they can only assume that this other person obtained it through his own labour. This socially accepted assumption that a private owner's property title stems from own labour is the **property laws of commodity production**.

When the capitalist initially appears on the market with 1000 and purchases means of production and labour-power at their value, those involved in the commodity and labour markets do not care how he came into possession of the 1000 in value, provided he is the proper owner of that sum. Those involved in the transaction all assume with regard to each other that commodities and money were obtained through their own labour, with each quite content to declare: «I worked

Premises:

- ❖ Being able to purchase the additional means of production necessary at their value on the commodity market.
- ❖ Being able to purchase the additional labour-power necessary at its value on the labour market.
- ❖ Capitalist accumulates one part of the surplus-value and consumes another part as revenue.

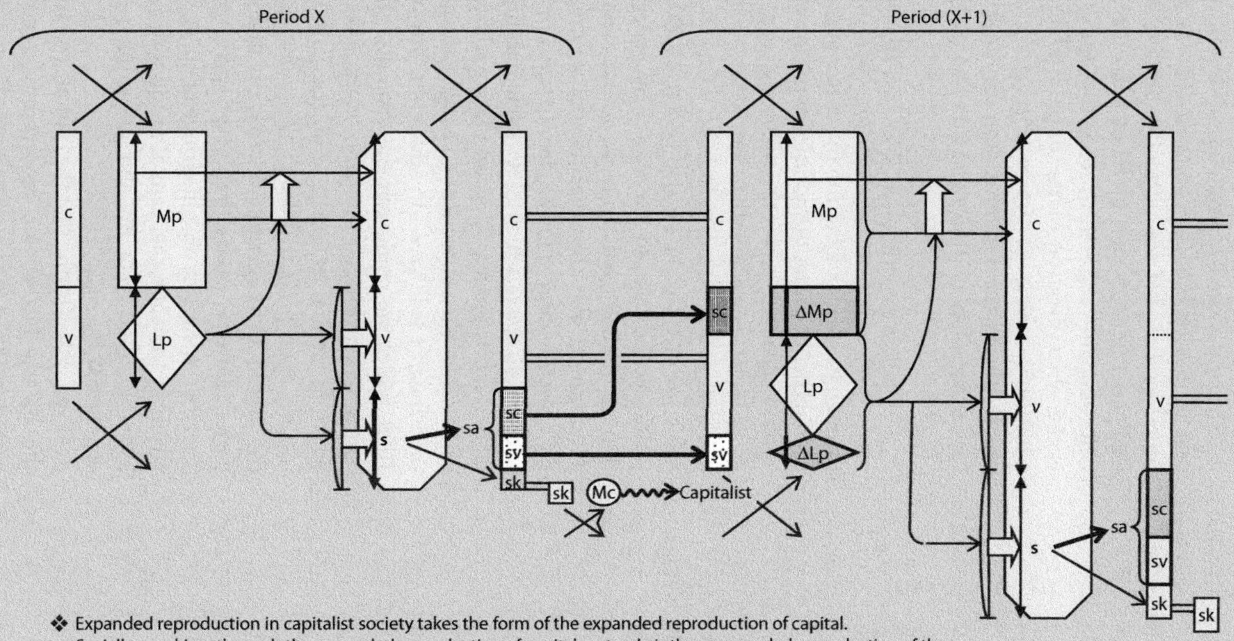

- ❖ Expanded reproduction in capitalist society takes the form of the expanded reproduction of capital.
- ❖ Socially speaking, through the expanded reproduction of capital, not only is there expanded reproduction of the products, and therefore of capital as well, but also expanded reproduction of the capital/wage-labour relation.

Fig. 9.2 Accumulation of capital = conversion of surplus-value into capital = expanded reproduction of the capital relation

to save up this 1000» or «It was obtained through my parents' hard work». And it seems that this is the only assumption that could be made, according to the property laws of commodity production.

Additional Capital Formed from Surplus-value Is the Objectification of Unpaid Labour

The situation is completely different, however, in the case of the 200 that the capitalist seeks to advance as additional capital. We are perfectly familiar with the process that generates this sum of value, knowing that it was originally surplus-value. This means that the 200 in its entirety is the objectification of the unpaid labour of others. The additional means of production and additional labour-power purchased with this sum are nothing more than a new form taken by this value *qua* objectification of unpaid labour.

Viewed as a transaction between the capitalist class and working class, we have a situation where the working class, through its surplus-labour in the current year, creates the new capital that becomes the additional means of production and additional labour-power the following year.

Appropriating the Labour of Others Through Objectifying Their Labour

Now let us assume that the 200 is advanced in the second year as additional capital and yields 40 in surplus-value. Since the original capital also generates 200 in surplus-value in the second year, by the third year, there is 440 (in addition to the 1000) that can be advanced as capital. Not only is 400 unmistakably the objectification of unpaid labour, 40 is the objectification of unpaid labour appropriated through the additional capital, which itself is the objectification of unpaid labour. If this process of accumulating all the surplus-value is repeated for the subsequent 4 years, by the end of that period the capitalist will have—in addition to his original capital of 1000, which we could call the «parent»—the surplus-value appropriated through the parent capital during the 4 years, which is the first to fourth «children» and the surplus-value in turn appropriated through this, which could be labelled the first to sixth «grandchildren», the first to fourth «great-grandchildren», and the first «great-great-grandchild». Together this forms an «offspring» of 1074. So if the capitalist advances the aggregate capital in the fifth year, there will be 2074 of capital («parent» and «offspring») in operation that year (*see* ◘ Fig. 9.3).

Even if we assume that the capitalist possessed the 1000 of the 2074 to begin with, he certainly cannot claim that the remaining 1074 in value was created through his own labour. As long as it is recognised that the 200 in surplus-value appropriated every year from the 1000 in capital is the objectification of surplus-labour, then this 1074 in value is, from top to

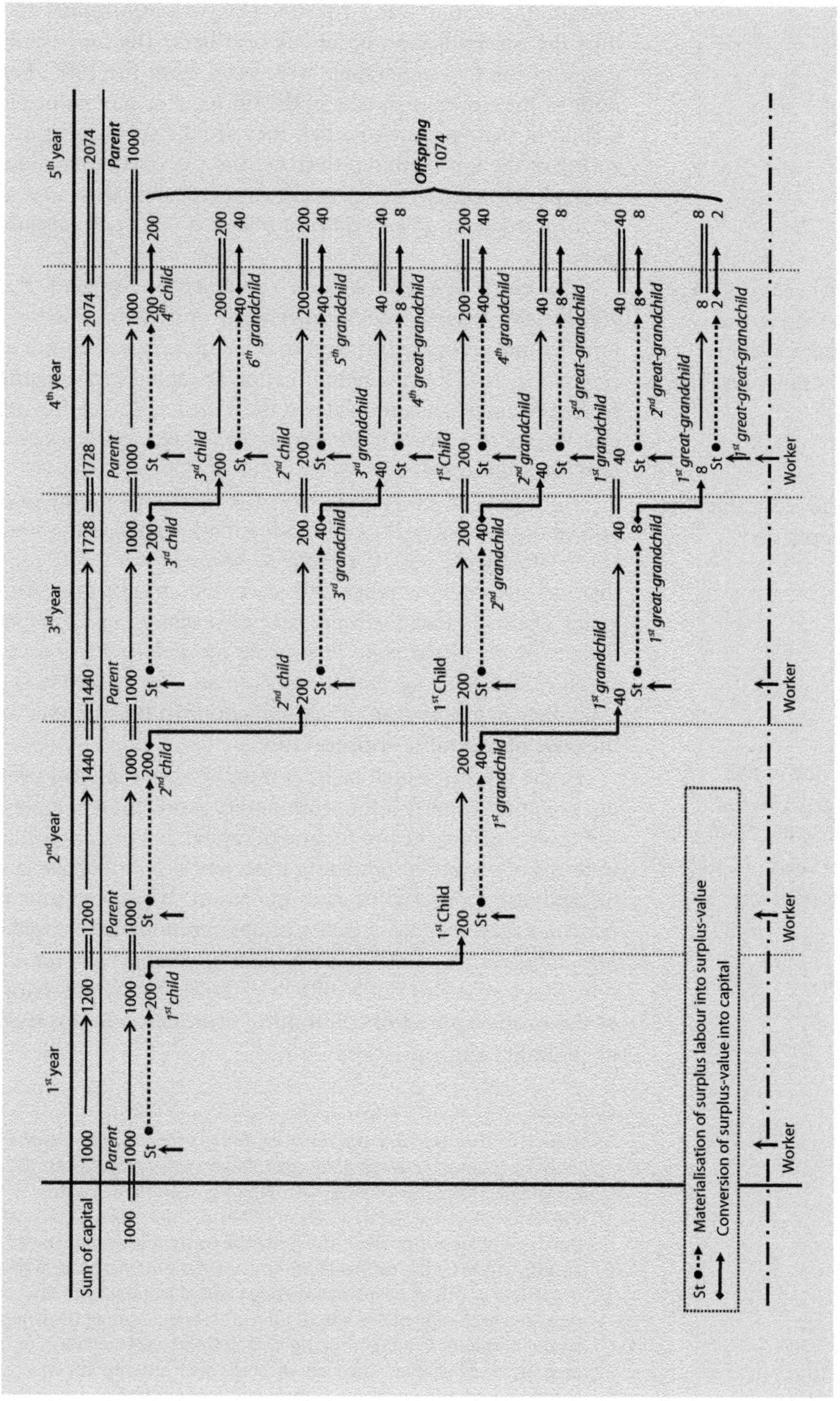

■ Fig. 9.3 Law of appropriation is inverted through the progression of accumulation

bottom, the surplus-value transformed back into capital and thus the objectification of labour of others. The four «children» in the first generation were born from the 1000, but none of the eleven members of the subsequent generations is a child of that «parent». Rather, they are the subsequent offspring of the four children that themselves constitute a mass of surplus-labour. In other words, we are dealing with *a mass of surplus-labour appropriated through a mass of surplus-labour.*

Capital-value Initially Possessed by the Capitalist Becomes Infinitesimal over Time

The more the reproduction of capital is repeated, the smaller the *original capital* advanced, until it becomes an *infinitesimal* amount. The *surplus-value transformed back into capital*, whether it is made to function as capital in the hands of the person who accumulated it or in the hands of someone else, comes to represent the *overwhelming part of the capital that currently exists.*

The Laws of Capitalist Appropriation

The capitalist every year buys the means of production and labour-power on the commodity market and labour market in accordance with the property laws of commodity production in order to repeatedly carry out production. The result of this is that *the capitalist appropriates unpaid living labour on an increasingly large scale by making the unpaid surplus-labour of others function as capital.* Marx refers to the capitalist's appropriation of unpaid labour in this manner as the **laws of capitalist appropriation.**

Inversion of the Property Laws of Commodity Production in the Laws of Capitalist Appropriation

In the market, which is the surface layer of capitalist production, the property law of commodity production operates. But if we consider the production of capital that underlies this in terms of social reproduction, it becomes clear that the law of capitalist appropriation is in operation. *Where the capital relation exists, the law of capitalist appropriation is the necessary consequence of the property laws of commodity production.* Marx expresses this reality by referring to **the inversion of the property laws of commodity production in the laws of capitalist appropriation.**[2]

2 Marx (1872) writes: «*The relation of exchange between capitalist and worker* becomes *a mere semblance belonging only to the process of circulation*, it becomes *a mere form*, which is alien to the content of the transaction itself, and merely mystifies it. The constant sale and purchase of labour-power is the form; the content is the constant appropriation by the capitalist, without equivalent, of a portion of the labour of others which has already been objectified, and his repeated exchange of this labour for a greater quantity of the living labour of others. Originally the rights of property seemed to us to be grounded in a man's own labour. Some such assumption was at least necessary, since only commodity-owners with equal rights

Behaviour of Labouring Individuals Within the Production Process Generates Capitalist Ownership

The surplus-value *qua* objectification of the surplus-labour of another person, which the capitalist appropriates in the production process, is turned into capital; and the *ownership of this capital value* is thus the *result of the appropriation of surplus-value* in the production process. The capitalist's appropriation of surplus-value in the production process precedes, and brings about, his ownership of capital. Here it is *precisely the production of surplus-value by the labouring individuals within the production process that generates capital-ownership.*

At first glance, there seemed to be a vicious circle with regard to capitalist ownership of the means of production by the capitalist and his appropriation of surplus-value, wherein the latter is only possible through the former, but the latter always generates the former. However, within this relation, the *active determining moment that continues capitalist production as such* is the constant reproduction of products within the production process by the labouring individuals and the constant production of surplus-value. Labouring individuals are the active subject of continual production, regardless of the form of society, but under capitalist production, we have a situation where *labouring individuals* completely separated from the conditions of labour *come into contact with the means of production in the production process as things belonging to others, which means that the resulting surplus-labour always belongs to others as well, and through this there is the continual reproduction of capital and wage-labour and the relation between them.* Thus, in terms of the capitalist ownership of the means of production, and the capitalists' appropriation of surplus-value, it cannot be said that the former is the immovable premise or even that it is a vicious circle where it cannot be said which of the two comes

---

confronted each other, and the sole means of appropriating the commodities of others was the alienation of a man's own commodities, commodities which, however, could only be produced by labour. Now, however, property turns out to be the *right*, on the part of the capitalist, to appropriate the *unpaid labour of others* or its product, and the impossibility, on the part of worker, of appropriating his own product. The *separation of property from labour* thus becomes the necessary consequence of a law that apparently originated in their *identity*.... / To the extent that commodity production, in accordance with its own immanent laws, undergoes a further development into capitalist production, the property laws of commodity production must undergo a dialectical inversion so that they become laws of capitalist appropriation» (Marx 1976, pp. 729–730 and 733–734; Marx's emphasis as in the first German edition).

first. Rather, *it is precisely the behaviour of the labouring individuals within the production process that is always generating the ownership of the means of production by the capitalist.*

This point can be well understood if we consider what would happen if the labouring individuals were to cease producing surplus-value in the production process. For example, if the working class, after sufficient preparation, were to carry out a nationwide general strike so that production throughout the country was halted or ceased over an extended period of time, not only would capitalists be unable to appropriate surplus-value, but the use-value of the means of production would gradually be lost, placing the ownership of the means of production in peril. This is exactly why a strike is an extremely powerful means of struggle for workers. Further, if the labouring individuals were to begin relating to the means of production in the production process not as belonging to others but rather as belonging to themselves, this would of course mean the end of capitalist appropriation as well as capitalist ownership, and what would subsequently emerge would be a different type of production than capitalist production.[3]

As we shall see later in ▶ Chap. 11, what forms the starting point of capitalist production is the separation of labouring individuals from the conditions of labour, and this separation generates the **bourgeoisie** on one side and the **proletariat** on the other. But this separation process itself is not yet the beginning of capitalist production. As Marx (1872) says, for capitalist production, «it is not enough that the conditions of labour are concentrated at one pole of society in the shape of capital, while at the other pole are grouped masses of men who have nothing to sell but their labour-power» (Marx 1976, p. 899), and capitalist production relations, i.e. relations between human beings *within production*, are first established when, *in the production process*, the latter behaves towards the conditions of labour *as dealing with capital*. And it is this initi-

3 With regard to the significance of a change in the consciousness of labouring individuals, Marx (1861–1863) writes: «The recognition of the product as its own, and its awareness that its separation from the conditions of its realisation is an injustice—*a relationship imposed by force*—is an enormous consciousness, *itself the product* of the capitalist mode of production and just as much the knell to its doom as the consciousness of the slave that he *could not be* the *property of another* reduced slavery to an artificial, lingering existence, and made it impossible for it to continue to provide the basis of production» (Marx 1975, p. 246; Marx's emphasis). We will further consider this issue in ▶ Sect. 11.2.2.

ated capitalist production and its repetition in the reproduction process that lead to the appropriation of the surplus labour of others by the capitalist and the resulting continual reproduction of the capitalist's ownership of the means of production.[4]

References

Marx K (1861-1863) Zur Kritik der politischen Ökonomie (Manuskript 1861–1863). MEGA II/3, Dietz-Verlag, Berlin 1976–1982. English edition: Marx (1975) Economic Manuscript 1861–1863. Collected Works, vol 34. Progress Publishers et al. New York.

Marx K (1872) Das Kapital. Kritik der politischen Oekonomie. Bd. 1. Buch 1: Der Produktionsprocess des Kapitals. 2. verb. Aufl. Hamburg. English edition: Marx K (1976) Capital. A Critique of Political Economy, vol 1 (trans: Howkes B). Penguin Books, Harmondsworth

4 From the above, the reader can grasp the fallacy of the common belief that the capitalist relations of production come down to the *capitalist's property relation towards the means of production*. It is a completely upside-down view to see the pivot of relations of *production* in the property relations, which is the relation of mutual recognition between economic persons *outside the production process*. Rather, what constitutes the core of the capitalist relations of production is that, in the production process, the labouring individuals relate to the means of production separated from them in the manner of dealing with capital, i.e. as something belonging to others. Capitalist ownership is a legal relation that is constructed on the basis of the relations of production.

We saw in ► Sect. 1.4.3 of the Introduction that in precapitalist forms of society—i.e. forms based on a community and the petty producer's mode of production—the ownership of the means of production is premised on the labour of labouring individuals. In the capitalist mode of production, this relation between ownership of the means of production and the labour of labouring individuals is completely inverted. Namely, what generates and reproduces the capitalist ownership of the means of production is precisely the relationship vis-à-vis the means of production by the labouring individuals who are separated from those means of production.

Accumulation of Capital and Relative Surplus Population

T. Otani, *A Guide to Marxian Political Economy*,
https://doi.org/10.1007/978-3-319-65954-1_10

10.1 Composition of Capital and Its Heightening

10.1.1 Composition of Capital

Composition of Capital

We have already seen that advanced capital is composed of constant capital and variable capital, with the constant capital becoming the means of production employed and the variable capital becoming the labour-power that should further become labour employed. It is vitally important to focus on the relative magnitudes of these two clearly distinguished parts of advanced capital when observing the *influence of capital accumulation on the working class*. The proportion between the two parts is called the **composition of capital** or the **capital composition** for short.

Value Composition of Capital

Capital, seen from the aspect of the value of the advanced capital, is composed of constant and variable capital. The magnitude of the constant capital is determined by the value of the means of production employed, while the magnitude of the variable capital is determined by the value of the labour-power employed. And the composition from this perspective is referred to as the **value composition of capital**.

Technical Composition of Capital

If we look at the aspect of the materials that function in the production process, capital is composed of the means of production and the labour-power employed. But the proportion between the two is technically determined by the quantity of the means of production employed and the quantity of labour necessary for their employment. The composition seen from this perspective is referred to as the **technical composition of capital** (*see* ◘ Fig. 10.1).

Organic Composition of Capital

The value composition of capital can change even if the technical composition of capital remains the same, through changes in the respective value or price of the means of

Technical composition of capital	Value composition of capital
Composition of capital seen from the aspect of the materials functioning in the production process	Composition of capital seen from the aspect of value
[Quantity of means of production employed] / [Quantity of labour employed]	[Constant capital (c) = Value of means of production] / [Variable capital (v) = Value of labour-power]

◘ **Fig. 10.1** Technical composition of capital and value composition of capital

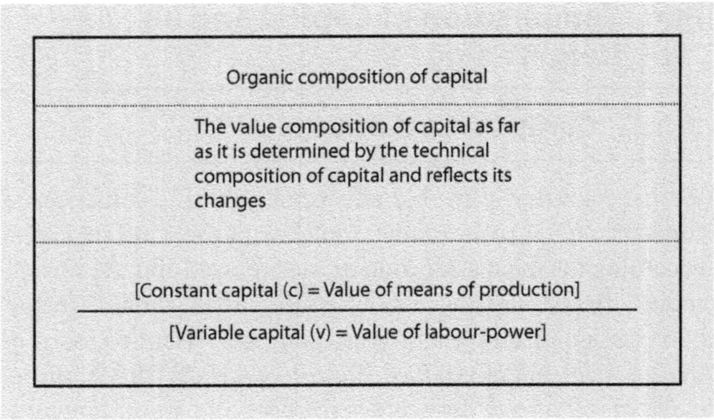

Fig. 10.2 Organic composition of capital

production and labour-power. However, if the value of the means of production and of labour-power remains unchanged, any change in the value composition of capital will reflect a change in the technical composition of capital. The most decisively important of the changes that emerge in the value composition of capital over the development of capitalist production are those that reflect a change in the technical composition of capital *brought about by the development of productive power*. The value composition of capital that is determined by, and reflects changes in, the value composition of capital is called the **organic composition of capital** (*see* Fig. 10.2). Hereinafter, unless some other indication is made, the term «composition of capital» will refer to the organic composition of capital.

10.1.2 Heightening of Capital Composition

Heightening of Capital Composition

An increase in the quantity of the means of production, or in their value relative to the quantity of labour or value of labour-power, is described as a **heightening of the capital composition**. Therefore, in terms of the technical composition, this is an increase in the quantity of the means of production employed by the same amount of labour, while in terms of the value composition or organic composition, this is an increase in the part c of advanced capital compared to the part v.

Manner of Expressing the Capital Composition

The capital composition can be expressed by setting the advanced capital at 100 and looking at the respective proportions of c and v (*see* Fig. 10.3).

$$60c + 40v \xrightarrow{\text{Heighten}} 70c + 30v \xrightarrow{\text{Heighten}} 80c + 20v \xrightarrow{\text{Heighten}} 90c + 10v$$

Fig. 10.3 Heightening of capital composition

10.2 Accumulation of Capital and Wage Fluctuations

10.2.1 Accumulation Under an Unchanged Capital Composition Increases the Demand for Labour-power at the Same Tempo as Accumulation

Accumulation Under an Unchanged Capital Composition Increases Demand for Labour

The individual capitals advanced in a particular branch of production have various compositions. The average of these compositions gives us the composition of the total capital in each branch of production. The average of all these average compositions for every branch of production gives us the **composition of the total capital of a society**, which is the topic that this chapter will exclusively concern itself with.

If capital accumulation (i.e. the conversion of surplus-value into capital ($s \to sc + sv$)) in a society progresses without any change in the capital composition, v will increase at the same tempo as the total social capital, which enhances demand for labour to the same degree.[1]

The Limit to Wage Rises Resulting from Increased Demand for Labour

There will be a rise in wages in the above case that accompanies the progression of accumulation (provided other conditions remain unchanged), but if accumulation continues, the rise in wages cannot continue unabated. This is because the rise in wages comes at the expense of a decrease in surplus-value. So unless prices are rising, at some point in time the **valorisation desire of capital** will decline, leading to sluggish accumulation.

10.2.2 Capital Accumulation Determines Wage Fluctuations

Lassalle's «Ironclad Law of Wages»

Various superficial explanations of wage fluctuations have been put forth. One typical mistaken view was the nineteenth

1 In reality, though, this «intermediate pause» only manifests itself during a certain phase of the industrial cycle.

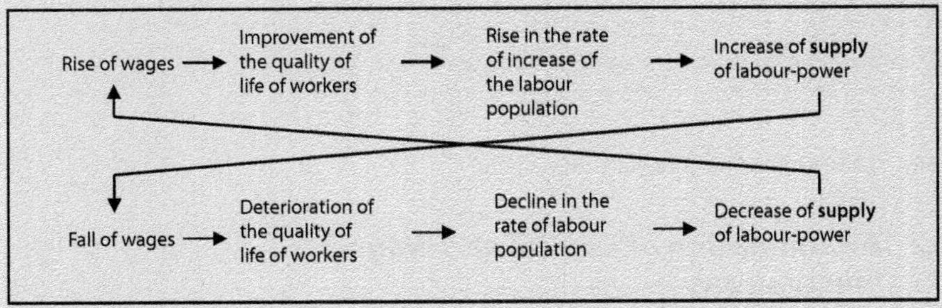

Fig. 10.4 Lassalle's view: Ironclad law of wages

century «**ironclad law of wages**» propounded by *Ferdinand Lassalle* (1825–1864), which exercised a considerable influence on the labour movement for a while. Lassalle said that an increase in wages would improve the lives of workers and raise the growth rate of the labour population, which in turn would increase the supply of labour-power, resulting in lowering of wages. Conversely, if wages were to be lowered, the living conditions of workers would worsen, so that there would be a decrease in the growth rate of the labour population that would decrease the supply of labour-power, resulting in a rise in wages. Viewing this cycle as inescapable, Lassalle argued that the effort to raise wages, even if successful, would be useless because one would end up again at the same point (*see* Fig. 10.4).

Error in the «Ironclad Law of Wages»

The groundlessness of Lassalle's argument is clear if we consider that it takes decades for an increase or decrease in the birth rate of workers to raise or lower the supply of labour-power and that it cannot be said that an improvement or worsening of workers' living conditions raises or lowers the number of members of a worker's family. However, Lassalle's *decisive error is to make wages an independent variable, treating the supply and demand for labour-power solely as a question of supply.* Wages are in fact a *dependent variable.* And what is decisively important to the supply and demand for labour-power is *capital's* demand for labour-power.

Capital Accumulation Determines Wage Fluctuations

The accumulation of capital is what determines wage fluctuations. Capital accumulation is the *independent variable* and must be taken as the starting point. Wage fluctuations arise as a result of fluctuating demand for labour-power,

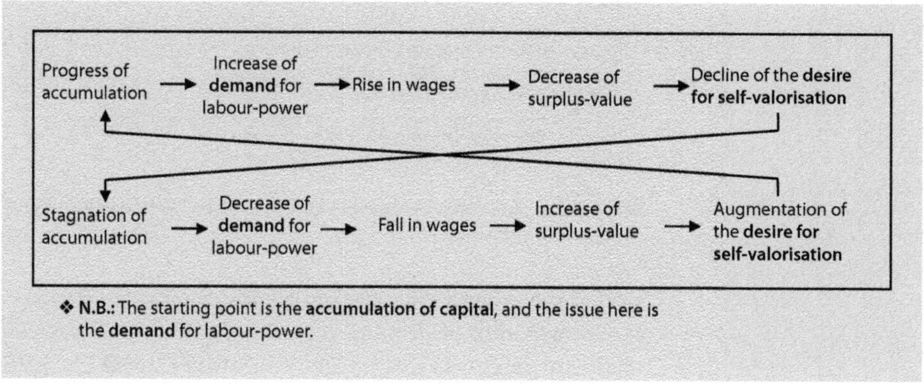

Fig. 10.5 Capital accumulation determines wage fluctuations (not *vice versa*)

which depend on the state of capital accumulation. Capitalist production, however, is the production of surplus-value, so the impulse for capital accumulation will necessarily change depending on an increase or decrease in surplus-value due to a decrease or increase in wages. *Wage fluctuations are determined by the production of surplus-value—and more concretely by the state of capital accumulation based on capital's desire for valorisation* (*see* Fig. 10.5).

10.3 Capital Accumulation Accompanying a Heightening of the Capital Composition and Fluctuations in Demand for Labour-power

10.3.1 Capital Accumulation Accompanying a Heightening of the Capital Composition and an Increase or Decrease in Variable Capital

As the Capital Composition Heightens, Variable Capital Increases at a Lower Rate than Capital as a Whole

As capital accumulation progresses, the development of the productive power of labour becomes a lever for accumulation. In this way, the capital accumulation and the development of the productive power of labour progress via mutual interaction. The inevitable result is a heightening of the capital composition. Because the capital newly advanced includes variable capital, accumulation absolutely increases the demand for labour-power to the same extent. But *when this is accompanied by a heightening of the capital composition*, the proportion of variable capital to constant capital will decrease relatively,

Development of productive power of labour
⇨ Heightening of technical composition of capital
⇨ Heightening of value composition of capital
⇨ Relative decrease in variable capital compared to constant capital

Fig. 10.6 Relative decrease in variable capital due to a heightening of capital composition

so that the growth rate of the variable capital—and therefore the *growth rate of demand for labour-power—will decrease relative to the growth rate for capital as a whole* (*see* Fig. 10.6). However, since the value of the means of production falls with the development of productive power, the heightening of the value composition does not progress at the same tempo as the heightening of the technical composition.

10.3.2 Centralisation of Capital and Increase or Decrease of Variable Capital

Demand for Labour Decreases Due to a Heightening of the Composition of Existing Capital via Centralisation of Capital

As accumulation progresses, there is a splitting or branching off of one part of the total social capital into many individual capitals, thereby increasing the number of individual capitals. But, at the same time, there is a **centralisation of capital** that progresses through the *amalgamation and merging of existing capitals* and the *absorption of bankrupted capitals*, resulting in the increased size of one segment of the individual capitals and a decrease in the number of individual capitals. One lever that powerfully accelerates this process is the *competition between capitals and the banking system*, as well as the *establishment of joint-stock companies* connected to the banking system. In this process, the productive power of capital increases rapidly, while the technical composition of capital heightens, thus decreasing demand for labour, absolutely as well relatively.

Centralisation of Capital Accompanying the Heightening of its Composition Brings About a Release of Workers

The enlargement of the scale of capital through the centralisation of capital does not change the magnitude of the total social capital. Therefore, the heightening of the capital composition via centralisation results in an *absolute decrease in the variable capital that causes workers to be released.*

Replacement of Fixed Capital Accompanying the Heightening of the Capital Composition Also Leads to Release of Workers

Furthermore, when **fixed capital is replaced**, the newest machinery and facilities are normally installed. Because the new equipment usually requires less labour to operate than the previous equipment, one segment of the workers who had been employed will no longer be needed. So this is another cause of the *workers being released due to a decrease in variable capital.*

❖ Heightening of composition of additional capital accumulated
⇨ Absolute increase of demand for labour at the lower increasing rate of capital via accumulation
❖ Heightening of composition of existing capital via centralisation
⇨ Absolute decrease of variable capital → Repulsion of active workers = Increase in supply in labour-power
❖ Heightening of composition of original capital during the replacement of fixed capital
⇨ Absolute decrease of variable capital → Repulsion of active workers = Increase in supply in labour-power

Fig. 10.7 Increase of demand for labour while active workers are released at the same time

10.3.3 Changes in the Supply and Demand of Labour-power Resulting from the Progress of Accumulation Accompanying a Heightening of the Capital Composition

Progress of Accumulation Increases Demand for Labour-power but Also Increases the Supply of Labour-power

We can see, then, that capital accumulation progresses along with (1) a heightening of the capital composition, (2) the centralisation of capital, and (3) the replacement of fixed capital, and this leads to an increase in demand for labour while also increasing the supply of labour-power (*see* Fig. 10.7).

10.3.4 Factors That Determine the Supply and Demand for Labour-power on the Labour Market

Progress of Accumulation Does Not Exert a Unilateral Influence in the Direction of Rising Wages

Changes in wages are directly determined by changes in the supply of and demand for labour-power. If we examine the *factors that lead to a change in the supply or demand for labour-power*, it becomes clear that the crucial factor is the progress in capital accumulation based on capital's desire for valorisation and that the progress of capital accumulation does not exercise a unilateral influence on wages with regard to either the demand for or supply of labour-power.

Fundamental Factor for Increase in Demand for Labour-power and Its Limit

Under capitalist production, the *fundamental factor that generally leads to an increase in demand for labour-power* is the *increase in the demand for labour that accompanies the progress of capital accumulation*. And the *limit of that capital accumulation is the restriction on capital's valorisation desire exercised by surplus-value*.

Factors That Relieve Increased Demand for Labour-power

First and foremost, a higher organic composition brings about a relative decline in the portion of variable capital within the additional capital.

Furthermore, demand for *labour* and demand for *labour-power* are not identical: An increase in demand for labour-power can be relieved by extending the working day or increasing the intensity of labour.[2]

Factors That Increase the Supply of Labour-power (i.e. Factors That Counter the Increase in Demand for Labour-power)

Under capitalist production, factors are always in operation that cause an increase in the supply of labour-power. And even in a case where the demand for labour-power increases, these factors operate as *countervailing factors* that prevent a unilateral rise in wages. The most important of these factors are the following:

1. Release of labour-power brought about by a heightening of the composition of existing capital through the centralisation of capital
2. Release of labour-power brought about by the heightening of the composition of replaced fixed capital
3. Increase in the working class (the cost of reproducing labour-power includes the cost of the expanded reproduction of this class)
4. Transformation of ruined small-scale capitalists and producers into wageworkers
5. Transformation of women and children into wageworkers

10.4 Production of a Relative Surplus Population and Its Forms of Existence

10.4.1 Production of a Relative Surplus Population or Industrial Reserve Army

Progress of Capital Accumulation Generates a Relative Surplus Population

The augmentation of aggregate social capital is accompanied by an augmentation of the portion of variable capital within it (i.e. labour-power incorporated into the aggregate capital). But the proportion of the latter is always decreasing relative to the former. As a result, the absolute augmentation in demand for labour-power due to the accumulation of capital is unable to absorb entirely the additional workers that emerge from the augmented working class or the workers set free because of the centralisation of capital and the replacement of fixed capital.

2 The demand for *labour* is the demand for labour employed in the production process, while the demand for *labour-power* is the demand with money on the labour market. When capital requires more labour for accumulation, the demand for labour certainly increases. But if the capital can manage to meet this demand by extending the working day or intensifying labour for the *labour-power already employed*, it will not be necessary to purchase additional labour-power on the labour market, so that there will be no increase in demand for labour-power. What is bought and sold on the labour market is labour-power, not its use-value (i.e. labour).

Hence, a **relative surplus population** or **industrial reserve army** emerges. This is *a labour population that is superfluous to a middling desire for valorisation on the part of capital.*

Production of Relative Surplus Population Is Inevitable Under Capitalist Production

The production of a relative surplus population is the *population law particular to the capitalist mode of production.*

The progress in capital accumulation under capitalist production that brings about a conspicuous augmentation of demand for labour-power is limited to one phase of the industrial cycle, where the profit rate and the expected profit rate are higher than average, so that the valorisation desire of capital also exceeds the average. This only occurs in the period stretching from a period of prosperous activity to the high point in a boom. The demand for labour-power is certainly higher during that period, which means that a lack of labour-power is felt, making it possible for wages to exceed the value of labour-power. In other periods, however, one does not see an augmentation in demand for labour-power that exceeds the augmentation of its supply, leading inescapably to a labour population that is superfluous to the valorisation desire of capital. The outcome, in other words, is a relative surplus population.

The *chronic* existence of an unemployed population that can be seen in advanced capitalist countries demonstrates the correctness of Marx's theory of a relative surplus population.[3]

---

3 The widely accepted theory of overpopulation is based on *Malthus' doctrine on population. Thomas Robert Malthus* (1766–1834) (1798) insisted that, whereas human beings tend to increase in geometric progression, their means of livelihood increase only in arithmetic progression, so that the result, sooner or later, is overpopulation. This overpopulation is an absolute surplus in every society, so that the problem cannot be solved unless the superfluous population is diminished (Malthus 1798, pp. 11–14).

The chronic unemployed population in advanced capitalist countries is certainly a surplus population, but not absolutely superfluous in relation to the means of consumption that sustain the population. This is because if that surplus population could make the huge quantity of idle means of production, which are generated by the limited effective demand for production or commodity stock, then production itself could be augmented to a great extent. This «surplus» is not absolute but rather a surplus compared with something. What, exactly? It is a surplus with regard to the «valorisation desire of capital»—and with regard not to its minimum level but to the valorisation desire of an average level or to the industrial cycle in its middling level of activity.

The surplus population in the advanced capitalist nations is clearly a relative surplus population since the number of unemployed only decreases significantly during a period of prosperity, whereas at other times, there is a constant level of mass unemployment.

[Middling activity ⇨ Prosperity ⇨ Over-production ⇨ Crisis ⇨ Stagnation] ⇨ [Middling activity ⇨ ...

Fig. 10.8 Industrial cycle: movement form of modern industry

10.4.2 Existence of a Relative Surplus Population Is a Living Condition for the Capitalist Mode of Production

Industrial Cycle

Capitalist production raises the productive power of society at a pace that far exceeds that of every preceding form of production, thus expanding the productive scale of society. This expansion of the scale of production does not proceed in a straight line, however. Capitalist production has a long-term tendency towards expansion, with a pattern of repetition between a rapid expansion in one period and a severe contraction in another. The expansion and contraction are repeatedly carried out by passing through the aspects of a middling activity, prosperity, overproduction, crisis, and stagnation—referred to as the **industrial cycle** (*see* Fig. 10.8).

Capital Itself Produces the Living Conditions of Capitalist Production

When a new market, for whatever reason, is opened up or there is a rapid augmentation of demand for new products, capital seizes on this opportunity and seeks to deliver commodities to the market through rapidly augmenting production. When this occurs, the procurement of the means of production necessary for the expansion of production can be provided to the market promptly through an enhancement of production stimulated by the rise of prices. In terms of the labour-power necessary for expanded production, however, unless there is elasticity in the amount of labour-power provided to the labour market, there is no way for it to be procured. This is because labour-power is not the sort of thing that can be rapidly mass-produced in a factory. Yet capital has not let such opportunities pass it by. And this has made possible a rapid expansion of capitalist production in periods of prosperity. This was possible thanks to the existence of a relative surplus population that is superfluous to a middling valorisation desire of capital. In other words, *the existence of the relative surplus population is a living condition for the capitalist mode of production, and this living condition is something that capital itself is always generating.*

Fluctuations in Capital Accumulation Regulate the Ratio of the Active Army and the Reserve Army

In most cases, the general movement of labour wages is restricted by the expansion or contraction of the industrial reserve army; in other words, *a rise or fall of labour wages* is not determined by the total number of the labour population but rather by changes in the *fluctuation in the ratio between the*

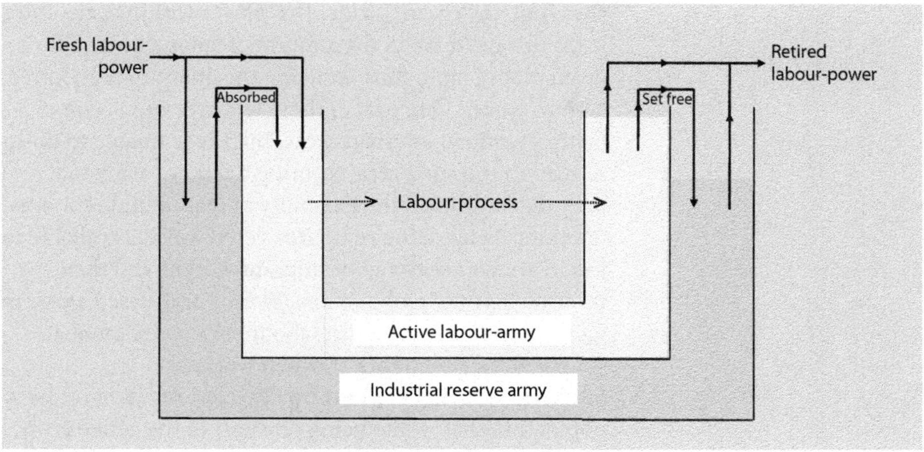

Fig. 10.9 Active labour-army and industrial reserve army

active army *and* **reserve army** *into which the working class is divided* and *by an increase or decrease in the scale of the surplus population that is employed*. The change in the ratio is itself regulated by the *magnitude of capital accumulation based on the valorisation impulse of capital at a particular time* (*see* Fig. 10.9).

10.4.3 Forms of Existence of the Relative Surplus Population

Three Existence Forms of the Relative Surplus Population

In addition to the *forms of the relative surplus population that appear periodically in the phases of the industrial cycle*, there are always more or less *three forms of the relative surplus population—as well as the population that is further below it in a state of pauperism*.

1. **Fluid Surplus Population**. The number of those employed in factories and other realms of modern industry is always decreasing relative to the scale of production, due to the heightening of the composition of capital, but generally the population is increasing in absolute terms. This increase, however, advances in a zigzag pattern and is not in equilibrium, so that large numbers of workers will either be released or drawn in at a given time. This means that a reserve army is always in existence, which corresponds to the temporary or part-time workers in various forms.
2. **Latent Surplus Population**. The accumulation of capital within agriculture generates an absolute surplus part of the agricultural population. This is because, generally

speaking, the rise in productive power within agriculture leads to a decrease in the amount of labour needed for a given plot of land, thus reducing the quantity of required labour-power. One part of these workers will become factory workers in urban areas. But those unable to do so remain in the rural area, forming a reserve army that may, depending on the flexibility of the natural economy, temporarily leave the rural area when work is available in urban areas as seasonal or migrant worker and then return when such jobs vanish. These rural-based workers, by increasing the supply of labour-power, are often a source of the low wages of urban workers.

3. **Stagnant Surplus Population**. This is a segment of the population that, while being one part of the active army, is subject to very irregular employment, thus forming a reservoir to regulate the number of workers for capital. The living conditions of this segment are lower than the average level for the working class; and they are always prepared to settle for the maximum labour-time at the minimum in wages. Because of this, they generally have a high birth rate and death rate and many family members. The workers who perform labour in the day-worker districts of large cities are one part of this type of relative population.

State of Pauperism

The lowest rung of the surplus population under the capitalist mode of production is occupied by those who, unable to obtain revenue via the sale of their labour-power, have to depend on the poor laws or those who have lost their will to work and live through begging or some other means. This segment is composed, firstly, of all those who have fallen into **pauperism** despite possessing labour-power; secondly, by orphans and poor children; and, thirdly, by the ruined and those unable to work. Most of the «homeless» population is in this layer.

Lumpenproletariat

Even lower than pauperism are those stuck within the **lumpenproletariat**, who are composed of vagrants, criminals, prostitutes, and the like.

10.4.4 General Law of Capitalist Accumulation

Relative Surplus Population Increases with Progress of Capital Accumulation

The labour population increases in line with the progress of capital accumulation and the increase in the amount of the total social capital. If there is no change in the proportion of the relative surplus population and the industrial reserve army within the labour population (i.e. no change in the rate of unemployment), there will be an increase in the absolute amount of the relative surplus population or industrial reserve army. In advanced capitalist countries, it is not unusual to have an unemployment rate of around 10%; and the rate often rises to an extremely high level during the stagnant phase of the industrial cycle, severely increasing the relative surplus population.

General Law of Capitalist Accumulation

When a large relative surplus population continuously exists in this manner, at its *bottom* always settles a large *fixed unemployed segment*, almost chronically unable to find jobs. Even though this segment is not subject to the hardships of production, its level of poverty is much greater. If this layer of unemployed expands, there will be a similar increase in the *stratum of the destitute* who cannot survive without aid from society. The *tendency towards increase of this sort of population is an expression of the fact that* the «**absolute general law of capitalist accumulation**» (Marx 1872: Marx 1976, p. 798) undergoes various transformations due to the particular conditions involved, wherein the accumulation of capital (i.e. the expanded production of capitalist production relations) is at the same time *the expanded reproduction of the subsumption of labour under capital and the alienation of labour.*

Methods for the Production of Surplus-value Are at the Same Time Methods of Accumulation

We already looked in ▸ Chap. 5 at the various methods for the development of productive power under capitalist production. There we saw that, under the capitalist system, the method to raise the social productive power of labour necessarily sacrifices individual workers, that the means of developing production necessarily become a means of dominating and exploiting workers, and that these means deform human beings by tying workers to a fixed division of labour in which they only perform some partial labour, making them a mere appendage of machinery and draining their labour of content so that it becomes a source of suffering. This means that the labour process, despite having been transformed into a scientific process, strips the workers within it of their mental capacities, limiting such capacities to specialised workers alone. And this also results in the working conditions of workers always being irregular, subjecting them to the tyranny of capital within the labour process and even turning their time for living into a part of the labouring time.

All of these methods of producing surplus-value are, at the same time, methods of accumulation, and in turn the progression of accumulation becomes a means to further develop those methods.

Accumulation of Misery Corresponding to the Accumulation of Capital

Thus, the outcome of the workings of the «absolute general law of capitalist accumulation», seen from the condition of the labour population as a whole, is *a tendency towards a worsening of the condition of the sedentary unemployed and the destitute, regardless of how the wage level of the active army of workers may change.*[4] One clear indication of this is the wretched state of those in the strata of pauperism and the lumpenproletariat—the bottom rungs in today's advanced capitalist countries.

References

Malthus TR (1798) (anonym) An essay on the principle of population. J. Johnson, London

Marx K (1872) Das Kapital. Kritik der politischen Oekonomie. Bd. 1. Buch 1: Der Produktionsprocess des Kapitals. 2. verb. Aufl. Hamburg. English edition: Marx K (1976) Capital. A critique of political economy, vol 1 (trans: Howkes B). Penguin Books, Harmondsworth

4 Marx (1872) writes: «The law which always *holds the relative surplus population* or *industrial reserve army in equilibrium with the extent and energy of accumulation* rivets the worker to capital more firmly than the wedges of Hephaestus held Prometheus to the rock. It makes an *accumulation of misery* a necessary condition, corresponding to the *accumulation of capital.* Accumulation of wealth at one pole is, therefore, at the same time accumulation of misery, the torment of labour, slavery, ignorance, brutalisation and moral degradation at the opposite pole, i.e. on the side of the class that *produces its own product as capital*» (Marx 1976, p. 799; Marx emphasis as in the first German edition).

Primitive Accumulation

T. Otani, *A Guide to Marxian Political Economy*,
https://doi.org/10.1007/978-3-319-65954-1_11

11.1 Primitive Accumulation and Its Methods

Section Structure

We examined the valorisation of capital in ▶ Chaps. 3, 4, 5, and 6, which is the process of how capital produces surplus-value. Our *premise* in those chapters was, first of all, that there exists on the one side capital, and therefore the ownership of capital value by capitalists, and on the other side labour-power as a commodity, and therefore property-less wageworkers separated from the means of production.

In ▶ Chaps. 8 and 9, however, where the valorisation process was examined as a repeating process (reproduction), we learned how the earlier premise regarding the capital and the ownership of capital value at one pole, and the labour-power commodity and property-less wageworkers at the other, is in fact continually reproduced through capitalist production itself. It thus became clear that once capitalist production is underway, both of those poles exist as the *outcome* of production itself.

But capitalist production had to start at some point. So what *needed to exist at the outset*—namely, the money necessary to advance for the means of production that are independent and separate from the labouring individuals as capital on the one hand and the labouring individuals free in a double sense on the other hand—could not have been the *outcome* of capitalist production at that point. The question, then, is how there came to emerge money transformed into capital and into means of production separate from the workers as well as labour-power as the workers' sole commodity, both of which could be purchased on the market. Up to now, we have placed this problem out of theoretical consideration as something that pertains to the **prehistory of capitalist production**.

Now that we know the fundamental mechanism of capitalist production, we can[1] and must address such problems that had been set aside earlier.

1 Why we *can* now, *after knowing the fundamental mechanism of production*, take up the prehistory of capitalist production? On this point, Marx (1857) left the following famous and pregnant remark: «Bourgeois society [i.e. capitalist society] is the most developed and many-faceted historical organisation of production. The categories which express its relations, an understanding of its structure, therefore, provide, at the same time, an insight into the structure and the relations of production of all previous forms of society the ruins and components of which were used in the creation of bourgeois society. Some of these remains are still dragged along within bourgeois society unassimilated, while elements which previously were barely indicated have developed and attained their full significance, etc. *The anatomy of man is a key*

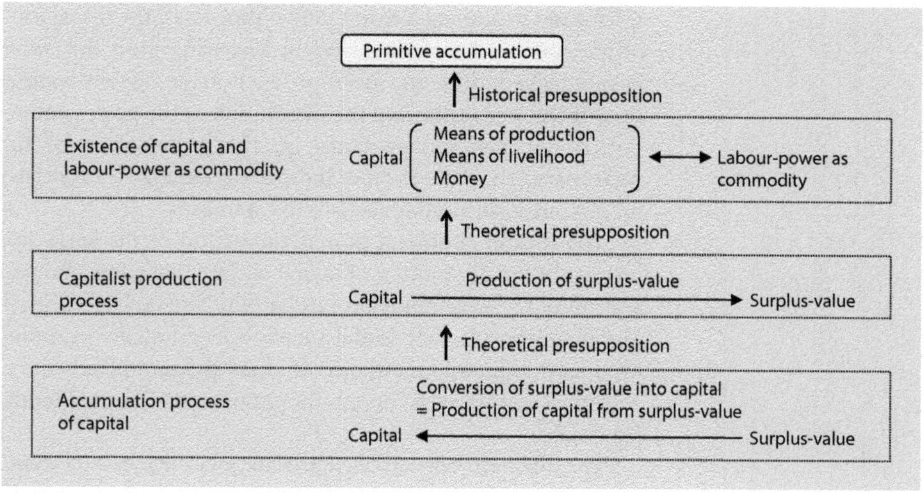

Fig. 11.1 Capital accumulation as the starting point of capitalist production = primitive accumulation

Adam Smith (1776) used the term *previous accumulation* (Smith 1937, p. 260) to refer to the initial formation of capital, which he explained in terms of diligent and capable producers emerging as capitalists from among a lot of independent producers, while the slothful and incompetent ones meet their downfall and became wageworkers. But was the genesis of capital in fact the sort of idyllic process described by Smith emerging as the result of differences in the abilities and diligence of individuals?

Here we will take a general look at the process that preceded capitalist production, which Marx referred to as **primitive accumulation**. This is the historical process that put in place the preconditions for the beginning of capitalist production, with capital on one side and the labour-power commodity on the other (*see* Fig. 11.1).

11.1.1 Economic Basic Process: Polarisation of Small Producers Under Commodity Production

Two Moments Within the Transition from Feudalism to Capitalism

Capitalist society emerged from the feudal society that had preceded it. Under capitalist production, labouring individuals are completely separated from the means of production. This

to the anatomy of the ape. On the other hand, *indications of higher forms in the lower species of animals can only be understood when the higher forms themselves are already known. Bourgeois economy thus provides a key to that of antiquity*, etc.» (Marx 1986, p. 42; my emphasis and brackets).

separation was formed through two processes: the dissolution of the system of serfdom wherein labouring individuals had been attached to the means of production, i.e. the **emancipation of the peasants**; and the dissolution of the petty production of independent peasants, i.e. the **polarisation of the peasantry**. The realisation of these two moments was decisive to the transition from feudalism to capitalism.

The former moment, the emancipation of the serfs, is a process of the dissolution of feudal society that came about as a result of the development of the productive power within it. The outcome was that feudal society was gradually uprooted by the widespread emergence of small peasants (*yeomanry*) within its womb, even though they continued to bear a feudal signboard.

The formation of capitalist production, *theoretically speaking*, is a process of the emergence of the capital relation via the *separation of the independent small producers and proprietors from their means of production*, which is to say, the *dissolution of small-scale production* (*see* ◘ Fig. 11.2).

Towards the historical end of feudal society, the small peasants whose surplus product was exploited by the landlords, in the form of money rent, were compelled to sell their products on the market as commodities (*see* ◘ Fig. 1.32). There was thus a necessary development of commodity production

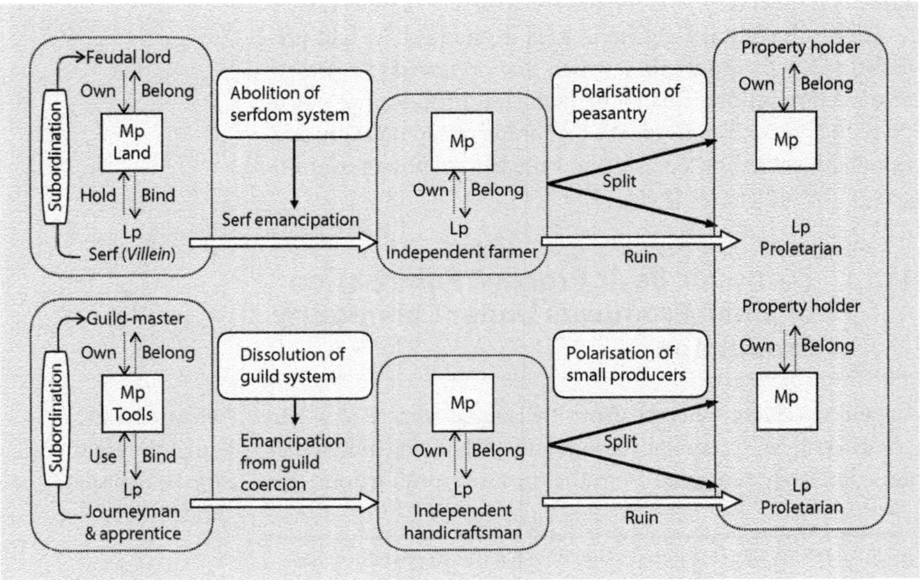

◘ **Fig. 11.2** Two moments of the process of separating labouring individuals from the means of production

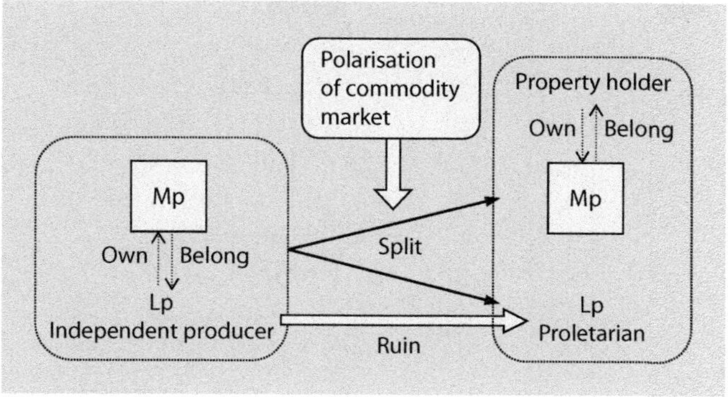

Fig. 11.3 Polarisation of small commodity producers

carried out by these peasants, as well as by independent peasant producers. The development of commodity production brought about a new situation.

Polarisation of Small Producers Under Commodity Production

The development of commodity production under those producers brought about their **polarisation**.[2] Among the independent commodity producers who possessed the conditions for their own labour (means of production), some accumulated sooner or later the wealth (means of production and means of livelihood or the money to purchase them) and rose to become the property holders, while the others, who lost what they had possessed, fell into the ranks of the property less, i.e. the proletariat (*see* Fig. 11.3).

The «Law of One Price»

The value of a commodity is determined by its socially necessary labour-time. This means that the same sort of commodity has the same value. The price of the same sort of commodity that expresses its value in money is also uniform in one market. This is the so-called «law of one price».

Formation of the «Wealth of the People» Through Accumulation of «Embryonic Profit»

We will assume here that the price of a commodity is equal to its value. Since the labour-time expended by the producer who produces under socially average conditions would therefore be equal to socially necessary labour-time, the expended labour-time is fully recouped by the producer in the form of money, and thus his surplus-labour-time also returns fully in the form of money. This corresponds to profit (surplus-value) in the case of the capitalist, so it is called «**embryonic profit**» (Marx 1981, p. 934), and if this is accumulated by the producer, it can form surplus wealth. In the first half of the fifteenth

2 Marx (1872a) writes: «With the *polarisation of the commodity-market* into these two classes, the fundamental conditions of capitalist production are present» (Marx 1976, p. 874; Marx's emphasis as in the first German edition).

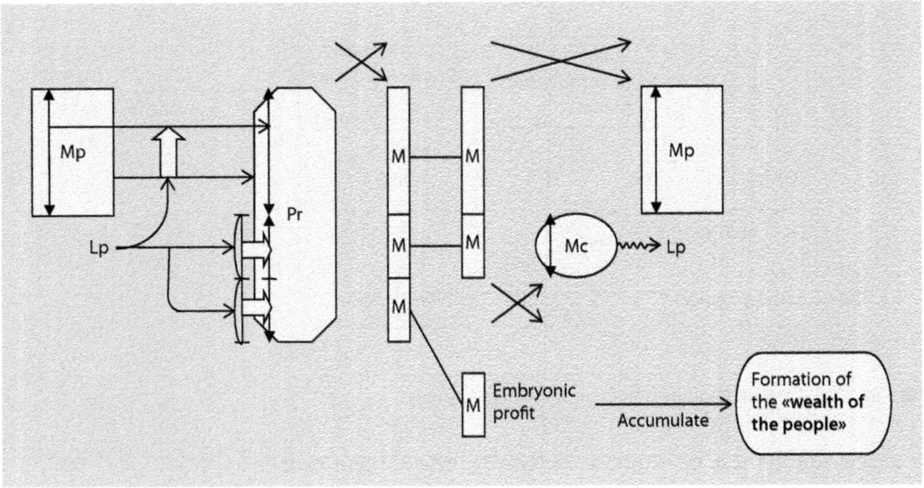

Fig. 11.4 Formation of embryonic profit and the «wealth of the people» under small commodity producers

century, *John Fortescue* (ca. 1394–1476) (1537) called this wealth the «**wealth of the people**» (*see* Fig. 11.4).

Becoming Rich by Accumulating Super Profits

The producers who produce under production conditions more favourable than the social average are also able to obtain an added amount of money that exceeds their surplus-labour (if their commodity is sold at its value), which can be called «embryonic super profits». This is because they can produce the same commodity using less labour-time. The producers who accumulate such super profits form the «wealth of the people» at a faster rate and on a larger scale and are thus able to enrich themselves. The means of raising the production conditions for individual producers is the development of productive power within their production. In this way, the competition between producers brings about a development of productive power.

Ruined Petty Producers Lose the Means of Production and Fall into the Ranks of the Property-less Proletariat

Meanwhile, those producers that produce under conditions less favourable than the average receive back less money than the labour-time they had expended if their commodity is sold at its value, because a greater amount of labour-time had to be expended on the production of the same commodity type. If the scale of losses for these producers increases, they will be incapable of even carrying out simple reproduction, thus forfeiting their means of production (most notably farmland) and slipping into the rank of the property-less *proletariat*.

Polarisation of Peasantry in Agricultural Districts

In the agricultural districts, this process takes the form of a breakdown of the peasantry into rich peasants and former peasants who are now landless. In other words, this is the **polarisation of the peasantry.**

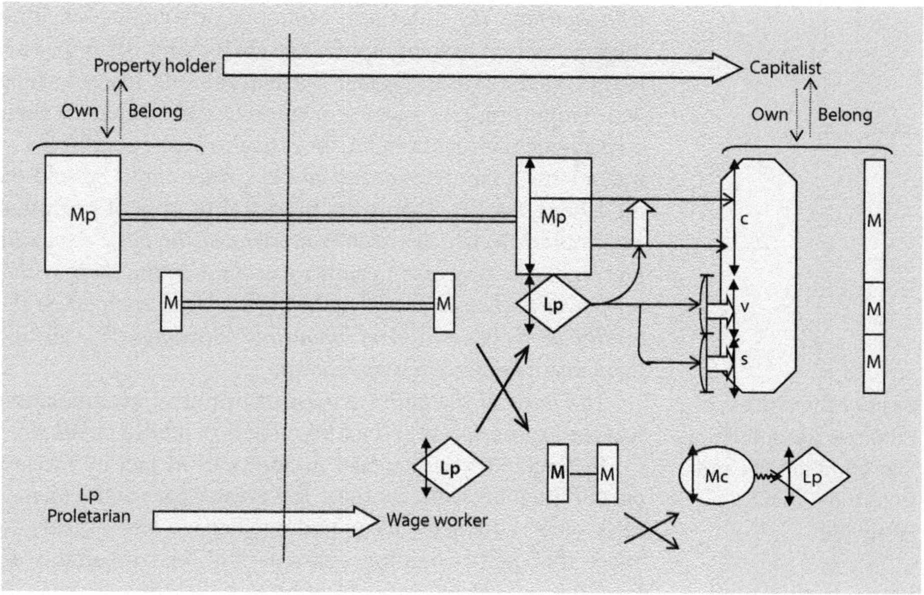

Fig. 11.5 Birth of capital/wage-labour relation

Birth of the Capital/Wage-labour Relation

The producers who formed the «wealth of the people» through raising their productive power buy the labour-power of the property-less who have lost their farmland and appropriate the surplus-labour of the latter as surplus-value. In this way, we have the formation of capitalists on the one hand and wage-workers on the other. Thus, in places where small commodity production is widely carried out, in line with the working of the *economic laws of commodity production*, sooner or later the capital/wage-labour relation must emerge. In the agricultural districts, the rich peasants become agricultural capitalists, while the former peasants without farmland are transformed into agricultural workers. In the urban districts, one part of the independent handicraftsmen freed from the guilds becomes industrial capitalists, while the vast majority are transformed into industrial workers (*see* Fig. 11.5).

11.1.2 Primitive Accumulation: Accelerating the Basic Economic Process Through Violent Methods

Primitive Accumulation and Its Methods

In the course of actual history, however, the people who formed wealth in some way or another to become capitalists were not content to simply wait for the outcome of the operation of *economic laws*, i.e. «the purely economic driving forces behind the agricultural revolution» (Marx 1872: Marx 1976, p. 883; Marx's emphasis as in the first German edition). Instead, along with employing *every sort of method* feasible to hasten their own augmentation of capital, they tried to create conditions so that a large quantity of cheap labour-power could be sold on the labour market. This is the historical process of **primitive accumulation**, which *violently accelerated the basic economic process*. In the process of primitive accumulation, *those wielding power freely used every method available to expropriate the conditions of labour from the labouring individuals, thus turning them into a property-less proletariat.*

Basis of the Process of Primitive Accumulation: Expropriation of Land from the Agricultural Population

The *basis of the entire process* of primitive accumulation was the *expropriation of land from the agricultural population.*

In England, serfdom had disappeared in fact by the last part of the fourteenth century. The greater part of the former serfs who remained *villein* under villenage was already in effect free, self-sustaining peasants with the possibility to form the «wealth of the people» through their own labour and thus enrich themselves. These **independent self-sustaining peasants** (yeomanry), who were in charge of **small production**, represented the bulk of the population from the fifteenth to seventeenth century. Throughout this period, however, there was the continual progression of a process whereby these peasants lost their land and fell into the position of wageworkers, thereby swelling the ranks of those in that position. This process accelerated rapidly in the seventeenth and eighteenth century, and by the mid-eighteenth century, the yeomanry had been nearly completely eliminated.

Simply put, these independent self-sustaining peasants—who once formed the bulk of the population—met their downfall and were transformed into a property-less proletariat through the **process of the violent expropriation of the masses of people** by those wielding power.

Both the peasants who still bore feudal trappings, and the small ranks of the true wageworker class that emerged as early as the fifteenth century, had small arable land and small cottages and also had the right to use the **common land**. Initially, they were able to live by relying on that common land, which was the last vestige of the **community**. That state of affairs persisted until the end of the seventeenth century, when the free self-sustaining peasants were finally wiped out. And by the early nineteenth century, even the memory of the relation between the farmers and the common land vanished.

The **usurpation of the common land** expedited the process of expropriation, which began at the end of the fifteenth century and progressed over the course of the next two centuries with a variety of forms. The plunder reached its peak in the eighteenth century with introduction the «Bills for Inclosures of Commons» and the final elimination of the yeomanry.

In the sixteenth century, the absolute monarchy that was being put in place created the Anglican Church and launched the Reformation in England, dissolving the monasteries in order to strengthen the monarchy and **usurp the Church's property**. The peasants were evicted from the land they had cultivated at the monasteries and churches, becoming vagrants. With the Glorious Revolution of 1688, the **theft of the state domains** began to be openly carried out.

The **first enclosure** carried out in the early sixteenth century involved the great feudal lords and new feudal aristocrats—who were tempted by the high price of wool amidst the booming wool industry in Flanders—driving the peasants from the cultivated land and turning it into sheep pastures. This was followed by the **second enclosure**, at the end of the eighteenth century: a large-scale enclosure of cultivatable land carried out under parliamentary approval by the large landowners and agricultural capitalists to increase the production of agricultural products. Both enclosures involved a large-scale effort to usurp the peasants' land and drive them off the land.

In the case of the «**clearing of the estates**» in Scotland, from the late eighteenth century to the nineteenth century, peasant cultivators were swept from the land, which was then turned into sheep pastures and later into hunting grounds.

This process of the usurpation of land from the residents of the rural villages gave birth to the modern landowners who created cultivatable land for capitalist agriculture, the small number of large-scale agricultural capitalists who integrated land and capital, and a large number of small-scale tenant farmers, while also creating for the sake of capital many helpless proletarians.

Forced Transformation of Proletarians into Wageworkers

The unprotected proletarians, however, did not immediately become wageworkers but rather wandered around each region as beggars, robbers, and vagabonds. Although the ranks of this proletariat increased in size, the proportion of wageworkers within it did not. Because of the lag in the supply of wageworkers compared to demand, there was a tendency for wages to rise.

Given this situation, the *unprotected proletarians were forcibly trained to become wageworkers*, on the one hand, through *bloody legislation against vagabondage*, while on the other hand there was a *forced lowering of wages and extension of the working day through legislation.*[3]

It was only after resigning itself to this destiny of having to sell labour-power as a commodity, and work for the person who purchases it, that the working class for the first time related to the conditions of labour within the production process as something belonging to another person. This was the point at which capitalist production could begin to stand on its own two feet.

Genesis of the Capitalist Farmer

The *agricultural capitalist*, i.e. *the capitalist tenant farmer*, was generated through a gradual process that took place over several centuries.

The first form that appeared was the **bailiff**, who was a serf who managed the land of the feudal lord. In the latter half of the fourteenth century, the bailiff was in turn replaced by the tenant producers, who were provided with farm implements, livestock, and seeds—although the conditions for those producers differed a little from those of the peasant. Soon after, the tenant producers evolved into the **metayer**, a semi-tenant farmer who advances capital along with the landlord. The metayer quickly disappeared, however, with the emergence of the **tenant farmer** in the proper sense of the term. These farmers augmented their own capital through employing wageworkers and paid landlords one part of their surplus product as ground-rent (either in money or in kind). Farmers prospered during the Agrarian Revolution, which spanned from the last third of the fifteenth century to the sixteenth century. The fall in the value of money in the sixteenth century lowered wages and decreased the burden of ground-rent, so that a class of wealthy **capitalist tenant farmers** could emerge.

Rise in Productivity Through Agrarian Revolution: Creation of Home Market for Industrial Capital

The transformation of the small-scale peasants into wageworkers created a market for capitalist agriculture by turning

3 Marx (1872a) writes: «It is not enough that the conditions of labour are concentrated at one pole of society in the shape of capital, while at the other pole are grouped masses of men who have nothing to sell but their labour-power. Nor is it enough that they are compelled to sell themselves voluntarily. The advance of capitalist production develops a working class which by education, tradition and habit looks upon the requirements of that mode of production as self-evident natural laws. . . . The rising bourgeoisie needs the *power of the state*, and uses it *to «regulate» wages*, i.e. to force them into the limits suitable for making a profit, to lengthen the *working day*, and to keep the worker himself at his normal *level of dependence*. This is an essential aspect of so-called *primitive accumulation*» (Marx 1976, pp. 899–900; Marx's emphasis as in the first German edition).

them into purchasers of agricultural products while at the same time creating a home market for industrial capital by destroying the subsidiary domestic industries in the rural districts and turning the residents into purchasers of industrial products. During the *manufacturing period in the proper sense of the term*, the process of splitting manufacture from agriculture progresses, but a broad basis of town handicrafts and domestic subsidiary industries still remains and is sustained.

Large-scale industry first provides a continual foundation for capitalist agriculture through the use of machinery—pillaging an enormous number of people in the countryside, radically uprooting the domestic and rural industries (both cotton and wool industries), and separating them from agriculture. In this manner, *large-scale industry was able to completely subordinate the entire home market to industrial capital.*

Genesis of the Industrial Capitalist

There were of course many guild masters, independent small artisans, and wageworkers who became small-scale capitalists, and then some of them, through their repeated exploitation and accumulation, became **bona fide** capitalists. Under that method, however, this process advances at a snail's pace, *which did not meet the commercial needs of the world market created by the great discoveries of the fifteenth century.*

The two forms of capital in the period prior to the era of the capitalist mode of production, **usurer's capital** and **merchant's capital**, had already formed moneyed capital through usury and commerce. That capital established the new manufactures in seaports and in parts of the countryside, where the regulations of the feudal system and guild organisations were lax, employing every means available to rapidly create industrial capital.

The dawn of the era of capitalist production is characterised by events that include *the discovery of gold and silver sources in the Americas, the extirpation and enslavement of indigenous populations and their entombment in the mines, the subjugation and plunder of India, and the turning of Africa into a commercial hunting ground for slaves.* These events are the *main moments within primitive accumulation.*

That was followed by the *commercial wars between European nations* that were fought throughout the world, beginning with Holland overthrowing Spanish rule, reaching a massive scale with England's Anti-Jacobin War, and continuing on with the Opium Wars against China.

The various moments of primitive accumulation followed chronologically from Spain and Portugal to Holland and then England. But in the case of England at the end of the seventeenth century, these moments are systematically combined as the **colonial system**, **national debt system**, **tax system**, and **protectionist system**. *Each of these methods employs the power of state, as the concentrated and organised force of society, to hasten, as in a hothouse, the process of transformation from the feudal mode of production to the capitalist mode, thereby shortening the transitional period.*

When an old society is pregnant with a new society, **force** acts as the midwife within the old society. Force itself is *an economic potency*. And herein lies the historical significance of primitive accumulation as well.

11.2 Historical Position of Capitalist Production

11.2.1 Laws of Movement of Capitalist Production

Tendencies of the Genesis, Development, and Annihilation of Capitalist Production

The previous section looked at primitive accumulation, i.e. the accumulation of capital up to the point where the capitalist mode of production is able to stand on its own two feet. This is the process of stripping the labouring individuals of their conditions of labour so that capital (i.e. capitalist private property based on the exploitation of others' labour) can be accumulated and the materials for the exploitation for capital (i.e. property-less wageworkers) can be created.

Now that we have familiarised ourselves with the genesis of capital within the prehistory of capital, we can turn our attention from primitive accumulation and the overall developmental tendencies of capitalist production (examined in ▶ Chaps. 5, 6, 7, 8, 9, and 10) to focus instead on the **laws of movement of capitalist production**—i.e. the **tendencies of the genesis, development, and annihilation of capitalist production**—and also pay particular attention to changes in the ownership forms of the means of production.

From Individual Private Property Based on One's Own Labour to Capitalist Private Property

Primitive accumulation was nothing but the *expropriation of the conditions of labour from the direct producers, which is to say, the dissolution of private property based on one's own labour.*

We will use the term **petty industry** to refer to cases where a worker utilises the conditions of labour that belong to him to carry out small-scale production. The **production mode of petty industry** exists not only in the process of the formation of the systems of slavery and serfdom but also continues to exist under them (*see* ◘ Fig. 1.35). However, this mode of production only flourishes and attains its classic shape in cases where the labouring individuals are the free proprietors of the conditions of labour that they utilise, i.e. only when peasants own the land they cultivate or when artisans are the free proprietors of the tools they employ (e.g., independent self-sustaining peasants or independent artisans in towns). Such petty industry is the *nursery that fosters the seedlings that subsequently develop into social production while at the same time the school that develops the workers' skilled hands as well as their free individuality*. It is here that *the labouring individuals as free individuals relate to the conditions of labour as something belonging to themselves*. This manner of relating to the conditions of labour is called **individual property**. Under individual property, the labouring individuals, by engaging as the subject, *have the potential to develop their own free individuality*.

However, the production mode of petty industry presupposes parcelling of the soil and the scattering of the other means of production. And this, along with excluding the concentration of the means of production, likewise hinders co-operation and a division of labour within the same production process as well as the social rule and control of nature. Because this mode of production prevents the free development of social productive powers, it is only in harmony with the narrow, naturally generated limits of production and society.

At a certain stage of development, this mode of production brings forth *the material means of its own destruction*. The polarisation of producers under commodity production progresses, necessarily bringing about a new *development of productive powers*. From that moment, new forces and passions spring up in the bosom of society; forces, and passions which feel themselves to be fettered by that mode of production. It must be annihilated—and it is annihilated. The individually dispersed means of production are transformed into socially concentrated means of production, so that the dwarflike property of the many is transformed into the enormous property of the few, and the great mass of people is expropriated from the soil, from the means of livelihood, and from the instruments of labour. Self-earned private property, based on the fusing together of the *independent labouring individuals with their conditions of labour*, is supplanted by **capitalist private property** based on the exploitation of the labour of others. And this is precisely the process of primitive accumulation.

Expropriation of a Large Number of Capitalists by a Small Number of Capitalists

As soon as this process of transformation has sufficiently decomposed the old society—so that workers have been turned into property-less proletarians and their conditions of labour into capital, making it possible for *the capitalist mode of production to stand on its own two feet*—then the further *socialisation of labour* and *transformation* of the land and other means of production into socially exploited and therefore *common means of production*, as well as the further *expropriation of private proprietors*, take a new form. What is now to be expropriated is not the self-sustaining labouring individuals but the capitalists exploiting many labouring individuals.

This expropriation is accomplished through the action of the immanent laws of capitalist production tending towards the centralisation of capital, so that **a few capitalists expropriate many others.**

Progress of the Socialisation of Production and the Development of the International Character of the Capitalist System

Hand in hand with the expropriation of many capitalists by the few, other developments take place, such as *co-operation within the escalating labour process, the conscious technical application of science, the planned use of land, an increase in the scale of the means of labour, and saving in the means of production through their common use.* This can be referred to as the **development of the social productive power of labour** and the **socialisation of labour**—or simply as the **socialisation of production**. Meanwhile, each nation in the world becomes *integrated within the network of the global market* so that there is a development of the *international character of the capitalist system.*

Bursting Asunder the Capitalist Integument That Has Become a Fetter to Productive Powers

Along with the continually decreasing number of big capitalists, who usurp and monopolise all of the benefits of this process of transformation, the subsumption of labour under capital progresses as does the alienation of labour. But with this there also grows the revolt *of the working class—a class always increasing in number and disciplined, united, and organised by the mechanism of the capitalist production process itself.*

The monopoly of capital becomes a *fetter upon the social productive powers* developed under it. Both the centralisation of capital and the socialisation of labour reach a point of being incompatible with the *capitalist integument. This integument is burst asunder. The knell of capitalist private property sounds. The expropriators are expropriated.*

Re-establishment of Individual Property and Actualisation of Social Property

The capitalist mode of appropriation, which stems from the capitalist mode of production, and therefore from capitalist private property as well, is a *negation of the private property of labouring individuals* that is based on their own labour. However, capitalist production itself begets, with inexorable necessity, *its own negation*. This is the *negation of the negation*. It does not re-establish the private property of

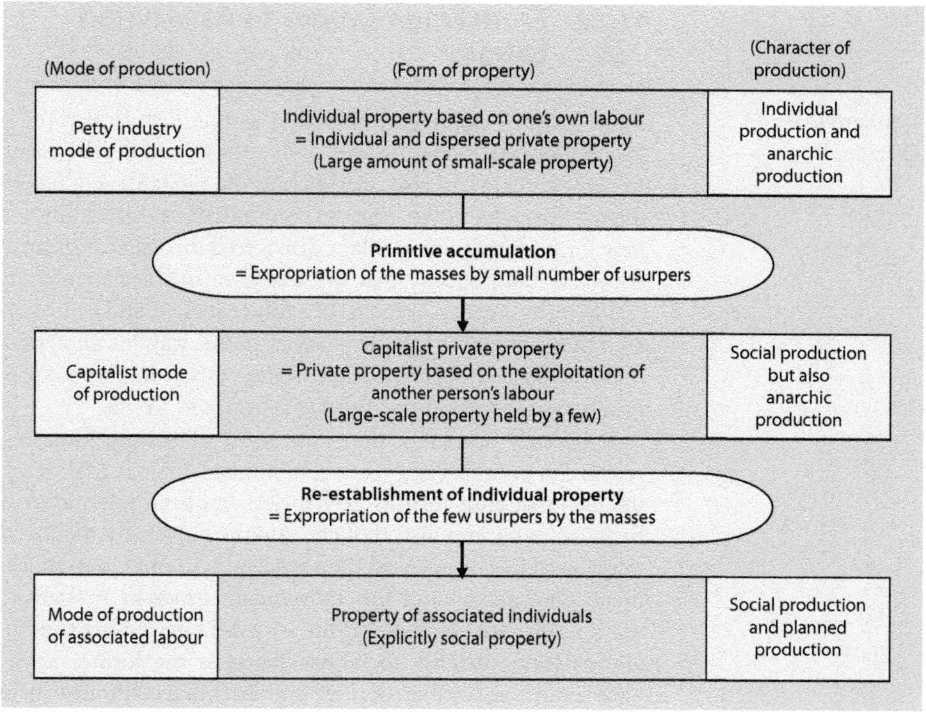

■ **Fig. 11.6** Primitive accumulation and the re-establishment of individual property

isolated, independent labouring individual, but rather the **property of associated individuals** based on the gains of the capitalist era, i.e. based on co-operation and the common holding of the land and all the other means of production. This is the **re-establishment of individual property**. Here we have *associated individuals*, rather than independent individuals. They *relate as free individuals to the conditions of labour as things belonging to themselves*, and these individuals actually acquire the requirements for cultivating their own free individuality. Only when the property of associated individuals is established, which is the final sublation of capitalist private property, *will the* **social property** *of the means of production that is already generated latently within the capitalist production—in the form of the common holding of means of production through labouring individuals within the labour process—becomes actual* (*see* ■ Fig. 11.6). The new mode of production that is established through this, as mentioned in ► Sect. 1.3.3 of the Introduction, is *Association* (*see* ■ Fig. 1.33).

11.2.2 From Wage-labour to Associated Labour

Problem to Be Discussed

Marx grasped capitalist production as one historical form of production, clarifying the laws of its genesis and development. In his analysis, Marx also clarified how the capitalist production form—through its own inherent contradictions—gives way to a new form of production. Marx discovered through his diagnosis of capitalist society that the womb of this society already contains the embryo or foetus of a future society, and he uncovered the nature of this future society. In this way, his *analysis of the capitalist mode of production* itself went beyond this mode of production to further clarify *what is within its womb*.

Generally speaking, that new form of society has been referred to as «socialism» (or «communism»). Since Marx's era, the idea that aims for this new society has been referred to as socialist (or communist) thought, and the movement that seeks to realise it has been called the socialist (or communist) movement. One outcome of this movement—generally thought to mark its terminal point—was the societies referred to as «**actually existing socialist societies**» (such as the former Soviet Union and East German or those countries that continue to bear the label «socialism» today like China, Vietnam, and Cuba).

However, these «actually existing socialist societies», despite advertising themselves as such, *are not, in any of their moments, socialist societies in the true sense.* One reason that the claim of these countries to be socialist could be taken at face value is that they were (or still are) a particular form of capitalism, known as «**state capitalism**», that has many characteristics that differ noticeably from the capitalism of «advanced capitalist states».

Given this situation, it is difficult to understand the nature of the «new society» elucidated by the analysis of the capitalist mode of production without touching on the nature of those «actually existing socialist societies». Yet to enter a concrete discussion of these societies goes far beyond the aim of this book, which is to examine the mechanism of the capitalist mode of production, so I will have to leave it to the reader to investigate some of the sources that examine this issue.[4] I will focus instead on the nature of the society Association, touched on earlier, whenever appropriate, and examine why capitalist society must give birth to this new society.

4 The author's views on Association and the social system of «actually existing socialism» in the USSR are presented in Otani (2011). An excellent exposition of the issue can also be found in Chattopadhyay (1994).

Association as a Free Human Society

Marx Called the New Society «Association»

It may be surprising to some to learn that Marx himself seldom referred to post-capitalist society as «socialism» or «communism». Rather, throughout his life, he overwhelmingly used the term «**Association**», calling the labour in this society «**associated labour**» and the mode of production the «**mode of production of associated labour**» (Marx 1894: Marx 1981, p. 743) or referring to it for short as the «associated mode of production» (Marx 1894: Marx 1981, p. 572). The subjects of this society are the «associated individuals» or «associated producers».[5] They are referred to as «individuals who treat social production as their own common capability» (Marx 1857a: Marx 1986b, p. 96), «individuals working together» (Marx 1857a: Marx 1986b, p. 398), «free men» (Marx 1872a: Marx 1976, p. 171), «socialised man» (Marx 1894: Marx 1981, p. 959), and «free and equal producers» (Marx 1872b: Marx 1988, p. 136).

Association Is Precisely a Society of Free Human Beings

This new society is thus «an association, in which the free development of each is the condition for the free development of all» (Marx and Engels 1847–1848: Marx and Engels 1976, p. 506), i.e. «a society in which the full and free development of every individual forms the ruling principle» (Marx 1872a: Marx 1876, p. 739). According to Marx, this is precisely a «free human society» (Marx 1861–1863: Marx 1975, p. 399).

Marx Later Used the Term «Co-operative Society» as Well

In his later years, Marx also characterised the new society as a «co-operative», using such expressions as «one large and harmonious system of free and co-operative labour» (Marx 1867: Marx 1985, p. 190), «the co-operative society based on common ownership of means of production» (Marx 1875: Marx 1989, p. 85), «the co-operative ownership of workers themselves» (Marx 1875: Marx 1989, p. 88), and «co-operative production» (Marx 1871: Marx 1986a, p. 335). Marx (1894) saw the «co-operative *factory*» or «co-operative *production*», which was a «new mode of production» that is «naturally formed» within capitalist society, as real examples

5 Of course, the term «associated individuals» does not refer to individuals *who are combined by any external cause* (e.g., by capital) but those *who associate* actively, consciously, and voluntarily *with each other* in pursuit of a common aim. Even in the present form of society we can see various kinds of associations everywhere, such as student groups, workers' organisations (e.g., International Workingmen's *Association*), and so on. In the nineteenth century, many reformers used that term with regard to society or the aim of social construction. Marx also seems to have felt that the word aptly expresses the active, conscious, spontaneous, and co-operative aspects of the undertakings of the individuals who form the new society.

indicating the possibility of realising an «association of free and equal producers» (Marx 1981, pp. 571–572).

What Kind of a Society Is Association?

What kind of a society, then, is the new society «Association» according to Marx? It is quite different from the image that people generally have had of «socialism» up to now.

Association of Free Individuals

This future society is, first and foremost, a society formed by the conscious and voluntary association of free *individuals*. The «ruling principle» is the «*full and free development of each individual*» (Marx 1872a: Marx 1976, p. 739), *through which a society can exist in which everyone is able to develop*, so that the society is practically synonymous with the *associated individuals* themselves. Unlike capitalist production, where the subjects are things (commodity, money, and capital), whereas individuals relate to each other as the mere personification of these things, in Association *individuals* become the *true subjects who consciously and spontaneously form society.*

Directly Social Labour of Free Individuals

The labour of these associated free individuals is *directly social labour* that reciprocally satisfies the needs of society's members through the individuals' products (*see* ◘ Fig. 2.32). In the case of commodity production, where labour is directly private, «the movement of the exchangers within society has for them the form of a movement made by things, and these things, far from being under their control, in fact control them» (Marx 1872a: Marx 1976, pp. 167–168), whereas in Association, *the individuals relate to the conditions of labour—and therefore to the products of labour as well—as the original subjects of the formation of the society.*

11

This associated labour is precisely what forms the deepest basis of Association. In other words, the *basis* of the new society is the *mode of production of associated labour.*

Common, Conscious, and Planned Control of All Production by Free Individuals

The *entirety of production (both social productive power and social relations) is controlled by the associated free individuals in a common, conscious, and planned manner.* «Socialised man, the associated producers, govern the human metabolism with nature, bringing it under their common control, instead of being dominated by it as a blind power» (Marx 1894: Marx 1981, p. 959).

Developed Social Production

In Association, there is further development of the social production that was established in the era of capitalism (i.e. large-scale production through co-operation among many individuals). The essential characteristic of large industry is the co-operation of a great number of individuals and the conscious application of science, but under capitalist production, this social nature and scientific character are subsumed within capital. In Association, however, *the free individuals as subject make nature their universal object and bring it under control through their co-operation.*

Re-established Individual Property: The Property of Associated Individuals

As we just saw in ► Sect. 11.1.1, in the petty industry that precedes capitalist production, the labouring individuals have the possibility to freely develop their own individuality by relating to nature as a subject possessing one's own conditions of labour, but this individual and private property based on one's own labour are negated by capitalist private property through the expropriation by the few. However, with the inevitability of a natural process, capitalist production negates itself, bringing about the expropriation of the few by the labouring masses, which is the negation of the negation. The property that is thereby newly established is the *property of the associated individuals*. That is to say, the individual property, or the property of the individual, is re-established, but the subject of the property is no longer the private individual but associated individuals. Through this re-establishment of individual property, the individuals—now the associated individuals—take back «a necessary condition for the development of social production and of the free individuality of the worker himself» (Marx 1872a: Marx 1976, p. 927), and therefore the individuals become able to *relate to the conditions of labour as the conditions of their own self-expression and the conditions for the creation of free individuality.*

Actualised Social Property

The establishment of the property of associated individuals marks the final elimination of capitalist private property. Thus, the social holding of the means of production through workers, which is already brought about by the social production as a matter of fact, yet concealed by the private property of capitalists, becomes actual as *social property*. «As soon as this contradictory form ceases to exit, it emerges that workers hold the means of production *socially*, not *as private individuals*» (Marx 1861–1863: Marx 1975, p. 108; Marx's emphasis). For Marx, *social property involves the large number of associated individuals relating to the large-scale means of production—and therefore to the social products produced through the utilisation of these means—as subjects vis-à-vis something belonging to themselves.*

Two Phases of Association

Marx (1875) distinguished two phases of Association (communist society) (Marx 1989, pp. 85–87). The first phase, «just as it emerges from capitalist society», is a way through which the Association must inevitably pass in order to reach a higher phase. In the higher phase, (a) the individual is no longer subservient to the division of labour, (b) the division between mental labour and physical labour has ceased to exist, (c) labour is no longer simply a «means of life» but «life's prime want» for individuals, and (d) individual's comprehensive development expands along with their productive power (capacity to labour) so that all of the sources of social wealth gush forth more abundantly. In other words, the higher phase is perfection of Association with regard to the manner and capacity of labour as well as to the necessity of the development of associated individuals.

While in the first phase the «part of the means of consumption which is divided among the individual producers» is distributed among them according to the quantity of social labour that each performs, in the higher phase each of the individuals receives the means of consumption from out of the overall product of society so as to meet their human needs as individuals seeking to fully develop themselves (*see* ◘ Fig. 1.33). This distinction between the two phases can be expressed by the following slogans: «**From each according to his abilities, to each according to his labour!**» (first phase) and «**From each according to his abilities, to each according to his needs!**» (second phase). But we should note that, with these slogans, Marx is not only speaking of the manner of distribution for the individual means of consumption but rather indicating that in Association, labour and human beings have developed to the high point where the latter slogan can be raised. In other words, this slogan implies that *labour*, regardless of the manner of distribution of the means of consumption, has *become «life's prime want» for individuals*, who labour in line with their own capabilities, according to their own awareness and volition, so as to develop into complete human beings.

A Highly Organic Organisation Composed of Various Associations

Association, moreover, is itself a *highly organic organisation* made up of various associations of individuals, rather than being a *monolithic «one country = one factory»* sort of *system where individuals are simply ordered to work by a single central organ*. Marx (1871) wrote: «*United co-operative societies* are to regulate national production upon a common plan, thus taking it under their own control» (Marx 1986a, p. 335; my emphasis). And Marx (1872b) spoke of «*A society composed of associations of free and equal producers*, carrying on the social business on a common and rational plan» (Marx 1988, p. 136; my emphasis). Needless to say, the social control of production does not mean control through the state or «society» or the like, as something distinguished from the associated individuals, nor would social property be a sort of special organ standing over them either.

Matters Eliminated in Association

In the higher phase of Association, the alienation of labour is overcome, thus eliminating various historical social forms that have caused suffering for labouring individuals. Concretely speaking this means the following:

1. Commodity production is eliminated, and therefore the commodity, money, and market cease to exist.
2. The reification of the relations of production and therefore the domination of human beings by value, money, and capital are eliminated, so that the fetishism in general also comes to an end.
3. The personification of things is eliminated, so that the individuals no longer relate with each other as persons representing various things, (commodity, money, capital, etc.).
4. The commodification of labour-power is eliminated, and therefore the labour market, wages, and wage-labour in general are also eliminated.
5. The alienation of labour is eliminated, and therefore the alienated consciousness of individuals within the labour process also ceases to exist.
6. A fixed division of labour is eliminated, and therefore the discriminated views towards concrete forms of labour, particularly the awareness of an opposition between physical and mental labour, is also eliminated.
7. Labour-time is greatly curtailed through the high development of productive powers, thus fundamentally eliminating the opposition between human beings and nature that leads to pollution and environmental destruction.
8. Every sort of class distinction and national conflict, as well as social oppression and discrimination (related to gender, race, physical disability, etc.) is eliminated.
9. The state as an apparatus of external force vis-à-vis individuals is eliminated.

Why Capitalism Inevitably Gives Birth to Association?

Marx, in analysing capitalist society, clarified that it already bears within its womb a new society and is preparing the way for that society's birth. According to Marx (1872a), *the actions of individuals aiming for Association play a role to «shorten and lessen the birth-pangs»* (Marx 1976, p. 92) *of this society* at the moment that capitalist society gives birth to its child. In other words, these individuals act as midwife to the birth of a new society.

We have already looked at Marx's view regarding *how the new society is prepared within capitalist society*. For instance, in ▸ Sect. 5.4.3, we saw how the contradictions of capitalist society deepen through the development of large-scale industry, thus developing the elements for the formation of a new society, and in ▸ Sect. 11.2.1, we saw that capitalist production itself generates the motive factors of the transition to a new form of production. But here, touching on this again, I would like to list the following three key points.

Capitalist Relations of Production Become a Fetter to the Development of Productive Powers of Society

First of all, capitalist production—by accomplishing its historical role of putting in place a high level of productive powers of society—itself becomes a limit to the further development of these powers, making necessary its replacement by a new form of production.

The concrete form for the high level of productive powers of society is *large-scale industry*, which has as its essential moments the *conscious technical application of natural science* and the *socialisation of labour*. In advanced capitalist countries, the development of productive powers proceeds to an extremely high level, as indicated by informatisation, electronisation, etc., and overall the productive powers become enormous. The so-called IT revolution that is proceeding at a pace that has exceeded expectations is not a new stage that is qualitatively different from large-scale industry but rather the development towards a new phase of the conscious technical application of natural science and the socialisation of labour. It is, in other words, a development towards a *new phase of large-scale industry*.

Capitalist production generates within itself *forms opposed to capitalist production itself that supersede private property*—such as joint-stock capital, financial capital, conglomerates, and multinational corporation—and through them obtains control of vast productive power that it then seeks to develop further. The fact that the capitalist relations of production themselves are no longer the form developing this enormous productive power is directly expressed by the fact that no developed capitalist nation *would be able to exist without the planning and regulation of the economy through the mobilisation of the state apparatus*. Without the development of a high degree of productive powers, the superseding of capitalist production is not possible, but a high level of productive powers of society, *which is the material precondition for the establishment of Association*, has already been generated in advanced capitalist countries as the fruit of capitalist production and continues to be further developed. This means that the *material conditions* for the establishment of a new society are ripening.

Results of the «Civilising Tendency of Capital» Demand the Elimination of Capital's Narrow Rule

Secondly, *capital, through the creation of a world market* and expansion and deepening of it, develops global exchange and relations of overall mutual dependence between the people of all nations, transforming human history into world history. Marx (1857–1858) called this the «**civilising tendency of capital**» (Marx 1986c, p. 336), which he saw as one *historical role played by capitalist production*. Through capital *developing labouring individuals into global citizens, its own narrow rule comes to be unsustainable*. This civilising tendency of capital is now advancing in every realm with the advancement of *internationalisation* or *globalisation*, although it takes a variety of upside-down forms. Increasingly, people of different nations are deeply enmeshed in global communication, in a variety of aspects, and their relations of interdependence are developing to an ever greater extent. One manifestation of this is the process whereby «actually existing socialism», as it has been known, is clearly revealed to be capitalism and the close connection of such countries to advanced capitalist nations via the world market. The fact that advanced capitalist nations have been forced to seriously address the task of environmental protection not only speaks to the intensity of environmental destruction but also symbolises the penetration of the civilising tendency of capital. In this way, the conditions are being put in place *for the individuals of the world—who support human society through their labour—to promote co-operation that extends beyond national boundaries*.

Capital Gives Birth to Individuals Aware of the Limitations of Capital

Thirdly, the revolutionary change of society is realised by *labouring individuals becoming aware of the limitations of the existing social system and by their conscious activity based upon that awareness*. The *necessity of the new society* thus encompasses the *necessity of the emergence and development of such awareness and action on the part labouring individuals*. Capital, meanwhile, necessarily demands that *labouring individuals—who are the bearers of large-scale industry that exists as a scientific-social process—achieve overall development so as to display their species capabilities by making nature their universal object*, and through the global communication it increasingly develops, capital drives *the individuals' awareness of being universal, global citizens*. Yet, at the same time, capital stands in the way of such overall development of labouring individuals, stifles their international solidarity, tries to keep them as separate and mutually isolated individuals and citizens of nations, and *seeks to contain these individuals within the old narrow limits*. This contradictory behaviour of capital necessarily generates and develops within the consciousness of individuals an awareness of the *limits of this mode of production and the need to break through these limitations*.

Role Played by Capitalism Within Human History Is Coming to an End

The three points listed above are *clarified by the development of the capitalist production itself when grasped through the scientific analysis of capitalism*. These points, as well as the prospect of Association resulting from them, should not be expressed in terms of a «conception» or «vision». *A familiarity with the capitalist system that forms the essence of modern society* involves, on the one hand, *appreciating the enormous role played within human history by this system*, which inevitably arose historically, while at the same time perceiving that the system generates the sort of forms that negate it and that it is losing the reasons to justify its continued existence. In other words, the *historical role that capitalism has played in preparing* the way for our *real history* as human beings to begin is reaching its end, which also marks the approaching end of what might be called the stage of human *prehistory*.

References

Chattopadhyay P (1994) The Marxian concept of capital and the soviet experience. Praeger Publishers, Westport et al

Fortescue J (1537) De laudibus legum Angliae, Companie of Stationers, London

Marx K (1857a) Einleitung zu den „Grundrissen der Kritik der politischen Ökonomie". English edition: Marx K (1986b) Introduction [to the outlines of the critique of political economy]. Marx-Engels Collected Works, vol 28. Progress Publishers et al. New York

Marx K (1857b-1858) Grundrisse der Kritik der politischen Ökonomie. English edition: Marx K (1986c) Outlines of the critique of political economy. Marx-Engels Collected Works, vol 28. Progress Publishers et al. New York

Marx K (1861–1863) Zur Kritik der politischen Ökonomie (Manuskript 1861–1863). English edition: Marx (1975) Economic Manuscript 1861–1863. Collected Works, vol. 34. Progress Publishers et al. New York

Marx K (1867) Instruktionen für die Delegierten des Provisorischen Zentralrats zu den eizelnen Fragen. English edition: Marx K (1985) Instruction for the Delegates of the Provisional General Council. The different questions. Marx-Engels Collected Works, vol 20. Progress Publishers et al. New York

Marx K (1871) The civil war in France. Address of the General Council of the International Working Men's Association. New English edition: Marx K (1986a) The Civil War in France. Marx-Engels Collected Works, vol 22. Progress Publishers et al. New York

Marx K (1872a) Das Kapital. Kritik der politischen Oekonomie. Bd. 1. Buch 1: Der Produktionsprocess des Kapitals. 2. verb. Aufl. Hamburg. English edition: Marx K (1976) Capital. A critique of political economy, vol 1 (trans: Howkes B). Penguin Books, Harmondsworth

Marx K (1872b) The Nationalisation of the land. New English edition: Marx K (1988) The Nationalisation of the land. Marx-Engels Collected Works, vol 23. Progress Publishers et al. New York

Marx K (1875) Kritik des Gothaer programms. English edition: Marx K (1989) Critique of the Gotha programme. Marx-Engels Collected Works, vol 24. Progress Publishers et al. New York
Marx K (1894) Das Kapital. Kritik der politischen Oekonomie. Bd. 3. Buch 3: Der Gesammtprocess der kapitalistischen Produktion. Hrsg. von F. Engels. Hamburg. English edition: Marx K (1981) Capital. A critique of political economy, vol 3 (trans: Fernbach D). Penguin Books, Harmondsworth
Marx K and Engels F (1847–1848) Manifest der kommunistischen Partei. English edition: Marx K and Engels F (1976) Manifesto of the Communist Party. Marx-Engels Collected Works, vol 6. Progress Publishers et al. New York
Otani T (2011) Marx's theory of association. In Japanese. Sakurai-Shoten Publishers, Tokyo
Smith A (1776) An inquiry into the nature and causes of the wealth of nations, vol 1. London. New English edition: Smith A (1937) The modern library. New York

The Process of the Circulation of Capital

Contents

The Circuit of Capital

T. Otani, *A Guide to Marxian Political Economy*,
https://doi.org/10.1007/978-3-319-65954-1_12

12.1 Theme of Part II and the Path of Investigation

Part I Assumed an Uninterrupted Circulation of Capital

Up to now, we have examined the production process of capital as the foundation of capitalism (▶ Chapters 3, 4, 5, 6, 7, 8, 9, and 10 in Part I) based on our understanding of the commodity and money (▶ Chap. 2 in Part I). But there we had to temporarily set aside the analysis of the circulation process of capital that is indispensable to the movement of capital, i.e. M–C (or more precisely, M–Mp and M–Lp) and C′–M′.

The premise in Part I, in other words, was that the circulation process proceeded smoothly, without any interruption. This assumption allowed us to focus on the production process. One exception was our examination of the buying and selling of labour-power, fundamental to capitalist production, in order to clarify the wage form assumed by the value of labour-power and consider the influence capital accumulation has on the sale and purchase of labour-power (in terms of its supply and demand and the level of wages).

In short, the formal metamorphoses that capital undergoes in the circulation process (M–C and C–M) have been premised up to now, so that our assumption has been that a capitalist is always able to purchase the necessary means of production at their value and also sell the resulting product at its value.

Examining Circulation Based on Our Understanding of the Production Process

The understanding of the production process of capital gained in Part I has put us in a position to now examine the circulation process of capital that had been set aside temporarily.

Path for Investigating Circulation Process of Capital

We will begin, in ▶ Chap. 12, by examining individual capital to consider the various forms it takes in its circuit and the various forms of the circuit itself, followed by a look at circulation time and circulation costs.

▶ Chapter 13 will then examine the «turnover» of capital, which is the circuit of capital as a cyclical process repeated within a given period of time. From that perspective, capital can be referred to as «fixed capital» or «circulating capital», depending on the differences of circulation form. These two concepts are employed to clarify how the valorisation process is affected by the ratio of production time to circulation time within the circuit and by the proportions between different elements of capital.

Finally, in ▶ Chap. 14, we turn to the circulation process of the total social capital, made up of individual capitals that are intertwined and interdependent. Our aim here is to analyse social reproduction under the capitalist mode of production: an analysis that encompasses the relations of production, circulation, and consumption. This analysis of the circulation of the total social capital is premised on our earlier study of the production process of capital, so it serves to clarify the total process of capital, both production and circulation.

Examining the Concrete Forms Within the Total Process

Once we have understood the total process of capital movement through the production and circulation processes, for both individual and social capital, we will be in a position, in Part III, to examine the concrete forms of capital and surplus-value within the total process of capital.

12.2 Circuit of Capital and Its Three Forms

12.2.1 Concept of the Circuit of Capital

Concept of Circuit

The term **circuit** refers here to starting off from a certain point and passing through a cyclical process to return to that initial point—so that the **departure point** becomes the **returning point** (*see* ◘ Fig. 12.1).

Circuit of Capital

Capital, in its movement, is continually assuming and shedding the forms of money, production element, and commodity. This circuit of capital is always a cyclical movement that returns to the given starting point, regardless of whether the starting point is money, the production elements, or the commodity. This movement of capital is called **circuit of capital**.

12.2.2 Three Forms Taken by Capital Within Its Circuit

Three Forms of Capital: Money Capital (M) → Productive Capital (P) → Commodity Capital (C)

The capital within the circuit of capital takes the form of money, the production elements, or commodity, which are referred to, respectively, by the terms **money capital**, **productive capital**, and **commodity capital** (*see* ◘ Fig. 12.2).

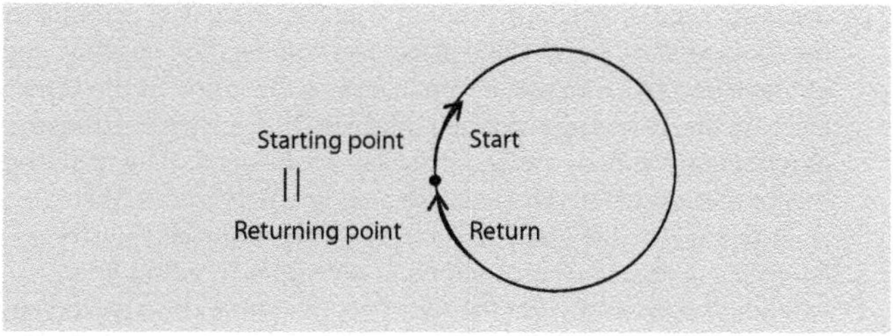

◘ **Fig. 12.1** Circuit

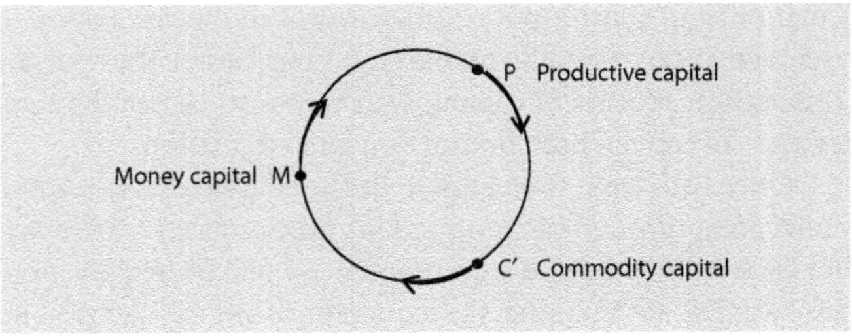

Fig. 12.2 Circuit of capital

Money capital, productive capital, and commodity capital are the three forms that capital assumes within the circuit of capital. The abbreviations for money, production element, and commodity are **M**, **P**, and **C**, but in our discussion of the forms taken by capital, these abbreviations will also indicate money capital, productive capital, and commodity capital, respectively.

Industrial Capital

Capital examined thus far included within its circuit the production process, wherein surplus-value is absorbed to augment capital (*see* Fig. 3.17). Expressed using abbreviations, this capital augments as in the formula below[1]. (In the formula, **Mp** stands for means of production, **Lp** for labour-power, **P** for the production process, and ... indicates an interruption of the circulation process.)

$$M\text{–}C\left\langle\begin{matrix}Mp\\ Lp\end{matrix}\right. \ldots P \ldots \; C'\text{–}M'$$

However, as we shall see, the circulation process includes two different types of capital: *commercial capital* (augmented in the form of M–C–M′) and *interest-bearing capital* (augmented simply through the movement of money going out

1 Mp and Lp in the formula express the fact that commodities (C) purchased by money (M) consist of labour-power (Lp) and the means of production (Mp). I should note that in *Capital,* contrary to the formula here, Marx (1885) places the abbreviation Lp above the abbreviation Mp, which is reasonable since the former is the active factor in the valorisation process (Marx 1978, p. 124). Nevertheless, as readers are already aware, I place labour-power (Lp) beneath the means of production (Mp) *in all the diagrams of this book.* This positioning was due solely to such technical reason, as I illustrate *labour* (or *labour-time*) proceeding as time goes by with a line extending *downwards.* For the sake of consistency, I also placed Lp beneath Mp in this formula.

and coming back as money, or M–M′). Distinct from those two types of capital is **industrial capital**, which is augmented through the absorption of surplus-value in the production process. The term «industrial» in this case encompasses *all production sectors operated capitalistically*. Industrial capital is capital that *moves by taking on and shedding the three forms of money capital, productive capital, and commodity capital*.

For the present, our analysis will be limited to industrial capital (*see* ▶ Chaps. 18 and 19 in Part III for a discussion of commercial capital and interest-bearing capital).

12.2.3 Three Circuit Forms

Significance of Examining the Three Circuit Forms

Three Forms of the Capital Circuit

With the repetition of the circuit of capital, it becomes possible to see that each of the *three circuits* (money capital, productive capital, and commodity capital) has a different point of departure/return:

Circuit of money capital: M–C...P...C′–M′
Circuit of productive capital: P...C′–M′–C...P
Circuit of commodity capital: C′–M′–C...P...C′

We can see that in the cyclical movement of capital as M–C...P...C′–M′, commodity (C) appears twice (as C and C′). The first C, however, is not the commodity to be realised through its transformation into money but rather consists of *elements of production that should shed the commodity form to be transformed into productive capital* P. In other words, in that circuit, the C in M–C is *not* an independent form within the circuit of capital. Because the C in M–C is converted into productive capital P, it would be meaningless to treat the circuit that takes this C as its departure/return point as a special circuit form. Therefore, M–C...P...C′–M′, as a circuit form, is M–(C=)P...C′–M′, and P...C′–M′–C...P, as a circuit form, is P...C′–M′–(C=)P.

Importance of Analysing Each of the Three Circuit Forms

It might seem formalistic to distinguish between the three circuits, since the actual movement of capital is a unity of them. However, when the movement of capital is viewed from the perspective of each particular circuit, various things immediately became apparent, and certain problems can be elucidated. Therefore, in examining the circulation process of capital, we need to first analyse the three circuits and then summarise the results of these analyses.

The mercantilists, Classical economists, and physiocrats each placed an emphasis on just one of the three circuits when analysing the movement of capital. Fruitful results did emerge from the analysis of each school, but the scope was limited given that one-dimensional approach.

Circuit of Money Capital (M...M′ Circuit: M–C...P...C′–M′)

Circuit of Money Capital

The circuit in which money capital is the departure/return point is the **circuit of money capital**, which can be diagrammed as below:

$$M\text{–}C\ldots P\ldots C' \begin{cases} C- \\ \delta c- \end{cases} -M' \begin{cases} M \\ \delta m \end{cases}$$

(Symbols c and m in δc and δm here signify respectively commodity and money.)

Circuit of Money Capital Clearly Expresses the Essence of Capital

The circuit M...M′ most generally and clearly expresses the *valorisation at the essence of capital.* In this circuit, the productive process appears as a means for, or intermediary point in, valorisation. Even if that intermediary point is ignored, the overall circulation process is M–C–M′, which expresses the circulation of capital.

Characteristic of M–C as the Circulation of Capital

Capital must, first of all, purchase labour-power (Lp), which is premised on the existence of a class of wageworkers and therefore the existence of the capital relation (i.e. the separation of Mp from Lp). Second, capital must buy sufficient Mp to absorb all of the labour, including surplus-labour. So there must be adequate M to make those purchases. This is the special trait of M–C as the circulation of capital.

Characteristic of C–M as the Circulation of Capital

First of all, C′ contains surplus-value, which makes C–M into C′–M′. Second, through this C′–M′, the capitalist can thus obtain from circulation a sum of money greater than the money advanced. And third, the capitalist must transform into M′ all of the C′ that contains surplus-value. Here we have the special trait of C′–M′ as the circulation of capital.

Industries in Which Capital Takes Distinctive Circuit Forms

In certain industries, such as the **transport industry**, capital takes the distinctive form of M–C...P–M′ because the products of capital do not take the form of independent commodities (C′). Likewise, in the **gold mining industry**, because the direct product is gold, which circulates directly as money, the circuit takes a similar form: M–C...P–M′.

Specific Traits of the Circuit of Money Capital

The current of money capital has the following specific traits:

1. Begins with the circulation process, passes through the production process, and ends up at the circulation process.
2. Circuit clearly reveals the aim and motive of the movement of industrial capital as the augmentation of capital.

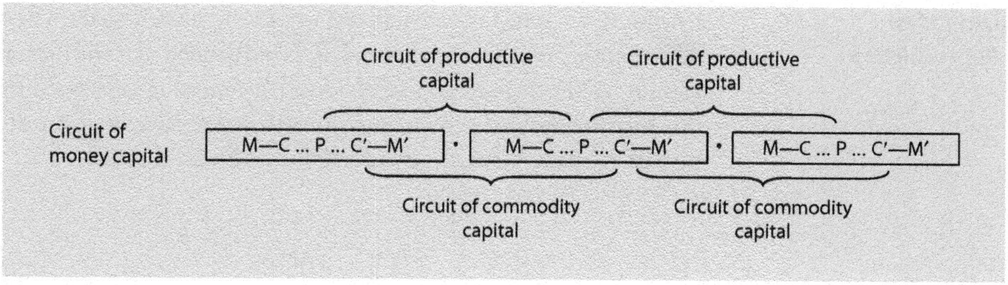

Fig. 12.3 Repetition of the circuit of money capital includes the circuit of productive capital and the circuit of commodity capital

3. The production process is manifested as an intermediate link (or necessary evil) for the augmentation of capital.

The circuit of money capital is the form that the *mercantilists* dealt with in their analysis of capital.

Three Circuit Forms of Capital

Capital is incessantly repeating its circuit to be self-augmenting value. Observing the circuit of money capital as a repeated process reveals the circuit of productive capital and the circuit of commodity capital (*see* Fig. 12.3).

Circuit of Productive Capital (P...P Circuit: P...C′–M′–C...P)

Circuit of Productive Capital

The circuit in which productive capital is the departure/return point is the **circuit of productive capital**. The productive capital at the point of departure is capital whose value is to be augmented in the production process. Therefore, the productive capital at the point of return is likewise productive capital whose value is to be augmented in the production process. This means that the return to the starting point is the return of the production process and its renewal. This circuit expresses the periodically repeating function of productive capital and thus represents reproduction.

Because the circuit of productive capital represents reproduction, we need to observe it in the case of both **simple reproduction** and **expanded reproduction**.

Simple Reproduction

The simple reproduction of productive capital is carried out when all surplus-value is consumed by the capitalist, rather than being used for further production. The formula below shows the circuit of productive capital under simple reproduction.

$$P \ldots C' \left\{ \begin{array}{l} C- \\ \delta c- \end{array} \right. -M' \left\{ \begin{array}{l} M-C \ldots P \\ \delta m-\delta c \end{array} \right.$$

(Symbol δ in δc and δm signifies 'increment', and c and m signify respectively 'commodity' and 'money'.)

Expanded Reproduction

Productive capital is reproduced on an expanded scale when all or some of the surplus-value is advanced as additional capital (ΔM). This circuit of productive capital is expressed by the formula below, which indicates the case in which a portion of surplus-value is advanced as additional capital.

$$P\ldots C'\left\{\begin{array}{l} C- \\ \\ \delta c- \end{array}\right. -M'\left\{\begin{array}{l} M == M-C \\ \quad\ \nearrow \Delta M-\Delta C \\ \delta m \longrightarrow \kappa m-\kappa c \end{array}\right\}\ldots P'$$

(Symbol Δ in ΔM and ΔC signifies 'added to capital'; κ in κm and κc signifies 'belonging to capitalist'.)

Circuit of Productive Capital Expresses the Repetition of Production Process

The circuit of P...P expresses the fact that the *production process is repeated through the mediation of the circulation process.* If we abstract from valorisation in the production process, overall circulation takes the form of simple commodity circulation: C–M–C. This circuit is suitable for elucidating the *conditions of circulation for the reproduction of capital.*

Conditions for Repetition of the Production Process

The circuit of productive capital shows that, under capitalist production, the circulation process C–M–C must proceed smoothly for the production process to repeat itself.

Development of a Possibility of Crisis

Simple commodity circulation already contains the **possibility of crisis**. This is because if C–M is not realised for a commodity, the subsequent M–C also becomes impossible and prevents, in turn, the realisation of C–M for another commodity. In this way, a *chain reaction can arise from the impossibility of a sale.* But the circuit of productive capital contains, *in a more developed form*, the possibility of crisis, which arises from a halt in circulation that makes it impossible to carry out production. This is because if *a capital* is unable to realise C–M, this makes it impossible for the M–C of this *capital* and the κm-κc of the *capitalist* involved to be realised. In turn, this makes it impossible to realise the C(Lp)–M–C(Rp) of the *workers* who buy their requisite products (Rp) after the sale of their labour-power (Lp) to this capitalist or to realise the C–M of other *capitals*. There is a possibility of this sort of *chain reaction of stagnation and constriction of reproduction.*

Reservation and Advance of Accumulation Funds

The advance of **additional capital** for expanded reproduction generally requires the expenditure of a large sum of money to purchase new plant facilities and equipment for them. Thus, in order to transform surplus-value into capital (accumulation), surplus-value must be saved up over a certain period of time as an accumulation fund. Money taken out of circulation to be reserved for an **accumulation fund** forms a money hoard, which can be advanced for actual accumulation either as a means of purchase or as a means of payment.

Specific Traits of the Circuit of Productive Capital

The circuit of productive capital has the following traits:

1. Circuit begins with the production process, passes through the circulation process, and ends up at the starting point of production.
2. Circulation process is a means and condition for the repetition of production.
3. Movement of capital presents itself as production for production's sake and accumulation for accumulation's sake.

The circuit of productive capital is the form that *Classical economists* dealt with in their analysis of capital.

Circuit of Commodity Capital (C′...C′ Circuit: C′–M′–C...P...C′)

Circuit of Commodity Capital

The circuit in which commodity capital is the departure/return point is the **circuit of commodity capital.**

This circuit of commodity capital must also be observed in the case of both simple and expanded reproduction.

Simple Reproduction

The simple reproduction of commodity capital, expressed in the formula below, is carried out when the capitalist consumes all of the surplus-value, rather than using it for production.

$$C' \begin{cases} C- \\ \quad -M' \begin{cases} M-C\ldots P\ldots C' \begin{cases} C \\ \delta c \end{cases} \\ \delta m-\delta c \end{cases} \\ \delta c- \end{cases}$$

Expanded Reproduction

Commodity capital is reproduced on an expanded scale when all or some of the surplus-value is advanced as additional capital (δM). The circuit of commodity capital for expanded reproduction is depicted in the formula below, which expresses the case in which a *portion* of surplus-value is advanced as additional capital.

$$C' \begin{cases} C- \\ \quad -M' \begin{cases} \left.\begin{array}{l} M == M-C \\ \quad \Delta M-\Delta C \end{array}\right\}\ldots P'\ldots C' \begin{cases} C \\ \delta c \end{cases} \\ \delta m \nearrow \longrightarrow \kappa m-\kappa c \end{cases} \\ \delta c- \end{cases}$$

Circuit of Commodity Capital Expresses the Reproduction of the Total Commodity Product

The circuit of C′...C′ expresses the *reproduction of the total commodity product, including surplus-value.* It begins with the circulation process of the total product and therefore includes not only productive consumption but also accumulation from surplus-value, the consumption of capitalists, and the consumption of workers. Thus, this circuit is suitable to observe *the capitalist circulation process directly and comprehensively.*

Intertwining of the Circulation of Capital and the Circulation of Revenue

The circuit of commodity capital suggests *the intertwining of capitals, the intertwining of production and consumption, and the intertwining of the circulation of capital and the circulation of revenue.*

Circuit Form for Observing the Reproduction and Circulation Process of the Total Social Capital

If we consider this circuit as the *circuit of the total social capital,* C′ is the total annual product of society, and this circuit encompasses all of the elements of social production and consumption. Observing the *reproduction and circulation of the total social capital* within this form makes it possible to clarify, in an integrated way, the overall movement of production and consumption under capitalist production (as will be done in ▶ Chap. 14).

Specific Traits of the Circuit of Commodity Capital

The circuit of commodity capital has the following traits:

1. Circuit begins with the circulation process and ends with the production process.
2. The process of capital must include the realisation of surplus-value.
3. Movement of capital presents itself as the intertwining between capital and capital, production and consumption, and the circulation of capital and the circulation of revenue.

The circuit of commodity capital is the form that the *physiocrats* (led by *Quesnay*) dealt with in their analysis of capital.

Concrete Movement Forms of Individual Industrial Capitals

Division into Three Capital Forms and Parallel Progression of the Three Capital Circuits

In the movement of individual capitals as well, each capital is divided into three parts to assume the forms of money capital, productive capital, and commodity capital. There is thus a parallel progression of three circuit forms: the money capital, productive capital, and commodity capital circuits (*see* ◘ Fig. 12.4).

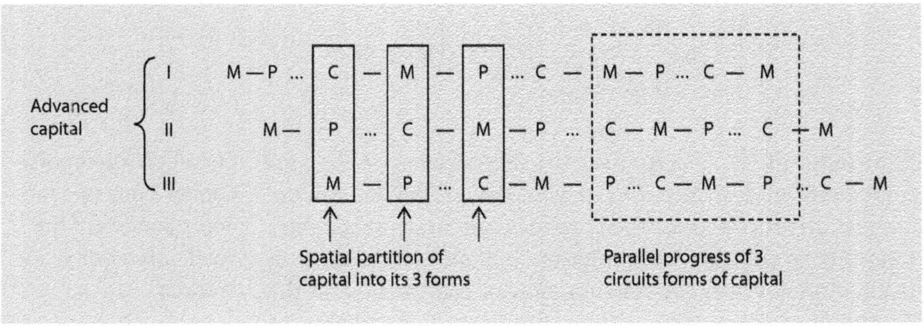

◘ **Fig. 12.4** Spatial partition of capital into its three forms and parallel progress of its three circuits

12.3 Circulation Time and Circulation Costs

12.3.1 Circulation Time

Production Time and Circulation Time of Capital

The circuit of capital, viewed from the time it takes to elapse, consists of the **production time** that capital passes through in the production process and the **circulation time** during which capital remains within the circulation process.

Production Time and Circulation Time

Circulation Time of Capital: Selling Time and Buying Time

The circulation time of capital consists of the **selling time** necessary for C′–M′ and the **buying time** necessary for M–C. Of the two, *selling time is of decisive importance to capital* because C′–M′ is a process, whereby a commodity must find a buyer on the market, whereas M–C is merely the process of purchasing a given product on the market by means of money (general equivalent).

Selling Time and Buying Time

Circulation Time and Valorisation

Circulation time is indispensable to capital, but it is a time during which the *production process is interrupted* and *capital remains in the commodity or money form*, so that no valorisation is carried out (*see* ◘ Fig. 12.5). Capital therefore tends to restrict circulation time to the absolute minimum (as we will examine in ► section ««Circulation Without Circulation Time»: A Necessary Tendency of Capital»).

Circulation Time Is a Period of Interrupted Valorisation

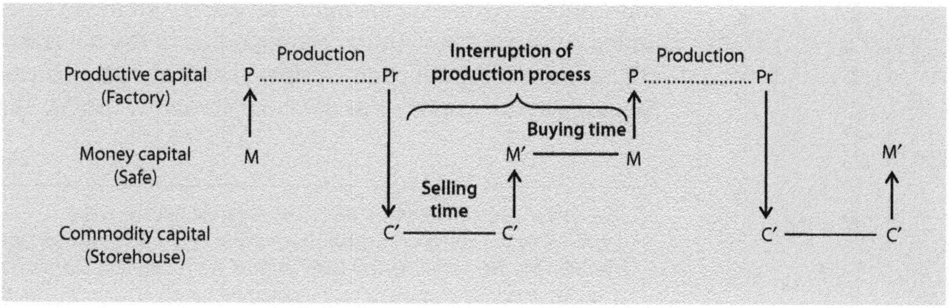

◘ **Fig. 12.5** Interruption of production process (valorisation) by circulation time

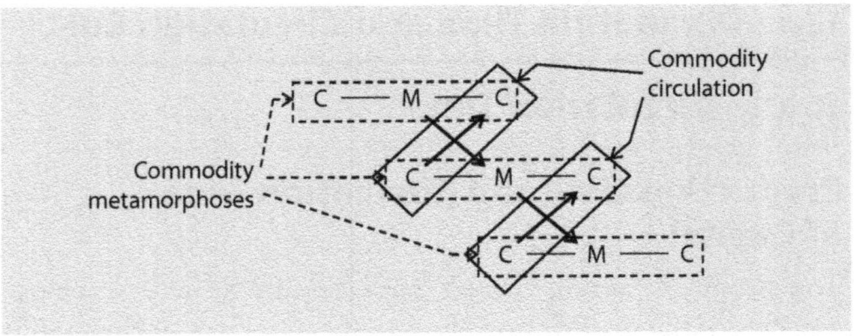

■ Fig. 12.6 Intertwining of commodity metamorphoses through commodity circulation

12.3.2 Circulation Costs

Circulation Process of Capital and Commodity Circulation

Capital Circulation Accompanies Commodity Circulation

In the circulation process of capital, commodity capital that bears surplus-value (C′) must be transformed into M′. This C′–M′, which corresponds to M–C from the side of the capitalists or workers, accompanies the circulation of money as well as the circulation of commodities, i.e. the changing of hands.[2]

Intertwining of Commodity Metamorphoses in Commodity Circulation

Let us begin by looking at how, within the commodity circulation examined in ▶ Chap. 1 in Part I (*see* ▶ Fig. 2.50), the *commodity metamorphosis of C–M–C* is mediated by and intertwined with the circulation of money (*see* ■ Fig. 12.6).

Intertwining of Capital Metamorphoses in Capital Circulation

The metamorphosis C–M–C also is included in the circuit of capital, so that it is simultaneously the metamorphosis of capital (capital value). Let us consider, then, how the *capital metamorphosis C–M–C is mediated by and intertwined with the circulation of money* (*see* ■ Fig. 12.7).

Intertwining of the Metamorphoses of Capital and Revenue

The M–C corresponding to capital C′–M′ includes not only the purchase of the means of production by capitalists but also the purchase of means of consumption by capitalists and workers, i.e. the circulation of revenue. And the M–C of capital consists of M–C(Mp) corresponding to the capitalist's sale of means of production C(Mp)–M and M–C(Lp) corresponding to the worker's sale of labour-power C(Lp)–M. The

---

2 The «circulation of commodities» that «change hands» is not identical to the «physical distribution» examined in the next section «▶ Two Moments of Physical Distribution: Transport and Storage». The circulation of commodities that change hands is accompanied by the transference of the property title of a commodity, whereas that is not necessarily the case for physical distribution. For instance, the circulation that occurs for the sale of a house is not accompanied by physical distribution.

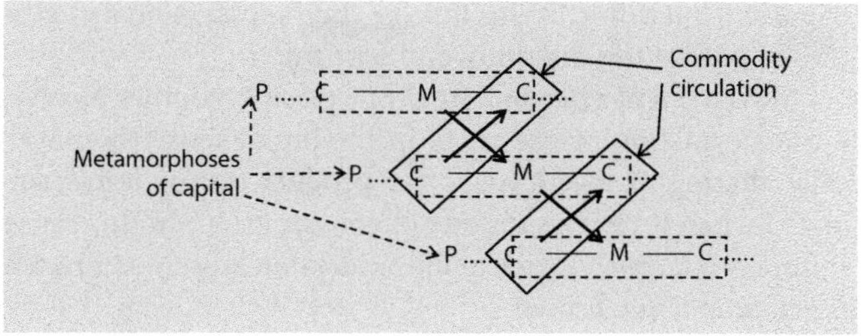

Fig. 12.7 Intertwining of capital metamorphoses through commodity circulation

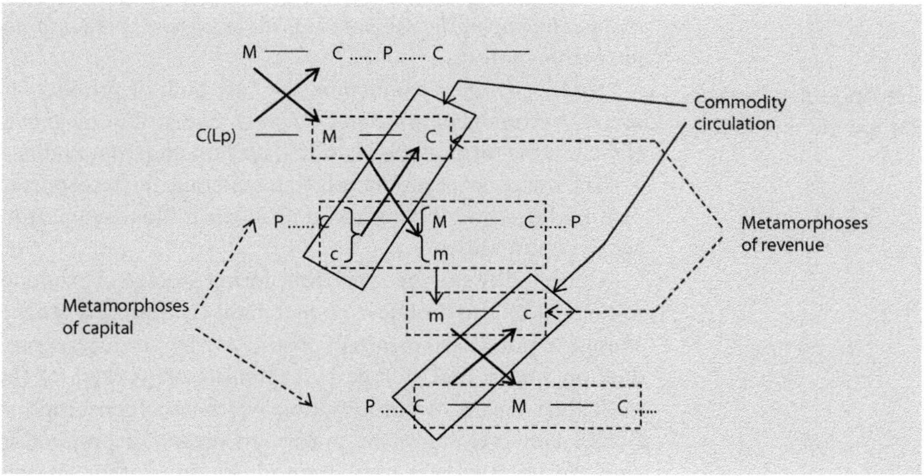

Fig. 12.8 Intertwining of metamorphoses of capital and revenue through commodity circulation

following diagram depicts how the metamorphosis of capital (M–C–M) is mediated by the circulation of money and intertwined with those purchases and sales (*see* Fig. 12.8).

Two Moments of Physical Distribution: Transport and Storage

Two Moments of Physical Distribution: Transport and Storage of Products

In any form of society, most of the *products* that emerge from the production process must pass through a *physical movement* (to a greater or lesser extent) prior to their consumption. This movement is broadly referred to today as **physical distribution**, which is a movement always accompanied by a temporal and spatial *inactivity*. Physical distribution requires two human activities: *transporting* the product from the site of production to the site of consumption and then the *storing* of the product in a stagnant or stocked condition. **Transport** and **storage** are the two main activities necessary for physical distribution, but they can also involve such supplementary activities of **packaging**, **loading**, and **sorting**.

Physical Distribution and the Production Process

Movement of a product from one place to another involves a transformation of use-value in the broad sense (by physically altering its location), so the product is only fully completed when it reaches the site of consumption. In this sense, *transport is a continuation of the production process* or an *additional production process*.

In contrast, storage does not bring about a change in the use-value of a commodity. It does, however, maintain that use-value, preventing its deterioration or depletion, and to this extent *storage* can be seen as *having the productive character of acting upon the use-value, as an extension of the original production process*.

Transport and Storage (Stock) of Commodities

Under capitalist production, the vast bulk of products in society becomes commodities, so physical distribution generally takes the form of the *physical distribution of commodities*.

The transport of products is thus generally the transport of commodities, and the storage of products is likewise the storage of commodities.

Commodity storage takes three forms: storage of products to be sold by the producer or merchant (commodity stock), storage of purchased means of production by producers (production stock), and storage by capitalists or workers of the individual means of consumption purchased (consumption stock). However, since the purchased means of production and consumption are not commodities, but rather latently part of the production or consumption process, only the first of those three forms (commodity stock) is *inherently the storage of commodities*.

Circulation Costs

Circulation Costs in the Broad Sense

Unlike production costs, which are made up of the objectified labour (value of the means of production) and the living labour expended in the production process, the **circulation costs** consist of the *objectified labour* (value of the material means) and the *living labour expended in the circulation process*.

The **production costs**, taken together, form the value of a commodity. The value of the means of production is transferred to the commodities, and all the living labour, objectified in the commodities, becomes new value. Since value is not produced in the realm of circulation, however, the necessary circulation costs do not add value to the product; their value is, in fact, a deduction from surplus-value.

Transport and storage, which are the two activities necessary for physical distribution, do have a productive character, however. As an extension of the original production process, the costs for physical distribution constitute quasi-production costs. Circulation costs thus can generally be divided into **physical distribution costs** and **pure circulation costs.**

Costs of Physical Distribution

Costs for physical distribution, i.e. transport and storage costs, *add to the value* of a commodity, as do the costs necessary for packaging, handling, sorting, etc. that accompany transport and storage. However, if these costs did not exist, the production of the product could be expanded by a corresponding amount, and *in this sense* they constitute the **faux frais of production**[3]. Moreover, storage costs that arise when the commodity metamorphosis is held up, resulting in an involuntary commodity stock, do not add value to the commodity.

Pure Circulation Costs

The costs for a solely formal change of value (C–M or M–C), particularly those costs necessary for the change of value from commodity form to money form (i.e. C′–M′ as the realisation of commodity capital), are pure circulation costs. Such costs *add absolutely no value to the commodity* and are a *faux frais of production* that is a *deduction from already existing value (surplus-value)* and must thus be compensated for by that surplus-value.

«Circulation Without Circulation Time»: A Necessary Tendency of Capital

Capital Seeks To Limit Circulation Time and Circulation Costs to the Minimum

The circuit of industrial capital encompasses the circulation process C–M–C. Of the C–M (sale) and M–C (purchase) in this circuit, it is C–M that poses the decisive difficulty. This involves the ultimate sale of the commodity value in C′ to transform it into M′. Industrial capital requires—to a greater or lesser degree—time (circulation time) and costs (circulation costs) for the sale. But this time limits production time, and the circulation costs must be deducted from the surplus-value. Circulation time and costs thus represent a *faux frais of production* for capital, and industrial capital seeks to limit such costs to the absolute minimum.

«Circulation Without Circulation Time»

Capital's tendency to limit circulation time and costs to the minimum can be, according to Marx (1857–1858), referred to simply as «**circulation without circulation time**» (Marx 1986, p. 49). Here «circulation time» refers more generally to the *time and costs that are both* needed for circulation. This tendency of capital for «circulation without circulation time» is

---

3 The concept «*faux frais of production*» was used by Classical political economists to refer to «incidental expenses» incurred in the productive advance of capital.

an indispensable moment for commercial capital's independence from industrial capital (*see* ► Chap. 18 in Part III) and for the establishment of the banking system (*see* ► Chap. 19 in Part III).

References

Marx K (1857–1858) Grundrisse der Kritik der politischen Ökonomie. MEGA II/1, Berlin 1976–1981. English edition: Marx K (1986) Outlines of the critique of political economy. Marx-Engels Collected Works, vol 28. Progress Publishers et al. New York

Marx K (1885) Das Kapital. Kritik der politischen Oekonomie. Bd. 2. Buch 2: Der Circulationsprocess des Kapitals. Hrsg. von F. Engels. Hamburg. English edition: Marx K (1978) Capital. A critique of political economy, vol 2 (trans: Fernbach D). Penguin Books

Turnover of Capital

T. Otani, *A Guide to Marxian Political Economy*,
https://doi.org/10.1007/978-3-319-65954-1_13

13.1 Turnover Time and Number of Turnovers

13.1.1 Concept of Turnover

Concept of Turnover

Whereas the term «circuit» in the circuit of capital (dealt with in ► Chap. 12) refers to a circular movement that returns to the point of departure, **turnover** signifies the repetition and continuation of a circuit until a certain point of time is reached. This, in other words, is the circuit viewed as a periodically repeating movement.

Turnover of Capital

As the term implies, the **turnover of capital** is the movement of capital as a process, whereby the capital advanced continues its circuit until it refluxes. As we shall see in ► Sect. 13.3, individual circuits also display a circular movement, but this does not mean that all the capital advanced in one circuit returns. The reflux of the advanced capital, generally speaking, requires the capital to pass through numerous circuits, which is why the concept of turnover is necessary.

13.1.2 Turnover Time of Capital

Turnover Time

The time that elapses for the entirety of the capital value advanced in the money form to flow back in the money form is called **turnover time**.

Turnover Time = Production Time + Circulation Time

Turnover time encompasses many repeating circuits. The time elapsing for each circuit consists of *production time* and *circulation time*. The sum of the production time and circulation time equals the turnover time.

13

Production Time = Labour-Time + Non-labour-Time

Production time is not identical to the **labour-time** during which labour is carried out because there can be times where labour is not applied to the object of labour in production. The time needed to make wine, for instance, involves an ageing process during which no labour is carried out and only the power of nature is applied to the raw materials. Production time can thus contain such **non-labour-time**.

Circulation Time = Selling Time + Buying Time

The circulation time of capital, as noted earlier, includes selling time and buying time, both of which are indispensable to the movement of capital. Of the two, however, differences in selling time, in particular, bring about differences in the turnover time.

Turnover Time Varies Among Production Spheres

Turnover time will vary depending on the production sphere in which capital is advanced.

13.1.3 Number of Turnovers of Capital

Turnover Time and Number of Turnovers

When comparing the turnover speed of different capitals, we can compare not only the absolute magnitude of **turnover time** but also the number of turnovers in a given period. **Number of turnovers** refers to how many times a turnover occurs in a given period of time, usually during 1 year. If we use the letter u to refer to the monthly turnover time and n to refer to the number of turnovers in a year, then we arrive at the equation $u = 12/n$; therefore, $n = 12/u$, or $n \times u = 12$.

13.2 Fixed Capital and Circulating Capital

13.2.1 Fixed Capital and Circulating Capital

Differences in the Reflux of Capital

If our point of focus is the reflux of the advanced capital, capital can be divided into two capitals that differ from the distinction between constant and variable capital.

Circulating Capital

One part of the advanced capital *reappears in its entirety in the value of the product during each individual circuit and then flows back in the money form through the sale of the product*. The value of the object of labour (raw materials) is all transferred to the product in the individual production processes. The value of *labour-power* is entirely reproduced within the product in the individual production processes. These portions of the capital—i.e. capital advanced in the object of labour and in labour-power—are called **circulating capital**.

Fixed Capital

In contrast, one part of the advanced capital *only transfers a portion of its advanced value to the product in each individual production process and then recovers that amount in the money form through the sale of the product, while the remaining value is fixed at the site of production*. Tools and machinery are the primary examples of this capital value advanced for the means of labour. The value of the capital advanced flows back little by little with each repeated circuit, eventually flowing back entirely after an extended period of time. We call this part of the capital **fixed capital**.

Fixed Capital and Circulating Capital

The difference between fixed capital and circulating capital is a *distinction of the constituent elements of productive capital from the perspective of the circulation mode of value* (see ◘ Fig. 13.1).

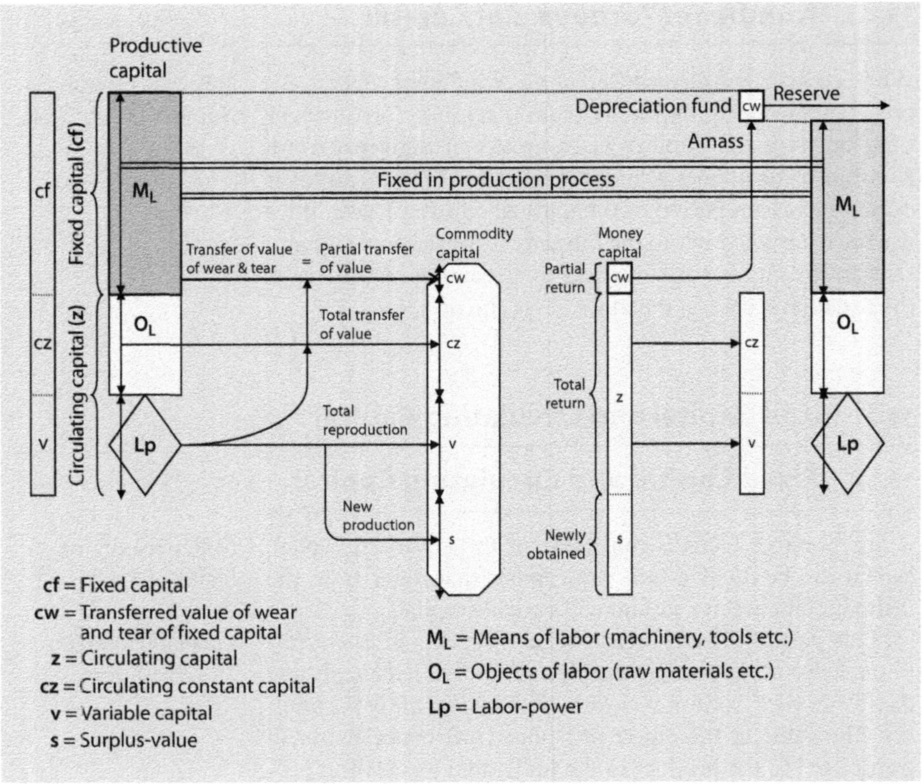

Fig. 13.1 Fixed capital and circulating capital

13

13.2.2 Distinction Between Fixed Capital and Circulating Capital and Distinction Between Constant Capital and Variable Capital

Different Perspective of the Two Categories and Their Interrelation

The *distinction between fixed capital and circulating capital* is a distinction that pertains to the concrete form of capital movement. Capitalists are always aware of this distinction in the course of their practical activities. In contrast, the *distinction between constant capital and variable capital*, examined earlier (*see* ▶ Sect. 3.1.5), does not reach people's everyday consciousness because it concerns the essential movement of capital concealed by surface phenomena. The latter is a distinction regarding capital from the perspective of valorisation, whereas the former centres on the circulation of capital value. We need to clearly grasp the difference between the two as well as their interrelation (*see* ■ Fig. 13.2).

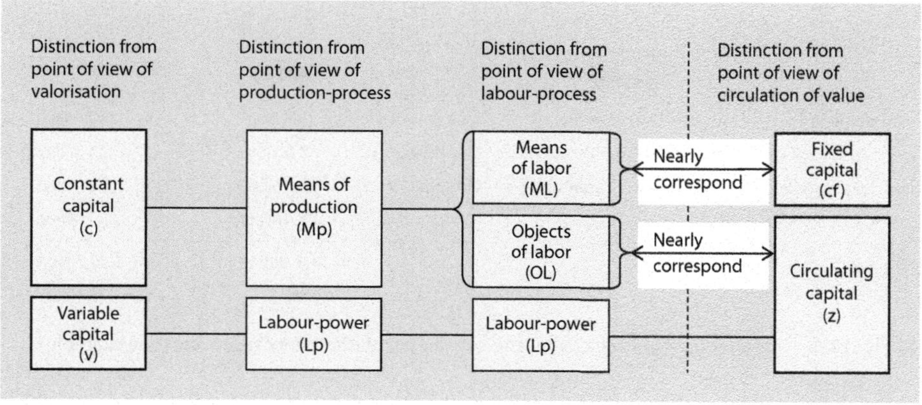

Fig. 13.2 Distinction between fixed capital and circulating capital and distinction between constant capital and variable capital

Cases Where Means of Labour Are Not Fixed Capital

The diagram above shows that the object of labour and labour-power are always circulating capital, but the means of labour are not necessarily fixed capital. For example, in the case of a pneumatic hammer used in shipbuilding, several hammers might be used up in the course of building one ship. The capital advanced for those hammers would thus be classified as circulating capital, rather than fixed capital. Such cases exist because the distinction between fixed capital and circulating capital is ultimately a distinction made from the perspective of the circulation mode of the value of productive capital, i.e. from the perspective of turnover.

13.3 Effects of Turnover of Capital on the Valorisation of Capital

13.3.1 Average Turnover of the Total Capital Advanced and Turnover Cycles

Average Turnover Time and Average Number of Turnovers

There is a difference in turnover time between fixed capital and circulating capital. And there are even differences within the category of fixed capital, such as the difference between factory buildings and machinery. The *turnover time of the entire capital advanced*, i.e. the *time for the entire sum of advanced capital to reflux*, is calculated by adding the weighted averages of the turnovers of each of the parts that compose this capital. For example, the following sort of calculation can be carried out (*see* Fig. 13.3).

In this example, the 4.3 billion yen advanced in total only has an average annual turnover of 3.95 billion yen. That is to

Elements of production	Turnover time		Annual number of turnovers		Invested value of capital		Annual sum of turnovers
Buildings	20 years (240 months)	→	1/20 times	×	¥ 1 billion	=	¥ 50 million
Machinery	10 years (120 months)	→	1/10 times	×	¥ 3 billion	=	¥ 300 million
Raw materials	1/12th of year (1 month)	→	12 times	×	¥ 200 million	=	¥ 2.4 billion
Labour-power	1/12th of year (1 month)	→	12 times	×	¥ 100 million	=	¥ 1.2 billion
					¥ 4.3 billion		¥ 3.95 billion

Fig. 13.3 Turnover time of total capital and calculation of number of turnovers (one example)

say, it takes about 1.09 years to complete one turnover of the entire 4.3 billion yen advanced.

Turnover Cycle

Regardless of the average turnover, the overall reflux movement of the total capital includes the repetition of the short-term turnover of the monthly reflux of capital value advanced in raw materials and labour-power but is at the same time a circular movement over a long period of time during which the full capital value advanced in the factory building finally flows back in the money form after 20 years, while the capital value advanced in the machinery flows back after 10 years. This circuit is called the **turnover cycle**. Both the average turnover time and the period of the turnover cycle are extremely significant for the valorisation of capital[1].

13.3.2 Quantity and Rate of Annual Surplus-value

13

Quantity and Rate of Annual Surplus-value

We saw earlier (*see* ► Sect. 3.2.1) that the degree of capital valorisation can be best grasped by the rate of surplus-value,

1 The significance of the turnover cycle for the actual movement of capitalist production can be grasped from the following observation by Marx (1885): «We can assume that, for the most important branches of large-scale industry, this *life cycle* [i.e. turnover cycle] is now on average a 10 year one. The precise figure is not important here. The result is that the cycle of related turnovers, extending over a number of years, within which the capital is confined by its fixed component, is *one of the material foundations for the periodic crises in which business passes through successive periods of stagnation, moderate activity, overexcitement, and crisis.* The periods for which capital is invested certainly differ greatly and do not coincide in time. But a crisis is always the starting point of a large volume of new investment. It is also, therefore, if we consider the society as whole, more or less a new material basis the next turnover cycle.» (Marx 1978, p. 264; my emphasis and brackets.)

Annual surplus-value: (Total surplus-value annually produced)	$S = s'vn = sn$
Annual rate of surplus-value:	$S' = \frac{s'vn}{v} = s'n$

s = Surplus-value v = Advanced variable capital
s' = Rate of surplus-value n = Annual number of turnovers

Fig. 13.4 Annual surplus-value and annual rate of surplus-value

which expresses the degree to which variable capital generates surplus-value. But even when the rate of surplus-value is the same, the quantity of surplus-value generated in a *given period* (*such as* 1 *year)* will differ if there are different numbers of turnovers. In considering turnover, we need to indicate the rate of augmentation of surplus-value in terms of how much surplus-value a given variable capital brings about in 1 *year*. If we indicate the surplus-value generated in one turnover by s and multiply this by the number of times it is repeated in a single year, indicated by n, we arrive at the yearly quantity of surplus-value sn. If variable capital is v, the rate of surplus-value (s') is s/v, but the annual rate of surplus-value (i.e. the rate at which variable capital generates surplus-value in a year) is $s'n$ (*see* Fig. 13.4).

Tendency of Capital to Shorten Turnover Time

The greater the annual turnovers of variable capital, the greater the annual rate and quantity of surplus-value. There is thus a tendency for capital to strive for «circulation without circulation time», manifested by its *tendency to seek to constrict turnover time and increase turnover speed.*

13.3.3 Need for Additional Money Capital and Formation of Idle Money Capital

Need for Additional Money Capital and Formation of Idle Money Capital

When capital leaves the realm of production to enter the realm of circulation, the production process for that capital must be halted during this time, thereby constricting it to that extent. *Avoiding this cessation and constriction* requires that a comparable amount of *additional money capital be advanced in the production process.* Generally speaking, if turnover time is reduced through increasing the speed of circulation, the amount of **additional money capital** that is needed will decrease. But there will still arise, to a greater or lesser extent, some need for additional money capital. At the same time, depending on the *proportion between the magnitudes of pro-*

duction time and circulation time for a given period, a certain quantity of money capital will depart from the realm of circulation to form idle capital.

Demand to Use Idle Money Capital as Additional Money Capital

Within the turnover of individual capitals, there is a need, on the one hand, for additional money capital, to a greater or lesser extent, while on the other hand, there is the greater or lesser formation of idle money capital. Both hinder valorisation for individual capitals, which thus seek to limit this burden to the greatest extent possible, even though it cannot be eliminated completely. A need arises here for capital to use *idle money capital* as *additional money capital.* What responds to this need is the banking system (*see* ► Sect. 19.2 in Part III).

Reference

Marx K (1885) Das Kapital. Kritik der politischen oekonomie. Bd. 2. Buch 2: Der circulationsprocess des Kapitals. Hrsg. von F. Engels. Hamburg. English edition: Marx K (1978) Capital. A critique of political economy, vol 2 (trans: Fernbach D). Penguin Books, London

Reproduction and Circulation of the Total Social Capital

T. Otani, *A Guide to Marxian Political Economy*,
https://doi.org/10.1007/978-3-319-65954-1_14

14.1 Aim of Chapter

► Chapters 12 and 13 looked at the circulation of capital in the case of an individual capital. However, the circulation of each individual capital is intertwined with, and conditioned by, not only the circulation of other individual capitals but also the sale of workers' labour-power and their revenue (and hence consumption) as well as the circulation of the revenue (consumption) of capitalists (*see* ◘ Figs. 12.7 and 12.8). The totality of these individual capitals forms the total social capital. Our aim here will be to examine *how the circulations of these individual capitals that are the constituent parts of the total social capital are intertwined and together constitute social reproduction.*

14.2 General Laws of Social Reproduction

General Laws of Social Reproduction

In any society, regardless of its historical form, general laws penetrate (*see* ◘ Fig. 1.26).

Means of Production and Labour-power Must Be Reproduced

The means of production and labour-power must be reproduced through social reproduction (*see* ◘ Figs. 1.21 and 1.22).

New Products Must Include the Required Products

The consumed means of production are replaced by the reappearing means of production in the social product. The new product (except for the reappearing means of production) must include, first and foremost, the means of consumption for the reproduction of labour-power, i.e. the required means of production (*see* ◘ Figs. 1.23 and 1.24).

New Products Must Include the Surplus Products

The new products must also include, beyond the required means of production, surplus products that fulfill various purposes (*see* ◘ Fig. 1.25).

Division of the Social Production into Two Great Departments

In the analysis of social reproduction, it is decisively important to break down social reproduction into two great departments (although this point was not touched on in the Introduction). Now we will expand on the general laws of social reproduction by looking at the laws in the case where social reproduction is divided into two great departments.

Production Department of Means of Production and Production Department of Means of Consumption

The total product of society ultimately enters either the production process as the means of production (Mp) or enters the individual consumption process as the means of consumption (Mc). This means that all of society's production can be categorised as either belonging to the production department for means of production (Department I) or the production department for means of consumption (Department II). *The*

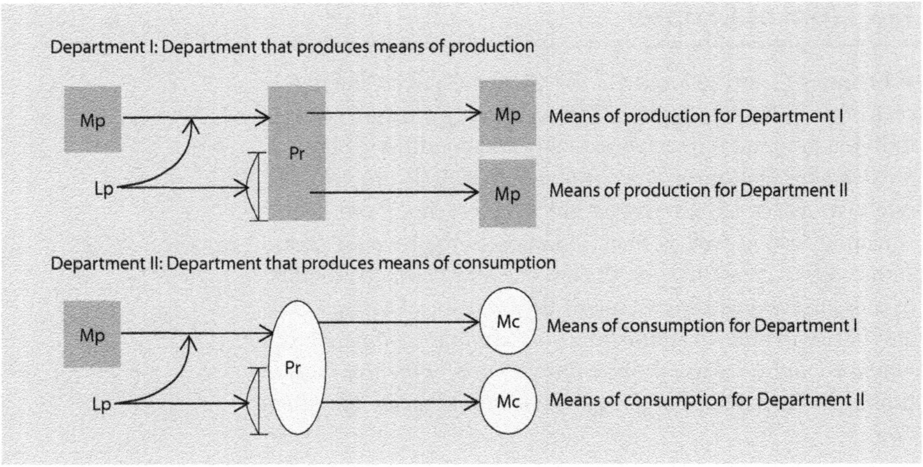

◘ Fig. 14.1 Two great production departments of society: Production Department I for means of production and production Department II for means of consumption

aggregate labour and means of production of society must, in some manner or another, be distributed into one of these two departments (see ◘ Fig. 14.1).

Internal Replacements of the Reproduction Elements Within Each Department and Reciprocal Replacement Between the Two Departments

In order for reproduction to be carried out, the means of production and labour-power needed for reproduction must be replaced in each department. Not only must *the means of production be replaced within Department I and the means of consumption within Department II (referred to as «internal replacement»),* but *the means of production needed in Department II must be replaced by the products of Department I and the means of consumption needed in Department I must be replaced by the products of Department II («reciprocal replacement») (see* ◘ Fig. 14.2).

Internal and Reciprocal Replacements of Elements Including the Surplus Products

In order to carry out social reproduction, whatever the form of society may be, it is necessary to replace the means of production of each department and to replace the means of consumption so that labour-power is reproduced. But it must also be possible, besides that, to secure products from the surplus products produced in each department to fulfill a variety of purposes (e.g., to provide for an accumulation fund or insurance fund to meet the consumption needs of those other than the direct producers, as we saw in ► Sect. 1.4.2). The task here is to examine *how the products of both departments, which include the surplus products, replace the means of production and the means of consumption for labour-power* (Rp: required means of livelihood) *of both departments, both inside each department and between them,*

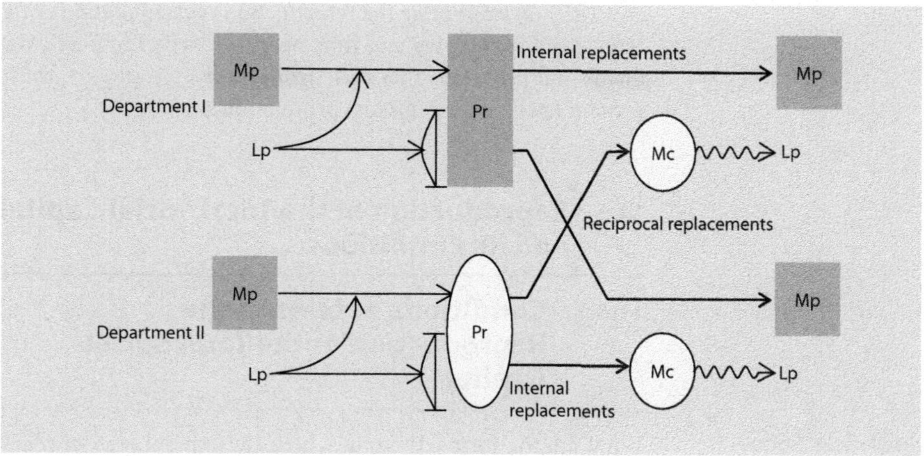

■ **Fig. 14.2** Internal and reciprocal replacements of the elements of reproduction

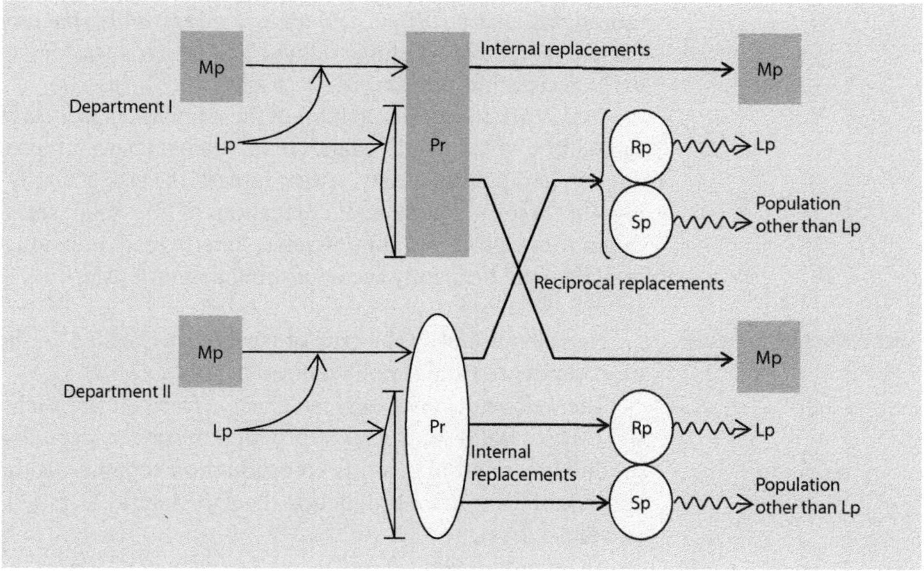

■ **Fig. 14.3** Internal and reciprocal replacements of the elements of reproduction that include the surplus products

and how the means consumption for the non-labour-power population are replaced. We can diagram these replacements based on the premise of simple reproduction (*see* ■ Fig. 14.3).

General Laws of Social Reproduction Take a Specific Form in Each Society

As we saw in ► Sect. 1.4.3.2, the *common, general laws of social reproduction* for every form of society penetrate each society in a specific form depending on the differences in the relations of production (*see* ■ Fig. 1.26, 1.29, 1.30, 1.31, 1.32, and 1.33). *In examining the reproduction and circulation of the total social capital*, we will thus need to clarify the particular forms and problems that arise from the penetration of those general laws under capitalist production.

14.3 Reproduction of the Total Social Capital and Its Conditions

14.3.1 Conditions or Laws of the Reproduction of the Total Social Capital

Analysis of Social Reproduction in Capitalist Society

What are the forms, then, in which the general laws of social reproduction penetrate under capitalist production? And what is the nature of the laws particular to capitalist production?

In the history of political economy, Marx was the first to thoroughly analyse the *particular forms and laws of social production within capitalist production*. This analysis was one of his greatest achievements.

In Part III of his examination of the circulation process of capital in *Capital*, vol. II, Marx (1885) analysed social reproduction in capitalist society, setting himself the task of clarifying the «reproduction and circulation of the total social capital» composed of innumerable, intertwined individual capitals—and brilliantly accomplishing that task (Marx 1978, pp. 425–599).

«Reproduction Schema»

Here, let us look at the crux of what Marx clarified, in the most condensed and simplified form possible.

The well-known two-row table below from Marx's analysis (Marx 1885) of social reproduction under capitalist production, referred to as his «**reproduction schema**», is the epitome of his entire reproduction theory (Marx 1978, p. 473) (*see* ◘ Fig. 14.4).

Meaning of the Reproduction Schema

The reproduction schema below, *in and of itself*, grasps the simple reproduction of the total social capital *from the perspective of the circuit of commodity capital*, indicating the total

$$\begin{array}{ll} \text{I} & 4000c + 1000v + 1000m = 6000 \\ \text{II} & 2000c + 500v + 500m = 3000 \end{array}$$

◘ **Fig. 14.4** Marx's reproduction schema (schema of simple reproduction)

social commodity capital[1] that is the departure/return point of this circuit.

The total social capital C′ in this example, which totals 9000 in value, is divided into two production departments: **Department I (production department for Mp)** and **Department II (production department for Mc).** The total commodity capital of 6000 in Department I includes the products with the use-value (natural form) possible to enter into the production process as means of production, while the total commodity capital of 3000 in Department II includes the products with the use-value (natural form) possible to enter into the individual consumption as means of consumption. Further, the total commodity value of both departments is divided into the three value components of **constant capital (c), variable capital (v),** and **surplus-value (s).** In other words, the total commodity capital (total social product) is divided from the **perspective of use-value** into the two components of means of production and means of consumption and from the **perspective of value** into the three components of constant capital, variable capital, and surplus-value. This is the key point of the reproduction schema.

On top of this, the schema also indicates that the capital of both departments, which set out at the beginning of the year with a total commodity capital C′, must pass through some sort of circulation and production prosesses in the course of the year to end up reproducing this exact commodity capital C′ by year's end. Let us take a closer look at the schema's content, using the same diagramming method used up to now (*see* ◘ Fig. 14.5).

Explanation of the Reproduction Schema Through Diagram

The circuit of commodity capital *of an individual capital* in the case of simple reproduction, as we saw in ► Sect. «Circuit of Commodity Capital (C′...C′ Circuit: C′–M′–C...P...C′)», progresses as follows. First, the advanced capital value C (= *c* + *v*) within the commodity capital C′ is transformed into production capital P by passing through the metamorphosis of C–M–C, while the surplus-value *s* is transformed into the capitalist's consumption fund by passing through the metamorphosis δc–δm–δc (c and m *here* signify, respectively, commodity and money, and δ the increment). These are both circulation processes. This is followed by the production

1 In order to fully understand the following explanation of the reproduction schema, it is necessary, above all, to correctly grasp the concept of the *circuit of commodity capital* explained in ► Chap. 12 (*see* ► Sect. «Circuit of Commodity Capital (C′...C′ Circuit: C′–M′–C...P...C′)»).

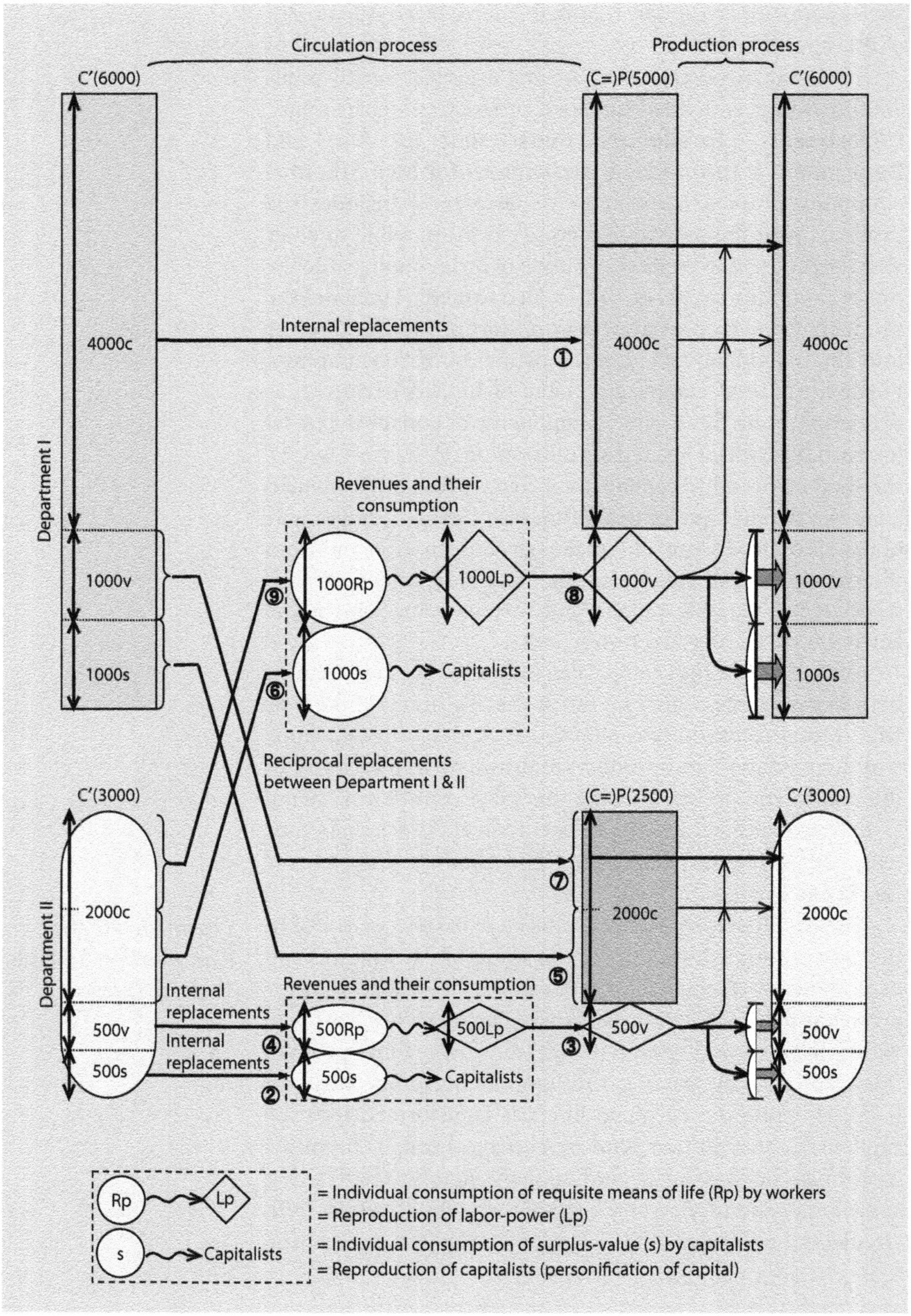

Fig. 14.5 Meaning of Marx's reproduction schema

capital P functioning in the production process to produce the product (commodity capital) C′ and to reproduce the capitalist through consumption of the consumption fund. It is in this manner that the circuit is completed.

The progress of the circuit of commodity capital is the same in the case *of the total social capital.* Commodity capital in each of the two departments is transformed into production capital and the capitalist's consumption fund by passing through the metamorphosis C–M–C. After this, the C′ of both departments and the capitalists are reproduced through the production process P and the individual consumption processes based on the consumption fund.

In the case of the total social capital, however, the reproduction of the total social capital progresses by means of the complicated **three intertwined metamorphoses in both departments**: the metamorphosis of capital C–M–C, of surplus-product δc–δm–δc, and of workers' labour-power C(Lp)–M–C(Mp). Here we need, therefore, to focus on a new question: *How do these three metamorphoses of both departments intertwine* so that the total social capital can be reproduced?

The circuit of commodity capital progresses through the circulation process and the production process, but since the production process proceeds solely within each of the individual capitals and within each production department, the intertwinement of metamorphoses of capitals and individual consumptions solely arises in the **circulation process.** The intertwinement in the circulation process is mediated by **sales and purchases of commodities.** If we look at ▫ Fig. 14.5, we can see that the boldfaced arrows indicate the *movement of commodities.* Money moves always in the opposite direction to that of commodities (i.e. in the direction running from the destination point of the arrow towards its starting point). So the *boldfaced arrows also indicate the movement of money.*

Although the circulation process and production process of the individual capitals that make up the total social capital are carried out separately at various points in time during the course of the year, for the sake of simplicity we have assumed that once the entire circulation process has been carried out at the beginning of the year, then the entire production process is carried out.

If we take a broad view of this diagram, we can grasp that the following three replacements are carried out through the intertwined movements of the elements of the total social capital:

- Internal replacements in Department I
- Internal replacements in Department II
- Reciprocal replacements between both departments

We need to analyse each of the three replacements realised through the movements of commodities and money. In the numbered headings below, we can trace the replacements that take place through the movement of commodities and money.

We can begin with the internal replacements in Department I in the diagram.

① **Replacement of the constant capital of Department I:** Capitalists in Department I replace their constant capital 4000*c*, which is used up in the production process of the preceding year in the form of means of production, by reciprocally buying and selling commodities of a value 4000 in the form of the commodity capital of Department I. The capitalists in Department I must advance the money required for this replacement, but this money refluxes necessarily to the capitalists who advanced it.

Next, turning to Department II, we can see two series of replacements.

② **Replacement of the revenue of capitalists of Department II:** Capitalists in Department II replace their consumption fund 500 *s*, which was consumed as income in the preceding year in the form of means of consumption, by reciprocally buying and selling commodities of a value 500 in the form of the commodity capital of Department II. The capitalists in Department II must advance the money required for this replacement, but this money refluxes necessarily to the capitalists who advanced it.

③ **Replacement of the variable capital of Department II** and ④ **Replacement of the revenue of workers of Department II:** Capitalists in Department II replace their variable capital, which was consumed in the production process of the preceding year as labour-power, by buying labour-power from workers in the same department. The workers use the wages received for their labour-power to buy commodities (means of consumption) of a value of 500 in the form of commodity capital Department II. So the money advanced by capitalists as wages refluxes to them.

The next point of focus is the two series of replacements between the two departments.

⑤ **Replacement of one part of the constant capital of Department II** and ⑥ **Replacement of the revenue of the capi-**

talists in Department I: Capitalists in Department II replace 1000*c* of their 2000*c* of the constant capital of Department II, which was used up in the production process of the preceding year as means of production, by buying from the capitalists of Department I means of production of a value of 1000 in the form of commodity capital of Department I. The capitalists of Department I who obtain money through this sale of means of production to the capitalists of Department II replace their consumption fund that had been consumed as revenue in the preceding year by buying means of consumption of a value of 2000 in the form of commodity capital of Department II. Thus, the money that capitalists in Department II advanced for buying the means of production refluxes to them.

The final series is the most complex, but needs to be understood precisely.

⑦ **Replacement of another part of the constant capital of Department II,** ⑧ **Replacement of the variable capital of Department I** and ⑨ **Replacement of the revenue of workers of Department I:** Capitalists in Department II replace the other 1000*c* of their constant capital in that department, which was used up in the production process of the preceding year as means of production, by buying from the capitalists of Department I means of production of a value of 1000 in the form of commodity capital in Department I. The capitalists of Department I who obtain money in this sale of the means of production to the capitalists of Department II replace their variable capital, which was consumed in the production process of the preceding year as labour-power, by buying labour-power from workers in the same department. The workers expend the wages received for their labour-power on buying means of consumption of a value of 1000 in the form of commodity capital in Department II. So the money advanced by capitalists of Department II for buying the means of production refluxes to them.

In this series of replacements, the capitalists in Department II replace their constant capital, the capitalists in Department I replace their variable capital, and the workers in Department I obtain their requisite means of life. The 1000 in money mediates these process flows from the capitalists in Department II to the capitalists in Department I, and from there to the workers in Department I, then returns to the capitalists in Department II.

We have seen, then, how all the elements of social reproduction under capitalist production are replaced.

Marx's «reproduction schema», sketched in a simple two-row table, turns out to have such rich content, as explained above. The schema expresses the specific characteristics of social reproduction under the capitalist mode of production,

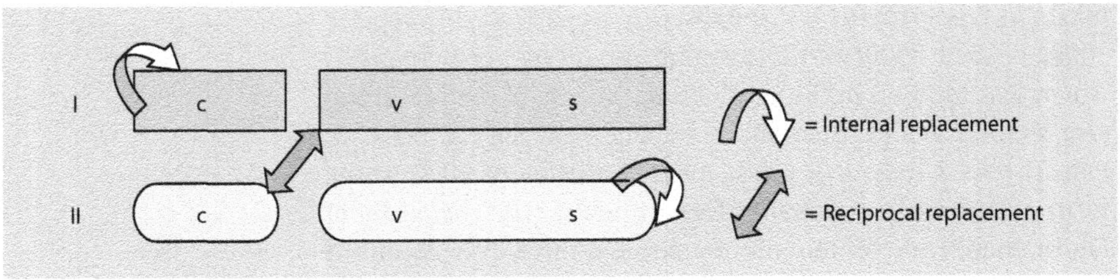

Fig. 14.6 Simplified version of the reproduction schema

wherein all the processes are mediated by **money circulation**, and social reproduction takes the form of the **reproduction of capital**. Under capitalist production, the general laws of the social reproduction operate in these specific forms.

Simplified Version of the Reproduction Schema

The main aim of the reproduction schema is to clarify, based on the premise of simple reproduction, how the commodity capital within the two departments that is the outcome of the previous year's production can replace the constant capital and variable capital necessary for the current year's production, both in material and value terms, while at the same time showing how the revenues of workers and capitalists in the current year are also replaced in material and value terms. This can all be depicted in a simplified form in the diagram above (*see* Fig. 14.6).

Movement of Three Streams = Laws of Simple Reproduction

Looking at the simplified diagram above, we can see that in the reproduction of the total social capital there are *three streams that mediate the replacement of capital and revenue in both departments*. The **movement of these three streams** can be called the **laws of simple reproduction**, because *without this movement capitalist production could not continue to exist* (*see* Fig. 14.7).

Meaning of the Conditions for Reproduction

The movement of the three streams within the production of the total social capital is referred to as the **conditions for reproduction** in the sense that *it is through this that the reproduction of the total social capital can proceed*. It is worth noting, however, that these conditions always penetrate as «laws» under capitalist production. The fact that these are conditions certainly does not mean they are absolute conditions for the progression of capitalist production and reproduction that must be always wholly fulfilled for reproduction to be possible (*see* Fig. 14.8).

14.3.2 Mediation of Reproduction by the Circulation of Money

Reproduction of the Total Social Capital is Mediated by Commodity Circulation

Capitalist production is commodity production. Moreover, commodity production becomes socially generalised under

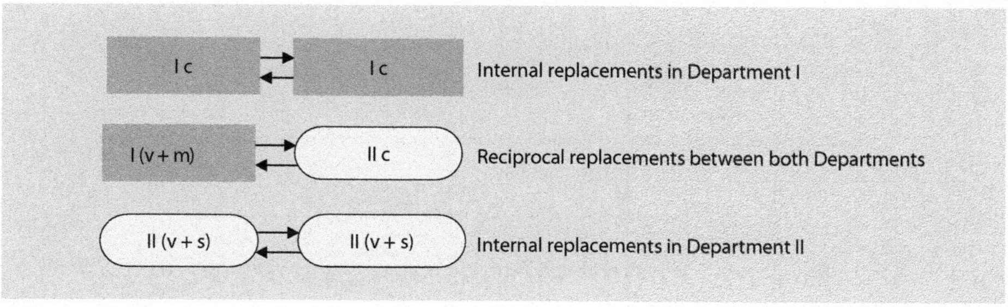

Fig. 14.7 Laws of simple reproduction (movements of the three streams)

$$\mathrm{I}\,(c+v+s) = \mathrm{I}c + \mathrm{II}c$$
$$\mathrm{II}\,(c+v+s) = \mathrm{I}\,(v+s) + \mathrm{II}\,(v+s)$$
$$\therefore\ \mathrm{I}\,(v+s) = \mathrm{II}c$$

Fig. 14.8 Conditions of simple reproduction

capitalist production. Therefore, the entirety of social reproduction is carried out through the sale and purchase of commodities (commodity exchange mediated by money).

Thus, *one of the decisive characteristics of social reproduction under capitalist production* is that it is *reproduction mediated by the circulation of money*. The intertwinement of the individual capitals that make up the total social capital is carried out in the form of the sale and purchase of commodities, and therefore the individual capitals, in their movement, always take the form of money capital.

Money Circulation Mediates the Replacement of All the Elements of Reproduction

Here we will take a fresh look at how the circulation of money mediates the internal replacements within Departments I and II, as well as the reciprocal replacements between them. In Fig. 14.9, Ct signifies the capitalists (ICt being the capitalists in Department I and IICt the capitalists in department II, while Ct1 and Ct2 refer to the two groups of capitalists within the same production department) and Wr refers to the workers (with IWr being the workers in Department I and IIWr the workers in Department II).

Advance of Means of Circulation by Capitalists and Its Reflux to Them

The replacements of the elements of reproduction are thus carried out through the mediation of money circulation, and in this case the circulating money is functioning as a means of circulation. So we need to recognise the three fundamental laws below concerning money as a means of circulation to mediate social reproduction.

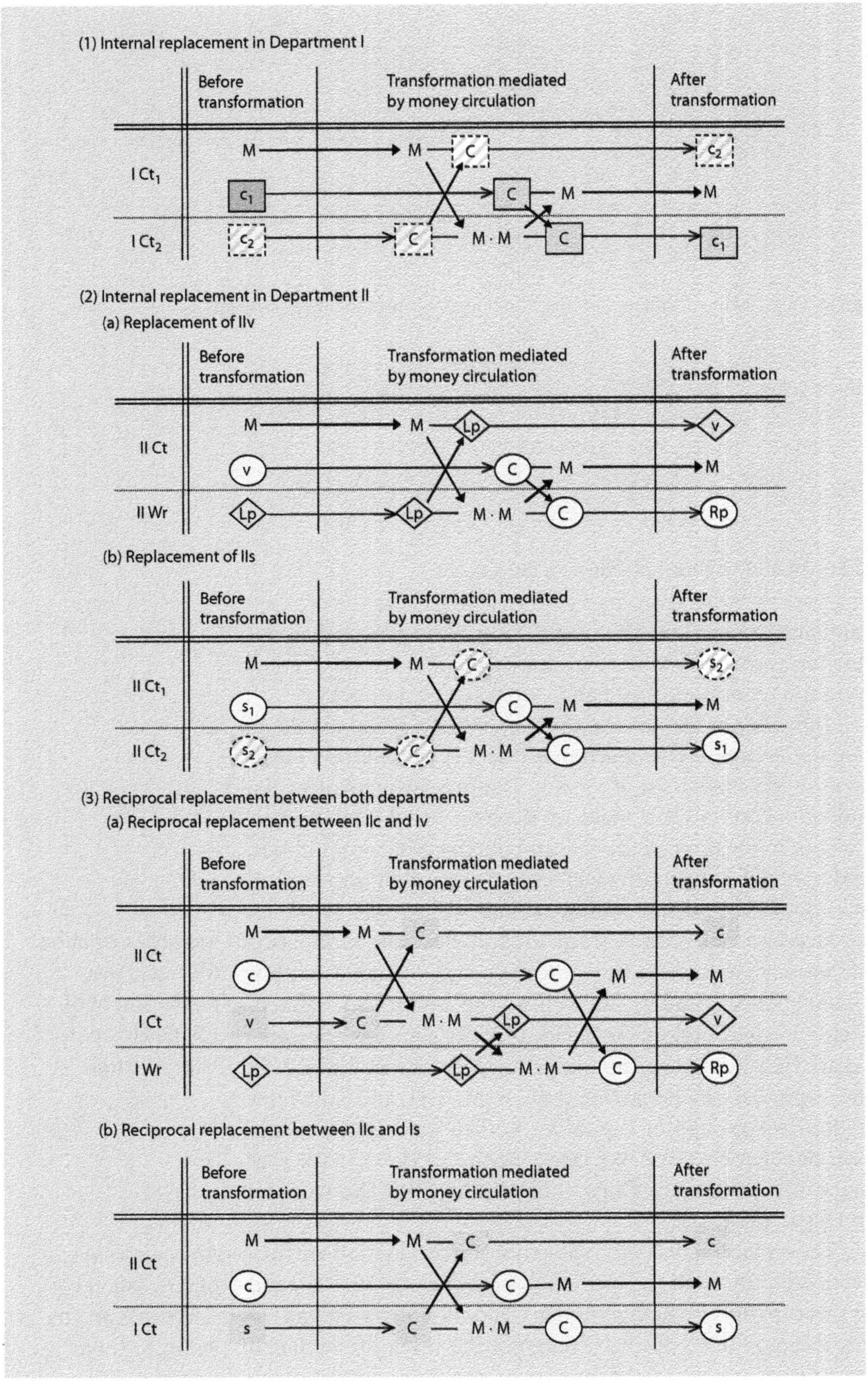

Fig. 14.9 Mediation of social reproduction replacements by money circulation

1. Someone within society must **advance**[2] the money as a means of circulation, to mediate the replacement of the elements of reproduction; therefore, that person must have, in addition to the elements of production, the money needed for the advance.
2. The workers possess nothing apart from labour-power, whereas the capitalists (in either Department I or Department II) have money in addition to the elements of reproduction, so it is the capitalists who advance money as a means of circulation.
3. The capitalists all have the commodity capital consisting of the products of the previous year, but some of them also have a hoard or coin reserve acquired in some manner or another, which can then be expended or advanced as a means of circulation to purchase the elements of reproduction. These capitalists, however, get back the money spent previously on purchases through the subsequent sale of their own products.

In this manner, the money advanced by the capitalists into circulation as a means of circulation always flows back to its starting point, thus flowing back to them.

14.3.3 *Marx's* Criticism of «*Smith's* Dogma of *v* + *s*»

Reproduction Elements to Be Replaced Consist of Old and New Value

The value contained in the aggregate product of the previous year (product-value) in both Department I and Department II consists of the old value transferred from the means of production consumed in the previous year through concrete labour (c) and the new value (value-product) created in the previous year by abstract labour ($v + s$) (*see* ◘ Figs. 2.18 and 3.18). The addition of these processes of the previous year to the earlier diagram demonstrating the replacements of the elements of both departments' aggregate commodities in the current year yields the diagram that follows (*see* ◘ Fig. 14.10). From this diagram it becomes clear that the value of the aggregate products (product-value), not only in Department II but in Department I as well, includes the value transferred from means of production consumed in the preceding year (c), so that the product-value consists of $c + (v + s)$. In order to

2 The term **advance** used here does not mean an «investment» of capital in expection of valorisation, but rather the «handing over of money in payment» in the expectation of a subsequent *reflux*.

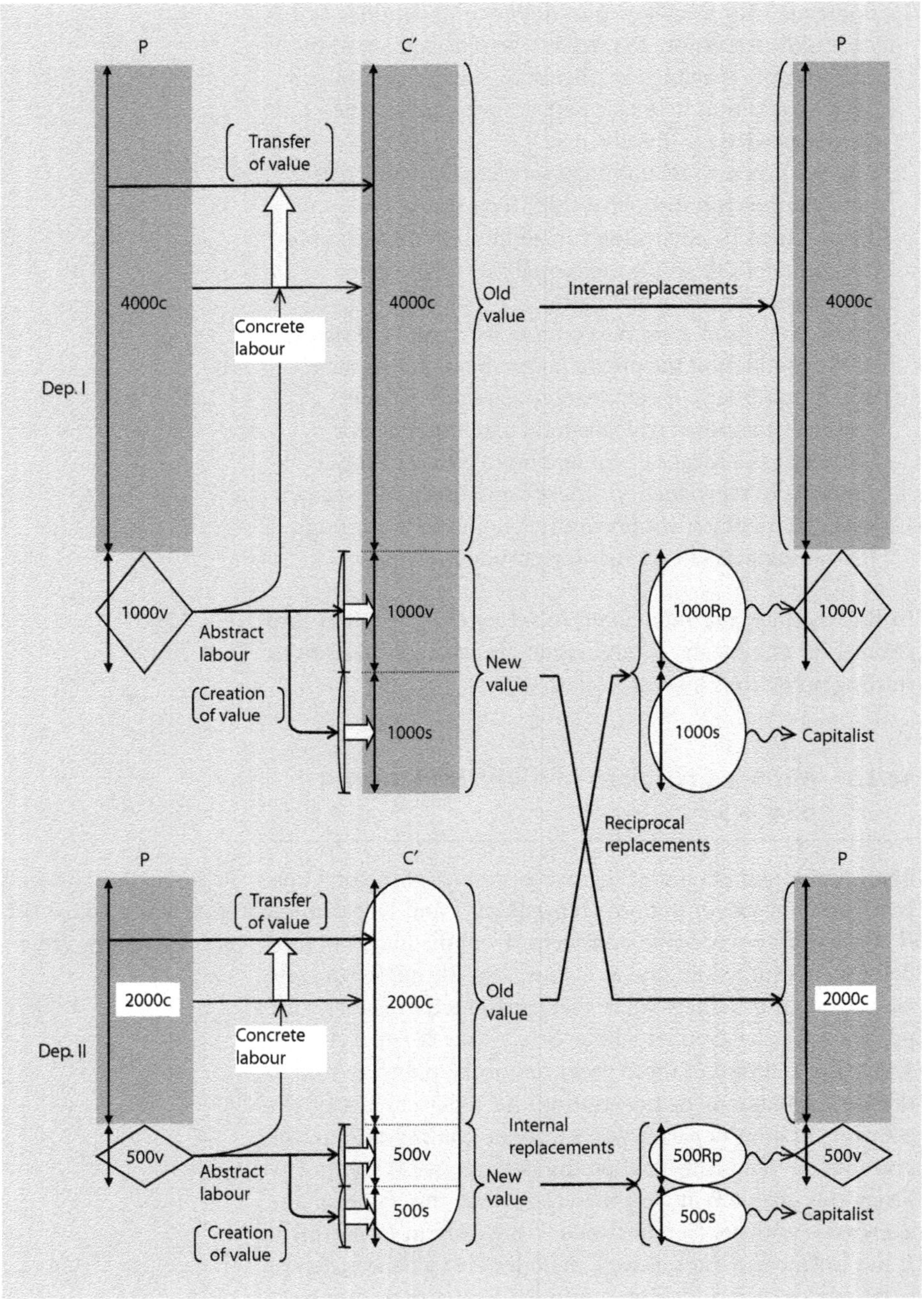

Fig. 14.10 Product-value ($c + v + s$) and value-product ($v + s$) of both departments

firmly grasp this fact, we need to precisely understand the respective functions of concrete and abstract labour—the two sides of the duality of labour. Incidentally, in ◘ Fig. 14.10, the relation of sale and purchase of labour-power between capitalists and workers is omitted, so that the means of consumption for the worker (Rp) are assumed to directly reproduce the purchased labour-power (v).

Smith's Dogma of $v + s$

Adam Smith took a different view of this issue, however. His reasoning was that, although the value of an individual capital consists of $c + v + s$, since the c of each capital is the $c + v + s$ of another capital, and the c of that capital is likewise that of yet another, it could be said that the entirety of c ultimately dissolves into $v + s$. Thus, no c is contained *in the aggregate product of the total social capital*—only $v + s$.

This idea, which was uncritically inherited as a dogma by economists who came after Smith and further refined, can be referred to as «Smith's dogma of $v + s$».

«Dogma of $v + s$» Seems to Conform with Superficial Facts

If we observe the appearance of social reproduction, the following plain facts are surely perceived. First of all, for every capitalist in Department II, their products are exchanged only with the money that represents revenue ($v + s$). Second, in the exchange between Department I and II, the products that represent the revenue of the former department replace the capital of the latter, and the products that represent the capital of latter department are purchased by the revenue of the former. The third and final point is that the reciprocal replacements within Department I bear no relation to the workers in both departments and the capitalists in Department II. *Having only these facts in view*, the reciprocal replacements between the capitalists in the Department I would be lost sight of, so that Smith's «dogma» could seem plausible.

Problems to Be Solved

We need to pose the following two questions in order to clearly grasp the error of Smith's dogma. If living labour composed of required labour and surplus-labour only produces variable capital and surplus-value ($v + s$), where is the labour that creates the value of constant capital (c)? And how is it possible for the used up means of production to be replaced (in material and value terms) from the value-product ($v + s$) created by society's aggregate labour?

Decisive Points for the Solution

Marx was the first economist to answer those questions so as to fully expose Smith's dogma. Three points, in particular, were crucial to Marx's solution. First, based on a clear grasp of the *two-fold character of labour*, he clarified that the product-value of the year's total social product is composed not only of the value-product but also the preserved old value that is transferred—i.e.

$c + v + s$. Second, in order to follow the material replacements between the constituent elements of social reproduction, from the viewpoint of use-value, he abstracted just two great production departments from various production spheres in society. The third contribution of Marx here was to clarify the *replacement relations between elements of social reproduction in material and value terms* and thus fully explain the reproduction of total social capital as a *totality of intertwined metamorphoses of individual capitals, workers' labour-power, and capitalists' revenue.*

14.3.4 Reproduction and Circulation of Fixed Capital

Amortisation and Replacement of Fixed Capital

Fixed capital is included within the total social capital, just as it is in the case of individual capital (*see* ◘ Fig. 13.1). The means of labour produced as one part of the total social product, when settled in the production process as fixed capital, circulate as commodities mediated by the money circulation, and that amount of money is advanced in the circulation process. However, during the period up until the durability of those means of labour expires, it remains as fixed capital within the production process, so it is only the value of the gradually worn-out part of the means of labour that is transferred to the yearly product, and only that portion of value is transformed into the money-form.

This money is not immediately thrown into circulation but rather is withdrawn from the circulation to be *reserved as an amortisation fund of fixed capital* in the hands of the capitalist. Once the durability period of the means of labour[3] has expired, the *replacement of fixed capital* is carried out, scrapping the means of labour that have lost their use-value, *throwing into circulation* an amount of money reserved as an *amortisation fund* equivalent to the original value of the means of labour, and transforming that money into new means of labour to be placed in the production process as

3 The durability period of the means of labour is not necessarily the period up to the point of time when it has physically lost its use-value because—under the pressure of competition between capitals or as the result of the «moral depreciation» of fixed capital (cf. footnote 4 of ▶ Chap. 5) arising from the development of productive powers—individual capital often replaces its means of labour before their physical durability has expired.

fixed capital. When the fixed capital is replaced, the money that remained outside the production process in the form of a hoard enters circulation as means of circulation. Thus, until this subsequent durability period of the means of labour expires, only the value of the worn-out part of the means of labour is transformed into the money-form, which remains idle outside of the production process as a hoard in the form of a reserved amortisation fund.

Unilateral Sales and Unilateral Purchases Are Inevitable

Next we can observe these relations from the perspective of the money circulation that mediates the social reproduction process. The *capitalists who replace their fixed capital* purchase the means of labour without selling their commodities of the same value as replaced fixed capital, so they are only making *unilateral purchases*, whereas the *capitalists whose fixed capital is in the amortisation process* must sell their commodities of the same value as the reserved amortisation fund and are therefore engaged in *unilateral sales*. These unilateral purchases on the one hand and unilateral sales on the other hand are intertwined in various ways through the circulation of money in the social reproduction process. Here, in order to depict such intertwining, it is sufficient to show two typical cases of how the capital of the capitalists replacing their fixed capital and that of the capitalists amortising their fixed capital are mutually intertwined (*see* ◘ Fig. 14.11).

In this figure, cf is the portion of value of the fixed capital within the production process, while cw indicates the part of the amortisation fund corresponding to the depreciating value. We need to bear in mind that there are multiple capitalists whose fixed capital is either replaced or depreciating. Diagram (1) shows a case where the money that is thrown into circulation by the capitalist in Department I to replace fixed capital is accumulated by another capitalist in Department I as an amortisation fund of fixed capital. Meanwhile, Diagram (2) is a case where the money thrown into circulation by the capitalist in Department II to replace fixed capital is accumulated by another capitalist in Department II as an amortisation fund of fixed capital. In both cases, we see that because the capitalist replacing fixed capital buys the means of labour that become fixed capital from the group of capitalists ICt (M_L) in Department I who produce them, their conversion necessarily involves ICt (M_L), with M_L representing the means of labour.

Intertwining of Amortisation and Replacement of Fixed Capital in Social Reproduction

As shown in ◘ Fig. 14.11, there are capitalists who throw money into circulation which up to that point had been preserved as idle money capital (and in the money-form this is a

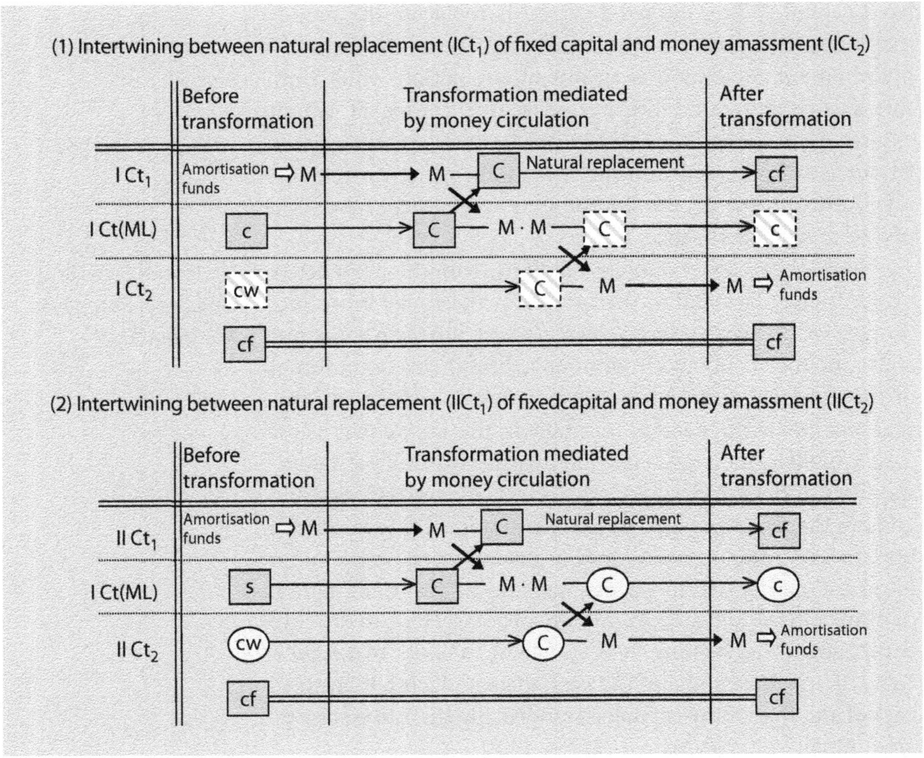

Fig. 14.11 Intertwinement between amortisation and replacement of fixed capital (reserve and advance of amortisation funds)

hoard), i.e. the transformation of a hoard into means of circulation; while, on the other hand, there are capitalists who preserve money withdrawn from circulation as idle money capital, i.e. the transformation of means of circulation into a hoard.

Conditions of Social Reproduction for the Turnover of Fixed Capital

Thus, in order for social reproduction to progress normally, *assuming that all other conditions have been met*, there must be an agreement between the replacement and accumulation of fixed capital and between each of their respective aggregate sums. This means that there must be an agreement between the sum of the hoard converted into means of circulation and the sum of the means of circulation converted into a hoard, as well as between the sum of unilateral sales and the sum of unilateral purchases. This is the condition for the social reproduction to proceed normally with regard to the depreciation and replacement of fixed capital.

14.3.5 Reproduction and Circulation of the Money Material

Wear and Tear of Circulating Money Replaced from Capitalists' Surplus-value

The money that mediates social reproduction is indispensable under commodity production, but it is a *faux frais of production* that is unable to enter either production or consumption, and must be borne by the capitalist class. The capitalist class, in some way or another, injects part of the surplus-value obtained annually into the circulation process, in the form of money.

Even if we assume that the money needed for circulation already exists, and that simple reproduction proceeds through its mediation, money in the realm of circulation will steadily be worn-out as it remains there, and this worn-out part must somehow be replaced. The replacement can only be done using one part of the surplus-value obtained by the capitalist class. Let us assume here that money is gold and that all the money to be replaced is borne equally by the capitalists. In this case, all the capitalists convert a certain portion of the surplus-value that is included within their own commodity capital into money *qua* gold, according to a certain rate, and this money is added, in that given state, to the circulation process.

Money Material Replaced Through Conversion Between Gold-producing Department and Other Departments

Meanwhile, since the replacement of new gold *qua* money is also a product made by gold-producing capital in gold-producing regions, it must first appear in the gold market as the commodity capital of that capital.

The question thus arises of how the capital other than the gold-producing capital converts one portion of its own surplus-value into the gold-money material that exists as the commodity capital of the gold-producing capital and how the gold-producing capital itself converts its capital and revenue into elements of production and means of consumption.

In the case of the conversion of gold *qua* money material into money, it is not the case that gold that has become money becomes the means of production or means of consumption. Thus, if we create a gold-producing Department III, separate from Department I (means of production) and Department II (means of consumption), the question could be expressed in terms of what conversions are made in the process of social reproduction between the elements of the aggregate commodity capital of Department III and the elements of the aggregate capital of Department I and II. The conversions, expressed numerically, can be depicted as follows (*see* ◘ Fig. 14.12).

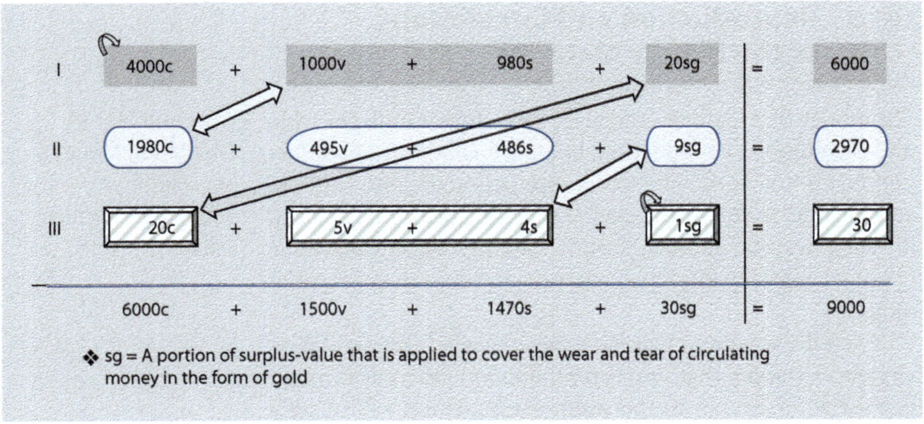

■ **Fig. 14.12** Reproduction of the money material

14.4 Accumulation of Capital and Reproduction on an Expanded Scale

14.4.1 Laws and Conditions of Expanded Reproduction

From Simple Reproduction to Expanded Reproduction

The most fundamental mechanisms and laws of social reproduction within capitalist production, which is the reproduction of the total social capital and the circulation that mediates it, become clear when we deal with simple reproduction. But now we need to observe the process of expanded social reproduction under capitalist production, which is the expansion of the reproduction of the total social capital via capital accumulation.

Capital Accumulation Through Transformation of Surplus-value into Capital

In ► Sect. 9.2 in Part I, we saw how individual capital is augmented through the accumulation of capital and learned that (1) the accumulation of capital is the transformation of surplus-value (*s*) into capital, (2) surplus-value (*s*) is divided into the consumption fund (*sc*) of the capitalist (because the capitalist consumes one part of surplus-value) and the accumulation fund (*sa*) that becomes additional capital, and (3) additional capital (*sa*) is further divided into additional constant capital (*sc*) and additional variable capital (*sv*) (*see* ■ Fig. 9.1). And this also fully applies to the total social capital and the aggregate capital of a given department.

Incorporating Transformation of Surplus-value into Capital Within Laws of Simple Reproduction

Next, let us introduce the mechanism of accumulation outlined above into the laws of reproduction under simple reproduction already examined, so that the latter is developed into the laws of expanded reproduction under social reproduction.

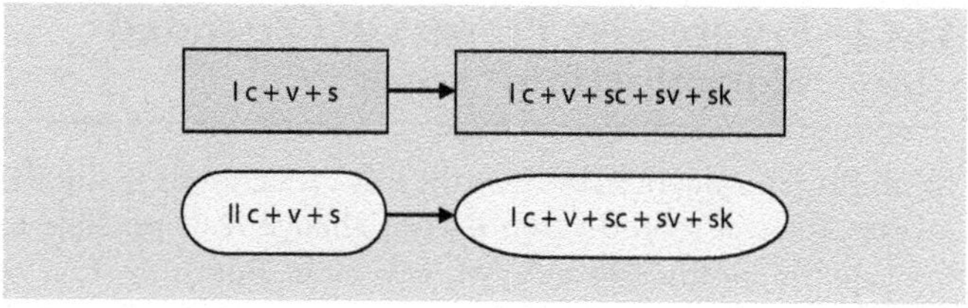

Fig. 14.13 Division of surplus-value for capital accumulation = expanded reproduction in both departments

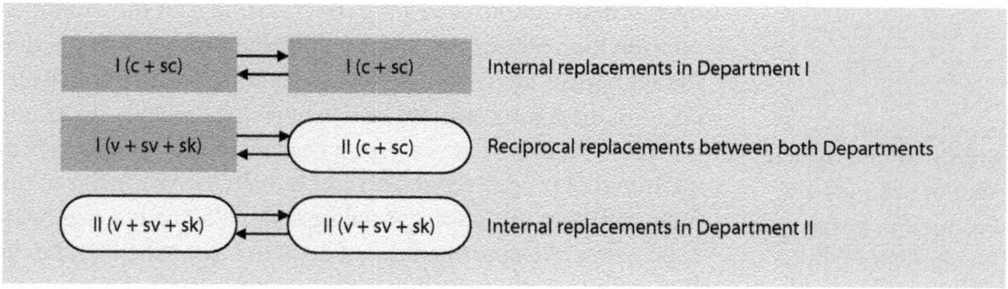

Fig. 14.14 Laws of expanded reproduction (movement of three streams)

$$\text{I}(c + v + sc + sv + sk) = \text{I}(c + sc) + \text{II}(c + sc)$$

$$\text{II}(c + v + sc + sv + sk) = \text{I}(v + sv + sk) + \text{II}(v + sv + sk)$$

$$\therefore \text{I}(v + sv + sk) = \text{II}(c + sc)$$

Fig. 14.15 Conditions of expanded reproduction

Division of Surplus-value Within Each Department

For simple reproduction, our assumption was that capitalists in Department I and Department II consume all the surplus-value. But now we will divide surplus-value (*s*) in Department I and Department II into additional constant capital (*sc*) + additional variable capital (*sv*) + capitalist's consumption fund (*sk*) (*see* Fig. 14.13).

Laws of Expanded Reproduction (Movement of Three Streams)

Additional constant capital (*sc*) must be transformed into means of production, additional variable capital (*sv*) into means of consumption, and the capitalist's consumption fund (*sk*) into the capitalist's means of consumption (means of livelihood + means of luxury). In the case of expanded reproduction, the movement of the three streams is transfigured as above (*see* Fig. 14.14).

Conditions for Expanded Reproduction

The conditions for expanded reproduction also are changed as above (*see* Fig. 14.15).

14.4.2 Progressive Process of Expanded Reproduction

Expanded Reproduction Must Be Expressed in a Linked Schema

In simple reproduction, because the value magnitude of the elements of social reproduction do not change, it is possible to indicate the mechanism in a two-row table. But in the case of expanded production, because the value magnitudes of the elements expand year after year, it can only be expressed as a linked schema with expanding numerical values. Here we can look at an example of this progressive process, in the form of a developed schema, in order to get a concrete image of the expanded reproduction of the total social capital. Please note, though, that the numerical figures are hypothetical and that the money circulation mediating each replacement is not explicitly depicted.

Starting Point of First Year of Expanded Production Is the Previous Year's Total Commodity Capital

Let us assume that year upon year there is expanded reproduction that progresses at a certain rate. In the year prior to the first year there was a total social capital of 7500 advanced, with 5500 going to Department I and 2000 to Department II. Let us also assume that production is carried out in both departments under the same organic composition of capital, with a *c*-to-*v* ration of 4:1 and a 100% rate of surplus-value (s/v). At the outset of the year, then, the total product of the previous year (aggregate commodity capital) is the 6000 of value in Department I in the form of means of production (including 1100 of surplus-value) and the 2400 of value in Department II in the form of means of consumption (including 400 of surplus-value).

Circulation Process and Production Process in the First Year

In Year 1, we will assume that 50% of the surplus-value in both departments is accumulated, so that the rate of accumulation is 50%. If the organic composition of the additional capital is the same as the original capital, the surplus-value of 1100 *s* in Department I must be divided into 440*sc* + 110*sv* + 550*sk*, while the surplus-value of 400 *s* in Department II must be divided into 160*sc* + 40*sv* + 200*sk*. Of this, the 440*sc* in Department I and 160*sc* in Department II must be transformed into means of production, while the 110*sv* + 550*sk* in Department I and 40*sv* + 200*sk* in Department II must be transformed into means of consumption. This is how the elements of the circulation process of Year 1 are transformed, and how the year's production process is advanced, so that by the year's end there emerges a new total product with an expanded magnitude of value. This aggregate product (aggregate commodity capital) becomes the starting point of circulation for Year 2.

We can illustrate what would happen by the beginning of Year 4 if the reproduction progresses from Year 2 without any change in the rates assumed above (*see* ◘ Fig. 14.16).

Department-proportion (proportion of total capital):	I (c + v) : II (c + v) = 11 : 4
Organic composition of capital (in both departments):	c : v = 4 : 1
Rate of surplus-value (in both departments):	$s' = \frac{s}{v} = 100\%$
Rate of accumulation (in both departments):	$\frac{sa}{s} = \frac{sc + sv}{s} = 50\%$

1st year C′	I 4400c + 1100v + 1100s = 6600 II 1600c + 400v + 400s = 2400
C′—M′—C	I 4400c + 440sc + 1100v + 550sk + 110sv II 1600c + 160sc + 400v + 200sk + 40sv
P	I 4840c + 1210v II 1760c + 440v
2nd year C′	I 4840c + 1210v + 1210s = 7260 II 1760c + 440v + 440s = 2640
C′—M′—C	I 4840c + 484sc + 1210v + 605sk + 121sv II 1760c + 176sc + 440v + 220sk + 44sv
P	I 5324c + 1331v II 1936c + 484v
3rd year C′	I 5324c + 1331v + 1331s = 7986 II 1936c + 484v + 484s = 2906
C′—M′—C	I 5324c + 532sc + 1331v + 666sk + 133sv II 1936c + 194sc + 484v + 242sk + 48sv
P	I 5856c + 1464v II 2130c + 532v
4th year C′	I 5856c + 1464v + 1464s = 8784 II 2130c + 532v + 532s = 3194

Fig. 14.16 Example of the progressive process of expanded reproduction

14.4.3 Amassment and Advance of Accumulation Fund Within Social Reproduction

Particular Monetary Factors Concerning Accumulation of Total Social Capital

Up to now, we have not separately considered the movement of money that mediates expanded reproduction. In the case of expanded reproduction, however, there is an additional specific condition regarding the movement of money that is not seen under simple reproduction. This specific money-related condition characterises the process of social reproduction under capitalist production and also has a tremendous impact on the actual progression of social reproduction.

Amassment and Advance of the Accumulation Fund

Even if surplus-value is transformed into additional productive capital in the reproduction of the social total capital, thereby expanding production year by year, not every individual capital is able to immediately convert the surplus-value acquired newly into additional productive capital. That is because the expansion of production requires, to a larger or lesser extent, the installation of substantial production facilities (e.g., factory buildings, machinery, etc.), thus requiring in turn a substantial accumulation fund. For individual capital, surplus-value can be converted into additional productive capital to expand production only when the *accumulation fund amassed* year after year from surplus-value has reached a suitably substantial size. Therefore, of the surplus-value acquired annually, only the part that has been accumulated to the size large enough to be advanced is actually converted into productive capital, whereas the rest of the accumulation fund is separated from the circulation process after being converted into money and becomes idle as is in the hands of the capitalist. In the accumulation process of the total social capital, there are thus two opposing movements with regard to money: *the withdrawal of money from circulation to amass the accumulation fund in the money-form* and *the throwing of money into circulation to advance the accumulation fund in the production process after it has been amassed.*

Now let us examine a few cases of how the amassing and advancing accumulation fund is carried out in Department I, and how those two processes are intertwined, as well as the intertwinement with Department II. We need to bear in mind that there are numerous capitalists who amass and advance an accumulation fund (*see* ◘ Fig. 14.17).

Intertwined Amassing and Advancing of Accumulation Funds Within Social Reproduction

As ◘ Fig. 14.17 illustrates, exactly as in the case of the amassment and replacement of fixed capital in the money-form, the capitalists on one side who have preserved money as idle money capital (a hoard in the form of money), throw it

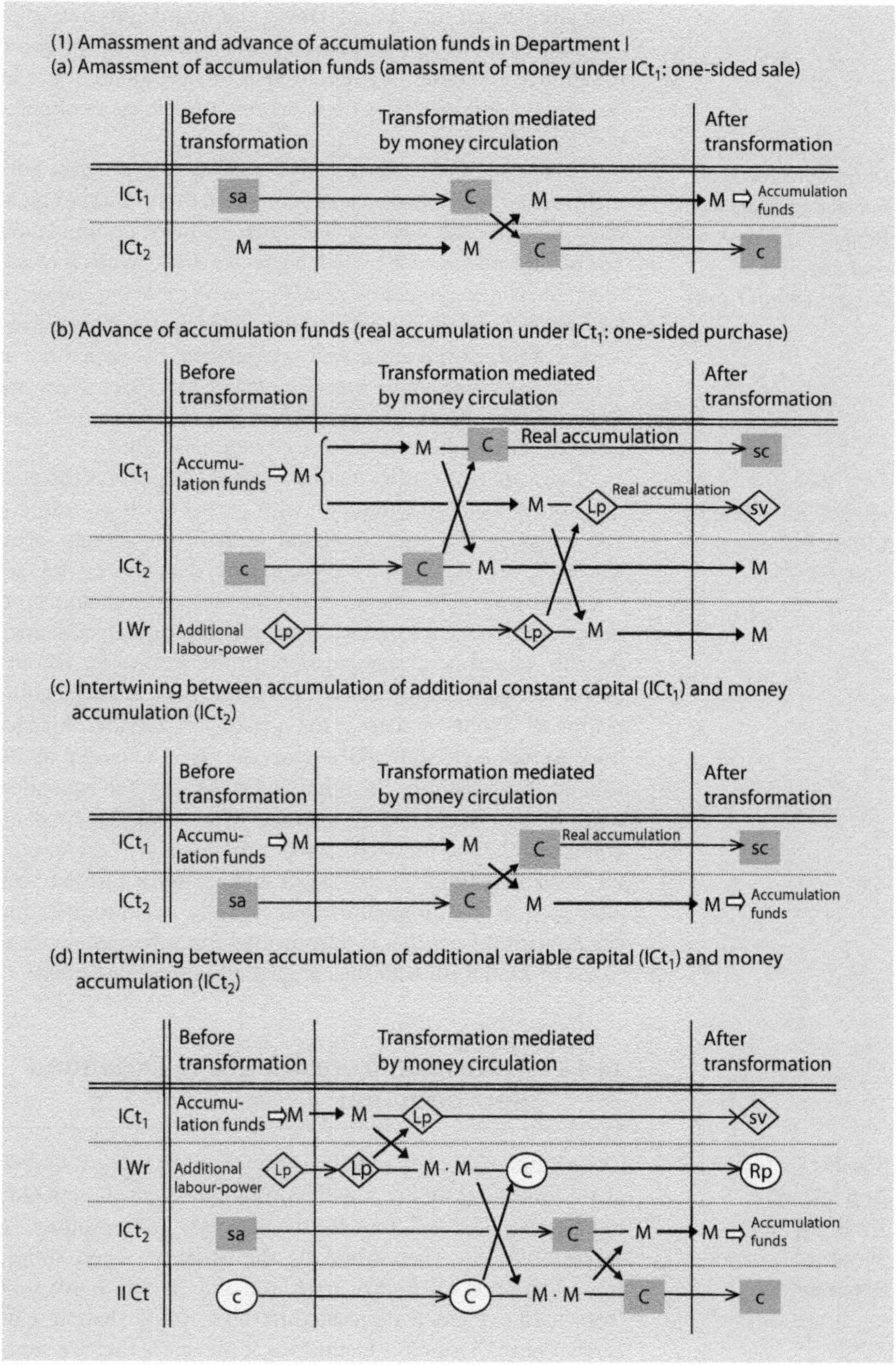

■ **Fig. 14.17** Amassment and advance of accumulation funds

into circulation, thus transforming the hoard into means of circulation, while the capitalists, on the other side, preserve the money taken out of circulation as idle capital (a hoard in the form of money), thus transforming the means of circulation into a hoard.

Conditions for Social Reproduction Regarding Amassment and Advance of Accumulation Funds

Therefore, in order for social reproduction to progress normally, *assuming all other conditions are met*, there must be agreement between the advance and amassment of accumulation funds and between each of their aggregate sums, which is to say, there must be agreement between the *sum of the hoard converted into means of circulation* and the *sum of the means of circulation converted into the hoard*, as well as agreement between the *sum of unilateral sales* and the *sum of unilateral purchases*. These are the *conditions of social reproduction for the amassment and advance of accumulation funds to proceed normally*.

Two Issues Concerning Movement of Money During Expanded Reproduction

There are two factors that have a great impact on the progression of social reproduction with regard to the amassment and advance of an accumulation fund in the money-form, although we cannot discuss them in great detail here. One factor, as shown in the diagram, is that the accumulation fund includes the advance of additional variable capital, and since variable capital is a wage payment to the worker for labour-power it is generally a deferred payment made after the completion of labour. So there is the question of whether this fact leads to particular difficulties when money is advanced at the time of accumulation. The other factor is that when expanded reproduction (including the amassment and replacement of an amortisation fund for fixed capital) progresses at a certain rate, the total magnitude of the accumulation fund formed year after year in the money-form exceeds the magnitude of the accumulation fund that is transformed from the money-form to the in-kind form with the completion of the amassment.

14.4.4 Transition from Simple to Expanded Reproduction

Specific Factors Underlying the Transition from Simple to Expanded Reproduction

The conditions for expanded reproduction that we just looked at are conditions for expanded reproduction when it is already in progress, i.e. conditions for the expansion of reproduction to continue. So what would be the situation when simple reproduction is still being carried out and there is then a shift from it to expanded reproduction: how would that shift be carried out? Distinctive factors are at play here that are separate from the conditions for expanded reproduction examined thus far.

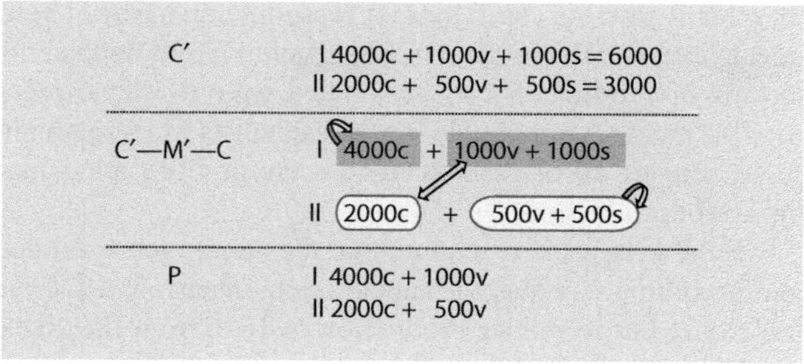

Fig. 14.18 Simple reproduction up to now

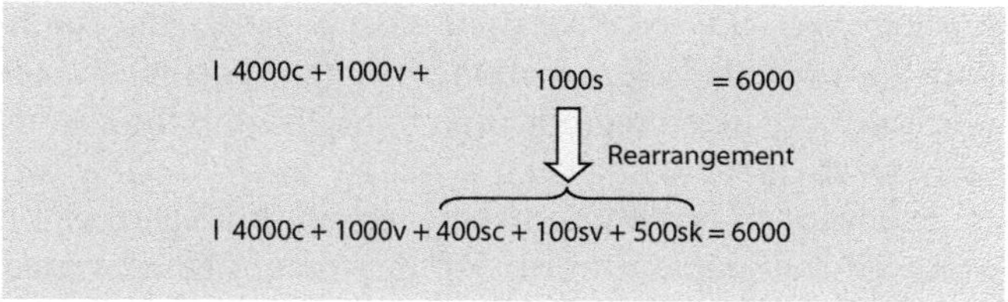

Fig. 14.19 Rearrangement for accumulation in Department I

Simple Reproduction Premised

We can begin by considering the value of the various elements listed above in the case of simple reproduction (*see* Fig. 14.18).

Department I Must Expand First

Now let us turn to the process of the shift from simple reproduction to expanded reproduction. As long as Department I does not constrict production, the maximum means of production that it is able to hand over to Department II would be 2000. So even if accumulation were carried out in Department II by transforming a part of the surplus-value into additional constant capital, it is not possible to obtain additional means of production from Department I. In short, for accumulation to be carried out in Department II, there must first be an expansion in Department I to provide the means of production to Department II. This means that accumulation must first be carried out in Department I to shift from simple to expanded reproduction.

Elements in Department I Are Rearranged for Accumulation

Our assumption here is a 50% rate of accumulation in Department I, which means that 500 is accumulated as half the sum of 1000. This 500*sa* is divided into constant and variable capital according to the same 4:1 organic composition as the original capital (*see* Fig. 14.19).

Department II Must Be Reduced as a Result of Rearrangement in Department I

The rearrangement in Department I for the sake of accumulation brings about the following result:

$$\mathrm{I}(1000v + 100sv + 500sk) < \mathrm{II}\,2000c$$

In other words, the conditions for reproduction have not been met because, of the product of Department I, only 1600 of the means of production can be handed over to Department II. This makes it impossible for the capitalists in Department II to convert all of their 2000*c* in commodity capital into means of production.

Thus, as long as we assume that the conversion is carried out according to value, the capitalists in Department II have no choice but to reduce production to 1600 from the 2000*c* they started off with in the previous year (*see* ◘ Fig. 14.20).

Beginning of Expanded Reproduction

The outcome is that the following conversions are made in both departments, diverging from those carried out in the previous year. These conversions already satisfy the conditions for expanded reproduction, making it possible for the process of expanded reproduction to begin from the current year (*see* ◘ Fig. 14.21)

Following this conversion, there remains in Department II means of consumption worth 500 that cannot be converted. These means of consumption that have become an excess either go to waste or are carried over into the following year as product stock, assuming they are not additionally consumed by the capitalists in that department during the course of the year.

The magnitude of the elements of the current year's productive capital and the commodity capital that is then produced in

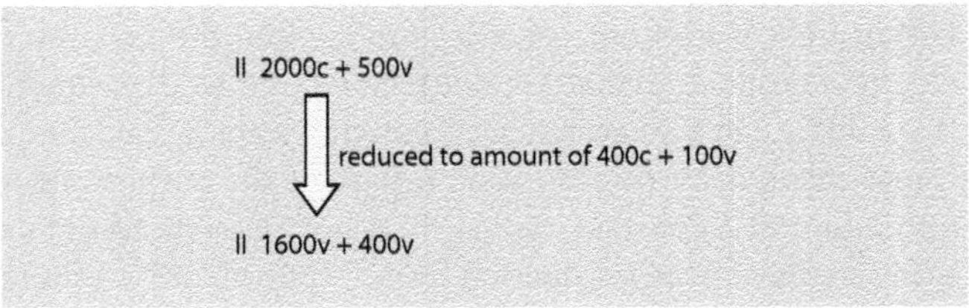

◘ **Fig. 14.20** Reduction of Department II

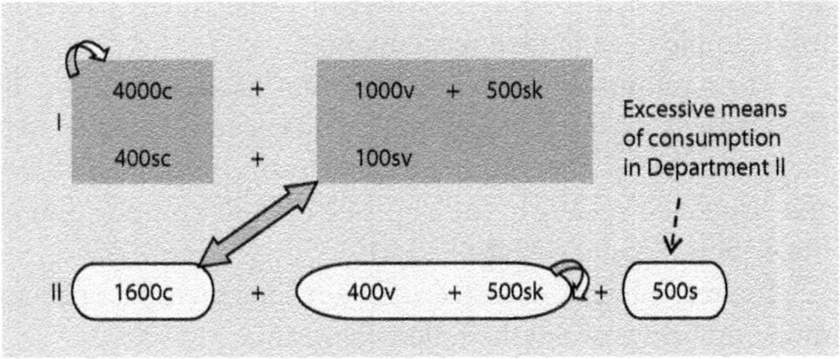

◘ **Fig. 14.21** Replacement of the elements of reproduction after reduction of Department II

1st year of expanded reproduction P	I 4400c + 1100v II 1600c + 400v
2nd year of expanded reproduction C′	I 4400c + 1100v + 1100s = 6600 II 1600c + 400v + 400s = 2400

Fig. 14.22 Expanded reproduction possible in both departments from the following year

the production process by that capital are listed above. Here Department I enters the process of expanded reproduction, which makes it possible for Department II to also enter expanded reproduction the following year (*see* Fig. 14.22).

What We Learn from the Transition from Simple to Expanded Reproduction

Examining the shift from simple to expanded reproduction clarifies the following two points:

1. The expansion of Department II necessitates as its material basis, first of all, the production of the additional means of production to be used in that department, which requires a prior expansion in Department I.
2. The shift from simple to expanded reproduction is accompanied by a constriction in the scale of reproduction in Department II that necessarily disturbs the reproduction process to some extent.

The points above show that, generally speaking, for the tempo of expanded social reproduction to rise, thus increasing the rate of accumulation, a prior expansion in Department I is necessary. If that has not yet occurred, a disturbance will arise to a greater or lesser extent within the process of reproduction.

Independent Variable Is the Rate of Accumulation; Dependent Variable Is the Proportion Between Departments

Under capitalist production, competition between capitals seeking to augment surplus-value increases relative surplus-value by raising the productive power of labour, on the one hand, and augments capital through the progression of capital accumulation, on the other hand. This process, socially speaking, proceeds in a completely unplanned and anarchic manner. There is an inequality in the development of the productive power of labour in each production department of society, so the organic composition of capital in each department rises unequally and the rate of surplus-value also changes in an unequal manner. Meanwhile, there is a lack of uniformity in the quantity and rate of capital accumulation in each department, so that the augmentation of the aggregate capital advanced in each department (and therefore the augmentation of the total commodity capital produced with this capital) occurs in an unequal manner.

The same is true if the aggregate social production is grasped by treating Department I and Department II as an inclusive whole. There are incessant changes in each department, independent of each other, with regard to capital composition, the rate of surplus-value, total advanced capital, and commodity capital. Through such changes, there are also incessant changes in the proportion between the two departments of the quantities of advanced capital and commodity capital. In short, the capital accumulation and accompanying development of productive power are the independent variables, while the proportion between the departments is the dependent variable. Thus, although actual social reproduction in Department I$(c + v + s)$ and Department II$(c + v + s)$ includes those six elements, it is extremely unlikely that there would be a convenient case where a sum of value allows replacements to be perfectly carried out between both departments.

This does not mean, however, that the conditions (laws) of expanded reproduction examined earlier lack significance. For example, in a case where Department I$(v + sv + sk)$ < Department II$(c + sc)$, the demand for Department I is greater than the demand for Department II, so there would be a relative rise in the prices of the commodities in Department I compared to the commodity prices in Department II. In turn, this will have an impact on capital accumulation and the development of productive power in both departments, bringing about a change in the quantity of advanced capital in both departments and thus altering the proportion of that quantity between the two departments. This in turn causes various movements of capital and surplus-value (to be discussed later), including the shifting of capital between departments, the banking system, and foreign trade. Indeed, understanding the motion and the direction, as well as the magnitudes of the movement of capital in both departments, absolutely requires a grasp of the conditions (laws) of expanded reproduction just examined[4].

4 Some Japanese researchers have advanced a «theory» that deduces an «equilibrium rate of accumulation» from the sum of capital accumulation possible under a premised reproduction schema in which the reproduction elements in both departments can be reciprocally replaced without any excess or deficiency. Furthermore, they go on to depict the progression of reproduction as it expands in accordance with that rate, which they call the «equilibrium trajectory of accumulation». But this conception, which they insist has theoretical significance, overlooks the real relations, wherein capital accumulation and the accompanying development of productive power are the independent variables, while the

14.5 Laws of Reproduction and the Developed Possibility of Crisis

Conditions for Reproduction Are Not Independent, Absolute Conditions

The various conditions for reproduction, clarified above, are not absolute limitations that would bring social reproduction to a stop if not met. Under capitalist production, the process of social reproduction is the comprehensive outcome of the actions of individual capitals that produce and accumulate anarchically for the sake of augmentation. The conditions for reproduction are complexly intertwined, so that some parts are mutually amplified while others negate each other, so that each of the conditions does not independently restrict the process. In the progress of capitalist production it is inevitable for equilibrium to penetrate as an incessant equalisation of incessant disequilibrium.

Conditions for Reproduction Are Also the Conditions for Crisis

As we have seen, however, capitalist production is commodity production, so that it must pass through various conversions in the process of circulation, mediated by money circulation. This means that there are many conditions for reproduction within social reproduction; and each condition, in and of itself, could become a moment that disturbs social reproduction. In other words, all of the conditions for reproduction, in their exact given state, are also the conditions for crisis[5].

Abstract Possibility of Crisis for Money as Means of Circulation and as Means of Payment

Money functions as a means of circulation, and since there is a broad intertwining of commodity circulation, if sales and purchases diverge at any point—so that the money received from a commodity sale is not subsequently expended—there

proportion between the departments is the dependent variable. These real relations have a decisive significance for an understanding of the conditions of expanded reproduction.

5 Marx (1885) writes: «In as much as one-sided conversions take place, a number of mere purchases on the one hand, and isolated sales on the other—the normal exchange of the annual product on the capitalist basis requires these one-sided metamorphoses—this balance exists only on the assumption that the values of the one-sided purchases and the one-sided sales cover each other. The fact that the production of commodities is the general form of capitalist production already implies that money plays a role, not just as means of circulation but also as money capital within the circulation sphere, and gives rise to certain conditions for normal exchange that are peculiar to this mode of production, i.e. conditions for the normal course of reproduction, whether simple or on an expanded scale, which turn into an equal number of *conditions for an abnormal course, possibilities of crisis*, since, on the basis of the spontaneous pattern of this production, this *balance is itself an accident*». (Marx 1978, pp. 570–571; my emphasis).

is the possibility that this will bring about a disturbance in commodity circulation. Money also functions as a means of payment, and when money circulates as such to settle a transaction that is not offset, in a situation where the sale of commodities has already been broadly established, the chain of payments will be broken if this payment is held up at any point, potentially resulting in the impossibility of continued payments. These possibilities constitute the abstract possibility for crisis.

Developed Possibility of Crisis for the Reproduction Process of the Total Social Capital

These abstract and formal possibilities, with regard to the various conditions of reproduction that are also the conditions of crisis, take on concrete content through the various elements of the reproduction of the total social capital, and in that sense they constitute the developed possibilities of crisis.

Disturbances Arising from Changes in the Accumulation Rate Constitute Part of the Developed Possibility of Crisis

Earlier we saw that in the shift from simple reproduction to expanded reproduction a change occurs that is characterised by the shift from a zero rate of accumulation to a positive one. This is just one particular case of a change of reproduction in terms of an increased rate of accumulation. That is, even when expanded reproduction is already being carried out, when the accumulation rate rises in Department I, the same case arises as in the shift from simple to expanded reproduction; and when the accumulation rate in both departments rises, there is the possibility for an even greater disturbance to occur. Thus, the analysis of the shift from simple to expanded reproduction also makes clear the nature of the disturbances that generally emerge when the rate of accumulation increases. The accumulation rate of capital is something that is independently determined by capitals through the competition between them and is thus merely the overall outcome of the accumulation rate in both departments within social reproduction and the accumulation rate of the total social capital. This is the most independent of the independent variables within the process of reproduction. Because the rate of accumulation is always in fluctuation, including cases where the rate of accumulation falls severely, a fluctuation always has the possibility to generate a disturbance within social reproduction. So the possible disturbance caused by a fluctuation in the rate of accumulation is an important aspect of the developed possibility of crisis.

14.6 Connections Between Production, Circulation, and Consumption Within Social Reproduction

Connections Between Production, Circulation, and Consumption Beneath the Surface of Society

We saw in ▶ Sects. 14.4.1 and 14.4.2 that the relations of conversion (replacement) of the elements of reproduction within the expanded reproduction of the total social capital also elucidate the intertwining of capital and revenue within the process of expanded reproduction and the reciprocal relation between production, circulation, and consumption that exists there. We can employ a single diagram here to show how capital and revenue are intertwined in the case where expanded reproduction progresses in both departments and to indicate the nature of the relation between the production and circulation processes of capitalists as well as the consumption of the capitalists and workers (*see* ◘ Fig. 14.23). If we contrast this diagram with ◘ Fig. 2.1 in ▶ Chap. 2, which depicted the «common image of the «circuit flow» of the economy», we can familiarise ourselves with the connections between production, circulation, and consumption that lie beneath (and differ from) the shape of the economy visible on the surface of society.

Significance of Grasping the Inner-Connections of Social Reproduction as a Totality of Conditions

◘ Figure 14.23 merely indicates the most fundamental of the replacements for the reproduction of capital and revenue within the two main departments from among the conditions for the reproduction and circulation of the total social capital. However, in this chapter we have also seen the various conditions of reproduction, and in analysing those conditions our assumption has been that all of the other conditions had been met. In the actual process of reproduction, however, the various conditions synergistically enhance disturbances or cancel each other out, thus making the resulting concrete profile of the movement of capital exceedingly complex. On the surface of society, each of these conditions does not manifest itself as an independent entity. Our investigation in this chapter, by clarifying each of the elements of the inner connections beneath the surface, has provided indispensable clues for clarifying complex phenomena that seem impenetrable at first sight.

Further, all the conditions of reproduction constitute the factors of the development of concrete forms of capital, and more particularly, of the credit system and the formation of the banking system (both examined in ▶ Sect. 19.2 in Part III).

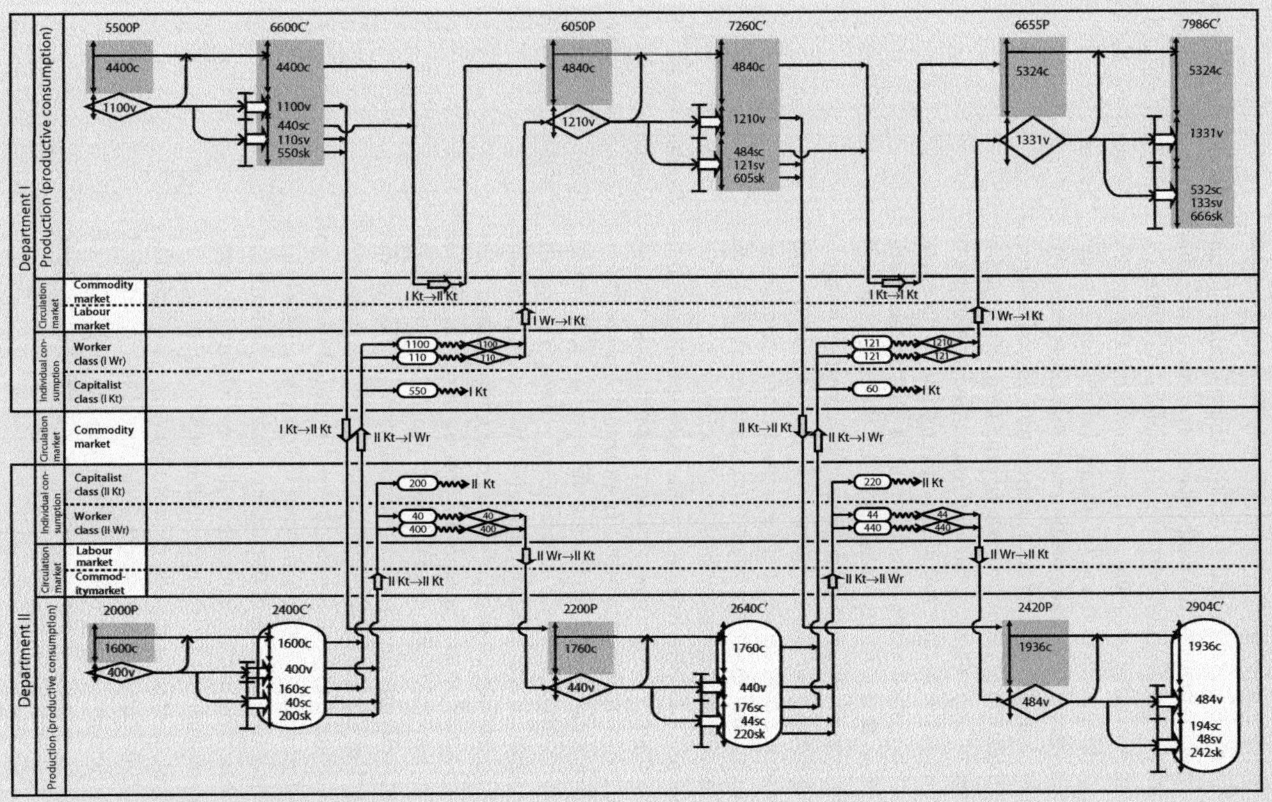

Fig. 14.23 Connections between production, circulation, and consumption within the process of social reproduction

Reference

Marx K (1885) Das Kapital. Kritik der politischen Oekonomie. Bd. 2. Buch 2: Der Circulationsprocess des Kapitals. Hrsg. von F. Engels. Hamburg. English edition: Marx K (1978) Capital. A critique of political economy, vol. 2 (trans: Fernbach D). Penguin Books, London

Various Forms of the Total Process of Capital

Contents

Capital and Profit

T. Otani, *A Guide to Marxian Political Economy*,
https://doi.org/10.1007/978-3-319-65954-1_15

15.1 Theme of Part III and the Path of Investigation

Focus Up to Now Has Been the Internal Relations of Capitalist Production

Starting from ► Chap. 3 («Capital and Surplus-value»), we familiarised ourselves with the most essential and fundamental mechanism of capitalist production by examining the production process of capital based on the premise that circulation proceeds normally.

Then, in Part II, we turned our attention to the circulation of capital, premised on that previous understanding of the production process of capital. In ► Chap. 12 («Circuit of Capital») and ► Chap. 13 («Turnover of Capital»), we became aware of the distinctive forms in the movement of circulating capital, while also appreciating the influences these forms exert on valorisation in the production process of capital. And in ► Chap. 14 («Reproduction and Circulation of the Total Social Capital»), we observed the reproduction of capital that progresses through the production and circulation processes as a social process, grasping how the movement of capitals are intertwined.

The investigations outlined above allowed us to complete our understanding of the internal relations within the total process of capital, which was something that the Classical economists had been unable to grasp as a totality.

Theme of Part III: Developing the Concrete Forms of Capital and Surplus-Value

Now we will move on to develop the various concrete forms assumed by capital and surplus-value in the total process of capital (i.e. the totality of the production and circulation processes passed through by individual capitals and the total social capital that they form), taking as the premise our essential understanding obtained thus far. This sphere was already explored in various ways by the Classical economists, so nearly all of the concrete forms had already been conceptualised. However, the Classical economists grasped phenomena separate from their essence, so they were unable, to unfold these concepts as phenomenal forms of the underlying essence. In contrast, we will set out from the knowledge at the level of essence, which has already been gained, and develop the concrete forms as the phenomenal forms of that essence.

Profit and Rate of Profit

► Chapter 15 will examine profit, which is the form surplus-value takes when grasped as an augmentation of the total advanced capital, as well as the particular forms the parts composing the value of individual commodities take when surplus-value is viewed as profit.

Average Rate of Profit and Production Price

In ► Chap. 16, we will become familiar with the tendency towards an equalisation of profit rates, resulting from the incessant movements of capitals seeking a higher rate of profit between spheres of production. And this, in turn, clarifies how the centre point within the fluctuating sales prices of individual commodities becomes the production price, which is the price that brings an average profit.

Tendential Fall in the Rate of Profit

► Chapter 17 clarifies that the heightening of the capital composition resulting from the development of production power acts to lower the rate of profit that is of decisive importance to both individual capitals and the total capital. This is phenomenally manifested as a tendential fall in the rate of profit.

Commercial Capital and Commercial Profit

► Chapter 18 looks at the capital that separates from industrial capital to become autonomous due to the tendency of capital towards «circulation without circulation time», which we learned by examining the circuit of capital (► Chap. 12 in Part II). This is the commercial capital that obtains profit by solely dealing in commodities and money within the circulation process of capital.

Interest-bearing Capital and Interest

Next, in ► Chap. 19, we turn to the distinctive forms of capital in the money form outside of the production and circulation process, existing in the hands of another person and mediating the movement of those processes in its role as capital. In other words, we will look at interest-bearing capital and the interest it obtains. This capital, in its developed form, is manifested as the distinctive «moneyed capital» that moves within the banking system, so our examination provides a rough overview of the banking system as well.

Landed Property and Ground-rent

► Chapter 20 deals with various issues that arise from the fact that, even though capitalist production subordinates the ownership of the specific production condition of land to the form of modern landed property, it is still necessary for a portion of surplus-value to be handed over to landowners in the form of ground-rent.

Forms of Revenue and Classes

After clarifying in those first six chapters in Part III the concrete forms taken by surplus-value (i.e. industrial profit and commercial profit, interest, and ground-rent), ► Chap. 21 turns to examine the mechanism, whereby the value generated by the workers' living labour forms the revenue of society's members as wages along with the other forms just listed. On the one hand, the starting point of our investigation was the common image people have of capitalist production (◘ Fig. 2.1), but we can now confirm that it has been transformed into an image that is explained according to the structure and laws that are at the deepest layer and also see that the members of society under such production necessarily constitute opposing social groups (i.e. classes).

15.2 Capital and Profit and the Rate of Profit

Capital Moves to Obtain Profit

The capital that we have familiarised ourselves with up to now has solely been *industrial capital* (*see* ► Sect. 12.2.2 in Part II). Starting from ► Chap. 18, however, we will begin dealing with other forms of capital: commercial capital, interest-bearing capital, and capital limited by landed property—in that order. But until then our investigation will be limited to industrial capital.

Everyone knows that what capital pursues through its movement is valorisation, or more concretely, the aim is to obtain the increment of capital value called **profit**.

Profit Manifests Itself as «Sales Price Minus Cost Price»

How, then, does capital obtain profit? Again, everyone knows that profit is obtained by means of selling the commodity produced, or more precisely, it is obtained when the *sales price* of the commodity is greater than its *cost*. That difference constitutes profit. The part within the sales price of a commodity that replaces its cost is called the commodity's **cost price**. So the profit obtained from an individual commodity is its *sales price minus cost price*. Viewed more concretely, in terms of the routine practices of capitalists, profit is the sum arrived at by subtracting from the «total sales revenue» the «expenses» (or «cost of goods sold») to cover wear and tear, raw materials, selling costs, and labour costs. The sum that remains is the «operating profit».

Rate of Profit as the Augmentation Rate of the Total Advanced Capital

From the perspective of individual commodities, profit is the excess part derived from the sales price exceeding the cost price. The proportion of profit to the *total advanced capital* (fixed capital plus circulating capital) is the **rate of profit**, which indicates the *degree of the capital augmentation*. If we make profit p and the total advanced capital K, the rate of profit p' is expressed in the following equation:

$$p' = \frac{p}{K}$$

15

15.3 Cost Price and Profit

Putting in Order the Common Image of Profit Based on Our Previous Theoretical Knowledge

The facts glanced at above regarding profit and the rate of profit which reach everyone's daily consciousness can now be put into order based on the theoretical knowledge we have obtained thus far by examining the production and circulation processes of capital.

In ► Chap. 2 in Part I, we saw that the cost necessary for the production of a commodity consists of (1) the value of the means of production consumed in its production (past labour objectified prior to the commodity's production) and (2) the living labour expended during the transforming and processing of the product using these means of production. The former is the old value transferred to the commodity, while the latter is the new labour objectified in the commodity. The value of a commodity is the sum of its old and new value. In other words, the value of the commodity expresses the production cost of a *commodity* (*see* ◘ Fig. 2.18).

Under capitalist production, as we saw in ► Chap. 3 in Part I, the old value transferred to a commodity takes the form of constant capital (c), while the living labour that is newly objectified takes the form of variable capital plus surplus-value ($v + s$). Thus the *cost of producing the commodity itself under capitalist production* is $c + v + s$ (*see* ◘ Fig. 3.18).

We saw in ► Sect. 13.2.1 in Part II, however, that whereas the circulating constant capital (cz) within the constant capital is always flowing back through the realisation of the commodity, the fixed capital (cf) remains within the production process so that only the value of its worn-out part (cw) is transferred to the commodity. Hence, the value of an individual commodity is the old value ($cw + cz$) transferred from the means of production and the newly objectified value ($v + s$). So that this can all be expressed as $cw + cz + v + s$ (*see* ◘ Fig. 13.1). This is the *real cost of the commodity*, whose magnitude is measured by the quantity of *objectified labour contained in the commodity.*

However, the surplus-value (s) within the value of the commodity ($cw + cz + v + s$) is the materialised surplus-labour expended by the worker, which is unpaid labour that does not cost the capitalist anything. The only part of the value of the commodity that the capitalist expends is the $cw + cz + v$ advanced as capital. *This is the cost of the commodity as far as the capitalist is concerned*, with its magnitude measured by the quantity of *capital advanced for the production of the commodity.*

What Presents Itself as «Cost Price + Profit» Is Really «Capital + Surplus-value»

We can see, then, that the *cost price* of a commodity is the part within its sales price that replaces the capitalist's costs. Therefore, profit is *value* minus the *cost price* of a commodity. In other words, what presents itself in the form of cost price and the profit that exceeds it is in fact *capital and the surplus-value it obtains.*

Essence of Surplus-value Concealed by the Forms of Cost Price and Profit

In the *phenomenal form* of cost price and of profit as the addition to cost price, however, their «essence» as capital and the surplus-value it obtains is not manifested at all. Instead these phenomenal forms completely conceal the *essential relations* wherein labour-power as the value creator generates surplus-value in the production process that exceeds its own value.

The first point to note is that when looking at cost price, what we see is that it is the part of the sales price needed to replace the capital expended by the capitalist as his cost; we cannot see at all what sort of relation each of its constituent parts (cw, cz, and v) have to the value that appears as profit. In short, we completely lose sight of the valorisation process.

Second, even though wages paid by the capitalist are in fact the price of labour-power, as seen in ▸ Chap. 6 of Part I, it appears that *wages are paid for labour*, or are the price of *labour*, so that this presents itself as the capital value paid for *all labour*, including the variable capital (v) advanced for labour and the *surplus-value* (s) generated in production (*see* ◘ Figs. 7.1 and 7.2). Given this, the advanced capital value and the value of the commodity produced thereby appear as follows, respectively:

Advanced capital = Capital value expended for means of production + capital value expended for labour

Commodity value = Cost price (price of means of production and of labour) + profit

Expressed in this way, the constant capital (c) and variable capital (v) manifest themselves as the «capital value expended on the means of production» and the «capital value expended on labour». Here the decisive difference between the two regarding their respective roles in the valorisation process is dissolved by only showing the material difference between the production elements each type of capital buys. We can no longer see at all how surplus-value (s), which takes the form of profit here, is augmented. Therefore, the cost price included within the commodity value is not only the exact return of the commodity value, i.e. the value expended on the means of production and labour, but it is also the *recovery of the cost expended* by capital, a *replacement* of the capital expended. Nevertheless, the commodity contains the sum of value called profit (surplus-value), which exceeds this cost price, but how that sum of value is generated remains a mystery[1].

---

1 Marx (1894) writes: «Profit, as we are originally faced with it, is thus the same thing as surplus-value, save in a *mystified form*, though *one that necessarily arises from the capitalist mode of production*. Because no distinction between constant and variable capital can be recognised in the apparent formation of the cost price, the

The third point is that, when calculating the cost price, the mental distinction made regarding the value composition of the advanced capital is between fixed capital and circulating capital. That is to say, among fixed capital within the production process, only the value *cw* that is the worn-out means of labour enters the value of the product, so only this part of fixed capital is recovered as one part of the cost price, whereas the constant capital advanced in the object of labour and the variable capital advanced in labour-power are all recovered as part of the cost price, with both seen as being the same as circulating capital. What is completely lost sight of is the decisively important difference of capital components in terms of the respective functions played by constant and variable capital in the valorisation process.

Fourth, since the entirety of the means of labour in the production process functions when a product is produced, it seems that the entirety of the capital value fixed in the production process is involved in the generation of the additional part of value.

Finally, the fifth point to note as the outcome of the foregoing is that the increment, profit, seems to emerge in quite the same way as the other value elements, i.e. it seems to arise from the means of production and labour. One thus has the impression that all the elements of capital, together, generate the additional part of value.

Profit Is Surplus-value Conceived of as Generated by the Total Advanced Capital

The fact that surplus-value is generated by labour-power and is an increment of the variable capital is overlooked. Instead, it seems that the augmentation is generated by the entire advanced aggregate capital (fixed capital plus circulating capital). **Profit** is generally thought of as an increment that capital brings about, but phrased in the correct terms of political economy, it is *surplus-value conceived of as being generated by the total advanced capital* and is thus *surplus-value in a mystified form*. This form, however, inevitably arises from the capitalist mode of production, and surplus-value must take this form, just as the value of labour-power must assume the wage form (*see* ◘ Fig. 15.1). We can compare that diagram, which presents the deceptive appearance of surplus-value, with ◘ Figs. 3.17 and 13.1, which indicate the actual process.

origin of the change in value that occurs in the course of the production process is shifted from the variable capital to the capital as a whole. Because the price of labour-power appears at one pole in the *transformed form of wages*, surplus-value appears at the other pole in the *transformed form of profit*.» (Marx 1981, p. 127; my emphasis).

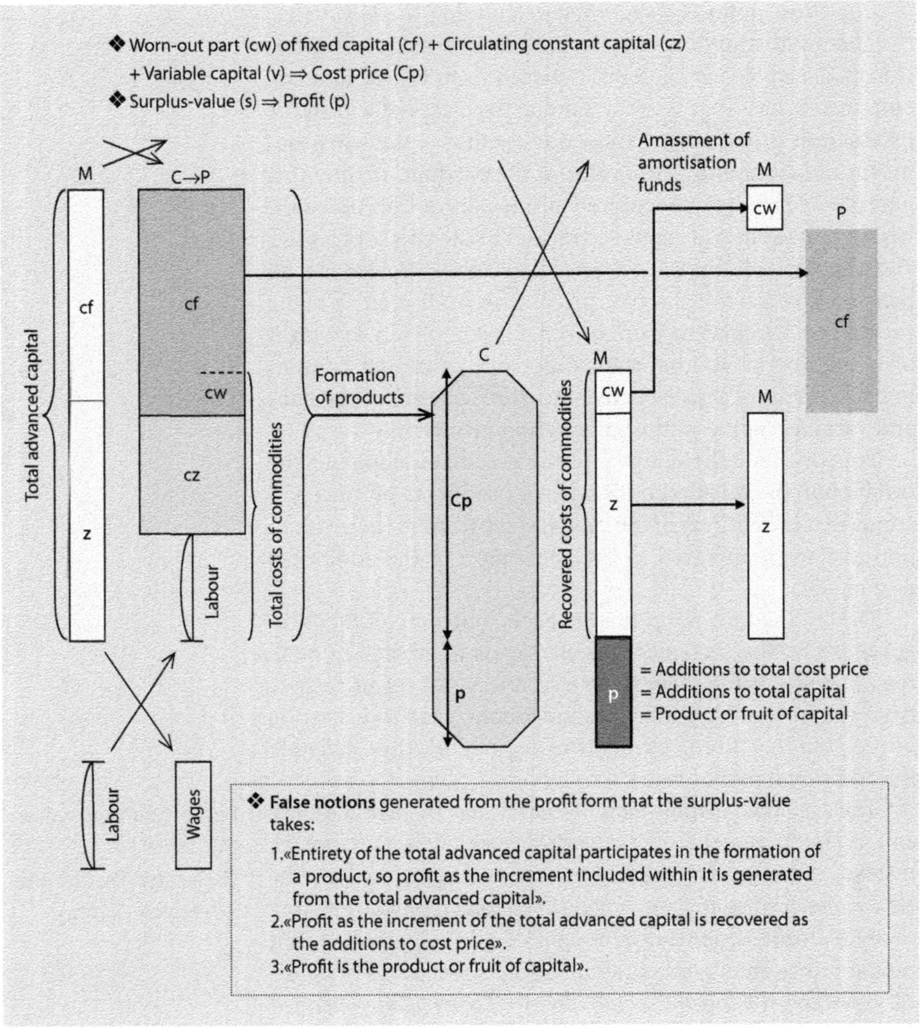

Fig. 15.1 Notions generated by the forms of cost price and profit

15

15.4 Mystification of Capital and Surplus-value in the Form of Profit

Rate of Profit Conceals the Rate of Surplus-value

We have just seen that profit (p) is surplus-value conceived of as «something generated by total advanced capital». But as the total advanced capital (K) is made up of constant capital (c) and variable capital (v), the **rate of profit** ($p' = \frac{p}{K}$) is essentially nothing more than:

$$p' = \frac{s}{c+v}$$

And since surplus-value is generated exclusively by the change in the value of variable capital, this rate of profit (p') must be grasped as:

$$p' = \frac{v}{c+v} \cdot \frac{s}{v} = \frac{v}{c+v} \cdot s' \left(s' = \text{rate of surplus} - \text{value} \right)$$

That is, the rate of profit is the product of the proportion of variable capital within the advanced capital ($\frac{v}{c+v}$) multiplied by the rate of surplus-value (s'). Therefore, the maximum rate of profit would be a case where constant capital is zero (although this could not occur in reality), which can be expressed as:

$$p' = \frac{v}{v} \cdot s' = s'$$

In other words, only in this case would the rate of profit be equal to the rate of surplus-value. This means that *the rate of profit is fundamentally restricted by the height of the rate of surplus-value*. But the greater the proportion of constant capital (c) within the total advanced capital (K), the greater the divergence of the rate of profit from the rate of surplus-value.

However, in the rate of profit (p'), only the total advanced capital and profit are seen, so it is impossible to discern from it the rate of surplus-value. This means that the *rate of surplus-value is decisively concealed by the rate of profit*.

Notion that Profit Comes from Selling Commodities Above Their Value

Our assumption up to now has been that the value of commodities produced by capital includes the profit (surplus-value) exceeding cost price that replaces the capital value expended, and that by selling commodities at their value a profit is realised in the form of money.

However, since profit for the capitalist presents itself as the difference between a commodity's cost price and its sales price, it is the cost price that clearly determines what must be spent on production of the commodity. Capital can be replaced as long as the cost price is recovered but not if the sales price falls below the cost price. Meanwhile, the sales price of a commodity is influenced by market conditions and also depends on the skill of the capitalist selling it. These facts lead the capitalist to believe that the value of a commodity does not contain profit to begin with and that rather *the cost price is the intrinsic value of the commodity*, so that profit arises from selling a commodity above its intrinsic value. In this way, the process that generates profit (surplus-value) already has been completely concealed, blocking from view the source of surplus-value. We are thus left with the concept that profit *emerges purely out of the circulation process*, as something generated by the sale of a commodity above the cost price thought to be its intrinsic value (*see* ◘ Fig. 15.2).

From that perspective, the commodity is sold above its value by the seller, so that the purchaser must buy it above its intrinsic value. The seller's profit thus always comes at the expense of the purchaser. If all the sales and purchases were considered together, gains and losses would cancel each other out, resulting in no aggregate profit at all. However, this fact does not trouble the upside-down logic of capitalists in the least.

At any rate, **capital** now is manifested as *the subject that generates profit while moving through the production process*

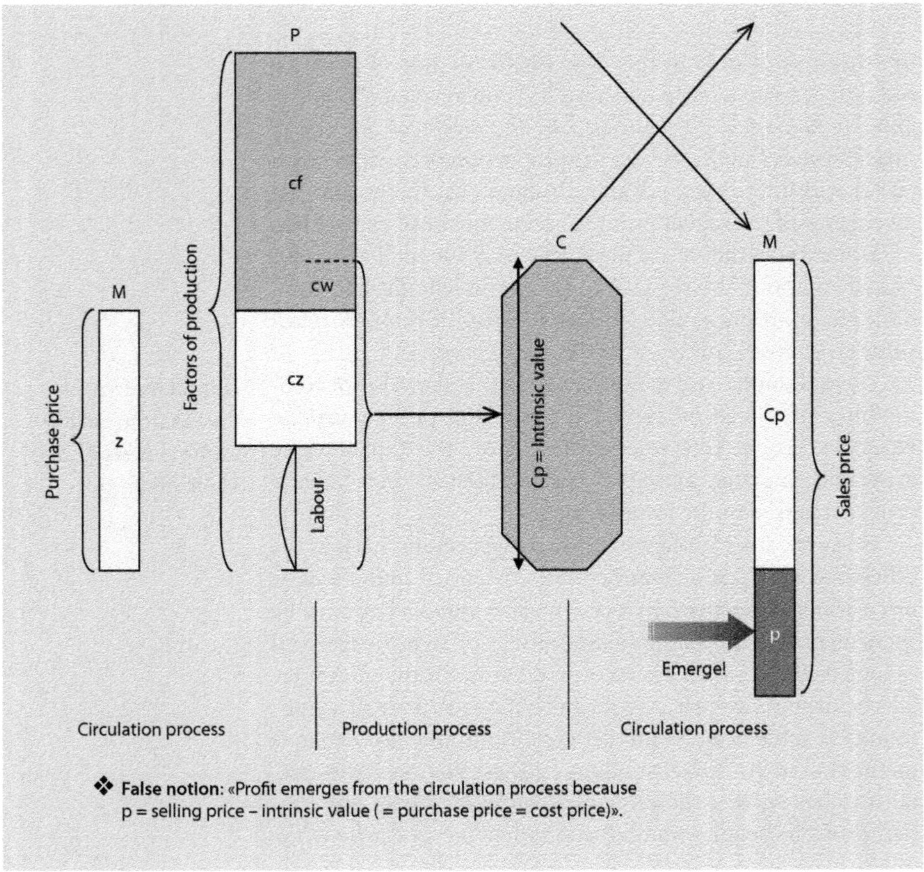

◘ **Fig. 15.2** False notion that profit emerges from the circulation process

and circulation process. Capital's relation to profit is akin to the relation between parents and the child they conceive. By generating a profit, capital is augmented by the magnitude of this profit. Because this augmented capital, in its entirety, is also capital, the profit as the increment is one part of the capital. This means that the relation between capital and profit is a relation of capital *qua* subject vis-à-vis capital itself. Indeed the rate of profit is nothing more than a *quantitative relation between «Capital the Father» and «Profit the Son»*. Once surplus-value takes the form of profit, one is no longer able to see that the true source of this increment of capital is generated by workers' surplus-labour. How this part actually emerges becomes completely incomprehensible and appears instead to derive from *some hidden, mystical quality that is inherent to capital.*

Rate of Profit Is a Quantitative Relation Between «Capital the Father» and «Profit the Son»

In ► Sect. 6.3 in Part I, we saw that in the production process of capital, the productive power of labour, i.e. the subjective productive power belonging to the labouring individual, presents itself as the productive power of capital. That is, it presents itself as the productive power belonging to the thing capital, which is personified in the form of the capitalist. From this inverted relation arises the upside-down notion that «the capitalist is subject, while the worker is a mere seller of labour who is provided employment by this subject». But now this consciousness develops into the idea that *capital as subject generates profit*. And the *personification of this capital as subject* is the **capitalist.**

Capital as Subject and the Capitalist as Its Personification

15.5 Profit Rate as the Determinant of the Action of Individual Capital

The rate of profit that is calculated by individual capital for practical purposes is a *rate of profit for a certain period of time* and, more concretely, the *rate of profit for* 1 *year*. The ratio of the quantity of profit obtained in 1 year to the total advanced capital is the **annual rate of profit.** This annual rate of profit is the product of the rate of profit multiplied by the yearly turnovers of capital that we looked at in ► Sect. 13.3.2 in Part II. If we designate the annual turnovers as n and the annual profit rate P', the latter is expressed as follows ($s'n$ is the annual rate of surplus-value; *see* ◘ Fig. 13.4 for more on this rate):

Annual Rate of Profit

$$P' = \frac{v}{c+v} \cdot s'n = \frac{1}{\frac{c}{v}+1} \cdot s'n$$

The fraction $\frac{c}{v}$ expresses the organic composition of capital. In short, the annual rate of profit rises in proportion to the rate of surplus-value (s') and the annual turnovers (n), while decreasing in line with heightening of the organic composition of capital ($\frac{c}{v}$).

The Determining Aim of Surplus-value Production Is Manifested as the Pursuit of Profit

We saw repeatedly in Part I that production of surplus-value is precisely the determining characteristic of capitalist production and thus the decisive aim of production for the capitalist, who personifies capital. And this fact is now manifested as *profit being the production aim for a capitalist*, so that the *pursuit of profit fundamentally determines his actions*.

The Capitalist Acts to Maximise the Rate of Profit

For the capitalist, the magnitude of profit is grasped, on the one hand, as an absolute quantity of profit and on the other hand as a relative rate vis-à-vis the total advanced capital, which is the rate of profit. However, since $p = Kp'$, the absolute quantity of profit (p) is determined by the absolute quantity of the total advanced capital (K) and the rate of profit (p'). For the capitalist, then, it is important to increase the total advanced capital (accumulated capital) and at the same time to raise the rate of profit to the greatest extent possible. The magnitude of the total advanced capital is determined by the degree of accumulation of individual capitals and the possibilities for accumulation, whereas the rate of profit is restricted by social factors that surround the individual capitals, such as competition between capitals and business conditions. Given this, *capital acts to maximise its own rate of profit, while keeping an eye on the rate of profit of society as a whole and the rate of profit within a specific department, which are constricted by competition and business conditions*. The question of the degree to which capital will be accumulated (advancing activities) is also related to these sorts of decisions. The rate of profit, or more exactly the «**expected rate of profit**», is the *greatest factor determining the actions of capital*.

15

Any Department Is Acceptable for Capital as Long as the Profit Rate Is High

The objective for capital is to obtain profit, so production of a particular product is merely a means to this end. So if a difference in the rate of profit exists between production spheres, capital will necessarily be further advanced in the sphere that brings a higher profit rate. This has important meaning, as we shall see in the next chapter, with regard to the equalisation of the average rate of profit and the formation of production price.

Reference

Marx K (1894) Das Kapital. Kritik der politischen Oekonomie. Bd. 3. Buch 3: Der Gesammtprocess der kapitalistischen Produktion. Hrsg. von F. Engels. Hamburg. English edition: Marx K (1981) Capital. A critique of political economy, vol 3 (trans: Fernbach D). Penguin Books, Harmondsworth

Average Rate of Profit and Production Price

T. Otani, *A Guide to Marxian Political Economy*,
https://doi.org/10.1007/978-3-319-65954-1_16

16.1 Market Value Established Through Competition of Capitals Within Each Production Sphere

This Chapter Deals with Competition Between Capitals

In ► Sect. 5.1 in Part I (cf. ■ Fig. 5.2), anticipatorily, we sought to understand the production of relative surplus-value by looking at the competition of capitals for extra surplus-value. Apart from that discussion, however, we have yet to examine the competition that develops between different capitals. This chapter will now elaborate in greater depth this *competition between capitals.*

Overview of the Market

The direct place where the competition between capitals unfolds is the **market**, and we will begin with a rough overview of the market.

From the perspective of the *spatial breadth* of the scene of transactions, distinctions can be made between the world market, foreign markets, the domestic market, remote markets, regional markets, the European or Asian market, etc.

When a specific *time period* or *place* pertains to a market, it can described using a special name that refers to the time or place, such as the annual fair, a Christmas market, morning market, riverside market, street market, etc.

The most important perspective from which to distinguish markets, however, is the *sort of commodity that is being sold.* Major differences in the nature of markets will arise depending on the different commodities sold. The primary distinction is between the commodity (product) market, money (capital) market, labour market, and land market.

The *commodity market* (product market) is the market for general commodities, excluding such special commodities as money (and capital), labour, land, etc. This market primarily consists of the market for products and the market for raw materials. The commodity market can be further divided into the production goods market for commodities destined to become means of production and the consumption goods market for commodities destined to become means of consumption. Then, depending on the particular commodity, there is the formation of markets for such specific products as vegetables, livestock, grain, fish, lumber, etc.

The *labour market*, as we saw at various points in Part I, is the market where labour-power is bought and sold, but this market takes its name from the notion of the «buying and selling» labour.

The *money market in the broad sense* is the market that deals with money as a commodity, seen to have the use-value of capital—i.e. the use-value as something that brings about an increment such as profit, interest, dividends, etc. Included within this market is the *money market in the narrow sense*, which is the market for short-term borrowing and lending between banks, and the capital market, securities market, stock market, dollar market, etc. We will discuss the money market later, in ▶ Chap. 19 («Interest-bearing Capital and Interest»), and the buying and selling of land will be looked at in ▶ Chap. 20 («Landed Property and Ground-rent»).

There are thus numerous sub-species and varieties of markets, with each market having its own characteristics. But if we were to speak of the market as a whole, it can be said that it is a *place where buyers and sellers come into contact and engage in the buying and selling of commodities*. A market usually is a place where *many* buyers and *many* sellers come into contact and carry out transactions, rather than just involving an individual transaction between a specific buyer and seller (i.e. *reciprocal transaction*).

Here we will only be dealing with the commodity market (product market). We have already touched on the labour market a number of times, and later we will take a closer look at the money market and land market.

Fundamental Difference Between Market Transactions and Reciprocal Transactions

The fundamental difference between the individual transactions carried out between a specific buyer and seller (reciprocal transactions) and transactions within a market (market transactions) is that, in the former, accidental and individual circumstances pertaining to the two parties in the transaction exert a major impact on the commodity price, whereas in the latter, such circumstances have almost no influence at all on the commodity price. Price fluctuation in the latter case is almost exclusively a matter of the *relative quantitative relation between the supply of and the demand for* the given commodity.

Supply and Demand

The totality of a particular commodity that appears in a particular market—regardless of the number of people in possession of it or the particular conditions related to them—always has meaning solely as a *commodity mass provided to the market*. Commodities in a market, from this perspective, are referred to as **supply**. Contrasted with this, the *totality of the desires for the commodity among the purchasers who appear on the market with the intent of buying the commodity depending on its price* is referred to as **demand**. Demand can also be expressed by the sum of money expected to be expended on the commodity, but the more fundamental determining factor is the quantity of commodities that are sought. However, demand is a relative magnitude since the quantity of the commodity and the sum of money expended on it can increase or decrease depending on changes in the price. Moreover, in the case of demand, regardless of the number of purchasers and the particular conditions pertaining to them, it always only has meaning as a *mass of money that appears in a market to make purchases*. In response to this quantitative relation between supply and demand (referred to hereinafter at times as the *supply and demand relation*), prices fluctuate. If supply is too great for demand or demand too small for supply, prices will fall, whereas if supply is insufficient to demand or demand too great for supply, prices will rise.

Price Fluctuations Due to Supply and Demand Result from Collective Bargaining over Price

The determination of price by the supply and demand relation could be described as a market version of the sort of price determination that occurs through the bargaining between an individual buyer and seller.

In such a transaction between individuals, the buyer presents a «bid price» against the seller's «asking price», and whatever the two parties agree to through their bargaining becomes the «selling price» or «sales price».

Compared to this, in a market mainly composed of numerous sellers who sell a large quantity of the same commodity to a large number of unspecified purchasers, price determination is carried out through *sellers raising or lowering their asking price while watching the response to each seller's asking price* (i.e. *the trends in the bid price*). If the number of sellers is greater, competition will arise among them in pursuit of having their own commodities bought through a lowering of the asking price, whereas if the number of purchasers is greater, competition will arise among them to make a purchase before others by raising the bid price to avoid paying even more later. This is how a sort of bargaining over price is carried out in the market between buyers and sellers[1].

«Law of One Price»

If such competition is freely carried out within the same market, a roughly identical price would be established for any one of the same commodities. This fact, which is clearly visible to anyone, has long been called the «**law of one price**».

Market Price

The price that is established in the market for each commodity in that manner is the **market price**. The market price is the real decided price, the real selling price of the commodity; it

16

1 Marx (1894) writes: «When we consider supply and demand, . . . the *supply* is equal to the *sum of commodities provided by all the sellers or producers of a particular kind of commodity,* and the *demand* is equal to the *sum of all buyers or consumers (individual or productive) of that same kind of commodity.* These totals, moreover, *act on one another as unities, as aggregate forces.* Here the individual has an effect only as part of a social power, as an atom in the mass, and it is in this form that *competition brings into play the social character of production and consumption.*» (Marx 1981, p. 295; my emphasis.)

is the price the seller can realise by selling the commodity. The market price of a commodity fluctuates up or down depending on changes in the supply and demand relation.

Social Value and Individual Value

The fact that each commodity has its own market price is in reality nothing more than the fact that any commodity unit of the same commodity will have the same value as a representative sample of this commodity, but expressed here in terms of price, which is to say, the expression of value through money. As we saw in ► Sect. 5.1 in Part I («Production of Relative Surplus-value»), the value of a commodity is determined by socially necessary labour-time; or more concretely, it is a **social value** decided by *socially necessary labour-time*, which differs from the **individual value** as the objectification of the *individual labour-time a capitalist actually requires to produce each commodity*. For individual capitalists, the *divergence between the individual value and social value* of their commodities is important. We have already seen that if this divergence is on the plus side, the capitalist can obtain **extra surplus-value**, whereas if it is on the negative side, he must lose a portion of surplus-value (*see* ◘ Fig. 5.2). It might seem, then, that the individual labour-time required by each individual capitalist and the individual value of each capitalist's commodities would only have significance for the capitalist in terms of determining the additional surplus-value gained or lost. But that is not in fact the case, since the *social value* of a given commodity sort that enters the market is the *social average of the individual values of all of the commodities, so the individual value of any commodity also constitutes one part that exerts an influence on the total social average.*

Value of the Commodity as Constituent Unit of the Total Quantity Is Average Value

The total quantity of a commodity in the market is what confronts, as the supply, the demand for that commodity. *In order to supply the commodity, society must use a portion of the totality of labour-time it can expend*; therefore, the total quantity of each commodity indicates a magnitude of this social labour-time. Of course, the total labour-time contains not only labour-time expended under socially average conditions of production but also labour-time expended under conditions that are more or less favourable than this average. Regardless of the production conditions for a commodity, the individual commodities belonging to this commodity mass are each an equally divided constituent unit of the total quantity of the commodity, so the *labour-time equally represented by these individual commodities on the market is obtained by dividing the total labour-time expended for the production of the mass of commodities by the quantity of commodities.* Indeed, the *socially necessary labour-time* of the commodity that appears on the market is this labour-time, so the social value of the individual commodities that appear on the market is determined by this labour-time as well. This social value, seen quantitatively, is the total average of the individual values of the individual commodities that appear on the market. If we designate three categories of production conditions, with one being mid-range conditions and the other two the conditions that are superior and inferior to this average level, then the social value is the *weighted average of the individual value of the commodities produced under each of these conditions.* Thus, if the total average of the individual values, or the magnitude of value determined by the weighted average of the individual values of commodities produced under different production conditions, is the **average value**, the *social value of the individual commodities appearing on the market is precisely this average value, quantitatively speaking.*

Market Value Is the Social Value of the Commodities Appearing on the Market

The value of a commodity at the time when it actually appears on the market—or the actual shape assumed by the social value of a commodity on the market—is the *value of a commodity as a constituent unit of the total quantity of the same sort of commodity*, and quantitatively this is the *average value*. The social value that takes such a concrete shape is called the **market value**[2]. The **market price** is actually the *money-expression of this market value.*

---

2 When we looked at the value of commodities in ▶ Sect. 2.2.2 in Part I («Value of a Commodity»), it was explained that because value is a *social attribute* of things, its quantity is determined by the labour-time *socially* required to produce a given commodity and that *socially* necessary labour-time is the labour-time required to produce the commodity under the normal conditions of production and with the average degree of skill and intensity of labour *for a given society*. At that starting level of our view, we still left out of consideration that the *totality of the same sort of commodity forms the supply on the market.* But now we have observed that each commodity is a *constituent unit (aliquot part) of the mass of the same commodity that forms the supply in the market.* So the entire labour-time required to produce the total mass of the commodity must be taken into consideration as a vital factor determining its value. And the value of the commodity as an aliquot part of the mass of the same commodity is its average value. In other words, the total labour-time required to produce the entire mass of the commodity divided by its total quantity.

However, the market value, which is fundamentally the average value, has an actual influence within the market on the market price in the following manner: The capital that supplies the market a large quantity of the same commodity sort, so its individual value is near to the market value, holds the initiative for determining price. Therefore, *when we observe the market value from the viewpoint of*

Competition Within a Sphere in Pursuit of Surplus Profit Establishes the Market Value

The **competition between capitals in the same production sphere** posits the social value in the shape of market value. As we saw in ► Sect. 5.1 in Part I («Production of Relative Surplus-value»), capitals with different production conditions compete in pursuit of *extra surplus-value*. We also saw in the previous chapter that because the surplus-value obtained by capital in the production process takes the form of profit, where surplus-value is conceived of as the «product of the aggregate capital», when extra surplus-value is viewed from the perspective of this conception, it must also take the specific form of profit. Given this, *extra surplus-value* takes the shape of profit obtained that exceeds the average profit within a production sphere and is thus called *surplus profit. Capitals within the same sphere compete in pursuit of surplus profit.* Through this competition, the three production conditions mentioned earlier—the middling conditions and those superior and inferior to them—are always undergoing a change to reach a higher level, which in turn raises the productive power of commodity-producing labour. Because the labour-time needed to produce individual commodities falls as the productive power of labour rises, the market value (average value) also falls. Thus, *competition in pursuit of surplus profit within a production sphere establishes a single, identical market value from out of the manifold individual values of individual commodities* produced under various production conditions.

Hence, we have known that competition within the same production sphere establishes a single, identical market value for a commodity and that the market price fluctuates around this market value. Given this, when we speak of the «value» of a commodity, it will be referring to this market value that is the average of the individual values (*see* ◘ Fig. 16.1).

Competition Between Capitals Executes the Intrinsic Laws of Capital

Various parties appear on the market. Along with buyers and sellers, these participants include capitalists or workers, producers or merchants, and moneyed capitalists or land-

---

which commodity should be taken as the average sample from out of the commodity mass so that its individual value can be considered as the representative to indicate the level of the market value, we can suppose the market value is determined by the individual value of the commodity produced by the capital that supplies a prodigious quantity of the commodity mass. Mathematically speaking, the average of the preceding average value was the weighted average, whereas the average of this average is a *mode* (the value that occurs most frequently in a given set of data). Although the two, quantitatively observed, are not identical, the latter determination, called the «mass determination of market value», is very useful when we must *concretely grasp the market price as the value of the representative commodity that determines the market price.*

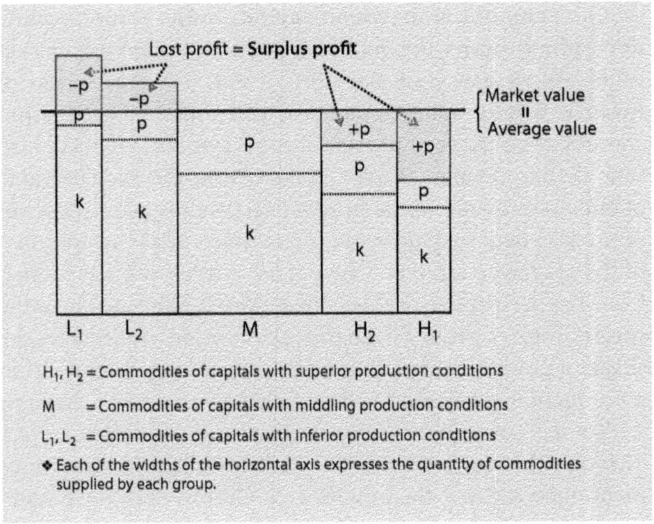

Fig. 16.1 Competition within a sphere establishes market value as the weighted average of individual values

owners. And the commodities or money brought in by these participants together constitute the supply and demand, whose relation causes fluctuations in the prices of commodities sold. These price fluctuations, in turn, can greatly alter the magnitude of the commodities or money brought in by the market participants. Within this continual movement, the participants are constantly exerting pressure, either between those in the same position or between those who confront each other. So the participants cannot remain aloof to this outside pressure, and they are always being driven in some direction by it. This *mutual pressure exerted* by the participants is **competition**. *The laws of capital are only first realised,* in fact, *through the participants being forcefully thrust ahead in a certain direction by competition.* In this sense, *competition as a compulsion exterior to individual capital* is the **executor of capital's intrinsic laws**. However, competition as executor does not create the laws themselves. So, when analysing capitalist production, one must proceed by first grasping the intrinsic laws of capital and then, on the basis of this understanding, study the manner in which competition executes these laws. We are able to deal with competition in this chapter because we already have the understanding of the intrinsic laws of capital necessary to address this topic. In this chapter, therefore, competition between capitals must be consistently grasped as the executor of the intrinsic laws.

16.2 Average Rate of Profit and Production Price

16.2.1 Profit Rates Will Differ by Sphere If All Commodities Are Sold at Their Value

Composition of Capital Varies by Sphere

The organic composition of capital varies depending on the sphere (*see* ◘ Fig. 16.2). (There are also differences in capital composition between capitals in the same sphere that produce the same commodity due to differences in production conditions, but here we will assume capital has an average capital composition within each production sphere.)

Because of Differences in Capital Composition, the Quantity of Profit and Rate of Profit Differ

If the rate of surplus-value is the same, the quantity of surplus-value (profit) will be proportional to the quantity of variable capital (*see* ◘ Fig. 16.3). (Here our assumption is that the rate of surplus-value is 100% at any time and place.)

Therefore, if the organic composition of capital differs, the rate of profit will also differ (*see* ◘ Fig. 16.4).

Thus, the rate of profit in each sphere (i.e. the particular rate of profit) will necessarily vary if all commodities *are sold at their value*.

There will also be differences in the rate of profit due to *differences in the turnover period of capital*, but this will be set aside in the explanation below for the sake of simplicity, so that our assumption will be that capital's *turnover is the same in all spheres*.

I. 95c + 5v Sphere with the highest capital composition (e.g., steel industry)
II. 85c + 15v Sphere with higher capital composition
III. 80c + 20v Sphere with middling capital composition (e.g., textile industry)
IV. 75c + 25v Sphere with lower capital composition
V. 65c + 35v Sphere with the lowest capital composition (e.g., rice cultivation)

◘ **Fig. 16.2** Different spheres have different organic compositions of capital

I. 95c + 5v ⇒ 5s Value = 105
II. 85c + 15v ⇒ 15s Value = 115
III. 80c + 20v ⇒ 20s Value = 120
IV. 75c + 25v ⇒ 25s Value = 125
V. 65c + 35v ⇒ 35s Value = 135

◘ **Fig. 16.3** Quantity of surplus-value differs depending on differences in capital composition

$$
\begin{cases}
\text{I. } 95c + 5v \Rightarrow 5s & 100K \Rightarrow 5p \quad p' = 5\% \\
\text{II. } 85c + 15v \Rightarrow 15s & 100K \Rightarrow 15p \quad p' = 15\% \\
\text{III. } 80c + 20v \Rightarrow 20s & 100K \Rightarrow 20p \quad p' = 20\% \\
\text{IV. } 75c + 25v \Rightarrow 25s & 100K \Rightarrow 25p \quad p' = 25\% \\
\text{V. } 65c + 35v \Rightarrow 35s & 100K \Rightarrow 35p \quad p' = 35\%
\end{cases}
$$

Fig. 16.4 Amount and rate of profit also vary depending on capital composition

16.2.2 Competition Between Capitals of Different Spheres Brings About Capital Transfers Among Spheres

The Crucial Issue for Capital Is the Realisation of a High Profit Rate

Capitalist production is the production of surplus-value, which is to say, production that aims to obtain profit. The crucial aspect for capital is the rate of profit. So what is at issue for capital is not what sort of commodity to produce or what production sphere to operate in but rather the realisation of a high rate of profit.

Transfers of Capital Necessarily Arises from a Difference in the Profit Rate Among Spheres

Every individual capital moves in pursuit of a higher rate of profit. Capitals compete within the same production sphere to obtain more surplus profit by introducing new techniques with greater productive power than those of other capitals to improve the production conditions. Further, capitals in different production spheres also compete in striving to achieve a higher profit rate. A **capital transfer between spheres** necessarily arises from the **pressure of this competition** if the profit rates differ between them. If all the commodities produced in the various production spheres are sold at their values, as we have just seen, differences arise in the rate of profit for each sphere. And there necessarily arises a transfer in capital from spheres with a lower rate of profit to those with a higher rate. Moreover, newly advanced capital will be directed towards these production spheres with a higher profit rate.

16.2.3 Market Prices of Commodities Fluctuate Around Their Production Price

Change in Supply and Demand Relation Due to Transfer of Capital Causes Fluctuation in Commodity Prices

The transfer of capital results in an *increase of capital* in production spheres with a higher rate of profit, thereby increasing the supply of commodities, while *capital decreases* in spheres where the rate of profit is lower, thereby contracting the *supply of commodities*. Through these changes in the magnitude of the supply of commodities, the *relation of supply and demand changes*, so that each commodity's *market price deviates from its value*.

Unceasing Capital Transfers and Price Fluctuations as Long as Profit Rates Differ

A *counteraction* arises—where a lowering of a commodity's price increases demand for it, while a price rise weaken this demand—but *the efflux and influx of capital begin anew* on the basis of the *new level of the profit rate*. This movement will never cease as long as there are differences in the rate of profit.

Average Rate of Profit Established Through Equalisation of the Profit Rate

As an outcome of the above, as long as the transfer of capital freely occurs, the market price of any commodity will necessarily come to fluctuate around a *price that allows the rate of profit in all production spheres to be the same*. The process that generates this state is called the **equalisation of the rate of profit**. The rate of profit obtained thereby is the **average rate of profit**, and the profit obtained through that average rate is the **average profit**. We can designate the average rate of profit as ap' and average profit as ap. The average profit ap for an individual capital is equal to its total advanced capital K multiplied by the average profit rate ap'.

$$ap = K \cdot ap'$$

Commodity Price that Yields an Average Profit for Capital Is the Commodity's Production Price

Commodities produced in any production sphere should have a price that yields an average profit for the capital that was advanced. This is the price that *capitalists are always aware of in their practical activities in terms of considering what price for their own commodity would allow them to obtain the socially average profit*, and there was already a clear understanding of this among the Classical economists. This price was called the «necessary price» by the *physiocrats*, the «natural price» by *Adam Smith*, and the «production price» or «production cost» by *David Ricardo*. Marx, for his part, adopted *Ricardo*'s term «production price» in the end —and here we will also use the term **production price** to refer to the *price that yields an average profit for capital*.

Production Price of a Commodity = Cost Price + Average Profit for the Single Commodity Unit

What is the nature, then, of this production price, which is the commodity price whereby the same rate of profit can be obtained in every production sphere? Simply put, it is the cost price (Cp) of the commodity plus the average profit vis-à-vis this cost price, or cost price plus the sum of cost price (Cp) multiplied by the average profit rate (ap'). If production price is Pp, this is expressed as follows:

$$Pp = Cp + Cp \cdot ap' = Cp\left(1 + ap'\right)$$

The capital advanced will be able to obtain average profit if all the commodities produced by this capital are sold at their production price.

Production Price of Individual Commodities Not Directly Related to Their Value

If commodities are sold at a price equal to their value, they will yield different rates of profit depending on the production sphere, so that the price of a commodity (apart from those whose capital composition happens to be the same as the socially average capital composition) will diverge from its value. What determines the production price is the cost price and the average profit per single commodity unit, but what is *uniformly fixed for each commodity* is only the *cost price*, which expresses the capital expended on it. The *average profit per single commodity unit* is arrived at by dividing the average profit calculated for the total advanced capital (i.e. total advanced capital multiplied by the average rate of profit) by the total quantity of commodities produced by the total advanced capital, while the average rate of profit is the *total social surplus-value divided by the total social capital.* Hence, the average rate of profit *is not directly related at all to a commodity's own value.*

16.3 Equalisation of the Rate of Profit Through Competition Between Capitals

Hypothetical Example to Trace the Equalisation of the Profit Rate

When all commodities are sold at their value, so that the rate of profit differs between production spheres with different organic compositions, individual capital will emigrate and immigrate among various spheres in pursuit of spheres with the highest rate of profit, provided that there is a free transfer of capital between spheres, and this results in the market prices of commodities in any of the spheres fluctuating around a price that yields a profit rate that becomes the average rate of profit, i.e. they fluctuate around the production price. In order to be able to visualise the nature of this process, let us create a **hypothetical example.**

The proportions of fixed capital and circulating capital differ among production spheres, and the magnitude of constant capital (amortised part of fixed capital + circulating constant capital) contained in individual commodities also varies. And this difference in constant capital influences the rate of profit through the influence posited by capital's turnover times. But here, to simplify matters, we will assume that *fixed capital does not exist at all.*

At the Starting Point, Commodities Are Sold at a Price Identical to Value

Let us assume, to begin with, that there are the following five production spheres, each utilising a capital of 100, and that products are sold at a price identical to value (*see* ◘ Table 16.1).

16

Table 16.1 Rate of profit varies by sphere of production due to difference in capital composition

Sphere of production	I	II	III	IV	V
1. Individual capital (C = c + v)	100	100	100	100	100
2. Total social capital (=Σ1)			500		
3. Capital composition (c:v)	95c + 5v	85c + 15v	80c + 20v	75c + 25v	65c + 35v
4. Constant capital (c)	95	85	80	75	65
5. Variable capital (v)	5	15	20	25	35
6. Rate of surplus-value (s′) (s/v)			100%		
7. Surplus-value (s) (=5 × 6)	5	15	20	25	35
8. Total social surplus-value (=Σ7)			100		
9. Particular rate of profit (p′) (=7/1)	5%	15%	20%	25%	35%
10. Total value of commodities (=4 + 5 + 7)	105	115	120	125	135
11. Total social value (=Σ10)			600		
12. Total cost price of commodities (=1)	100	100	100	100	100
13. Total price of commodities (=Σ10)	105	115	120	125	135
14. Total social prices (=Σ13)			600		
15. Realised profit (p) (=13–12)	5	15	20	25	35
16. Total social profit (=Σ15)			100		
17. Realised rate of profit (p′) (=15/1)	5%	15%	20%	25%	35%

Capital Transfer Arises in the Pursuit of Higher Rate of Profit

At this starting point, given the differences in capital composition, the rate of profit will be higher or lower depending on the sphere. Now let us assume capital in the amount of 20 and 10 flows out of spheres I and II, where the rate of profit is low, and into spheres IV and V, respectively, where the rate of profit is high. Based on the assumption that the aggregate demand of society is equal to the amount of value produced and that the proportion of distribution of aggregate demand to each sphere remains unchanged, the commodity prices determined by that demand will rise in spheres I and II and fall in spheres IV and V—as depicted in ◘ Table 16.2[3].

Outcome of Capital Transfer: Demand/ Supply Relation Changes in Each Sphere and Prices Fluctuate

The amount of total social value (total social demand) can increase from 600 to 607, despite the unchanged quantity of total social capital, because of the increased capital advanced in spheres with a low capital composition, so that the total social surplus-value increases compared to its previous level. As we can see, the situation in spheres I and II is «supply < demand», whereas in spheres IV and V, it is «supply > demand». The result is that prices necessarily rise in I and II and fall in IV and V.

Since the amount of total demand (total value) remains the same here, demand for commodities in I and II decreases by 9.11 and 7.08, respectively, while demand for commodities in IV and V increases by 7.08 and 9.11. As a result, the prices of the former decline and those of the latter increase. For the sake of convenience, we will assume that the magnitude of these price fluctuations is the same as the breadth of the fluctuations in demand, thus yielding the results in ◘ Table 16.3.

Demand/Supply Relation Established Whereby Market Prices Anywhere Identical to Production Prices

As seen above, the rate of profit comes to be equal in all spheres. This rate is equal to the average rate of profit, which is the proportion of total surplus-value (total profit) to the total capital. As long as this condition remains unaltered, there is no reason—from the perspective of the profit rate—for the capital to move from one sphere to another, and therefore no transfer of capital occurs. Under such a situation, the price of a commodity is equal to its production price. And the results of this are summarised in ◘ Table 16.4.

What Occurs in Reality Is the «Constant Equalisation of Incessant Inequalities»

Under capitalist production, however, there is absolutely no way to establish such an ideal relation of price equilibrium, wherein the influx and efflux of capital ceases. This is not merely because numerous individual capitals anarchically

3 Marx (1894) writes: «If commodities were sold at their values this would mean very different rates of profit in the different spheres of production, as we have already explained, according to the differing organic composition of the masses of capital applied. Capital withdrawn from a sphere with a low rate of profit and wends its way to others that yield higher profit. This *constant migration*, the *distribution of capital between the different spheres* according to where the profit rate is rising and where it is falling, is what produces a *relationship between supply and demand* such that the average profit is the same in the various different spheres, and values are therefore transformed into prices of production.» (Marx 1981, p. 297; my emphasis.)

■ **Table 16.2** Outcome of capital transfer: change of demand/supply relation in each sphere and the price fluctuations

Sphere of production	I	II	III	IV	V
1. Individual capital (C = c + v)	80	90	100	110	120
2. Total social capital (=Σ1)			500		
3. Capital composition (c:v)	95c + 5v	85c + 15v	80c + 20v	75c + 25v	65c + 35v
4. Constant capital (c)	76	76.5	80	82.5	78
5. Variable capital (v)	4	13.5	20	27.5	42
6. Rate of surplus-value (s′) (m/v)			100%		
7. Surplus-value (s) (5 × 6)	4	13.5	20	27.5	42
8. Total social surplus-value (=Σ7)			107		
9. Particular rate of profit (=7/1)	5%	15%	20%	25%	35%
10. Total value of commodities (=4 + 5 + 7)	84	103.5	120	137.5	162
11. Total social value (=Σ10)			607		
12. Total social demand (=Σ11)			607		
13. Demand for each sphere (=12 × (10/11 of ■ Table 16.1))	106.23	116.34	121.4	126.46	136.57
14. Total price of commodities (=13)	106.23	116.34	121.4	126.46	136.57
15. Total social price (=Σ14)			607		
16. Total cost price of commodities (=1)	80	90	100	110	120
17. Realised profit (p)(=14–16)	26.23	26.34	21.4	16.46	16.57
18. Realised rate of profit (p′) (=17/1)	32.78%	29.27%	21.4%	14.96%	13.80%
19. Sum of changed price (=14–10)	+22.23	+12.84	+1.4	−11.04	−25.43
20. Rate of change of price (=19/10)	+26.46%	+12.4%	+1.17%	−8.03%	−15.7%

Table 16.3 Changes in demand arise through price fluctuations, yielding an equalisation in the rate of profit between all spheres

Sphere of production	I	II	III	IV	V
21. Change in demand	−9.11	−7.08	0	+7.08	+9.11
22. Demand = total price (=13 + 21)	97.12	109.26	121.42	133.54	145.68
23. Total social price (=Σ22)			607		
24. Total cost price of commodities (=1)	80	90	100	110	120
25. Realised profit (=22–24)	17.12	19.26	21.4	23.54	25.68
26. Total social realised profit (=Σ25)			107		
27. Realised rate of profit (=25/1)	21.4%	21.4%	21.4%	21.4%	21.4%

Table 16.4 In a state of equilibrium, commodities in every sphere are sold at their production prices

Sphere of production	I	II	III	IV	V
1. Individual capital (C = c + v)	80	90	100	110	120
2. Total social capital (= Σ1)			500		
3. Surplus-value (s)	4	13.5	20	27.5	42
4. Total social surplus-value (= Σ3)			107		
5. Average rate of profit (ap′) (= 4/2)			21.4%		
6. Total value of commodities (= 1 + 3)	84	103.5	120	137.5	162
7. Total social value (= Σ6)			607		
8. Average profit (ap) (= 1 × 5)	17.12	19.26	21.4	23.54	25.68
9. Total social average profit (= Σ8)			107		
10. Total cost price of commodities (= 1)	80	90	100	110	120
11. Total production price of commodities (= 10 + 8)	97.12	109.26	121.4	133.54	145.68
12. Total social production price (= Σ11)			607		
13. Total production price – total value (= 11–6)	+13.12	+5.76	+1.4	−3.96	−16.32
14. Sum of 13 (= Σ13)			0		

16

produce numerous types of commodities. In addition, there is capital's *internal impulse towards valorisation*, which penetrates as the *external law of competition* between the capitals in each production sphere that are pursuing surplus profit. Each individual capital is thus *compelled to continually develop the productive power of labour*. This occurs in a completely unequal manner, driving down the market price in each production sphere by heightening the composition of capital, which lowers each product's market value. Furthermore, *capital accumulation among individual capitals* seeking to augment their amount of profit also quite unevenly increases the quantity of production and supply of commodities. All of this means that, *under actual capitalist production, it is quite impossible from the outset for relations of complete equilibrium to be established*. What can be seen in reality is the constant turbulence, where supply and demand progress towards a state of equilibrium but always goes too far and recede, so that disequilibrium is always arising from the fluctuations in the new market value and changes in supply and demand. The actual market prices are constantly fluctuating around the production price, which is the equilibrium price (central price), and these fluctuations bring about a change in the magnitude and direction of the transfer of capital, thus altering the production price that is the equilibrium price. In short, what exists in reality is in essence nothing but the «**constant equalisation of incessant inequalities**» (Marx 1894: Marx 1981, p. 298). Moreover, there are various *restrictions* and *obstacles* to the efflux and influx of capital, so even if it is known that the rate of profit is higher in some other sphere, this does not necessarily mean that *capital can be transferred between spheres in an absolutely free manner*. From this perspective as well, it is clear that *a perfect equalisation of the profit rate is not possible in reality*.

Laws and the Concept of Production Price Must Be Grasped to Understand Reality

This movement of «continual equalisation of incessant disequilibrium» is a fact that would be hard to deny. The problems raised here are how and why this phenomenon occurs, its direction and magnitude, as well as the influence that restrictions on capital transfer has on price fluctuations and what sort of differences remain between the rate of profit between spheres. None of these problems can be dealt with at all without understanding the law of the equalisation of the profit rate through competition as well as the concepts of production price and the average rate of profit, which are established through the movement of equalisation. In other words, without that understanding there is no way for us to analyse the concrete processes of reality.

16.4 Penetration of the Laws of Value and Surplus-value

Does Value Lose Its Significance as the Regulator of Price?

As seen earlier, production price does not coincide with value in any production sphere apart from those rare spheres whose organic composition happens to be equal to the average organic composition of the total social capital. Thus, once production prices are established, the production price becomes the point around which the market price fluctuates. So as long as we are dealing with individual commodities, value is no longer the centre point of market price fluctuations. And the production prices of individual commodities themselves have no *direct* relation at all to value. Does this mean, then, that with the establishment of production prices, commodity value no longer has significance as the regulator of price?

Production Price Is Still Determined by the Value of a Commodity and Surplus-value

Let us take a closer look at ◘ Table 16.4, which was referred to earlier. The «total production price of commodities» (11) of each sphere is arrived at, *directly speaking*, by adding the «average profit» (8)—which is the sum of the «total capital» (1) multiplied by the «average rate of profit» (5)—to the «total cost of commodities» (10). And total production price has no *direct* relation to the «total value of commodities» (6), which is the sum of the «total capital» (1) added to «surplus-value» (3). However, the level of the «average rate of profit» (5) is the «total social surplus-value» (4) divided by the «total quantity of social capital» (2). This «total social surplus-value» (4) is the sum of the «surplus-value» (3) contained within the «total value of commodities» (6) produced in each of the five spheres. This can be expressed in terms of the following relation of determination: Value and surplus-value of individual commodities → total social surplus-value → average rate of profit → average profit → total production price of each production sphere → production price of each commodity. In other words, *the value and surplus-value of individual commodities determine the absolute quantity of the production prices of individual commodities*, so that changes in the former, no matter how minimal, necessarily influence the latter. That is to say, *the magnitude of production prices and of the average rate of profit are premised on the value of the commodities and the specific rate of profit in each production sphere that is determined by this* (as the sum of the total surplus-value of each sphere divided by the total amount of capital in each sphere)[4].

16

4 Marx (1894) writes: «Since it is the total value of the commodities that governs the total surplus-value, while this in turn governs the level of average profit and hence the general rate of profit—as a general law or as governing the fluctuations—it follows that the law of value regulates the prices of production» (Marx 1981, p. 289).

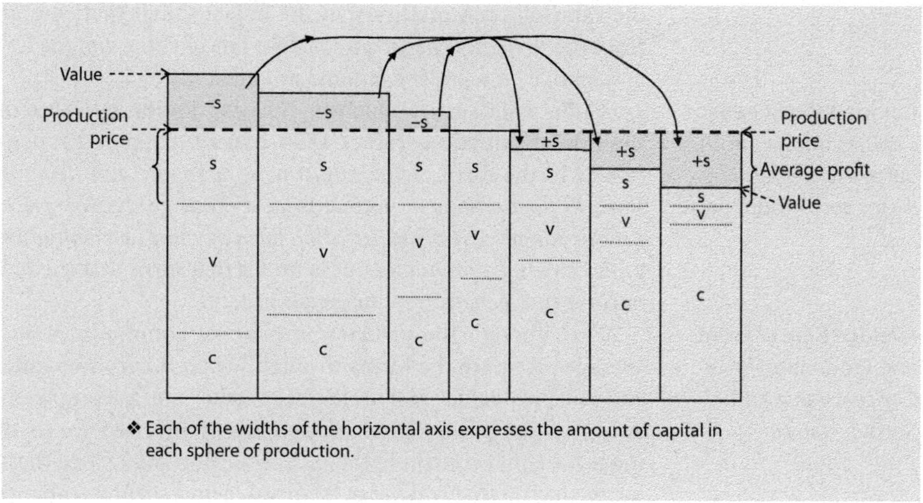

Fig. 16.5 Average profit is what distributes the total surplus-value according to the magnitude of capital

Equalisation of the Profit Rate Is the Mechanism for Proportionally Distributing the Total Surplus-value

Let us express this in more general terms. If commodities are sold at their production prices, capital in any production sphere will be able to obtain average profit in proportion to its own amount. This *average profit* is precisely *what proportionally distributes the total surplus-value of society among the total capital of society in proportion to the magnitude of each individual capital.* In other words, if products are sold at their production prices, the surplus-value produced in production spheres where the production price is lower than value will flow to those spheres where production price exceeds value. Thus, *what determines the level of the average rate of profit and the sum of average profit* is precisely *the total value of commodities and the total surplus-value contained therein.* Marx ironically refers to the outcome, whereby the total surplus-value obtained by all of the capitalists is divided among them, in proportion to the magnitude of each capital, as «**capitalist communism**» (Marx 1868. Marx 1988, p. 23) (*see* Fig. 16.5).

Establishment of Production Prices Is the Outcome of the Penetration of the Laws of Value and Surplus-value

The establishment of an average rate of profit and production prices stems from the penetration of the intrinsic laws of capitalist production. This is the penetration of the intrinsic law that compels individual capitals to pursue the greatest valorisation possible, i.e. the «law of surplus-value», which is itself based on the «law of value», whereby prices fluctuate around the centre point of value through the changes in the supply and demand relation caused by price diverging from value. Thus, far from the average rate of profit and production price of a commodity having no relation to the surplus-value generated by workers' surplus-labour or the value of a commodity, they are in fact things that emerge from the *inevitable penetration of the law of value and the law of surplus-value under capitalist production.*

Competition Between Capitals Brings About Value's Regulation of Aggregate Production

Under capitalist production, the «**regulation by value of the total production**» (Marx 1894. Marx 1981, p. 1020) penetrates in the form of the *adjustment of supply and demand through fluctuations in market price around production price. Production price is the penetration form of value determination under capitalist production.* It is under that form that the *law of value* first *penetrates throughout society.*

Average Rate of Profit and Production Price Conceal Value and Surplus-value

Even though the production price of commodities and average profit are the forms through which the laws of value and surplus-value penetrate, they take on a completely *estranged appearance from those laws* as inverted *forms* of those laws that constitute their *essence.* Moreover, since these forms quantitatively diverge from value and surplus-value in the case of individual commodities and individual capitals, we are completely unable to directly grasp from these forms that their essence is value and surplus-value. Thus, production price and the average rate of profit, even more than the forms cost price and profit, utterly conceal the *value and surplus-value at their essence,* leaving us quite unable to glimpse the secret of capital valorisation.

Average Rate of Profit and Production Price Must Be Explained from Value and Surplus-value

Both the average rate of profit and production price are *facts* of capitalist production as well as *forms* that are visible to the eye. Capitalists are unable to grasp these forms conceptually, but they are conscious of them when actually engaging in competition and thus when carrying out the transfer of capital. The task for political economy is *not* to confirm the reality of this average rate of profit and production price. What must be done, rather, is to theoretically explain this reality of which people are more or less conscious—these forms that completely conceal their own essence from people's vision—on the basis of unfolding the underlying laws of value and surplus-value and in accordance with the value and surplus-value of the commodity. Ultimately, the visible phenomenal world of the average rate of profit and production price must be explained by the underlying *world of labour formed by labouring individuals.*

References

Marx K (1868) Letter to Friedrich Engels, 30 April 1868. English edition: Marx K (1988) Marx-Engels Collected Works, vol 43. Progress Publishers et al. New York

Marx K (1894) Das Kapital. Kritik der politischen Oekonomie. Bd. 3. Buch 3: Der Gesammtprocess der kapitalistischen Produktion. Hrsg. von F. Engels. Hamburg. English edition: Marx K (1981) Capital. A critique of political economy, vol 3 (trans: Fernbach D). Penguin Books, Harmondsworth

Law of the Tendential Fall in the Rate of Profit

T. Otani, *A Guide to Marxian Political Economy*,
https://doi.org/10.1007/978-3-319-65954-1_17

17.1 Fall in the Rate of Profit and the Classical School of Political Economy

Recognition of the Falling Profit Rate Accompanying Capitalist Development

In the eighteenth and nineteenth centuries, the gradual fall in the rate of profit, which is of fundamental significance to capital, was recognised as a *fact*. Moreover, the rate of profit, and therefore the interest rate as well, was relatively lower in countries where capitalist production had developed. The Classical economists sought to explain this phenomenon, and their explanation was applied to various policy objectives.

Smith Sought the Cause in Increased Competition

Adam Smith argued that the fall in the rate of profit resulted from increased competition among capitals, which raises wages and lowers commodity prices. His explanation was used as a weapon of criticism against the mercantilists. As we have seen, however, competition is only able to equalise the rate of profit—not lower the level of profit itself.

Ricardo Sought the Cause in the Diminishing Returns on Land

David Ricardo argued that the cause of the fall in the rate of profit was a rise of wages from the increased grain prices that result from the operation of the law of diminishing returns on land. He used this argument to criticise the demands of landowners for a policy maintaining high grain prices. Not only was Ricardo's law of diminishing returns vacuous in itself, but his argument also confused the rate of profit with the rate of surplus-value, since a wage only lowers the rate of surplus-value.

17.2 Law of the Tendential Fall in the Rate of Profit

17.2.1 *Marx's* Explanation: Fall in the Rate of Profit Is Due to a Heightening of Capital Composition

Marx Clarified the Cause as a Heightening of the Capital Composition

Marx was the first within the history of political economy to clarify the fundamental cause that lowers the rate of profit as a heightening of the organic composition of capital accompanying the accumulation of capital. In this way, he showed that the fall in the rate of profit is a manifestation of the development of productive power under capitalist production.

17

If the organic composition of capital ($\frac{v}{c}$) is indicated by k', then the quantitative relation between the rate of profit (p') and the organic composition of capital (k') can be expressed as follows:

$$p' = \frac{s}{c+v} = \frac{1}{\frac{c}{v}+1} \cdot \frac{s}{v} = \frac{s'}{k'+1}$$

That is, the rate of profit (p')—conceived of here as the average rate of profit—increases in proportion to the rate of surplus-value (s') and decreases in proportion to the heightening of the (socially average) organic composition of capital ($k' = \frac{c}{v}$). If the rate of surplus-value remains the same, the rate of profit will fall with the heightening of the organic composition of capital. Because productive power develops as capital accumulation progresses, the organic composition of capital heightens. Thus, with the development of capitalism, there is necessarily a fall in the rate of profit.

Marx thus clarifies that *the heightening of the organic composition of capital, which accompanies the development of productive power under capitalist production, is precisely the fundamental cause of the fall in the rate of profit* (*see* ◘ Fig. 17.1).

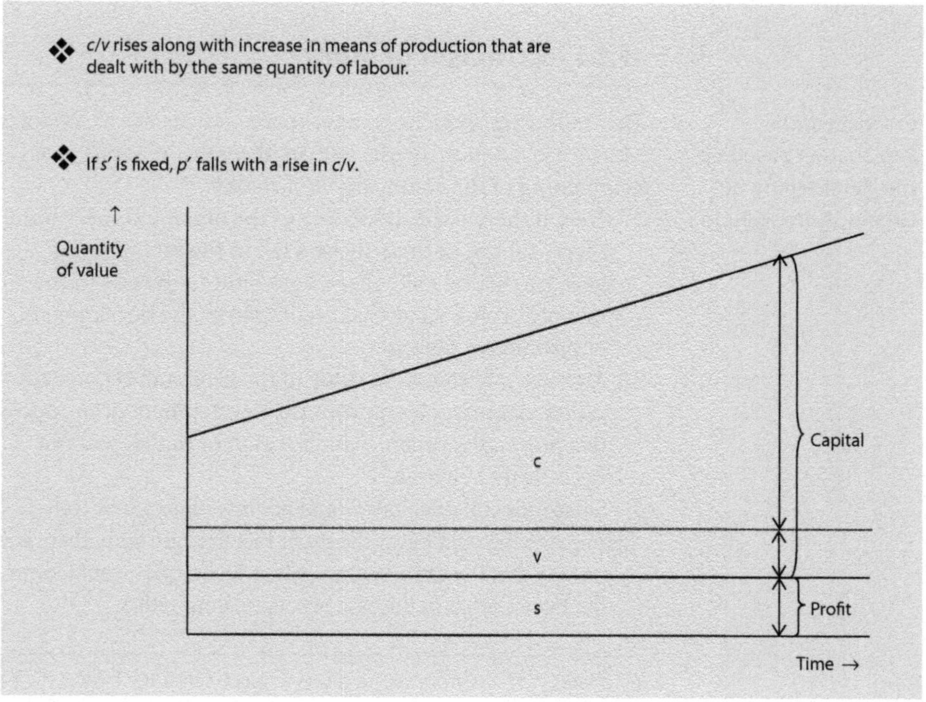

◘ **Fig. 17.1** Fall in the rate of profit accompanying the heightening of the organic composition of capital

Capital Seeks to Cover the Fall in the Rate of Profit by Increasing the Quantity of Profit

Marx did not merely clarify the necessity of a fall in the rate of profit due to a heightening of the organic composition of capital. He also showed that the total quantity of profit can augment even if the profit rate falls in cases where the increase in the quantity of capital advanced exceeds the fall in the profit rate, so that individual capitals are compelled to augment their quantity of profit in that way. In other words, the fall in the rate of profit generates a *necessary tendency wherein capital strives to augment the quantity of profit to cover the fall in the rate of profit*. The fall in the rate of profit necessarily *propels the accumulation of capital*, so that the total amount of profit under capitalist production must tendentially increase—albeit passing through periods where it decreases temporarily. The same law, from the perspective of the total social capital, thus generates *an increase in the quantity of capital* and *a decrease in the rate of profit*.

Marx Referred to the Law as the «Most Important Law of Modern Political Economy»

Marx referred to the «**law of the fall in the rate of profit**», which contains the *two-sided action of a decline in the rate of profit and an augmentation of its quantity*, as the «most important law of modern political economy»[1].

17.2.2 Criticism of *Marx*

Criticism of the Explanation Based on the Heightening of Organic Composition

The following criticisms have been advanced to counter Marx's explanation of the fall in the rate of profit from a heightening of the composition of capital:

1. Even if there is a heightening of the organic composition, there will not necessarily be a fall in the rate of profit because theoretically there is no limit to the rise in the rate of surplus-value that accompanies the development of productive power.
2. Moreover, because the value of the elements of constant capital decreases along with the development of productive power, the organic composition of capital will not necessarily heighten.
3. Since individual capitals would not introduce a new technique that would lower the profit rate to begin with, there is no way that the introduction of new techniques would lower the rate of profit in the case of social capital either.

1 Marx (1857–1858) writes: «In every respect, this is the *most important law of modern political economy*, and the *most essential one for comprehending the most complex relationships*. It is the *most important law from the historical viewpoint*. Hitherto, *despite its simplicity, it has never been grasped and still less has it been consciously formulated*» (Marx 1986, p. 133; my emphasis).

17.2.3 Maximum of Rate of Profit Falls Through Development of Productive Power

First Criticism

Let us first consider the idea that the rate of profit will not necessarily fall because there is no theoretical limit to the rise in the rate of surplus-value accompanying the development of productive power.

Ratio of Living Labour to Transferred Past Labour

Marx stated clearly[2] that what precisely *limits the augmentation of the quantity of profit*—independently of the height of the surplus-value rate—is the *total quantity of living labour that generates new value in the production process*, and that this, therefore, also *limits the rate of profit.*

Given this fact, instead of the organic composition of capital, which is the proportion of constant capital to variable capital (value of labour-power), let us take the ratio between the value of the means of production (i.e. past objectified labour) transferred to the product in the production process and the quantity of *living labour* applied in the production process to be *objectified as new value*. These two amounts of labour—viewed in terms of the value of *commodity capital* that is the product of capital—are the *old value* of the previously objectified labour transferred to the product (i.e. the value of constant capital or c) and the *new value* from the labour newly objectified in the production process (i.e. the value of variable capital plus surplus-value or $v + s$).

«New/Old Value Composition of Capital» and «Rate of New Value»

We will use the term «**new/old value composition of capital**» to refer to the ratio between the two value components of commodity capital that express the ratio of living

2 Marx (1894) writes: «The law of the falling rate of profit, *as expressing the same or even a rising rate of surplus-value*, means in other words: taking any particular quantity of average social capital, ... an ever greater portion of this is *represented by means of labour* and an ever lesser portion *by living labour*. Since the total mass of *living labour added* to the means of production falls in relation to the value of these means of production, so too does *the unpaid labour, and the portion of value in which it is represented*, in relation to the value of the total capital advanced. Alternatively, an *ever smaller aliquot part of the total capital laid out is converted into living labour*, and hence the *total capital absorbs ever less surplus labour in relation to its size*, even though the *ratio of the unpaid to paid parts of the labour applied may at the same time be growing*» (Marx 1981, p. 322; my emphasis). Needless to say, here the «ratio of the unpaid to paid parts of the labour applied» refers to the rate of surplus-value.

labour to transferred past labour. If the new value ($v + s$) is called N, the ratio of N to the old value (c), indicating the new/old value composition of capital, is $\frac{N}{c}$. We can call this ratio the «**new value rate**» or n'. Thus, a **rise in the new/old vale composition of capital** comes to be expressed through a decrease in the new value rate (n').

New/Old Value Composition Not Affected by Changes in the Rate of Surplus-value

The value composition of capital, which expresses the ratio of the value of constant to variable capital, necessarily rises when the value of variable capital decreases due to an increased rate of surplus-value, even if the technical composition remains the same. In contrast, *the new/old composition of capital* $\left(\frac{N}{c} = \frac{v+m}{c}\right)$ *is not at all affected by a change in the rate of surplus-value.* Therefore, this rate more exactly reflects changes in the technical composition of capital than the value composition of capital. This is because *a heightening of the technical composition of capital necessarily brings about a decrease in the new value rate* $\left(n' = \frac{N}{c}\right)$, regardless of the rate of surplus-value—i.e. it necessarily leads to a *rise in the new/old composition of capital.*

New Value Rate Is the Maximum Rate of Profit

The quantitative relation between the new value rate n' and the rate of profit p' can be expressed as follows (assuming $c > 0$, $v > 0$, and $s > 0$):

$$p' = \frac{s}{c+v} < \frac{v+s}{c} = \frac{N}{c} = n'$$

As is clear from the equation above, when variable capital (value of labour-power) is zero, so that the entire new value created by living labour becomes surplus-value, the rate of profit $\left(p' = \frac{s}{c+v}\right)$ equals the new value rate $\left(n' = \frac{v+s}{c}\right)$. The rate of profit cannot be more than this upper limit, so the *new value rate is the maximum rate of profit.*

Maximum Rate of Profit Falls Through Development of Productive Power

17

With a heightening of the technical composition of capital, there is a rise in the old/new value composition of capital and a fall in the new value rate, so that the maximum rate of profit also falls in turn. Ultimately, over the long-term, the rate of profit will necessarily fall because *the heightening of the technical composition of capital through the development of productive power that accompanies capital accumulation causes the new/old value composition of capital to rise, thereby continually lowering the maximum rate of profit.* This point can probably be grasped more intuitively by looking at ◘ Fig. 17.2.

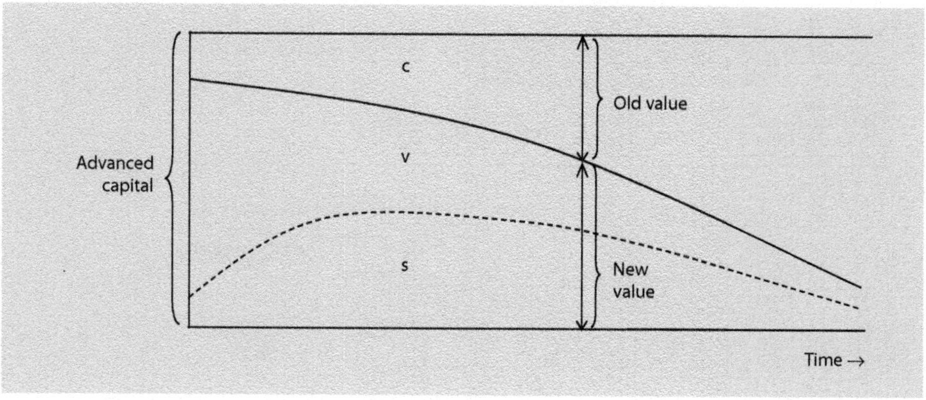

Fig. 17.2 Rise in rate of surplus-value cannot offset the fall in the new value rate (maximum of *p'*)

17.2.4 Fall in the Rate of Profit Takes Tendential Form Due to Counteracting Factors

Phenomena that Appear to Contradict the Law Can Only Be Explained on the Law's Basis

The following three points are at the *crux* of an understanding of the law of the tendential fall in the rate of profit:

1. The development of productive power under capitalist production *at all times* acts in the direction of heightening the organic composition of capital.
2. The heightening of the organic composition will unilaterally lower the profit rate *if the other conditions remain the same.*
3. The *given fact of a fall in the rate of profit* is fully elucidated by the two points above.

Even recognising the phenomenon of profit rates that do not fall over an extended period of time, what must be clarified are the *factors that prevent a falling profit rate despite the operations of the law of a tendential fall.* Such an explanation, needless to say, is impossible unless we take the operations of the law as our premise. To conclude the non-existence of the law from that phenomenon is akin to rejecting the law of the earth's gravitational force because an artificial satellite can be launched into orbit.

Rather, it is precisely because the law of the falling rate of profit is in operation that capitalist production must seek—as a means of alleviating that fall—to make the means of production (particularly raw materials) less expensive, which requires the development of productive power in each production sphere, thereby heightening the organic composition of capital.

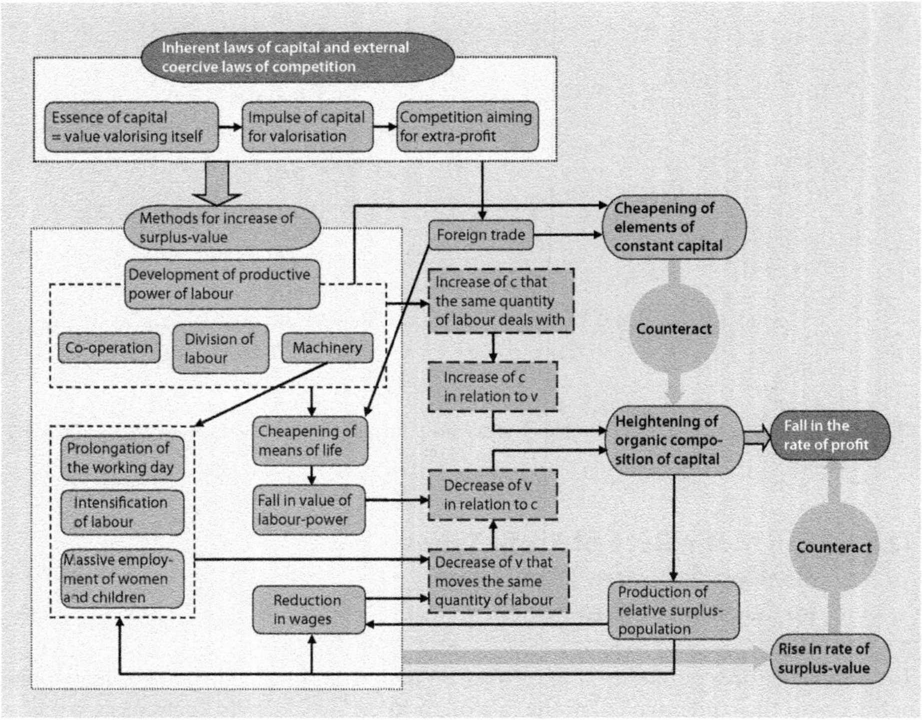

■ **Fig. 17.3** Factors lowering the rate of profit and countering factors

Law of the Falling Rate of Profit Takes a Tendential Form Due to the Action of Counteracting Factors

Marx, in addition to explaining the phenomenon of the fall in the rate of profit from the heightening of the organic composition of capital, raises the question of *why this phenomenon manifests itself as a tendency*[3]. *Marx notes the factors that operate in opposition to the fall in the profit rate to bring down the cost of the constituent elements of constant capital and to lift the rate of surplus-value.* He shows that these factors cause the operation of the law of the falling profit rate to be *tendential* (*see* ■ Fig. 17.3).

Second Criticism

Given the above, let us now consider the criticism of Marx's theory mentioned earlier, which claims a heightening of the organic composition of capital will not necessarily

3 Marx (1894) writes: «If we consider the enormous development in the productive powers of social labour over the last 30 years alone, compared with all earlier periods, and particularly if we consider the enormous mass of fixed capital involved in the total process of social production quite apart from machinery proper, then *instead of the problem that occupied previous economists, the problem of explaining the fall in the rate of profit*, we have the *opposite problem of explaining why this fall is not greater or faster*» (Marx 1981, p. 339; my emphasis).

occur because there is a cheapening of the elements of constant capital.

Certainly, if productive power rises for the production of certain means of production, thus lowering their value, the capital that uses these means of production will have its constant capital (c) lowered by that same amount. Thus, if $v + s$ remains the same, the value composition of capital will fall by this amount, resulting in a rise in the rate of profit. One might think, therefore, that the continual cheapening of the elements of constant capital resulting from the development of productive power would (from a social perspective) prevent the heightening of the organic composition of capital and thus raise the rate of profit.

Cheapening of the Elements of Constant Capital Cannot Prevent the Heightening of Composition

The heightening of the technical composition of capital through the development of productive power, however, must continually progress in the form of a heightening of the composition of new/old value (as just seen in ▶ Sect. 17.2.3). Compared to this, the cheapening of the elements of constant capital only arises when there is generalised use of new technique that can lower product-value in the spheres where the constant capital is produced, and until that point in time is reached the heightening of the capital composition is already progressing. Thus, the cheapening of the elements of constant capital is incapable of directly preventing the heightening of capital composition. Instead, it merely operates counter to the progressing heightening of capital composition, acting to slow the pace of that increase.

17.2.5 Competition Between Capitals Spurs Introduction of New Technologies That Lower the Profit Rate

Third Criticism

The third criticism of Marx's theory, mentioned earlier, states that individual capital would not introduce technology that would lower the profit rate, and so it also would be impossible in the case of social capital. This is plausible at first glance, but completely misses the mark. If this were indeed true, the phenomenon of a falling rate of profit, which was happening right in front of the eyes of the Classical economists, who struggled to explain it, would have had no reason to occur in the first place.

Competition Between Capitals Leads to the Adoption of New Technologies That Lower the Profit Rate

Then why does the rate of profit fall despite individual capitals introducing new technologies in order to raise that rate?

An individual capital introduces a new technology because it makes it possible—amidst the competition with other capitals in the same production sphere—to obtain a surplus profit by reducing the individual value of the commodity produced by the capital below its market value, so that the rate of profit for the individual capital can rise. However, if the new technology is generalised within the production sphere, so that the market value is lowered to the same level as that of such individual capitals, the surplus profit and the particularly high rate of profit will disappear. The outcome is that the new technology heightens the capital composition throughout the production sphere, which drives down the average rate of profit of that sphere.

It is precisely the competition among individual capitals over surplus profit that spurs individual capitals to adopt new technologies that bring down the rate of profit by heightening the capital composition. Here we have the intrinsic law of capital penetrating as the external forced law of competition among capitals.

17.3 Law of the Tendential Fall in the Rate of Profit and the Movement of Capital

Contradiction Between Falling Profit Rate and Accelerated Accumulation Is Manifested as a Collision of Various Agents

Capital must push ahead accumulation in pursuit of an expanding volume of profit, even if the profit rate falls. But because the rise in productive power causes the profit rate to fall, the movement of capital, which bears that contradiction between a falling profit rate and accelerated accumulation, manifests itself as a *collision of agents that are difficult to reconcile.*

Excess of Capital

The centralisation of capital advances through large capital toppling and absorbing small- and medium-sized capitals. Those capitals that are unable to offset the fall in the profit rate by increasing the magnitude of profit are no longer able to continue functioning as capital. The mass of small, fragmented capitals are forced onto the adventurous path of speculation, credit swindles, and the like. From a social perspective, this means an **excess of capital**—i.e. an **overproduction of capital**. The result of the excess is a **competitive struggle** for survival among such capitals, leading wages to temporarily rise, which temporarily lowers the profit rate. The removal of *superabundant capitals* becomes inevitable. What is revealed here is the *limitation of production by profit (capital).*

Excess of Commodities

The rise in productive power and the rapid accumulation of capital expand the quantity of products, but the sale of commodities is limited by the distribution and consumption relations particular to capitalist production. Although the workers of other capitals are important to a given capitalist as purchasers of commodities, each capital keeps to a minimum the payment it makes to its own workers who sell their labour-power and the payment by capitalists are also limited by their own consumption and the desire to accumulate capital. The outcome is that the *restrictions of capitalist distribution and consumption relations* are manifested as an **excess of commodities produced**—i.e. as an **overproduction of commodities.**

Excess Population

The excess production of capital thus includes the excess production of commodities. But this arises from the capitalist form of production, not from an absolute excess of production itself, as is clear from the fact that there also arises an **excess population** that coincides with these other excesses. That is, there is also an enormous relative surplus population of those without jobs or a means of livelihood, as well as an enormous amount of idle means of production. The *same capital accumulation and development of productive power* also brings about a fall in the rate of profit and the creation of a relative surplus population.

Crisis as the Explosion of Contradictions

When the cumulative contradictions that gather in the course of capital's development of productive power and promotion of accumulation reach their limit, they explode, recovering various relations. These are the **crises**, which occurred roughly every 10 years during the nineteenth century. The moments of capital accumulation that surface when the law of the falling profit rate penetrates are at the same time the *moments that turn the possibility of crisis* (touched on earlier) *into its actuality.*

References

Marx K (1857–1858) Grundrisse der Kritik der politischen Ökonomie. English edition: Marx K (1986) Outlines of the critique of political economy. Marx-Engels Collected Works, vol 28. Progress Publishers et al. New York

Marx K (1894) Das Kapital. Kritik der politischen Oekonomie. Bd. 3. Buch 3: Der Gesammtprocess der kapitalistischen Produktion. Hrsg. von F. Engels. Hamburg. English edition: Marx K (1981) Capital. A critique of political economy, vol 3 (trans: Fernbach D). Penguin Books, Harmondsworth

Commercial Capital and Commercial Profit

T. Otani, *A Guide to Marxian Political Economy*,
https://doi.org/10.1007/978-3-319-65954-1_18

18.1 Commercial Capital Becomes Independent of Industrial Capital

18.1.1 Commercial Capital Becomes Independent of Industrial Capital

Commercial Capital and Commercial Profit

The term **commercial capital** refers to capital that is augmented in the sphere of circulation by carrying out the movement of selling after buying, i.e. the movement of M–C–M′. The increment of this capital is profit, just as in the case of industrial capital, but we refer to it as **commercial profit**, in distinction from the profit of industrial capital, which is referred to as **industrial profit**.

Commercial Capital Becomes Independent of Industrial Capital

Commercial capital is *capital that reduces circulation costs by shortening the circulation time of industrial capital by taking over from it the function of selling commodities*. As capital that belongs to the **commercial capitalist** (merchant), who is a separate person from the **industrial capitalist** (producer), this is *capital that becomes independent of industrial capital.*

One Part of Industrial Profit Becomes Commercial Profit

Circulation time is curtailed through the function of commercial capital, thereby reducing circulation costs so that industrial capital can, first of all, augment surplus-value by transforming circulation time into production time and, secondly, avoid deducting circulation costs from surplus-value. Industrial capital *uses one part of the surplus-value augmented in this way to pay for the functions of commercial capital*. This is the *commercial profit*, which makes it possible for commercial capital to become independent as one divided branch of the social capital.

Functions of Commercial Capital

As far as the producer is concerned, his *commodity value has been realised* as soon as the product is sold to a merchant. But the *commodity itself* has yet to be sold. It is the function of commercial capital to ultimately sell this commodity to the final purchaser (for either productive or individual consumption).

Thus, commercial capital is established when the *function of commodity capital* becomes autonomous as an *exclusive function of a specific capital in the circulation process* and is fixed as a function allotted to one specific sort of capitalist through the division of social capital.

18.1.2 Movement Form of Commercial Capital

Movement Form of Commercial Capital Is M–C–M′

Commercial capital is advanced in the purchase of a commodity, and this refluxes to the starting point through the sale of the commodity. The commercial capital is always within the repetitive movement of M–C–M′ that is the circulation process, i.e. «buying and then selling» (*see* ◘ Fig. 18.1).

Even though commercial capital is established and takes over the sale of commodities for industrial capital, the sales time and its cost for industrial capital are not reduced to zero. This is because industrial capital itself still must be able to at least sell the commodity to commercial capital. Moreover, commercial capital may also carry out functions that are an extension of the production process if it is engaged in physical distribution along with its strictly sales functions.[1] In order to purely grasp the matter, however, we will be setting aside such facts here to assume that commercial capital bears the time and cost connected to the circulation of commodities produced by industrial capital but does not perform any productive functions that could be viewed as an extension of the production process.

1 The circulation of commodities is usually accompanied with the physical distribution of commodities. In ▸ Sect. 12.3.2 («circulation costs»), we referred to transport and storage as moments of physical distribution and also clarified that transport is a continuation of the production process or an additional production process, just as storage is as an extension of the original production process, so that the transport and storage costs enter into the value of a commodity. Therefore, the capital of the transportation business that specialises in transporting commodities and the capital of warehouse business that is engaged in storing commodities belong to industrial capital in the broad sense, not commercial capital, whereas the fundamental function of commercial capital is to perform operations of buying and selling, with the vital task being to find purchasers in order to sell commodities. Therefore, generally speaking, commercial capital entrusts the transport and storage of commodities to those specialised industrial capitals. Commercial capital or merchants also engage, however, to varying degrees, in operations related to physical distribution. From the obtaining of stock until the handing over of commodities, merchants perform the operation of packing and sorting commodities, as well as unpacking or subdividing commodities at the stage of the final sale to the consumer. These operations belong to the production process in the broad sense, as a continuation of the production process, because they transform the products into a consumable state. The «commercial labour» of the commercial workers expended in those operations is also objectified in the commodities, adding value to them.

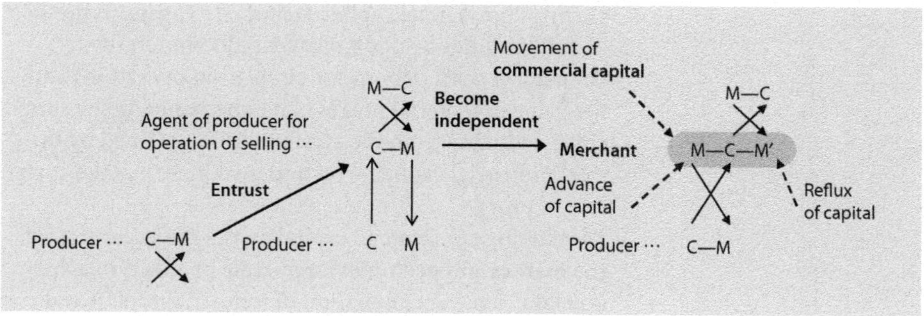

Fig. 18.1 Commercial capital becomes independent

18.1.3 Significance for Capitalist Production of Commercial Capital's Separation from Industrial Capital

Significance of Separation of Commercial Capital

For *industrial capital*, and therefore for *capitalist production*, there is the following positive significance of commercial capital separating from industrial capital to become independent:

1. Shortening sales time for industrial capital accelerates the turnover of capital, both individually and socially, thereby raising the annual rate of profit.
2. Having commercial capital take over the function of industrial capital's realisation of commodity-value allows industrial capital to reduce the sum of capital that must be advanced for the circulation process in the money-form and the sum of money capital that must be reserved to prepare for any stagnation in or cessation of the reproduction process. This makes it possible to carry out the same scale of production using less capital, which raises the rate of profit.
3. Having commercial capital exclusively engaged in the sale of commodities accelerates the metamorphoses of commodity-capital, so that a much smaller sum of capital is needed compared to a situation where industrial capitalists handle this function themselves. Thus, the total quantity of capital advanced for handling commodities is reduced compared to a case where industrial capitalists themselves would carry out these functions. Seen from the perspective of society, there is a proportional reduction in the money capital involved in the circulation process relative to the total capital. Therefore, the proportion of capital advanced in the production process expands, resulting in a rise in the average rate of profit, which is the proportion of total surplus-value to social total capital.

4. Having commercial capital exclusively engage in the sale of commodities brings a relative reduction in the circulation costs (labour for circulation operations and the value of material means), thereby reducing the sum of value deducted from the surplus-value obtained by the total industrial capital, which in turn increases the social rate of profit.
5. Developing commercial capital assists the expansion of the market and promotes large-scale production, which accelerates the accumulation of industrial capital and spurs productive power.

18.2 Commercial Profit

18.2.1 Price Differences in Sale and Purchase Are Source of Commercial Profit for Commercial Capital

Commercial Capital Obtains Profit Through Price Differences in Sales and Purchases

The commercial capitalist must extract his profit from the price differences of his commodity, i.e. the source of his profit is clearly the *excess of sales price over purchase price*. And in cases where commercial capital covers the *operating expenses* (value of material means and wages), in addition to the *purchase of the commodity*, the replacement of this expenditure also clearly stems from that difference. Thus, for the commercial capitalist, the purchase price must always be below the sales price. When commercial capitalists exist, a dual price is socially and generally established for the same commodity (*see* ◘ Fig. 18.2).

Given the above, the question centres on how this dual price can be generally established for any given commodity and what decides the level of the purchase price and sales price, respectively, for the commercial capitalist.

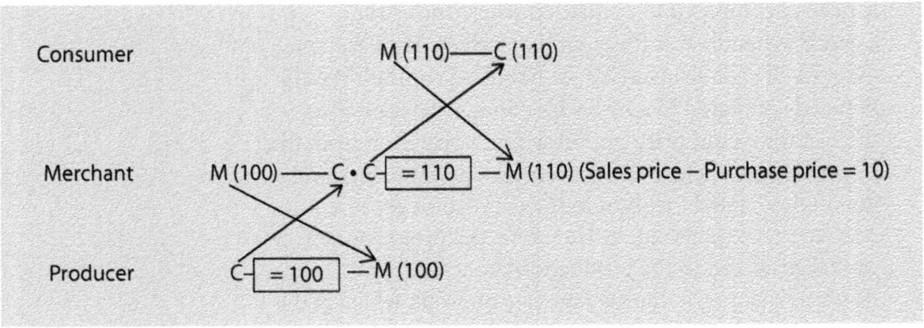

◘ **Fig. 18.2** Price difference as source of commercial profit: sales price > purchase price

18.2.2 Fundamental Relation: Buy Below Value and Sell at Value

Commodity Purchased Cheaper than Value from Industrial Capital and Sold at Its Value

As already seen, commercial capital obtains one portion of the surplus-value of industrial capital by carrying out sales functions for it, and this distributed portion becomes commercial profit. *How, then, is commercial capital able to receive one part of surplus-value from industrial capital?*

Let's suppose, to begin with, if commercial capital did not exist, commodities would be sold at their value rather than production price. Into this situation, the commercial capitalist then appears, and the industrial capitalist sells his commodity to the commercial capitalist at a price below the commodity's value. This price is the sales price for the industrial capitalist and the purchase price for the commercial capitalist. The commercial capitalist sells the commodity to the consumer at a price that is identical to its value. In this way, the commercial capitalist receives, from the industrial capitalist, the difference between the purchase price of a commodity and its value. In this case, the commercial capitalist has *purchased the commodity below its value and sold it at its value* (*see* ◘ Fig. 18.3).

If the Equalisation of the Rate of Profit Is Premised, a Commodity Is Sold at Its Production Price

However, as we have already seen, once the rate of profit is equalised through the movement of industrial capital between production spheres, thereby establishing production price, the market price of each commodity fluctuates around its production price. Thus the sales price for the commercial capitalist as well must be determined by production price, not value. In short, the commercial capitalist *must purchase the commodity below what its production price would have been in the case where there was no commercial capital and sell it at this production price.*

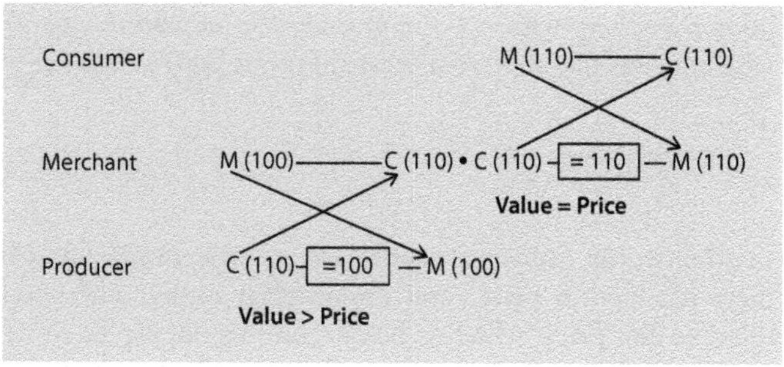

◘ **Fig. 18.3** Commercial capitalist purchases a commodity below its value and sells it at its value

18.2.3 Both Industrial Capital and Commercial Capital Sell the Commodity at Production Price

Commercial Capital Also Participates in the Equalisation of the Profit Rate

How much lower is commercial capital's purchase price (or industrial capital's sales price) than the production price of industrial capital in a case where commercial capital does not exist? Depending on this level, the rate of profit for industrial capital would be greater than that of commercial capital—or vice versa.

If the profit rate of commercial capital is higher than that of industrial capital, a movement would arise for industrial capital to be converted to commercial capital, assuming that capital can move freely between production spheres, just as the opposite movement of conversion would occur when the profit rate of industrial capital is higher. On top of this, the commercial realm is one in which the influx and efflux of capital can be carried out most easily. The outcome, then, is that *commercial capital also participates in the equalisation of the rate of profit established for the totality of industrial and commercial capital.* And the *rate of profit for commercial capital* also comes to *fluctuate around the average rate of profit.*

Production Price Established that Generates an Average Rate of Profit in Common

Given the above, a production price is also established for the commercial capitalist's sales price. And the commercial capitalist's purchase price (industrial capitalist's sales price) and sales price must be able to generate an equal average profit for both the commercial capitalist and industrial capitalist. In short, prices come to fluctuate around *production prices.*

Industrial Capital and Commercial Capital Sell at Their Respective Production Prices

The average rate of profit here is not the rate of total surplus-value to total industrial capital but rather the rate of total surplus-value to total capital (sum of both industrial and commercial capital). If commercial capital is g, the total capital is $c + v + g$ (with $c + v$ *expressing the industrial capital*), which means that the average rate of profit (ap') would be:

$$ap' = \frac{s}{c+v+g}$$

In other words, industrial capital sells its own commodities at their production price, and commercial capital purchases them at that price, which is below commercial capital's own production price; then commercial capital sells the commodities, in turn, at its own production price (*see* ◘ Fig. 18.4).

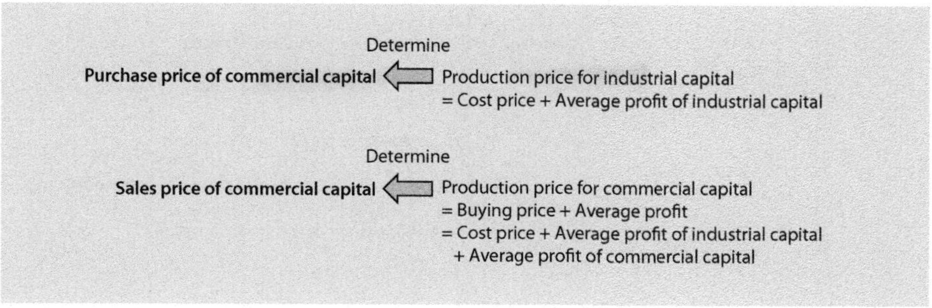

Fig. 18.4 Purchase price and sales price of commercial capital

Surplus-Value Obtained by Industrial Capital Is Distributed to Industrial Capital and Commercial Capital

The total surplus-value obtained by industrial capital is thus distributed to the totality of industrial and commercial capital in accordance with the magnitude of capital.

Amount of Average Profit Within Commodity Price Differs Between Industrial and Commercial Capital

It must be noted, however, with regard to the two formulas in the diagram above that the magnitude of average profit within the price of the same commodity unit will be completely different between industrial capital and commercial capital due to their completely different *turnover velocity of capital.* In the case of commercial capital, whose turnover is far faster than that of industrial capital, *far less average profit is contained within a commodity unit than in the case of industrial capital.*

18.2.4 Commercial Costs Also Form One Part of Commercial Capital and Demand Profit

For Commercial Capital, Commercial Costs Are Also an Advance of Capital

To carry out its operations, commercial capital employs various material means, which must be purchased, and labour, for which labour-power must be purchased. For capital, these purchases are also an advance of capital. But these commercial costs are *pure circulation costs.* These *faux frais of production* must be deducted from the surplus-value of the total capital because the costs are fundamentally borne by the total capital—as noted in ▶ Sect. 12.3.2 in Part II («Circulation Costs»).

However, the *commercial costs* are all expended by commercial capital, and *for commercial capital, this is manifested as an advance of capital.* Commercial capital is advanced not only in the purchase of commodities but also for commercial costs. And commercial capital requires an average profit for that totality. If the commercial costs are added as one part of the commercial capital advanced, the purchase price and sales price of commercial capital become the following (*see* ◘ Fig. 18.5).

Purchase price	= Production price for industrial capital
	= Cost price + Average profit of industrial capital
Sales price	= Production price for commercial capital
	= Purchase price + **Commercial costs per commodity unit**
	+ Average profit of commercial capital

Fig. 18.5 Commercial costs included in the sales price of commercial capital

Profit and Production Price for Industrial Capital and for Commercial Capital

If the constant capital of the total industrial capital is designated as c, its variable capital as v, and the surplus-value produced as s, while the commercial capital advanced for commodity purchase is designated as g, the material expenses of commercial capital as a, and its personnel expenses (value of labour-power purchased) as b, then the average rate of profit, total industrial profit, total commercial profit, total production price of industrial capital, and the total production price of commercial capital will be as follows:

$$\text{average rate of profit}: ap' = \frac{s-(a+b)}{c+v+g+a+b.}$$

$$\text{total industrial profit}: p = (c+v)ap'$$

$$\text{total commercial profit}: h = (g+a+b)ap'$$

$$\text{total production price of industrial capital}: \\ Pp = (c+v)(1+ap')$$

$$\text{total production price of commercial capital}: \\ Pk = (g+a+b)(1+ap')$$

Looking at the total industrial capital and total commercial capital, the total commercial capital purchases the total commodities from total industrial capital [total value – (commercial profit + commercial costs)] and then sells the commodities at their total value to the end consumers (W). We can confirm this using the following equation:

$$Pk = (g+a+b)(1+ap') = c+v+s = W$$

A. Turnover of Industrial Capital:
Profit increases in proportion to the number of turnovers.

(1) M ———————— C .... P .... [C ———————— M
δc ———————— δm]

(2) M—C ... P ... [C—M · M—C ... P ... [C—M · M—C ... P ... [C—M · M—C ... P ... [C—M
δc—δm | δc—δm | δc—δm | δc—δm]

❖ In the case (2) the profit of four times of (1) is produced.

B. Turnover of Commercial Capital:
Profit per turnover decreases in inverse proportion to the numbers of turnovers.

(1) M ———————————————— C · [C ———————————————— M
δc ———————————————— δm]

(2) M—C · [C—M · M—C · [C—M · M—C · [C—M · M—C · [C—M · M—C · [C—M
δc—δm | δc—δm | δc—δm | δc—δm | δc—δm]

❖ The total amount of profit by five turnovers in (2) is equal to profit by one turnover in (1).

Fig. 18.6 Difference between the turnover of industrial and of commercial capital

18.3 Turnover of Commercial Capital

The Greater the Turnover Velocity for Commercial Capital, the Less Profit in Each Commodity

Commercial capital sells a commodity at a price that makes it possible to obtain an average profit *over a certain period of time*. If we *look at the totality of commercial capital* in the same commercial sphere, the greater the turnover velocity, the smaller the average profit obtainable through one turnover, so that there is less average profit contained in one commodity (*see* Fig. 18.6).

Quantity of Profit Increasable Through «SPQR»

Individual commercial capital, however, is able to *sell more cheaply than capital with an average turnover* by means of accelerating the turnover. This acceleration increases the quantity of commodities sold, thereby expanding market share and increasing total profit so that a *surplus profit* can be obtained that surpasses the average profit. This is the benefit of «**small profits and quick returns**»—or SPQR.

18.4 External Autonomy of Commercial Capital and the Re-establishment of the Inner Connections of the Reproduction Process

Industrial Capital's Scale of Production Increases Through Autonomy of Commercial Capital

When commercial capital becomes independent of industrial capital, so as to exclusively assume the function of selling the commodities produced by industrial capital, commodity sales can be greatly expanded through a wide circulation network that encompasses everything from wholesale to retail markets. And the sale of commodities even extends beyond a country's boundaries to include the world market. All of this makes it possible for industrial capital to colossally increase its scale of production.

Elasticity of Reproduction Process Through Production and Storage Capabilities

Commercial capital must at all times be in possession of commodity stock to some extent. Even though the commodities in this stock have already been sold as far as industrial capital is concerned, these are commodities that still need to be sold by commercial capital. However, because commercial capital operates independently from industrial capital, outside the production process, it can expand its stock of commodities by buying a huge quantity from industrious capital. The *enormous production capacity of industrial capital and the production process* combined with the *storage capacity of commercial capital* creates an *enormous* **elasticity** for the *process of reproduction*. Through the mediation of commercial capital, the connection between the *production sphere and the consumption sphere* becomes *quite indirect*, so that both spheres *operate in relative independence of each other* (*see* ◘ Fig. 18.7).

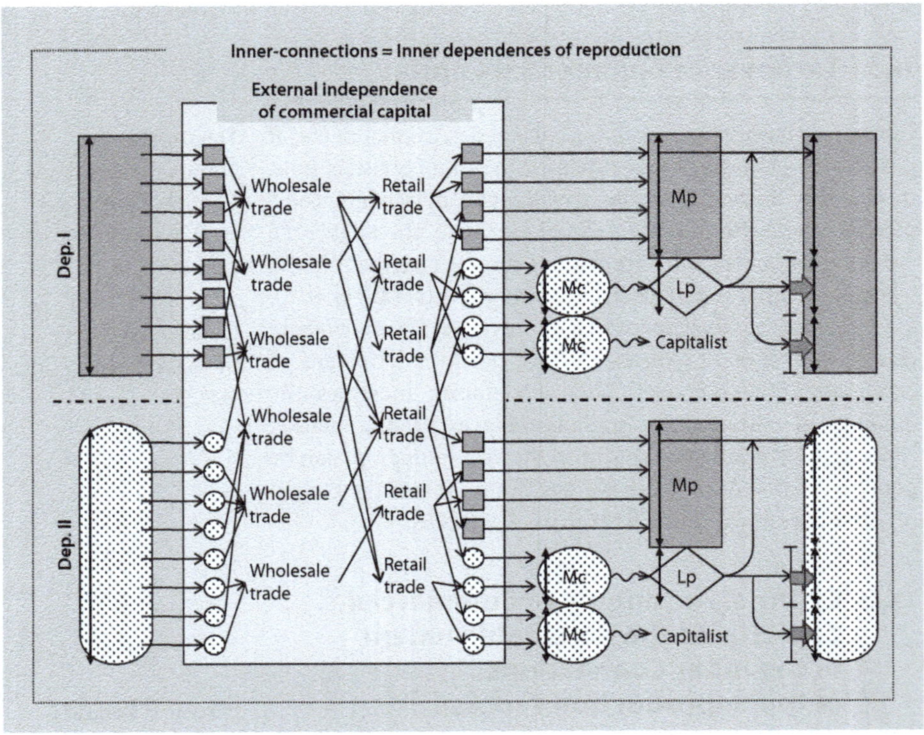

◘ **Fig. 18.7** Inner-connections of reproduction process and external autonomy of movement of commercial capital

During the prosperous phase of the industrial cycle, commercial capital creates **fictive demand** vis-à-vis industrial capital—*independent of final demand.* If this process progresses, *stock accumulated* under commercial capital will exceed final demand. When it is finally perceived that this is an *excess inventory*, the *phenomenon of crisis arises in the wholesale sphere.* Sales become impossible as a result, which in turn results in failures to pay, clearance sales, and ultimately bankruptcy. The **apparent prosperity**, which was supported by fictive demand, comes to an end, shedding light on the **overproduction of commodities** that had been hidden in the shadows. *The inner-connections within the reproduction process that had been concealed by the external autonomy of commercial capital are finally re-established.*[2]

Inner Connections of the Reproduction Process Re-established Through Crisis

18.5 Money-dealing Capital

18.5.1 Money-dealing Capital

Money-dealing capital is capital that makes a profit from **fees** for performing money dealing. Since money-dealing capital solely functions in the realm of circulation, it belongs to commercial capital in the broad sense. The commercial capital observed in the preceding section may be called «commodity-dealing capital», in distinction from «money-dealing capital».

Capital Obtaining Profit Through Money Dealing

Commercial capital in the broad sense
- Commodity-dealing capital (Commercial capital in the *narrow sense*)
- Money-dealing capital

2 Marx (1894) writes: «Given the *tremendous elasticity of the reproduction process*, which can always be driven beyond any given barrier, he finds no barrier in production itself, or only a very elastic one. Besides the separation of C–M and M–C, which follows from the nature of the commodity, an *fictive demand* is now therefore created. Despite the autonomy it has acquired, the movement of commercial capital is never anything more than the movement of industrial capital within the circulation sphere. But by virtue of this autonomy, its movement is *within certain limits* independent of the reproduction process and its barriers, and hence it also drives this process *beyond its own barriers*. This *inner dependence in combination with external autonomy* drives commercial capital to a point where the *inner connection is forcibly re-established by way of a crisis*». (Marx 1981, p. 419; my emphasis.) Incidentally, in this passage of the Penguin books edition, the decidedly important keyword «fictive demand» is *fatally mistranslated* as «active demand».

18.5.2 Money-dealing Capital Acquires Independence from Industrial Capital and Commodity-dealing Capital

Money-dealing Operations and Cost

Money dealing involves technical operations related to money, such as the payment and receipt of money, settlement of balances, keeping of current accounts, storage of money, and bookkeeping. As these are all operations within the circulation process, they do not create surplus-value. Rather, the costs necessary for these operations are *circulation costs deducted from surplus-value.*

Money-dealing Capital Becomes Independent of Industrial Capital and Commodity-dealing Capital

Both industrial capital and commodity-dealing capital require money-handling operations in the circulation process. By having money-dealing capital exclusively carry out these operations, they can be performed at a lower cost than when industrial capital and commodity-dealing capital handle the operations themselves. For this reason, industrial capital and commodity-dealing capital hand over to money-dealing capital a part of their profits, which originally stem from the surplus-value that industrial capital obtained. By so doing, they are able to reduce, by that degree, the circulation costs necessary for their money-related operations.

In the form of money-dealing capital, the *money-dealing operations of industrial capital and commodity-dealing capital in the circulation process become independent as a function of a specific capital that has separated from the total capital to become independent.* Just as commodity-dealing capital is capital derived from industrial capital, money-dealing capital *is capital derived from industrial capital and commodity-dealing capital.*

However, even after the establishment of money-dealing capital, which comes to perform the money-dealing operations of industrial capital and commodity-dealing capital, those two capital forms do not completely give up their money-dealing operations.

18.5.3 Movement Form of Money-dealing Capital

18

Movement-Form of Money-dealing Capital Is M–M′

The money-dealer advances a certain amount of material costs and labour for money-dealing operations. This labour is obtained by paying wages to purchase workers' labour-power. The *capital advanced by money-dealing capital* is no more than these material costs and personnel costs. These expenditures are recovered along with profit through the fees received from industrial and commodity-dealing capital.

Thus, the movement-form of money-dealing capital is M–M′, i.e. «capital – capital + profit».

18.5.4 Profit of Money-dealing Capital

Money-dealing Capital Also Participates in the Equalisation of the Profit Rate

Money-dealing capital, like commodity-dealing capital, *participates in the competition that forms the average rate of profit.* Therefore, the greater the proportion represented by money-dealing capital within the total capital, the lower will be the average rate of profit. However, the function of money-dealing capital reduces the circulation costs of industrial capital and commodity-dealing capital, thereby raising the average rate of profit. For capitalist production, the significance of money-dealing capital is fundamentally the same as commodity-dealing capital.

Since money-dealing capital also demands average profit, the fee for the dealing of money comes to fluctuate around a level that will generate «capital (material costs + personnel costs) + average profit (capital × average rate of profit)» for money-dealing capital over a given period of time.

18.5.5 Establishment and Development of Money-dealing Capital

Money-dealing Capital Emerges from Exchange Dealing and Bullion Trade

Money-dealing capital, historically speaking, develops out of international trade. The *spontaneous basis of money-dealing capital* is **exchange dealing**, which involved the conversion of the local coins into bullion as world money or changing world money into local coins; and the **bullion trade**, which dealt with gold and silver as world money. These are the *most fundamental forms of money-dealing capital.* Upon this foundation, the **exchange banks** emerged and in England the «**goldsmiths**» were active.

Money Reserve of Entire Capitalist Class Is Centralised in Money-dealing Capital

The *reserve fund for means of purchase and payment as well as idle money capital* gradually becomes centralised within money-dealing capital, which performs such functions as exchange transaction, bullion-dealing, and money transfers. Thus, money-dealers come to deal with a great quantity of money capital, but this is the money capital of industrial capital and commodity-dealing capital. Through this centralisation, the *reserve fund for means of purchase and payment required by the entire capitalist class* decreases in size compared to when it was reserved by the individual capitalists themselves.

Money-dealers Become Bankers and Money-dealing Operations Become Banking Operations

Given the above, money-dealers set about to utilise the money at their disposal for interest-based lending. Thus, the aforementioned functions of money-dealing operations come to be combined with the managing of interest-bearing capital and credit dealings. This is the means through which money dealing is fully developed, but what we have here is already the modern banking system, so the capital in movement here is no longer simply money-dealing capital but rather has become banking capital. We will soon address this issue in more detail when discussing bank capital in ▶ Sect. 19.2.

Reference

Marx K (1894) Das Kapital. Kritik der politischen Oekonomie. Bd. 3. Buch 3: Der Gesammtprocess der kapitalistischen Produktion. Hrsg. von F. Engels. Hamburg. English edition: Marx K (1981) Capital. A Critique of Political Economy. Vol. 3 (trans: Fernbach D). Penguin Books

Interest-bearing Capital and Interest

T. Otani, *A Guide to Marxian Political Economy*,
https://doi.org/10.1007/978-3-319-65954-1_19

19.1 Interest-bearing Capital

Course of Investigation in This Chapter

As its name suggests, **interest-bearing capital** is capital whose increment takes the form of interest. Interest-bearing capital is the most fundamental form of capital that is in motion within the so-called financial world.

In ► Sect. 19.1, the essence of interest-bearing capital and interest, as well as the fundamental movement forms of this capital, will be clarified. This is followed, in ► Sect. 19.2, with a glance at the mechanism of the banking system, which is centre stage for the activities of interest-bearing capital, and the elucidation of the fictitious character of the forms of interest-bearing capital under the banking system. Finally, we will offer an overview of the necessity of the formation of the banking system and the role it plays within capitalist production.

19.1.1 Interest-bearing Capital and Interest

Moneyed Capital and the Money Market

The place where the *rate of interest* fluctuates as a result of changes of the quantitative relation between supply of and demand for «**moneyed capital**» is called the **money market**. The term directly expresses *the common notion people have that the commodity money is bought and sold in this case.* A price must be paid in return for a commodity, and here the price for the commodity «money» is **interest**, which is paid in the same money-form.

«Money as Capital» Is Bought and Sold as a Commodity

As we saw in ► Sect. 2.3 in Part I («Value-Form and Money»), money is a special commodity with the power of being immediately exchangeable with any commodity (i.e. a commodity that monopolises the function of general equivalent), and price is the money expression of a commodity's value. What does it mean exactly, then, for «**money to become a commodity**»? And how is it that money can be paid for a «commodity» that is also «money»?

For a given thing to become a commodity, it must have some sort of use-value as far as the buyer is concerned. What is *the use-value of money bought and sold on the money market*? According *to the view of the market participants themselves,* this money *possesses the quality of being useful as capital,* so they often refer to the interest that is seen as this commodity's price as the *«price of capital»*.

We can understand from this that what people view as a «commodity» in this case is not money as «something with the character of functioning as general equivalent», but rather as «something with the character of functioning as capital». Money has become a *commodity with the particular use-value of functioning as capital.* Simply put, «money as capital becomes a commodity»—or «as capital money has become a commodity».

Buying and Selling of «Money as Capital» Takes the Form of Loan and Repayment

The «commodity» money, however, cannot be sold in the manner of normal commodities handed over to another person after payment is made. This is because the person who buys this «money» and consumes its «use-value», which is the ability to function as capital, will be able to recover this money along with profit after the money is advanced and made to function as capital. Thus, the «use-value» of being capital is the use-value of being able to obtain profit. Obtaining profit by having money function as capital requires a certain period of time to elapse. For this reason, the «commodity» money is sold in the manner of the seller entrusting the money to the buyer for a period of time, after which the buyer returns the money to the seller. This is precisely the *temporary sale and purchase of a commodity* discussed in the examination of the sale and purchase of labour-power in ▸ Sect. 3.1.3 in Part I («Sale and Purchase of Labour-power»).

The transaction whereby A sells money as capital to B is carried out in the particular form of A allowing B to freely use the money during a fixed period of time. In this temporary sale and purchase of the «commodity» money as capital, the term **loan** is used to refer to *letting go of money for the promise of its return after a fixed period of time*, and *this return* is called **repayment**. In other words, the «seller» here is the *lender* and the «buyer» is the *borrower.* Through the action of loan and repayment, the «use-value» of money as capital is handed over from the seller (lender) to buyer (borrower).

The *value received for the commodity* handed over is the **interest** paid for a loan over a certain period of time. Interest is the value received for the special commodity that is money as capital; it is seen as «price» of this commodity and therefore as the «price of capital».

Interest-bearing Capital

The money of the lender goes through the metamorphosis of M–M′. Value is quantitatively augmented by simply letting go of money for a certain period of time and then having it returned. Needless to say, the valorised value is *capital.* In the form of M–M′, the *self-valorisation of capital* appears in a completely pure shape, without the process of valorisation. Capital *augmented solely through this movement of being advanced and then returning* is **interest-bearing capital**. And, if we focus on the movement in the form of loan and repayment, it can also be called **loan capital**. What people call «**moneyed capital**»[1] in the money market is the *concrete form of interest-bearing capital.*

What Is the Function of Capital as «Use-Value»?

What exactly, then, is the *function of capital* thought of as the use-value of the «commodity» money? This question can be fully answered, easily, on the basis of our investigation up to this point.

Under capitalist production, as we have seen, if money is advanced as capital in the production and circulation processes, it returns along with profit (industrial profit and commercial profit)—and brings an average profit when the rate of profit has been equalised. Money, by being put into motion as industrial or commercial capital, is able to generate an average profit. Therefore, in addition to money's attribute of functioning as general equivalent, it further has the *attribute here of functioning as capital so as to be able to generate an average profit.*

The use-value as «capital» that the «commodity» money possesses is thus the *potential or potency to generate an average profit* if it functions as capital for a certain period of time *for the person who makes it function as such.*

The Substance of Interest and the Preconditions for Interest-bearing Capital

«Money» does not from the outset have the potential or potency to generate an average profit. So when does it come to have this sort of use-value?

It is only once production is carried out in a capitalistic manner, upon the establishment of the capitalist mode of production, that money first acquires this use-value.

The borrower obtains average profit by making the borrowed money function as capital, and one part of the average profit is used to pay the lender in the form of interest. In this way, the borrower obtains a sum of value that is the average profit minus interest. The person who makes money function as capital is the **functioning capitalist** (either the **industrial capitalist** or **commercial capitalist**), whereas the person who loans the money to augment it is a capitalist of a different sort: a **moneyed capitalist**[2]. In capitalist society, therefore, **interest**

1 *Nota bene:* The concept «moneyed capital» must be clearly distinguished from the concept «money capital». Whereas «money capital» refers to the form industrial or commercial capital can take in its metamorphoses (M and M′ in M–C...P...C′–M′ or M–C–M′) (*see* ► Sect. 12.2 in Part II and ► Sect. 18.1.2 in Part III), the «moneyed capital» discussed here is the capital in a money-form that is centralised in a bank and is thus in the state of being loanable as interest-bearing capital.

2 The term «moneyed capitalist» should be understood to include not only personal moneylenders, rentiers, pensioners, etc. but also personal bankers and banks as well as joint-stock banks and central banks.

is the part of the *average profit obtained handed over* to the moneyed capitalist by the functioning capitalist who made the borrowed *money function as capital*; therefore, the *substance of interest is surplus-value.*

Money, and therefore the means of production purchased by it, can function as capital due to capitalist relations of production, wherein *labour is separated from and opposes the means of production as wage-labour.* And the *ownership of capital expresses this separation.* These relations give money the power to command the labour of another person, making it possible to appropriate surplus-labour, so that money as such, in its attribute as capital, becomes a commodity. This generates the specific capital form of interest-bearing capital.

Confusion Surrounding Concepts of Commodity, Money, Capital, etc.

Those involved with the money market are also aware of the fact that in this market money becomes a commodity as capital. What they are able to see, however, is only the superficial phenomenon of the owner of money obtaining interest solely through the simple movement of «loan followed by repayment». They only see that interest is the «price» of the «capital» that is the «commodity», but are totally unaware that the substance of this is surplus-value. Moreover, because they are quite ignorant of the essence of the commodity, money, capital, etc. and cannot understand price by starting from value, they are unable to clearly grasp the nature of the «commodity» that is «money as capital»—and fall into all sorts of **confusion** when they use these concepts to address an issue.

19.1.2 Division of Profit and Rate of Interest

Upper and Lower Limit for Fluctuation of the Interest Rate and the Determinant of the Interest Rate

Since interest is the portion of average profit that the functioning capitalist pays to the moneyed capitalist, the upper limit of interest is average profit itself, while the lower limit is zero. The **rate of interest** (i.e. the rate to loan capital) fluctuates between the upper and lower limit through *changes in the supply and demand relation for interest-bearing capital*, which are the *fluctuations in competition between lenders and borrowers. Nothing exists apart from this to determine the level of the interest rate.*

Supply of and Demand for Loanable Moneyed Capital

With the development of the banking system, interest-bearing capital on the money market takes the form of **loanable moneyed capital** concentrated in banks. The rate of interest fluctuates due to the *power relationship between the supply of and demand for this loanable moneyed capital.* Here, *moneyed capital consolidated en masse* presents itself as the *common* *capital of the capitalist class*[3]. Therefore, the rate of interest, at any point in time, always presents itself as a definite, socially uniform magnitude.

Fluctuation Tendencies for the Rate of Interest

Along with the development of capitalist production, there is a tendential fall in the average rate of profit. With this, the upper limit of the rate of interest also falls, so that there is a *tendential fall in the rate of interest*. The *changes in the successive phases of the industrial cycle*—progressing from a state of quiescence to growing animation, prosperity, overproduction, crisis, stagnation, and then returning to quiescence—*bring about certain recurrent changes in the supply and demand for interest-bearing capital*, so there is a roughly corresponding relationship between those phases and the rate of interest. During a period when animation is growing and then prosperity continues, the rate of interest rises gradually but is still relatively low, but when prosperity reaches its peak and the overproduction generated during that phase but concealed by the prosperity begins to be exposed, the rate of interest rises rapidly and reaches its peak at the moment when everyone is seeking money to settle past transactions. Then, during the period of stagnation, the rate of interest again falls, eventually reaching its lowest level.

3 Marx (1894) splendidly depicts moneyed capital *en masse* as *the common capital of the capitalist class* in the following passage: «In the money-market it is only lenders and borrowers who face one another. The commodity has the same form—*money*. All particular shapes of capital, arising from its advance in particular spheres of production or circulation, are obliterated here. It exists in the undifferentiated, homogeneous shape of independent value, i.e. money. Competition between particular spheres here ceases. They are all thrown together as *borrowers of money*, and capital confronts them all in a form still indifferent to the specific manner and mode of its application. Here capital really does in the *demand for capital* according to its weight emerge as the *common capital of the class*, whereas industrial capital appears like this only in the movement and competition between the particular spheres. On the other hand, moneyed capital in the money-market actually possesses the shape, in which, indifferent to its specific employment, it is divided as a common element among the various spheres, among the capitalist class, according to the requirements of production in each particular sphere may dictate. Moreover, with the development of large-scale industry moneyed capital, so far as it appears on the market, is not represented by *some individual* capitalist, not the owner of one or another fraction of the capital in the market, but assumes the nature of a concentrated, organised mass, which, quite different from real production, is subject to the control of bankers representing the social capital. The result is that, as far as the form of demand, capital for loan is faced with the entire weight of a class, while, as far as supply goes, it itself appears *en masse* as loanable capital» (Marx 1981, pp. 490–491; Marx's emphasis as in his manuscript).

19.1.3 Interest and Profit of Enterprise

Division of Profit into Interest and Profit of Enterprise

Interest must be paid on the borrowed capital that is made to function by the functional capitalist, so the capitalist's profit is divided into two parts: *interest* and *what remains after interest is deducted*. The latter part is called **profit of enterprise**. The proportion between the two divided parts will change depending on fluctuations in the rate of interest. This is a purely quantitative division of capital because the rate of interest is decided by the relation between the quantity of loanable moneyed capital (supply) and the size of the portion of functional capital seeking to borrow (demand).

Distorted Notions: «Interest = Fruit of Capital-ownership» / «Profit of Enterprise = Fruit of the Function of Capital»

Once the category of interest is established, however, the false notions emerge that «interest is the fruit of capital-ownership» and that «profit of enterprise is remuneration for making capital function» (or the «fruit of the function of capital»). As a result, even though the rate of interest is not influenced at all by the magnitude of the self-owned capital within the total functioning capital, even those *functioning capitalists who only use their own capital* conceive of the profit obtained as being composed of the two parts of «interest» for the «ownership» of their capital and «profit of enterprise» for the «functioning of their capital». There thus come to be established two *hard-to-escape*, distorted notions: «interest = fruit of the ownership of capital», on the one hand, and «profit of enterprise = fruit of the function of capital», on the other hand. A *purely quantitative division of profit* into interest and profit of enterprise, between two sorts of capitalists, is turned into a division between two separate categories from completely different sources, so that it becomes a *qualitative division*. The notion of *interest* as the «fruit of the ownership of capital» makes it appear *totally unrelated to the production process* and therefore *unrelated to the exploitation of the surplus-labour of the working class*—even though interest is in fact one part of the surplus-value obtained by functioning capital in the production process. Meanwhile, the *profit of enterprise*, which is also one part of the same surplus-value, appears to be unrelated to capital, and to *arise from the production process itself* and *from the labour process in general, without any relation to a social form.*

Notion Also Established that the «Worker Makes Capital Function»

The notion thus arises that the capitalist in general is outside the production process and that *it is not the capitalist but only the worker who makes capital function in the production process.*

When the labour of direction and superintendence within the production process is entrusted to specific workers, who receive wages for performing those functions, the labour of the directors of the combined social labour originally needed in a mode of production where a large number of workers labour in co-operation (like the labour of an orchestra conductor) and the labour of the superintendence of workers for the exploitation of surplus-value are directly and inseparably fused, making it impossible to distinguish between the two types of labour or even distinguish between the labour of direction and superintendence and the labour carried out by exploited workers.

Thus, *the capitalist vanishes from the scene where capital is functioning, so that there are ordinary workers and the high-grade workers with special skills called managers who direct and superintend them in return for wages.* In this way, the opposition between capital and labour is completely dissolved, generating the *notion that two completely different sources of income—capital and labour—generate, respectively, interest and wages.*

Superfluity of the Capitalist Is Revealed by the Joint-Stock Company

In the case of the **joint-stock company**, all of the substantial functions pertaining to the functioning capitalist are performed by **managers**, who do not own capital. These simple functionaries are the only ones who function in the production process, while the capitalist fades completely from the scene of production. The development of the joint-stock company thus *clarifies that the capitalist is a superfluous person, totally unnecessary for the process of production.* This brings into view the fact that *capital's profit is nothing more than congealed unpaid labour from other people.*

19.1.4 Completion of the Fetish Character and Fetishism of Capital in Interest-bearing Capital

Completion of the Fetish Character and Fetishism of Capital in Interest-bearing Capital

In the movement of interest-bearing capital, M–M′, we have only the *form of valorisation of capital completely without content*, whereby a certain sum of money bears «fruit» after a given period of time. The notion takes full shape that capital itself (whether borrowed or one's own), as such, produces an offspring and augments itself. This is precisely the **completion of the fetish character of capital** that is generated by the **completion of the reification of capital relations**. The essential, intrinsic relations of capitalist production are thus concealed, only presenting themselves in a completely distorted manner.

Development of Relations of Production and the Development of Fetish Character

In a society where labour is performed as private labour and the social division of labour is spontaneously carried out, so that products of labour necessarily take the commodity form, the social relations of human individuals also take a reified form and are concealed by the relations between commodities = things (*see* ▪ Fig. 2.35). This results in the distorted notion that «the vital issue for human beings is to possess things». This is the fetishism attached to the world of commodities that emerges from the undeniable fact that one cannot receive any part of the wealth of society without possessing things; i.e. this is the domination of human individuals by things (*see* ▪ Fig. 2.36).

Furthermore, with the development of the commodity form, a specific commodity (gold) becomes money. Money is a form that is only posited in a society of private labour and a spontaneous social division of labour, so its power (as general equivalent) is a completely social attribute. Despite this, the notion arises that «money is the most essential thing in society» from the fact that without money (congealed value), one is unable to receive anything at all from society, whereas with it one can obtain whatever one likes—so that money comes to exercise domination over human individuals.

Under social relations where labouring individuals are separated from the means of production and can only live by selling their own labour-power, money and the means of production are transformed into capital. And once capitalists come to be split into functioning capitalists and moneyed capitalists through the development of capitalist production, profit is divided into interest and profit of enterprise. In other words, interest is precisely the product of such social production relations. But with the establishment of such forms, the *notion arises that money as a thing automatically augments, producing its own offspring,* leading ultimately to the idea that the most essential thing in the world is to «make money» by advancing capital in the most lucrative «financial commodity» put up for sale. This idea is the **completed fetishism of capital**. Anything that offers any opportunity to «make money» comes to be sold as a commodity and is called a «financial commodity», so that, for instance, even the deposits accepted by banks as their debt are turned into a «financial commodity» that the banks put up for sale[4] (*see* ▪ Fig. 19.1).

Even though economic categories and ideas are nothing more than forms posited to things under specific historical relations of production, this fact is concealed by the fetish character of the commodity, money, and capital.

4 Marx (1894) clearly writes: «Interest-bearing capital always is the *mother of every distorted form*, so that *debts* [i.e. deposits!], for example, can appear as commodities in the mind of the banker» (Marx 1981. p. 596; my emphasis and brackets).

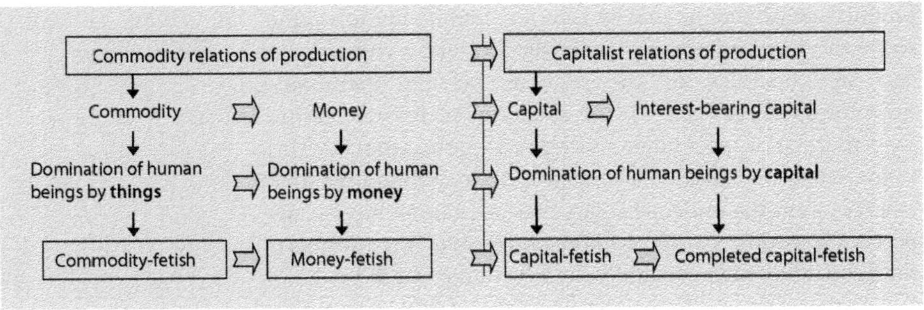

Fig. 19.1 Development of relations of production and development of fetish character and fetishism

Development of Forms of Capital Reveals the Self-contradictions of Capital

The capital fetish is thus completed in the form of interest-bearing capital, but capital in the course of its development escalates, at the same time, the **split between ownership and labour**, exposing *in the form of the joint-stock company that capital's obtainment of surplus-value is unjustified*. In this way, the development of capitalist production advances, on the one hand, the reification of production relations and completes the capital fetish, while at the same time necessarily giving birth to *forms that negate its own justification*. This indicates, clearly, that the development of capital is precisely the *development of the contradictions of capital itself*.

19.2 Bank Capital and Banking System

Banking System

The *main stage for the activities of interest-bearing capital* under developed capitalist production is the **banking system**. Within the banking system, money and money capital are centralised in banks, taking the peculiar shape of **moneyed capital** lent as interest-bearing capital.

The banking system is a *social institution artificially created within capitalist production to centralise and distribute moneyed capital*.

Banking System = Credit-dealing System + the Management Institution of Interest-bearing Capital

19.2.1 Two Aspects of the Banking System

The banking system has two aspects: the credit-dealing system and the institution for the management of interest-bearing capital.

19

Banking System as a Credit System

Credit System

The banking system is above all *a system to handle credit*. The **credit system** has significance as the *system through which credit circulates in lieu of money with real value*.

First, we need to grasp the most fundamental meaning of the credit system itself.

Formation of the Credit System

In ► Sect. «Sale on Credit and Function of Money as Means of Payment» in ► Sect. 2.6.1, we saw that **credit** is originally the claims and debts under **sales and purchases on credit** that are established spontaneously in the course of the development of commodity circulation. Even when only metallic money is in circulation and banknotes have yet to appear, a mechanism arises where credit is widely substituted for money on the basis of those credit-based transactions, signifying the emergence of the credit system.

Commodity Credit

Even under simple commodity circulation, owing to a variety of circumstances, there spontaneously arises among producers sales and purchases on credit in lieu of cash transactions. A credit transaction involves the seller, at the first point of time, alienating the commodity, and the buyer paying money at the second point of time. The seller alienates the commodity, transferring the rights of ownership to the buyer, based on the promise by the buyer, at the first point of time, to pay the seller money at the second point. At the first point in time, the price of the commodity possessed by the seller is converted to the promise to pay money of the buyer, *which brings the sale and purchase to an end*, with the seller becoming creditor and the buyer debtor. In this way, instead of money itself, the seller alienates the commodity in exchange for a promise to pay money, which is referred to as *giving credit* to the buyer, who is *receiving credit*. In short, «credit» is a promise to pay money, and here the relation between creditor and debtor that emerges is the *credit relation* (*see* ◘ Figs. 2.55, 2.56, and 2.57).

Because the seller gives credit to the buyer in the form of a commodity, this credit could be called **commodity credit**. This commodity credit is precisely *what constitutes the foundation of the entire credit system*, and all credit in a developed form arises on this basis.

Commercial Credit

The totality of social reproduction under capitalist production becomes mediated by commodity circulation, so the commercial capital moving within the realm of circulation also develops. *Commodity credit expands and is generalised as it comes to be handled by functioning capitalists* (industrial and commercial capitalists). Among these capitalists, commodities are generally sold in exchange for a *promise to pay* at a certain date, rather than for money. Such written promises to pay are called **commercial bills**. These bills repeatedly circulate up to the point of their due dates among functioning capitalists, who endorse and hand them over. Rather than simply expressing the promise to pay money (i.e. credit) for a single transaction, these bills circulate in place of money for multiple transactions.

For this reason, such commercial bills are referred to as **commercial money**. If the claims and debts that arise when commercial money circulates are settled by «offsetting» each other, there is no need for money to make an appearance at any point. In such a case, commercial money (i.e. credit) functions absolutely as money (*see* ◘ Figs. 2.58, 2.59, and 2.60).

Commodity credit in a developed form under capitalist production that is given and received in the commodity form among functioning capitalists is called **commercial credit** or, more recently, **inter-business credit**.

Credit Dealing as One Aspect of the Banking System

Here we need to return to the banking system, which was first formed on the basis of commercial credit. With the establishment of the banking system, *credit received by banks* is widely substituted for money in every sphere of circulation. Concretely speaking, banks discount commercial bills. This involves the replacement of the circulating commercial bills (*promissory notes* drawn by debtors and *bills of exchange* drawn by creditors and accepted by debtors) with banknotes or deposits. **Banknotes** are created on the basis of the bills circulating within commercial circulation. These are promissory notes that indicate the bank's promise to pay at sight, thus expressing *credit received by the bank*. But these banknotes can exit commercial circulation to enter general circulation, where they are widely used in place of money. Under the banking system, the *fundamental forms of credit received by banks* are banknotes (promissory notes of banks) and **current deposits** that circulate via **cheques** (bills of exchange drawn by depositors on a bank). We will see later that *banks give credit in various money-forms to customers*, but the money actually used for such credit-giving operations is *the credit received by banks*, in the form of banknotes or deposits.

Banking System Is the Superstructure of the Credit System

Handling the various types of credit that circulate is thus the first aspect of the banking system. In other words, the banking system forms one part of the credit system. The banking system, while formed on the basis of commercial credit, itself has the aspect of handling credit, so that it constitutes one part of the credit system.

Whereas *commercial credit is the foundation of the credit system*, the *banking system is its superstructure*, and together are the two constituents of the credit system under capitalist production (*see* ◘ Fig. 19.6).

Banking System as the Management Institution of Interest-bearing Capital

19

Management of Interest-bearing Capital

One other aspect of the banking system is the **management of interest-bearing capital**. This aspect is formed on the *basis and is the developmental outcome of money-dealing capital.*

Centralisation of Money Under Money-dealing Capital and the Formation of Idle Capital

As we have seen, there comes to be centralised under money-dealing capital the technical operations for handling money required by functioning capital (industrial and commercial capital), as well as the idle money capital that inevitably forms in the reproduction process and the reserve funds of functioning capital for purchase and payment. Because money-dealing capital makes it possible to minimise the reserve funds for purchase and payment vis-à-vis the totality of functioning capital, one portion of the reserve funds of functioning capital under the money-dealing capital becomes superfluous as a reserve fund for purchase and payment, thus becoming money in an idle state. Thus, under money-dealing capital, there is an accumulation of *idle money that forms one part of functioning capital's reserve funds for purchase and payment* and of a *large quantity of idle money capital necessarily brought about by functioning capital* (*see* ◘ Fig. 19.2).

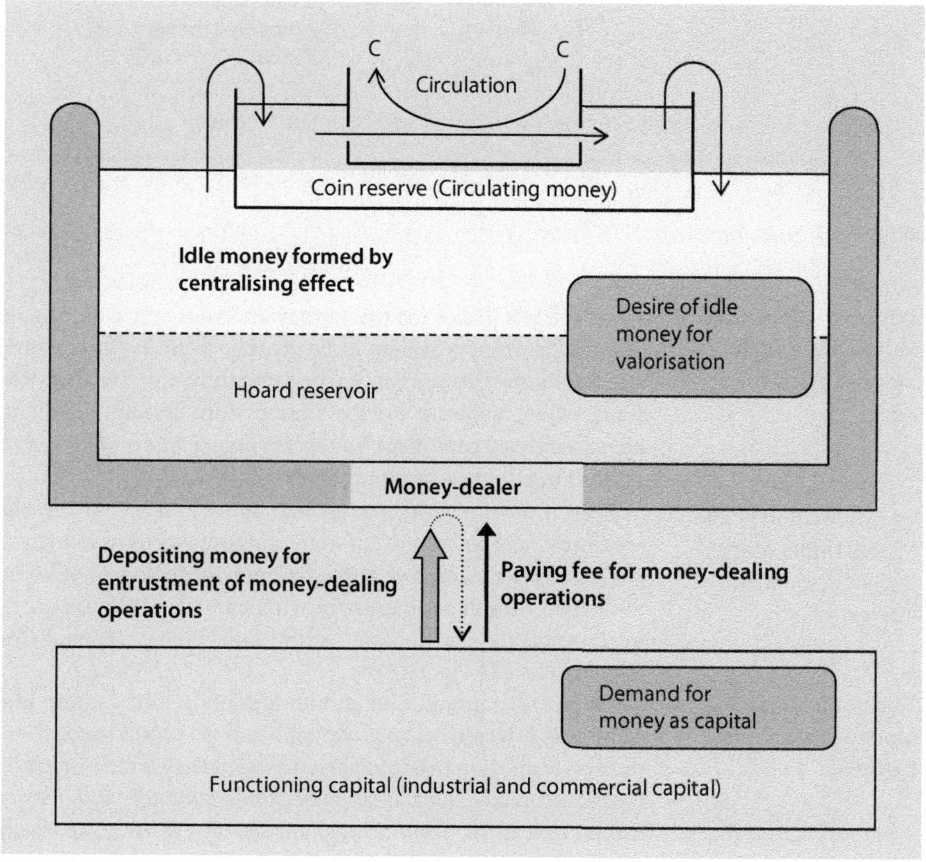

◘ **Fig. 19.2** Centralisation of money under money-dealing capital and the formation of idle money on this basis

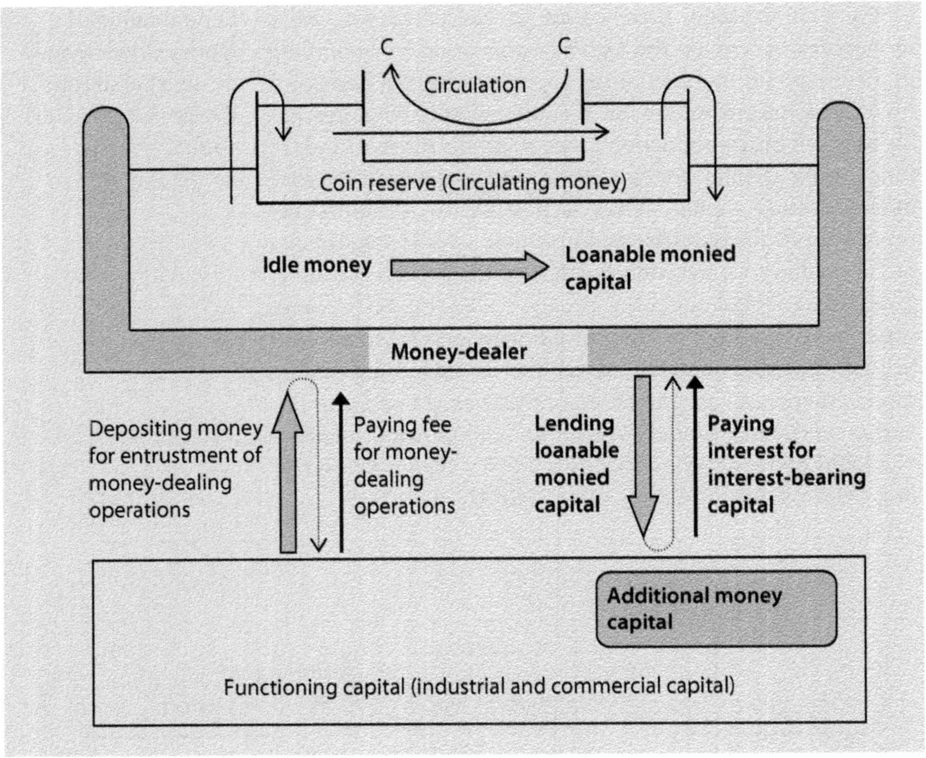

Fig. 19.3 Transformation of idle money under money-dealing capital into interest-bearing capital

Desire to Valorise Idle Money and Obtain Money Capital for Advances

There is a desire for the money and money capital that is idle under money-dealers *to be awoken from its barren state and be valorised as capital.* At the same time, there is always to some extent a desire on the part of functioning capital to *increase money capital for advances (money to be advanced as capital)* in pursuit of more surplus-value.

Transformation of Idle Money Under Money-dealing Capital into Interest-bearing Capital

Given the above, *money-dealers come to lend out the idle money in their possession to functioning capitalists in return for interest.* This makes it possible for money-dealers to valorise their own capital as interest-bearing capital, while functioning capitalists can obtain additional money capital for advances (*see* Fig. 19.3).

Transformation of Money-dealers into Bankers

When the practice of money-dealers lending their idle money as interest-bearing capital becomes regularised, these money-dealers, in order to valorise the money lent as interest-bearing capital, *come into possession of money and money capital that is idle from throughout society (either temporarily or over the long term) by paying interest*—in addition to the money deposited to them by functioning capital for the money-dealing operations. In this way, money-dealers *take*

19

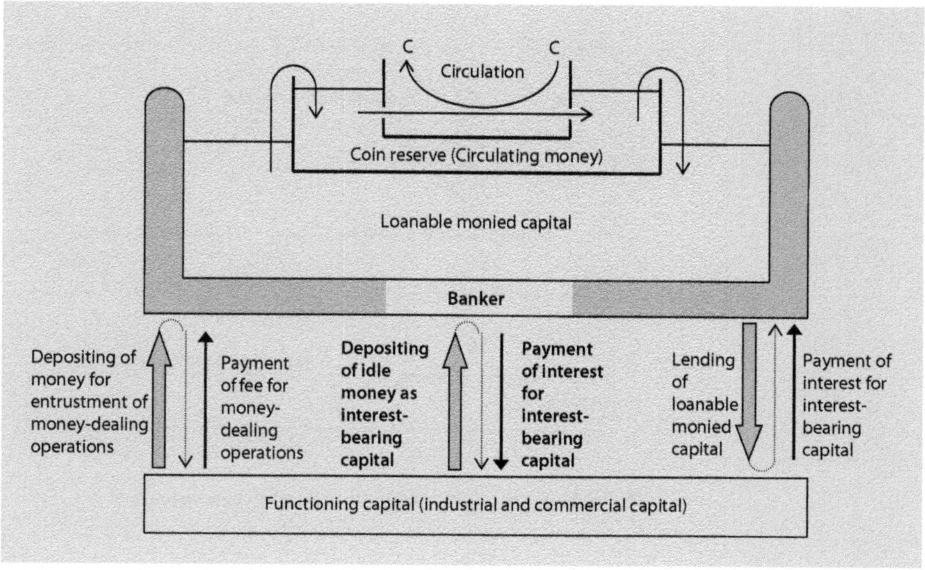

Fig. 19.4 Banking capital: Capital that performs money-dealing operations plus management of interest-bearing capital

on as one of their particular operations—in addition to their money-dealing operations—*the lending and borrowing of money*, thus becoming **bankers**.

Functioning capitalists deposit not only their own *reserve funds* to these bankers, who are entrusted with the money-dealing operations, but also *deposit all of the money capital* that is idle in their possession, *receiving interest in return from the bankers* (*see* Fig. 19.4).

Banks as the Centraliser, Mediator, and Manager of Interest-bearing Capital

From a social perspective, bankers, on the one hand, as the *representatives of borrowers, centralise the money and money capital of society as a whole that is idle* by paying interest to borrow not only the money and money capital idle under functioning capital but also the money possessed by *original* moneyed capital as well as the reserves for purchases and payments by workers and all other strata of society. On the other hand, *as representatives of lenders*, bankers loan out this large amount of loanable moneyed capital that is formed to *borrowers among functioning capital who seek additional moneyed capital*, thus playing the role of *intermediary between lenders and borrowers of moneyed capital*[5] (*see* Fig. 19.5).

5 *See* again Marx's description of supply and demand of the common capital for the capitalist class in footnote 3 of this chapter. The same situation can be seen in *a concrete shape in the banking system.*

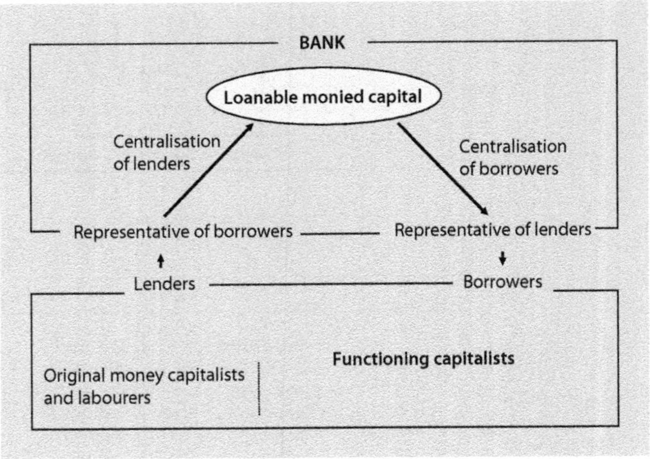

Fig. 19.5 Banks as mediators of interest-bearing capital

Management of Interest-bearing Capital Is One Aspect of the Banking System

What precisely distinguishes bankers from pure money-dealers, therefore, is that they *make the borrowing and lending of money their own proper function and mediate and manage moneyed capital as interest-bearing capital.* These are the *most essential aspects of the banking system.*

Two Aspects of the Banking System and Two Constituents of the Credit System

We can see, then, that the banking system is a constituent part of the credit system in its aspect of handling credit, while at the same time having the aspect of mediating and managing interest-bearing capital in connection to money-dealing operations. Thus, with the establishment of the banking system, the *credit system* comes to be composed of two constituent parts: *commercial credit* as the fundamental constituent part and the *banking system* built upon this foundation as its superstructure. This is diagrammed in Fig. 19.6.

With the development of capitalist production, in addition to banks, various «financial institutions» emerge that are involved with money and credit, also becoming constituent parts of the credit system. The term «financial system» used today can be viewed as basically signifying the totality of the «credit system» that encompasses such institutions, but this does not alter the fact that the basic constituent part of this system is the commercial credit between functioning capital (industrial and commercial capital) and that its pivot is the banking system that arises upon this foundation.

19.2.2 Profit and Capital of Banks

Bank Profit = Margin of Interest Plus Dealing Fees

In performing their banking operations, bankers obtain profit, known as **bank profit**.

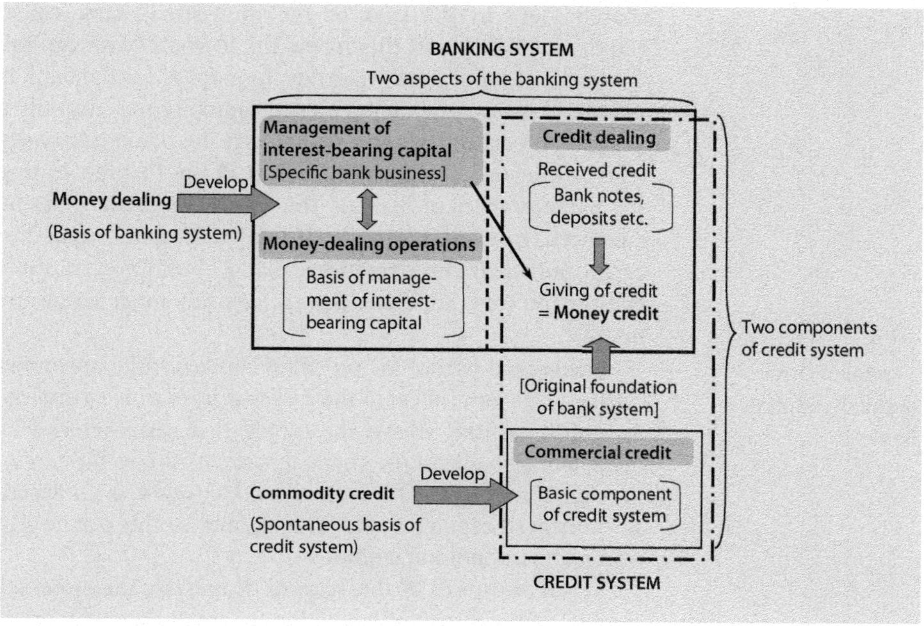

Fig. 19.6 Two aspects of the banking system and two constituent parts of the credit system

Two elements of **bank business**		Two sources of **bank profit**
Management of interest-bearing capital	→	Margin between received and paid interests based on spread between lending and borrowing rates
Money-dealing operations	→	Fee for money-dealing operations

Fig. 19.7 Business of banks and their profits

The profit of bankers arises, first of all, from the **margin of interest** when functioning as mediator between lenders and borrowers, i.e. the higher interest that a bank receives from its loans than the interest it pays when for borrowing. Secondly, banks also receive **dealing fees** from functioning capital in return for taking over the operation of money- and credit-dealing operations from functioning capitalists in the bankers' capacity as money-dealers.

Therefore, *bankers are not simple moneyed capitalists who solely receive interest from lending capital as interest-bearing capital, nor are their gains definitely limited to interest (see* Fig. 19.7).

Bank-owned Capital = Original Bank Capital

The capital of a bank is composed of two parts. The first part is the **owned capital** of the bank. This is the *capital owned by the bankers themselves* (or the capital paid in by the shareholders in the case of the joint-stock bank called «equity capital»), and this forms the *original* **bank capital**. The proportion of profit vis-à-vis this capital for the bank is its **rate of profit**. The bank's owned capital represents only a very small part of the total capital that the bankers manage (this is the «owned capital» listed in ◘ Fig. 19.9 illustrating the balance sheet of banks). The «owned capital» must be advanced, first and foremost, in the fixed capital needed to carry out banking operations (land, buildings, durable equipment, etc.), but this is a part that does not generate any interest.

Capital of Others (Banking Capital) of Banks

The second part of the capital of bankers is the **borrowed capital**. This term refers to the *credit received from customers*, i.e. **credit capital**. This is the capital that earns interest by being lent by bankers. This capital part constitutes the core of the *capital managed in the original banking business* (indicated as «borrowed capital» in ◘ Fig. 19.9), and so this part is also referred to as **banking capital**.

When we speak of the «capital of banks», therefore, we need to clearly distinguish whether we are dealing with original «bank capital» (owned capital), «banking capital» (borrowed capital), or the total of both.

Bank Capital Valorises as Money-dealing Capital and as Interest-bearing Capital

A bank advances its combination of owned and borrowed capital in the operations of money dealing and the management of interest-bearing capital to obtain a profit made up of money-dealing fees and the margin of interests. The capital operating under banks, from the perspective of the fundamental capital forms, thus operates in the forms of *money-dealing capital* and *interest-bearing capital*, so that *bank capital has the characteristic of combining the two types of capital*.

Further, because of the special character of the capital of bankers, *the bulk of it* actually put into operation to generate a profit is customarily *borrowed capital*, which *distinguishes it from ordinary functioning capital*.

Balance Sheet and Profit/Loss Statement

The movement of bank capital and the activities of banks can be understood well by looking at a bank's balance sheet (B/S) and profit/loss statement (P/L). Let us take a look here, first, at the general relation between the **balance sheet**, which indicates the *status of capital at a given point in time*, and the **profit/loss statement**, which shows a *bank's profits and losses for a given period of time* (*see* ◘ Fig. 19.8).

Balance sheet and profit/loss statement in the case of banks are as follows (*see* ◘ Fig. 19.9).

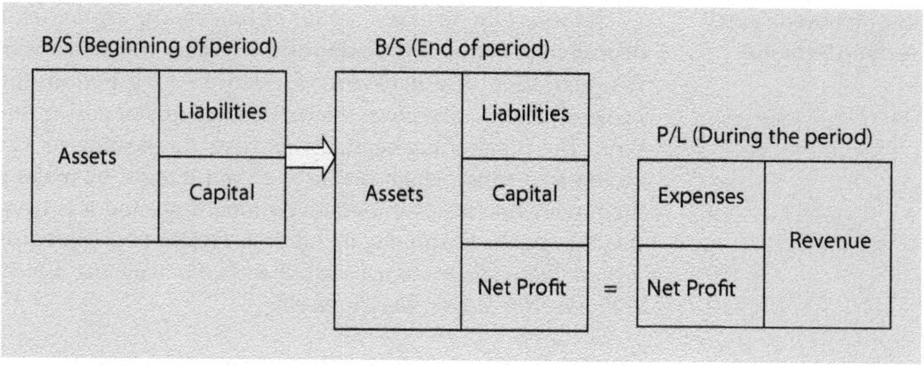

Fig. 19.8 Balance sheet (B/S) and profit/loss statement (P/L)

B/S of bank

Assets	Capital & Liabilities
Cash in hand and deposits in the central bank	Borrowed capital
	Issued bank notes
	Deposits
Lending	Owned capital
Discounted bills	Starting capital
Loan	Current profit
Securities	
Fixed property	

P/L of bank

Expenses	Revenue
Paid interest	Received interest
Costs	Received fees
Current profit	

Fig. 19.9 Balance sheet and profit/loss statement of banks

19.2.3 Sources of Loanable Moneyed Capital of Banks (Sources of Deposits)

Money and Idle Money Capital of Functioning Capitals Centralised Under the Banks

Reserve Funds for Purchase and Payment → Current Deposits

First, the *reserve funds for purchase and payment in the world of commerce* are centralised within the **current deposits** of banks.

By this becoming a common reserve fund within the banks, it is reduced to the minimum required. Bankers must always keep a *reserve funds for payments* to handle the part constantly entering and exiting, but the *sum of money exceeding this reserve* can be transformed into *loanable moneyed capital*, which can *be made to function as interest-bearing capital.*

Idle Moneyed Capital → Time Deposits

Second, *idle moneyed capital of functioning capitalists* is deposited in banks as **time deposits**. Because this remains in the possession of a bank over a relatively long period, the bank can make it *operate as interest-bearing capital* during this time. The functioning capitalist entrusts the dealing of idle money to a bank, which is able to obtain interest by making the money operate over a relatively long time, and it is from this that the bank can pay its interest. *Functioning capitalists deposit their idle moneyed capital in banks with the aim of obtaining this interest that is offered.*

Centralisation of the Idle Moneyed Capital of Original Moneyed Capitalists

Centralisation of the Moneyed Capital of Rentiers

The **proper moneyed capitalists**, in distinction from functioning capitalists, are *those capitalists who live on their interest revenue obtained from lending their own money exclusively as interest-bearing capital*. These **rentiers**, as they are also known, deposit money in banks with the aim of obtaining interest. These capitalists entrust the advance of their own capital as interest-bearing capital to a bank, and the bank pays them interest from out of the interest obtained for advancing this capital. Here the bank is acting as mediator between moneyed capitalists and functioning capitalists.

Deposits of Money for the Consumption of Consumers of All Classes

Centralisation of Money as a Consumption Fund for All Consumers

With the development of the banking system and particularly the practice of paying interest on bank deposits, all of the consumers in society deposit their consumption funds in banks. These *consumers*, first of all, deposit a hoard for future consumption in banks, over the long or short term, and secondly deposit a reserve fund for everyday purchases and payments.

Concentration of Small Sums of Money Is a Particular Operation of the Banking System

In the case of the loanable moneyed capital from the three sources listed above, *small sums of money that would not be able to function on their own as moneyed capital are collected together to form a massive moneyed capital*. This function of collecting small sums *is one of the particular operations performed by the banking system.*

19.2.4 Forms of the Advance of Moneyed Capital by Banks

Banks obtain profit by advancing loanable moneyed capital as interest-bearing capital. The fundamental forms of this advance are lending and investment in securities.

Lending in the Broad Sense

Lending in the Broad Sense

The **lending** by banks, in the broad sense, includes the discounting of bills and other forms of lending.

Discounting of Bills

The primary type of lending by ordinary commercial banks is the **discounting of bills**. Banks discount the commercial bills that express commercial credit between functioning capitalists. The discounting of a bill involves *a bank purchasing a bill and receiving a discount charge. From the view of banks, this discount charge is nothing but the interest for advanced capital up to the current day*. The payment due, i.e. the face value of the bill minus discount charge, is paid in the form of either banknotes or a deposit in a current account.

Other Forms of Lending: Loan on Deeds, Loan on Bills, and Overdrafts

Other forms of loans include **loan on deeds**, the «deeds» being various sorts of certificates other than commercial bills; **loan on bills**, which involves lending in the form of discounting bills as a matter of processing convenience; and the **overdrafts** that occur when a depositor has overdrawn his account.

Secured Loans and Unsecured Loans

Loans are further classified into **secured loans** and **unsecured loans**, depending on whether the loan is covered with collateral security or not. Contrary to the popular impression, unsecured loans (e.g., loan based on personal security) may actually involve less risk than those secured with collateral security.

Securities Investment

Obtaining Interest and Dividends from Investment in Bonds or Stocks and Obtaining Marginal Profit Through Differences Between Sales Price and Purchase Price

Banks advance moneyed capital as interest-bearing capital in various securities other than commercial bills, obtaining *interest and dividends* generated as a result. The objects of securities investment include a variety of bonds, such as public bonds (national and local bonds) and corporate bonds, as well as the stocks of various joint-stock companies. The aim of securities investment by banks is not only to obtain interest and dividends but also to obtain at times a *margin profit through the difference between sales price and purchase price, which is a sort of speculative activity.*

19.2.5 Bank Credit and the Forms of Credit a Bank Receives

Bank Credit or Money Credit

By lending out loanable capital, a bank obtains a claim on the customer who becomes a debtor, thereby *giving the customer credit*. The credit given to customers by banks is **bank credit**, in popular parlance. It is also referred to as **money credit** because such *credit is given in some form of money*, rather than a commodity form as in the case of commodity or commercial credit.

Banks Give Credit in the Form of the Credit They Themselves Receive

When a bank gives credit, by lending out loanable moneyed capital, what the customer receives is not money as real value, but *some form of circulatable credit*, the main forms of which are banknotes, bank drafts other than banknotes, and deposits. These all express **credit that the bank itself has received**, so *the bank gives credit in the form of credit that it has received itself.*

The main forms of the credit that banks receive are the following:

Banknotes

At one time in England as well as in Japan, every bank could issue its own banknotes. Later, the issuing of banknotes was centralised in the central bank or national bank.

Banknotes are nothing more than bank-issued promises to pay that are payable on sight. This is an obligation that the bank has to the holder of the banknotes, expressing the credit that *the bank has received.*

Banknotes, typically, are handed over to a functioning capitalist when a bank gives the capitalist bank credit, and these notes exit circulation between functioning capitalists (commercial circulation) when they are paid by a functioning capitalist to workers as wages, thus entering general circulation where they also function as money.

When the **central bank** emerges that *monopolises the issue of banknotes*, these notes, while remaining banknotes, become *legal tender that is given mandatory (legally stipulated) circulating power*, so that they spread throughout the circulation of a given country. Despite this, however, as long as *convertibility is in effect*, it is clear that the notes represent *credit received by the banks.*

Banknotes are the most noticeable type of credit received by banks.

Bank Draft

Besides banknotes, banks can give customers credit received by banks themselves in the form of a **bank draft.**

Deposits

Of comparable importance to banknotes, among the credit received by banks, are **deposits**. All deposits represent a debt *of the bank to depositors*. For the depositor as well as for the bank, current deposits and time deposits each have their respective significance.

Interest and Dealing Fee for Current Deposits

In the case of **current deposits**, the depositor places his own money in a bank and entrusts it with the money-dealing operations. The bank must expend costs on these operations, so the depositor is obliged to pay a fee to the bank for the consignment of those operations. However, because the average daily withdrawal by depositors is much smaller than the total amount of money they have deposited, the banks only need to set aside a comparatively small reserve to cover the withdrawals, leaving them free to advance the bulk of the current deposits as interest-bearing capital to obtain interest. We can compare the sum of money that the bank must expend on money-dealing operations to the sum of interest obtained thereby. If the former sum is smaller than the latter, the bank would likely pay the depositors' interest so as to expand the sum of deposits, whereas in a case where the latter sum is smaller, the bank would likely seek a fee from depositors for handling their money. Whether banks pay some interest, zero interest, or require a fee for current deposits will differ considerably among countries. Banks in Japan, for example, had for a long time overwhelmingly adopted the policy of zero interest and no dealing fees because there was still some margin for the banks even though the two cancel each other out. More recently, it has become common for Japanese banks to charge fees for money-dealing operations and also for current deposits. This issue should be taken into consideration when evaluating the «zero-interest-rate policy» of central banks in recent years.

Credit Creation = Lending by Deposit Setting

In the case of current deposits, a bank is able to provide *credit to a customer of a certain amount by writing it in the customer's deposit account*, thereby granting the customer a loan. This is referred to as **lending by deposit setting**. The customer can then pay a third party by issuing a cheque, which is an order to pay to the bearer from the deposit that was set up. Like a banknote, a cheque is payable on sight, *representing the claim of its possessor on the bank* and thus expressing credit received by the bank. Thus, when a bank grants a loan by setting a deposit, it *creates credit of the same amount that is received by the bank* and is thus referred to as **credit creation**. Incidentally, a reserve for payment is needed when there is a lending by deposit setting, so the magnitude of such lending is also limited by the magnitude of the reserve funds that can be secured.

Deposit Currency

Because *the credit received by a bank as deposits can also circulate in place of money*, current deposits viewed from this perspective are called **deposit currency**.

Time Deposits

Contrasted with the above, **time deposits** involve a depositor placing his idle capital in a bank as interest-bearing capital, with the aim of obtaining interest. The bank is able to receive such deposits because it advances the money deposited as interest-bearing capital so as to earn a margin based on obtaining more interest than the interest paid.

In addition, when a central bank comes to monopolise the issuing of banknotes, the *main form of credit received by* **commercial banks** becomes deposits.

19.2.6 Bank's Reserve for Payment and Bank Administration

Reserve Funds for Conversion of Banknote and Repayment of Deposits

As just seen, the loanable moneyed capital of banks is formed through deposits of various sources, one part of which is made up of the current deposits of functioning capitalists and of a variety of consumers. Meanwhile, the main forms of credit received by banks, which are used when it gives credit, are banknotes (in the case of convertible banknotes) and current deposits. Because both banknotes and current deposits (as well as cheques made out to those deposits) are payable on sight, the bank must always have on hand a **reserve for payment** for this purpose. When the issue of banknotes is centralised within a central bank, *the central bank must have reserve funds for convertibility of banknotes and for payment of deposits* (which are deposits made by commercial banks to the central bank), while *commercial banks must have payment reserve funds for deposits.*

Stability and Profitability in Bank Administration

The demands for the conversion of banknotes or repayment of deposits do not involve a request for the entire sum at once. Usually, there is only a need for a reserve fund that is a *relatively small sum* compared to the *level of banknotes issued and the sum of deposits received.* For the banks, the portion of the banknotes issued and deposits received that remains after setting aside that reserve fund becomes a *non-reserve debt* for the bank. Therefore, the greater the magnitude of the reserve fund for payment, the greater the stability of the bank administration. Meanwhile, because the money that is dormant in the bank's vaults as a reserve fund for payment is idle money, which is not advanced as interest-bearing capital, the smaller the amount of this idle money, the greater the bank's profit and the higher its profitability.

Given this, *one important issue of bank administration is determining how to reduce the reserve fund for payment without harming stability.*

19.2.7 Fictitious Capital and Its Forms

Fictitious Capital

Creation of Fictitious Capital Through Capitalisation

Because money lent as interest-bearing capital brings about interest at the given rate of interest settled on in the market, a *regularly obtainable money revenue* is conceived of as *interest* on some sort of «capital», and in turn, the *revenue source* generating this «interest» is conceived of as *capital.* For instance, if the annual rate of interest is 5% and 1 million yen of money is advanced as interest-bearing capital, this capital will generate an annual interest of 50,000 yen. Given this, an annual revenue of 50,000 yen is seen as the «interest» on a capital of 1 million yen, and the thing that brings about this revenue is seen as the interest-generating «capital» of 1 million yen. *The term* **capitalisation** refers to *this way of thinking or calculation whereby one arrives at a magnitude of capital by multiplying the amount of revenue that has been settled by the given rate of interest*. The «capital» conceived of through this capitalisation is neither actually functioning capital nor actually loaned interest-bearing capital, but rather *a purely illusory entity that is simply imagined*. This sort of imagined «capital» is called **fictitious capital**.

Commodification of Fictitious Capital

This distorted way of thinking reaches its pinnacle with the conception of labour-power as capital through the capitalisation of wages. The stupidity of this conception becomes immediately apparent if one considers that the worker must work to obtain this «interest» and is quite unable to liquidate the value of this «capital» of his. Under capitalist production, however, *the various types of fictitious capital that are formed through capitalisation are bought and sold as commodities*. The price of land, which we will examine in ▶ Sect. 20.5 («Land Price»), is likewise created through the capitalisation of ground-rent, so that the land bought and sold is a sort of fictitious capital.

Financial Market

The *financial market* is a *comprehensive term to refer to the markets where various sorts of fictitious capital are commoditised and bought and sold.*

Forms of Fictitious Capital and Their Accumulation

National Bonds

A **national bond** is a *bond that expresses a claim vis-à-vis the state*. The owner of a national bond is paid a fixed amount of interest every year by the state, so *national bonds* are seen as *capital* that generates interest, and these *national bonds as capital* are sold on the bond market. The market price to express the «value» of this «capital» is arrived at through capitalisation based on the interest fixed at the time of issue and the rate of interest of the time, so the value falls with a rise in the interest rate and rises when the interest rate falls. The actual sales price will fluctuate around this «value» in line with supply and demand. The money paid by purchasers to buy national bonds on the bond market—even if conceived of by the purchasers as «capital that generates a fixed interest»—is *certainly not func-*

tioning as real capital, but rather is merely money transferred to the hands of the seller. The money paid by the person who initially buys the national bond from the state is used up in the state's expenditures and is certainly not valorising capital. What remains is merely the debt of the state, and the national bond itself is nothing more than an *order for a portion of future tax revenue*. Despite this, the fictitious capital of national bonds becomes the *object of securities investment by banks, forming a component part of banking capital*. The other bonds sold on the financial markets have this same fundamental nature.

Stocks

We have already suggested that the banking system generates the associated capital that is joint-stock capital. The **stocks**, which are the securities that express the ownership of this capital, themselves represent one part of the capital advanced by the given company. Stocks, however, are actually nothing more than a *nominal right to one part of the surplus-value created by this capital*. So stocks are also a typical case of fictitious capital. An annual *dividend* is paid to the owner of the stock by the joint-stock company in accordance with business performance. The conceived *value of the stock* («theoretical price») is the *capitalisation of this dividend based on the rate of interest of the time*, so that it rises or falls in inverse proportion to the rate of interest. The actual price on the market fluctuates around this «value» depending on the supply and demand for each stock. The money paid for the stock on the stock market merely moves into the hands of the seller and certainly does not become real capital. Despite this, *stocks also become an important object of a bank's securities investments*, forming *a constituent part of banking capital*.

Price Formed Through Speculative Action

In the manner above, the ownership rights that are a source of income become commodities as capital, but since these commodities cannot be consumed productively or individually, their purchasers, including banks, buy them in the hope of either having the revenue they generate income or obtaining a marginal profit in the future through their sale on the market. The price of this sort of commodity is essentially *speculative* and is always fluctuating through *supply and demand based on speculative moments. One part of the bank's capital takes the form of this sort of speculative, fictitious capital.*

Moneyed Capital in Banks as Fictitious Capital

Fictitious Character of Securities Held by Banks

One part of the loanable moneyed capital of banks is advanced in various forms of securities that are fictitious capital as stated above. But in addition to this, the overall securities held by banks, including commercial bills and banknotes of other banks, are merely orders for payment of money, so that it is also *fictitious in the sense of not being money with its own intrinsic value.*

Fictitious Character of Deposits

Furthermore, the bulk of the capital of banks is credit received by banks, which is to say, customers' capital deposited in banks. The deposits received from customers, not to mention the deposits settled to be lent out, are for the most part *non-reserve debts* that only exist on paper and are therefore *fictitious.* In this sense, the *accumulation of loanable moneyed capital in banks* is really nothing more, in essence, than the *concentration of a fictitious capital.*

Fictitious Character of Payment Reserve

Lastly, even most of the *reserve funds* of a bank for deposits in the case of *commercial banks* take the form of *deposits in the central bank*, the bulk of which constitute *non-reserve debt* that is also fictitious.

Disturbances in the Banking System Through Exposure of the Fictitious Character of Banking Capital

Thus, the *totality of the capital of banks* is essentially fictitious. When, *for whatever reason*, one part of the fictitious capital seeks to be transformed into real value, the fictitious character of this enormous totality of capital is immediately brought to light, and the banking system itself undergoes a disturbance to a greater or lesser extent. This became clearly visible in the 1990s in the case of Japan's banking system, as many large banks faced collapse due to the exposure of an enormous **amount of bad loans.**

Accumulation of «Money» as Accumulation of Fictitious Capital

«Accumulation of Money» Is an Accumulation of Fictitious Capital (Nothing but an Accumulation of Claims)

In countries where capitalist production has developed, an enormous amount of moneyed capital exists in the form of fictitious capital through capitalisation. The «money» referred to today when saying that «money flies around world» is this sort of fictitious moneyed capital. What is thought of when referring to the «accumulation of money» is, at best, the *accumulation of claims on one part of the surplus-value generated by the labour of labouring individuals* or the *accumulation of the prices of these claims as commodities on the market.* The money flying around world is said to be four or five hundred times the total amount of worldwide trade, but the «money» spoken of in such cases is precisely the fictitious capital described above.

Abnormal Expansion of Fictitious Capital Necessarily Generates «Casino Capitalism»

If one is taken in by the magnitude of this accumulated «money» or of money assets, it will necessarily appear that the wealth of a country during a certain period (such as a financial bubble) is also rapidly expanding. But the expansion of such fictitious capital is merely an expansion of claims, so the swelling or contraction of this money does not correspond to a change in the *wealth* of a country or in its *production and circulation*. Rather, the *expansion of claims vis-à-vis a certain magnitude of surplus-value lowers the average augmentation rate of fictitious capital*, thus intensifying the competition within this world of «money», as everyone *scrambles for prey*. The source of gain for individual capital in this case is not so much the common prey of surplus-value but rather the carcasses of the other capitals that fall by the wayside. The term «**gambling capitalism**» or «**casino capitalism**» expresses the condition where the abnormal proliferation of fictitious capital is like a pack of hyenas fighting bitterly over the limited prey (surplus-value) and eating up each other in the process[6].

19.2.8 Necessity of the Formation of the Banking System Under Capitalist Production

The banking system is an *extremely organised and therefore artificial instrument created by capital*.

Prehistory of the Modern Bank

What lied before the eyes of the rising industrial and commercial capital was the old usury capital that monopolised the precious metals and earned high interest through usury. In order to promote capital accumulation and expand capital production, the emergent capital had to subordinate interest-

6 In his manuscript for volume III of *Capital*, Marx analysed in great detail moneyed capital as the concrete form of interest-bearing capital under the banking system. The most important and brilliant discussion there concerns the elucidation of the accumulation of moneyed capital in relation to the accumulation of real capital (industrial and commercial capital). Because the spectacular phenomenal movements of moneyed capital are in fact ultimately conditioned by the movement of real capital, Marx's examination of this issue gives many valuable suggestions for also clarifying the «financialisation» in developed countries today, which symbolises the noticeable separation and independence of moneyed capital from real capital. The dynamic relationship between moneyed capital and real capital can be explained only in connection with the phases of the industrial cycle, as Marx did. This book, however, cannot enter into a direct discussion of the industrial cycle itself. For more on Marx's elucidation of the relation between the accumulation of moneyed capital and the accumulation of real capital, one can consult Miyata (2016). I have also written a comprehensive work (Otani 2016) examining Marx's study of the interest-bearing capital in volume III of *Capital*.

profiteering capital and lower the rate of interest to a level where it could be paid from out of the industrial and commercial profit. The banking system was created to attain this aim. The banking system broke the money monopoly of usury capital by *gathering all the idle hoards and advancing them in the money market,* on the one hand, and by *creating credit money (convertible banknotes),* on the other hand. At the beginning of the seventeenth century, some **exchange banks** came into existence, such as the Bank of Amsterdam and the Bank of Hamburg, but the historical landmark in the formation of the banking system was the **establishment of the Bank of England** in 1694. From that point, the *proper history of modern banking begins.*

Grasping the Banking System from the Intrinsic Nature of Capital Itself

Here, based on the intrinsic nature of capital examined thus far, we will grasp the *necessity of creating the banking system for capital,* including its moments and direct motives. And, on the basis of that understanding, ▶ Sect. 19.2.9 will seek to summarise the *role that the banking system plays within capitalist production.*

Necessary Tendency of Capital to Seek «Circulation Without Circulation Time»

Because circulation time is a period of time that yields neither value nor surplus-value, industrial capital necessarily *aims to limit circulation time to a minimum.*

Capital also necessarily seeks to minimise the circulation costs expended by industrial capital in the circulation process, which include the costs for money itself, the buying and selling of commodities, and money dealing, because such costs are a deduction from surplus-value. Money itself as a circulation cost, first of all, involves the coin reserve for purchases and payments that capitalists keep on hand as the means of circulation that must be advanced by them to replace the elements of reproduction. An intrinsic tendency of capital is to *seek «circulation without circulation time»,* with the term «circulation time» in this specific expression involving the circulation costs.

Money as a circulation cost for capital refers, secondly, to the amortisation fund for fixed capital and the accumulation fund that must be compiled and exist as *idle capital* in the hands of someone among the capitalists.

Commodity-dealing Capital Becomes Autonomous

Commodity-dealing capital comes to specialise in handling the C–M operation of capital, thus becoming independent of industrial capital, and this shortens circulation time for industrial capital and reduces circulation costs.

Despite this, however, the reproduction of functioning capital (industrial and commodity-dealing capital) still requires circulation time and circulation costs, and there is an inevitable tendency to seek to reduce both.

Expansion of Commercial Credit and Need to Break Through Its Limitations

The development of capitalist commodity credit, i.e. commercial credit, reduces both circulation time, by hastening the metamorphoses of functioning capital, and money as a circulation cost, by increasing transactions without money through the offsetting of claims and debts and by replacing money with commercial bills (circulating credit) that are commercial money (*see* ▶ Sect. «Banking System as a Credit System»). However, because obligations not offset must be settled with money, individual capitals have to keep reserve funds on hand for payment in such cases and for payment in times of emergency. Functioning capital has a desire to reduce these reserve funds while also seeking to convert its bills (circulating credit) into cash as quickly as possible.

Establishment of Money-dealing Capital and the Formation of Idle Moneyed Capital Under It

Following commodity-dealing capital, money-dealing capital also becomes independent of functioning capital as something that reduces the cost of money dealing for functional capital.

The centralisation under money-dealing capital of the reserve fund for purchase and payment of functioning capital, so that it becomes a common reserve fund, reduces the fund's magnitude. But there still remains a need for this reserve fund, and the idle money formed through this reduction under money-dealing capital also remains in a dormant state here along with the idle moneyed capital that is centralised there.

Money-dealing capital necessarily has a strong intention to have the idle money and moneyed capital self-valorised by moving from an idle to an active state.

Need to Break Through the Quantitative Limitations of Individual Capital Posited by Competition Between Capitals

Because individual capitals are compelled by competition—i.e. by the external pressure that capitals exert upon each other—to transfer to spheres with a high rate of profit, there is an equalisation of profit rates between spheres, provided that capital is able to move freely. This results in the establishment of an average rate of profit and production prices.

There are various obstacles to the moving of capital, however, so differences in the rates of profit between spheres do not easily disappear. Capitals in spheres with a lower rate of profit than the average rate will reduce the scale of production, so that a portion of capital in these spheres is inevitably removed from a functioning state to become idle. Meanwhile, capitals in spheres with a higher rate of profit expand the scale of production, but the decisive limit to that expansion is the sum of the surplus-value produced in that a particular sphere. There thus arises a need for the capitals in the latter spheres to utilise the latent capital that remains idle in the former spheres so as to *break through their own quantitative limitations and expand production.*

Furthermore, the fall in the rate of profit due to the heightening of organic composition posits an impulse, via competition, for individual capitals to respond by obtaining an absolute increase in the quantity of profit through expanding the amount of capital advanced. But this also cannot be done without individual capitals breaking through their own quantitative limitations set by the surplus-value produced in their sphere.

Thus, the *impulse of individual capitals to seek to break through their own quantitative limitations* inevitably generates a strong need to use the idle money and moneyed capital as functioning capital.

Formation of Interest-bearing Capital as the Mediating Form of the Transformation of Idle Money into Functioning Capital

Under the capitalist mode of production, money is able to generate average profit by functioning as capital. Money as capital thus becomes a commodity, with interest paid as the «price of capital». With this formation of interest-bearing capital, the owners of idle money and moneyed capital become able to valorise their money by entrusting it as interest-bearing capital to someone else. Meanwhile, the functioning capitalists, by paying out one part of the profit as interest, become able to advance money owned by another person as functioning capital in the production process. The capital form of interest-bearing capital thus creates the possibility of realising both the *need to activate idle money and moneyed capital from its dormant state so that it self-valorises* as well as the *impulse of industrial capital to break through its own individual quantitative limitations by making use of the idle money and moneyed capital of others as functioning capital.*

However, for this possibility to be socially realised, the idle money and moneyed capital of society must *be provided as a bulk of centralised moneyed capital*, and *the demand of functioning capitals for this moneyed capital must likewise appear as a mass of centralised demand*—and a *social structure is needed to mediate these two sides.* The mediating structure is precisely the **banking system** and the **money market** within it.

Establishment of the Banking System and Money Market

The money-dealers, in whose hands the idle money and moneyed capital seeking valorisation has been concentrated, discount bills—by replacing the commercial credit circulating between functioning capitalists (in the form of bills) and their own received credit (banknotes and current deposits)—and in that sense give customers credit from the credit received from other customers. In so doing, the money-dealers become bankers, and the banking system is established.

Once the banking system has been established, a money market centres around banks as the mediator. Banks bring together not only the idle money and moneyed capital of functioning capital but also all the idle money and moneyed capital of society. The supply of moneyed capital provided by lenders and the demand for moneyed capital of borrowers oppose each other through the mediation of the banks.

Thus, *all the disposable capital of society comes to be distributed to the production spheres corresponding to the needs of production, bringing about an equalisation of the rate of profit mediated by the movement of capital between the spheres.* Furthermore, the banking system as a totality, along with commercial credit, forms the *credit system*, thereby *greatly reducing circulation time and circulation costs.*

19.2.9 Role of the Banking System Within Capitalist Production

Role of the Banking System Within Capitalist Production

Mediation of the Distribution of Total Social Capital

From the above, it should be clear that the banking system performs a vital role within capitalist production. The role of the system can be briefly summarised as follows.

The banking system mediates the equalisation of the rate of profit by bringing together all the latent capital of society, making it the common capital, *en masse*, of the capitalist class, and distributing this mass of loanable moneyed capital to the various spheres in line with the needs of production. Thus, *even though banking capital is a particular type of capital*, it is also *capital in the general form* vis-à-vis the total functioning capitals, or *the capital of the entire capitalist class*, and in this sense it has a *social character*. The movement of the equalisation of the profit rate is the foundation of capitalist production, making capitalist production feasible as one form of social production. So the banking system that mediates this movement is, itself, an *intrinsic form of the capitalist mode of production.*

Reduction of Circulation Time and Circulation Costs

The banking system along with the commercial credit that forms its foundation constitutes the credit system, bringing about a *reduction in circulation time and circulation cost* through various means.

The banking system, first of all, accelerates commercial credit through the discounting of bills and shortens circulation time by hastening the metamorphoses of commodities. This, in turn, accelerates the circulation of currency (means of circulation), which reduces the quantity of money needed for circulation. Meanwhile, the acceleration of commercial credit economises money by expanding the amount of moneyless transactions. Under the banking system, money is economised because banknotes and cheques replace money. And the development of money-dealing techniques, such as the development of a settlement system connected to the dealing of current deposits, also reduces the amount of circulating banknotes. Finally, the banking system reduces—for both individual capital and capitalist production as a whole—the reserve fund for purchases and payments as well as the idle moneyed capital.

The summary above explains the necessity of the banking system, but once the system has been established, it plays the following role within capitalism that has a decisive effect on the outcome of production.

Mediation and Promotion of the Formation of Joint-stock Companies

The banking system, through its role of distributing the total social capital to the various production spheres, becomes *a means of developing capitalist production into the highly advanced forms that are possible*. The most advanced form is the specific type of enterprise called a **joint-stock company**, which presupposes the existence of the **stock market**, and **share capital** is the corresponding form of capital that is in movement.

Capital is concentrated through the accumulative process of capital, manifesting itself as a large individual capital. However, it is in the form of the joint-stock company that truly enormous capital appears. In the case of such companies, capital is advanced through the purchase of stock shares having the same unit of value, and profit is distributed through the dividends allotted to each share. In this way, a great diversity of different capitals are able to equally earn profit in line with their magnitude. This structure, which is a sort of «*capitalist communism*», links together a great number of individual capitals, generating a single «**associated capital**».

The *formation of joint-stock companies* leads, first of all, to a tremendous expansion in the scale of production, giving birth to large-scale companies that could not have been formed through individual capital. Prior to the emergence of joint-stock companies, production on that scale could only be accomplished by the state.

The second key point about joint-stock companies is that capital takes the form of social capital (i.e. the capital of directly associated individuals), in opposition to private capital. So the enterprises of capital appear as social enterprises opposed to private enterprises. This is the sublation, within the capitalist mode of production itself, of capital as private ownership.

Thirdly, under joint-stock capital, functioning capitalists are turned into mere managers, and the owners of capital become mere money capitalists. As a result, on the one hand, these managers merely receive a «wage» for their type of skilled labour, while on the other hand, the owners of capital in the joint-stock company are in a relation of opposition to all the «producers» (from the managers all the way down to the lowest ranking workers) and appear as superfluous, outside individuals who merely appropriate the surplus-labour of others.

In these ways, *the joint-stock company is the sublation of the capitalist mode of production within the capitalist mode of production, encompassing a contradiction that itself must be sublated and constituting an inevitable point of transition for capital to be transformed into the ownership of associated labouring individuals.*

The banking system performs the role of advancing capitalist production up to this point.

References

Marx K (1894) Das Kapital. Kritik der politischen Oekonomie. Bd. 3. Buch 3: Der Gesammtprocess der kapitalistischen Produktion. Hrsg. von F. Engels. Hamburg. English edition: Marx K (1981) Capital. A critique of political economy, vol 3 (trans: Fernbach D). Penguin Books, Harmondsworth

Miyata K (2016) Karl Marx's theory—the relation between the accumulation of monied capital and the accumulation of real capital. *Marx-Engels-Jahrbuch* 2015/16. 10–27. De Gruyter Akademie Forschung, Berlin/Boston

Otani T (2016) Marx's theory of interest-bearing capital, 4 vols. Sakurai-Shoten Publishers, Tokyo. In Japanese

Landed Property and Ground-rent

T. Otani, *A Guide to Marxian Political Economy*,
https://doi.org/10.1007/978-3-319-65954-1_20

20

20.1 Capitalist Production and Landed Property

20.1.1 Modern Landed Property and Capitalist Agriculture Management

Capitalist Production Transforms the Long-Established Landed Property into Modern Landed Property

Capitalist production first became the dominant mode of production in the industrial sphere, whereas in the agricultural sphere, it confronted the forms of premodern landed property, namely, *feudal landed property* and *small peasant landed property*. Capital was unable to do away with landed property altogether, but *by transforming long-established landed property into a form appropriate to capitalist production*, it was able to first *subordinate agriculture to itself*. The new landed property that was created was *landed property that coincides with the property laws of commodity production*, referred to as **modern landed property**.[1] In this way, the capitalist production generated large landed property in place of the small-scale landownership by peasants who farm their own land[2] (*see* ► Sect. 11.1 in Part I: «Primitive Accumulation and Its Methods»). In the case of modern landed property, the

1 Needless to say, this transformation of landed property by the capitalist mode of production had great historical significance, as Marx (1894) explains: «It is one of the great results of the capitalist mode of production that on the one hand *it transforms agriculture from a merely empirical set of procedures, mechanically handed down and practiced by the most undeveloped portions of society, into a conscious scientific application of agronomy*, in so far as this is at all possible within the conditions of private property; that on the one hand *it detaches landed property completely form relations of lordship and servitude*, while on the other hand *it completely separates the land as a condition of labour from landed property and the landlord*, for whom moreover this land represents nothing but a certain monetary tax that his monopoly permits him to extract from the industrial capitalist, the farmer. . . . *Landed property thus receives its purely economic form*. . . . The *rationalisation of agriculture, which enabled this to be pursued for the first time on a social scale*, and the *reduction of landed property to an absurdity*—these are the *great services of the capitalist mode of production*». (Marx 1981, pp. 754–755; my emphasis).

2 Marx (1894) describes how large landed property «produces conditions that provoke an *irreparable rift* in the interdependent process of social metabolism, a *metabolism prescribed by the natural lows of life itself*. The result of this is a squandering of the vitality of the soil, which is carried by trade far beyond the bounds of a single country». (Marx 1981, p. 949; my emphasis.) *See* also footnote 5 of ► Chap. 5.

landowners, who privately own the land, enter a leasing contract with the tenant farmers who are the agricultural capitalists and receive ground-rent from the tenant farmers in return for the use of the land over a certain period of time. The farmers themselves hire agricultural workers and engage in capitalist agriculture on the land.

20.1.2 Capitalist Ground-rent

Ground-rent Is Demanded as Repayment for Land Use

In commodity production society, landowners possess the *right of private ownership* vis-à-vis the land,[3] meaning they have been *socially recognised* as having the right to exclusively hold, use, and dispose of the land. When these landowners allow another person to hold or use the land for a period of time, repayment, called **ground-rent**, is demanded for its economic utilisation.

Tenant Farmers Must Pay a Capitalist Ground-rent

Capitalist tenant farmers who carry out capitalist production in the agricultural sphere are compelled to temporarily lease the land from landowners because they do not possess the land that is the indispensable means of production for agricultural products. The money form paid for this is **capitalist ground-rent** within agriculture.

Two Fundamental Forms of Capitalist Ground-rent: Differential Rent and Absolute Rent

If we look at the ground-rent paid by tenant farmers to landowners, we can notice that it has *two fundamental forms*. First of all, higher rent is paid for land with better fertility, location, and other conditions than for land with worse conditions, so we can see that there is rent of differing magnitudes depending on the differences in land conditions. Economists refer to this form of rent as **differential rent**. However, no matter how bad the conditions of a plot of land may be, the landowner will not lease it for free. The rent that is paid even in the case of the **worst land** is called **absolute rent**. Of course, both types of rent are paid in the form of money, with the tenant farmer handing over to the landowner a sum of value in the form of money.

---

3 Regardless of the historical form of society, the surface of earth provides human beings with the place for living and producing, as well as their means of livelihood and of production, constituting their natural base and ready-made depot. This surface of the earth is also called «land». But when we say, «my land», «the land of landowner», «state land», etc., this is understood as signifying the artificial demarcation of a piece of the earth, so that it is of a certain size and is occupied, possessed, owned, or monopolised by an individual, group, or social organisation. In this book, I use the word in both senses, but the distinction can be easily grasped from the given context.

Explaining the Fundamental Forms of Ground-rent on the Basis of the Law of Value and Law of Surplus-value

What is at issue for political economists is the question: From where, exactly, is *the sum of value* derived that tenant farmers pay landowners as either differential or absolute rent?

In the «common image of the «circular flow» of the economy», presented in the introductory chapter (*see* ◘ Fig. 2.1), land is conceived—along with capital and labour—as a production element that itself generates «value added» within production. This supposed value added by land is thought of as an enterprise's payment to a landowner for the «commodity» that is the land's service. In other words, land itself is thought of as generating value, which becomes rent.

However, it is clear from our study up to this point that value is the materialisation of abstract labour, so land itself cannot possibly generate value. Where exactly, then, does the sum of value that becomes ground-rent come from? How is it generated? Where is the materialised labour in this case?

In order to clarify these points, we must *base ourselves on the law of value and the law of surplus-value developed up to now, so as to explain the issue in terms of the penetration of these laws.*

When attempting to methodically deal with ground-rent, the usual approach is to first elucidate differential rent and then proceed to discuss absolute rent. But here, to make things easier to understand, we will look at rent from the reverse order.

20.2 Absolute Rent

Tenant Farmer Must Also Pay Ground-rent for the Worst Land

Even in the case of the worst land, provided it has an owner, the capitalist tenant farmer must pay the landowner ground-rent in order to be able to use the land for capitalist agriculture. This ground-rent is **absolute rent**.

But the Tenant Farmer Must Also Secure Average Profit

Because the tenant farmer is a capitalist, if there is a sphere of production that brings a higher rate of profit, he would shift his capital from the agricultural sphere to that sphere. Therefore, the tenant farmer only pays absolute rent to a landowner to engage in farming on the worst land if it is possible to secure an average rate even after paying that rent.

Prices of Agricultural Products Must Be at a Level That Brings Average Profit plus Absolute Rent

The fact that the tenant farmer is able to more or less obtain an average profit even after paying absolute rent is because the market price of the agriculture product he produces and sells fluctuates around the level of «cost price + average profit + absolute rent». Since «cost price + average profit» is the production price, the level of market price exceeds production price by an amount equivalent to the absolute rent. The fact that the prices of agricultural products are more or less at this level means that the *supply of and demand for these products fluctuates around a proportion that brings about this price.*

Market Price Is Higher than Production Price Because Capital Cannot Freely Flow In

As we have seen, however, production spheres have different rates of profit, and if the movement of capital is not restricted, the free movement of capital will cause market prices to become equal to «cost price + average profit», i.e. the establishment of a supply/demand relation under which the market price fluctuates around production price, thus equalising the rate of profit. Thus, the price level for agricultural products is one at which absolute rent can still be paid in the case of the worst land. This suggests, therefore, that *capital is not able to flow freely into the agricultural sphere.* In other words, capital does not flow into the agricultural sphere in pursuit of a higher than average rate of profit, even though market prices in the agriculture sphere are above production prices by an amount equivalent to absolute rent.

Limitation by Landed Property Forms a Barrier to the Influx of Capital

Capital does not flow into the agricultural sphere freely because capitalist tenant farmers cannot utilise land without paying landowners absolute rent, so even if the rate of profit in this sphere exceeds the average rate of profit, a capitalist who pays absolute rent is unable to obtain a higher than average profit. In short, the existence of *landed property* (personified by landowners) *restricts the free utilisation of land, thereby restricting the influx of capital.*

This **limitation by landed property** forms a **barrier** *that prevents the movement of capital from industrial spheres into the agricultural sphere,* thus hindering an increase of supply of capital that would lower the level of market prices to the production price. One could express this by saying that the limitation of landed property keeps the price of agricultural products high, at the level of «production price + absolute rent».

What Is the Source of the Value that Becomes Absolute Rent

But what is the source of the difference between the price level of agricultural products and their production price? Where is the value that becomes absolute rent actually produced?

Agricultural Product Sold at Its Value Generates a Surplus Profit

Of all production spheres, the organic composition of capital is lowest in the agricultural sphere. This is an area of production that is «labour intensive». This is due not only to the great restrictions arising from natural conditions but also the difficulty for capital to flow in from other spheres, which hinders the rapid accumulation of capital and its accompanying rapid rise in the productive power of labour. Generally, the productive power of labour lags behind the level in the industrial sphere and therefore the organic composition of capital in

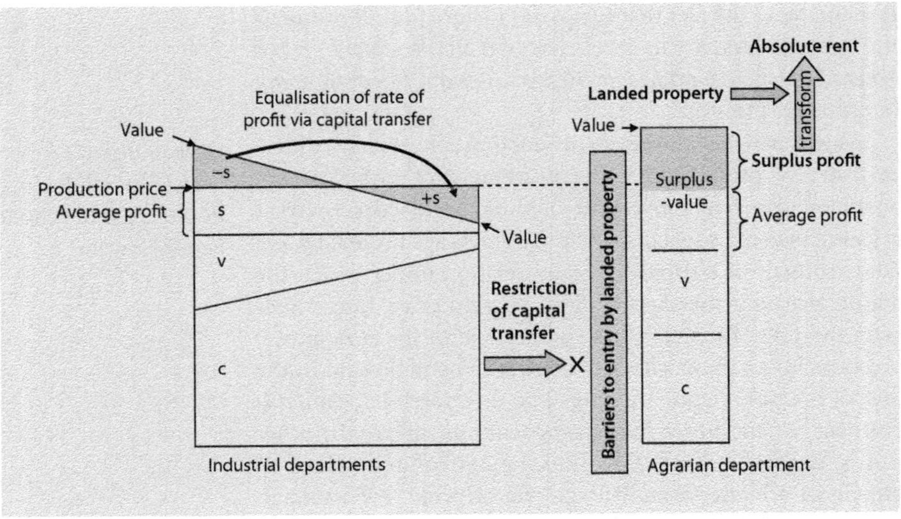

Fig. 20.1 Surplus profit arising from the limitation of landed property is transformed into absolute rent

the agricultural sphere are also lower. As we saw in ▶ Sect. 16.2 («Average Rate of Profit and Production Price»), the rate of profit will be higher in such spheres with a lower composition, if the rate of surplus-value is the same as in the spheres of a higher capital composition, so that *products sold at their value* will yield a higher than average profit. If products in such spheres are sold at their value, capital is able to obtain the difference between value and production price, as a **surplus profit.**[4] The agricultural sphere is precisely such a sphere.

Surplus Profit Due to the Limitation of Landed Property Is Transformed into Absolute Rent

This surplus profit, which is the *difference between the value and production price of an agricultural product*—and therefore a part of value that is nothing more than the *surplus-value produced in the agricultural sphere*—becomes absolute rent. The surplus-labour of the workers in the agricultural sphere is the **substance of absolute rent.** This is the pivot of the understanding of absolute rent. In the case of *absolute rent*, because the free flow of capital into the agricultural sphere is hindered by the barrier of landed property, one part of the surplus-value obtained in this sphere becomes surplus profit that is transformed into rent because of landed property. In ■ Fig. 20.1, the industrial sphere on the left is the same

4 This surplus profit is referred to as the **second form of surplus profit** to distinguish it from the *surplus profit that arises from differences in the productive power of capital within a sphere.*

as ◘ Fig. 16.5. Because the barrier of landed property prevents an equalisation of the rate of profit, surplus profits arise in the agricultural sphere, which is turned into absolute rent (*see* ◘ Fig. 20.1).

Absolute rent does not always completely absorb this surplus profit, however. The magnitude of rent will depend on the *power relation between the landowner and the tenant farmers prepared to enter the agricultural sphere* and on the related fluctuations of supply and demand for *agricultural products.*

Monopoly Rent Can Arise from Abnormal Demand for Agricultural Products

Furthermore, it is possible for the market price of agricultural products to rise above their value due to the demand determined *solely by the desire of the buyer and the capacity to pay*[5] in relation to some accidental, external factor. In this case, the tenant farmer, even after paying the entirety of the difference between value and production price to the landowner as absolute rent, is still able to obtain a surplus profit above this amount. If the landowner can be paid all or part of this surplus profit by the tenant farmer, as rent, the value that makes up this rent would differ from absolute rent in terms of being value produced in another department that was obtained through a monopoly situation, rather than being surplus-value produced in the agricultural sphere. For this reason, such rent is called **monopoly rent.**

20.3 Differential Rent

All but the Worst Land Generates Differential Rent

Now let us turn our attention to differential rent, whose magnitude differs depending on the land conditions. **Differential rent** is a ground-rent paid by tenant farmers to landowners for the use of all but the worst land.

As noted in the previous section, the market price of an agricultural product fluctuates around value, not production price, because of the limitation of landed property in the agricultural sphere. *Here we can thus think in terms of the market price of the agricultural product being fundamentally determined by its value.* We will also assume that all tenant farmers, regardless of the quality of their land, pay landowners surplus profit, which is the difference between value and production price, in the form of absolute rent.

5 Marx (1894) writes: «Rent can derive only from a *genuine monopoly price*, which is determined neither by the price of production of the commodities nor by their value, but rather by the *demand of the purchasers and their ability to pay*» (Marx 1981, p. 898; my emphasis).

In the Agricultural Sphere Competition Also Establishes Market Value from Out of the Individual Values

The magnitude of differential rent differs depending on the differences in land conditions. But even in the agricultural sphere, independent of those differences in land conditions, there are various individual values of agricultural products that arise from differences in production conditions that are created or adopted by capital.

Even if the land conditions are identical, and the same amount of capital is advanced for the same size of land, there will inevitably arise differences in the quantity of a harvest produced depending on the skill level of the agricultural techniques applied, mechanisation, and the level of the organisation for workers (e.g., co-operation or the division of labour), as well as the operational scale. Thus, the individual value of a product unit will be lower for capital with better production conditions and higher in the case of capital with worse production conditions. The differences in these production conditions pertain to individual capital itself, but *any capital can employ the better conditions—and competition does in fact compel every capital to adopt more advanced production conditions*. Such conditions are referred to as **capital conditions**.

The competition between the capitals within a sphere over production conditions leads to the establishment of a market value that is the weighted average of the various individual values. The outcome of this is that a surplus profit or a lost value is generated among capitalists who produce a commodity whose individual value differs from the market value, with that surplus profit or loss borne by the particular capital involved (*see* ◘ Fig. 20.2). In the industrial sphere, depicted on the left of diagram, the capital conditions differ, and through the products of each capital within a sphere being sold at their value, surplus profit is generated on one side and a loss of value on the other.[6]

In the agricultural sphere as well, the capital conditions vary among individual capitalists, and the market value of an agricultural product is established as the average of the various individual values. But since this is exactly the same situa-

6 Strictly speaking, the «individual value», «market value», and «surplus-value» of the industrial spheres in ◘ Fig. 20.2 should be, respectively, «individual production price», «market production price», and «average profit». Here I have avoided adding those new terms («individual production price» and «market production price»), however, because the relation between individual production price and market production price is theoretically identical to the relation between individual value and market value.

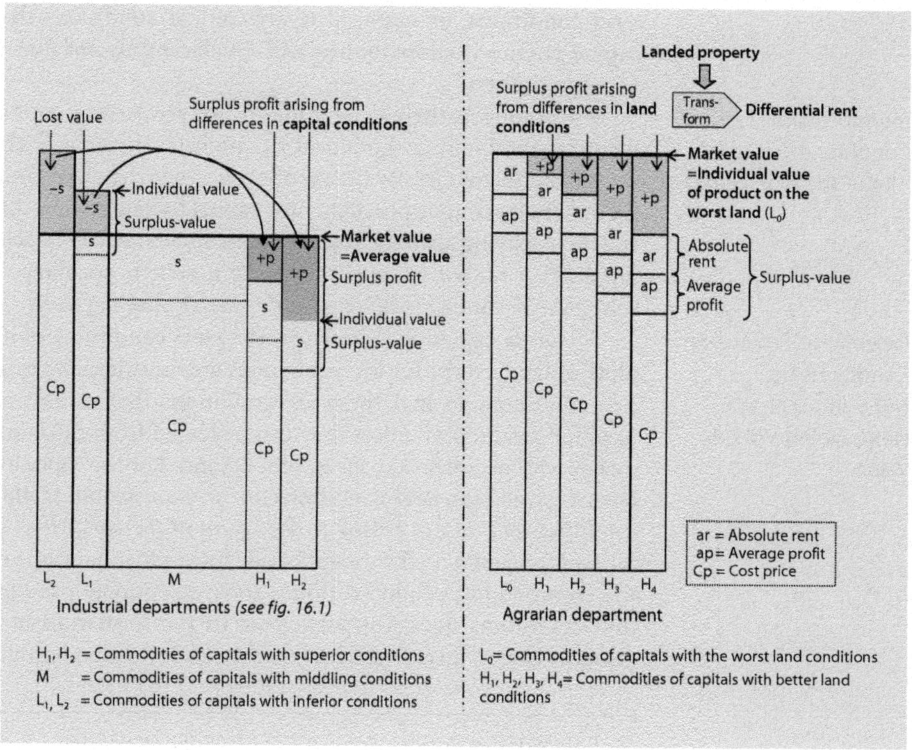

Fig. 20.2 Transformation of surplus profit arising from differences of land conditions into differential rent

tion as in the industrial sphere, we can *set aside the differences in individual values that arise from varying capital conditions* and assume that such differences do not exist.

Farming Is Inevitably Accompanied by Different Land Conditions

However, in the agricultural sphere, even if we set aside the capital conditions, another extremely important difference in production conditions exists.

For capital engaged in farming, even though land is an indispensable means of production, each plot of land has its own *particular natural fertility and proper geographical location*, and it is not possible to artificially create land of the same fertility or forcefully change the location. These production conditions based on the situation particular to land, especially *fertility* and *geographical location*, cannot be created anew by individual capital. At the same time, because of this fact, *individual capitals are able to monopolise the use of these production conditions*. Such production conditions are referred to as

20

land conditions, as opposed to the capital conditions that capital can newly adopt for use, and which are thus not able to be monopolised.[7]

Monopolisable Land Conditions Belong to All but the Worst Land

But as long as there is land that is not yet used by capital whose natural and geographical situation is the same as the worst land that is already in use, or even worse than that land, then there is always a possibility for capital to newly enter this sphere by paying absolute rent. Thus, *monopolisable land conditions that cannot be newly created are*, strictly speaking, *a condition pertaining to all land that is better than the worst.*

Exceptional Production Conditions Do Not Contribute to Determining Market Value

As far as capital is concerned, the land conditions of all plots of land except for the worst ones are an externally posited condition, so that these are conditions that cannot be used for production unless they can be leased from the landowner who possesses the given plot of land. For the capitalist tenant farmer, the land conditions *are an external production condition that do not belong to the realm of the conditions of mutual competition*. The exceptionally low individual value of the commodities produced under such exceptional production conditions does not participate in the formation of a market value in this sphere, and neither the level of individual

7 It should be noted that under certain circumstances capital conditions can change into land conditions. During the stipulated lease period of land, the capitalist farmer invests his constant capital in the means of production in various ways: both transiently, as is the case of chemical improvements, use of fertiliser, etc. and more permanently, as with drainage ditches, the use of irrigation, levelling of land, construction of farm buildings, etc. When these means of production are effectual over a longer period, which is to say, more permanent, the capital is in fact fixed capital that incorporated into each, which Marx (1894) referred to as «earth-capital» (Marx 1981, p. 756). But as soon as the lease stipulated in the contract has expired, the improvements made to the land fall to the landowner as his property, treated as an inseparable attribute of the object, the land. Here the *capital conditions for the capitalist farmer convert into the land conditions for the landowner.* This is one of the secrets of the increasing enrichment of landowners, the constant increase of their rents and the growing money value of their estates as economic development progresses. Thus, they are able to pocket the result of a social development achieved without their participation. And this is one of the reasons why landowners seek, as capitalist production develops, to shorten the terms of a lease to a minimum. But this is also *one of the greatest obstacles to a rational agriculture*, since the farmer avoids all improvements and outlays which are not expected to give their full return during the duration of his lease. Here is «one of the forms expressing the *contradiction between the private ownership of land and a rational agriculture, the normal social use of the land*». (Marx 1894: Marx 1981, p. 948; my emphasis).

value nor the quantity of commodities exerts any influence on that market value.

Market Value Is Determined by the Individual Value of Commodities Produced on the Worst Land

What sort of commodity, then, has its individual value participate in establishing and determining the level of market value? This is the individual value of *commodities produced under production conditions that are neither monopolisable nor exceptional.* Since our assumption here is that no differences in capital conditions exist, this would only be *commodities produced on the worst* of the land utilised. In short, here the *market value is fundamentally determined by the individual value of the commodities produced on the worst land*, which is to say, the market value around which the market prices of agricultural products fluctuate is equal to the individual value of the commodities of the worst land. Thus, even if the worst land only accounts for 1% of the total products in the sphere, the individual value of the commodities produced on this worst land will determine the market value. There could thus arise a case where the individual values of the other 99% of the products are below this market value. What is depicted on the right of ◘ Fig. 20.2, with regard to the agricultural sphere, are the various individual values of agricultural products produced by capitals using land of differing conditions (other than the worst land), having set aside the variation in individual values arising from differences in capital conditions, and also the market value determined by the individual values of the products of the worst land. And, as we saw in ▸ Chap.16, when the individual value is below the market value, a surplus profit is generated. In the example just given, if all the commodities in this sphere are sold at their market value, all but the worst land will generate surplus profit for capital.

Surplus Profit Generated from Differences of Land Conditions Becomes Differential Rent

However, the private ownership of land is socially recognised in capitalist society, and for each plot of land there exists a **landowner** as the **personification of landed property**. Capital is not permitted to use land without handing over to landed property (the landowner) the surplus profit that arises from the land conditions adhering to the land that is owned. The Landowner requires the tenant farmers to hand over this surplus profit because the profit is the fruit of his land. Meanwhile, because average profit can be obtained even if the entire surplus profit is handed over, there will always be capitals that seek to use the land despite the need to forfeit the surplus profit. In this way, the surplus profit is transformed into ground-rent belonging to landed property—or **differential rent**, to be exact (*see* agricultural sphere on the right of ◘ Fig. 20.2).

Surplus Profit Generated as the Outcome of the Penetration of the Law of Market Value

This surplus profit is not based on the differences in the capital conditions, but rather arises from differences in land conditions, so at first glance it would seem that what generates this is the better land, which is to say, nature itself. However, this surplus profit is also brought about in this production sphere as the outcome of the penetration of the **law of market value**, whereby the *same market value for a unit of any commodity—and therefore the same market price—is necessarily established through competition within a given sphere*. Clearly, then, this *surplus profit is a completely social attribute*, not something that emerges from the land itself.

If Market Value Is Average Value, Surplus Profit Is the Surplus-value Within a Sphere

We saw in ► Chap. 16 that in the industrial sphere, where competition is carried out over capital conditions, the surplus profit obtained within a sphere by capitals with advantageous production conditions comes from transferred surplus-value produced by capitals with disadvantageous conditions, so that the substance of the value that becomes surplus profit is the surplus-value produced within a sphere. In other words, as can be seen on the left side of ◘ Fig. 20.2, the «plus» of surplus profit and the «minus» of lost value offset each other within the same sphere.

If the market values in the agricultural sphere were determined (as in the case of those capital conditions) by the average value obtained as the weighted average between the various individual values of the better or worse land, then the surplus profit obtained by the capital producing on better land would stem from the transferred surplus-value produced by the capital on the worse land and would correspond to the latter's lost value, so that the substance of value that becomes surplus profit would be the surplus-value produced within the agricultural sphere.

Value That Becomes Differential Rent Produced by Labour in Other Sectors

However, surplus profits based upon differences in land conditions in the agricultural sphere are obtained by all capitals apart from those that produce on the worst land, so this is not offset in the agricultural sphere. There is, in other words, no «minus» (lost value) vis-à-vis the «plus» of surplus profit within this sphere. So if agricultural products are sold at their *market value* to other production spheres, the agricultural sphere will receive from those spheres a sum of value equivalent to the surplus profit of the capital that produces on the better lands. This means that the *surplus profit transformed into differential rent* is *transferred value from other spheres* by means of agricultural products being sold at their market value. ◘ Figure 20.2 shows that there is no «minus» vis- à-vis the «plus» of surplus profit generated from differences in land conditions.[8]

The agricultural sphere, by selling agricultural products to other production spheres, is able to receive a greater sum of value, which is surplus profit received from other spheres purchasing these products. So the sum of value received from the other spheres stems from «society, considered as a consumer, paying too much for agricultural products», with the result becoming a «plus for the landowners». In other words, *the private ownership of the land, which is an external force vis-à-vis the movement of capital, appropriates this amount of value from society to make it the revenue of the landowners, who are the personification of landed property.*[9]

First and Second Form of Differential Rent

The sort of differential rent that arises from the parallel advance of equal capitals in various plots of land with different conditions for fertility and location is called the **first form of differential rent.**

This form is distinguished from the case where additional capital is successionally advanced into the same plot of land, so that the market price rises because the productivity of this advance is lower than the productivity until now, resulting in the emergence of a surplus profit, which is also demanded by the landowner and handed over as differential rent. Such differential rent is called the **second form of differential rent.** In this case as well, surplus profit is based on a difference in land conditions, so it is fundamentally a modification of the first form.

---

8 Marx (1894) writes: «This is *determination by a market value brought about through competition* on the basis of the capitalist mode of production; this determination produces a *false social value*. This results from the *law of market value* to which agricultural products are subjected. The *determination is based on the exchange-value of the product and not on the soil and the differences in its fertility*». (Marx 1981, p. 799; my emphasis). The expression «false social value» here means a value without the substance of value, i.e. without materialised abstract labour and in this sense a feigned value.

9 Marx (1894) writes: «The *identity of the market price for commodities of the same kind* is the manner in which the social character of value is realised on the basis of the capitalist mode of production and in general of production depending on commodity exchange between individuals. *What society (considered as a consumer) pays too much for agricultural products, what is a minus for the realisation of its labour-time in agricultural products, is now a plus for one portion of society, for the landowners*». (Marx 1981, p. 800; my emphasis).

20

20.4 Capital and Landed Property

Landed Property Is External Force to Capital

As we have already noted, landed property is *an external force to capital* and is *completely unnecessary to the movement of capital itself.* Despite this, when capitalist production emerges, capital is unable to abolish the private landed property it confronts, only being able rather to subordinate this property to itself by transforming it from a precapitalist to a «modern» form.

Capitalist Production Cannot Abolish Private Land Property

Why, then, was capital unable to abolish landed property? The reason is, first of all, that capital production is a developed commodity production. Under commodity production, the property laws of commodity production penetrate the sphere of commodity exchange, with the private property of commodity and money owners socially recognised and established as a legal right. This society, *expressed in legal terms, exists on the basis of the recognition of private property and of its title to property rights.* Such a society could not abolish private property only for land. What could be done was only to establish property and property rights that conform to the property laws of capitalist production. And it is precisely such **modern landed property** that was established.

Secondarily, as we saw in ► Sect. 11.1 in Part I («Primitive Accumulation and Its Methods»), the capitalist mode of production was established through the separation of labouring individuals from the land that was their fundamental means of production. Therefore, the «*private ownership of land,* and thus the expropriation from the land of the direct producers—private ownership for some, involving non-ownership of the land for others—*is the basis of the capitalist mode of production*». (Marx 1894: Marx 1981, p. 948; my emphasis).

As long as this is the case, in the course of the development of capitalism, capital is unable to cast aside landed property, even though it perceives it as a nuisance.

National Ownership of Land Is Still a Form of Private Property

At the same time, however, under capitalist production there are various forms of private land ownership. The direct conception people generally have when they hear the term «landed property» is the form in which individuals, as living personalities, become landowners. But in modern society, *juridical persons* such as joint-stock companies, which are not living individuals, become landowners. Everyone recognises that the property of such juridical persons is also a form of private property. Furthermore, there is property owned by *local governments* and by *the state*, i.e. **national landed property**. Everyone also knows that in every advanced capitalist nation a vast area of land is nationally owned. This property owned by the state is not only *private property vis-à-vis other states* but also *vis-à-vis the individuals who are cut off from this land.* These individuals include not only labouring individuals but also capitalists (the personification of capital). In a case where a capitalist leases land from the state to carry out some operation upon it, paying rent in return, the relation between the state and capitalist is a relation between two private owners.

National Landed Property Is the Ideal Form for Capital

There is certainly nothing particularly strange, therefore, for the «*overall nationalisation of the land*» to be proposed within capitalist society as a policy to alleviate the burden placed on capital by landed property. Indeed, the *ultimate form of private landed property within capitalist society* is national landed property. For the capitalist class, national landed property is the best possible form of landed property. Nationalising land takes differential rent out of the hands of the landowner class and places it at the disposal of the capitalist state, while also abolishing absolute rent, thus making possible the overall development of the capital/wage-labour relation within the agricultural sphere.

The Capitalist Class on its Own Cannot Fully Nationalise the Land

However, when living individuals and private juridical persons dominate landed property, it is quite impossible for the state that represents the interests of the capitalist class to carry out the overall nationalisation of the land. Such an attempt *would touch on the very essence of the legal superstructure of private property that corresponds to capitalist production*, going so far as to even call into question *the very legitimacy of capital property itself.*

Landed Property Under State Capitalism Is Also a Form of Private Property

It can be seen from various historical experiences, however, that general national landed property has existed under capitalism and that there are still countries today where this form of ownership exists. In the states referred to as «actually existing socialism», land in many cases has been fundamentally state owned (although given various juridical names, such as the «ownership of the people», etc.), and this remains the case in a number countries today. The economic structure in countries claiming to be «socialist» is essentially a system of capitalism that can be referred to as **state capitalism**, where economically speaking the state landed property was private property, vis-à-vis both the labouring individuals and the various forms of capital moving within the system (*see* ► Sect. 11.2.2). Also, in the case of many developing countries, the nationalisation of the land was declared along with agrarian reform, but it is perfectly clear today that this was not social property in opposition to private property.

Requirement for the Overall Nationalisation of the Land Calls into Question the Legitimacy of Private Property

Land nationalisation is thus a reform within the framework of capitalist production, but when the working class is advancing toward overcoming capitalist production, raising this demand and struggling for it can have great significance. This struggle—by clarifying the *penetration of the property laws of commodity production* and the *penetration of the laws of capitalist appropriation* as their outcome—calls into question **the legitimacy of private property itself.**[10] Moreover, the nationalisation of the land clarifies that this step is not yet the sublation of the framework of private property as long as it does not proceed beyond that point.

20.5 Land Price

Land Without Value Is Also Bought and Sold

Land is not the product of labour and therefore has no intrinsic value, and yet land on which no human being has laid a finger may be sold at a high price. What is it that determines price in this case?

Is Land Price Solely Determined by Supply and Demand?

Needless to say, in developed capitalist society, every sort of thing becomes a commodity, and there are any number of commodities whose price has no basis apart from accidental circumstances and bears no relation to economic laws. These are cases where «price is determined by the demand among purchasers and their ability to pay», examples of which include a costume worn by *Michael Jackson* or the «price» of a

10 Marx (1894) denounces the title of private property to the earth as follows: «This surplus profit . . . is transformed into rent and accrues in this form to the landowner *by virtue of his title* to the portion of the earth endowed with these special properties. . . . *it is only the title a number of people have to property in the earth that enables them to appropriate a part of society's surplus labour as tribute, and in an ever growing measure as production develops. . . .* It was *entirely created by the relations of production. Once these have reached the point where they have to be sloughed off, then the material source, the economically and historically justified source of the title that arises from the process of life's social production, disappears, and with it all transactions based on it. From the standpoint of a higher socio-economic formation* [i.e. society of associated labouring individuals], *the private property of particular individuals in the earth will appear just as absurd as the private property of one man in other men. Even an entire society, a nation, or all simultaneously existing societies taken together, are not the owners of the earth. They are simply its possessors, its beneficiaries, and have to bequeath it in an improved state to succeeding generations, as boni patres familias*». (Marx 1981, pp. 910–911; my emphasis and brackets).

vote in an election. Is land likewise determined solely by supply and demand? In fact, that is not the case.

Land Price Is a Fictitious Price Formed Through Capitalisation of Ground-rent Based on the Interest Rate

No matter how much share prices on the stock market may diverge from prices in actual markets, it is generally recognised that the «appropriate price» of each share is the capitalisation of the dividend it generates, calculated according to the interest rate at the particular time, and its magnitude should reflect the profit of the joint-stock company that issues the share (*see* ▶ Sect. 19.2.7.2). Likewise in the case of land, leasing land on a temporary basis generates a certain amount of ground-rent for the landowner, and to the extent that this economic law prevails under capitalism, when land is bought and sold, the magnitude of ground-rent will necessarily determine the land price. As the previous chapter noted, a source that generates a certain regular revenue is seen as interest-bearing capital and capitalised to establish a fictitious price. **Ground-rent**, as well, because it is a revenue for the landowner, is **capitalised** *based on the given rate of interest*, and the result is *seen as the* **price of land**. So land price is one sort of fictitious price. The buying and selling of land is carried out while considering the degree that the actual price diverges from this «capitalised ground-rent». In a case where the market price noticeably diverges from this «theoretical price» because of particularly strong demand compared to supply, even if the need is felt to clarify the circumstances or cause that brings about this divergence, this certainly does not negate the existence of the «theoretical price» itself.

Tendency for Land Price to Rise with the Development of Capitalist Production

In ▶ Chap. 17 («Law of the Tendential Fall in the Rate of Profit») we saw that capitalist production encompasses a tendency for the rate of profit to fall. We then saw in ▶ Sect. 19.1.2 («Division of Profit and Interest Rate») that because the limit for the rate of interest is set by the rate of profit, this limit will fall along with a fall in the rate of profit and that therefore a fall in the level of the rate of interest necessarily arises. If the rate of interest falls, the fictitious prices of the various sources of income, which are established through capitalisation according to the rate of interest, will in turn rise. The same is true of land price, which is a fictitious price capitalised on the basis of the rate of interest. This means that the development of capitalism necessarily encompasses a trend towards a fall in the rate of interest and a tendency for land price to rise. Moreover, with the development of capitalist production, the actual fee paid by the leaser to the landowner comes to contain various elements in addition to the ground-rent in the original sense that we just examined (although we cannot address the topic of those elements here), so that land price is a fictitious price that is the capitalisation of the total sum of the fees from all the elements involved and thus has a tendency to rise further. What all this means is that the portion of social wealth appropriated by landowners—those individuals with no relation whatsoever to production, whose possession of one part of the surface of the earth is socially approved—expands with the development of capitalist production, so that the «value» of the partitions of the surface of land that they own also rises.

20.6 Land Fetish

Notion Established that Land Is Acquired Through One's Own Labour

Private property of the land is a situation where it is possible, given social recognition, *to exclusively use and dispose one part of the artificially partitioned surface of the earth,* and *the* **personification of this private landed property** is the **landowner**. In capitalist society, as a society of developed commodity production, the property laws of commodity production penetrate the market. This means that the transactions between the commodity owner and money owner are based on the mutual recognition that what they bring to market was obtained through their own labour. In such a society, the notion is also established that owned land has been «obtained through one's own labour» by some means, such as a purchase using money acquired through one's own labour. Moreover, as noted in ▶ Sect. 20.5, this notion reaches its completion in land having a price and being bought and sold. This is because the landowner who buys land at its price is able to feel assured that it was acquired through his «own money» and was thus the «result of his own labour».

Notion Established That Land Is a «Tree» That Bears «Fruit» for the Landowner

The landowner can obtain ground-rent only by entrusting the land that belongs to himself to a capitalist for a certain period of time. For the landowner, his land is *a fruit tree that bears the fruit of ground-rent.* The notion is thus established that it is «natural for land legitimately acquired through one's own labour to generate ground-rent and that it should indeed bear ground-rent in reality».

Notion Established That Ground-rent Is a Production Cost That Enters Cost Price

The land that is temporarily leased by a capitalist is one of his indispensable production conditions, but the ground-rent he pays to lease it (as we have seen) does not constitute any production cost for him. However, based on the superficial fact that *ground-rent is paid to use land for a period of time,* the capitalist necessarily thinks that ground-rent is a payment for *the price of land use itself over a certain period of time,* so that it constitutes one part of the *production cost,* or more concretely, one part of the *cost price*. And because this temporary use of land is related to the product as a condition of production, the notion arises that the cost price recovered through the product's sales price also contains a price corresponding to ground-rent.

Completion of the Trinity Formula Through «Land–Ground-rent»

Economists have incorporated, as is, the idea of those involved in market transactions that land, as a production factor, is a source of revenue that generates the fruit of ground-rent. This element of *«land–ground-rent»*, along with «labour–wages» and «capital–interest», which we already examined, completes the *trinity formula*.

Land Fetish Enthrals Those Involved in Production

Within the world of such upside-down notions, the money fetish and capital fetish are joined by the land fetish—even though land is nothing but a partition of the surface of the earth. One concrete manifestation of the land fetish took place in the late 1980s in Japan, when everyone from giant banks to individual «salarymen» was caught up in the mania of this delusional belief.

Reference

Marx K (1894) Das Kapital. Kritik der politischen Ökonomie. Bd. 3. Buch 3: Der Gesammtprocess der kapitalistischen Produktion. Hrsg. von F. Engels. Hamburg. English edition: Marx K (1981) Capital. A Critique of Political Economy. Vol. 3 (trans: Fernbach D). Penguin Books

Revenue Forms and Classes

T. Otani, *A Guide to Marxian Political Economy*,
https://doi.org/10.1007/978-3-319-65954-1_21

21.1 Revenue and Its Sources

Revenue

The word **revenue** has the meaning of *value that can be obtained repeatedly from a certain source and consumed without ruining the source*, as well as *the products that are measured by its magnitude*.

Ultimate Source of the Total Revenue of Capitalist Society Is Workers' Living Labour

Our study thus far has clarified the *fundamental forms of revenues under the capitalist mode of production*, which are **wages** of *wage workers*, **profit of enterprise** of *functioning capitalists* (industrial and commercial capitalists), **interest** of *moneyed capitalists*, and **ground-rent** of *land owners*.

We have also become well aware of the true source of each type of revenue.

The most important point is that they all stem from *part of the value created by the new living labour of workers*. Apart from this, there is no source from which revenue can arise.

Wages → Wageworker

Wage workers, who are the creators of the new value that is the source of all revenue, only receive from out of this new value, as repayment for their labour-power commodity, the objectified required labour, which is equivalent to the value of the variable capital advanced by the capitalist. This is the capitalist form of the labour fund that must be consumed by labouring individuals in any form of society. Wage workers receive the objectification of their own required labour from the capitalist, and this becomes their revenue.

Profit of Enterprise → Functioning Capitalist

The functioning capitalists (industrial and commercial capitalists) advance the money they possess as capital in the production or circulation processes and thereby obtain average profit. This average profit is the share distributed to each functioning capitalist from out of the total profit of industrial capitalists, in accordance with the given quantity of capital. The profit of industrial capitalists is originally surplus-value, which is to say, it is the objectification of the surplus-labour of workers that is obtained in the production process by industrial capitalists. However, functioning capitalists do not consume all of the average profit obtained as revenue. First, in a case where a capitalist has borrowed all or part of his capital from a moneyed capitalist, interest must be paid to this moneyed capitalist. Second, when the capitalist leases land from a landowner as one of the conditions for production, the landowner must be paid ground-rent. What remains after deducting these two items is the profit of enterprise of a functioning capitalist (industrial profit and commercial profit). Third, one part of the profit of enterprise is turned into an accumulation fund for the sake of capital accumulation (and one part of this accumulation fund is transformed back into

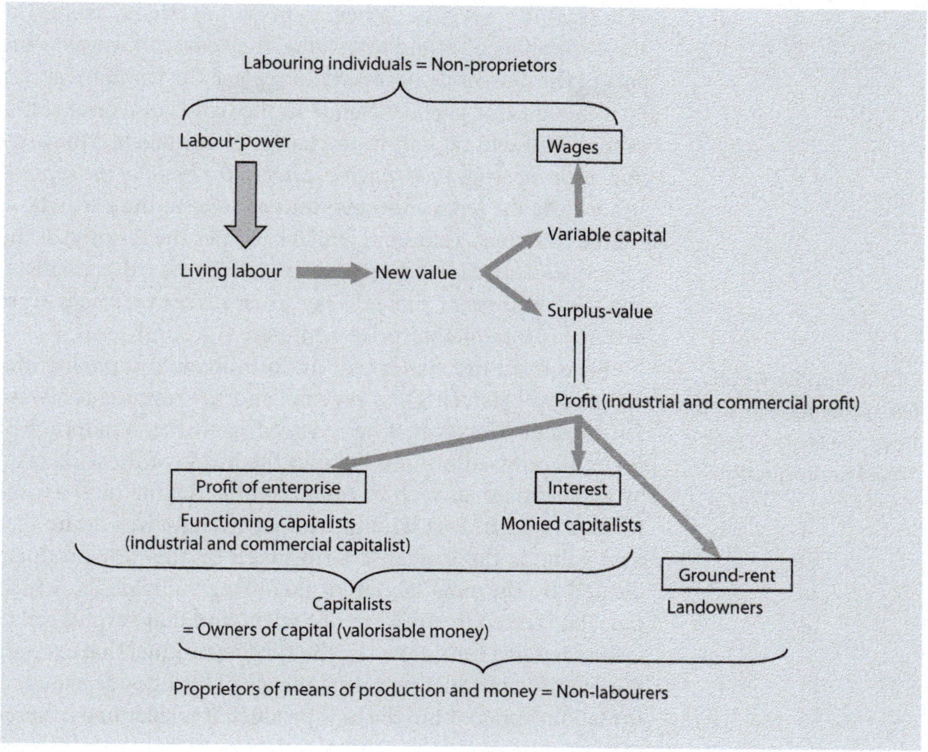

Fig. 21.1 Forms of revenue in the capitalist mode of production and their true sources

the labour fund). The remaining value finally forms the capitalist's consumption fund, i.e. the revenue that he can personally consume.

Interest → Moneyed Capitalist

Moneyed capitalists, who possess valorisable money, receive one part of the functioning capitalists' average profit in the form of interest by means of lending money to them as capital.

Ground-rent → Landowner

Landowners, whose property title to a portion of the earth is socially recognised, are able to obtain part of the average profit of functioning capitalists, in the form of ground-rent, by leasing their land to them. This becomes the revenue of landowners (*see* Fig. 21.1).

Total Revenue Is Divided into Wages and Net Revenue

Out of the total value contained in the products of capital (i.e. total product-value), it is only the *new value*—the *objectification of the new living labour of wage workers*—that is the source of all these types of revenue. The new value part that becomes wages, profit of enterprise, interest, and ground-rent—or the products that contain this value—is referred to as «**gross revenue**». There is, however, an *essential distinction* between the wages of wage workers and the other revenues.

Whereas the revenue other than wages stems from the surplus-value out of the new value, the source of wages is the part of the new value necessary to replace the variable capital. So although this part is revenue in the hands of workers, it is capital (variable capital) in the hands of capitalists. Thus, *setting aside the wage part that is capital in the hand of the capitalists*, we use the term «**net revenue**» to refer to the part whose source is surplus-value and which becomes the revenue of the capitalists (functioning capitalists and moneyed capitalists) and the landowners, that is to say: gross revenue = wages + net revenue (profit of enterprise + interest + ground-rent).

Distinction Between Gross Revenue and Net Revenue Is also Clear in Social Reproduction

Seen from the standpoint of an individual capitalist, the distinction between gross revenue and net revenue is always self-evident. However, when viewed from the standpoint of society, confused notions arise in the heads of those dazzled by appearances, as seen in Adam Smith's dogma of $v + s$ (*see* ► Sect. 14.3.3 in Part II). But we have become well aware that new value is the capitalist form taken by the new products created by the new labour of labouring individuals, which must be created in any form of society, and that surplus-value is the capitalist form taken by the surplus product that exceeds the required product (required means of livelihood), which is the labour fund within the new product. It is clear to us, therefore, *even from the viewpoint of society as a whole*, that the new value within the total product, except for the value of total constant capital, forms the gross revenue, so that surplus-value becomes net revenue.

21.2 National Income

Value Composition of the Total Social Product = $c + v + s$

As we saw in detail in ► Chap. 14 in Part II («Reproduction and Circulation of the Total Social Capital»), under the capitalist mode of production, the value of the total social product is the value of the product of the total social capital, which can be divided into the constant and variable capital advanced in production and the surplus-value that is the increment of this capital. But whereas the value of the constant capital is the transferred old value, which is the past labour objectified in the means of production, the value of the variable capital and surplus-value is the new value formed through the objectification of the workers' new labour. This portion of new value is divided into the various forms of revenue as well as the *accumulation fund* for the new expansion of production and of capital (a part of which is then further transformed into the *labour fund for additional workers*). The value of the variable

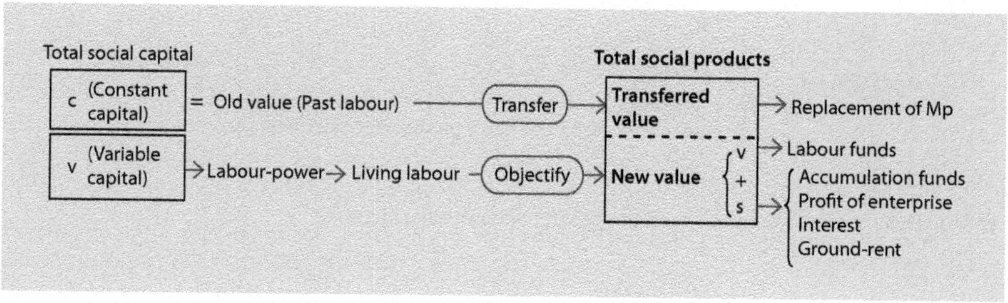

Fig. 21.2 Two constituent parts of the value of the total social product and the division of new value

capital, on the one hand, replaces the variable capital advanced by the capitalist, and on the other hand, in the hands of workers, becomes the wages that are the wage workers' labour fund, while surplus-value becomes the revenue of capitalists and landowners (*see* Fig. 21.2).

Gross Domestic Production (GDP)

The *total social product produced in 1 year in a given country* is called the «**Gross Domestic Production**» (GDP). From the material perspective, which is the *perspective of use-value*, GDP is composed of infinitely varied means of production and infinitely varied means of consumption, and from the *perspective of value*, it combines the transferred value of constant capital and the new value. Further, the new value can be divided into variable capital and the surplus-value that exceeds it.

National Income

Out of the GDP, the transferred value of constant capital needed to replace the means of production consumed over the past year cannot become revenue, even in the case of simple reproduction. In contrast, the new value part can be transformed into revenue, and in the case of simple reproduction, all of it becomes revenue. *The part of the «gross domestic production»* (GDP) *that can be disposed of by each nation as revenue is called* its «**national income**»[1] (*see* Fig. 21.3).

Primary Distribution of National Income

New value is the new labour reified in the *production process of the material product* and in the *logistical process that is its extension*. The capital that engages in this production is *industrial capital*. The national income is thus generated by the capitals in production spheres such as manufacturing, processing, and construction; agriculture, forestry, and fishing; mining, electricity, gas; and water, transport, storage, communication, etc.

1 In this case, the word *income* is ordinally used instead of *revenue*, but there is no difference between the two in their economic meaning.

Gross Domestic Production (GDP) {
- Transferred value = Value transferred/preserved from the previous year = c
- **National Income** = Value newly produced in the current year = v + s

Fig. 21.3 Gross Domestic Production (GDP) and national income

The labour under capital that is solely involved in the circulation process, which is *labour under commercial capital*, does not form new value and therefore does not generate national income. Examples of this labour include such activities as wholesaling and advertising.

Also, no new value is created or national income generated by the *labour of the labour-power that is purchased by money-dealing or interest-bearing capital*. Such labour includes the activities performed at various financial institutions in the fields of banking, insurance, trusts, securities, etc.

Even in the spheres not engaged in production, various material means are advanced as capital that represents one part of the total annual product or as payment for the wage workers that carry out the labour in these spheres, and this subsequently flows back along with profit to the capitalists engaged therein. *This capital and profit are all value that is produced in the production spheres, from whence it flows into the other spheres in a variety of ways*, and all of this is the *redistribution of the national income produced in the production spheres*.

Original Incomes

The national income generated in the production spheres is distributed or redistributed to commercial capital and the capital in financial institutions. The process whereby this ultimately becomes the revenue of wage workers, financial capitalists, moneyed capitalists, and landowners is called the «**primary distribution of national income**», while the various sorts of revenue formed in this process are called «**original income**».

Secondary Distribution of National Income

The original income obtained by wage workers, functioning capitalists, moneyed capitalists, and landowners, respectively, flows out of their hands in a variety of forms, and this comes to constitute the various types of derivative revenue. This process is called the «**secondary distribution of national income**».

One part of original income is paid for *services sold with prices attached to them just as in the case of original commodities*. Such services include art, entertainment, medical treatment, travel, dining, hairdressing, etc. Today, most of the sellers of services in this sphere are **service capital**, managed in a capitalistic manner through the purchase of the labour-power of wage workers. *Because the labour in the service* *industry is not objectified to become value, the capital in this sphere also does not generate national income.* The capital therein and therefore the wages and profit as well are merely the secondary distribution of the original income.

Derivative Income

The *labour under state organisations* (such as the national government, parliament, courts, armed forces, police, and local governments)—conceived by some schools of *economics* as «public services sold» as in the case of service capital—is in fact *not objectified to create value* (if we set aside labour involved in the production and logistical processes of commodities sold) and *does not form national income.* Fundamentally speaking, the financial source here is the **taxes** collected from peoples' revenue, and this **fiscal spending** is the *redistribution of national income.* The *revenue of government workers* is one type of derivative income, and the *expenditure of the state* also forms various types of derivative income.

The distribution of national income, including redistribution to the service sphere, is illustrated in ◘ Fig. 21.4. This figure omits the redistribution through the public sphere.

Concepts of National Income in the Current Statistics on National Accounts

In order to see the totality of activity in a country, it is extremely important to precisely grasp the gross domestic product and national income, both quantitatively and qualitatively. The governments of capitalist countries annually publish national statistical reports compiled according to the **System of National Accounts** (SNA). And there are methods for preparing statistics that are internationally comparable.

We must bear in mind, however, that it is difficult to correctly grasp the process of the distribution and redistribution of the *value objectified in the production sphere* over the course of a year through these statistics because they are premised on the *concept of national income*, which is *distorted by various unscientific notions.*

21.3 Formula of the «Economic Trinity»

Trinity Formula

In ▶ Chap. 7 in Part I («Wages»), we saw that the value of labour-power appears in the eyes of those involved as the value or price of labour, thus appearing in the form of wages for labour. Here we have *labour—wages.*

In ▶ Chap. 19 in Part III («Interest-Bearing Capital»), we also saw that the interest paid to moneyed capital from out of the surplus-value of functioning capital presents itself as the value of the commodity «capital» and that this is conceived of as the «fruit of capital-ownership»; while the profit of enterprise corresponding to this is conceived of not only as «payment for

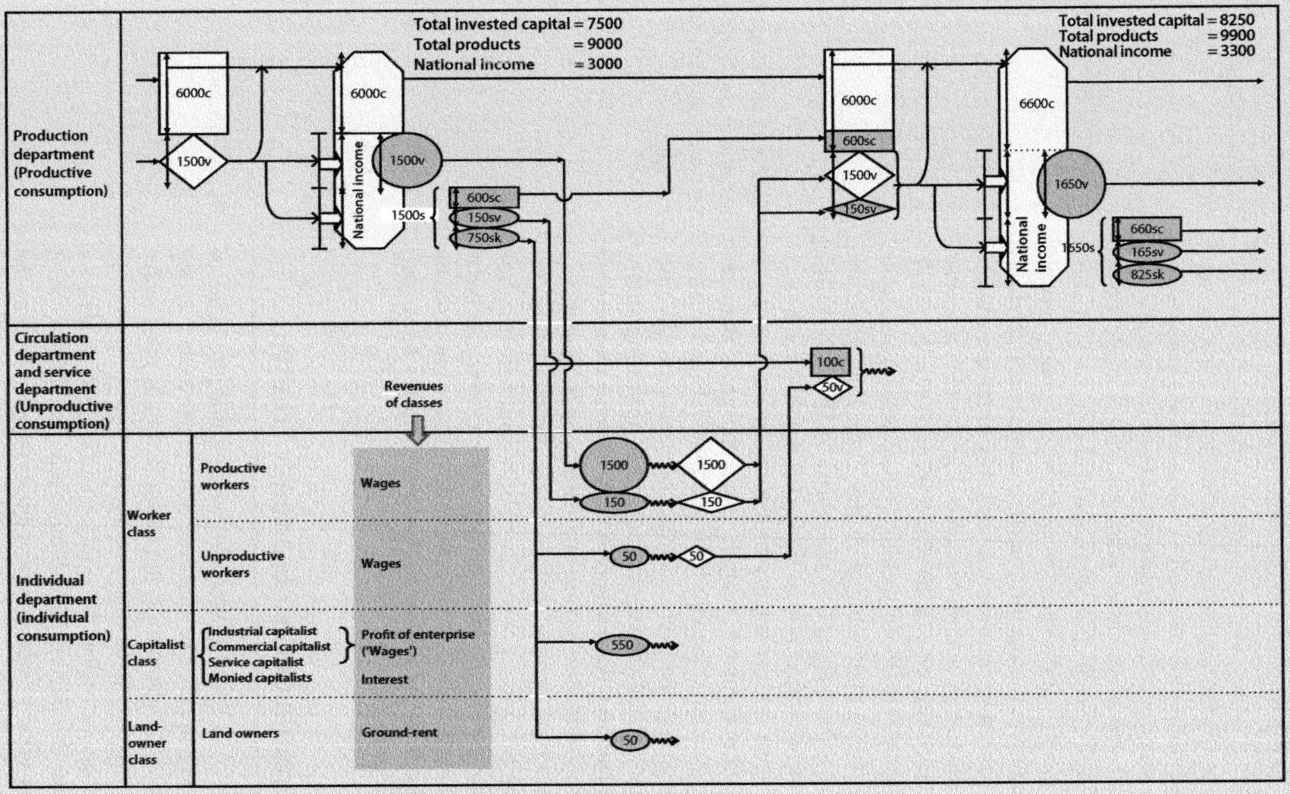

■ **Fig. 21.4** National income and its distribution among classes in capitalist society

3 factors of production = 3 sources of income { Labour → Wages; Capital → Interest; Land → Ground-rent } 3 revenues

Labour	→	Wages
Capital	→	Interest
Land	→	Ground-rent

Fig. 21.5 Formula of «economic trinity»

the function of capital» but further as the «wages of superintendence of labour» paid to the «manager» within the production process. As a result, even the concept of profit as revenue disappears, so only the person who receives the revenue of interest for the ownership of capital is seen as being the capitalist. This is *capital—interest.*

Next, in ▶ Chap. 20 in Part III («Landed Property and Ground-Rent»), we saw that, through the monopoly of the particular production condition of land, the surplus profits in the agricultural sphere are handed over as ground-rent from functioning capitalists to landowners. But this is conceived of in the distorted form of the «production element land generating value that becomes ground-rent, which the landowner appropriates as the fruit of landownership». Hence, *land—ground-rent.*

In those investigations, we arrived at a profound understanding of the *establishment grounds and structure of the* **trinity formula**, *which states that the*«**three elements of production**»—**labour**, **capital**, *and* **land**—*are the* **three sources of revenue** *and compose the* **value added** *to the product* (*see* Fig. 21.5).

Returning to the «Common Image» of the Capitalist Economy

At the beginning of ▶ Chap. 2 in Part I, we presented the «common image» that people have of the capitalist economy, in the diagram titled, «The Common Image of the «Circular Flow» of the Economy» (*see* Fig. 2.1). And now we have returned to this image, but it had undergone a complete transformation under our eyes.

What we saw at the beginning was merely the image that people have of the capitalist economy when they observe its surface without any economic analysis. But now we are well aware of what lays hidden beneath the surface and how that is significantly different from the surface phenomena. That is, we now know the internal mechanism beneath the surface. And we are aware of how and why such a common image is necessarily generated from the various forms of capitalist production.

This is exactly as if one first observed a car's hood that conceals its internal mechanism, so that one would only see that a peculiar object runs by consuming a specific sort of liquid. But after training at a school for mechanics to learn about the structure of an automobile, one would be able, from the appearance of an operating car, to mentally reproduce its internal mechanism—from the driving force of its motor, which the hood conceals, to the transmission that reaches the axels—and to understand how this mechanism determines the hood's shape, etc.

Let's now carefully compare ◘ Fig. 2.1 at the starting point («The Common Image of the «Circular Flow» of the Economy») with ◘ Fig. 14.23 in Part II («Connections Between Production, Circulation, and Consumption Within the Process of Social Reproduction»), ◘ Fig. 21.4 in this chapter («National Income and Its Distribution to Classes in Capitalist Society»), and ◘ Fig. 21.5 just presented («Formula of Economic Trinity»). Let's also examine how ◘ Fig. 2.1 at the beginning was an *amalgam of the various distorted conceptions of the capitalist economy.* In making such comparisons, we can confirm that what is vitally important to our entire analysis of capitalist production is, first of all, grasping the secret of capital valorisation—depicted in ◘ Fig. 3.17 («Valorisation Process»)—and second, on that basis, grasping the mechanism of total reproduction within capitalist production using the reproduction schema—depicted in ◘ Fig. 14.5 («Meaning of Marx's Reproduction Schema»).

We thus began with the analysis of the simplest, most general phenomena, grasped from our common image of the capitalist economy, before advancing our study to analyse one element after another of the most essential mechanism of this economy—moving from the general to the specific and from the abstract to the concrete. And now we have finally returned to the surface of the economy. We have thus *finished tracing* the «ascending way» suggested in ► Sect. 1.5.2 of the introduction (*see* ◘ Fig. 1.40). More concretely, we have now reached the «arrival point» of ◘ Fig. 2.2 («Starting and Arrival Points of the Presentation») of ► Chap. 2 in Part I, which is to say, here in the final chapter of this book, we have reached the point of «mentally reproducing» the total figure of our object.

21.4 Classes of Capitalist Society

Relations of Distribution and Classes

Not all of the *individuals who comprise capitalist society* are engaged with nature and society as *labouring individuals.* In this society, in addition to wage workers, who are the personification of labour-power and wage-labour, there are capitalists, who personally represent capital—the functioning capitalists (industrial and commercial capitalists) and moneyed capitalists, as well as landowners, who personally represent landed property. The *things represented by these economic persons* are inevitably generated from the *social relations of individuals under the capitalist mode of production*, but these economic personifications *seem to be* distinguished according to their respective *position within distribution* and *the source and manner in which they obtain their revenue*. In other words, the *distribution relations of capitalist society and the individual economic personifications are connected.*

Individuals of the same economic personification share *common economic interests* and have common *interests that conflict* with those individuals of different economic personifications. Because of this, individuals that possess the same economic personifications necessarily form *social groups*, which are **classes**. This means that classes, *first of all*, can be called *groups of individuals that share in common the same position within the* **distribution relations** *of capitalist society. From this perspective*, the fundamental classes of capitalist society are the **working class, capitalist class**, and the **landowner class.**[2]

Relations of Distribution Determined by Relations of Production

However, what *determine these* are the *social relations people form within production*, i.e. the **relations of production.**

The production relations within capitalist society, as we have already examined in detail, are the commodity production relations in which labour that is privately performed and mutually independent constitutes, in its entirety, the social division of labour. Upon this basis, there is the relation between wage workers and capitalists—i.e. between labouring

---

2 Marx (1894) writes in the last chapter of vol. III of *Capital*: «The owners of mere labour-power, the owners of capital and the landowners, whose respective sources of income are wages of labour, profit and ground-rent—in other words wageworkers, capitalists and landowners—form the three great classes of modern society based on the capitalist mode of production. . . . The question to be answered . . . is: «What makes a class?», and this arises automatically from answering another question: «What makes wageworkers, capitalists and landowners the formative elements of the three great social classes?» / *At first sight*, the *identity of revenues and revenue sources*. For these are three great social groups whose components, the individuals forming them, live respectively from wages, profit and ground-rent, from the utilisation of their labour-power, capital and landed property». (Marx 1981, pp. 1025–1026; my emphasis). To the question posed, Marx responds with «identity of revenues and revenue sources» as his answer. But be careful to note that he says, «At first sight . . .» and his manuscript breaks off thereafter. Clearly, Marx had the intention to offer a more profound answer to the question in what was to follow.

individuals separated from the labour conditions who are compelled to sell their labour-power as a commodity, on the one hand, and those who personify the labour conditions and do not engage in labour themselves. This is the *capital/wage-labour relation*. Meanwhile, the landowners, who personify the labour condition of land, are not in direct opposition with wage workers, having only a relation with them via the capitalists who represent and personify the labour conditions (*see* ◘ Fig. 21.1).

These are the *production relations* that *determine the relations of distribution in capitalist society*. The specific forms of distribution relations are merely an expression of the specific historical relations of production. Relations of distribution are historical because the relations of production are historical. Thus, if capitalist production were to end, capitalist relations of distribution would likewise cease to exist.

Capitalist Relations of Production (Capital/Wage-labour Relation) Determine Fundamental Class Relation

From the perspective of the relations of production, therefore, the opposition between the capitalist class and the landowner class is the opposition within the relations of production between two types of economic personifications which both represent labour conditions. In that sense, it is merely a *secondary opposition* as compared to the *fundamental opposition that is the relation between the labouring individuals separated from the labour conditions and those who personify those labour conditions.*

Under the capitalist mode of production, the *most fundamental class relation* is that between the class of labouring individuals who do not own the means of production (**wage-worker class**) and the class of individuals who do not labour and own the means of production and money (**capitalist class** and **landowner class**) (*see* ◘ Fig. 21.6).

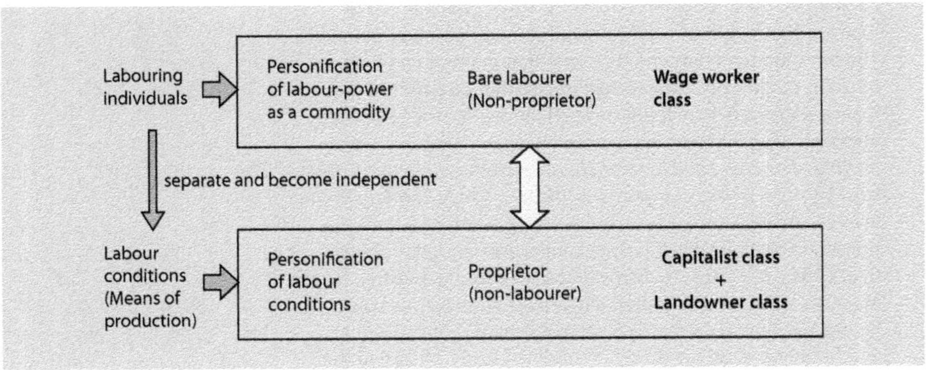

◘ **Fig. 21.6** Fundamental class relations within capitalist society

Classes and Class Struggle

It hardly bears mentioning at this point that those on either side of this fundamental class relation have **economic interests** that are in direct opposition on every point. So as long as capitalist production relations continue to exist, the **class struggle** will unfold without cease between the wage worker class and the capitalist class as well as the landowner class, centring on the conflict between wage workers and capitalists. There also arises an opposition or collision of interests between the capitalist class and the landowning class, but this is only a secondary matter.

With the development of capitalist production, it is precisely the wage worker class, made up of the labouring individuals within capitalist society, that is the subjective power that breaks through the limitations of capitalist production to assist the birth of the new society gestating the womb of capitalist production (*see* ▶ Sect. 11.2.2: «From Wage-Labour to Associated Labour»).

Labouring Individuals Are the Subject to Form and Transform Society

From the introduction up to here, the term «labouring individual» has been consistently used to refer to those who sustain society by producing social wealth with their own labour. Some readers may have wondered why it was necessary to use such a peculiar expression, rather than simply saying «human being» or «individual», or why the people who comprise the working class could not be referred to as «workers». The reasons may already be evident by this point, but for the sake of clarity, I would like to list them here.

First of all, the word «worker» overwhelmingly conjures the image of the «wage worker». But wage workers are the alienated shape, assumed under modern capitalist society, of the «labouring people» who have supported human society through their labour during every historical period. Always being able to perceive such «labouring people» within the modern shape of the «wage worker» is an indispensable key to understanding the mechanism of modern society.

Second, even though these «labouring people» cannot fully develop their own individuality and capabilities as long as they are «wage workers», each of them remains an «individual» with his or her own unique individuality and capabilities. The working class is the mass of these diverse individuals who share a common economic interest. They are not a mere constituent organ of the living totality that is «society». Rather, each is a living individual subject, an «individual», who reproduces, maintains, and forms the actual society—which today is a capitalist society—through their daily actions.

The third reason is that the movement of the working class to revolutionise present-day society is, therefore, a movement carried out consciously through the solidarity of these diverse «individuals», who thereby first display their actual strength. Precisely because this is a movement that aims for the creation of *association*, consciously formed by *associated free individuals*, it can only be carried out by self-aware *individuals* acting in solidarity.

These labouring individuals comprise the subject that every day reproduces and forms society and which one day will also transform society.

Reference

Marx K (1894) Das Kapital. Kritik der politischen Oekonomie. Bd. 3. Buch 3: Der Gesammtprocess der kapitalistischen Produktion. Hrsg. von F. Engels. Hamburg. English edition: Marx K (1981) Capital. A Critique of Political Economy. Vol. 3 (trans: Fernbach D). Penguin Books

Concluding Remarks: Arrival Point of Our Investigation and Remaining Tasks

T. Otani, *A Guide to Marxian Political Economy*,
https://doi.org/10.1007/978-3-319-65954-1_22

In ▸ Chap. 21 («Revenue Forms and Classes»), we finally summarised the mechanism whereby the outcome of the labour of the individuals comprising society is distributed under capitalist production as the national income and its sources. And we confirmed that, ultimately, the true content of this distribution is necessarily concealed by the trinity formula: «labour—wages», «capital—interest», and «land—ground-rent», so that the parts of surplus-value necessarily present themselves as being completely independent of each other. Finally, we spoke of how the fundamental production relation of capitalist production—the capital/wage-labour relation—necessarily manifests itself as the class relation between the wage worker class composed of labouring individuals and the capitalist/landowner class that personifies the labour conditions that those individuals are separated from and how the opposition of class interests between them necessarily develops into a class struggle between those two classes.

Up to this point, we have performed a «**general analysis of capital**» (Marx 1894. Marx 1981, p. 342), which is to say, a «**general investigation of capitalist production**» (Marx 1894. Marx 1981, p. 242), and the ultimate point of arrival of our analysis is as sketched above.[1]

We took as our clue the superficial image of capitalist society, presented in ▸ Chap. 2 in Part I («Commodity and Money»), and proceeded in analysing this surface layer, grasping the essential laws hidden beneath it. And based on these laws, we then elucidated why the external appearance at the surface layer is necessarily distorted.

We now know that the external movement of capitalist society arises from the laws of movement that penetrate its foundation and from the internal relations at its deepest layer and that the former cannot be understood without an understanding of the latter.

However, only being aware of this does not yet constitute an explanation of the **various concrete forms in which the laws of capitalist production penetrate**, which can only occur, essentially, as a continual equalisation of incessant disequilibrium. Understanding this requires us to advance towards the **investigation of concrete problems**, based on the understanding of the internal relations and laws that we obtained through our general analysis of capital. This is a task that lies beyond the framework of this book, but here I would

1 My views on Marx's characterisation of *Capital* as the «general analysis of capital» are presented in Otani (2015).

like to briefly indicate four of the most important tasks to pursue.

First of all, in the general analysis of capital, the main task is to grasp the internal relations of the capitalist mode of existence as well as internal organisation and general phenomenal forms of these relations, so we did not enter into a full discussion of the concrete forms of movement when those laws penetrate. This is why we never took as our direct object of investigation the *dynamic form through which capitalist production develops in the course of time:* the **industrial cycle** that passes through the phases of a middling activity, prosperity, overproduction, crisis, and stagnation (*see* ► Sect. 10.4.2 in Part I and ► Sect. 17.3 in Part III). Such an investigation is dealt with in the *theory of industrial cycle*[2] (the so-called business cycle) and the *theory of crisis*[3], to borrow the classifications of political economy.

Second, in the general analysis of capital, capitalist society is mainly dealt with solely as a single society. Although the analysis of capitalist production is not looking at a specific country, it can be thought of as an analysis within a one-nation framework. Actual capitalism, however, can only exist as the intertwined capitalist production of many coexisting countries. Moreover, capitalist production also has an intrinsic impulse to create and expand the **world market**, creating a single world, so one must clarify how the *capitalist relations of production brought together in the form of the capitalist state develop into international movement that goes beyond this nation state*. Such issues are dealt with in the field that political economy terms the *study of the world economy*.

Third, in order to be useful in elucidating and solving the concrete contemporary problems, and thereby move forward the gears of history, political economy must clarify the *specific forms and concrete movement of capitalist production in different countries and at different periods of time* based on a systematic, theoretical understanding of capitalist production gained through the general analysis of capital and present this *to the labouring individuals in each given country*, showing them fundamental tasks that must be solved. This is the *theoretical analysis of current situation*, in other words, the **analysis of the status quo**.

---

2 Marx's elucidation of industrial cycle in Marx (1894) discussed in Otani (2016). Cf. Kuruma (1976).

3 A comprehensive and theoretically reliable guidance to Marx's theory of crisis was compiled by Kuruma (1972–1975).

Finally there is one more concrete task, whose elucidation is particularly pressing with regard to addressing the previous three tasks. This is the question of how to understand the current state of world capitalism in which the **inconvertibility system** has been generalised throughout the world, with central banks of capitalist countries issuing inconvertible banknotes, and the inconvertible currency of a particular country, the US dollar, circulating as an «international currency» under this system. This issue concerns the questions: *Has the monetary system based by on gold as money lost its significance, and does the sort of a credit system that strictly speaking should only be able to exist on the basis of such a monetary system no longer exist?* This issue was not touched on in this book because it goes beyond the general analysis of capital, but it is one of the most important theoretical issues for the analysis of the contemporary economy. An attempt to deal with this issue[4] requires us to take a step forward by engaging in the *theoretical study of credit and the banking system*, including such issues as *finance and international finance.*

Here, I have only listed four topics that remain to be examined, but the various branches of political economy have addressed almost every issue related to the capitalist economy, so I would encourage the reader to engage in the study of the more concrete forms of the capitalist economy, from a variety of analytical approaches, based on a firm grasp of the basic theory of capital.

In this sense, the reader has only reached the top of the first summit that affords a view of the summits of the surrounding mountains. My firm hope is that the day will come when my fellow explorers have traversed all of the peaks in this magnificent mountain range.

References

Konishi K (2014) Maturity and transformation of capitalism—contemporary credit and crisis. In Japanese. Sakurai-Shoten Publishers, Tokyo

Kuruma S (1972–1975) Marx-Lexikon der Politischen Ökonomie, vol 6–8. Otsuki-Shoten Publishers, Tokyo

Kuruma S (1976) Marx-Lexikon der Politischen Ökonomie, vol 9. Otsuki-Shoten Publishers, Tokyo

Marx K (1894) Das Kapital. Kritik der politischen Oekonomie. Bd. 3. Buch 3: Der Gesammtprocess der kapitalistischen Produktion. Hrsg. von

4 One recent stimulating work that has examined this issue is Konishi (2014).

F. Engels. Hamburg. English edition: Marx K (1981) Capital. A Critique of Political Economy. Vol. 3 (trans: Fernbach D). Penguin Books
Otani T (2015) Zur Entstehung des ‚Kapital' als ‚allgemeine Analyse des Kapitals'. *Marx-Engels-Jahrbuch* 2014. 141–158. Berlin/Boston
Otani T (2016) Marx's theory of the interest-bearing capital, vol III. Sakurai-Shoten Publishers, Tokyo

Supplementary Information

T. Otani, *A Guide to Marxian Political Economy*,
https://doi.org/10.1007/978-3-319-65954-1

Name Index

Subject Index

A

B

C

H

I

J

L

M

S

T

U

V

W

Y

The manufacturer's authorised representative in the EU is Springer Nature Customer Service Centre GmbH, Europaplatz 3, 69115 Heidelberg, Germany. If you have any concerns regarding our products, please contact ProductSafety@springernature.com

Printed and bound by CPI Group (UK) Ltd, Croydon, CR0 4YY
30/09/2026
02225587-0010